Kültepe at the Crossroads between Disciplines

SUBARTU LI

Subartu — a peer-reviewed series — is edited by the European Centre for Upper Mesopotamian Studies.

General Editor

Marc Lebeau

Editorial Board

M. Conceição Lopes
Lucio Milano
Adelheid Otto
Walther Sallaberger
Véronique Van der Stede

With the support of the following institutions

Università Ca' Foscari Venezia
Université Libre de Bruxelles
Universidade de Coimbra
Ludwig-Maximilians-Universität München

Subartu is a part of The ARWA Collection

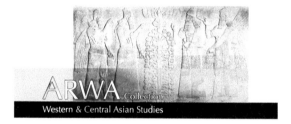

Cover image: Detail of the lyre player on the decorated pithos from the Stone Building, Kültepe mound. © Kültepe Archaeological Mission.

VOLUME 51

Previously published volumes in this series are listed at the back of the book.

Kültepe at the Crossroads between Disciplines

Society, Settlement and Environment from the Fourth to the First Millennium BC

Edited by

Fikri Kulakoğlu & Cécile Michel

(With the collaboration of Guido Kryszat)

KIM Editors
Fikri Kulakoğlu & Cécile Michel

KIM Editorial Board
Gojko Barjamovic, Guido Kryszat, Luca Peyronel & Aslıhan K. Yener

KIM 5 — KÜLTEPE INTERNATIONAL MEETINGS 5

BREPOLS

British Library Cataloguing in Publication Data

A catalogue record for this book is available from the British Library.

Keywords: Kültepe/Kaneš, Central Anatolia, Old Assyrian, Bronze Age in Western Asia, Politics, Religion, Women, Letters, Glyptic, Zooarchaeology, Ceramics, Architecture, Chronology, Türkiye.

© 2024, Brepols Publishers n.v., Turnhout, Belgium

All rights reserved. No part of this publication may be reproduced, stored in a retrieval system, or transmitted, in any form or by any means, electronic, mechanical, photocopying, recording, or otherwise, without the prior permission of the publisher.

D/2024/0095/18
ISBN: 978-2-503-60941-6
e-ISBN: 978-2-503-60942-3
DOI: 10.1484/M.SUBART-EB.5.135809
ISSN: 1780-3233

Printed in the EU on acid-free paper

Table of Contents

List of Illustrations vii

Acknowledgements xvii

CÉCILE MICHEL
   1. Kültepe at the Crossroads between Disciplines 1

Politics, Law and Religion

JAN GERRIT DERCKSEN & JACOB JAN DE RIDDER
   2. A City-State's Diplomacy in the Early Middle Bronze Age Near East 13

ADELHEID OTTO
   3. Law and Justice in Kaneš and its Depiction on Cylinder Seals: A New Interpretation of the Motifs 'Ball-Staff' and 'Pot' 33

YORAM COHEN
   4. The Origins and History of the God Šarra-mātān 55

AMIR GILAN
   5. The Cult of Aškašepa in Hittite Sources 63

Women, Family and Correspondence

ANITA FATTORI
   6. Keeping in Touch: Language and Mobility of Assyrian Women in the Old Assyrian Period.............75

WIEBKE BEYER
   7. The Hand of a Woman? 93

MATTHIAS ADELHOFER
   8. Invoking Relations in Old Assyrian and Old Babylonian Letters 109

AGNETE W. LASSEN
   9. The Seals of the Šalim-Aššur Family (94/k) 117

Of Humans and Animals

DONALD KALE, HANDAN ÜSTÜNDAĞ, SEMIH ÖZEN, DORUK CAFER ÖZGÜ & FIKRI KULAKOĞLU
    10. A First Attempt to Assess Activity Patterns at Kültepe: Studying Entheseal Changes in the Bronze Age Skeletal Sample 135

KAMERAY ÖZDEMIR, HANDAN ÜSTÜNDAĞ, TURHAN DOĞAN, FURKAN KULAK & FIKRI KULAKOĞLU
    11. Reconstructing Bronze Age Diet from Stable Isotopes Analysis: Preliminary Results from Kültepe-Kaneš 151

FIKRI KULAKOĞLU, LUCA PEYRONEL & CLAUDIA MINNITI
    12. Of Lions and Sheep: Animal Exploitation at Kültepe and in Central Anatolia during the Middle Bronze Age: New Data from Recent Excavations 167

Recent Discoveries at Kültepe and its Vicinity

FIKRI KULAKOĞLU, RYOICHI KONTANI & YUJI YAMAGUCHI
    13. Discovering the Late Chalcolithic Period at Kültepe: Excavation of the Central Trench (2021–2022) 179

YILMAZ RIDVANOĞULLARI, GÜZEL ÖZTÜRK, CIHAN AY, ELIF GENÇ & FIKRI KULAKOĞLU
    14. Changes in the Settlement Plan at the End of the Third Millennium BC in Kültepe-Kaneš: New Data on the Transition from Public Buildings to Private Workshops 185

FIKRI KULAKOĞLU, LUCA PEYRONEL, VALENTINA OSELINI & AGNESE VACCA
    15. The Settlement Sequence of Kültepe from the Late Early to the Middle Bronze Age: Stratigraphic and Ceramic Periodization from Recent Excavations in the Southern Sector of the Mound 207

ANDREAS MÜLLER-KARPE
    16. Šamuha and Kaneš 227

ADAM ANDERSON
    17. Two New Tablets from the House of Kuliya, Son of Ali-abum, and One Broken Envelope: 2022 Kültepe Texts (Kt 22/k 02–03, 05) 249

FIKRI KULAKOĞLU & LUCA PEYRONEL
    18. Recent Excavations on the Mound of Kültepe: A New Public Building from the End of the Karum Period at Kaneš-Neša 257

BURCU TÜYSÜZ & YILMAZ RIDVANOĞULLARI
    19. Studies on Kültepe Hellenistic Period: Preliminary Evaluations on 2022 Excavations 275

Index 297

List of Illustrations

1. Külterpe at the Crossroads between Disciplines: An Introduction — *Cécile Michel*

Figure 1.1	Participants to the Fifth Kültepe International Meeting, Kültepe, 30 July–1 August 2022.	1
Figure 1.2	The KIM 5 participants in the Lower Town of Kültepe, 1 August 2022.	2
Figure 1.3	Mont Erciyes as seen from the mound of Kültepe, 2014.	3
Figure 1.4	The participants of the 5th KIM visiting Ḫattuša.	7

2. A City-State's Diplomacy in the Early Middle Bronze Age Near East — *Jan Gerrit Dercksen & Jacob Jan de Ridder*

Figure 2.1	Kt 85/t 17: obverse.	29
Figure 2.2	Kt 85/t 17: lower edge.	30
Figure 2.3	Kt 85/t 17: reverse.	31

3. Law and Justice in Kaneš and its Depiction on Cylinder Seals — *Adelheid Otto*

Figure 3.1	Kültepe seals and sealings depicting the ball-staff and pot.	35
Figure 3.1b	Anatolian style cylinder seal.	35
Figure 3.1c	Impression of recut Babylonian cylinder seal, Ktn/k 1698A, 1709A*. CS 73.	35
Figure 3.1d	Impression of Anatolian stamp seal, Ktn/k 1740C. St 110.	35
Figure 3.1e	Impression of Assyrian style seal, Ktn/k 1845B. CS 629.	35
Figure 3.2a	Impression of Assyrian style seal Ktn/k 1949. CS 806.	36
Figure 3.2b	Impression of seal of Puzur-Ištar, son of Šu-Anum, the steward, Kt n/k 1811B, 1961–2009.	36
Figure 3.2c	Impression of Assyrian style cylinder seal, Ktn/k 1966B. CS 822.	36
Figure 3.2d	Impression of Assyrian style seal in two registers, Ktn/k 1793A. CS 518.	36
Figure 3.3a	Impression of Anatolian style cylinder seal, Ktd/k 13A, v/k 150B. CS 270.	37
Figure 3.3b	Impression of Anatolian style seal, Ktn/k 1786E. CS 502.	37
Figure 3.4a	Impression of Syro-Cappadocian style cylinder seal, Ktn/k 1837B, 1898A. CS 609.	37
Figure 3.4b	Impression of Syro-Cappadocian style cylinder seal, Ktn/k 1911A. CS 744.	37
Figure 3.5	Number of depictions of the ball-staff on seal impressions from Karum Kaneš II, collected by Teissier 1994.	38
Figure 3.6	Percentage of depictions of the ball-staff on seals of various styles.	38
Figure 3.7	Impression of Old Syrian (Shakkanakku style) seal.	39

Figure 3.8	Worshippers carrying 'ball-staff' and 'pot' on Syrian and Anatolian seals.	40
Figure 3.8a	Kt n/k 1861C.	40
Figure 3.8b	Kt c/k 1636A.	40
Figure 3.8c	Kt n/k 1865B.	40
Figure 3.8d	Anatolian style cylinder seal in the Louvre, AO 4796.	40
Figure 3.8e	Syrian style haematite seal in Fribourg, Institut Biblique, ex-Schmidt Collection.	40
Figure 3.9a	Seal impression on envelope Kt 93/k379.	41
Figure 3.9b	Sketch of the detail of the god with saw and the case containing ball-staff, pot, and another object.	41
Figure 3.10	Seal impression of Erum, the merchant.	42
Figure 3.11	Akkadian/Post-Akkadian cylinder seals.	43
Figure 3.11a	Seal depicting weighing and measuring. Drawing A. Otto & M. Lerchl after Boehmer 1965, no. 1105, fig. 458.	43
Figure 3.11b	One of the first depictions of the ball-staff: introduction scene to Shamash.	43
Figure 3.11c	Lapis lazuli seal Kt 82 t. 224.	43
Figure 3.11d	Seal depicting grain deities carrying the capacity measuring vessel towards the grain goddess.	43
Figure 3.11e	ED III-early Akkadian cylinder seal depicting the grain measuring procedure.	43
Figure 3.12	A strickle from the eighteenth century AD in use.	44
Figure 3.13	Mosaic from the Aula dei Mensores in Ostia, AD 230.	44
Figure 3.14a	Larsa pot containing scrap silver, weight stones, and sealed closures of sacks.	46
Figure 3.14b	Tentative reconstruction of a 'sack of sealed silver'.	46
Figure 3.14c	The sack with horizontal striations and serrated upper end. Detail from Fig. 3.1b.	46
Figure 3.14d	Seal impression Kt n/k 1870B showing the sack closed with a cord in front of the supreme authority.	46
Figure 3.15	Lapis lazuli cylinder seal Kte/t 180 belonging to a high-ranking Assyrian officer.	47

4. . The Origins and History of the God Šarra-mātān — *Yoram Cohen*

Table 4.1	Erišum 1, Erišum 14, and Šamšī-Adad 1.	58

6. Keeping in Touch — *Anita Fattori*

Figure 6.1	Elamma's family.	76
Figure 6.2	Women mobility in Elamma's family.	77
Table 6.1	Shipping of silver from Lamassutum to the city of Aššur.	79
Table 6.2	Lamassutum as a receiver of merchandise.	79

LIST OF ILLUSTRATIONS

Table 6.3	Lamassutum receiving metals, textiles, and objects in Kaneš.	79
Table 6.4	Lamassutum acting as creditor.	80
Table 6.5	Shipping from Ummī-Išhara to the city of Kaneš.	80
Table 6.6	Ummī-Išhara receiving silver in Aššur.	80
Table 6.7	Šalimma receiving silver in Aššur.	81
Table 6.8	Shipping from Šalimma to the city of Kaneš.	81
Table 6.9	Šalimma as a receiver of merchandise.	81
Table 6.10	Šalimma acting as creditor.	81
Table 6.11	Šalimma's own business.	82
Table 6.12	Letters sent and/or received by women from Elamma's family.	84

7. The Hand of a Woman? — *Wiebke Beyer*

Figure 7.1	The second line on the obverse of KT 8, 165 shows many irregular or uneven elements, such as the different heights of the line and uneven spacing between signs and wedges. Anadolu Medeniyetleri Müzesi.	94
Figure 7.2	Comparison of KT 8, 165 (right) and 206 (left). Anadolu Medeniyetleri Müzesi.	94
Figure 7.3	The second line on KT 8, 206. Anadolu Medeniyetleri Müzesi.	94
Figure 7.4	Examples of the sign AM on tablets of Ummī-Išhara (KT 8, 165 and 206), Ennam-Aššur (KT 8, 190), and Elamma (KT 8, 80). Anadolu Medeniyetleri Müzesi.	95
Figure 7.5	Examples of the sign DÍ with the protruding first upper *Winkelhaken* on KT 8, 165, 206, 190, and 79. Anadolu Medeniyetleri Müzesi.	95
Figure 7.6	Examples of the signs DÍ, GA, ḪA, MA, and TIM on KT 8, 165 and tablets of Ennam-Aššur (KT 8, 190, 189, 190, 189, 189). Anadolu Medeniyetleri Müzesi.	96
Figure 7.7	Examples of IM on Kt 93/k 143, 198, 301, 352, 543, 564, and 722. Anadolu Medeniyetleri Müzesi.	97
Figure 7.8	The sign combination *um-ma* on Kt 93/k 303 (Ali-ahum), Kt 93/k 489 (Aššur-taklāku), and Kt 93/k 143 (Tariša). Anadolu Medeniyetleri Müzesi.	97
Figure 7.9	Two variations of the sign AM on Kt c/k 127. Anadolu Medeniyetleri Müzesi.	98
Figure 7.10	Examples of sign variants: the sign LI on Kt c/k 272, ZI on Kt c/k 266, NA on Kt c/k 272, and Ù on KT c/k 44. Anadolu Medeniyetleri Müzesi.	99
Figure 7.11	The typical edges of the tablets of Ali-ahum (Kt c/k 249), Aššur-bēl-šadue (Kt c/k 208), Aššur-malik (Kt c/k 801), and Šīmat-Ištar (Kt c/k 272). Anadolu Medeniyetleri Müzesi.	99
Figure 7.12	Examples of DÍ on KT 6a 237 und KT 6b 533, and IM on KT 6a 235 and 245; in both cases, the number of wedges differs, but not their arrangement. Anadolu Medeniyetleri Müzesi.	100
Figure 7.13	The sign AM on KT 6a, 236 shows the gap between the small *Winkelhaken* and the large one at the top. Anadolu Medeniyetleri Müzesi.	100

Figure 7.14	The sign AM with the gap on KT 6a, 236 (Lamassī), KT 6a, 136 (Šalim-Aššur), and KT 6a, 231 (Ennam-Aššur). Anadolu Medeniyetleri Müzesi.	101
Figure 7.15	The different corner types of Anna-anna's tablets: KT 6a, 239 vs. KT 6a, 238 + KT 6b, 314 vs. KT 6b, 299 + 302. Anadolu Medeniyetleri Müzesi.	102
Figure 7.16	The signs IM, LI, and ZI on KT 6b, 302 (Anna-anna), KT 6b, 314 (Anna-anna), and KT 6a, 151 (Šalim-Aššur). While the signs on Anna-anna's tablets are written with very common and simple variants, the ones on Šalim-Aššur's tablets are more complex. Anadolu Medeniyetleri Müzesi.	103
Table 7.1	Sign variants according to letter authors and tablets.	104

9. The Seals in the Šalim-Aššur Family (94/k) — *Agnete W. Lassen*

Figure 9.1	The Šalim-Aššur family house, excavated in 1994.	117
Figure 9.2	The Šalim-Aššur family tree. Individuals with identified seals are marked in bold.	118
Figure 9.3	Drawing of the seal of Issu-arik.	119
Figure 9.4	Drawing of the seal of Iddin-abum s. Issu-arik, CS 606.	119
Figure 9.5	Seal impression of Iddin-abum's seal on A 847/TC 1, 64 held at the Louvre Museum.	120
Figure 9.6	Left, crop of the inscription of Iddin-abum's seal from A 847 and kt n/k 1836, flipped horizontally and turned 90 degrees counterclockwise.	120
Figure 9.7	Statue mentioning Šakkanakku of Mari, Puzur-Ištar. Museum of the Ancient Orient, Istanbul.	121
Figure 9.8	Drawing of the seal of Ennam-Aššur, CS 222.	122
Figure 9.9	Drawing of Ennam-Aššur's other seal, CS 1317.	122
Figure 9.10	Drawing of the seal of Šāt-Anna, Šalim-Aššur's youngest daughter, CS 1293	123
Figure 9.11	Drawing of the seal of Kukuwa, CS 1310.	123
Figure 9.12	Left: drawing of CS 42. Right: drawing of CS 88, the seal of Šu-Kūbum s. Qayātum.	123
Figure 9.13	Left: drawing of the seal of Šalim-Aššur, CS 1278. Right: impression of CS 1278 on KT 6, 141A.	124
Figure 9.14	Drawing of the seal of Lamassī, Šalim-Aššur's oldest daughter, CS 1308.	124
Figure 9.15	Drawing of the seal of Anna-anna, CS 1269.	125
Figure 9.16	Drawing of the seal of Ali-ahum, CS 1270.	125
Figure 9.17	Left: drawing of the seal of Šu-belum, CS 1283. Right: drawing of the seal of Anuli, CS 1355.	126
Figure 9.18	Left: Drawing of the seal of Enna-Suen, CS 1280. Right: Impression of Enna-Suen's seal on KT 6, 71.	127

10. A First Attempt to Assess Activity Patterns at Kültepe — *Donald Kale, Handan Üstündağ, Semih Özen, Doruk Cafer Özgü & Fikri Kulakoğlu*

Figure 10.1	A simple inhumation from the Lower Town.	137
Figure 10.2	A stone cist burial from the Lower Town.	137
Figure 10.3	A jar burial from the Lower Town.	138

Figure 10.4	A bathtub burial from the Lower Town.	138
Figure 10.5	An example of entheseal changes in radial tuberosity: bone formation in Zone 1 (black-filled arrow with white border), bone formation in Zone 2 (white-filled arrow with black border), fine-porosity in Zone 2 (white arrow), and macro-porosity in Zone 2 (back arrow).	139
Table 10.1	Sex and age-at-death distribution of the sample group.	138
Table 10.2	The observed entheses and related muscles of the upper and lower limbs and the pelvic gridle, and their actions (anatomical descriptions adapted from Standring 2021).	140
Table 10.3	Number (n) of observed entheses (Z: zone).	140
Table 10.4	Significant results for correlation between EC scores and age groups (Z: zone, n: number, MS: mean score).	141
Table 10.5	Significant results for correlation between EC scores and sex (Z: zone, n: number, MS: mean score).	141
Table 10.6	Significant results for correlation between EC scores and chronological periods (Z: zone, n: number, MS: mean score).	142
Table 10.7	Significant results for correlation between EC scores and individuals from different burial types, both sexes pooled (Z: zone, n: number, MS: mean score).	143
Table 10.8	Significant results for correlation between EC scores and individuals from different burial types, only males (Z: zone, n: number, MS: mean score).	143

11. Reconstructing Bronze Age Diet from Stable Isotopes Analysis — *Kameray Özdemir, Handan Üstündağ, Turhan Doğan, Furkan Kulak & Fikri Kulakoğlu*

Figure 11.1	Adult individuals and local fauna scatter plot graph. Mean values with standard deviation.	157
Figure 11.2	Scatter plot graph by sex groups. Mean values with standard deviation.	157
Figure 11.3	Scatter plot graph by age groups. Mean values with standard deviation. YA: Young Adult; MA: Middle Adult; OA: Old Adult.	157
Table 11.1	List of Kültepe samples for carbon and nitrogen analysis.	153
Table 11.2	Distribution of Kültepe samples according to the variables used in the study (samples that do not meet the collagen quality criteria are not included). N: number of samples.	154
Table 11.3	$\delta^{13}C$(‰) and $\delta^{15}N$(‰) results of Kültepe adult human and animal samples. EBA: Early Bronze Age; MBA: Middle Bronze Age.	156
Table 11.4	Descriptive statistics of Kültepe carbon and nitrogen results according to the studied variables. N: number of samples; SD: standard deviation value; Max.: maximum value; Min.: minimum value.	158

12. Of Lions and Sheep: Animal Exploitation at Kültepe and in Central Anatolia during the Middle Bronze Age — *Fikri Kulakoğlu, Luca Peyronel & Claudia Minniti*

Figure 12.1	Goat (above) and sheep (below) mortality profiles according to the model of Helmer et al. (2007). Age classes according to Payne (1973). Total goat mandible/teeth: 63; total sheep mandible/teeth: 361.	169

Figure 12.2	Representation of bear anatomical elements found in the monumental Stone Building at Kültepe.	170
Figure 12.3	Two fragmented left lion mandibles.	171
Figure 12.4	Representation of lion anatomical elements found in the monumental Stone Building at Kültepe.	171
Table 12.1	Numbers of identified animal remains (NISP) per species.	168

13. Discovering the Late Chalcolithic Period at Kültepe — *Fikri Kulakoğlu, Ryoichi Kontani & Yuji Yamaguchi*

Figure 13.1	Location of central trench (north on the right).	180
Figure 13.2	Plan of large zigzag building.	180
Figure 13.3	Black burnished pottery with white-filled incision.	181
Figure 13.4	Burial jar from south-west part of Room 1.	181
Figure 13.5	Burial jar from north-east part of Room 1.	181
Figure 13.6	Horseshoe-shaped hearth in Room 1 (north on the right).	182
Figure 13.7	Burial jar in eastern small room.	183
Figure 13.8	Canaan blades from eastern small room.	183
Table 13.1	AMS ^{14}C dates from Central Trench.	182

14. Changes in the Settlement Plan at the End of the Third Millennium bc in Kültepe-Kaneš — *Yılmaz Rıdvanoğulları, Güzel Öztürk, Cihan Ay, Elif Genç & Fikri Kulakoğlu*

Figure 14.1	Kültepe-Kaneš mound, view from the east.	186
Figure 14.2	Centres mentioned in the text.	188
Figure 14.3	Palatial complex of level 13. Orthomosaic produced by Yuichi Hayakawa, 2015.	189
Figure 14.4	A view of the south-western part of the 'Idol Room' with its plastered walls and benches.	191
Figure 14.5	Kültepe-Kaneš Late EBA III Modest Workshops. The earliest phase of the complex (in violet). Rooms A1 and A2.	192
Figure 14.6	A clay crucible containing metal slag found in Room A1.	193
Figure 14.7	Kültepe-Kaneš Late EBA III Modest Workshops with oven installations. *Room is labelled as 'B' in the Figure.	193
Figure 14.8	Handmade buff slipped bowl found in the early phase of Room B3.	194
Figure 14.9	Gritty Ware sherds found in the middle phase of Room A1.	194
Figure 14.10	'Local Anatolian Type' plate fragments.	194
Figure 14.11	A clay crucible containing metal slag found in the middle phase of Room A1.	194
Figure 14.12	The so-called tandoor unearthed in Room B1.	195
Figure 14.13	Kültepe-Kaneš Late EBA III Modest Workshops. The multi-phase rooms in the south-west part of the complex excavated in 2019–2021. *Room is labelled as 'B' in the Figure.	195

Figure 14.14	A ceramic group found on the floor of the late phase of Room B5.	195
Figure 14.15	Paint decorated sherds of vessel with Intermediate tradition, found on the floor of the late phase of Room B5.	195
Figure 14.16	Alişar III ware cup and a vessel fragment found on the floor of the late phase of Room B5.	196
Figure 14.17	The multi-phase unused oval kiln and a pile of baked and unbaked pottery over northern upper wall.	196
Figure 14.18	The multi-phase unused oval kiln. View of the exterior of the structure from the east.	197
Figure 14.19	A pot with painted decoration in Intermediate style from 'Unused Oval Kiln'.	197
Figure 14.20	Alabastron-shaped Syrian bottle from 'Unused Oval Kiln'.	197
Figure 14.21	Stone idol from 'Unused Oval Kiln'.	198
Figure 14.22	Stone amulet (?) from 'Unused Oval Kiln'.	198
Figure 14.23	Schematic plan of Kültepe Late EBA III workshops and other later level buildings.	198
Figure 14.24	The cell-type underground room of level 12.	199
Figure 14.25	Round and cell-planned stone structures of EBA III.	200

15. The Settlement Sequence of Kültepe from the Late Early to the Middle Bronze Age — *Fikri Kulakoğlu, Luca Peyronel, Valentina Oselini & Agnese Vacca*

Figure 15.1	Kültepe, southern terrace complex, mound levels/periods 8–9 with indication of Açma/Operations excavated by the PAIK in 2019–2022.	208
Figure 15.2	Kültepe, mound Açma/Areas 01 and 08, excavations 2020–2022 with the Burnt Room (periods/levels 8–9/10) and the Stone Building (period/level 7).	209
Figure 15.3	Pottery from the Burnt Room: Simple Ware, open and closed shapes (1–12); Slip and Burnished Ware (13–18).	213
Figure 15.4	Pottery from the Burnt Room: Painted Ware, open and closed shapes (1–11); Cooking Ware, closed shape (12–14).	214
Figure 15.5	Pottery from the Stone Building: Simple Ware, open shapes.	216
Figure 15.6	Pottery from the Stone Building: Simple Ware, closed shapes.	218
Figure 15.7	Pottery from the Stone Building: an applied bull's head decoration on a Simple Ware jar.	219
Figure 15.8	Pottery from the Stone Building: Red Slip Ware.	220
Figure 15.9	Pottery from the Stone Building: Red Slip *hydria* and jar (1–2), fragment with the motif of the *signe royal* (3); and a fragment with plastic animal's head (4).	221
Figure 15.10	Pottery from the Stone Building: Cooking Ware.	222
Figure 15.11	A detail of the plastic geometric decoration applied on pithos 20.t 08.mk17_647.	222

16. Šamuha and Kaneš — *Andreas Müller-Karpe*

Figure 16.1	Reconstruction of the caravan route between Šamuha and Kaneš with intermediate stops (daily stages).	228

Figure 16.2	Kayalıpınar level 5.	229
Figure 16.3	Kayalıpınar level 5, isometric view with bronze sockets of door hinges from the 'House of Tatali'.	229
Figure 16.4	Kayalıpınar, level 5 (grey) and Kültepe, level *kārum* Kaneš II, house of Šalim-Aššur (black after T. Özgüç 2003).	230
Figure 16.5	Kayalıpınar level 5. Virtual reconstruction of the situation at sunrise at the summer solstice. The walls of the houses are exactly in line with the first rays of the sun.	231
Figure 16.6	Kayalıpınar level 5, pottery in situ during the excavation.	232
Figure 16.7	Kayalıpınar level 5, pottery after restoration.	232
Figure 16.8	Kayalıpınar level 5, beak-spouted pitchers and drinking bowls.	233
Figure 16.9	Kayalıpınar level 5, pithoi, cooking pots, and vessels.	233
Figure 16.10	Impressions of stamp seals with geometrical motifs: 1, 2, 4 Kayalıpınar level 5 (Kp 06/152; 07/74); 3, 5, 6 Kültepe, level *kārum* Kaneš Ib.	234
Figure 16.11	Impressions of stamp seals with depictions of animals: 1 Kayalıpınar level 5 (Kp 08/5); 2 Kültepe, level *kārum* Kaneš II.	234
Figure 16.12	Impressions of stamp seals and cylinder seals with depictions of a hunter with a lance and wild animals: 1, 2 Kayalıpınar level 5 (Kp 07/44); 3–5 Kültepe, level *kārum* Kaneš II.	235
Figure 16.13	Impressions of stamp seals and cylinder seals with depictions of animals, among others seen from above: 1, 2 Kayalıpınar level 5 (Kp 08/101); 3, 4 Kültepe, level *kārum* Kaneš II.	236
Figure 16.14	Impressions of stamp seals with depictions of a double-headed eagle: 1, 2 Kayalıpınar level 5 (Kp 08/6); 3–5 Kültepe, Waršama Saray.	236
Figure 16.15	Impressions of cylinder seals, Classic Old Assyrian Style: 1, 2 Kayalıpınar level 5 (Kp 08/109); 3, 4 Kültepe, level *kārum* Kaneš II.	237
Figure 16.16	Impressions of cylinder seals, Old Assyrian Style (top left) and Old Assyro-Cappadocian Style (bottom left and top right) with the motif God of War on Lion: 1, 2 Kayalıpınar level 5 (Kp 08/16. 17. 108); 3 Kültepe, level *kārum* Kaneš II (N. Özgüç 2006, pl. 60 Kt.n/k 1851 CS 641). Parallels of the motif: 4 gold folio from Kültepe (Kulakoğlu 2008); 5 Yazılıkaya.	238
Figure 16.17	1–5 Cylinder seal from Kayalıpınar level 5 (Kp 07/45); 6, 7 Kültepe.	239
Figure 16.18	Distribution of cylinder seals like Fig. 16.17.	240
Figure 16.19	Kayalıpınar level 6, radiocarbon dates from three samples of charred grains.	241
Figure 16.20	Kayalıpınar level 5, radiocarbon dates of four different annual rings of a charred wooden beam. The light grey area indicates the calibrated age without wiggle matching, the dark grey area the calibrated age with wiggle matching.	242

18. Recent Excavations on the Mound of Kültepe — *Fikri Kulakoğlu & Luca Peyronel*

Figure 18.1	Kültepe mound. Aerial view of the southern sector with the area investigated by the Italian Archaeological Project (PAIK) of the University of Milan.	258
Figure 18.2	Schematic plan of the Middle Bronze I–II (mound levels/periods 7–8) building in the central-southern sector of the Upper Town of Kültepe. (A) Southern Terrace Building Complex, (B) Stone-Paved Plaza, (E) Warehouse, (F) Square Building, (C–D) Temple I and II.	259

Figure 18.3	Plan and view from the north of Temple II of Kültepe.	260
Figure 18.4	Kültepe mound. The Stone Building in the southern sector of the Upper Town.	261
Figure 18.5	Kültepe mound. Plan of the Stone Building of the Upper Town.	262
Figure 18.6	Kültepe mound. Stone Building. View of Room L.79 from the north.	263
Figure 18.7	Kültepe mound. Stone Building. Section with the level of collapsed stones in Room L.79 from the north.	263
Figure 18.8	Kültepe mound. Stone Building. The bench in Room L.79 from the south.	258
Figure 18.9	Kültepe mound. Stone Building. Detail of the mat over the floor in Room L.79.	264
Figure 18.10	Kültepe mound. Stone Building. Detail of bowl over the floor in Room L.79.	265
Figure 18.11	Radiocarbon datings calibrated 2-sigma of samples (animal bones and charred seeds) from the filling layers of the Stone Building.	266
Figure 18.12	Kültepe mound. Stone Building. The pithoi in Room L.78 from the west.	266
Figure 18.13	Pithos Kt.22.t 01.Mk4.P_2 from Room L.78.	267
Figure 18.14	Decorated pithos Kt.20.t 08.Mk17.P_647 from the Stone Building.	268
Figure 18.15	Decorated pithos Kt.20.t 08.Mk17.P_648 from the Stone Building.	268
Figure 18.16	Detail of the figurative frieze of decorated pithos Kt.20.t 08.Mk17.P.647.	269
Figure 18.17	Detail of the lyre player of the Inandik vase and Kültepe pithos Kt.20.t 08.Mk17.P.647.	269

19. Studies on Kültepe Hellenistic Period — *Burcu Tüysüz & Yılmaz Rıdvanoğulları*

Figure 19.1	Sites excavated in 2009–2020 and geophysical studies in 2022.	276
Figure 19.2	Goddess statue and bull's head.	276
Figure 19.3	Sites with intense anomaly in geophysical surveys.	277
Figure 19.4	Trench 4 excavation site.	278
Figure 19.5	Trench 4 architectural remains.	279
Figure 19.6	Ceramic samples unearthed in the late phase, drawings and photographs.	280
Figure 19.7	In situ pithos unearthed in the late phase.	282
Figure 19.8	Loom weights uncovered in pithos.	283
Figure 19.9	Beads.	283
Figure 19.10	Ceramic samples unearthed in the early phase, drawings and photographs.	284
Figure 19.11	Goat-figured appliqué.	286
Figure 19.12	Coins.	286
Figure 19.13	Plan of Hellenistic period architectural remains unearthed in 2009, 2020, and 2022.	288

Acknowledgements

This fifth Kültepe International Meeting (KIM) would not have been possible without the help of people and institutions to whom we would like to address our warmest thanks. The Turkish Republic Ministry of Culture and Tourism (T. C. Kültür ve Turizm Bakanlığı), which has supported the Kültepe excavations since the mid-twentieth century; the General Directorate of Cultural Assets and Museums (Kültür Varlıkları ve Müzeler Genel Müdürlüğü); the Governor of Kayseri; the Rector of Ankara University; the Dean of the Faculty of Languages and History-Geography in Ankara; the President of the Turkish Historical Society; Dr Memduh Büyükkılıç, Mayor of the Kayseri Metropolitan Municipality for important moral, material, and financial support; the Kültepe team; all contributors and participants of the KIM 5 conference; and the institutions who sponsored the conference, including Ankara University, the Faculty of Languages and History-Geography, the French National Centre for Scientific Research, the Turkish Historical Society.

We also address our warmest thanks to Andreas Schachner who welcomed us at Boğazköy, the ancient Ḫattuša, and offered us a guided tour through this marvellous site. Last but not least, we thank the members of the KIM series editorial board; all reviewers and proofreaders who graciously devoted their time to this volume; Rosie Bonté, publishing manager at Brepols publishers, Tim Barnwell, copy editor, Jelmar Meynckens, typesetter, and Marc Lebeau, editor of the SUBARTU series.

For the opening day of KIM 5, several events took place in Kayseri. An exhibition sponsored by the Metropolitan Municipality of Kayseri and directed by Siret Uyanık was opened, featuring works of art inspired by Kültepe, objects and cuneiform tablets discovered there. We thank them warmly for this event. Afterwards, in the auditorium of the new Kayseri Archaeological Museum, conference participants were invited to the premiere of the Turkish version of the documentary film *Thus Speaks Tarām-Kūbi, Assyrian Correspondence*, a film by Cécile Michel and Vanessa Tubiana-Brun, CNRS, 2020 (English version online: <https://images.cnrs.fr/en/video/7315>; Turkish version online: <https://lecture2go.uni-hamburg.de/en/l2go/-/get/v/67290>).

Having just completed this manuscript, on 28 July 2023, we were deeply saddened to learn of the death of Klaas Veenhof. With Klaas, we have lost a great scientist who inspired several generations of Assyriologists and a very dear friend.

1. Kültepe at the Crossroads between Disciplines

An Introduction

Cécile Michel

Figure 1.1: Participants to the Fifth Kültepe International Meeting, Kültepe, 30 July–1 August 2022. © Kültepe Archaeological Mission.

For the fifth time since 2013, scholars carrying out research on Kültepe and the surrounding region have come together on the archaeological site to present their work, share ideas, and discuss advances in the disciplines of archaeology, ceramology, archaeometallurgy, zooarchaeology, anthropology, palaeogenetics, aerial archaeology, history, philology, art history, and digital humanities (Fig. 1.1). For three days, from 30 July to 1 August 2022, more than seventy attendants followed and commented on twenty-eight presentations, in the cool of a large tent specially fitted out for the occasion.

The model set up ten years ago is working perfectly. The main goal of the Kültepe International Meetings is to encourage interdisciplinary dialogues between researchers working on the same site but from very different perspectives, and to forge relationships between doctoral students and professors. During the late afternoons, participants visited Kültepe mound and discovered the history of the Bronze Age buildings recently unearthed thanks to guided tours given by archaeologists. They also wandered through the streets of the Lower Town of ancient Kaneš, listening to philologists reconstructing the stories of the families living in the different houses (Fig. 1.2).

Cécile Michel (cecile.michel@cnrs.fr) Director of Research at CNRS, ArScAn-HAROC, Nanterre, France and Professor at Hamburg University, Germany

Kültepe at the Crossroads between Disciplines: Society, Settlement and Environment from the Fourth to the First Millennium BC, ed. by Fikri Kulakoğlu and Cécile Michel, Subartu, 51 (Turnhout, 2024), pp. 1–10.
DOI 10.1484/M.SUBART-EB.5.136336

Figure 1.2: The KIM 5 participants in the Lower Town of Kültepe, 1 August 2022. © Kültepe Archaeological Mission.

This volume brings together eighteen of the papers presented at the conference, many of them focusing on recent discoveries made on the site or on artefacts found there. The contributions are divided into four sections dealing respectively with the political role of Aššur in Anatolia and religion through the study of gods, the family and the role of women documented by their correspondence, analyses of human and animal skeletons, and a final section presenting the most recent research (up to 2022) on the archaeological excavations of Kültepe mound from the Chalcolithic to the Hellenistic period. Other contributions could not be included in the volume because they presented preliminary research, work from PhD theses not yet defended, or for other reasons.

Politics, Law and Religion

The Assyrians originating from Aššur succeeded in establishing themselves in the Anatolian trade by supplying the local elite with luxury goods such as textiles imported from Babylonia or woven by the women of Aššur. The treaties signed between the representatives of the Assyrian authorities in Kaneš and the local kings enabled these long-distance exchanges to flourish in a generally calm political climate during the nineteenth century BC. The situation was presumably different during the eighteenth century, after the death of King Šamšī-Adad, when the Assyrians in Anatolia became more independent. A fragment of a letter discovered in the foundations of a public building on Kültepe mound is published here for the first time. According to its editors, it is a letter combining diplomacy and trade perhaps sent by the king of Aššur to the king of Kaneš, making it as a unique document (Kt 85/t 17, Dercksen & de Ridder in this volume). It is not impossible that other testimonies of this importance can be found among the thousands of tablets preserved in the Museum of Anatolian Civilizations in Ankara.

The study of the texts goes hand in hand with that of the seal impressions that appear on the envelopes. The scenes depicted according to the Assyrian, Anatolian, Syrian, and Babylonian stylistic canons bear witness to social, cultural, religious, and economic life during the nineteenth century BC. Some of the elements give rise to very different interpretations. Those relating to cultic activities have often dominated, however recent studies have shown that everyday activities were more often present than previously thought, especially on the fourth- and third-millennium cylinder seals (Breniquet 2008). An element depicting a kind of stick with a central bulge has generally been considered to represent the upper part of a balance, an object which bears witness to trade activities of merchants negotiating mainly metals. A re-examination of all the attestations of this element would suggest that it could be interpreted differently: it could be the strickle used in capacity measurement procedures. It would then be a symbol of law and justice, and therefore linked to the god Šamaš (Otto in this volume).

Divine elements predominate on the seals, with scenes of adoration, introduction, or audience with the gods. However, the divinities depicted are not always as easily identifiable as Aššur, represented on a mountain (Kryszat 1995; Lassen 2017) or the goddess Ištar, her feet resting on a lion. The correspondence between the gods depicted on seals and those attested in the texts may be difficult to establish. Also, for certain deities, interpretations sometimes appear divergent, as is the case for Šarra-mātān, whose meaning is debated, whether it is a dual form confused with the plural form, a doubling of the name inspired by the Sumerian plural, or both at the same time. This deity was already attested in the Sargonic period, but the dual form was a creation of Aššur, where it played an important role, appearing alongside the great gods in the treaty concluded between Apûm and Aššur (Eidem 2011, 417–26 and 604–09; Cohen in this volume).

Some deities attested during the early centuries of the second millennium at Kaneš, are better documented by the Hittite texts. This would be the case with the deified Mount Aškašepa, which appears alongside other Anatolian gods in the treaty concluded between the Assyrian merchants and the king of Kaneš (Kt 00/k 6, Günbattı 2004). Anyone who has visited Kültepe immediately understands the importance of this mountain, which is identified with Mount Erciyes, an old volcano located 25 km south of Kayseri, that rises to almost four thousand metres, and dominates the landscape. It must certainly have served as a landmark for Assyrian caravans arriving on the Anatolian plateau, itself a thousand metres high (Fig. 1.3).

The identification of Aškašepa with this mountain has been questioned by some Hittitologists, as only a small number of attestations use the determinative of the mountain. In reality, although the site of Kültepe is no longer inhabited, the Hittites would have retained Aškašepa in their pantheon, the god of forests, as a reminiscence of the mountain. Mount Erciyes itself would then be known as Harhara (Gilan in this volume).

Women, Family and Correspondence

The second section of this volume gathers four contributions linked to the archives unearthed in the Assyrian merchant houses in the Lower Town of Kaneš. During

Figure 1.3: Mont Erciyes as seen from the mound of Kültepe, 2014. Photo: C. Michel.

the last decade, two large archives were published by Klaas Veenhof and Mogens Larsen, respectively the archive of Elamma in 1991 and 1992 (KT 8), and the archive of Šalim-Aššur in 1994 (KT 6a-e). These very rich documents make it possible to reconstruct the activities of the members of these two families over several generations and have given rise to numerous studies on the family, the place and role of women (Michel 2020a), the style and language of letters (Adelhofer 2022), literacy (Michel 2008; Beyer 2021), and the iconography of seals used by members of the same family (Lassen 2012).

The Kaneš archives provide exceptional documentation on Assyrian women, their integration into society, and their contribution to long-distance trade between Aššur and Kaneš. A study based on the women of Elamma's family shows that they were well integrated into commercial networks, and as such enjoyed a degree of mobility in geographical space. Some of these women learned to read and write within their families, which enabled them to communicate by letter, thus creating new networks beyond the family (Fattori in this volume).

Assyrian merchants, often on the road, had to be able to read and write in order to carry out their transactions and keep their families informed. Some women were also able to read, write, and keep accounts (Michel 2009; 2020a, 333–38; 2023). In order to determine more precisely the women who were literate, a palaeographic study is required. The identification of writers' hands is based on letters and takes into account many different aspects linked to the tablet shape and layout, including ruling, use of signs and their construction, the quality of the impression of wedges and slant, the position of wedges in relations to ruling and spacing between signs, selected diagnostic signs and their variants, as well as the use of different signs (Beyer 2019). Detailed analyses of the letters sent by a selection of women is not necessarily conclusive insofar as it concerns few texts and when these show the same handwriting, it is not easy to determine whether it is that of the woman author of the letters or that of a professional scribe. Nevertheless, it seems that the letters sent by women from Aššur are more homogeneous than those sent by women living in Anatolia, which show different hands (Beyer in this volume).

The long distance between Aššur and Kaneš explains the large number of letters in the archives of the Lower Town of Kaneš: on average, more than a third of the tablets are letters (Michel 2018). Their content was primarily commercial, and in some cases could even be used in a legal context, but they also touched on everyday life. Relationships between correspondents use rhetorical expressions that may, for example, use terms of kinship, such as 'you are my brother', when addressing a business relation of equal rank, or 'you are my father' when the correspondent was of a higher rank. The relationship between correspondents is also indicated in the letter headings, with the most important person being quoted first. The urgency of a request is often accompanied by a multiplication of such figures of expression (Adelhofer in this volume).

Letters, as well as contracts and other texts with legal value, were enclosed in a clay envelope on which seals were unrolled: that of the sender in the case of letters, and those of the parties and witnesses for texts with legal value (Michel 2020b). Seal impressions are also found on *bullae* used to close containers and doors. Major studies have been carried out on seals and seal impressions to identify the various stylistic influences (Tessier 1994; Özgüç & Tunca 2001; Özgüç 2006; Lassen 2014). These impressions are now being analysed in their archaeological context, and particular attention is being paid to seals used by members of the same family (Lassen 2012). Among the impressions found on the envelopes and *bullae* of the Šalim-Aššur house excavated in 1994, a dozen seals have been identified as belonging to his family members. The themes depicted and the styles are unrelated and do not allow the seals to be linked to this particular family, a mixture that confirms the great mobility of the Assyrians and the cosmopolitan nature of the families settled in Kaneš (Lassen in this volume).

Of Humans and Animals

In addition to the numerous cuneiform tablets discovered mainly in the Lower Town, the excavations at Kültepe yielded a wealth of archaeological material that is systematically studied. This third section is devoted to the human and animal bones discovered both in the Lower Town and more recently on the mound. Research on human bioarchaeology at Kültepe really took off around fifteen years ago, particularly on the bones discovered in tombs from 2006 onwards (Üstündağ 2009; 2014). These analyses make it possible to assess the average ages at which individuals died according to gender, type of diet, or recurring pathologies. The different activities performed by individuals during their lifetime can sometimes be suggested by studying certain parts of the human body, such as the vertebrae, or the enthesis of the inferior and superior members. The latter corresponds to the area where tendons, ligaments, and joint capsules are anchored in the bone. Its alterations might suggest repetitive and intensive movements. Entheses were analysed on around twenty skeletons dating from the Early and Middle Bronze eras, broken down by age at death, sex, period, and type of burial. Results seems to indicate that individuals buried simply in the ground had physical activities that put a lot of strain on their hip muscles. Some skeletons suggest a repeated movement of the left arm, probably linked to a particular craft activity (Kale, Üstündağ, Özen, Özgü & Kulakoğlu in this volume).

Some isotope analyses have also been carried out on skeletons exhumed at Kültepe, showing, for example, that one of the individuals discovered in a tomb dated to the end of the third millennium may have been the son of an immigrant woman (Yazıcıoğlu Santamaria 2017). New research is now focusing on the stable carbon and nitrogen isotopes in the collagen of human and animal bones from the Early and Middle Bronze Age, making it possible to determine certain dietary habits. The results indicate a mixed diet of animal and vegetable proteins, with no discernible difference between male and female or between adults and children. However, this is only a preliminary study based on a limited sample (Özdemir, Üstündağ, Doğan, Kulak & Kulakoğlu in this volume). DNA analyses are underway and the forthcoming study will involve a larger number of human and animal skeletons.

The fauna unearthed between 2020 and 2022 was systematically analysed. A large number of animal remains were discovered in a monumental building located in the south-western part of the mound and dating from the last phase of occupation of the site in the Middle Bronze (level 7). In addition to domestic animals raised for their meat and fleece, mainly sheep and goats, or for transport, such as equids, the wild species are particularly varied, and the discovery of faunal remains of large felids, such as lions, suggests that the local ruler was a hunter (Kulakoğlu, Peyronel & Minniti in this volume). Excavations carried out in the same area during the early 2023 season have completed certain skeletons of a lion and a bear, and broadened the range of wildlife that was hunted in the vicinity of Kültepe.

Recent Discoveries at Kültepe and Vicinity

The last and larger section of this volume, arranged chronologically, includes the most recent discoveries made at Kültepe, including some results of 2022 excavations which took place just after the fifth Kültepe International Meeting. The stratigraphy of the Early and Middle Bronze Age levels has been partially reconstituted thanks to a survey carried out on the mound between 2015 and 2017 (Kulakoğlu et al. 2020). However, we do not know much about the occupation of the site before the Early Bronze Age. A survey carried out in the southern part of the Waršama Palace (Central Trench) between 2021 and 2022 revealed a building with a zigzag plan dated to the end of the Late Chalcolithic (end of the fourth millennium) and thus provided a better understanding of the material culture of this period. In 2023, the Turkish-Japanese team hopes to reach the virgin soil of this level and possibly discover an earlier level (Fikri Kulakoğlu, Ryoichi Kontani & Yuji Yamaguchi in this volume).

Excavations carried out at Kültepe over the last decade have especially made it possible to reassess the evolution of occupation of the mound between the second half of the third millennium and the beginning of the second millennium. The simple buildings of the Early Bronze I and II, were replaced during the next phase by large constructions testifying to the importance acquired by the site in the network of international exchanges (Kulakoğlu 2017). In the last centuries of the third millennium, buildings on level 11a located in the Central Early Bronze Age Trench, in the south-west of the mound spread southwards and were connected to form a district of workshops and private houses, indicating an evolution in the occupation plan of this area (Rıdvanoğulları, Öztürk, Ay, Genç & Kulakoğlu in this volume). Consequently, as the population of the Lower Town grew with the arrival of the Assyrians, individuals settled on the outskirts of the mound, as evidenced by the presence of a few tablets with private contents discovered during previous excavations (Donbaz 1998; Michel 2019, 128–30).

Since 2019, the Turkish-Italian team has been carrying out excavations in the south-western sector of the mound, an area that is helping to refine the chronology of levels 10 to 6. Excavations have focused on the south terrace complex (designated as the Palace on the South Terrace by Özgüç 1999, 106–16). Archaeologists have uncovered a room referred to as the 'Burnt Room' (levels 10–18), belonging to that complex, and to the north of the latter, a large semi-underground building, the 'Stone Building' (level 7). Radiocarbon analysis of the Stone Building indicates that this complex should be dated to the eighteenth century BC (Kulakoğlu &

Peyronel in this volume). A large number of ceramic assemblages discovered in the Stone Building provide a better understanding of the evolution of material culture during this period (Kulakoğlu, Peyronel, Oselini & Vacca in this volume).

With regard to the Lower Town of Kültepe at the beginning of the second millennium, comparisons with other contemporary central Anatolian sites belonging to the same ceramic cultural area show certain similarities in their architectural planning. Thus, in level 5 of Kayalıpınar, west of Sivas, the buildings have a similar orientation to those of the Lower Town of Kültepe levels II and Ib, suggesting similar urban planning perhaps linked to the point of sunrise on the day of the summer solstice (Müller-Karpe in this volume).

The site of Kayalıpınar, the ancient Šamuha, has so far yielded two Old Assyrian tablets (Sommerfeld 2006; Kryszat 2019). But it is attested more than twenty times in the texts from Kültepe, and the town included an Assyrian settlement: it was relatively small during the nineteenth century (*wabartum*), but was upgraded to a *kārum* during the eighteenth century (Barjamovic 2011, 151).

Since 2006, excavations at Kültepe have focused on the mound, where only forty cuneiform tablets have been unearthed during the earlier excavations. However, the regular clean-up operations carried out in the Lower Town, to remove the fast-growing vegetation, are often accompanied by the discovery of a few tablets. Just after the 5th KIM, Tarik Öğreten, who is writing a PhD thesis at the University of Ankara on the architecture of the Lower Town level II, incorporating the archives of the Kültepe archaeological mission and his observations in the field, while trying to define the outline of the walls of Kuliya's house in the company of Adam Anderson and Anita Fattori, discovered two tablets and an envelope belonging to this merchant's archive.[1] These tablets were probably inserted into the wall of the house, perhaps reused as a building material, as is the case, for example, in some houses of Old Babylonian Nippur where school tablets were used to build a basin or in the pavement of a courtyard (Robson 2001). It has been decided to include an edition of these three texts, discovered in 2022, in this volume as they complement the edition of the Kuliya archive published by Klaas Veenhof in 2010 (KT 5). The two loan contracts record silver and goods that Kuliya has lent to other merchants and are connected to other texts of his archive (Anderson in this volume).

The last phase of occupation in the Middle Bronze Age, contemporary with the last three kings of Kaneš, Pithana, Anitta, and Zuzu (second half of the eighteenth century), in the southern zone of the mound, has been the focus of particular attention in recent years. The Stone Building discovered by the Turkish-Italian team is located to the west of Temple II. In the basement of this building, one of the rooms was used for storage, with very high-capacity pithoi (up to 2000 litres), and in the next room, the archaeologists discovered an abundance of ceramic vessels, including two exceptional pithoi with applied geometric and figurative decorations (see the photo on the cover of this volume). These discoveries, along with the numerous faunal remains unearthed (see above), suggest that feasts must have been held here on a regular basis, and confirm the interpretation of a ceremonial area (Kulakoğlu & Peyronel in this volume).

During the Hellenistic period, Kültepe, known as Anisa, was a small town in Cappadocia, depending on the capital Eusebia (Barjamovic 2015). The Hellenistic levels of the site, explored in recent years, show continuous occupation between the end of the fourth century and the end of the first century BC. Discoveries made in a partially excavated building revealed in the upper layers of the main Early Bronze Age Trench, which has been systematically explored since 2020, suggest that it was used for religious purposes. It is not impossible that it was a place of worship for a goddess, as a figurine of this deity holding a pomegranate has been unearthed. In 2022, the northern part of the building was excavated, showing two very distinct phases, both of which produced a substantial number of ceramics, typical of this period; two coins were unearthed, probably dating from the third century BC (Tüysüz & Rıdvanoğulları in this volume).

Some Promising Current Research

Other papers presented at this 5th KIM herald important results for the coming years. Some of the most important research in progress for both the archaeologists and philologists working on Kültepe is a detailed architectural study of the Lower Town level II. Among other things, this involves reconstructing the plan of the area excavated between 1948 and 2005, and attributing the tablets and other objects found there to each of the houses (T. Öğreten). The plan reconstructed by

---

1 Another tablet was found in the house of the family of Ali-ahum and his son Aššur-taklāku excavated in 1993 (Kt 22/k 4). It is a loan contract and Aššur-taklāku is the creditor. This tablet will be published together with the archive of this family in the series *Kültepe Tabletleri*.

T. Hertel (2014) was based on scattered publications of certain houses, or quarters; the new work is also based on archive plans, excavation notebooks, and photographs, as well as the remains of walls still visible on the ground. This long-awaited work by Kültepe specialists should make it possible to complete the identification of the individuals and families who lived in these houses.

In addition, preliminary DNA analyses have been carried out on more than a hundred Middle Bronze Age individuals in order to determine their genetic pattern, highlight individuals with similar genetic heritages, and then compare them with data known from elsewhere. Initial results have made it possible to identify members of the same family and have revealed the existence of a few individuals from the Levant and the Caucasus (A. Akbaba, S. Özen, S. Yorulmaz, M. Somel & H. Üstündağ).

Pending the publication of this ongoing research, this new volume in the KIM series makes available to researchers the results of the most recent works carried out on the site of Kültepe and the surrounding area.

After three intensive days of presentations, on 2 August 2022, the participants enjoyed an exciting guided tour of the site of Boğazkale, the ancient Ḫattuša, capital of the Hittites, led by director of the excavations, Andreas Schachner, with kindness and patience, for which he is greatly thanked (Fig. 1.4).

Figure 1.4: The participants of the 5th KIM visiting Ḫattuša. © Kültepe Archaeological Mission.

Abbreviations

KIM	Kültepe International Meetings.
KT 5	Veenhof, Klaas R., *Kültepe Tabletleri*, 5. Türk Tarih Kurumu Basımevi, Ankara, 2010.
KT 6a-e	Larsen Mogens, Trolle, *Kültepe Tabletleri*, 6. Türk Tarih Kurumu Basımevi, Ankara 2010/2013/2014/2018/2021.
KT 8	Veenhof, Klaas R., *Kültepe Tabletleri*, 8. Türk Tarih Kurumu Basımevi, Ankara, 2017.

Bibliography

Adelhofer, Matthias

2022 'On the Old Assyrian Letter Heading. Playing with Social Hierarchy for Rhetorical Effect', *Chatressar* 3/2: 5–18.

Barjamovic, Gojko

2011 *A Historical Geography of Anatolia in the Old Assyrian Colony Period* (Carsten Niebur Institute Publications 38). Museum Tusculanum Press, Copenhagen.

2015 'Kültepe after Kaneš', in Fikri Kulakoğlu & Cécile Michel (eds), *Proceedings of the 1st Kültepe International Meeting: Kültepe, 19-23 September, 2013; Studies Dedicated to Kutlu Emre* (Kültepe International Meetings 1, Subartu 35). Brepols, Turnhout: 233–42.

Beyer, Wiebke

2019 'The Identification of Scribal Hands on the Basis of an Old Assyrian Archive' (unpublished doctoral thesis, University of Hamburg) <https://ediss.sub.uni-hamburg.de/handle/ediss/8815> [accessed 1 November 2023].

2021 'Teaching in Old Babylonian Nippur, Learning in Old Assyrian Aššur?', in Stefanie Brinkmann, Giovanni Ciotti, Stefano Valente & Eva Maria Wilden (eds), *Education Materialised: Reconstructing Teaching and Learning Contexts through Manuscripts* (Studies in Manuscript Cultures 23). Berlin: De Gruyter: 15–32.

Breniquet, Catherine

2008 *Essai sur le tissage en Mésopotamie, des premières communautés sédentaires au milieu du IIIe millénaire avant J.-C.* (Travaux de la Maison René-Ginouvès 5). De Boccard, Paris.

Donbaz, Veysel

1998 'Tablets from the Palace of Waršuma', in Hayat Erkanal, Veysel Donbaz & Ayşegül Uğuroğlu (eds), *XXXIV Uluslararası Assiriyoloji Kongresi (Istanbul 1987)* (Türk Tarih Kurumu Yayınları 26 D-Sa.3). Türk Tarih Kurumu Basımevi, Ankara: 413–19.

Eidem, Jesper

2011 *The Royal Archives from Tell Leilan: Old Babylonian Letters and Treaties from the Lower Town Palace East* (Publications de l'Institut historique-archéologique néerlandais de Stamboul 117). Nederlands Instituut voor het Nabije Oosten, Leiden.

Günbattı, Cahit

2004 'Two Treaty Texts Found at Kültepe', in Jan Gerrit Dercksen (ed.), *Assyria and Beyond: Studies Presented to Mogens Trolle Larsen* (Publications de l'Institut historique-archéologique néerlandais de Stamboul 100). Nederlands Instituut voor het Nabije Oosten, Leiden: 249–68.

Hertel, Thomas

2014 'The Lower Town of Kültepe: Urban Layout and Population', in Levent Atıcı, Fikri Kulakoğlu, Gojko Barjamovic & Andrew Fairbairn (eds), *Current Research at Kültepe-Kanesh: An Interdisciplinary and Integrative Approach to Trade Networks, Internationalism, and Identity* (Journal of Cuneiform Studies Supplemental Series 4). Lockwood, Atlanta: 25–54.

Kryszat, Guido

1995 'Ilu-šuma und der Gott aus dem Brunnen', in Manfried Dietrich & Oswald Loretz (eds), *Vom Alten Orient zum Alten Testament: Festschrift für Wolfram Freiherrn von Soden zum 85. Geburtstag am 19. Juni 1993* (Alter Orient und Altes Testament 240). Butzon & Bercker, Kevelaer: 201–13.

2019 'Bemerkungen zu den altassyrischen Fragmenten KPT 1.2 und KPT 1.35', in Elisabeth Rieken (ed.), *Keilschrifttafeln aus Kayalipinar, I: Textfunde aus den Jahren 1999-2017* (Documenta antiqua Asiae Minoris). Harrassowitz, Wiesbaden: 111–12.

Kulakoğlu, Fikri

2017 'Early Bronze Age Monumental Structures at Kültepe', in Fikri Kulakoğlu & Gojko Barjamovic (eds), *Movement, Resources, Interaction: Proceedings of the 2nd Kültepe International Meeting; Kültepe, 26-30 July 2015; Studies Dedicated to Klaas Veenhof* (Kültepe International Meetings 2, Subartu 39). Brepols, Turnhout: 215-24.

Kulakoğlu, Fikri; Kontani, Ryoichi; Uesugi, Akinori; Yamaguchi, Yuji; Shimogama, Kazuya & Semmoto, Masao

2020 'Preliminary Report of Excavations in the Northern Sector of Kültepe 2015-2017', in Fikri Kulakoğlu, Cécile Michel & Güzel Öztürk (eds), *Integrative Approaches to the Archaeology and History of Kültepe-Kaneš: Kültepe 4-7 August 2017* (Kültepe International Meetings 3, Subartu 45). Brepols, Turnhout: 9-97.

Lassen, Agnete Wisti

2012 'Glyptic Encounters: A Stylistic and Prosopographical Study of Seals in the Old Assyrian Period; Chronology, Ownership and Identity' (unpublished doctoral thesis, University of Copenhagen).

2014 'The Old Assyrian Glyptic Style: An Investigation of a Seal Style, its Owners, and Place of Production', in Levent Atıcı, Fikri Kulakoğlu, Gojko Barjamovic & Andrew Fairbairn (eds), *Current Research at Kültepe-Kanesh: An Interdiciplinary and Integrative Approach to Trade Networks, Internationalism, and Identity* (Journal of Cuneiform Studies Supplemental Series 4). Lockwood, Atlanta: 107-22.

2017 'The "Bull-Altar" in Old Assyrian Glyptic: A Representation of the God Assur?', in Fikri Kulakoğlu & Gojko Barjamovic (eds), *Proceedings of the 2nd Kültepe International Meeting: Kültepe, 26-30 July 2015; Studies Dedicated to Klaas Veenhof* (Kültepe International Meetings 2, Subartu 39). Brepols, Turnhout: 177-94.

Michel, Cécile

2008 'Écrire et compter chez les marchands assyriens du début du IIe millénaire av. J.-C.', in Taner Tarhan, Aksel Tibet & Erkan Konyar (eds), *Muhibbe Darga Armağanı*. Sadberk Hanım Müzesi, Istanbul: 345-64.

2009 'Les femmes et l'écrit dans les archives paléo-assyriennes (XIXe s. av. J.-C.)', in Françoise Briquel-Chatonnet, Saba Fares, Brigitte Lion & Cécile Michel (eds), *Femmes, cultures et sociétés dans les civilisations méditerranéennes et proches-orientales de l'Antiquité* (Topoi, Suppl. 10). Maison de l'Orient et de la Méditerranée, Lyon: 253-72.

2018 'Constitution, Contents, Filing and Use of Private Archives: The Case of the Old Assyrian Archives (19th Century BC)', in Alessandro Bausi, Christian Brockman, Michael Friedrich & Sabine Kienitz (eds), *Manuscripts and Archives: Comparative Views on Record-Keeping* (Studies in Manuscript Cultures 11). Berlin: De Gruyter, 43-70.

2019 'Palaces at Kaneš during the Old Assyrian Period', in Dirk Wicke (ed.), *Der Palast im antiken und islamischen Orient: 9. Internationales Colloquium der Deutschen Orient-Gesellschaft 30. März - 1. April 2016*. Harrassowitz, Wiesbaden: 121-38.

2020a *Women of Aššur and Kaneš: Texts from the Archives of Assyrian Merchants* (Writings from the Ancient World 42). SBL Press, Atlanta.

2020b 'Making Clay Envelopes in the Old Assyrian Period', in Fikri Kulakoğlu, Cécile Michel & Güzel Öztürk (eds), *Integrative Approaches to the Archaeology and History of Kültepe-Kanesh, Kültepe, 4-7 August, 2017* (Kültepe International Meetings 3, Subartu 45). Brepols, Turnhout: 187-203.

2023 'Gendered Private Letters: The Case of the Old Assyrian Correspondence (Nineteenth Century BC)', in Madalina Dana (ed.), *La correspondance privée dans la Méditerranée antique: sociétés en miroir*. Ausonius, Bordeaux: 223-41.

Özgüç, Nimet

2006 *Kültepe-Kaniš/Neša: Seal Impressions on the Clay Envelopes from the Archives of the Native Peruwa and Assyrian Trader Uṣur-ša-Ištar Son of Aššur-imittī* (Türk Tarih Kurumu Yayınları 5/50). Türk Tarih Kurumu Basımevi, Ankara.

Özgüç, Nimet & Önhan, Tunca

2001 *Kültepe-Kaniš: Sealed and Inscribed Clay Bullae* (Türk Tarih Kurumu Yayınları 5/48). Türk Tarih Kurumu Basımevi, Ankara.

Özguç, Tahsin

1999 *Kültepe-Kaniş/Neşa Saraylari ve Mabetleri / The Palaces and Temples of Kültepe-Kaniš/Neša* (Türk Tarih Kurumu Yayınları 5/46). Türk Tarih Kurumu Basimevi, Ankara.

Robson, Eleanor

2001 'The Tablet House: A Scribal School in Old Babylonian Nippur', *Revue d'assyriologie et d'archéologie orientale* 93: 39–66.

Sommerfeld, Walter

2006 'Ein altassyrisches Tontafelfragment aus Kayalıpınar', in Andreas Müller-Karpe, 'Untersuchungen in Kayalıpınar 2005' with contributions by Vuslat Müller-Karpe, Elisabeth Rieken, Walter Sommerfeld, Gernot Wilhelm & Manuel Zeiler, *Mitteilungen der Deutschen Orient-Gesellschaft* 138: 231–33.

Tessier, Béatrice

1994 *Sealing and Seals on Texts from Kültepe Kārum Level 2* (Publications de l'Institut historique-archéologique néerlandais de Stamboul 120). Nederlands Instituut voor het Nabije Oosten, Leiden.

Üstündağ, Handan

2009 'Kültepe/Kanesh (Turkey), Season 2007', *Bioarchaeology of the Near East* 3: 31–35.

2014 'Human Remains from Kültepe-Kanesh: Preliminary Results of the Old Assyrian Burials from the 2005–2008 Excavations', in Levent Atıcı, Fikri Kulakoğlu, Gojko Barjamovic & Andrew Fairbairn (eds), *Current Research at Kültepe-Kanesh: An Interdisciplinary and Integrative Approach to Trade Networks, Internationalism, and Identity* (Journal of Cuneiform Studies Supplemental Series 4). Lockwood, Atlanta: 157–76.

Yazıcıoğlu Santamaria, G. B.

2017 'Locals, Immigrants, and Marriage Ties at Kültepe. Results of Strontium Isotope Analysis on Human Teeth from Lower Town Graves', in Fikri Kulakoğlu & Gojko Barjamovic (eds), *Movement, Resources, Interaction: Proceedings of the 2nd Kültepe International Meeting Kültepe; 26-30 July 2015* (Kültepe International Meeting 2, Subartu 39). Brepols, Turnhout: 63–84.

POLITICS, LAW AND RELIGION

2. A City-State's Diplomacy in the Early Middle Bronze Age Near East

Jan Gerrit Dercksen & Jacob Jan de Ridder

Introduction

The city-state of Aššur seems to have largely led a peaceful existence until it was conquered by Šamšī-Adad I in 1808 BC. At least, this is the picture that emerges from the evidence largely excavated at Kaneš (modern Kültepe). There is one potential mention of warfare during the reign of Ilu-šūma; an otherwise unknown tradition preserved in a Late Babylonian chronicle connects this king with 'warfare'.[1] Otherwise, there are no references that lead us to assume that pre-Šamšī-Adad Aššur possessed any military capacity. Whereas other, more powerful states, relied on a combination of military power and diplomacy to achieve their political goals, Aššur did so by means of diplomacy and its economic potential. The mercantile capacities of the city-state, its skilled merchants, and in general the interdependency of the city-state and its merchants, provided it with a strong position in negotiations with foreign kings, whose merchants did not travel to Anatolia or who depended on Assyrian import of tin.

The careful analysis presented by Larsen (1976) of the political structure of the Old Assyrian city-state and the role of the envoys of the city as diplomats has not lost its significance, although written nearly fifty years ago. Since then, several tablets with international treaties, whose content was reconstructed by Larsen, have been identified. In this article, we will review the most salient evidence presently available on diplomatic activities by Aššur, loosely arranged chronologically, including the discussion of a fragmentary letter excavated at Kültepe.

The Political Landscape of Anatolia during the Level II Period

During the Old Assyrian Colony Period Anatolia was fragmented in kingdoms of varying power.[2] The most powerful among these was no doubt Burušhattum, where the ruler was being referred to as *rubāʾum rabium* 'great king' (e.g. TTC 27:7, see Barjamovic 2011, 378). These city-states were frequently at war with each other and this could have serious consequences; for example, during the late level II period the Assyrian merchants suddenly had to leave Wahšušana after which the town was destroyed and the Assyrian tablets were looted and offered for sale.[3]

It is not entirely clear how and when Assyrian caravans started to travel to Anatolia, where several trade colonies were founded. According to a recent theory

---

1 The Chronicle of Early Kings ll. 37–38: 'Ilu-šūma was king of Assyria in the time of Su-abu. Battles (?)', see Grayson 1975, 155, no. 20A:37–38; Glassner 2004, 271.

Jan Gerrit Dercksen (j.g.dercksen@hum.leidenuniv.nl) Lecturer in Assyriology at the Leiden Institute of Area Studies, Leiden University

Jacob Jan de Ridder (jacob_jan.de_ridder.2@uni-leipzig.de) Privatdozent at Leipzig University

2 The word colony denotes a group of persons living abroad but continuing to have political, religious, economic, and social ties with their city of origin. See also Michel 2014, 70–71.

3 For this event in Kt 87/k 40 following KT 5, 15, see the initial edition in Hecker 2003 and the studies by Dercksen 2004, 116, 143–44; Veenhof 2008, 136–40; Barjamovic 2011, 349; de Ridder 2021a, 74–75.

trade first began in the Syrian region, with the early colony of Hahhum as starting point for traders selling their merchandise in Anatolia before the foundation of a new trading centre in Kaneš, as Hahhum is frequently mentioned in the Ur III documentation while Kaneš is virtually absent.[4] The main Assyrian colony was Kaneš, in part due to its central location, where the Assyrian office was the main authority over the other colonies and the smaller trading stations (*wabartum*) in the region. For important affairs communication between the traders and the city-state of Aššur as well as with the local Anatolian king passed through this colony.

The Role of the King of Aššur (*waklum*) in the Level II Period

Before the political unification under Šamšī-Adad, northern Mesopotamia was also home to various smaller city-states of which the city of Aššur was only one. Aššur in this period seems to have been led by a city assembly, with the ruler (*waklum*) acting as its chairman rather than possessing absolute power. At least this was the case until Šamšī-Adad took over. The *waklum* would send letters on behalf of the city assembly to Kaneš, communicating verdicts and other decisions they had taken. However, in addition to being sent to the colony, copies were also sent to some of the more important traders who archived them, but would take them out when they were required to add weight to legal affairs (Veenhof 2019, 442–46). More rarely, the *waklum* wrote directly to traders when he had to communicate legal affairs in which they were involved (Hertel 2013, 36; Veenhof 2019, 447–48). There is very little evidence for the Assyrian ruler sending messages to Anatolian kings, but we cannot exclude this, for the official archives of the Anatolian and Assyrian palaces are missing. The Hurmeli letter from the Ib period, to be discussed below, seems to be the only surviving remnant of the diplomatic correspondence that once existed between the government of Aššur and foreign rulers. From the late level II period, the Liepsner tablet offers another perspective on diplomacy between Aššur and an Anatolian ruler (de Ridder & Kryszat 2023). Despite is fragmentary state, that letter suggests that the *waklum* was giving instructions to a party of Assyrians on behalf of the city council with the goal of solving their dispute with the Anatolian ruler caused by the murder of a group of his subjects. Since many of the details of the letter are lost, it seems that the solution of the *waklum* was to follow the demand of the *rubāʾum* and pay the blood money in gold. The extraordinary fact of this unusual document remains that, despite apparently having murdered some of his subjects, the Anatolian king only asked for financial compensation rather than the heads of the Assyrian culprits. A similar case is the legal *waklum*-letter Kt 91/k 100 (Veenhof 2019), which is also fragmentary, but has the *waklum* providing legal counsel on a caravan belonging to Puzur-Aššur which had been detained in Zalpa for over eight months, presumably due to its involvement in smuggling. Finally, the fragmentary letter TC 1, 40 must be mentioned (Larsen 1976, 251 n. 7; Michel 2001, 78–79 no. 17). The letter was written by the envoys from Aššur and *kārum* Kaneš to other envoys, presumably those from *kārum* Kaneš. The letter itself discussed what is expected from a local king (*rubāʾum*). The affairs may very well relate to the renegotiations of an oath, which will be discussed below and suggests that the government of Aššur played a large and direct role in these diplomatic affairs of Anatolia.

Treaties

For the most part, the Assyrian traders were operating independently of the Assyrian government. In the letters exchanged between the colony of Kaneš and Anatolian kings, the Assyrians never invoke any authority of the city of Aššur. Yet, the existence of the trade colonies was the result of treaties which Aššur concluded with local kings (Veenhof 2008, 183–218; 2013). Only three treaties have survived, all from the level Ib period. These are the treaties with the rulers of Kaneš (Kt 00/k 6) and Hahhum (Kt 00/k 10), published by Günbattı (2004). The third treaty is one with the kingdom of Apûm in northern Mesopotamia (L.T. 5 in Eidem 2011). A document from the level II period contains part of the text of a treaty (Kt n/k 794 in Çeçen & Hecker 1995). The responsibility for negotiating a treaty was carried fully by the colony of Kaneš, which would lead the procedures on behalf of the smaller colonies or trading posts. The role of the government of Aššur in such procedures remains obscure. It is imaginable that the other trade colonies apart from *kārum* Kaneš, such as that of the powerful local kingdom of Burušhattum exercised similar diplomatic tasks for smaller trading posts in their vicinity, but this cannot be confirmed with the evidence available from Kültepe. Each treaty was concluded with an individual ruler and lasted as long as his reign. This meant that upon the death of any local king a new treaty had to be concluded between the new

---

4 See Larsen 2010, 8; Barjamovic et al. 2012, 62; Dercksen 2022, 82.

ruler and the Assyrian colonial authorities. The procedure is best described in KTP 14 concerning the king of Wašhaniya, who upon deposing his father from the throne asked the Assyrian *wabartum* of his town to conclude a new oath. As per the usual praxis, the *wabartum* of Wašhaniya fell under the authority of the colony of Kaneš, therefore a delegation consisting of two men was sent from Kaneš to take the oath from the new king.[5]

The goal of renewed negotiations on a treaty is clear: it allowed both sides to adjust the conditions to the current circumstances, and thus pressure could be exercised to force compromises on the other party. This tactic is attested in Kt h/k 317 (Albayrak 2008), a letter by a new Anatolian king (*rubāʾum*) addressed to the colony of Kaneš. There may be two separate issues at play in these negotiations. The first lines suggest there was an ongoing lawsuit and the king seems to suggest that he can withdraw himself altogether, but the colony cannot (presumably as this would cease all trade): 'What oath are you requesting me (to accept)? I can withdraw myself from the legal proceedings, (but) you cannot withdraw!'[6] On the reverse of this tablet, the king mentions an Anatolian named Anupiya bringing merchandise that must be bought by the colony before taking the oath. However, not only the Anatolian side tried to manipulate the negotiations in order to arrive at a treaty more favourable for them. In KT 8, 274 it is openly said that the oath is supposed to help the Assyrians control the Anatolian ruler:[7]

> We will make the man of Kukrin, the ruler, swear the oath so that we may control him.

Negotiations did not always go smoothly, as can be observed from the palace revolt in Hahhum which is described in a number of letters to Innāya.[8] In CCT 4, 30a (ll. 13–15) this revolt is mentioned (*šarrum dāmē ētapaš-ma* 'the king committed bloodshed'), and as his throne is not secure (*kussīšu lā taqnat*) the agreements are suspended (*šiknātum ahhurā*).[9] According to Larsen (1976, 271) the Assyrian *ešartum* 'ten-man board' at Hahhum was leading the negotiations with the palace. Copies of the treaty (*mehrāt māmītem* ll. 8–9) were written for the colony and a settlement was agreed on, but the local nobles (*awīlū* l. 12) changed their mind, which possibly refers to events prior to the revolt. In CCT 6, 15b, another letter dealing with the revolt in Hahhum, it is discussed how the nobles (*rubāʾū*) of the city refused to hear letters from the colony brought by the *ešartum* 'ten-man board'.[10]

Diplomatic Gifts

Following the agreement on the conditions of the proposed treaty the Anatolian ruler formally accepted it by taking an oath (*māmītum*). Usually the colony of Kaneš was responsible for taking the oaths of the new rulers, as can be observed in the following letter:[11]

> Speak to the Kaneš colony, thus the colony of Hurama: The king of Hurama has issued an oath.

In order to smooth the process of subjecting the king to the oath, gifts could be sent, as in Kt f/k 183 (Larsen 1976, 274 n. 64; Barjamovic 2011, 310 n. 1260). In this level Ib letter the colony of Tawiniya wrote to Kaneš, when the colony of Durhumit sent gifts to the king, yet the king refused them and insisted on taking the oath from the envoys of Kaneš. According to Larsen, this letter is a sign of shifting political landscapes as the colony of Kaneš was not the only authority anymore for having local kings swear an oath, as also a lesser colony such as that in Durhumit could send envoys to carry out the procedure.

---

5 KTP 14:1–22, see the discussion in Barjamovic 2011, 325 n. 1341.

6 Kt h/k 317:5–10 *mīnam māmītam ša terrišanni anāku ramīnī ina dittem šalāham aleʾʾe attūnu šalāham lā taleʾʾeā*.

7 KT 8, 274:9'–11' *Kukrinīam rubāʾum lū nutammī[ma] qātni lukaʾʾilšu*. Only the lower part of this large letter remains, so that the context of this phrase remains vague. The town Kukrin is otherwise unknown. See Veenhof 2017a, 388–89.

8 See Larsen 1976, 271; Michel 1991, 183–84; Garelli 1998; Barjamovic 2011, 106.

9 The revolt is also mentioned in CCT 4, 40a (*sihītum* l. 19), see Barjamovic 2011, 106 n. 300.

10 Perhaps not directly related to the negotiation of a commercial treaty are a few references with regard to the oath for the rulers of Kaneš and Wašhaniya. In ATHE 66 (ll. 9–11) Puzur-Aššur mentions that an oath was brought to the rulers of Kaneš and Wašhaniya, but until the new oath was sworn trade was effectively brought to a halt. Another letter, Kt n/k 1251 (Sever & Çeçen 1993), seemingly relating to the same events (Barjamovic 2011, 325–26) features a request of some Assyrian colleagues to travel to Wašhaniya, but not to enter it until things calm down. It therefore seems that the 'oath' between Kaneš and Wašhaniya may well refer to a peace treaty between both Anatolian states rather than to a commercial treaty with the Assyrians. Note also the king of Wašhaniya returning from war (*ina sikkātem itūranni*) in Kt g/k 185:3–6 (Barjamovic 2011, 324 n. 1137).

11 Kt m/k 134:1–5: *ana kārem [Kaneš] qibīma umma k[ārum] Huramama rubāʾum Hura[maium] māmītam iddi[nma]*. The remainder of the letter is only fragmentarily preserved. See also Barjamovic 2011, 184 n. 640.

The word for gift in this period was *erbum* (< *irbum, Kouwenberg 2017, 124 § 4.2.2.6). These gifts could be presented by Assyrian envoys to the local king on other occasions as well, as is the case in the letter TC 3, 85, where the king of Zalpa received an *erbum*-gift of 9 shekels of gold during an audience about lost silver. Barjamovic (2011, 310) suggested that the *erbum* was part of a ceremonial exchange where neither party would state the value of the *erbum* beforehand.[12] He based himself on two texts concerning the exchange of gifts with the ruler of Tuhpiya (see Dercksen 2007, 197): TC 1, 39 and Kt 85/k 27 (Günbattı 1996). Kt 85/k 27 was sent by the king himself where he lists several *erbum*-gifts from different Assyrians while stating what he gave these traders in return. The ruler concluded that he had fulfilled his obligations and that there was nothing to claim from his palace for the traders.

It seems from Kt n/k 388 (Günbattı 1996) that one of the purposes of giving an *erbum*-gift was to receive an audience with the king as the local ruler of Tawiniya discussed several diplomatic affairs upon receiving his gift.[13] Later in the same letter it becomes clear that the king and queen had already specified what they would receive as an *erbum* on the next occasion: a white robe and a *kutānum*-textile. In this regard KT 11a, 31 may be mentioned, where a textile of fine quality was already bought to serve as a gift, but it could not yet be given to the Anatolian king as a problem arose (probably during the negotiations of a treaty) and the ruler sent an Assyrian envoy to *kārum* Kaneš with his terms. More garments were given as *nišʾum* 'gift' (l. 6) on an unidentified occasion to the queen of Wahšušana in KTS 50 (EL 150, see Veenhof 1989, 522). From the level Ib period, the Assyrian elders sent a humble letter and a gift (*tāmartum* l. 61) of one hundred textiles to Hurmeli king of Harsamna to persuade him to reopen the roads for trading.[14]

The Safety of Assyrian Traders

As the Assyrians traded in foreign lands their personal safety and that of their merchandise fell under the responsibility of the rulers of the various local kingdoms. This was one of the main points of the treaties concluded between Assyrians and Anatolian kings, as can be observed in the first lines of the level Ib treaty with Kaneš:[15]

> If the blood of a citizen of Aššur is shed in your city or in your land (and) a loss will occur, you shall pay the fixed amount for the blood money to us and we will kill him (i.e. the murderer).

Similar phrases are found in the treaty from level Ib with Hahhum (Kt 00/k 10:15'–18') and a treaty quoted in the draft Kt n/k 794:1–11 (Çeçen & Hecker 1995). The main point always being, the killers of any Assyrian shall be handed over and be put to death, and lost merchandise is to be restored by the Anatolian ruler, who also has to pay blood money. The amount of a payment as blood money is not specified, but does not seem to be equal to the lost property (*huluqqāʾum*) as can be seen in KT 6a, 146 (ll. 7–10). There are a few cases where we learn of the practicalities of the blood money.[16] According to Kayseri 1830 (Hecker 1996), two Assyrians were killed in the land of Luhusattiya. However, as these Assyrians were killed somewhere remote in the mountains, there was no one who could identify the killed merchants. There was no colony in this state and therefore the *wabartum* of Kuššara wrote to the envoy of Aššur and to the colony of Kaneš, thus applying to the two main centres of Assyrian political power (Barjamovic 2011, 27 n. 118).

The best-known case about blood money is found in the Šalim-Aššur family archive, in the dossier about his son Ennam-Aššur, who was murdered in the kingdom Tawiniya (texts KT 6c, 523–33, analysed in Hertel 2013, 297–98). His brother Ali-ahum intended to extract blood money from the local king for his murdered brother. When Ennam-Aššur was murdered, he had been selling meteoritic iron from another Assyrian named Itūr-ilī in Tawiniya to the king; details of this trading enterprise are described in KT 6c, 524. Ennam-Aššur had concluded

---

12 For the reciprocity of ceremonial gift exchange in the ancient Near East, see Zaccagnini 1987.

13 A similar audience is granted by a ruler upon receiving a gift in Kt 87/k 249, although as we will see, things did not go as planned for the Assyrian trader: *u ša [er]bēka apallaska* 'concerning your gift I will look (friendly) at you' ll. 12–13 (Hecker 1996, 157).

14 The reconstruction of the sender follows Dercksen 2015. The word *tāmartum* is not attested elsewhere in the Old Assyrian period (already Günbattı 2014, 21), but is common in Old Babylonian texts where it can serve to receive an audience (Durand 1988, 103) or to conclude an agreement (de Ridder 2021b, 92); a gift made by the merchant Innaya to the king of Tell Leilan is called *tāmartum* (Vincente 1991, no. 153, dated to REL 224).

15 Kt 00/k 6:39–44 *inūmi dāmum [ša mār] Aššur ina ālēka [ū māt] ēka innepušūni [hulu]qqāʾum ibaššiūni [an]a dāmē šīmtam [tadd]ananniātima nidu(w)ākšu* (Günbattı 2004).

16 Only a few cases of blood money being extracted from an Assyrian party are known: Kt b/k 162a-b (Çeçen 1998, 293–94; Hecker 2007, 83 n. 30) with related Kt b/k 12; TC 2, 12; VS 26, 2.

his transactions and was on the way back when he was killed. This means that the murder was not only the concern of Ali-ahum and the family, but also of Itūr-ilī, whose money was gone. The colony in Kaneš sent Ali-ahum as one of the envoys to meet the king in person as we learn from the draft of a letter (KT 6c, 527).

It seems to be common practice for the colony in Kaneš to send envoys to the cities where Assyrians were killed, in order to negotiate with the local ruler how to handle the affair. This happened according to Kayseri 1830 (see above) and is also attested in KT 6, 146 where Karwāʾu and the well-known Pūšu-kēn are sent to Burušhattum because of the murder of an Assyrian, the blood money, and the lost silver. In case of the murder of Ennam-Aššur, it is noticeable that his brother Ali-ahum was sent as an envoy, as he would also be the beneficiary of the payment of blood money. This may have presented an unwanted conflict of interest and in one letter Idnaya questions Ali-ahum for having accepted the role of envoy (KT 6c, 526). According to Larsen (2014, 35), Ali-ahum may have taken up the position of envoy as an earlier mission sent from Kaneš included his colleague Damiq-pî-Aššur, who when in the presence of the king of Tawiniya read a message of Itūr-ilī, the rival of Ali-ahum. No blood money was paid and Ali-ahum had Damiq-pî-Aššur removed from the affair (KT 6c, 525).

When Ali-ahum and the second envoy went to the king of Tawiniya in order to request help in finding the murderer the ruler refused to help in a reply that is unfortunately partly broken (KT 6c, 527). The king seems to have motivated his rejection by the costs he had already incurred from the affair. One wonders whether anything Damiq-pî-Aššur arranged on behalf of Itūr-ilī may have spoiled the chances of Ali-ahum obtaining financial compensation in Tawiniya. The situation was hostile or the lands in general were not safe as Ali-ahum complains that the affair had endangered his life. The refusal of the king of Tawiniya to assist Ali-ahum in obtaining blood money is a direct violation of the treaty. It may suggest that Ennam-Aššur had been smuggling when he was killed, but there is no evidence for this. The ruler's refusal may not have been without consequences, as one reference in a judicial document appears to state that nobody may cross through Tawiniya (*ebar Tawiniya*) until blood money is extracted (KT 6c, 530). This would in effect impose an embargo on trade with that city as the king had broken the law.

Punishment for Smuggling and Other Crimes

The protection granted to Assyrian traders by the Anatolian rulers required the Assyrians to declare their merchandise openly by registering it at the palace in Kaneš. Without this, it would not be possible to compensate anything that was robbed when the traders travelled through the local kingdom. Moreover, undeclared merchandise could not be taxed, which is effectively smuggling (*pazzurtum*), a practice rigorously prosecuted by the local Anatolian government, often in cooperation with the Assyrian authorities.[17] As the treaties never directly mention smuggling, the illegal character of the activity was well understood as is evident by the strong measures the Anatolians took to counter it.[18] These measures were effective in discouraging some culprits as is illustrated by the following example:[19]

> Errāya sent his smuggled goods to Pūšu-kēn, but his smuggled goods were seized. The palace threw Pūšu-kēn in jail. The guard posts are strong. (ATHE 62:30–33)

The letter continues discussing how the queen of Kaneš had written to several neighbouring cities for assistance in combatting the smuggling by the traders. The measures had the desired discouraging effect as ATHE 62 ends with the conclusion that they should give up smuggling and any *ašium*-meteoritic iron that was already smuggled should be safely deposited until things would cool down. Further proof of the effectiveness of the alliance between Kaneš and the other cities can be found in letters from other archives where the severe guarding of the smuggling routes is discussed, e.g. KT 6d, 771 (Barjamovic 2011, 175–76). The campaigns against smuggling affected all Assyrians, whether they smuggled or not, as in general the illegal act of smuggling spoiled the relations with the local palace. As we already discussed, the *waklum*-letter Kt 91/k 100 (Veenhof 2019) is a rare case where the Assyrian ruler involved himself in such diplomatic affairs by writing to the Assyrians about the detainment of a caravan in Zalpa, that was suspected of smuggling.

---

17 See for instance KTH 13 (ll. 4–10): 2 *miʾat* 12 túg sig₅ diri *Abu-ilī našʾakkunūti šumma pazzuršunu taleʾʾā pazzirāšunu šumma pazzuršunu lā taleʾʾā ana ekallem šēliāšunūma e*[*kallum*] *nishātīšunu li*[*lq*]*ēma* 'Abu-ilī is bringing you 212 good textiles. If you can, smuggle them! (But) if you are unable, bring them to the palace and the pa[lace] shall take its *nishātum*-tax.'

18 The act of smuggling and the common routes have been discussed extensively in the past. Most notably by Veenhof 1972, 305–44 and Barjamovic 2011, 169–80.

19 The seizure of smuggled goods is further attested in I 509.

However, the local colony offices would also attempt to discourage smuggling, with some success as is evident from letters where Assyrians were asking each other to stop the smuggling attempts (CTMMA 1, 72:28–32). It is possible that the *kārum* would imprison its own merchants when they found out that smuggling had taken place: this seems a possibility for WAG 48.1465 (Larsen 1978) where the reason of imprisonment was the sale of meteoritic iron (*amūtum*) in Burušhattum. Throwing people into jail (*kišeršum*), as happened to Pūšu-kēn, was not uncommon as it is known to have happened to a few other traders.[20] One of these was Ilīya as described in KT 8, 180:25–26. His crime is not mentioned, but involvement in smuggling is likely. We can be certain that Ilīya was in a prison of the Anatolian authorities, as his ransom was paid by a local businessman (*nuwāʾum*) named Lullu, his father-in-law (ll. 26–31). As we do not hear anything from Ilīya afterwards, except for his family's estate, it seems possible that he died in prison. The best-known case of an Assyrian prisoner is the dossier on Aššur-taklāku, which is prepared for publication by Cécile Michel; parts of it were already discussed extensively, with the charges being espionage and breaking a trade embargo with the ruler of Tawiniya with whom the alliance of Kaneš and Wašhaniya was at war (Michel 2008a, 64; 2008b; Barjamovic 2011, 304–05). This diplomatic incident caused the city assembly of Aššur to become involved, as emerges from the protocol which contains the discussion between the *kārum* delegation and the king and queen.[21]

Aššur after the Conquest by Šamšī-Adad and Afterwards

The Old Babylonian letters and other documents excavated in the palace at Tell Hariri, the ancient city of Mari in eastern Syria demonstrate that around 1765 BC there was intense diplomatic activity with envoys travelling across the region from the Mediterranean coast to Iran (Lafont 2001). They were bringing oral or written messages ('tablets') to or from their lords to other kings, were involved in the negotiations about treaties, and so on. The arrival of these envoys in the territory of the king of Mari and the purpose of their visit were announced to the palace and the envoy was given food and a present if his destination was Mari.

A good example of the geographical range is provided by ARM 6, 23, a letter in which governor Bahdī-Lîm reports from Mari to King Zimrī-Lîm about messengers arriving from Babylon, Ešnunna, Ekallatum, Karana, Qabra, and Arrapha and on their way to Yamhad, Qaṭna, Haṣor, and Karchemiš. Aššur is not mentioned in this particular letter, because at the time it fell under the domination of Ekallatum, ruled by Išme-Dagan, son of Šamšī-Adad. There was, therefore, no ruler of a city-state Aššur who could have his own foreign policy after the Old Assyrian dynasty had been overthrown by Šamšī-Adad in 1808. This leads to the question of how key elements of the earlier Old Assyrian diplomatic system were continued, specifically the concluding of treaties and the role of envoys of the city attested for the first half of the nineteenth century. Considering that Šamšī-Adad reigned over Aššur for thirty-three years, there must have been multiple instances where treaties with kings in Syria and Anatolia, possibly even with the king of Kaneš, were renewed. Unfortunately, not a single piece of evidence has survived from this period, as the few extant Assyrian treaties from the level Ib period found at Kültepe all date to period after Šamšī-Adad's death. Thus, we lack information of whether those earlier treaties were concluded with the city of Aššur, as customary before and after Šamšī-Adad and his successors ruled the city, or whether the king himself acted as treaty party.

Yet we know from a single source that a major part of the political establishment in Aššur did remain active after the conquest by Šamšī-Adad. This source is the so-called Hurmeli letter, published by Cahit Günbattı (2014). The letter dates from shortly after the death of Šamšī-Adad in 1776/1775 BC. It is written against the background of an armed conflict between Zalpa and Harsamna, two regional powers in northern Syria. Šamšī-Adad had provided military support to Zalpa and the king of Harsamna retaliated by seizing an Assyrian caravan. Having seized the Assyrian caravan, the king of Harsamna deemed his negotiating position to be strong

---

[20] Another trader being imprisoned at the palace was Innāya (ICK 1, 1 ll. 29–30). Unclear are the circumstances of an Assyrian being jailed in TC 2, 49 (EL 285), see the discussion in Veenhof 1972, 125. Nūr-Ištar relates in the letter Kt b/k 95 (Balkan 1967) how the recipient, Šu-Bēlum, saved him and his son in the past from prison by speaking for his case. It is uncertain whether this was an Anatolian prison and how this event relates to the rest of the letter. The second section of the letter also involves the chief of the staircase (*rabi simmiltem*). Further attestations of prisons occur in RA 59, 16:28 (MAH 16205); RA 59, 32:17 (MAH 19602); RC 1749 C:18 (edited as OAA 1, 51). For prison in the Old Assyrian period, see Riemschneider 1977, 115–17.

[21] Kt 93/k 145:39–41 (Michel & Garelli 1996) and its duplicate Kt n/k 504:44–46 (Günbattı 2001): *ammala ṭuppem ša ālem kārum Kaneš (ṣaher rabi) iddinniātima* 'In accordance with the tablet of the city the Kaneš colony in plenary session gave us to testify.'

enough to send two envoys, not to Šamšī-Adad, but to what remained of the city-state of Aššur, urging them to interfere on his behalf with Šamšī-Adad. A delegation of merchants had an audience with Šamšī-Adad, but the king gave them a scolding. This may be rather unsurprising information when reading letters from the Mari palace, but by Old Assyrian standards, an account of a discussion with a king is extremely rare. More important is how Šamšī-Adad addresses the delegation. In translation:

> We took this plea to our lord and fell at his feet. But he said: 'You are merchants, my (own) servants. And (are you) also the servants of the man of Harsamna? Truly, you (would then be) carrying a weapon and keep following me. (But) you are merchants. Well then, make business trips as well as you can to conduct your trade! What are you meddling with us, the important kings?' (ll. 35–49)

Šamšī-Adad does not regard the members of the delegation as representatives of a city-state of Aššur, as a political body, because he does not acknowledge any political representation from Aššur. Instead, he sees them as that which constituted the very essence of Aššur: as merchants. Yet, the members of the delegation consider themselves to be the true representatives of Aššur's interests. Their own political position is clear from the address of the letter they sent to the king of Harsamna, but unfortunately the line identifying them is partly broken and what remains is 'of the city of Aššur'. Günbattı restored 'the envoys of the city of Aššur' in his publication of this letter. This seems odd, since the senders are in Aššur and later in the letter write that they are dispatching two other men 'from the Elders, our peers'. For this reason, we should restore the name of the sender as 'the Elders of the city of Aššur' (Dercksen 2015).

During the preceding period of political independence (level II), the Elders (*šēbūtum*) were part of the 'city' (*ālum* in TC 1, 1), the general term for the governing body which also comprised the king of Aššur and the city assembly; the Elders could be appealed to and pass a verdict, which was then communicated to *kārum* Kaneš by the king (AKT 3, 37; Kt c/k 261). They could also receive complaints about a foreign dignitary and take appropriate diplomatic measures (as threatened in Kt m/k 14, Hecker 1996, 148 and Hecker 2007, 89–90). From the Hurmeli letter, written during Aššur's dependence, it seems the Elders still were part of the city's elite.

What is even more interesting is the fact that the two envoys which the Elders are sending to the king of Harsamna and are identified by their name and patronym, are Elders themselves — and a few years later both would be appointed year-eponym in Aššur. Their mission is to appease the ruler of Harsamna with words and a rich gift of textiles, making a small caravan of at least six donkeys for the men and the textiles, which could travel incognito with a caravan bound for Kaneš. Even though Aššur was part of the Kingdom of Upper Mesopotamia, this letter shows that the elite of Aššur was a partner for foreign kings and that envoys were sent to other rulers. It is unclear whether Šamšī-Adad employed such envoys from Aššur in matters pertaining to the Assyrian trade colonies, but if so, it is likely that he described them as 'my envoys' instead of 'envoys of the city'.

A few texts from Mari inform us that Assyrian trade colonies abroad also engaged in diplomatic activity by sending an envoy to Zimrī-Lîm, the king of Mari. From about 1768 BC there is a short reference to the visit of Aššur-bāni, an Assyrian envoy from Kaneš, who receives 5 shekels of silver on the same day as two envoys from Ešnunna (ARM 7, 173 from 13?/vii/ZL7). A letter from about five years later announces the arrival in Mari of a group including Aššur-šaduni, envoy, from Uršum (FM 3, 293 no. 139). The names of the envoys make it practically certain that they are not representing the kings of the cities of Kaneš and Uršum, but rather the Assyrian *kāru*s in those towns. As the city of Mari was not part of the Old Assyrian trade network, there must be other motives to send such envoys. For example, to discuss measures taken by the king of Mari, Zimrī-Lîm, which impacted on Assyrian caravans or individual traders travelling through the northern periphery of his realm. See, for example, the dossier studied by Guichard (2008) about Zimrī-Lîm's attempt to obtain compensation for gifts he had sent to the king of Kaneš by confiscating assets of Assyrian merchants travelling through Nahur.

A Fragmentary Diplomatic Letter

Returning now to the treaties found in Kültepe, we want to draw attention to a fragmentary text, photos of which were published in *Kültepe-Kaniş* II (Pl. 135, 2a–c) (for new photos, see Fig. 2.1–3 below).[22] Tahsin Özgüç (1986) added the following details about Kt 85/t 17:[23]

---

22 New photos by Jan Gerrit Dercksen, by kind permission of Fikri Kulakoğlu.
23 See Özgüç 1986, 93.

A small fragment of a large tablet came to light among the foundation stones of a large Ib period building on the mound. The break is ancient; the fragment was put among the foundation stones with the mortar.

The fragment was discovered on the mound among the foundation stones of a large building dating to level 7, which corresponds to level Ib in the Lower Town. T. Özgüç did not identify which building this was. According to excavation reports, Temple 2 and the Large Storehouse belong to level 7. The find-spot suggests that the tablet dates to the early level 7 period and perhaps even as a piece of waste to the level 8 period (contemporaneous with Lower Town level II).

As far as one can infer from the broken state of the tablet, the text is written in standard Old Assyrian, with use of mimation as was customary during the level II and part of the level Ib period. The scribe employed the word divider to separate words, but did not put a dividing wedge between preposition + noun, negation + verb, and relative pronoun *ša* + noun; this closely resembles the use of the word divider in Kt g/t 35, a letter sent by King Anum-hirbi to King Waršama (Balkan 1957).

The fragment's dimensions are given as 5.2 cm by 5.2 cm wide and 2.7 cm thick, which led Tahsin Özgüç to remark: 'to judge by its thickness, this must be one of the largest tablets from Kaniš'. The thickness of 2.7 cm was measured about 5 cm from the edge and will have increased near the middle of the tablet. How much more is uncertain, as that part of the tablet has been lost. To give an idea of the tablet's possible original dimensions, it may be compared to some other tablets. From the eighteenth century we have first of all the letter sent to King Hurmeli by the elders of Aššur, Kt 01/k 217, which measures 20 × 8.5 × 4.2 cm and has thirty-three lines on the obverse, three on the lower edge, thirty-four on the reverse, four on the upper edge, and one on the left edge. Kt 00/k 6 (a treaty with a king of Kaneš) measures 15.3 × 7.1 × 3 cm and has thirty-seven lines on the obverse, five on the lower edge, and thirty-six on the reverse. The list Kt g/t 42+z/t 11 is 10 × 6.3 × 2.9 cm with twenty-five lines on the obverse (Günbattı 1987, 3 n. 1). It is remarkable that two tablets from level II that contain an exceptional number of lines are thinner than the examples just mentioned, which all date to level Ib: the protocol CTMMA 1, 84a measures 16.9 × 7.3 × 2.5 cm with forty-seven lines on the obverse, four on the lower edge, forty-eight on the reverse, five on the upper edge, and two on the left edge. The *Sammelmemorandum* Kt c/k 839 measures 18.9 × 10.1 × 2.6 cm with 113 lines. Also the fragmentary *waklum* letter Kt 91/k 100, although inscribed with large writing, fits here: 7.1+ × 7.0 × 2.4 cm (courtesy K. R. Veenhof). Although this may suggest that the shape of tablets changed after level II, the broken state of Kt 85/t 17 makes any estimate of its original dimensions uncertain. For practical purposes, however, it may be compared with the formats of Kt 00/k 6 and Kt 01/217. This means that the extant part of Kt 85/t 17 possibly is merely one-third of the original tablet, with nine lines on the obverse and eleven lines on the reverse of the original thirty or so lines per side partly preserved. In addition, the beginning and the end of every line have been lost, and as a result not a single complete sentence survives.

The text runs in transliteration and translation as follows:

Obv. (about two-thirds of the obverse missing)
1' [...] x -pu-tí-k[à-ma : h]e-⌈er-ma-am⌉
[... t]a-⌈ma⌉ : dí-in : šu-ma : ú-nu-ša-am [(x)]
[up-ta]-zu-ru : ṣú-ha-ar-kà : a-na ma-m[ì-tim]
[ta-da-an ša lu-qú]-a-tim : up-ta-zu-ru-ma : ú-[x x]
5' [... a-ḫi] ⌈a⌉-ta a-ni : e-na-ni-<<NI>>-šu : a[l-qé x]
[... i-na] 20-ta túg.hi.a 1-ta túg.hi.a : ni-[is-ha-tí-kà]
[ta-lá-qé ší-tí túg.hi.a] a-šar : li-bi₄-šu-nu : i-ma-k[u-ru (x)]
[(x) da-tám š]a a-ḫi-⌈a⌉ : áš-ta-ú-lu ni-[x x]
[... i]m-gu₅-ru : iš-tù : sà-aḫ-ra-[tí-ni (x)]
l.e.10' [...] ⌈a⌉-na kà-ni-iš : ub-lá-[kum...]
[... a]-ni : a-wi-lu-ú : ša u₄-m[a-am i-na]
[... w]a-áš-bu-ni : ma-tí-ma : a-n[a ...]
[... -r]i-a : lá iš-ku-nu : ni-[...]
[... p]á-na-nu-um : ša-ru-[ú ...]
15' [... dumu.meš] ⌈a⌉-šur : lá-am-ni-i[š e-pu-šu]
Rev. [...] im : a-na ú-ri-i[m ...]
[... a-ší]-ú-šu-nu : na₄.gìn.za : si[g₅ ...]
[ša a-na ší-mì]-im : ú-šé-lu-ú : ⌈e⌉-[ki-mu ...]
[...]-nu : a-ni : a-na-ku [...]
20' [...] x : e-pu-uš : iš-t[ù x x x x]
[...] ⌈i⌉-dí-na-ni : i-nu-mì : [x x x x]
[... a-ḫi]-⌈i⌉ : kà-ra-nàm : a-na ṣ[é-ri-a]
[lu-bi-il₅] x i-na ša-re-e : š[a-ni-ú-tim]
[ra-bi₄]-ú-tim : ma-nu-um : mì-[ma (lá)]
25' [x x] x x-[k]à : ú ni g[a ...]
[x x x x x x x] ma [x x x x x]
(remainder broken off)

Translation
(1'–2') [...] your [...] [*Make a copy*] *of the envelope* and give (it to me)!
(2'–4') If they go [into hiding] because of the *unuššum* duty [you will let] your servant [take] an oath. [He who] conceals [merch]andise and [...]
(5'–7') [...] You [are my brother!] Now, I pardoned him. [...] [You can take] one textile [from] every twenty textiles as [your] le[vy]. They (i.e. Assyrian merchants)] will (then) trade [the other textiles] wherever they wish.

(8'–9') [You know] I frequently enquired [after the well-being] of my brother. [...] agreed.

(9'–10') Ever since [you] were young I brought [*the goods you wished*] to Kaneš.

(11'–13') [...] Now, the men who are sitting [...] today, never placed [... be]fore me [...]

(14'–19') Previously, the kings [of ...] mal[treated] Assyrians. [...] to the *roof* [...] Their meteoritic [ir]on (and) the fine lapis lazuli that they had brought up to sell [they took] away. [...]

(19'–23') Now, I did [...]. After [...] he gave me [...]. When [...], [may] my [brother bring me] wine.

(23'–26') Who among the other great kings [...] you? [...] (remainder broken off)

Commentary

1'. The traces of the first sign suggest MA or RU, not A or ŠÍ. The first preserved sign is BU, followed by DÍ and the beginning of GA.

2'. Perhaps to be restored [*šu-ba-al-ki-t*]*a-⌈ma⌉*; for the meaning 'to copy (a tablet)' of *šubalkutum*, see Larsen, KT 6b, p. 378. Note the sequence *šubalkitā*+ventive+ma – *dinā*+ma – *ṭurdā*+ventive+acc.suffix in KT 6b, 231:15–18, translated 'Have a copy made (of my father's will) [...], and give this cleared tablet to A. and send him'.

3'.]-*zu-ru* : either a verbal form or the name of the servant of the addressee (attested male names are *hu-zu-ru*, Kt k/k 14; *ki-zu-ru*, Kt b/k 21).

5': The sequence E NA NI NI ŠU is difficult. A personal name Enna(m)-ilīšu does not exist in Akkadian, and *ēnā ilīšu* 'the eyes of his god' makes little sense in the context.

6'. Restored from Kt 00/k 6: (69) *i-na* 10-*ta pá-ra-kà-ni : pá-ra-kà-nam* (70) *ni-is-ha-tí-kà : ta-lá-qé*. The 10 per cent mentioned in this treaty with Kaneš refers to the *pirikannum*, a well-known Anatolian type of woollen textile. The palace of Kaneš levied a *nishātum* of 5 per cent on textiles imported by Assyrian merchants during level II, as illustrated by Kt c/k 454:7–10, according to which 210 textiles entered the palace and 10½ were taken as *nishātum*. In addition, about 10 per cent of the imported textiles were subject to a pre-emption, which could be taken at the *kārum* office. A levy of 5 per cent on textiles was then an existing feature at the time of writing of Kt 85/t 17.

13': Possible restoration: [igi-*r*]*i-a*; the level Ib logogram occurs in, for example, Kt 01/k 219:39 (Günbattı 2014, 31).

16 f.': It is unclear whether *ana ūrim* is to be connected with the expression in TC 3, 93: (12) *ṣú-hu-ur-kà : a-na* (13) *ú-ri-im : kà-šu-ud*, translated by Larsen as 'your children have been chased into destitution!' (Larsen 2002, 21 with commentary p. 23); booked under *ūru* A 'roof' in CAD U and W, 264b. The lines may have contained a description of the maltreatment, in which case]-*ú-šu-nu* in line 17' is the end of a verbal form. Alternatively, the first readable signs in line 17' can be read [*aši*]*ušunu* as suggested by the treaty with Kaneš line 30, where meteoritic iron and lapis lazuli occur in the same context.

We do not claim to fully understand the contents of this fragment and will refrain from speculations on how to restore the broken parts. The occurrence of the word 'your servant' and the imperative form 'give!' and several verbal forms in the first person singular make it clear that the text was a letter. That this was not a letter exchanged between merchants appears from the fact that the sender refers to a service duty (*unuššum*), several trade items (meteoritic iron and lapis lazuli), and to the levy of tax. The last feature is phrased in nearly the same way as in the treaty with Kaneš. We know that during the level II period, the palace of Kaneš already levied a *nishātum* of 5 per cent on textiles imported by Assyrian merchants, after which the remaining textiles could be sold elsewhere. The objects of trade mentioned here, textiles, meteoritic iron, and lapis lazuli, would fit the assortment of Assyrian merchants. The sender of the letter refers to the recipient as his 'brother' (line 8'). The levy on textiles, the topic of gift exchange, and the mention of 'other great kings' (23') makes it likely that the sender and addressee were both kings. The sender asks for wine, which is often used as a royal gift.[24]

The mixture of diplomatic and commercial topics with personal remarks feels slightly odd and gives this text the character of a school exercise in letter writing. Yet, one does not expect to find a school text on the mound. The recipient of this letter is in our view the king of Kaneš, the town mentioned in line 10', and who would be interested in the subject matter. But who is the sender? Another king in Anatolia? The letters from Anum-hirbi of Mama to Waršama of Kaneš (Kt g/t 35, see Balkan 1957) and from Wiušti king of Ḫattuša to a king of Harsamna (KBo 71, 81, see Schwemer & Barjamovic 2019) demonstrate that rulers of Anatolia and adjacent regions communicated with each other by means of letters written in Old Assyrian script and dialect. The town of Mama might be on the route by which lapis lazuli and other commodities reached Kaneš, and the letter from Anum-hirbi shows that he had held back a caravan heading for (or coming from) Kaneš — probably an Assyrian caravan. But a ruler of Mama or another Anatolian state would have no interest in discussing the practice of a service duty in Kaneš and the levy of tax on textiles there unless it regarded his own subjects, and we lack any proof for non-Assyrian merchants regularly travelling to Kaneš. Therefore, it is unlikely that an Anatolian king is the sender of Kt 85/t 17.

---

24 Barjamovic & Fairbairn 2018, 253; jars of wine as royal gifts also in IM 49222, edited in de Boer 2021, 59–60.

The alternative is that the sender is the ruler of Aššur. The items of trade mentioned and the levy on textiles as well as the Assyrian focus in general make it probable that a ruler of Aššur sent this letter. As far as the presently available documentation allows, there is no positive evidence to the effect that an Old Assyrian ruler entered into direct contact with his counterpart in Kaneš; diplomatic messages were transmitted through the envoys of the city (*šiprū ša ālem*) and the Assyrian colony in Kaneš itself. This does not mean that such contacts may not have existed, but we lack any evidence.

The fragment seems to date from the last decades of the nineteenth century BC. It refers to the maltreatment of Assyrians in the (recent) past and the sender claims that he already sent goods to Kaneš when the recipient of this letter was still a young man (reading *ṣahrāku* instead of *ṣahrāti*, which would have the sender sent goods as a young man, is unlikely). This might mean that the addressee had only recently become king of Kaneš and that the letter must be seen in the context of negotiations to renew the treaty between Aššur and the king of Kaneš.

The maltreatment of Assyrians hardly refers to the destruction of Kaneš Lower Town level II around 1835 BC and must refer to abuses that happened after the rebuilding of the city and the resumption of Assyrian life there. At Aššur, the period between 1835 and 1809 is filled with the second half of the reign of Narām-Sîn and the reign of Erišum II, followed by the reign of Šamšī-Adad 1808–1776. To the sequence of kings of Kaneš known from the *iqqātē* formula as reconstructed in *Ups and Downs* can now be added a certain Bahanu (Günbattı 2014 texts 1–3), who will have reigned round 1800.

The sealed *bullae* found in the Sarıkaya palace at Acemhöyük are important evidence of the diplomatic and commercial links between this city and Syria in the first decades of the eighteenth century. Several of the *bullae* are impressed with one of the seals of Šamšī-Adad that identify him as ruler of Aššur (N. Özgüç 2015, 37–48; Veenhof 2017b, 249–53). It appears unlikely that he only sent consignments to Acemhöyük and would have ignored the key city of Kültepe.

This means that Kt 85/t 17 may have been sent by Narām-Sîn or Erišum II of Aššur to an unknown king of Kaneš, or by Šamšī-Adad (employing an Assyrian scribe) to Hurmeli or Bahanu. Unfortunately, comparative evidence is lacking; no letters are known from Narām-Sîn (with the exception of the *waklum* letter ICK 1, 182 mentioning the eponym of 1869 BC, see Kryszat 2004, 356) and Erišum II and the surviving letters sent by Šamšī-Adad are written in Old Babylonian and addressed to his son Yasmah-Addu or to a vassal (Kuwari, see Eidem & Læssøe 2001), but not to another king as part of a diplomatic process.

Concluding Remarks

Diplomacy, or the management of international relations, was of crucial importance to the economic success of the city-state of Aššur. Its leverage rested on its ability to regularly provide tin and elite goods such as lapis lazuli, meteoritic iron, and sought-after garments, as well as silver and gold, due to its entrepreneurs whose caravans crossed the lands between Aššur and central Anatolia. This economic influence had the political effect that treaties could be concluded with foreign rulers to their mutual benefit: the Assyrians obtained security guarantees and freedom of movement, the rulers were permitted to levy taxes and pre-empt certain merchandise and got access to luxury goods.

Due to the overwhelming amount of textual evidence from part of the nineteenth century BC, we have a fairly good insight into the mechanisms of Old Assyrian diplomacy. The Assyrian merchants did not conduct trade individually but were tied into the network of larger and smaller Assyrian trade organizations, the *kārus* and *wabartus*. Although self-governed on a local scale, these Assyrian organizations in Anatolia were all directed from *kārum* Kaneš with regard to supra-regional affairs. And *kārum* Kaneš was the pivotal institution that received pertinent instructions from Aššur itself. It is important to keep in mind that all actions by Assyrian merchants could potentially disrupt the balance and cause trouble which sooner or later would jeopardize the Assyrian trading system as such. Examples have been mentioned above: the smuggling of merchandise, trade in restricted commodities, providing commercial services for enemy kings — all these incidents called for action from the highest authorities, the king and the city assembly. Multiple letters addressed to *kārum* Kaneš or also directly to individual Assyrian merchants document how the king of Aššur relayed decisions taken by the city assembly on legal and political matters. On the international scene, the so-called envoys of the city acted as ambassadors equipped with written instructions.

By contrast, the following period of Assyrian involvement in Anatolia, dating to the level Ib period of the Lower Town of Kaneš, yielded very few texts that inform us about diplomacy. Exceptions are the treaties with a king of Kaneš, with the rulers of Hahhum, and the treaty text excavated at Tell Leilan. Another important exception is formed by the copy of a letter which the elders of Aššur had sent to the king of Harsamna and which contains the wording of a discussion they had with the then-ruler of Aššur, Šamšī-Adad. Other evidence shows that the Assyrian colonies had acquired a larger degree of independence by the time Šamšī-Adad had died: they engaged in diplomatic activities of their own and we find Assyrian envoys from Kaneš and from Uršum travelling to Mari — which lay outside of the customary trade routes. The whole Assyrian community was connected by the exchange of letters, as is demonstrated by a copy of an alarming letter found in Kültepe (Kt 98/k 118, Dercksen & Donbaz 2001), which was sent by merchants of Karakin near the Zagros Mountains and addressed to divine Aššur and the city, dealing with political unrest in Niqqum which could endanger the supply of merchandise to Assur.

None of the published texts informs us about messages exchanged between the rulers of Aššur and Kaneš, but such correspondence may still await excavation. For that reason, Kt 85/t 17 may be all that remains of a letter sent by an Assyrian ruler to his counterpart in Kaneš.

Abbreviations

AKT 3 — Bilgiç, Emin & Cahit Günbattı, *Ankaraner Kültepe-Texte*, III: *Texte der Grabungskampagne 1970* (Freiburger Altorientalische Studien, Beihefte: Altassyrische Texte und Untersuchungen 3). Steiner, Stuttgart, 1995.

ARM 6 — Kupper, Jean-Robert, *Correspondance de Bahdi-Lim préfet du palais de Mari* (Archives royales de Mari 6). Imprimerie nationale, Paris, 1954.

ARM 7 — Bottéro, Jean, *Textes économiques et administratifs* (Archives royales de Mari 7). Imprimerie nationale, Paris, 1957.

ATHE — Kienast, Burkhart, *Die altassyrischen Texte des orientalischen Seminars der Universität Heidelberg und der Sammlung Erlenmeyer*. De Gruyter, Berlin, 1960.

CCT 4 — Smith, Sidney, *Cuneiform Texts from Cappadocian Tablets in the British Museum*, IV. British Museum, London, 1925.

CCT 6 — Garelli, Paul & Dominique Collon, *Cuneiform Texts from Cappadocian Tablets in the British Museum*, VI. British Museum, London, 1975.

CTMMA 1 — Larsen, Mogens Trolle, *Tablets, Cones and Bricks of the Third and Second Millennium B.C*, ed. by Ira Spar (Cuneiform Texts in the Metropolitan Museum of Art 1). Metropolitan Museum of Art, New York, 1988, 92–143, 177–92, pls 66–109, 129–56.

FM 3 — Charpin, Dominique & Jean-Marie Durand (eds), *Florilegium marianum*, III: *Recueil d'études à la mémoire de Marie-Thérèse Barrelet* (Mémoires de N.A.B.U. 4). Société pour l'Étude du Proche-Orient Ancien, Paris, 1997.

ICK 1 — Hrozný, Bedrich, *Inscriptions cunéiformes du Kültepe*, I. Statni Pedagogicke Nakladatelstvi, Prague, 1952.

KT 5 — Veenhof, Klaas R., *Kültepe Tabletleri, 5: (Kt 92/k 188-263)* (Türk Tarih Kurumu Yayınları 6/33c). Türk Tarih Kurumu Basımevi, Ankara, 2010.

KT 6a — Larsen, Mogens Trolle, *(Ankara) Kültepe Tabletleri, 6a: The Archive of the Šalim-Aššur Family*, I: *The First Two Generations* (Türk Tarih Kurumu Yayınları 6/33d-a). Türk Tarih Kurumu Basımevi, Ankara, 2010.

KT 6b — Larsen, Mogens Trolle, *Kültepe Tabletleri, 6b: The Archive of the Šalim-Aššur Family*, II: *Ennam-Aššur* (Türk Tarih Kurumu Yayınları 6/33d-b). Türk Tarih Kurumu Basımevi, Ankara, 2013.

KT 6c — Larsen, Mogens Trolle, *Kültepe Tabletleri, 6c: The Archive of the Šalim-Aššur Family*, III: *Ali-ahum* (Türk Tarih Kurumu Yayınları 6/33d-c). Türk Tarih Kurumu Basımevi, Ankara, 2014.

KT 8 — Veenhof, Klaas R., *Kültepe Tabletleri, 8: The Archive of Elamma, Son of Iddin-Suen, and his Family (Kt 91/k 285-568 and Kt 92/k 94-187)* (Türk Tarih Kurumu Yayınları 6/33f). Türk Tarih Kurumu Basımevi, Ankara, 2017.

KTH	Lewy, Julius, *Die Kültepetexte aus der Sammlung Frida Hahn, Berlin*. Hinrichs, Leipzig, 1930.
KTP	Stephens, Ferris J., 'The Cappadocian Tablets in the University of Pennsylvania Museum', *Journal of the Society of Oriental Research* 11 (1927): 101–36.
OAA 1	*The Aššur-nādā Archive* (Old Assyrian Archives Studies 1; PIHANS: Uitgaven van het Nederlands Instituut voor het Nabije Oosten te Leiden 96). Nederlands Instituut voor het Nabije Oosten, Leiden, 2002.
TC 1	Contenau, Georges, *Tablettes cappadociennes du Louvre* (Textes cunéiformes du Louvre 4). Geuthner, Paris, 1920.
TC 2	Thureau-Dangin, François, *Tablettes cappadociennes du Louvre* (Textes cunéiformes du Louvre 14). Geuthner, Paris, 1928.
TC 3	Lewy, Julius, *Tablettes cappadociennes du Louvre* (Textes cunéiformes du Louvre 19–21), 3 vols. Geuthner, Paris, 1935–37.
TTC	Contenau, Georges, *Trente tablettes cappadociennes*. Geuthner, Paris, 1919.
VS 26	Veenhof, Klaas R. & Evelyn Klengel-Brandt, *Altassyrische Tontafeln aus Kültepe: Texte und Siegelabrollungen* (Vorderasiatische Schriftdenkmäler der Staatlichen Museen zu Berlin, n.s. 10 (26)). Mann, Berlin, 1992.

Bibliography

Albayrak, Irfan
2008 'A *Rubāʾum* Letter sent to *Kārum Kaneš*', in Cécile Michel (ed.), *Old Assyrian Studies in Memory of Paul Garelli* (Publications de l'Institut historique-archéologique néerlandais de Stamboul 112). Nederlands Instituut voor het Nabije Oosten, Leiden: 111–15.

Balkan, Kemal
1957 *Letter of King Anum-Hirbi of Mama to King Warshama of Kanish* (Türk Tarih Kurumu Yayınlarından 7/31a). Türk Tarih Kurumu Basımevi, Ankara.

Barjamovic, Gojko
2011 *A Historical Geography of Anatolia in the Old Assyrian Colony Period* (Carsten Niebuhr Institute Publications 38). Museum Tusculanum Press, Copenhagen.

Barjamovic, Gojko & Fairbairn, Andrew
2018 'Anatolian Wine in the Middle Bronze Age', *Welt des Orients* 48: 249–84.

Barjamovic, Gojko; Hertel, Thomas Klitgaard & Larsen, Mogens Trolle
2012 *Ups and Downs at Kanesh: Chronology, History and Society in the Old Assyrian Period* (Publications de l'Institut historique-archéologique néerlandais de Stamboul 120). Nederlands Instituut voor het Nabije Oosten, Leiden.

Boer, Rients de
2021 *The Ikūn-pîša Letter Archive from Tell ed-Dēr* (Publications de l'Institut historique-archéologique néerlandais de Stamboul 131). Nederlands Instituut voor het Nabije Oosten, Leiden.

Çeçen, Salih
1998 'Yeni delillere göre Kültepe'de "kan parası"', in Hayat Erkanal, Veysel Donbaz & Ayşegül Uğuroğlu (eds), *XXXIV Uluslararası Assiriyoloji Kongresi: 6–10/VII/1987-Istanbul*. Türk Tarih Kurumu, Ankara: 291–96, pls 71–73.

Çeçen, Salih & Hecker, Karl
1995 '*ina mātika eblum*: Zu einem neuen Text zum Wegerecht in der Kültepe-Zeit', in Manfried Dietrich & Oswald Loretz (eds), *Vom Alten Orient zum Alten Testament: Festschrift für Wolfram Freiherrn von Soden zum 85. Geburtstag am 19. Juni 1993* (Alter Orient und Altes Testament 240). Butzon & Bercker Kevelaer, Neukirchen-Vluyn: 31–41.

Dercksen, Jan Gerrit
2004 *Old Assyrian Institutions* (Publications de l'Institut historique-archéologique néerlandais de Stamboul 98). Nederlands Instituut voor het Nabije Oosten, Leiden.
2007 'Die altassyrischen Handelsabgaben in Nordmesopotamien und Anatolien im 19.–18. Jh. v. Chr. in Verträgen und Praxis', in Hilmar Klinkott, S. Kubisch & Renate Müller-Wollermann (eds), *Geschenke und Steuern, Zölle und Tribute: Antike Abgabenformen in Anspruch und Wirklichkeit* (Culture & History of the Ancient Near East 29). Brill, Leiden: 187–211.
2015 'The Government of Assur during the Rule of Samsi-Addu', *Nouvelles assyriologiques brèves et utilitaires* 8: 11–12.
2022 'The Golden Interval of Old Assyrian Trade (2000–1700 BC)', in David A. Warburton (ed.), *The Earliest Economic Growth in World History: Proceedings of the Berlin Workshop* (Publications de l'Institut historique-archéologique néerlandais de Stamboul 133). Nederlands Instituut voor het Nabije Oosten, Leiden: 79–108.

Dercksen, Jan Gerrit & Donbaz, Veysel
2001 'Merchants in Distress. An Old Assyrian Text Mentioning habbātu', *Jaarbericht Ex Oriente Lux* 35–36 (1997–2000): 103–10.

Durand, Jean-Marie

1988 'La mission matrimoniale', in *Archives épistolaires de Mari* (Archives royales de Mari 26). Éditions Recherche sur les civilisations, Paris: I.1: 95–117.

Eidem, Jesper

2011 *The Royal Archives from Tell Leilan* (Publications de l'Institut historique-archéologique néerlandais de Stamboul 117). Nederlands Instituut voor het Nabije Oosten, Leiden.

Eidem, Jesper & Læssøe, Jørgen

2001 *The Shemshara Archives*, I: *The Letters* (Det Kongelige Danske Videnskabernes Selskab Historisk-filosofiske Skrifter 23). Det Kongelige Danske Videnskabernes Selskab, Copenhagen.

Garelli, Paul

1998 'Hahhum un relais assyrien sur la route commerciale de la Cappadoce', in Hayat Erkanal, Veysel Donbaz & Ayşegül Uğuroğlu (eds), *XXXIV Uluslararası Assiriyoloji Kongresi: 6-10/VII/1987-Istanbul*. Türk Tarih Kurumu, Ankara: 451–56.

Glassner, Jean-Jacques

2004 *Mesopotamian Chronicles* (Writings from the Ancient World 19). Society of Biblical Literature, Atlanta.

Grayson, A. Kirk

1975 *Assyrian and Babylonian Chronicles* (Texts from Cuneiform Sources 5). Augustin, New York.

Günbattı, Cahit

1987 'Yeniden işlenen Bir Kültepe Tableti (Kt.g/t 42+z/t ll)', *Belleten* 51: 1–10.

1996 'Two New Tablets Throwing Light on the Relations between Anatolian Kings and Assyrian Merchants in the Period of the Assyrian Colonies', *Archivum Anatolicum* 2: 25–37.

2001 'The River Ordeal in Ancient Anatolia', in Wilfried H. van Soldt, Jan Gerrit Dercksen, N. J. C. Kouwenberg & Theo J. H. Krispijn (eds), *Veenhof Anniversary Volume: Studies Presented to Klaas R. Veenhof on the Occasion of his Sixty-Fifth Birthday* (Publications de l'Institut historique-archéologique néerlandais de Stamboul 89). Nederlands Instituut voor het Nabije Oosten, Leiden: 151–59.

2004 'Two Treaty Texts Found at Kültepe', in Jan Gerrit Dercksen (ed.), *Assyria and Beyond: Studies Presented to Mogens Trolle Larsen* (Publications de l'Institut historique-archéologique néerlandais de Stamboul 100). Nederlands Instituut voor het Nabije Oosten, Leiden: 249–68.

2014 *Harsamna Kralı Hurmeli'ye Gönderilen Mektup ve Kaniš Kralları: The Letter Sent to Hurmeli King of Harsamna and the Kings of Kaniš* (Türk Tarih Kurumu Yayınları 5/3). Türk Tarih Kurumu, Ankara.

Guichard, Michaël

2008 'Nahur et la route des marchands assyriens à l'époque de Zimri-Lîm', in Jan Gerrit Dercksen (ed.), *Anatolia and the Jazira during the Old Assyrian Period* (Publications de l'Institut historique-archéologique néerlandais de Stamboul 111). Nederlands Instituut voor het Nabije Oosten, Leiden: 43–53.

Hecker, Karl

1996 'Rechtlos in der Fremde?', *Anadolu Medeniyetleri Müzesi Konferansları* 1995: 145–59.

2003 '*kunuk kārim ṣaher rabi*', in Gebhard J. Selz (ed.), *Festschrift für Burkhart Kienast: Zu seinem 70. Geburtstage dargebracht von Freunden, Schülern und Kollegen* (Alter Orient und Altes Testament 274). Ugarit, Münster: 183–96.

2007 'Altassyrische Briefe', *Texte aus der Umwelt des Alten Testaments. Neue Folge* 3: 77–100.

Hertel, Thomas Klitgaard

2013 *Old Assyrian Legal Practices, Law and Dispute in the Ancient Near East* (Publications de l'Institut historique-archéologique néerlandais de Stamboul 123). Nederlands Instituut voor het Nabije Oosten, Leiden.

Kouwenberg, Norbert J. C.
2017 *A Grammar of Old Assyrian* (Handbook of Oriental Studies 118). Brill, Leiden.

Kryszat, Guido
2004 'Wer schrieb die Waklum-Briefe?', in Jan Gerrit Dercksen (ed.), *Assyria and Beyond: Studies Presented to Mogens Trolle Larsen* (Publications de l'Institut historique-archéologique néerlandais de Stamboul 100). Nederlands Instituut voor het Nabije Oosten, Leiden: 353–58.

Lafont, Bertrand
2001 'Relations internationales, alliances et diplomatie au temps des royaumes amorrites', in Jean-Marie Durand & Dominique Charpin (eds), *Amurru*, II: *Mari, Ébla et les Hourrites dix ans de travaux*. Éditions Recherche sur les civilisations, Paris: 213–328.

Larsen, Mogens Trolle
1976 *The Old Assyrian City-State and its Colonies*. Akademisk Forlag, Copenhagen.
1978 'Four Letters from the Walters Art Gallery, Baltimore', in Blahoslav Hruška & Géza Komoróczy (eds), *Festschrift für Lubor Matouš*. Eötvös Loránd Tudományegyetem, Budapest: 113–37.
2002 *The Aššur-nādā Archive* (Old Assyrian Archives 1; Publications de l'Institut historique-archéologique néerlandais de Stamboul 96). Nederlands Instituut voor het Nabije Oosten, Leiden.
2010 *The Archive of the Šalim-Aššur Family*, I: *The First Two Generations* (Kültepe Tabletleri VI-a). Türk Tarih Kurumu, Ankara.
2014 *The Archive of the Šalim-Aššur Family*, III: *Ali-Ahum* (Kültepe Tabletleri VI-c). Türk Tarih Kurumu, Ankara.

Michel, Cécile
1991 *Innāya dans les tablettes paléo-assyriennes I Analyse*. Éditions Recherche sur les civilisations, Paris.
2001 *Correspondance des marchands de Kanish* (Littératures anciennes du Proche-Orient 19). Éditions du Cerf, Paris.
2008a 'The Alāḫum and Aššur-taklāku Archives Found in 1993 at Kültepe Kaniš', *Altorientalische Forschungen* 35: 53–67.
2008b 'Nouvelles données de géographie historique anatolienne d'après des archives récentes de Kültepe', in K. Strobel (ed.), *New Perspectives on the Historical Geography and Topography of Anatolia in the II and I Millennium B.C.* LoGisma, Vicchio: 235–52.
2014 'Considerations on the Assyrian Settlement at Kanesh', in Levent Atici, Fikri Kulakoğlu, Gojko Barjamovic & Andrew Fairbairn (eds), *Current Research at Kültepe-Kanesh: An Interdisciplinary and Integrative Approach to Trade Networks, Internationalism, and Identity* (Journal of Cuneiform Studies Supplemental Series 4). Lockwood, Atlanta: 69–84.

Michel, Cécile & Garelli, Paul
1996 'Heurts avec une principauté anatolienne', *Wiener Zeitschrift für die Kunde des Morgenlandes* 86: 277–90.

Özgüç, Nimet
2015 *Acemhöyük-Burušḫaddum*, I: *Silindir Mühürler ve Mühür Baskılı Bullalar / Cylinder Seals and Bullae with Cylinder Seal Impressions*. Türk Tarih Kurumu, Ankara.

Özgüç, Tahsin
1986 *Kültepe-Kaniš*, II: *Eski Yakındoğu'nun Ticaret Merkezinde Yeni Araştırmalar. New Researches at the Trading Center of the Ancient Near East*. Türk Tarih Kurumu, Ankara.

Ridder, Jacob Jan de
2021a 'Assyrian-Anatolian Relations Observed through Ethnic Designation', in Fikri Kulakoğlu, Guido Kryszat & Cécile Michel (eds), *Cultural Exchange and Current Research at Kültepe and its Surroundings: Kültepe, 1-4 August, 2019* (Kültepe International Meeting 4, Subartu 46). Brepols, Turnhout: 65–81.

2021b 'HS 200B: A Bridal Gift (Tuppu Bibli) from the First Sealand Dynasty', *Journal of Cuneiform Studies* 73: 89–102.

Ridder, Jacob Jan de & Kryszat, Guido

2023 'Murder in Anatolia – an Urgent Letter from the Ruler of Aššur', *Altorientalische Forschungen* 50: 51–62.

Riemschneider, Kaspar K.

1977 'Prison and Punishment in Early Anatolia', *Journal of the Economic and Social History of the Orient* 20: 114–26.

Schwemer, Daniel & Barjamovic, Gojko

2019 'Textfunde der Kampagne 2018', 84–89 in Andreas Schachner, 'Die Ausgrabungen in Boğazköy-Hattuša 2018', *Archäologischer Anzeiger* 2019/1: 42–117.

Sever, Huseyin & Çeçen, Salih

1993 'New Developments about Anatolia's History according to the II. Level Documents in Kültepe', *Belleten* 57: 41–49.

Veenhof, Klaas R.

1972 *Aspects of Old Assyrian Trade and its Terminology*. Leiden, Brill.

1989 'Status and Offices of an Anatolian Gentleman. Two Unpublished Letters of Huharimataku from Karum Kanish', in Kutlu Emre, Barthel Hrouda, Machteld Mellink & Nimet Özgüç (eds), *Anatolia and the Ancient Near East: Studies in Honour of Tahsin Özgüç*. Anadolu Medeniyetleri Arastirma ve Tanitma Vakfi Yayinlari, Ankara: 515–25.

2008 *Mesopotamia: The Old Assyrian Period* (with Jesper Eidem) (Orbis biblicus et orientalis 160/5). Academic Press Fribourg, Göttingen.

2013 'New Mesopotamian Treaties from the Early Second Millennium BC from kārum Kanesh and Tell Leilan (Šehna)', *Zeitschrift für altorientalische und biblische Rechtsgeschichte* 19: 23–57.

2017a *The Archive of Elamma, Son of Iddin-Suen, and his Family (Kt. 91/k 285-568 and Kt. 92/k 94-187)* (Kültepe Tabletleri 8). Türk Tarih Kurumu, Ankara.

2017b 'Acemhöyük: Seals, Chronology and History', in Fikri Kulakoğlu & Gojko Barjamovic (eds), *Proceedings of the Second Kültepe International Meeting, 26-30 July 2015: Studies Dedicated to Klaas Veenhof* (Kültepe International Meetings 2, Subartu 39). Brepols, Turnhout: 243–57.

2019 'A Verdict of the Assembly of the Old Assyrian City-State', in Doris Prechel & Hans Neumann (eds), *Beiträge zur Kenntnis und Deutung altorientalischer Archivalien: Festschrift für Helmut Freydank zum 80. Geburtstag* (Dubsar 6). Zaphon, Münster: 439–64.

Vincente, Claudine Adrienne

1991 *The 1987 Tell Leilan Tablets Dated by the Limmu of Habil-kinu (Volumes I and II)*. ProQuest Dissertations and Theses.

Zaccagnini, Carlo

1987 'Aspects of Ceremonial Exchange in the Near East during the Late Second Millennium BC', in Michael Rowlands, Mogens Trolle Larsen & Kristian Kristiansen (eds), *Centre and Periphery in the Ancient World*. Cambridge University Press, Cambridge: 57–65.

Figure 2.1: Kt 85/t 17: obverse. Photo by Jan Gerrit Dercksen, by kind permission of Fikri Kulakoğlu.

Figure 2.2: Kt 85/t 17: lower edge. Photo by Jan Gerrit Dercksen, by kind permission of Fikri Kulakoğlu.

Figure 2.3: Kt 85/t 17: reverse. Photo by Jan Gerrit Dercksen, by kind permission of Fikri Kulakoğlu.

3. Law and Justice in Kaneš and its Depiction on Cylinder Seals

A New Interpretation of the Motifs 'Ball-Staff' and 'Pot'

Adelheid Otto

Introduction

Kültepe seals have such an amazingly rich iconography and are so extremely elaborate and detailed that they can deliver more than one clue for understanding ancient social, cultural, religious, and economic concepts. Some original seals but especially thousands of seal impressions on tablets from the Lower Town of Kaneš level II constitute by far the most important source of Anatolian, Assyrian, and Syrian imagery of the nineteenth century. Step by step, the iconography can be better understood and more depictions deciphered. Nevertheless, many elements of the extremely varied and dense depictions on these masterpieces of art are still difficult to be interpret.

The period investigated in this paper is Karum Kaneš level II or more precisely the rather short period from which the majority of sealed tablets originate. This corresponds more or less — due to the chronological distribution of the texts in the merchants' archives — to the first half of the nineteenth century (c. 1900–1860 BC), roughly corresponding to the Isin-Larsa period in Babylonia and to the Late Šakkanakku period in Syria.[1]

The majority of the seals impressed on Karum Kaneš II tablets, tablet cases, or clay closures depict adoration, introduction, and audience scenes where mortal and immortal men and women were approaching or standing in front of a seated person, who is evidently the 'supreme authority' in this scene.[2] These veneration scenes are attested in a multitude of styles which indicate numerous origins of the seals and many workshops in various regions that were involved in cutting these seals, today classified roughly into Anatolian, Assyrian, Syrian, and Babylonian styles.

However, contrary to what has been commonly assumed, seals were not only depicting narrative scenes, but there was much more depicted on a seal's surface despite its tiny size. This indicates that seal images must be understood today and were meant in ancient times as statements, wishes, prayers, or markers of identity — sometimes all this together encapsulated in a single seal. Seals were the mass media of the ancient Near East, disseminating pictorial motifs and ideas over vast areas. They were small, easy to transport, worn close to the body, and every legal person possessed at least one, not to speak of institutions (Otto 2019).

---

1 Kulakoğlu 2011; Barjamovic et al. 2012.

Adelheid Otto (aotto@lmu.de) is Professor for Near Eastern Archaeology at LMU Munich (Germany)

2 This designation 'supreme authority' is chosen, because in our opinion it expresses well the hierarchical position, but does not want to commit itself in the interpretation of the main person, because this is not always completely clear. A figure wearing a horned crown can be identified without doubt as a deity. A figure wearing only a flounced garment and no horned crown could be either a deity or a deified ruler or ancestor. If the depiction is an (often modified) form of the motif of the (deified) king, which was popular in the Ur III period, it also cannot be said with certainty that this concept was also intended to be expressed here.

Therefore, the meaning inherent in a seal was not only embedded in the main scene usually depicting human or divine protagonists, but also in the countless tiny motifs which are especially frequent on seals attested at Kültepe. These are often called 'filling motifs' (Collon 1995), but they were clearly no meaningless fillers of free space, but implied an added value for the seal owner. Some of them even contained information about the seal owner's profession, belief, or major concern. Since many 'filling motifs' were rarely depicted on large-scale works of art, they must have had a symbolic or amuletic meaning specific for the seal owner. Even so-called decorative bands expressed the concerns of the seal owner and were not merely decorative adornments, e.g. the guilloche, frequently attested also on stamp seals from Kültepe (Özgüç & Tunca 2001, pls 18–19) served as a symbol of fertility (Otto 2016).

The choice of a seal motif was dependent on the status and position of the seal owner, and it was particularly influenced by whether the person acted as part of an institution or as a private person. The motifs for private seals could obviously be freely chosen, whereas official or institutional seals had to follow the motif commanded by the institution, which was given the value of an official coat of arms.[3]

The 'Ball-Staff' and 'Pot' on Assyrian, Anatolian, Syrian/Syro-Cappadocian, and Babylonian Seals

Let us focus on a pair of these small motifs which was depicted frequently on seals dating to the first half of the second millennium, but has not yet been understood properly: the 'ball-staff' and the 'pot'. The enigmatic object called in English literature most frequently 'ball-and-staff' or 'ball-staff', but which carries many other names as well (see below), is a vertical bar with a round or semicircular excrescence halfway up the staff, nearly always depicted as a lateral protrusion, rarely as a central protrusion. The 'pot' is a small globular object with a narrow neck. Its lower body and the opening of the top are sometimes rendered as linear, smooth surfaces, sometimes as wavy lines. These two objects occur nearly always as a pair, only sometimes alone, on numerous seals of every style group in Kaneš. In the following, I will analyse these objects on the basis of the seal impressions from Kültepe published so far, focusing especially on the two major 'source books' by Teissier (1994) and Özgüç (2006).

Figure 3.1 illustrates examples of the varying depictions of every style. The adoration scene of the Syrian style cylinder (Fig. 3.1a) shows the ball-staff and pot placed horizontally above the altar between the supreme authority and the worshipper, i.e. in the centre of the scene. The Anatolian style cylinder seal (Fig. 3.1b) depicts both motifs in a similarly central position at the focal point of the scene, beside and above the altar. Note that the ball-staff bears a kind of loop at its upper end, and that the upper edge of the pot is rendered as a zig-zag line. The recut Old Babylonian seal with an original audience scene (Fig. 3.1c) had the ball-staff added immediately in front of the face of the supreme authority, i.e. in a most prominent position. The Anatolian stamp seal (Fig. 3.1d) shows a large female and smaller male worshipper in adoration towards the seated goddess, between them only the ball-staff and the pot. Also the Assyrian style cylinder seal had the objects placed in direct connection to a female and a male worshipper, both of them being introduced by a goddess (Fig. 3.1d).

However, the meaning of these objects has been a matter of debate over the past decades. Common interpretations include:[4] a vertical loom and a comb, a gatepost and aryballos (connected with water deities); while the pot alone has most often been interpreted as a small vessel, called pot or vase, the interpretations of the ball-staff are varied and sometimes imaginative: a balance, a measuring instrument, a dropping tube for removing wine from a container, a case for holding drinking tubes, a spouted jar for libations, toiletry equipment, or even a water-pipe for smoking. Nimet Özgüç used to call them an elixir vase and a vase.

None of these previous interpretations is convincing. This is also because most scholars studied only the representations on Old Babylonian seals, most of which are much more stereotypical and abbreviated than Old Anatolian or Old Syrian ones. Because 'ball-staff' and 'pot' were placed as isolated elements between figures without any relation to the scene, this led to the general belief that these objects were more or less irrelevant filling motifs. In contrast, on Kültepe seals of the Anatolian and Syrian groups, these objects were depicted in a much more varied way, often as relevant elements of whole scenes, which sheds new light on their meaning.

---

3 The contrast between motifs on official and private seals has already been discussed several times for Old Syrian and Old Babylonian seals (Otto 2000, 173–78; 2013; 2017, 30–33), but it needs to be studied systematically for other periods and regions.

4 The basis of this enumeration are the collections by Dominique Collon (1986, 49–51) and Elisa Roßberger (2018, 120–21).

Figure 3.1: Kültepe seals and sealings depicting the ball-staff and pot.

3.1a: Impression of Syrian style cylinder seal, Ktd/k 22D, 34A, g/k 6B, n/k 8. CS 292. Özgüç 2006, pl. 8.

3.1d: Impression of Anatolian stamp seal, Ktn/k 1740C. St 110. Özgüç 2006, pl. 28.

3.1b: Anatolian style cylinder seal. Özgüç 2005, 271, fig. 358.

3.1c: Impression of recut Babylonian cylinder seal, Ktn/k 1698A, 1709A*. CS 73. Özgüç 2006, pl. 21.

3.1e: Impression of Assyrian style seal, Ktn/k 1845B. CS 629. Özgüç 2006, pl. 58.

Three main questions will be addressed in the following: What are these elements, what is their meaning, and where and when did they originate?

The usual explanation for nearly every element which occurs on Assyrian, Anatolian, and Syrian seals and on Babylonian seals, is that this element originated in Babylonia.[5] Indeed, there were a few Old Babylonian seals with this motif impressed on Kültepe tablets where the motifs could have belonged to the original seal (e.g. Kt n/k 1814A; CS 548; Özgüç 2006, pl. 195). However, it is visible in most instances that these elements had been added later when the Old Babylonian or Ur III seal was recut in Kültepe, see e.g. Fig. 3.1c. Another example is CS 560 (Kt n/k 1818), a recut Old Babylonian seal which was used by the Assyrian Aššur-idī, son of Amur-Aššur (Özgüç 2006, 182, pl. 48). But is this pair of enigmatic objects just another motif which was taken over by Assyrian, Anatolian, and Syrian seal-

---

5 The appearance of 'ball-staff' and 'pot' on Mesopotamian seals is considered one of the surest indications that a seal with an introduction or presentation scene dates to the Isin-Larsa and not to the Ur III period. Nevertheless, the occurrence on Isin-Larsa seals is much rarer than on seals from Kültepe.

Figure 3.2a: Impression of Assyrian style seal Ktn/k 1949. CS 806. Özgüç 2006, pl. 82.

Figure 3.2c: Impression of Assyrian style cylinder seal, Ktn/k 1966B. CS 822. Özgüç 2006, pl. 84.

Figure 3.2b: Impression of seal of Puzur-Ištar, son of Šu-Anum, the steward, Kt n/k 1811B, 1961–2009. Özgüç 2006, pl. 46.

Figure 3.2d: Impression of Assyrian style seal in two registers, Ktn/k 1793A. CS 518. Özgüç 2006, pl. 42.

cutters from Babylonian prototypes? Isin-Larsa and Old Babylonian seal impressions originating from the Diyala region, Sippar, Larsa, Isin, and Ur show the motif, but not very frequently.[6] On Ur III period seals the motif was usually not depicted[7] (for Akkadian seals see below).

Many Assyrian style seals depict the 'ball-staff' and 'pot'. On some seals the motif occurs several times, between each worshipper and the supreme figure, thus emphasizing the importance of the objects (Fig. 3.2a). Another Assyrian style seal depicts ball-staff and pot between the supreme figure and the inscription case, thus emphasizing the close connection of the central figure and the two

objects (Ktn/k 1718*, 2056; CS 79, Özgüç 2006, 318, pl. 20). This seal is property of the famous Uṣur-ša-Ištar, son of Aššur-imittī, whose house delivered the large archive of which the sealings were published by Nimet Özgüç in 2006. The seal CS 545 (Fig. 3.2b) belonged to Puzur-Ištar, son of Šu-Anum, the steward (nu-bandà) overseer and was used by his brother Buziya, son of Šu-Anum (Özgüç 2006, 176). It is interesting to note that possibly the steward himself — holding a position of high authority[8] — and his father or brother are depicted, both framing the adoration scene. The fact that ball-staff and pot are directly placed in front of one of them, possibly the steward, could indicate the relevance of these objects for his profession.

On some Assyrian style seals the 'ball-staff' and 'pot' are depicted in direct connection with the peculiar bull-altar with the cone on his back, placed exactly below or in front of him (Figs 3.2c, 3.2d). This bull-altar, frequently depicted on Assyrian and Anatolian style seals, can be interpreted today — following the suggestion by Agnete Lassen (2017)

---

6 Only a single Isin-Larsa period seal impression out of 112 ones from Isin, Larsa, and Ur collected by Blocher (1992a, 54, dated to year Sumu-el 14) shows the ball-staff. Contemporary seal impressions from Sippar show the ball-staff and pot more frequently (Blocher 1992b, 131–32); nevertheless, the percentage of 10 per cent (twenty out of approximately two hundred impressions which are reasonably well preserved) is considerably lower than on Kültepe seal impressions.

7 The motifs are found on only two Ur III seals from the very large Umma corpus comprising several thousand seal impressions: Mayr 2005, 73, fig. 47; 384, no. 834C; 444, no. 1081A.

8 Cécile Michel informs me that the nu-bandà, written as logogram, usually worked for the city hall and held a post of authority, in a rank perhaps just below the eponym.

Figure 3.3a: Impression of Anatolian style cylinder seal, Ktd/k 13A, v/k 150B. CS 270. Özgüç 2006, pl. 4.

Figure 3.4a: Impression of Syro-Cappadocian style cylinder seal, Ktn/k 1837B, 1898A. CS 609. Özgüç 2006, pl. 55.

Figure 3.3b: Impression of Anatolian style seal, Ktn/k 1786E. CS 502. Özgüç 2006, pl. 40.

Figure 3.4b: Impression of Syro-Cappadocian style cylinder seal, Ktn/k 1911A. CS 744. Özgüç 2006, pl. 73.

— as the supreme Assyrian god Aššur. The position of the objects in the scenes' focal point and next to the bull-altar shows that they were of highest relevance and were visibly placed under the protection of the god Aššur.

Ball-staff and pot on Anatolian style seals are often depicted in the centre of the scene, placed in front of the enthroned supreme authority (Fig. 3.3a) or in front of the bull-altar (Fig. 3.3b). Several Anatolian style seals show a small worshipper next to ball-staff and pot directly in front of the bull-altar, while more of these objects were depicted in front of other, larger worshippers (e.g. Fig. 3.3b).[9] These seals show that the emblem of the god Aššur was deliberately placed in close connection with these enigmatic objects. It is clear that these objects were of major importance also for the owner of Anatolian style seals. Even a seal of purely Anatolian iconography, certainly not originating from Kaneš but from a trade station somewhere else in Anatolia, depicts the ball-staff with a loop handle between the supreme authority and the loaded altar in front of him (Özgüç 2006, pl. 34, CS 453).

Ball-staff and pot appear also on Syrian style and Syro-Cappadocian seals. On these seals they are most frequently placed directly in the centre of the scene between the supreme authority and the first worshipper (Figs 3.4a, 3.4b). The Syro-Cappadocian and Syrian seals are specifically inventive as concerns the position of the ball-staff: it can be depicted horizontally in front of the main god, floating over his lap, with the globular protrusion either turned up or down;[10] sometimes it is depicted lying on the altar in front of the supreme authority (see Fig. 3.1a),[11] or is depicted above the hand of the seated figure (Özgüç 2006, CS 308).

The quantitative distribution of these motifs on seals of the different style groups which is presented here certainly needs to be revised in future, since it is based on the seal impressions which have been published to date — clearly only a part of what has been brought to light so far. Nevertheless, the relations may be relatively reliable since the study is based on a fair number of impressions (Figs 3.5, 3.6).

---

9 A similar seal showing one small and two large worshippers worshipping the bull-altar with a ball-staff in front of each, is Ktd/k 32A, g/k 1E; Özgüç 2006, 82, Lev. 11, pl. CS 310.

10 e.g. Özgüç 2006, CS 390, 744, 608.

11 See also Özgüç 2006, pl. 55, CS 608.

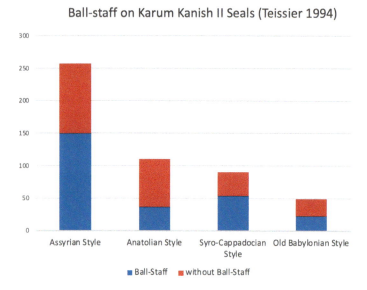

Figure 3.5: Number of depictions of the ball-staff on seal impressions from Karum Kaneš II, collected by Teissier 1994.

Figure 3.6: Percentage of depictions of the ball-staff on seals of various styles.

In total, if we count only the depictions of the ball-staff on the 677 seal impressions on Lower Town Kaneš level II texts, which Beatrice Teissier collected in 1994, we see that the motif is extremely frequent and occurs on approximately 50 per cent of the seals (Fig. 3.5).

The majority of the Assyrian style seals, i.e. 58 per cent show this motif (Fig. 3.6).[12] Twenty-nine of these seals show it in front of the seated figure, eleven behind the seated figure, three in front of the bull-altar, the remaining show it between the worshipper and the goddess. On many Assyrian seals, the ball-staff and the pot are the only 'filling motifs'.

This number is approximately the same or even slightly higher on Syrian and Syro-Cappadocian seals where the ball-staff appears on 59 per cent of them (Fig. 3.6).[13] Of these, three show the ball-staff behind and twenty-seven in front of the seated figure.

The percentage on Anatolian style seals is lower, but still a third of those seals shows this motif.[14] Seventeen of these seals show it in front of the seated figure, two behind the seated figure. Four show it in front of the bull-altar of which two seals show the ball-staff before both the seated figure and the bull-altar.

The occurrence of the ball-staff on 46 per cent of the Old Babylonian seals seems quite high at first glance; however, a careful consideration shows that most of the motifs had been added when the seals were recut in Anatolia or Assyria.[15] Four of these seals show the ball-staff in front of the seated figure, two behind the seated figure.

The Identity of 'Ball-Staff' and 'Pot': New Clues from the Seals from Kaneš

Let us come back to the crucial and often discussed question: What are these objects, what do they stand for? The Syrian and Anatolian seals, which are much more elaborate and detailed in their depictions than Babylonian seals, can possibly provide the clue to this enigma.

Since the ball-staff is sometimes depicted placed horizontally on top of an altar, some scholars interpreted it as a balance (see lastly Müller-Karpe 2021). Seals like

---

12 The catalogue of Teissier 1994 lists 282 Assyrian style seal impressions in total. Twenty-four are too fragmentary. Of the remaining 258 seal impressions, 150 show the ball-staff = 58 per cent.

13 Teissier 1994 lists 102 Syrian and Syro-Cappadocian style seal impressions. Eleven are too fragmentary. Of the remaining ninety-one seal impressions, fifty-four show the ball-staff = 59 per cent.

14 Teissier 1994 lists 137 Anatolian style seal impressions. Twenty-six are too fragmentary. Of the remaining 111 seal impressions, thirty-seven show the ball-staff = 33 per cent.

15 Teissier 1994 lists sixty-three Old Babylonian style seal impressions. Thirteen are too fragmentary. Of the remaining fifty, twenty-three show the ball-staff. Most of them seem to be recut, but only the study of the original or the photo will make it possible to distinguish in every case between an original ball-staff or one added later.

Figure 3.1a show a central protrusion and thickened ends. They are interpreted as a balance beam with a central loop for hanging it and attachments for the pans.

However, the Kaneš archives have provided the image of one of the finest Old Syrian seals which clearly shows that the ball-staff cannot be a balance (Fig. 3.7). This delicately carved seal must have originated in a north Syrian town and belongs to a group of seals which has been attributed to the Syrian Šakkanakku rulers of the first two centuries of the second millennium (Teissier 1993). Two scenes are depicted, one shows the Syrian Šakkanakku king pouring a libation to the rain goddess, and the second scene illustrates — in an exceptionally elaborate manner — the process of weighing by the supreme authority. The seated supreme authority wearing the royal broad rim cap and a flounced garment is holding with his right hand a balance. This consists of two balance-pans being attached with three strings each from the ends of a balance beam — the most detailed depiction of weighing which has been reported so far from the second millennium.

However, the interest of this seal goes much further. A small worshipper is standing below the balance act. He is holding in one hand the pot, and the ball-staff is hanging down from the wrist of his other hand. If the ball-staff was a balance, it would not have been depicted in the same scene in two completely different ways.

Another question arises from the depicted scene: Why is this small man equipped with ball-staff and pot depicted directly below the weighing procedure and not somewhere else between the three large figures of the audience scene? This certainly had a meaning in a carefully designed seal image like this, and I will argue in the following that the balance, the pot, and the ball-staff are objects closely related to each other.

Additional arguments against the identification of the ball-staff as a balance is the fact that the object never shows balance-pans at the two ends, that it is nearly always depicted vertically, and that one loop for hanging is frequently seen at one end, but never at both ends.

The depiction of a man carrying ball-staff and pot is not unique on the Syrian seal (Fig. 3.7), but occurs on several other seals of Syrian, Syro-Cappadocian, and Anatolian style. There are several seals where the mortal or the divine worshipper approaching the supreme authority is holding the ball-staff in his hands (Teissier 1994, nos 521, 522, 523). Other Syrian style seals depict a worshipper holding both ball-staff and pot in his hands and standing in front of the supreme authority (Teissier 1994, no. 472).

Figure 3.7: Impression of Old Syrian (Shakkanakku style) seal.

3.7a: Özgüç 2006, pl. 263, CS 767.

3.7b: Teissier 1994, no. 533.

The Syrian style seal impression Kt n/k 1861C (Fig. 3.8a) shows again a small man holding the pot in the right hand and the ball-staff in the left hand standing immediately in front of the supreme authority, who is in this case a bearded god associated with birds.

The Anatolian style seal Kt c/k 1636A (Fig. 3.8b) shows two worshippers approaching the bull-altar. The first one is raising both hands in adoration, the second one is holding the pot in his right hand, the ball-staff is hanging down the wrist of his left hand, suspended by a cord.

A seal cut in a different Anatolian style which is characterized by tall and slender, finely cut figures, depicts two worshippers advancing towards the seated supreme authority in front of which stands a table loaded with bread and meat. The first worshipper is raising both hands, the second holds a large, globular 'pot' in his left hand. Hanging down from the wrist of his same hand is a ball-staff, attached with the help of a leash or loop (Fig. 3.8c). A very similar seal, probably cut by the same artist, depicts a similar scene and shows even better how the hanging ball-staff was suspended at his wrist.[16]

The Anatolian style seal in the Louvre[17] (Fig. 3.8d) shows again two worshippers approaching the bull-

---

16 Ktb/k 305a. Özgüç 1965, 84, pl. XXV:75a.

17 Bought in 1911, primary publication by Delaporte 1923, 188–89, pl. 94:25 (A.871; AO 4796).

Figure 3.8: Worshippers carrying 'ball-staff' and 'pot' on Syrian and Anatolian seals.

3.8a: Kt n/k 1861C. Özgüç 2006, CS 662.

3.8b: Kt c/k 1636A. Özgüç 2006, CS 345.

3.8c: Kt n/k 1865B, Özgüç 2006, CS 668, drawing and photo.

3.8d: Anatolian style cylinder seal in the Louvre, AO 4796 (<https://collections.louvre.fr/en/ark:/53355/cl010165593> [accessed 1 July 2022]).

3.8e: Syrian style haematite seal in Fribourg, Institut Biblique, ex-Schmidt Collection. Collon 1987, 42, no. 139.

altar, the first one raising his hands in adoration and the second one presenting the 'pot' in his left hand and firmly holding the 'ball-staff' in his right hand. The slaughtering of a bull accompanying the scene underlines the ritual act and the seal owner's concern for the divine protection of the presented objects.

The Syrian style cylinder seal (Fig. 3.8e) shows, besides a second scene with divine protagonists, two human figures approaching the supreme authority. In this case the large bearded worshipper is carrying the 'ball-staff' in his left hand, while the small worshipper in front of him is carrying a small 'pot' in his left hand and a staff in his right hand.

These are just a few examples of numerous Syrian and Anatolian seals showing worshippers carrying 'ball-staff' and 'pot' towards the supreme authority. One of the worshippers is depicted larger than the other on some seals, but the meaning of this eludes us. However, it is evident that both elements are real, stable objects which can be held in both hands and which are presented by humans to the supreme authorities for a certain purpose.

A fascinating seal impression was recently published in an excellent photo by Cécile Michel (2020a, 192) (Fig. 3.9) which allows to recognize more details than an earlier photo.[18] The Anatolian style seal depicts a worshipper holding a staff-like object in his hand, followed by a suppliant goddess, approaching a seated god. The 'ball-staff' and 'pot' are rendered below the raised hand of the god. The 'pot' shows horizontal lines around its neck, which can in all probability be interpreted as cords strung around the neck of the object (for a similar depiction e.g. Fig. 3.1b).

The figure which is of prime interest for this research is the bearded god standing on a bull and holding it on a leash attached to a nose-ring. He is holding a saw in his right hand. In front and above his hands is a rectangular case which contains three objects: a 'ball-staff', a 'pot' with cords strung around its neck, and another elongated object with horizontal striations (Fig. 3.9b).

The god on the bull, holding the saw, and the case with these enigmatic objects, are clearly a coherent unit. But who is this god and what is the case? In Mesopotamia, the saw was associated with the Mesopotamian Sun God and god of justice since the Akkadian period. Among the Kültepe seal impressions there are several Syrian and Babylonian ones depicting the Sun God with his saw associated with ball-staff and pot.[19] But the bull was associated in Anatolia with weather gods and with the god Aššur. The meaning of the saw has been often debated, but most probably it expressed the act of decision and the sphere of jurisdiction.[20] Therefore, whatever god is depicted here, he was associated with justice, and it is reasonable to assume that the 'tool kit' in front of him was part of his seminal equipment. If this explanation seems too simple at first sight, we must take into account that Anatolian and Syrian seal imagery is much more narrative and explicit than the highly condensed and symbolic Babylonian imagery.

Hints for the Interpretation of the 'Ball-Staff'

The seal of Erum, the merchant, gives further hints (Fig. 3.10). It shows the supreme authority weighing silver on a balance. The first god with a saw in his hand, probably the god associated with justice, is standing in front of this weighing procedure, thus indicating his concern with the correctness of this economic proce-

Figure 3.9a: Seal impression on envelope Kt 93/k379. Michel 2020a, 192, fig. 10.2; photo courtesy C. Michel / Kültepe Archaeological Mission.

Figure 3.9b: Sketch of the detail of the god with saw and the case containing ball-staff, pot, and another object. A. Otto / M. Lerchl.

---

18 The seal was also impressed on Kt n/k 1847A and published by Özgüç 2006 as CS 631, but the photo on pl. 224 cuts the upper edge and the drawing omits this important detail.

19 Seal impression on a *bulla*, Kt 86/k 158: Özgüç & Tunca 2001, 210, pl. 90, CS 136. Özgüç thinks that ball-staff and pot were recut, but the style seems very similar and could be original. A seal that was definitely recut with an elaborate depiction of the enthroned Sun God is CS 644 (Özgüç 2006, pl. 60).

20 For the saw as judicial tool see Woods 2009, 218.

dure. Behind him, another deity is introducing a worshipper who is holding the 'ball-staff' in his right hand.

It is certainly not by chance, that merchant Erum stressed his concern about the correctness and the righteousness of metrological procedures in economic transactions in this very elaborate way, since this is the heart of any successful economic system. The Assyrian trade and the connected financial affairs meant in the first place: counting, weighing, and measuring goods; paying (i.e. weighing silver), guaranteeing and checking (i.e. writing and sealing) (Veenhof 1999). This seal is another hint for the meaning of the 'ball-staff': it must be somehow related to the concept of righteousness and justice.

Figure 3.10: Seal impression of Erum, the merchant. Teissier 1994, no. 532.

These detailed renderings of weighing on two Kültepe seal impressions are remarkable (Figs 3.7, 3.10), since this type of economic action was extremely rarely depicted in every period and in any kind of imagery. It can only be explained by the fact that the merchants of Kaneš were so very much concerned about the correctness of the financial transactions that they had their concern expressed in their seals' imagery.

Weighing metal on a handheld balance with the help of weight stones originated in the Near East in the late fourth millennium and spread throughout the Old World in the Bronze Age (Rahmstorf & Stratford 2019; Hafford 2019). Unfortunately, too few weight stones have been identified in the archaeological record because not every weight had the sphendonoid or conical shape which is considered typical for Near Eastern weight stones (Peyronel 2019). One of the earliest depictions of the act of weighing with a handheld balance can be found on an Akkadian cylinder seal (Fig. 3.11a). The scene shows two bearded men approaching the seated Sun God and god of justice Šamaš, characterized by the sun-rays and the saw in his right hand. One of the two men is holding a balance above the altar in front of the Sun God, with the other hand he is holding a staff. The man behind him is carrying a kid and raising one hand in adoration.

Not only the handheld balance, but also the 'ball-staff' was depicted for the first time on Akkadian cylinder seals, although not frequently. On this seal from the art market (Fig. 3.11b), the worshipper carrying a kid is introduced by a deity to the Sun God, in front of which the ball-staff is placed vertically. Clearly the object is deliberately associated with the god of justice already on this early representation. A very similar seal (Fig. 3.11c) is said to have been found at Kültepe and was purchased by the Kayseri Museum (Öztürk 2019, seal 6). The lapis lazuli seal may have belonged to a Mesopotamian merchant who was actively involved in the trade with Anatolia already in the late third millennium. It also shows the introduction of a kid-carrying worshipper to the ascending Sun God with the saw in hand. The ball-staff is this time depicted between the worshipper and the introducing goddess, but again it is related somehow to the god of justice. In fact, the first depictions of the ball-staff in the Akkadian period are always connected with the Sun God.

But let us come back to the fascinating and so far unique seal Figure 3.11a. The scene shows as the fourth person another man, depicted much smaller, behind the two larger men. He is bent forward and seems to take a step forward, in this way expressing his involvement in the action. But what is he doing? He is holding a staff-like instrument and is busily working with it above a cylindrical vessel. This scene has not been understood so far, but we will propose in the following a new interpretation.

Similar cylindrical vessels appear on Akkadian seals in direct relation to the harvesting of grain and the grain measuring procedure (Fig. 3.11d): a female grain goddess (possibly Nisaba) sitting on top of a grain heap is approached by a god carrying a plough and two male gods, characterized by ears of grain sprouting from their shoulders; they carry on a barrow a large cylindrical vessel which must be understood as the measuring vessel for grain. A slightly earlier seal (Fig. 3.11e) shows a similar vessel involved in the elaborately illustrated grain measuring procedure: two individuals measure together grain from a large heap between them, other people are bringing more grain in containers which they are carrying on their heads (Amiet 1972, 80, pl. 196c).

Therefore, we can assume that the cylindrical vessel was used for measuring grain. There have been no archaeological remains of those capacity measuring vessels because they were made of organic substances. However, they are well known from countless texts, which mention the *sūtu* or the *bariga* in use, the cor-

Figure 3.11: Akkadian/Post-Akkadian cylinder seals.

3.11a: Seal depicting weighing and measuring. Drawing A. Otto & M. Lerchl after Boehmer 1965, no. 1105, fig. 458.

3.11b: One of the first depictions of the ball-staff: introduction scene to Shamash. Porada 1948, no. 254.

3.11d: Seal depicting grain deities carrying the capacity measuring vessel towards the grain goddess. Collon 1987/2005², no. 106.

3.11e: ED III-early Akkadian cylinder seal depicting the grain measuring procedure. Amiet 1972, pl. 196c.

3.11c: Lapis lazuli seal Kt 82 t. 224. Öztürk 2019, fig. 7.

rectness of which was frequently guaranteed by civil authorities such as the palace, the city house, or the market overseer, or by deities, e.g. 'the *bariga* of (the Sun God) Šamaš' (Veenhof 1985).[21] The capacity measures which were in use in Syria at that time have also been studied in detail (Chambon 2011), the capacity measures from Ur III Mesopotamia by Sallaberger (2022).

In Anatolia, the Assyrian merchants were dependent on the regular supply of the staple food barley, from which their main diet, bread and beer, was produced. Grain, especially barley and wheat, was traded by Assyrians and Anatolians (Veenhof 2008, 87–88). But grain also had another meaning in Kültepe: the merchants' payment terms were designated after the agricultural year with a special focus on grain, from the ploughing of the fields until the growing, harvesting, and threshing (Veenhof 2008, 238–45). Wheat and barley were the most frequently mentioned foodstuffs, and in addition to their consumption in large quantities as the staple foods, they also functioned as capital in payments, interest in loans, and object of debts (Atici 2014, 238; Dercksen 2008). The 'chief of the barley' (*rabi še'ē*) was among the high-ranking officials at Kaneš (e.g. Dercksen 2004, 166–67) and even a *limum ša še'im* is attested (Veenhof 2008, 88).

But what was the small man on Figure 3.11a doing with the staff on top of the grain measuring container? Grain was measured in Europe until the nineteenth century AD in a wooden cylindrical measuring container, and was either heaped, or smoothed flat with a strickle, consisting of an elongated tool of hard wood with a handle in the middle. A cord was added on one side, which served as an easy means of suspension when the tool was out of use.[22]

This method was apparently also used in the Near East. As J. N. Postgate shows in a recent article (Postgate 2023), Old Babylonian and Middle Assyrian texts indicate that measuring grain needed a measuring container and the implement *mešēqum*, known in English as a strickle, with which the grain was smoothed flat, level with the rim.[23] The texts mention a thick (*kabrum*), medium (*birûyum*), or thin (*raqqum*) strickle which refers to the size of the wooden tool.[24] There were actually different ways of filling a grain container: either the grain was horizontally flush with the rim, or it was heaped up to a conical mound, which explains the differences in measuring procedures.

Figure 3.12: A strickle from the eighteenth century AD in use <https://fdmf.fr/les-mesures-a-grains-du-xviiieme-siècle> [accessed 1 July 2022].

Egyptian measuring vessels in the Old and Middle Kingdom (i.e. the third and early second millennium) are known from depictions, models of granaries and original measuring vessels (Pommerening 2005). These cylindrical vessels were usually made from wood or leather. Capacity measuring vessels were made from stone only if they were kept in temples as reference vessels, e.g. the stone measuring vessel with inscription of Thutmosis III from the Karnak temple.[25]

In the Roman economy, the measuring container (*modius*) and the strickle (*rutellum*) were important tools for measuring capacities. Numerous depictions — the one illustrated here covering the floor in the 'hall of the grain measurers' in Ostia — show a man with a staff (strickle) in one hand working on the capacity container (Fig. 3.13).

Figure 3.13: Mosaic from the Aula dei Mensores in Ostia, AD 230. Berg 2020, 85, fig. 4.

---

21 For more details, see Chambon & Otto 2023.

22 I owe this idea to Grégory Chambon with whom I have been working on metrological issues for a long time. The results have been published recently, see Chambon & Otto 2023.

23 For the Old Babylonian texts see Wilcke (1983, 55–56) who translates it as 'Glattstreich-Holz'.

24 For the discussion see Postgate 2016 following Veenhof 1985.

25 Volume 1 oipe = 19.2 litres. Pommerening 2005, 363–64, M09.

This depiction on the Akkadian seal (Fig. 3.11a) is to our knowledge unique in showing the act of weighing with a small handheld scale and the filling and levelling of a measuring container. Because scenes on cylinder seals from the third millennium sometimes have clear allusions to the task or profession of the seal owner, we may assume that this seal (unfortunately without provenance) belonged to a merchant or to a weighing office which was either associated with a temple of the Sun God or made allusion to the guarantee of the procedures by the Sun God. In any case, this seal shows in a very explicit way the Sun God's role as the protector of weighing and measuring.

To sum up: there is ample evidence that the 'ball-staff' was an instrument like the staff called a strickle today which was used to smooth the contents in capacity measuring vessels. The capacity units at Kaneš are well known (Michel 2020b, 43 with further literature), and also the method of measuring with measuring pots *karpatum* (Dercksen 2021, 333), and certainly a designation similar for *mešēqum* will be found in the Kültepe texts in future.

The Interpretation of the 'Pot'

In Babylonia, weighed and sealed silver (*kaspum kankum*) was the obvious early currency the weight and quality of which had been checked and guaranteed by the relevant authorities (Marti & Chambon 2019, 59). Evidently, the silver itself was not sealed (this was invented later, in the first millennium, in the form of minted coins), but silver pieces were stored in little pots, when deposited, and in sacks, when transported. The silver sack was closed with a cord, then weighed on a balance, and clay labels or clay were attached to the knot of the cord closing the sack. These clay pieces were then impressed with seals, and this was described as *kīsum qadum kunukkiša*.[26] There is one archaeological proof for it: an Old Babylonian clay pot filled with scrap silver and gold, sets of weight stones, and sealed sack closures, which was found in the Ebabbar of Larsa (Fig. 3.14a) (Arnaud et al. 1979). It contained the equipment of the office for weights and measures (*bīt kittim*) which was housed in the temple of the Sun God (Charpin 2017). Every leather sack had contained a few shekels of silver the amount of which was written on the clay sealing which had been sealed by the responsible weighing officer. We propose that the sacks would have looked like the reconstruction on Figure 3.14b.

In the Assyrian trading colonies in Anatolia the controlling institutions were different ones, but clearly they existed. Silver is mentioned as 'refined' (*ṣarrupum*), 'good' (*dammuqum*), 'checked' (*ammurum*), or in various other forms; possibly the checking meant the establishment of the correct weight which seems at least in some instances to have been checked by the 'House of the Market'; possibly also 'marked, verified' (*uddu*) silver designates silver which had been controlled by the local trade office at the Karum; Dercksen (2021, 334–35) summarized: 'It is never stated who marked or verified the silver, but it is possible that this was done on behalf of the local Office of the Colony.' Silver and gold could be packed in packets (*nēpišum*) containing between 10 and 20 mina or 'bundles' (*riksum*) containing between 1 shekel and 1 mina, to which sealed clay tags were attached (Dercksen 2021, 335). Jars containing hacksilver were excavated in contemporary levels at Acemhöyük (Öztan 1997).[27]

If we compare the visual appearance of the sacks filled with silver with the depictions of the 'pot' on Kültepe seals, we can see striking similarities. The horizontal striations around the very narrow neck and the serrated upper end (Figs 3.14c, 3.14d) can be much better explained if we assume that a sack was depicted rather than a pot. The objects contained in the sack, i.e. the numerous, often angular pieces of hacksilver, could have caused the uneven, wavy outline of the sack on some seal images, which led to the not infrequent interpretation of the 'pot' as a serrated 'comb'.

Sacks containing silver, i.e. money purses, were the subject of many letters from Kaneš. One letter (Kt 01/k 219) mentions that someone's purse or sack of silver (obv. 4: *ki-sí-i*) was stolen in the palace (Günbattı 2014, 101–04). However, there are more possible identifications for the sack depicted on the seals. The term 'leather bag' (*naruqqum*) in fact meant a long-term joint-stock capital — one of the innovations of the bankers and traders at Kaneš (Dercksen 2022, 85–86). Some of these 'bags' are reported to have contained up to 30 pounds of gold, the equivalent of 120 pounds of silver. Silver was not only a crucial commodity but also the central currency of Old Assyrian trade (Veenhof 1999). Dercksen (2022, 88–89) calculated that 600 kg on average was shipped to Aššur every year and that about 1000 kg silver was yielded through the sale of tin and

---

26 AEM I/2 387 no. 463 rev. 8; Stol 2004, 884–85.

27 Marked moulds for producing metal ingots and nipples for easier division of such ingots were found in Kültepe and other Anatolian sites, Müller-Karpe 1994, 138–41.

Figure 3.14a: Larsa pot containing scrap silver, weight stones, and sealed closures of sacks. Arnaud et al. 1979, fig. 5.

Figure 3.14c: The sack with horizontal striations and serrated upper end. Detail from Fig. 3.1b.

Figure 3.14d: Seal impression Kt n/k 1870B showing the sack closed with a cord in front of the supreme authority. Özgüç 2006, CS 679.

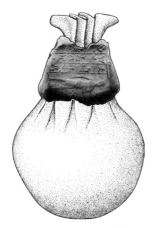

Figure 3.14b: Tentative reconstruction of a 'sack of sealed silver'. Closure: Arnaud et al. 1979, pl. I,2; reconstruction by A. Otto / M. Lerchl.

textiles, which underlines the fundamental importance of silver for these trading communities.

Taking all the evidence together, we are inclined to interpret the 'pot'-like element so frequently depicted on the Kültepe seals as a silver sack or purse.

The Kültepe Merchants' Concern for Legal Regulations Expressed in Seals

Law and justice were the backbone of the Assyro-Anatolian trading system and the century-long success of the merchants' community at Kaneš with a sophisticated administrative and economic structure.

All commercial activities of the inhabitants of Kaneš such as credit and investment, securities, cooperation with the business partners, regulation of taxes and wages, and much more depended directly on the legal regulations and their control (Veenhof 2008, 93–96), as well as family legal affairs such as marriage, adoption, divorce, and inheritance (Michel 2020b), which were more complicated than in Babylonia due to the considerable distances between the parties involved. Countless texts from Kültepe dealing with all aspects of legal affairs have been reported and studied over the past decades.

The merchants' houses of the Lower Town contained many artefacts connected with economic transactions, the most stable ones being weight-stones of stone and metal. Fikri Kulakoğlu, who published many weight stones and scale-pans from Kültepe, recently stressed the importance of standardized units and their correctness for the inhabitants of Kaneš in these words:

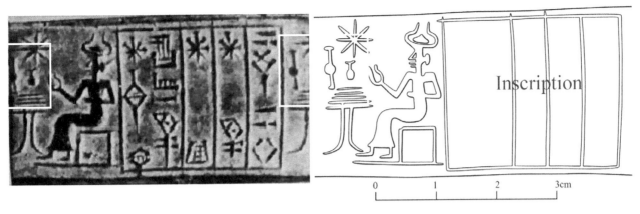

Figure 3.15: Lapis lazuli cylinder seal Kte/t 180 belonging to a high-ranking Assyrian officer. Öztürk 2019, fig. 5.

Artifacts and written documents provide important information about weighing procedures and the importance of standardized units in trade. Almost every tablet concerning business activities documents units of weight, which differed according to owner, institution, or region. The texts also indicate the existence of official standard weights in Anatolia as well as in Mesopotamia. (Kulakoğlu 2017, 341)

The currencies in use were metal, especially silver which was the general standard of value, but also gold, copper, and tin on the one hand and grain on the other hand (Dercksen 2021). The control of their mass and quality was of utmost importance for everyone.

The concern for law and justice — including on the social and on the commercial level — was expressed also in the seals of the people at Kaneš, Aššur, and other areas involved in the Assyro-Anatolian-Syrian trading system. Seals were foremost legal tools crucial in testifying the correctness of legal processes and written contracts. Sealed legal documents and closures of goods are the archaeological remains of these procedures.

However, the depiction of abstract concepts is a most difficult task for any artist. In Greek and Roman iconography there existed a whole set of symbols, attributes, and personifications which expressed positive abstract concepts of the society and its ruling class, e.g. for illustrating *pax*, *libertas*, *spes*, *virtus*, *securitas*, *concordia*, *justitia*, and many more (Hölscher 1967). Until today, the icon for justice or a law-court is the balance; but no one seems to have investigated how far back the origin of this motif might go.

In the Near East, rod and ring symbolize divine order and were depicted when a deity symbolically awarded it to a ruler (Wiggermann 2006–2008). This motif was also derived from a concrete set of simple instruments which were used to measure length. Rod and ring expressed — not unlike 'ball-staff' and 'pot' — the humans' concern for divine protection of the correctness of juridical and economic procedures.

The ultimate guarantee for the righteousness of trade and exchange was only possible with the support of the supreme authorities in the divine sphere. This explains why the strickle and the purse, the symbols for law and justice, became such extremely important motifs on seals within this trade-centred community, and why they were often prominently depicted in front of the supreme authority, or more precisely under its direct protection.

Most remarkable in this respect is a lapis lazuli cylinder seal found in a late third-millennium context on the Kültepe mound (Öztürk 2019, fig. 5). The image is outstanding (Fig. 3.15): only an enthroned god and his most essential tools or symbols — strickle and purse — are depicted above an altar and below a star. The name of the seal owner, designated as 'the beloved of (the city of) Aššur'[28] must have been a high-ranking Assyrian officer on duty in Kaneš in order to monitor compliance with law and order.

Conclusions

Legal certainty has been the basis of most functioning societies. In Near Eastern societies of the Bronze Age, texts on the one hand and depictions in various pictorial media on the other hand emphasize the role metrology played with respect to the ancient concepts of law, justice, and righteousness. Since every economically active person at ancient Kaneš owned at least one cylinder or stamp seal in order to sign and validate written docu-

---

[28] 'Abu-aḫi, Adad is his god, beloved of / who loves (the city of) Aššur', Schwemer 2001, 238.

ments and letters and the closures of goods and doors, it is not too far-fetched to claim that the concern for justice may also have entered the imagery of their seals.

We suggest to identify the 'ball-staff' with the strickle which was an essential tool in capacity measuring procedures, and the 'pot' with the purse or sack containing silver. Gradually these motifs, which were initially depicted as actively used tools and commodities, developed into abstract symbols of law and justice. More than 50 per cent of the seal images known from Kaneš so far contain these symbols, most frequently depicted under direct protection of the supreme authority or in close connection with a worshipper, i.e. with the seal owner who perpetuated his concern for legal processes in these little symbols.

These pictorial motifs — for the first time attested in the Akkadian period in clear connection with Šamaš, god of justice — may have come to Assyria or to Kültepe via Syria already in the Anatolian Early Bronze Age, and were developed here further, depicted in lively actions on seals. An impressively high number of seals of all styles — Assyrian, Anatolian, Syrian, and even recut Old Babylonian seals — show these symbols. They may have returned into the Babylonian imagery from Anatolia or Assyria in the Isin-Larsa period. But in Babylonia they never became equally important icons or symbols like in Assyria and Anatolia, where the lives of the vast majority of those people who used seals revolved around private trade, and where the plea for law and justice was therefore a major concern.

Acknowledgements

My sincere thanks are due to Professors Fikri Kulakoğlu, Cécile Michel, and Guido Kryszat for inviting me to participate at the 5th Kültepe International Meeting which was not only enriching in every respect but showed clearly the added value of interdisciplinary cooperation. My interest in Kültepe seal impressions goes back to the time when, writing my dissertation, I was fascinated by the endless ideas present in Old Syrian and Anatolian seals; my fascination has endured ever since, and I am glad that I can contribute here a token to this most meaningful art in miniature.

Bibliography

Amiet, Pierre
1972 *Glyptique susienne, des origines à l'époque des Perses Achéménides* (Mémoires de la Délégation archéologique en Iran 43). Geuthner, Paris.

Arnaud, Daniel; Calvet, Yves & Huot, Jean-Louis
1979 'Ilšu-ibnišu, orfèvre de l'E.BABBAR de Larsa. La jarre L.76.77 et son contenu', *Syria* 56: 1–64.

Atici, Levent
2014 'Tracing Inequality from Assur to Kültepe/Kaneš: Merchants, Donkeys, and Clay Tablets', in Benjamin S. Arbuckle & Sue Ann McCarty (eds), *Animals and Inequality in the Ancient World*. University Press of Colorado, Colorado: 231–50.

Barjamovic, Gojko; Hertel, Thomas & Larsen, Mogens Trolle
2012 *Ups and Downs at Kaneš: Chronology, History and Society in the Old Assyrian Period* (Publications de l'Institut historiquearchéologique néerlandais de Stamboul 120). Nederlands Instituut voor het Nabije Oosten, Leiden.

Berg, Ria
2020 'Iconography of the Modius Measure in Ostia: The Visualizing of Economic and Cultural Exchange', in Alice Landskron & Claudia Tempesta (eds), *Trade and Commerce in the Harbour Town of Ostia* (Keryx 7). University of Graz, Graz: 79–106.

Blocher, Felix
1992a *Siegelabrollungen auf frühaltbabylonischen Tontafeln in der Yale Babylonian Collection* (Münchener Vorderasiatische Studien 9). Profil, Munich.
1992b *Siegelabrollungen auf frühaltbabylonischen Tontafeln im British Museum* (Münchener Vorderasiatische Studien 10). Profil, Munich.

Boehmer, Rainer Michael
1965 *Die Entwicklung der Glyptik während der Akkad-Zeit* (Untersuchungen zur Assyriologie und Vorderasiatischen Archäologie 4). De Gruyter, Berlin.

Chambon, Grégory
2011 *Normes et pratiques: l'homme, la mesure et l'écriture en Mésopotamie, I: Les mesures de capacité et de poids en Syrie Ancienne, d'Ébla à Émar* (Berliner Beiträge zum Vorderen Orient 21). PeWe-Verlag, Gladbeck.

Chambon, Grégory & Otto, Adelheid
2023 'New Perspectives in the Study of Weights and Measures of the Ancient Near East', in Grégory Chambon & Adelheid Otto (eds), *Weights and Measures as a Window on Ancient Near Eastern Societies* (Münchener Abhandlungen zum Alten Orient 9). PeWe-Verlag, Gladbeck: 1–23.

Charpin, Dominique
2017 *La vie méconnue des temples mésopotamiens*. Collège de France, Paris.

Collon, Dominique
1986 *Isin-Larsa and Old Babylonian Periods* (Catalogue of the Western Asiatic Seals in the British Museum 3). British Museum Publications, London.
1987/2005[2] *First Impressions: Cylinder Seals in the Ancient Near East*. British Museum Press, London.
1995 'Filling Motifs', in Uwe Finkbeiner, Reinhard Dittmann & Harald Hauptmann (eds), *Beiträge zur Kulturgeschichte Vorderasiens: Festschrift für Rainer Michael Boehmer*. Von Zabern, Mainz: 69–76.

Delaporte, Louis

1923 *Musée du Louvre, Catalogue des Cylindres Orientaux*, II: *Acquisitions*. Hachette, Paris.

Dercksen, Jan Gerrit

2004 *Old Assyrian Institutions* (MOS Studies 4, Publications de l'Institut historique et archeologique neerlandais de Stamboul 98). Nederlands Instituut voor het Nabije Oosten, Leiden.

2008 'Subsistence, Surplus and the Market for Grain and Meat at Ancient Kaneš', *Altorientalische Forschungen* 35/1: 86–102.

2021 'Money in the Old Assyrian Period', in Lorenz Rahmstorf, Gojko Barjamovic & Nicola Ialongo (eds), *Merchants, Measures and Money: Understanding Technologies of Early Trade in a Comparative Perspective* (Weight and Value 2). Wachholtz, Kiel: 331–59.

2022 'The Golden Interval of Old Assyrian Trade (2000–1700 BC)', in David A. Warburton (ed.), *The Earliest Economic Growth in World History* (Publications de l'Institut historique archéologique néerlandais de Stamboul 133). Peeters, Leuven: 75–104.

Günbattı, Cahit

2014 *Harsamna Kralı Hurmeli'ye Gönderilen Mektup ve Kanis Kralları: The Letter Sent to Hurmeli King of Harsama and the Kings of Kaniš*. Türk Tarih Kurumu, Ankara.

Hafford, William B.

2019 'Accounting for Civilization: Early Weights and Measures at Tepe Gawra', in Lorenz Rahmstorf & Edward Stratford (eds), *Weights and Marketplaces from the Bronze Age to the Early Modern Period: Proceedings of Two Workshops Funded by the European Research Council (ERC)*. Wachholtz, Kiel: 15–34.

Hölscher, Tonio

1967 *Victoria Romana: Archäologische Untersuchungen zur Geschichte und Wesensart der römischen Siegesgöttin von den Anfängen bis zum Ende des 3. Jahrhunderts n. Chr.* Von Zabern, Mainz.

Kulakoğlu, Fikri

2011 'Kültepe-Kaneš: A Second Millennium B.C.E. Trading Center on the Central Plateau', in Sharon R. Steadman & Gregory McMahon (eds), *The Oxford Handbook of Ancient Anatolia*. Oxford University Press, Oxford: 1012–30.

2017 'Balance Stone Weights and Scale-Pans from Kültepe-Kaneš: On One of the Basic Elements of the Old Assyrian Trading System', in Çiğdem Maner, Mara T. Horowitz & Allan S. Gilbert (eds), *Overturning Certainties in Near Eastern Archaeology: A Festschrift in Honor of K. Aslıhan Yener* (Culture and History of the Ancient Near East 90). Leiden, Brill: 341–402.

Lassen, Agnete Wisti

2017 'The "Bull-Altar" in Old Assyrian Glyptic: A Representation of the God Assur?', in Fikri Kulakoğlu & Gojko Barjamovic (eds), *Movement, Resources, Interaction: Proceedings of the Second Kültepe International Meeting, Kültepe 27–31 July 2015* (Kültepe International Meetings 2, Subartu 46). Brepols, Turnhout: 177–94.

Marti, Lionel & Chambon, Grégory

2019 'Identifying Weights in Cuneiform Texts from Mari and Assyria: Management and Circulation of Silver', in Loren Rahmstorf & Edward Stratford (eds), *Weights and Marketplaces from the Bronze Age to the Early Modern Period: Proceedings of Two Workshops Funded by the European Research Council (ERC)*. Wachholtz, Kiel: 51–66.

Mayr, Rudolf H.

2005 'Seal Impressions on Tablets from Umma' (unpublished doctoral thesis, Yale University).

Michel, Cécile
2020a 'Making Clay Envelopes in the Old Assyrian Period', in Fikri Kulakoğlu, Cécile Michel & Güzel Öztürk (eds), *Integrative Approaches to the Archaeology and History of Kültepe-Kaneš* (Kültepe International Meetings 3, Subartu 45). Brepols, Turnhout: 187–203.

2020b *Women of Assur and Kaneš: Texts from the Archives of Assyrian Merchants* (Writings from the Ancient World 42). Society of Biblical Literature, Atlanta.

Müller-Karpe, Andreas
1994 *Altanatolisches Metallhandwerk* (Untersuchungen aus dem Institut für Ur- und Frühgeschichte der Christian-Albrechts-Universität, Kiel, und dem Archäologischen Landesmuseum sowie dem Zentrum für Baltische und Skandinavische Archäologie in der Stiftung Schleswig-Holsteinische Landesmuseen Schloss Gottorf, Schleswig und dem Archäologischen Landesamt Schleswig-Holstein, Schleswig 75). Wachholtz, Neumünster.

2021 'Siegel hethitischer Kaufleute', in Michael Herles, Claudia Beuger, Jörg Becker & Simone Arnhold (eds), *Von Syrien bis Georgien – durch die Steppen Vorderasiens: Festschrift für Felix Blocher anlässlich seines 65. Geburtstages* (Marru 13). Zaphon, Münster: 427–47.

Otto, Adelheid
2000 *Die Entstehung und Entwicklung der Klassisch-Syrischen Glyptik* (Untersuchungen zur Assyriologie und Vorderasiatischen Archäologie 8). De Gruyter, Berlin.

2013 'Königssiegel als Programm – Überlegungen zum Selbstverständnis altorientalischer Herrscher und zur Deutung der Tierkampfszene', *Zeitschrift für Assyriologie* 103: 45–68.

2016 'Much more than just a Decorative Element: The Guilloche as Symbol of Fertility', in Julie Patrier, Philippe Quenet & Pascal Butterlin (eds), *Mille et une empreintes: un Alsacien en Orient; mélanges en l'honneur du 65ᵉ anniversaire de Dominique Beyer* (Subartu 36). Brepols, Turnhout: 379–93.

2017 'Private and State in the Second Millennium B.C. from an Archaeological Perspective', in Rients de Boer and Jan Gerrit Dercksen (eds), *Private and State in the Ancient Near East: Proceedings of the 58th Rencontre Assyriologique Internationale at Leiden, 16–20 July 2012*. Eisenbrauns, Winona Lake: 21–42.

2019 'Glyptic', in Ann C. Gunter, *A Companion to Ancient Near Eastern Art*. Wiley, Hoboken: 411–31.

Özgüç, Nimet
1965 *The Anatolian Group of Cylinder Seal Impressions from Kültepe* (Türk Tarih Kurumu Yayınları 22). Türk Tarih Kurumu, Ankara.

2006 *Kültepe-Kaniš / Neša: Seal Impressions on the Clay Envelopes from the Archives of the Native Peruwa and Assyrian Trader Uṣur-ša-Ištar son of Aššur-imittī* (Türk Tarih Kurumu Yayınları 50). Türk Tarih Kurumu, Ankara.

Özgüç, Nimet & Tunca, Önhan
2001 *Kültepe-Kaniš: Sealed and Inscribed Clay Bullae* (Türk Tarih Kurumu Yayınları 48). Türk Tarih Kurumu, Ankara.

Özgüç, Tahsin
2005 *Kültepe, Kaniš / Neša*. Yapı Kredi Yayınları, Istanbul.

Öztan, Aliye
1997 'Acemhöyük gümüş hazinesi', *Türk Tarih Kurumu Belleten* 61: 231, 233–71.

Öztürk, Güzel
2019 'Post-Akkadian and Ur III Features on Cylinder Seals from Kültepe-Kaneš: An Iconographic and Stylistic Analysis', *Adalya* 22: 45–67.

Peyronel, Luca

2019 'Weighing Silver on the Scales. An Overview of Silver Hoards and Balance Weights during the Middle Bronze Age (ca. 2000–1600 BC) in the Near East', in Loren Rahmstorf & Edward Stratford (eds), *Weights and Marketplaces from the Bronze Age to the Early Modern Period: Proceedings of Two Workshops Funded by the European Research Council (ERC)*. Wachholtz, Kiel: 67–86.

Pommerening, Tanja

2005 *Die altägyptischen Hohlmaße* (Studien zur Altägyptischen Kultur, Beihefte 10). Buske, Hamburg.

Porada, Edith

1948 *Corpus of Ancient Near Eastern Seals in North American Collections*, I: *The Pierpont Morgan Library*. Pantheon, New York.

Postgate, John Nicholas

2016 'Measuring Middle Assyrian Grain (and Sesame)', in Gilda Bartoloni & Maria Giovanna Biga (eds), *Not Only History: Proceedings of the Conference in Honor of Mario Liverani Held in Sapienza-Università di Roma, Dipartimento di Scienze dell'Antichità, 20-21 April 2009*. Eisenbrauns, Winona Lake: 21–241.

2023 'On Some Middle Assyrian Metrological Points', in Grégory Chambon & Adelheid Otto (eds), *Weights and Measures as a Window on Ancient Near Eastern Societies* (Münchener Abhandlungen zum Alten Orient 9). PeWe-Verlag, Gladbeck: 87–94.

Rahmstorf, Lorenz & Stratford, Edward (eds)

2019 *Weights and Marketplaces from the Bronze Age to the Early Modern Period: Proceedings of Two Workshops Funded by the European Research Council (ERC)*. Wachholtz, Kiel.

Roßberger, Elisa

2018 'What's Inside this Jar? Actual and Iconic Use of Vessels in Early Mesopotamia', *KASKAL* 15: 111–38.

Sallaberger, Walther

2022 'Measuring Grain in Early Bronze Age Mesopotamia: Form, Use, and Control of the *bariga* Container in the Twenty-First Century BCE', in Karine Chemla, Agathe Keller & Christine Proust (eds), *Cultures of Computation and Quantification in the Ancient World* (Why the Sciences of the Ancient World Matter 6). Springer, Cham: 171–96.

Schwemer, Daniel

2001 *Die Wettergottgestalten Mesopotamiens und Nordsyriens im Zeitalter der Keilschriftkulturen: Materialien und Studien nach den schriftlichen Quellen*. Harrassowitz, Wiesbaden.

Stol, Marten

2004 'Wirtschaft und Gesellschaft in altbabylonischer Zeit', in P. Attinger, W. Sallaberger & M. Wäfler (eds), *Mesopotamien: Die altbabylonische Zeit* (Orbis biblicus et orientalis 160/4). Academic Press, Fribourg: 641–975.

Teissier, Béatrice

1993 'The Ruler with the Peaked Cap and Other Syrian Iconography on Glyptic from Kültepe in the Early Second Millennium B.C.', in Machteld Mellink, Edith Porada & Tashin Özgüç (eds), *Aspects of Art and Iconography: Anatolia and its Neighbours; Studies in Honor of Nimet Özgüç*. Türk Tarih Kurumu, Ankara: 601–12.

1994 *Sealings and Seals on Texts from Kültepe Karum Level 2*. Nederlands Historisch-Archaeologisch Instituut te Istanbul, Istanbul.

Veenhof, Klaas R.

1985 'SAG.ÍL.LA = saggilû, "Difference Assessed". On Measuring and Accounting in Some Old Babylonian Texts', in Jean-Marie Durand & Jean-Roberts Kupper (eds), *Miscellanea Babyloniaca: Mélanges offerts à Maurice Birot*. Éditions Recherche sur les civilisations, Paris: 285–306.

1999 'Silver and Credit in Old Assyrian Trade', in Jan Gerrit Dercksen (ed.), *Trade and Finance in Ancient Mesopotamia* (Publications de l'Institut historiquearchéologique néerlandais de Stamboul 84). Nederlands Historisch-Archaeologisch Instituut te Istanbul, Istanbul: 55–83.

2008 'The Old Assyrian Period', in Klaas R. Veenhof & Jesper Eidem (eds), *Mesopotamia: The Old Assyrian Period* (Orbis biblicus et orientalis 160/5). Vandenhoeck Ruprecht, Göttingen: 13–264.

Wiggermann, Frans A. M.

2006–2008 'Ring und Stab', in Michael P. Streck (ed.), *Reallexikon der Assyriologie und Vorderasiatischen Archäologie*, XI: *Prinz, Prinzessin - Samug*. De Gruyter, Berlin: 414–21.

Wilcke, Claus

1983 'Nachlese zu A. Poebels Babylonian Legal and Business Documents from the Time of the First Dynasty of Babylon Chiefly from Nippur (BE 6/2), Teil 1', *Zeitschrift für Assyriologie* 73: 48–66.

Woods, Christopher E.

2009 'At the Edge of the World: Cosmological Conceptions of the Eastern Horizon in Mesopotamia', *Journal of Ancient Near Eastern Religions* 9: 183–239.

4. The Origins and History of the God Šarra-mātān

Yoram Cohen

Introduction to the Problem

Guido Kryszat's work in the past decade or more (although see as early as 2003) has mainly concentrated on an ongoing effort to distil the essence of Old Assyrian religion.[1] In multiple studies, Kryszat asks: What is Assyrian and what is not Assyrian in Aššur in the early phase of the city's history? While Aššur's distinctiveness is always acknowledged in the literature — the nature of kingship at the city, the city's social institutions, and its venerated god, Aššur — it is difficult to unravel the strands of which it is made, especially considering the major influence Babylonia had had, which had begun already in the Sargonic period (if not before) and continued throughout the city's life under the Ur III kingdom. A crucial point of Kryszat's scholarship considered the identity of the god Šarra-mātān.

Following Dercksen (2011), Kryszat (2018) succeeded in crystallizing the identity of the god Šarra-mātān. Šarra-mātān appears in the Apûm-Aššur Treaty, in oaths, in letters, and once as a theophoric element in a PN: *ni-mar-ša-ra-ma-té*, 'the appearance of Šarra-mātān' (without nunation; but see footnote 2 and further below).[2] He appears to be an individual god, and not an epithet of Aššur, because both gods are mentioned together in an inventory list.[3] What is clear is that the ending of the second element of the god's name is in the dual case (nom.: -*mātān*, oblique: -*mātēn*).

Kryszat understood the name to mean as 'The King of both Lands'. In this divine name he saw a reflection of the socio-historical situation of Aššur. The divine name, so he claimed, was a deliberate artificial creation of a force which was meant to give articulation to the composite make-up of early Assyrian society. The two lands included the newly integrated population from the west and the Assyrians in Aššur, included as one under this god's presence.[4]

---

1 e.g. Kryszat 2003, 2006, 2018, 2020, and 2021. This paper is a response of a non-specialist to Guido Kryszat's work on early Assyrian religion. I offer an opinion neither as an expert of Old Assyrian life and society nor as a scholar of ancient Anatolia, but as an onlooker who has studied the West Semitic world in the Bronze Age. It is to be understood that since this is to be taken as a *responsum*, my citations of the sources and secondary literature are limited. Fuller details can be found in Kryszat's papers, all of which are cited.

Yoram Cohen (ycohen1@tauex.tau.ac.il) Professor, Department of Archaeology and Ancient Near Eastern Cultures, Tel Aviv University

2 OIP 27, no. 2: *ni-mar-ša-ra-ma-té*; the texts from Alişar are considered to belong to Kültepe Lower Town Level Ib period; see Dercksen 2001. According to Kouwenberg 2017, 66, in the construct state the final -n of dual forms is dropped. This is also noticed when the dual noun is in the oblique case, i.e. -*ē*. The loss of the final -n in the oblique dual resulting in -*ē* makes the form 'indistinguishable from the oblique plural, and may represent a replacement of the dual by the plural'. Hence the analysis of the name *ni-mar-ša-ra-ma-té* as *mātē(n)* is not without its difficulties, as it may also represent *šarra-mātē*, 'King of the Lands', or even possibly *šarra-māte/i*, 'King of the Land'. For lack of distinction in the OA syllabary between /i/ and /e/, see Kouwenberg 2017, 94–95.

3 Barjamovic & Larsen 2008, 153–54 (Kt 94/k 670): '[x] tables that were before his gods, one chair that was before Aššur, one cup that was before Šarru-mātēn (*ša-ru-ma¹-té-en*).' See discussion in Michel 2020, 340.

4 Kryszat 2018, 198 and 200: '(h)e [Šarra-mātān] might be a deity invented by the rulers of the city of Aššur to create a common religious focus for two originally ethnic different groups inhabiting the city.' Kryszat 2021, 249: 'Šarra-mātān poses an enigma, which might partly be solved by accepting the hypothesis of a dichoto-

In what follows I will consider more closely the name of the god Šarra-mātān, his origin, and his history.

The Name Šarra-mātān and the Ambiguous Morphology of the Dual

What is first to be considered is the dual form in the name, -mātān/-mātēn. While in Old Assyrian the dual form was productive, its state was rather fluid.[5] There are cases in which the dual was used for nouns that were counted in multiples above '2'. For example: 4 šiprēn, 'four messengers', in dual oblique. One also recalls that in Old Assyrian oaths, found at the end of many letters, as well as in royal inscriptions, any number of subjects above '2' attracted a dual verb, but not a plural verb, as would have been expected. This unclear situation of the dual may have caused confusion for the Assyrian scribes themselves. Let us consider this oath in the letter KT 4, 42:22–23 (Dercksen 2011): ša-ra-ma-ta-an i-lu-a ù Ištar lu i-de₈-ú. The form of i-lu-a is 'my gods', given in the nom. pl. and not dual form, which would have been ilāya, if it were an attribute of Šarra-mātān, standing in apposition to it. One is confounded by this. How is one to translate this phrase? Here are three suggestions by Dercksen, Veenhof, and Kryszat.

1. Dercksen (2011) suggests thus: 'Šarramatān, my gods, and Ištar surely know!', in which 'my gods' refers to Š., a pair of deities, or a sort of double-duty deity. Thus, Dercksen sees in the form two gods.

2. Veenhof (2018, 71 and n. 111) follows with this translation: 'May Šarra-mātān, my gods, and Ištar know.' He explains that because one's personal god is always given in the singular (ilī), ilū'ā must stand in apposition to Šarra-mātān. In his words, 'I assume that ilū'ā is in apposition to Šarra-matān, so that two gods are invoked and not three. An independent plural would be exceptional, leave the identity of the gods unknown and is unlikely since a man had only one family god.' Veenhof (2018, 80) concludes that 'the meaning of his name and his identity remain unclear.' It seems that he closely agrees with Dercksen's opinion, but suggests that the god is a plural form deity.

3. Kryszat (2018, 203) translates the oath phrase as 'Šarra-mātān, my gods, and Ištar may know [...]'. Kryszat treats 'my gods' as a separate subject, and not in apposition to Šarra-mātān, whom he considers as a singular subject. He translates the name Šarra-mātān as the 'King of the two/both lands/people'.

The uncertainty regarding the actual meaning of the dual in the name despite the morphology leads me to consider the following possibility. We can think of the name Šarra-mātān as a reflection of the common Sumerian epithet of Enlil: lugal kur-kur-ra, which is documented since Early Dynastic times (Second Dynasty of Uruk). The doubling of 'kur' in Sumerian, meant for expressing plurality, was picked up (although perhaps not directly, see below) in Old Assyrian as the dual form. In Babylonian sources of the period, the epithet was never pluralized, expressed solely as Bēl mātim.[6] This epithet may have belonged to Dagan (or to Enlil, or even to both). So, it is possible, I contend, that the name is to be understood as the 'King of the Lands', or the 'King of all the Lands'. Here in the Assyrian attestations, the dual simply expresses plurality or totality. In the oath phrase, the plural ilū'ā was an attraction, because of a misanalysis of the name's ending -an, as a plural, this said in consideration of what we surmised about the status of the dual in Old Assyrian morphology. Hence, in the oath, one god is meant. Thus, I translate the phrase as follows, 'the King of the Lands, my¹ god, and Ištar may know.'

Before continuing with Šarra-mātān, it is worth considering for the sake of what I have described now a somewhat similar use of the dual case, although it is not attested in Aššur proper. Note the dual form attested in a month name from Mari of the so-called 'Šakkanaku' period.[7] We find the month of ma-al-kà-né-en. The name is attested multiple times written as a dual but sometimes also as ma-al-kà-ni, which is probably its plural form but not a dual without nunation.[8] This month name can paralleled (by placing it in sequence) with another month however from a different but near contemporary calendar, the month of šarrāni, which obviously

---

mous society in Aššur before the arrival of Šamšī-Adad and his followers.'

5 Kouwenberg 2017, 168 n. 28, 259–60 n. 29–30, 275 n. 9, 686–87; Hecker 1968, 92, 95, 198, 220, and passim.

6 In Mari, the title lugal ma-tim is to be understood as Bēl-mātim, and not *Šar(ra)-mātim; Feliu 2003, 58 n. 127, with previous literature, although this may require reconsideration, based on what follows.

7 Durand 1985, who assigns most of the 'Šakkanakku' documents to the times of Yaḫdun-Lim's reign.

8 Limet 1976, 10–12, and passim.

4. THE ORIGINS AND HISTORY OF THE GOD ŠARRA-MĀTĀN

means '(the month of) the Kings'.[9] Hence *malkānēn* and *malkānē* does not mean *'(the month of) the Two Kings' (dual), but obviously '(the month of) the Kings (pl.)'. It is certainly possible to assume that the use of the dual *malkānēn* was either because 1.) the dual and plural were already quite interchangeable, as in the Old Assyrian situation, or because 2.) the dual form was influenced by a logographic writing of the month as *lugal-lugal. It is relevant to note that in Zimrī-Lîm's and Šamšī-Addu's calendar we find the month name now written as (iti) *malkānim* (*ma-al-ka-nim*), hence reanalysed as singular, as if its sg. form was **malkānum*.[10] When I analyse how the name of Šarra-mātān in Šamšī-Adad's Aššur inscription was written, this observation will be useful.

Origin and History

Coming back to consider the origin and history of Šarra-mātān, we see that a very similar name or epithet is attested elsewhere in two non-Assyrian sources: an Old Babylonian hymn to the god Pap-ul-e-gar-ra and a Hurro-Hittite ritual.

In the Old Babylonian hymn to the god Pap-ul-e-gar-ra, the god is given the epithet *šar-ra-am-ma-tim*, an obvious spelling of Šarra-mātim.[11] The strange spelling may show that the meaning of the epithet was not properly understood by whoever wrote it. Thus, it possibly was lifted from an archaic source. It is hardly likely that this source was Old Assyrian. An early Old Babylonian or even an Old Akkadian source are more likely candidates.

The god pap-ul-e-gar-ra can be associated with Ninurta.[12] Hence it is possible that the epithet originally belonged to Enlil's circle, although any definite evidence is lacking.

In the Hurro-Hittite cleansing ritual (CTH 471, The Ritual of Ammiḫatna),[13] a deity called ᵈ*ša-a-ri-im-ma-ti* appears. The origin of the deity is not clear, but certainly it is not Hittite or Hurrian. Although a unique appearance, in some way or the other, it is obviously connected, as previous scholars have noted, to Šarra-mātān/-mātēn, or Šarra-mātim.[14] This should not come as a surprise, because in this Kizzuwatnean ritual, as in other such rituals, deities of various origins are met, sifted through a Hurrian sieve. The bizarre spelling, very similar to the one of the Hymn to Pap-ul-e-gar-ra (with the doubling of the -m), eventually suggests a Babylonian origin. Even when passing through Hurrian mediation, on occasion Hittite rituals betray their Babylonian origins.[15] But there is more to this than this observation.

In the Hittite ritual, the god ᵈ*ša-a-ri-im-ma-ti* is offered a blood libation. After him, comes his consort, *ša-a-lu-uš-bi-i-te-in-ḫi*, who also receives a blood libation.[16] The goddess Šaluš-bitenḫi was the consort of Kumarbi. She was in origin a Syrian goddess, identified with Dagan's consort, Šala(š).[17] Dagan, in turn, was identified with Kumarbi. Hence, the epithet in the Hittite ritual ᵈ*ša-a-ri-im-ma-ti* was Kumarbi's, although originally, Dagan's.

Thus, to conclude, the seemingly exclusively Assyrian divine name Šarra-mātān may ultimately have had its origins in Babylonia or at least took its aspiration from that deity or divine epithet.[18] One may perhaps venture to say that the name or epithet was a leftover from the Sargonic period. The little evidence we have indicates that the epithet served either Enlil or Dagan. The recent publication of the remarkable Amorite vocabularies, neatly shows us that in the Amorite world the two gods Enlil and Dagan were thought of as the same god.[19]

Šamšī-Adad's Aššur Inscription: From -mātān to -mātim

One final point can be made. In his Aššur inscription dedicated to Enlil, who by this time was wholly syncretized with Aššur, Šamšī-Adad calls in the curse section upon a god called Šarru-mātim.[20] As Kryszat (2018, 199) had surmised, Šamšī-Adad's scribe did not recognize a god called Šarra-mātān, and, when composing Šamšī-Adad's inscription, changed Šarra-mātān's name to Šarru-mātim, with *mātum*, 'land', given in the gen. sg.,

---

9 Cohen, M. 2015, 206 and 318.

10 Arkhipov 2012, 192 (from the times of Yasmaḫ-Addu, i.e. Šamšī-Addu's calendar), 218, 291, 292 (from the reign of Zimri-Lim), and passim, for attestations.

11 Beaulieu & Mayer 1997, 167; Streck & Wasserman 2008, 340 (v. 6).

12 Krebernik 2005, 329–30.

13 Strauß 2006.

14 Laroche 1980, 216. *Pace* Kryszat 2018, 201, n. 22–23.

15 Schwemer 2013.

16 Strauß 2006, 223–24, and 41.

17 Schwemer 2008; Archi 1995.

18 For other epithets (of Enlil), adopted in Assyria (standing for Aššur), see Cohen, Y. 2017.

19 George & Krebernik 2022, 115 and 118.

20 Grayson 1987, 47–51 = Šamšī-Adad I; A.0.39.1. See Krebernik 2011.

Table 4.1: Erišum 1, Erišum 14, and Šamšī-Adad 1.

Erišum 1 (ll. 50–51)		Erišum 14 (ll. 29–31)		Šamšī-Adad 1 (ll. 114–17)	
	[--]		[--]	114	ᵈUTU
50	[a-šùr]	29	a-šùr^{ki}	114	ᵈen-líl
50	ᵈIŠKUR	29	ù ᵈIŠKUR	114	ᵈIŠKUR
50	ú be-l[u-um i-li]	30	[ù] be-lúm ì-lí	115	ù ᵈšar-ru-ma-a-tim
51	[za-ra-šu]	31	[za-r]a-šu	116	pé-re-é'-šu
51	[li-i]l₅-qú-ta	31	⌈li-ik-sú-ma⌉	117	li-il-qú-tu

possibly, so I wish to add, as an analogy with Mari's lugal *mātim* (see footnote 6).

It is worth dwelling a bit longer on Šamšī-Adad's inscription. Šamšī-Adad tells us that he restored the temple of Enlil/Aššur that was built by Erišum but was eventually abandoned by him. He says thus: é ᵈ*en-líl ša e-ri-šum dumu dingir-šum-ma i-pu-šu é i-na-ah-ma ú-ša-as-sí-ik-su-ma*, 'the temple of Enlil, which Erišum, son of Ilušumma, had built — the temple was dilapidated, and he abandoned it.' It seems logical from this statement that Šamšī-Adad, or his scribe, divulged the information regarding the building of the Enlil/Aššur temple at the times of Erišum from Erišum's own inscriptions. Furthermore, a comparison between two of Erišum's inscriptions (nos 1 and 14) and Šamšī-Adad's inscription point to sufficient similarity so as to suggest that Šamšī-Adad's scribe saw a similar inscription of Erišum, which actually mentioned the god Šarra-mātān. It was this inscription, no longer available to us, which served as an inspiration for Šamšī-Adad's Aššur inscription.[21]

In the 'lost' inscription, there appeared Šarra-mātān. The name was misunderstood by Šamšī-Adad's scribe, who changed it to Šarru-mātim. Such a correction is apparently not innovative or unique, if one considers the month name from Mari we saw before, where the forms *malkānēn* and *malkānē*, a dual and probably a plural, were reanalysed as the singular *malkānim*.[22] At any rate, if this putative inscription of Erišum is given any consideration, it can stand as reconstructed evidence for Šarra-mātān's elevated position in Old Assyrian royal inscriptions. Thus, the god Šarra-mātān may have been mentioned by Erišum in the company of Šamaš, Aššur, and Adad.

Conclusion

In this paper I have considered the meaning, form, origin, and history of the god Šarra-mātān. First, the appearance of the god in Old Assyrian sources was presented and analysed. Then, a discussion about the morphology and meaning of the dual form in his name was offered. Two hypotheses, perhaps complementary and not conflicting as it seems at first glance, were offered as starting points for the analysis of the name: the first was that the dual was already conflated or confused with the plural form, and the second was that close contact with Sumerian plural formation, i.e. the doubling of the nouns, in divine or royal epithets may have given rise to the dual form. The example of the month name from Mari, *malkānēn* and *malkānē* was illuminating in this respect. The next section of the paper considered the origin and history of the god in question. It was seen that similar divine names or epithets were in circulation in the Mesopotamian and north Syrian pantheons. The god Pap-ul-e-gar-ra, of Ninurta's circle was given the epithet *šar-ra-am-ma-tim*, and a god called ᵈ*ša-a-ri-im-ma-ti* was proven to be linked to Kumarbi, and from here to Dagan and Enlil. This demonstrates that while the dual form was unique to Aššur, the basic formation of the divine name probably had its origins elsewhere, and perhaps as early as the Sargonic era. This, incidentally, necessitates a reconsideration of the epithet lugal *mātim* in Mari, usually understood as *Bēl mātim*. Should we read here *Šar(ra)-mātim*?

Finally, Šamšī-Adad's Aššur inscription was brought in order to show how the name *Šarra-mātān* was reinterpreted. We have sought to demonstrate how the reanalysis of the name into *šarra-mātim* arose from a direct written encounter of *Šarra-mātān*, as per our reconstruction, in one of Erišum's inscriptions. In spite of the wrong rendering or reinterpretation of the god's name in Šamšī-Adad's Aššur inscription, Šarra-mātān maintained his important role at Aššur. He is mentioned as

---

[21] Grayson 1987, 19–21 and 36–37 = Erišum I; A.0.33.1 and A.0.33.14.

[22] Consider also footnote 2, discussing the analysis of the name *ša-ra-ma-té*, whose form is difficult to determine.

one of the chief gods in the Apûm-Aššur treaty, in the company of Anu, Enlil, Dagan, Adad, Suen, and Šamaš. His place and role in the treaty demand further discussion and investigation.[23]

Acknowledgements

I am most grateful to Guido Kryszat for sharing his work with me, and, specifically for this paper, for allowing me access to his database and notes of Old Assyrian names. Without his generosity this paper would never have been written.

---

[23] See Kryszat 2021 and Eidem 2011.

Abbreviations

KT   *Kültepe Tabletleri* (Ankara).

OIP   *Oriental Institute Publications* (Chicago).

Bibliography

Archi, Alfonso

1995   'Šalaš Consort of Dagan and Kumarbi', in Theo P. J. van den Hout & Johan de Roos (eds), *Studio historia ardens: Ancient Near Eastern Studies Presented to Philo H. J. Houwink ten Cate on the Occasion of his 65th Birthday* (Publications de l'Institut historique-archéologique néerlandais de Stamboul 74). Nederlands Instituut voor het Nabije Oosten, Leiden: 1–6.

Arkhipov, Ilya

2012   *Le vocabulaire de la métallurgie et la nomenclature des objets en métal dans les textes de Mari: matériaux pour le Dictionnaire de Babylonien de Paris tome 3* (Archives royales de Mari 32). Peeters, Leuven.

Barjamovic, Gojko & Trolle Larsen, Mogens

2008   'An Old Assyrian Incantation against the Evil Eye', *Altorientalische Forschungen* 35: 144–55.

Beaulieu, Paul-Alain & Mayer, Werner R.

1997   'Akkadische Lexikographie: Chicago Assyrian Dictionary, $Š_2$ und $Š_3$', *Orientalia* 66: 157–80.

Cohen, Mark E.

2015   *Festivals and Calendars of the Ancient Near East*. CDL Press, Bethesda.

Cohen, Yoram

2017   'An Assyrian Teacher at Ugarit? A New Reading of the Colophon of *Šimâ Milka* ("Hear the Advice") from the Maison aux Tablettes', *Bibliotheca Orientalis* 74: 274–83.

Dercksen, Jan Gerrit

2001   '"When We Met in Ḫattuš": Trade according to Old Assyrian Texts from Alishar and Boğazköy', in Wilfred H. van Soldt (ed.), *Veenhof Anniversary Volume: Studies Presented to Klass R. Veenhof on the Occasion of his Sixty-Fifth Birthday* (Publications de l'Institut historique-archéologique néerlandais de Stamboul 89). Nederlands Instituut voor het Nabije Oosten, Leiden: 39–66.

2011   'The Double God Šarramat(t)an', *Nouvelles assyriologiques brèves et utilitaires* 75/4: 91.

Durand, Jean-Marie

1985   'La situation historique des Šakkanakku: nouvelle approche', *Mari: Annales de recherches interdisciplinaires* 4: 147–72.

Eidem, Jesper

2011   *The Royal Archives from Tell Leilan: Old Babylonian Letters and Treaties from the Lower Town Palace East* (Publications de l'Institut historique-archéologique néerlandais de Stamboul 117). Nederlands Instituut voor het Nabije Oosten, Leiden.

Feliu, Lluís

2003   *The God Dagan in Bronze Age Syria* (Culture and History of the Ancient Near East 19). Brill, Leiden.

George, Andrew & Krebernik, Manfred

2022   'Two Remarkable Vocabularies: Amorite-Akkadian Bilinguals', *Revue d'assyriologie et d'archéologie orientale* 116: 113–66.

Grayson, A. Kirk
1987 *Assyrian Rulers of the Third and Second Millennia B.C. (to 1115 B.C.)* (The Royal Inscriptions of Mesopotamia, Assyrian Periods 1). University of Toronto Press, Toronto.

Hecker, Karl
1968 *Grammatik der Kültepe-Texte* (Analecta orientalia 44). Pontifical Biblical Institute, Rome.

Kouwenberg, N. J. C.
2017 *A Grammar of Old Assyrian* (Handbuch der Orientalistik 118). Brill, Leiden.

Krebernik, Manfred
2005 'Pa(p)-ule-ĝara', *Reallexikon der Assyriologie* 10: 329–30.
2011 'Šar(ra)-mātin, Šarru-mātim', *Reallexikon der Assyriologie* 12: 73.

Kryszat, Guido
2003 'Zur Liste der Schwurgötter im Aššur-Apûm-Vertrag', *ISIMU* 6: 99–102.
2006 'Die Altassyrischen Belege für den Gott Amurru', *Revue d'assyriologie et d'archéologie orientale* 100: 53–56.
2018 'Towards the Understanding of Old Assyrian Šarra-mātā/ēn and Šarru-mātim', in Kai Kaniuth, Daneil Lau & Dirk Wicke (eds), *Übergangszeiten: Altorientalische Studien für Reinhard Dittmann anlässlich seines 65. Geburtstags*. Zaphon, Münster: 195–205.
2020 'Some Comments on Amurrum and Old Assyrian Family Religion', *Nouvelles assyriologiques brèves et utilitaires* 50/2: 110–12.
2021 'Gods, Names, and the Question of Western Elements in Early Assyrian Religion', in Fikri Kulakoğlu, Guido Kryszat & Cécile Michel (eds), *Cultural Exchange and Current Research at Kültepe and its Surroundings: Kültepe, 1-4 August, 2019* (Kültepe International Meetings 4, Subartu 46). Brepols, Turnhout: 235–55.

Laroche, Emmanuel
1980 *Glossaire de la langue hourrite*. Klincksieck, Paris.

Limet, Henri
1976 *Textes administratifs de l'époque des Šakkanakku* (Archives royales de Mari 19). Geuthner, Paris.

Michel, Cécile
2020 *Women of Aššur and Kanesh: Texts from the Archives of Assyrian Merchants* (Writing from the Ancient World 42). Society of Biblical Literature Press, Atlanta.

Schwemer, Daniel
2008 'Šāluš, Šālaš', *Reallexikon der Assyriologie* 11: 590.
2013 'Gauging the Influence of Babylonian Magic. The Reception of Mesopotamian Traditions in Hittite Ritual Practice', in Eva Cancik-Kirschbaum, Jorg Klinger & Gerfried Müller (eds), *Diversity and Standardization: Perspectives on Ancient Near Eastern Cultural History*. Munich: Akademie-Verlag, 145–71.

Strauß, Rita
2006 *Reinigungsrituale aus Kizzuwatna: Ein Beitrag zur Erforschung hethitischer Ritualtradition und Kulturgeschicht*. De Gruyter, Berlin.

Streck, Michael P. & Wasserman, Nathan
2008 'The Old Babylonian Hymns to Papulegara', *Orientalia* 77: 335–58.

Veenhof, Klaus
2018 'The Family God in Old Babylonian and Especially in Old Assyrian Sources', *Revue d'Assyriologie et d'archéologie oriental* 112: 49–90.

5. The Cult of Aškašepa in Hittite Sources

Amir Gilan

Mount Aškašepa famously appears next to the deities of the land of Kaneš in a treaty between the king of Kaneš and the Assyrian merchants (Kt 00/k 6). The mountain was consequently identified with Mount Argaeus (Erciyes Dağı). Mount Aškašepa, and more often a deity by that name, continued to be venerated by the Hittites long after Kaneš itself was deserted, often in connection with other deities affiliated with Cappadocia. The present contribution will survey these attestations and explore some of the questions that emerge from the evidence.

Introduction

Mount Aškašepa (KUR *a-áš-kà-ši-pá*) famously appears together with the gods of the land of Kaneš (DINGIR.MEŠ is reconstructed) in a treaty between the great king of Kaneš and the Assyrian merchants. The text, Kt 00/k 6, was edited by Günbattı in 2004 and by Donbaz in 2005 and consequently treated by Veenhof (2008, 190–93). Both Günbattı and Veenhof read KUR *a-áš-kà-ši-pá* in line 2 and their reading is generally accepted.

The identification of Mount Aškašepa with Mount Argaeus (Erciyes Dağı), majestically towering above the site of Kültepe is as good as self-evident to anyone who has visited the site.[1] The summit of the volcano, the highest mountain in Anatolia, was famously described by Strabo (in his *Geography*, XI.2.7) as covered with snow all year round, adding that when visibility was good, both the Black Sea and the eastern Mediterranean were visible from its summit. Strabo noted that there were forests all around Mount Argaeus, a remarkable phenomenon in an otherwise woodless Cappadocia. He also reported that 'the region that lies beneath the forests also contains fires in many places and at the same time has an underground supply of cold water, although neither the fire nor the water emerges to the surface; and therefore most of the country is covered with grass'.[2]

The identification of Mount Aškašepa with Mount Argaeus was first suggested, to my knowledge, by Haas in his voluminous *Geschichte der hethitischen Religion* (1994a, 614), a decade before the publication of Kt 00/k 6 by Günbattı. Haas was not a clairvoyant: Mount Aškašepa is well attested in Hittite sources, often in connection with other deities that are affiliated in modern scholarship with Kaneš. In the present contribution, I will survey these attestations and explore some of the questions that arise from them.

The Meaning of the Name Aškašepa

Perhaps the most striking feature of the Hittite evidence pertaining to Aškašepa is the fact that only *c.* 20 per cent of the fifty or so attestations of the name are written with the HUR.SAG (mountain) determinative.

---

1 For other identifications of the mountain in earlier scholarship see in detail Forlanini 2009, 42–44 with previous literature. These include the names Harka/BABBAR 'White' and Harhara. The latter, a Luwian name, appears in the two hieroglyphic inscriptions from Hisarcık as well as in the hieroglyphic inscription of Tekirderbent, all found in the immediate vicinity of the mountain.

Amir Gilan (agilan@tauex.tau.ac.il) Professor at Tel Aviv University

2 Cited from Strabo [1928], 360–63. On the continuity of the cult of Mount Argaeus in the ancient world, see Börker-Klähn 1989 and Casabonne 2006. Casabonne 2007 proposes to identify the mountain on Old Assyrian seals originating from Kaneš but see Lassen 2017.

Most of the time, Aškašepa is written with the DINGIR sign, as deified Aškašepa. Certainly, deified mountains may appear occasionally with the DINGIR determinative instead of the HUR.SAG determinative, but the ratio here is odd. In comparison, Mount Puškurunuwa, a deified mountain of great religious importance throughout Hittite history, situated only a two-day walk away from the capital Hattuša, is also attested *c.* fifty times in Hittite sources. Yet it is overwhelmingly written with the HUR.SAG determinative while only rarely with the DINGIR sign.[3] This situation has led most scholars to assume the existence of another deity by the name Aškašepa, independent of Mount Argaeus. Disproving this is one of the main hypotheses of this contribution, suggesting instead that the available Hittite sources only document one Aškašepa, indeed the deified Mount Argaeus.

The prevalent analysis of the name Aškašepa may have contributed to the assumption that we are in fact dealing with more than one deity. The suffix or compound endings *-šepa-* or *-zipa-* have a long history of research.[4] They frequently appear in divine names and are conventionally considered to denote something like 'genius' or 'spirit', even though these translations are often unsatisfactory (as convincingly argued by Mouton 2014). Laroche (1946, 67–68) identified these endings and considered them feminine endings. Aškašepa, constructed with *aška-* 'gate', thus hardly constitutes a unique entity that could have indeed been imagined in different settings. Goetze (1953, 265) erroneously concluded that Aškašepa was a female, *IŠTAR*-like, deity, based on the appearance of Aškašepa next to *IŠTAR MULTARRIHU* in duplicate A (KBo 1.1 rev. 45–46) of Šuppiluliuma's treaty with Šattiwaza of Mittani. Aškašepa appears next to the planet Venus (MUL DIL.BAD) in the same position in duplicate B of the same treaty (KBo 1.2 rev. 23). As already established by Mouton (2014, 23), there is nothing to suggest that Aškašepa was a female deity, as Hittite divinized mountains were gendered as male deities.[5] The intriguing question as to why the inhabitants of Kaneš considered the Argaeus as a 'gate' must remain unanswered at this point.

Mount Aškašepa in the Festival of the Month

The best place to begin the search for Mount Aškašepa in Hittite sources is the Festival of the Month (EZEN$_4$.ITU, CTH 591), an elaborate, complex three-day-ritual. It was celebrated by the Hittite king on the occasion of a new moon, marking the transition from one lunar cycle to the next (the festival is edited by Klinger 1996, 286–614). More than eighty fragments were identified so far as belonging to the Festival of the Month, representing numerous manuscripts. Most of them date to the Late Empire period but some are written in Middle Hittite script. Aškašepa often appears here alongside other deities, all receiving offerings to the accompaniment of chants sang in Hittite by the 'singers of Kaneš' (LÚ(.MEŠ)NAR URU*KA-NI-EŠ* or URU*KA-NI-IŠ*) and are therefore sometimes designated in Hittite scholarship as the 'circle of Kaneš'.[6]

The Empire period duplicate KUB 2.13 ++ iii 17-iv 3, containing a well-preserved offering ceremony to the deities belonging to the 'circle of Kaneš', may serve as an example. There, the overseer of the cooks breaks bread for a sequence of deities, beginning with Aškašepa (written in plene-writing) and followed by the 'Queen' (DMUNUS.LUGAL), Pirwa, the Heptad, Maliya, the male deities of the Stag God, the male deities of 'Day', the 'gods of Kaneš', DHaš(š)ammeli, DHilašši, DU.GUR and the rivers.[7]

The 'singers of Kaneš' appear in various cultic settings in Hittite texts and their existence triggered a lively scholarly debate concerning the alleged correspondence between the language of the liturgy chosen for the cult of certain deities and the 'origin' of the deities involved.[8] As shown by Archi (2004), the cult of a

---

3 For the mountain and its cult see Galmarini 2014.

4 See Mouton 2014 and now Warbinek 2022 for a full list of all divine names ending with *-šepa-* or *-zipa-*. In their Hittite grammar, Hoffner & Melchert (2008, 61–62) list as examples daganzipa- (from *dagan-* 'earth'), Hantašepa- (from *hant-* 'forehead'), Hilanzipa- (from *hila-*'court'), Išpanzašepa- (from *išpant-* 'night'), and Miyatanzipa- (from *miyatar* 'fruitfulness').

5 *Pace* Warbinek 2022, 3. Another mountain deity ending with *-zipa-* is Halalazipa appearing twice with the determinative HUR.SAG and once with the determinative KUR in the cult inventory text KUB 38.26, edited by Cammarosano (2018, 229–46).

6 See for instance Haas 1994a, 412–13; Beckman 1984, 310; Taracha 2009, 28–30 and already Goetze 1953, 264–66. For a critic of this notion of 'circle' see now Warbinek 2022, 12–13 with previous literature.

7 Other offering sequences in the Festival of the Month involving the deities of the 'circle of Kaneš' include KUB 56.45 + obv. ii 4'–8', in which a goat is sacrificed to them. Later on in the festival (VSNF 12.28 iii 9'–14') bread is broken for a similar list of deities. The plene-writing *a-aš-ka-še-pa*, reminiscent of the writing in the Kaneš treaty Kt 00/k 6, is also attested in KBo 67.186, 5' and in KBo 49.54, right col. 7', both belonging to the Festival of the Month; both written with the DINGIR determinative.

8 On the 'singers of Kaneš' see already Forrer 1922, 191, 196–98; Güterbock 1958 but see especially the detailed study by Archi 2004. See more recently Steitler 2017, 181–84 and Gilan 2021. As noted by Güterbock (1958, 50), the LÚ.MEŠNAR URU*KA-NI-EŠ* is the logographic

fairly large and heterogeneous group of Anatolian deities was accompanied by recitations in the Hittite language by the 'singers of Kaneš'. More recently, Steitler (2017, 181–84) argues for more confidence in the veracity of the information found in the Hittite sources, suggesting that the language of the liturgy may indeed, in many cases, be indicative of the 'cultural-linguistic provenance' of the deity worshipped. Following earlier scholars, Steitler also attributes the continuity between the pantheon of Kaneš and the pantheon of the Hittite kingdom, to the presence of Hittite and Luwian speakers in both kingdoms.

However, most of the deities belonging to the circle of deities customarily associated with Kaneš in Hittite texts are not attested in Kaneš itself during the Old Assyrian period.[9] Thus, the 'circle of Kaneš' represents a Hittite innovation, not necessarily epitomizing the pantheon of Kaneš itself during the Old Assyrian period. If at all, the 'circle' consists of deities that were worshipped in Cappadocia. The deity Pirwa, whose name is often attested in the onomasticon of Kaneš, is perhaps the most notable representative of this group. Pirwa is also amply attested in Hittite texts. Most significantly, there is evidence for an Empire-period restoration of the cult of Pirwa in the same area, the middle Kızılırmak region, in the vicinity of Kaneš. The re-establishment was carried out by King Muršili III, but is only mentioned in a Late Empire period cult inventory text, IBoT 2.131, dating to Tudhaliya IV, correcting the neglect of the vineyards of Pirwa (IBoT 2.131, § 5').[10] Pirwa is famously related to horses and Anatolian horse-breeding is traditionally located in Cappadocia.[11]

The edition of some of the deities of the 'circle of Kaneš' into a manuscript of the Festival of the Month is in fact documented in KUB 1.17, a six-column tablet belonging to the festival.[12] The tablet is remarkable as it contains several, often completely preserved recitations in the Hattian language that were integrated in the drinking ceremonies. Hittite festival texts often refer to Hattian recitations but their full wording is only rarely documented in them. As shown by Steitler (2014), column five also contains a sequence of drinking ceremonies with the participation of the king and the cup-bearer (LÚSAGI.A) but with an important difference. There are no recitations in Hattian. In that column, the king is drinking, standing up, deities that belong to the 'circle of Kaneš'. These include Kapukkuzi, only attested in this tablet, who is sang to by the Singer of Kaneš, that is, in Hittite. Next are drinking ceremonies to the Sun God of Heaven and to Aškašepa, to which the king is drinking, standing up, from a lion-shaped, golden rhyton. The drinking is accompanied by singing, probably in Hittite, while a performer recites and the *kita*-man calls (KUB 1.17 rev. v 28'-32'). The column breaks off after the drinking ceremony to Mount Aškašepa but as suggested by Yoshida (1996, 133, also Steitler 2014, 306), it probably also contained a drinking ceremony to ᴰMUNUS.LUGAL (Haššušara). The question, whether this addition was merely a scribal copy-paste, or whether it was motivated by more vigorous theological reflexion, religious convergence, or by other cultic, 'real-life' necessities, must remain open.

Aškašepa, Pirwa and the 'Queen'

Mount Aškašepa frequently appears together with Pirwa and with ᴰMUNUS.LUGAL (Haššušara, 'the Queen'). These three deities form the so called 'triad of Kaneš' (Haas 1994a, 614), representing perhaps the core of the extended 'circle of Kaneš'. Local pantheons in Hittite Anatolia often consisted of a god, a goddess, and a deified mountain. The triad appears already in texts dating to the early phases of Hittite history.[13] Thus, it appears in the fragmentary right column of the Old Hittite festival text KBo 25.88 (+)

---

equivalent of the less frequently attested Hittite designation LÚ.MES*ne-šu-me-ni-eš* ('Nešians'), likewise attested singing in various cultic settings. As the Hittite language was named after the town, the designation 'Singer(s) of Kaneš' or 'Nešian' (singers) denotes the language that was sung, not the provenance of the performers, especially as the town of Kaneš was already a ghost town, centuries before most of the festivals were performed in which the 'singers of Kaneš' were chanting.

9 Kryszat 2006 with previous literature. See also Taracha 2009, 25–32; Steitler 2017, 181–84 and most recently Hutter 2021, 43–50.

10 For the text, the cult inventory IBoT 2.131, see Cammarosano 2018, 258–70.

11 Pirwa is described as a man on a horse, holding a whip and two rings of black iron in the cult inventory text KUB 38.4, edited most recently by Cammarosano 2018, 329–31, pertaining to the cult image of Pirwa of Šippa, a town in central Cappadocia. A *BIBRU*-vessel shaped like a horse is also mentioned in the inventory. See also the pitcher depicted in Kulakoğlu & Kangal 2011, 194. Horse herders are specifically allocated to the cult of Pirwa in the town Tenizidaša according to KBo 12.53+, edited by Cammarosano 2018, 271–90, obv.

36–37, 280–81, 289. The cult inventory also mentions cults for Pirwa in other towns. For the tradition of breeding of horses in Cappadocia see Balza 2013. For Pirwa see Otten 1953; Haas 1994b and Ünal 2019.

12 Edited by Klinger (1996, 422–54) see especially Steitler 2014.

13 Aškašepa, if Otten's reconstruction is correct, appears next to ᴰMUNUS.LUGAL in the little-known Middle Hittite ritual KBo 42.5 obv. 3.

KBo 7.38, where 'he (the king) takes place and drinks three times: [Aškašepa], ᴅMUNUS.LUGAL and Pirwa. The Kanešites sing'. Since the king drinks three deities and the list seems to end with Pirwa, it is very plausible to reconstruct Aškašepa in the gap before the two other members of the 'triad'.[14] The three deities occur in a similar drinking ceremony, likewise accompanied by chants in Hittite, in KBo 30.56 iv 19–22, an Empire period copy of an Old Hittite festival text.[15] The three deities also appear in one of the Late Hittite festivals of Karahna, KUB 25.32 ++, in a long list of deities receiving sacrificial animals: a billy-goat for Pirwa, sheep for Aškašepa and for the 'Queen' (ᴅMUNUS.LUGAL), if the reconstruction of the text is indeed correct.[16] Incidentally, the town of Karahna, possibly identified as modern Sulusaray on the Çekerek River, is already attested in the Old Assyrian period, as a station on the smugglers route leading to the town of Durhumit (Durmitta), known as the 'the narrow path'.[17]

Mount Aškašepa also received offerings accompanied by chants in Luwian. Such is the case of KUB 35.2 + KUB 35.4 (CTH 670), where someone, perhaps the chief of the gardeners (GAL ᴸᵁ́.ᴹᴱˢ̌NU.ᴳᴵˢ̌KIRI₆) is drinking Peruwa (Pirwa) and Aškašepa from an earthenware cup while sitting. The singers sing in Luwian, not in Hittite.[18] The festival, including also the parallel text KUB 35.1, contains many chants in Luwian.[19] Beside Peruwa (Pirwa) and Aškašepa, the Storm God of Heaven (*ne-pí-ša-aš* ᴅ10), receives offerings as well (KUB 35.4 rev. iii 11'; KUB 35.1 obv. 11'). The most noteworthy feature of the festival, however, is the frequent appearance of gardeners (ᴸᵁ́.ᴹᴱˢ̌NU.ᴳᴵˢ̌KIRI₆), led by the chief of the gardeners (GAL ᴸᵁ́.ᴹᴱˢ̌NU.ᴳᴵˢ̌KIRI₆). Significantly, Aškašepa is linked to gardens or to forests in several other texts as well, recalling Strabo's famous remark (in his *Geography*, XII.2.7) about the existence of forests around Mount Argaeus in an otherwise woodless Cappadocia.

Aškašepa, often accompanied by other members of the 'triad', appear in various contexts in combination with other deities as well. Beside appearing in Šuppiluliuma's treaty with Šattiwaza of Mittani, mentioned above, Aškašepa is also listed in the witness section of the Middle Hittite treaty with Hayaša (KUB 26.39 iv 14) and in two Empire period treaties with Amurru (KBo 22.39 iii 23 and KUB 8.82 + rev. 13). A deified Aškašepa appears after Hašammeli and Pirwa and before Telipinu in a drinking ceremony to a very long and heterogeneous list of deities held during a festival in honour of Teššob and Hebat.[20] A deified Aškašepa is also found next to Pirwa and to several other mountains in the long list of the gods of all the lands in Great King Mutawalli's prayer. They are listed there in the second section of the entry dedicated to the gods of Hattuša (KUB 6.45 i 54–56, Singer 1996, 33–34):

§ 13 (i 54–56) *IŠTAR* of Haddarina, Pirwa, Aškašepa, Mount Puškurunuwa, male gods, female gods, mountains and rivers of Hattuša, Karzi, Hapandaliya, Mount Tatta, Mount Šummiyara.

According to Singer (1996, 55), Aškašepa and Pirwa represent the Nešite religious layer in Hattuša in what seems a very heterogenous list of deities. Yet as suggested earlier, the existence of such a layer is highly doubtful. There are, however, other Hittite traditions that connect Aškašepa and *IŠTAR* of Haddarina.

Aškašepa in Other Festivals

The tablets of the great AN.DAH.ŠUM spring festival provide another connection between *IŠTAR* of Haddarina and ᴅAškašepa. According to one of the outline tablets of the AN.DAH.ŠUM festival, on the twenty-second day of the festival, the royal couple allegedly went to a temple of Aškašepa while the seers (ᴸᵁ́.ᴹᴱˢ̌HAL) were invoking *IŠTAR* of Haddarina (see Galmarini 2015 for the latest discussion of the passage).[21] The reading was based on traces of the sign É that were indicated by Güterbock and Otten in their hand-copy of the text in KBo 10, and

---

14 KBo 7.38, 8'–9': *ta-aš ti-e-ez-zi* 3 *e-ku-⸢zi⸣*[...] ⁽⁹⁾ ᴅMUNUS.LUGAL-*an* ᴅ*Pé-ru-*an*-na* x[...] ⁽¹⁰⁾ ᴸᵁ́.ᴹᴱˢ̌*ne-šu-me-né-eš* ⸢SÌR⸣-[RU ...]. See already Haas 1994a, 614. For the dating to the Old Hittite period see Groddek 1995, 327.

15 KBo 30.56 iv 19–22: LUGAL-*uš* 3-ŠU *e-ku-z*[*i*] ⁽ᴵⱽ ²⁰⁾ ᴅ*A-aš-ka-še-pa-an* ᴅ⸢MUNUS.L[UGAL] ⁽ᴵⱽ ²¹⁾ ᴅ*Pí-ir-wa-*[*an*] ⁽ᴵⱽ ²²⁾ ᴸᵁ́.ᴹᴱˢ̌NAR ᵁᴿᵁKA-NI-EŠ SÌ[R-RU]. See Klinger 1996, 160, 234 and Archi 2004, 14. Duplicate is KUB 51.79.

16 KUB 25.32 i 11', edited by McMahon 1991, 53–77: 1 MÁŠ.GAL A-NA ᴅ*Pí-ir-wa* 1 UDU ᴅ*Aš-ka-ši-pa* 1 UDU ⸢ᴅ⸣[MUNUS.LUGAL]. See now the HFR edition.

17 For the localization see Mouton 2011, Barjamovic 2017, 316.

18 KUB 35.2 Vs. I 8'–10': EGIR-*an-da-*[*m*]*a* ᴅ*Pé-ru-wa-an* ⸢ᴅ⸣*Aš-ka-ši*⸢-⸣*pa-an-na* TUŠ-*aš* ⁽ⱽˢ.¹⁹⁾ ⸢IŠ-TU⸣ GAL GIR₄ *e-ku-zi* ᴸᵁ́NAR *lu-⸢ú⸣-i-li* ⁽ⱽˢ.¹ ¹⁰⁾ ⸢SÌR-RU⸣.

19 Edited by Starke 1985, 354–57. The tablets date to the Empire period.

20 KUB 10.92 v 19, edited by Wegner 2002, 228–31 (no. 114).

21 KBo 10.20 iii 23–25, edited by Güterbock 1960 [1997], see now the online transliteration by the HFR team): ⸢*lu*⸣-*uk-kat-ti-ma* ⸢LUGAL MUNUS.LUGAL I-NA ᴳᴵˢ̌K[IRI₆] ⸢*AŠ-KA-ŠI*⸣-*PA* ⁽ᴿˢ.ᴵᴵᴵ ²⁴⁾ ⸢*pa*⸣-*a-an-zi* ᴸᵁ́.ᴹᴱˢ̌HAL-*m*[*a*] ⸢ᴅ*IŠTAR*⸣ ᵁ[ᴿᵁ*H*]*A-*⸢*AT-TA-RI*⸣-*NA* ⁽ᴿˢ.ᴵᴵᴵ ²⁵⁾ [*mu-u-ga-an-z*]*i* ⸢UD 22⸣ᴷᴬᴹ. A fragment representing another duplicate or a parallel outline tablet, KBo 47.242 rev.? 3', also mentions Aškašepa.

in Güterbock's subsequent edition. However, Charles Steitler convincingly suggests now a new reading of the traces, reading garden (ᴳᴵˢKIRI₆) instead of temple. Thus, there is currently no evidence for a temple of Aškašepa in Hittite sources.[22] According to the outline tablet KBo 10.20, the seers continue to invoke *IŠTAR* of Haddarina, one of the most prominent *IŠTAR* avatars in Hittite Anatolia, over the next four days. The invocation of the goddess continues uninterrupted up to the twenty-sixth day of the AN.TAH.ŠUM festival (Güterbock 1960 [1997] 97–98; Galmarini 2015, 50). During that time the royal couple is visiting other temples and is engaged in various rites. Thus, the royal visit to the garden of Aškašepa and the invocation of *IŠTAR* of Haddarina were two independent events, taking place simultaneously.[23] The question as to why the royal couple would spend the day at the garden of ᴰAškašepa at the beginning of a long invocation session of *IŠTAR* of Haddarina remains unanswered.

Another outline tablet of the great AN.DAH.ŠUM festival, VSNF 12.1, edited by Houwink Ten Cate (2003, 205–19), also mentions a garden. The outline tablet lists a different sequence of days: on the twenty-fourth day festivities were held for *IŠTAR* of Nineveh and other deities. On the next day (VSNF 12.1 rev. 2'–7', Galmarini 2015, 50), festivities for LAMMA of Tauriša, Ea, and another deity, took place on the occasion of the festival for *IŠTAR* of Haddarina in the ᴳᴵˢKIRI₆ *har-wa-ši-ia-aš*, translated by the HW² (H, 385) and Galmarini (2015, 50) as the 'garden of secrecy'.[24] Later on, the outline tablet VSNF 12.1 also establishes a new locality in relation to Aškašepa, written here without any determinative, also in relation to a garden:

(Rs. 17') [*lu-u*]*k-*[*k*]*at-ti-ma-za* LUGAL-*uš A-NA* ᴳᴵˢKIRI₆ *AŠ-KA-ŠI-PA* EZEN₄ AN.⌈DAH⌉.ŠUMˢᴬᴿ *i-i*[*a-zi*] (Rs. 18') [Š]À-*ta ši-ia-an-na* UD 31ᴷᴬᴹ

([On the ne]xt day the king cel[berates] himself the AN.DAH.ŠUM-festival to the garden/forest of Aškašepa. To be taken to [he]art. Day 31.)

It is important to note that the king is celebrating the festival to the garden/forest of Aškašepa; the garden/forest of Aškašepa is the entity being celebrated, not merely the location of the festival. The garden/forest of Aškašepa also appears in KUB 28.108 (CTH 744), a tiny fragment of a festival intriguingly containing recitations in Hattian and chants by a choir of *zintuhi*-girls, another characteristic of the Anatolian Hattian cult tradition. A further fragment attributed to the great AN.TAH.ŠUM festival, KBo 45.27, contains a more conventional occurrence of Aškašepa, listing bread offerings to Pirwa, to ᴰAškašepa, and to ᴰMUNUS.LUGAL as well as to Maliya (obv. 9'–11'), among other deities.[25]

Several festivals that were solely dedicated to Aškašepa are attested in Hittite sources, among them the cult inventory text KUB 38.19, listing, among other festivals, also a festival of Aškašepa.[26] The fragmentary section (§ 5') notes the men of the palace of the town of Šukziya and Bronze-bowl holders among the provisions' providers. Another fragmentary cult inventory text, KUB 58.15 iv 4–5, likewise documents a festival of Aškašepa, written here without a determinative, in some relation to a golden cult statue of a man standing. KBo 12.135, a text relating to the administration of the cult, lists Aškašepa twice, once in relation to the town of Šalušna, otherwise unattested in Hittite sources, and once in relation to the town of Atarmapa.[27] The 'triad' receives offering in the fragmentary cult inventory text KUB 54.61, now indirectly joined to KUB 54.90. Interestingly, the pertinent section seems to offer different combinations of deities, including Pirwa, ᴰMUNUS.LUGAL (Haššušara), and a third, or more, deities.[28] A festival of Aškašepa is mentioned in KBo 24.118 (CTH 586), oracular inquiries concerning local festivals relating to the *nuntarriašha*-Festival, the great autumn festival, and to the AN.DAH.ŠUM festival, the great spring festival mentioned above. The text is probably dating to the reign of Great King Muršili II.

---

22 Aškašepa appears once with the determinative URU. The reverse of the fragmentary ritual/inventory text KUB 59.6 lists several towns, among them ᵁᴿᵁ*Aš-ka-š*[*i-pa-* ...] (iv 9'). See Forlanini 2009, 44 for the geography of the text.

23 As the particle *-ma* and Güterbock's translation (1960 [1997], 97) may suggest.

24 Note however the É.GAL ᵁᴿᵁ*Har-wa-ši-ia-aš* mentioned in the cult inventory text KUB 57.108 + KUB 51.23 ii 9', edited now by Cammarosano 2021, 150–57, interestingly concerning the cult of Pirwa.

25 These four deities receive together offerings of bread, liver, and groats in the festival for all the titulary deities (KBo 38.50 + KBo 40.210 + iii 23–24).

26 KUB 38.19 i 8': 1 EZEN₄ GURUN 1 EZEN₄ *AŠ*¹-*KA-ŠE-PA* EZE[N₄ ...].

27 Atarmapa may be attested once more elsewhere, in KBo 31.69 (+) KBo 18.25, a letter of Tudhaliya IV to Tukulti-Ninurta, but the reading is more than uncertain (Mora & Giorgieri 2004, 103). Forlanini (2009) suggests that the text may list towns in the vicinity of Mount Erciyes.

28 KUB 54.61: 2'–7', edited now by M. Cammarosano (ed.), hethiter.net/: CTH 528.116 (TX 2016-06-03). Aškašepa should probably be reconstructed in line 3': [...]ᴰ*Pí-ir-wa-aš* ᴰMUNUS.LUGAL ᴰ*Aš-x*[...].

Mount Aškašepa appears once in a secular context. It is mentioned as a hiding place, or as a place of refuge, in a fragmentary Late Hittite letter, KBo 18.56 (edited by Hagebuchner 1989, 100), citing an earlier communication concerning two households that were previously hiding in the midst of the lands of Hattuša but are now present on Mount Aškašepa. The mountain also appears in KUB 17.8+, a highly fragmentary *Sammeltafel*, containing a magic ritual for increasing manliness, perhaps before going to war.[29] The name of the mountain appears in an invocation of the Storm God, most probably Teššob, as the appearance of Kumarbi (i 4) may suggest. Other entities that are mentioned beside Mount Aškašepa (KUB 17.8 + i 8) include the sea, the deity Miyatanzipa, and possibly also the Sun Goddess of Arinna.

Conclusion

The Hittite evidence pertaining to Aškašepa is puzzling. Only a fraction of the fifty or so attestations of the name in Hittite sources are written with the HUR.SAG determinative whereas in most cases, the name appears with the DINGIR determinative, sometimes in contexts far removed from Mount Argaeus. The evidence has led scholars to surmise the existence of another deity by the name Aškašepa, independent of Mount Argaeus. The available Hittite sources support, however, even if not conclusively, another interpretation of the evidence.

The identification of Mount Aškašepa, appearing together with the gods of the land of Kaneš in Kt 00/k 6, the treaty between the great king of Kaneš and the Assyrian merchants, with Mount Argaeus, majestically overlooking Kültepe, is highly probable. The identification is also supported by the Hittite textual evidence surveyed here. Mount Aškašepa is well attested in Hittite sources, very persistently appearing together with other deities 'affiliated', at least according to Hittite religious imagination, with Cappadocia, most notably Pirwa and the 'Queen'.

The city of Kaneš did not survive the transition into the Old Hittite period. The town never fully recuperated from the destruction documented at the end of the Ib stratum. Layers 6 in Kültepe and Ia at the *kārum*, roughly contemporary with the Old Hittite kingdom, reveal only a very modest settlement. Kültepe was completely deserted shortly afterwards and remained uninhabitable for about eight hundred years, throughout the entire history of the Hittite kingdom, possibly due to environmental causes (Kulakoğlu 2014). It is thus not surprising that the demise of Kaneš itself also led to the decline of the cult of Aškašepa, the deified Mount Argaeus. Its religious significance waned. Knowledge about the cult did, however, linger on in Hattuša, especially in scholarly and scribal circles, but the 'living' memory of Aškašepa as the deified Mount Argaeus, intrinsically related to the town of Kaneš, must have faded. The ancient name of the mountain survived but it no longer clearly signified the mountain, becoming an unspecified deity, receiving offerings within long, often repeating, cultic sequences. If this interpretation is indeed correct, the first-millennium name Harhara, appearing in the hieroglyphic inscriptions from Hisarcık as well as in the hieroglyphic inscription of Tekirderbent, found in the immediate vicinity of Mount Erciyes, may denote the mountain after all.

Several occurrences of Aškašepa, however, may have preserved 'genuine' cultic moments in connection with the cult of Mount Erciyes. Such, perhaps, is the connection between Aškašepa and gardens/forests, attested in several texts, such as the 'Luwian' festival KUB 35.2 + KUB 35.4 (CTH 670), mentioned above, where Peruwa (Pirwa) and Aškašepa receive offerings in a festival celebrated by gardeners ($^{LÚ.MEŠ}NU.^{GIŠ}KIRI_6$) and led by the chief of the gardeners (GAL $^{LÚ.MEŠ}NU.^{GIŠ}KIRI_6$). As noted earlier, Aškašepa's link to gardens or to forests recalls Strabo's description of Mount Argaeus, cited above. The garden/forest of Aškašepa also occurs in VSNF 12.1, one of the outline tablets of the AN.DAH.ŠUM festival. The seal of Wališra and Šiwašme'i, the gatekeepers of the *addahšu*-gate, mentioned in an Old Assyrian *Selbstverkauf-Urkunde* edited by Farber (1990), may hint at the great antiquity of this festival, and its affiliation to the town (Kryszat 2004, 22). However, this remains to this day, to the best of my knowledge, the only evidence for such a connection in the Old Assyrian records.

Acknowledgements

I warmly thank Charles Steitler for sharing his new reading of KBo 10.20 with me. The contribution was supported by the Israel Science Foundation, grant no. 1911/19, 'The Religious World of King Ḫattušili "III" as Reflected in his "Autobiography" and in Related Texts'.

---

29 Edited now by Fuscagni 2012.

5. THE CULT OF AŠKAŠEPA IN HITTITE SOURCES

Abbreviations

Abbreviations follow the Chicago Hittite Dictionary.

Bibliography

Archi, Alfonso

2004 'The Singer of Kaneš and his Gods', in Manfred Hutter & Sylvia Hutter-Braunsar (eds), *Offizielle Religion, lokale Kulte und individuelle Religiosität: Akten des religionsgeschichtlichen Symposiums 'Kleinasien und angrenzende Gebiete vom Beginn des 2. bis zur Mitte des 1. Jahrtausends v. Chr.' Bonn, 20.-22. Februar 2003* (Alter Orient und Altes Testament 318). Ugarit, Münster: 11–26.

Balza, Maria E.

2013 'Horses and Horse Husbandry in Central Anatolia during Hittite and Neo-Hittite Periods', *Res antiquae* 10: 1–14.

Barjamovic, Gojko

2017 'A Commercial Geography of Anatolia', in Mark Weeden, Lee Z. Ullmann & Zenobia Homan (eds), *Hittite Landscape and Geography* (Handbook of Oriental Studies 1/121). Brill, Leiden: 311–18.

Beckman, Gary

1984 'Pantheon. A. II. Bei den Hethitern', *Reallexikon der Assyriologie und Vorderasiatischen Archäologie* 10/3–4: 308–16.

Börker-Klähn, Jutta

1989 'Mons Argarius und Papana "Die Berge"', in Barthel Hrouda, Kutlu Emre, Machteld J. Mellink & Nimet Özgüç (eds), *Tahsin Özgüç'e Armağan: Anatolia and the Ancient Near East; Studies in Honor of Tahsin Özgüç*. Türk Tarih Kurumu Basımevi, Ankara: 237–53.

Cammarosano, Michele

2018 *Hittite Local Cults* (Writings from the Ancient World 40). SBL Press, Atlanta.

2021 *At the Interface of Religion and Administration: The Hittite Cult Inventories* (Studien zu den Boğazköy-Texten 68). Harrassowitz, Wiesbaden.

Casabonne, Olivier

2006 'La divinité du mont Argée', *Res antiquae* 3: 191–98.

2007 'Le dieu-taureau et la montagne divinisée: brèves remarques à propos d'un groupe de sceaux de Kültepe-Kaneš', in Metin Alparslan, Meltem Doğan-Alparslan & Hasan Peker (eds), *Belkıs Dinçol ve Ali Dinçol'a Armağan: VITA; Festschrift in Honor of Belkıs Dinçol and Ali Dinçol*. Ege Yayınları, Istanbul: 133–35.

Donbaz, Veysel

2005 'An Old Assyrian Treaty from Kültepe', *Journal of Cuneiform Studies* 57: 63–68.

Farber, Walter

1990 '*Hanum kauft Gadagada*: Eine altassyrische Selbstverkaufs-Urkunde', *Aula Orientalis* 8: 197–205.

Forlanini, Massimo

2009 'On the Middle Kızılırmak, II', in Franca Pecchioli Daddi, Giulia Torri & Carlo Corti (eds), *Central-North Anatolia in the Hittite Period: New Perspectives in Light of Recent Research* (Studia Asiana 5). Herder, Rome: 39–69.

Forrer, Emil

1922 'Die Inschriften und Sprachen des Hatti-Reiches', *Zeitschrift der Deutschen Morgenländischen Gesellschaft* 76/1: 174–269.

Fuscagni, Francesco

2012 'Mythos und Beschwörung des Feuers (CTH 457.1)' <https://hethiter.net/>: CTH 457.1 [accessed 1 November 2023].

Galmarini, Niccolò

2014 'The Festivals for Mount Puškurunuwa', in Piotr Taracha & Magdalena Kapełuś (eds), *Proceedings of the Eighth International Congress of Hittitology, Warsaw, 5-9. Sept. 2011*. Wydawnictwo Agade, Warsaw: 277-95.

2015 'The Veneration of LAMMA of Taurisa and the Discrepancies between Versions of the AN.TAH.ŠUM Festival', in Anacleto D'Agostino, Valentina Orsi & Giulia Torri (eds), *Sacred Landscapes of Hittites and Luwians: Proceedings of the International Conference in Honour of Franca Pecchioli Daddi; Florence, February 6th-8th 2014* (Studia Asiana 9). Firenze University Press, Florence: 49-55.

Gessel, Ben H. L. van

1998 *Onomasticon of the Hittite Pantheon*, I (Handbuch der Orientalistik 33). Brill, Leiden.

Gilan, Amir

2021 'A City Shrouded in Myth: Kaneš in Hittite Texts', in Fikri Kulakoğlu, Guido Kryszat & Cécile Michel (eds), *Cultural Exchange and Current Research at Kültepe and its Surroundings, Kültepe, 1-4 August 2019* (Kültepe International Meetings 4, Subartu 46). Brepols, Turnhout: 259-73.

Goetze, Albrecht

1953 'The Theophorous Elements of the Anatolian Proper Names from Cappadocia', *Language* 29/3: 263-77.

Groddek, Detlev

1995 'Fragmenta Hethitica dispersa II', *Altorientalische Forschungen* 22/2: 323-33.

Günbattı, Cahit

2004 'Two Treaty Texts Found at Kültepe', in Jan Garrit Dercksen (ed.), *Assyria and Beyond: Studies Presented to Mogens Trolle Larsen* (Publications de l'Institut historique et archéologique néerlandais de Stamboul 100). Nederlands Instituut voor het Nabije Oosten, Leiden: 249-68.

Güterbock, Hans Gustav

1958 'Kaneš and Neša: Two Forms of One Anatolian Place Name?', *Eretz Israel* 5: 46-50.

1960 [1997] 'An Outline of the Hittite AN.TAH.ŠUM-Festival', *Journal of Near Eastern Studies* 20: 80-89 (repr. in Harry A. Hoffner Jr. (ed.), *Perspective on Hittite Civilization: Selected Writings of Hans Gustav Güterbock* (Assyriological Studies 26). University of Chicago, Chicago: 91-98).

Haas, Volkert

1994a *Geschichte der hethitischen Religion* (Handbuch der Orientalistik 1/15). Brill, Leiden.

1994b 'Das Pferd in der hethitischen religiösen Überlieferung', in Bernhard Hänsel & Stefan Zimmer (eds), *Die Indogermanen und das Pferd: Akten des Internationalen interdisziplinären Kolloquiums, Freie Universität Berlin, 1.-3. Juli 1992. Bernfried Schlerath zum 70. Geburtstag gewidmet* (Archaeolingua 4). Archaeolingua, Budapest: 77-89.

Hagebuchner, Albertine

1989 *Die Korrespondenz der Hethiter: Die Briefe mit Transkription, Übersetzung und Kommentar* (Texte der *Hethiter* 16). Winter, Heidelberg.

Hoffner, Harry A. Jr & Melchert, Craig H.

2008 *A Grammar of the Hittite Language*, I: *Reference Grammar* (Languages of the Ancient Near East 1). Eisenbrauns, Winona Lake.

Houwink ten Cate, Philo H. J.
2003 'A New Look at the Outline Tablets of the AN.TAH.ŠUM^{SAR} Festival: The Text-Copy VS NF 12.1', in Gary Beckman, Richard Beal & Gregory McMahon (eds), *Hittite Studies in Honor of Harry A. Hoffner Jr. on the Occasion of his 65th Birthday*. Eisenbrauns, Winona Lake: 205–19.

Hutter, Manfred
2021 *Religionsgeschichte Anatoliens: Vom Ende des dritten bis zum Beginn des ersten Jahrtausends* (Die Religionen der Menschheit 10/1). Kohlhammer, Stuttgart.

Klinger, Jörg
1996 *Untersuchungen zur Rekonstruktion der hattischen Kultschicht* (Studien zu den Boğazköy-Texten 37). Wiesbaden, Harrassowitz.

Kryszat, Guido
2004 'Herrscher, Herrschaft und Kulttradition in Anatolien nach den Quellen aus den altassyrischen Handelskolonien. Teil 1: Die *sikkātum* und der *rabi sikkitim*', *Altorientalische Forschungen* 31: 15–45.
2006 'Herrscher, Herrschaft und Kulttradition in Anatolien nach den Quellen aus den altassyrischen Handelskolonien – Teil 2: Götter, Priester und Feste Altanatoliens', *Altorientalische Forschungen* 33/1: 102–24.

Kulakoğlu, Fikri
2014 'Kanesh after the Assyrian Colony Period: Current Research at Kültepe and the Question of the End of the Bronze Age Settlement', in Levent Atici, Fikri Kulakoğlu, Gojko Barjamovic & Andrew Fairbairn (eds), *Current Research at Kültepe-Kanesh: An Interdisciplinary and Integrative Approach to Trade Networks, Internationalism, and Identity* (Journal of Cuneiform Studies Supplemental Series 4). Lockwood, Atlanta: 85–94.

Kulakoğlu, Fikri & Kangal, Selmin
2011 *Anatolia's Prologue, Kültepe Kanesh Karum, Assyrians in Istanbul* (Kayseri Metropolitan Municipality Cultural Publication 78). Avrupa Kültür Başkenti, Istanbul.

Laroche, Emmanuel
1946 'Recherches sur les noms des dieux hittites', *Revue hittite et asianique* 7/46: 7–139.

Lassen, Agnete Wisti
2017 'The "Bull-Altar" in Old Assyrian Glyptic: A Representation of the God Assur?', in Fikri Kulakoğlu & Gojko Barjamovic (eds), *Proceedings of the 2nd Kültepe International Meeting: Kültepe, 26-30 July 2015; Studies Dedicated to Klaas Veenhof* (Kültepe International Meetings 2, Subartu 39). Brepols, Turnhout: 177–94.

McMahon, Gregory
1991 *The Hittite State Cult of the Tutelary Deities* (Assyriological Studies 25). University of Chicago, Chicago.

Mora, Clelia & Giorgieri, Mauro
2004 *Le lettere tra i re ittiti e i re assiri ritrovate a Hattuša* (History of the Ancient Near East/Monographs 7). S.a.r.g.o.n. Editrice e Libreria, Padua.

Mouton, Alice
2011 'Sulusaray/Sebastopolis du Pont (Province de Tokat): la Karahna des textes hittites?', *Anatolia antiqua* 19: 101–11.
2014 'Terre divinisée et autres "genies" de l'Anatolie hittite', *Semitica et classica* 7: 19–29.

Otten, Heinrich
1953 'Pirva – der Gott auf dem Pferd', *Jahrbuch für kleinasiatishe Forschung* 2: 62–73.

Singer, Itamar

1996 *Muwatalli's Prayer to the Assembly of Gods through the Storm-God of Lightening (CTH 381)*. Scholars Press, Atlanta.

Starke, Frank

1985 *Die keilschrift-luwischen Texte in Umschrift* (Studien zu den Boğazköy-Texten 30). Harrassowitz, Wiesbaden.

Steitler, Charles W.

2014 'Sakralsprache gelöst vom ursprünglichen Kontext? Das Beispiel einer Tafel des hethitischen Monatsfestes', *Die Welt des Orients* 44/2: 301–08.

2017 *The Solar Deities of Bronze Age Anatolia: Studies in Texts of the Early Hittite Kingdom* (Studien zu den Boğazköy-Texten 62). Harrassowitz, Wiesbaden.

Strabo

Geography, V: *Books 10-12*, trans. Horace L. Jones, 1928 (Loeb Classical Library 211). Harvard University Press, Cambridge, MA.

Taracha, Piotr

2009 *Religions of Second Millennium Anatolia* (Dresdner Beiträge zur Hethitologie 27). Harrassowitz, Wiesbaden.

Ünal, Ahmet

2019 'New Insights into the Nature and Iconography of the Hittite Horse Deity Pirwa', in Natalia Bolatti Guzzo & Piotr Taracha (eds), *'And I Knew Twelve Languages': A Tribute to Massimo Poetto on the Occasion of his 70th Birthday*. Agade Bis, University of Warsaw, Warsaw: 690–702.

Veenhof, Klaas R.

1972 *Aspects of Old Assyrian Trade and its Terminology* (Studia et documenta ad iura Orientis antiqui pertinentia 10). Brill, Leiden.

2008 'The Old Assyrian Period', in Markus Wäfler (ed.), *Mesopotamia: The Old Assyrian Period* (Orbis Biblicus et Orientalis 160/5). Vandenhoeck & Ruprecht, Göttingen: 13–268.

Warbinek, Livio

2022 'The -šepa Theonyms in the Hittite Pantheon', *Vicino Oriente* 26: 1–19.

Wegner, Ilse

2002 *Hurritische Opferlisten aus hethitischen Festbeschreibungen, II: Texte für Teššub, Hebat und weitere Gottheiten* (Corpus der hurritischen Sprachdenkmäler 1/3-2). CNR, Istituto di Studi sulle Civiltà dell'Egeo e del Vicino Oriente, Rome.

Yoshida, Daisuke

1996 *Untersuchungen zu den Sonnengottheiten bei den Hethitern: Schwurgötterliste, helfende Gottheiten, Feste* (Texte der Hethiter 22). Winter, Heidelberg.

WOMEN, FAMILY AND CORRESPONDENCE

6. Keeping in Touch

Language and Mobility of Assyrian Women in the Old Assyrian Period

Anita Fattori

> L'espace est un doute : il me faut sans cesse le marquer, le désigner ;
> il n'est jamais à moi, il ne m'est jamais donné, il faut que j'en fasse la conquête.
>
> (George Perec 1974, 179–80)

Introduction

Early in the 1990s, the archive of the Assyrian merchant Elamma was excavated by Tahsin Özgüç in the Lower Town of Kaneš. About two decades later, the 372 cuneiform documents found in Elamma's house were edited and published by Klaas R. Veenhof in the volume KT 8 (2017). The publication of these documents gives us a unique opportunity to gain considerable insights into the organizational aspects of an Assyrian family and the involvement of their members, including women, in the far-reaching trading networks of the Old Assyrian period (Fig. 6.1).

Elamma's archive documents many aspects of the lives of his wife Lamassutum, his daughters Ištar-lamassī, Ummī-Išhara, and Šalimma and his granddaughter Šīmat-Ištar. Among them, the transmission of the female patrimony, the social role of religious women, and the insertion of Assyrian women living in Aššur and Kaneš in trade networks. The aim of this study is to discuss the mobility and insertion of these women in the long-distance trade network between Aššur and Kaneš from the perspective of one chief matrix of social relations and sociability in premodern societies, the family. To this end, I consider Assyrian merchant families as Communities of Practices (from now on CoPs), a concept developed at the heart of the social theory of learning (Lave & Wenger 1991; Wenger 1998).

In the first section, the concept of CoP is introduced and defined for interpreting Old Assyrian social organization. An Assyrian merchant family can be considered as a CoP for at least two main reasons. For one thing, family is the main background for socialization and learning of trade practices. For another, family is the locus where the member of a trading family could access the means of mobility necessary to insert themselves and engage in trade networks in increasing spatial degrees of social interaction between Mesopotamia and Anatolia. As recognized members of a trading family, Lamassutum, Ištar-lamassī, Ummī-Išhara, Šalimma, and Šīmat-Ištar engaged on a regular basis in social activities shared by members of the same family group. In the hope of contributing to a more complete view of women's mobility in trade networks, later in this section I analyse the activities performed by women in Elamma's family.

One of the most important shared practices in the family context is literacy, as literacy in the Old Assyrian period could be learned within the kinship *milieu*. In a socio-geographic context of high mobility and physical distance brought about by commerce, the

---

Anita Fattori (anitafattori@usp.br) PhD candidate at Universidade de São Paulo and Université Paris 1 — Panthéon Sorbonne. Fellowship of São Paulo Research Foundation (FAPESP grantee no. 2019/12945-6 and 2020/07395-4)

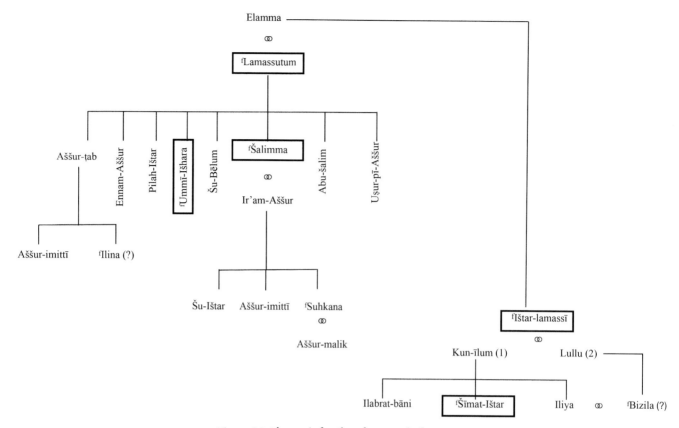

Figure 6.1: Elamma's family. After Veenhof 2015, 77.

maintenance of contact, mainly carried out by letter exchange, was quintessential for the success of trade operations. With that in mind, in the second part of this paper, I shed a light on how women use writing language through letters in order to participate in the dynamics of trade and reinforce their position both in the family groups and trading networks they were part of.

Family: Mobility and Community of Practices

A family in Mesopotamia can be described as a group of people connected through kinship ties that include parentage and alliances (marriage or other affinity bonds) (Rede 2007, 22; 2009, 21). Veenhof (2014), developing on Larsen (2007), considers that an Old Assyrian merchant family parallels a traditional Assyrian family, but the presence of trade and the accumulation and circulation of movable goods can change its dynamics.[1] The family would be maintained especially but not exclusively by ties of consanguinity, given that kinship is a set of categories and statutes that often contradict bio-genetic relationships. Long-distance trade between Assyria and Anatolia in the early second millennium BC was based on the organization of merchant groups into family associations. Although capital accumulation was individually pursued in this context (Larsen 2007, 98), the arrangement of family associations was essential to foster networks of collaboration and solidarity, which are very important for the maintenance of trade networks (Veenhof 2014, 348–49). A general conceptualization of family will suffice to place our main focus on the understanding of kinship not as a static unit, but as a lived practice.[2]

To corroborate my point, I define a merchant's family as a Community of Practices (CoP), adopting in our discussion the approach of Lave & Wenger (1991, 89–117; Wenger 1998), summarized by Eckert

---

1 In Larsen's (2007) article, the nature of the Old Assyrian family and the meaning of the *bēt abim* institution are explored. The author mainly discusses the interface between commercial and kinship structures to determine what function this socioeconomic unit played within the Assyrian society of the early second millennium BC.

2 This tendency arises from David Schneider's (1984) critique of the anthropological field, originating the so-called *new kinship studies* (notably the contribution of Janet Carsten, cf. 1995; 2000; 2004). The implementation of this approach to ancient societies in Egypt and Mesopotamia can be seen in Olabarria 2020, Nielsen 2011, Garcia-Ventura 2014, and Kogan 2014.

6. KEEPING IN TOUCH

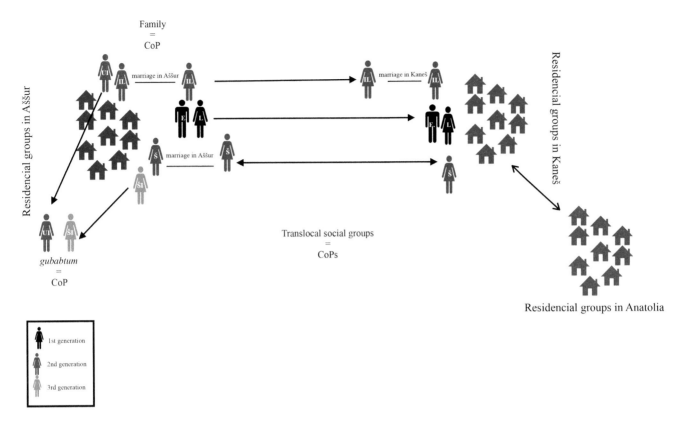

Figure 6.2: Women mobility in Elamma's family. After Furholt 2018, 307.

& McConnell-Ginet (1992, 464) in three main key points: a CoP is (1) 'an aggregate of people who come together around mutual engagement in an endeavor', in our case, long-distance trade; (2) they share common practices that 'emerge in the course of this mutual endeavor'; (3) its idiosyncratic 'idiom' is the result of a relational construction 'defined simultaneously by its membership and by the practice in which that membership engages'. Individuals, as part of CoPs, negotiate actively on a daily basis, and through varied active strategies, their insertion and degree of membership in these communities. A merchant family can be considered as the primary CoP in which an individual engages since early stages of life. This is because participating in commerce implies participating in the family. As family groups are the base of trade organization, CoPs are essential for fostering partnerships and for establishing support networks. By belonging to these families, women could have had extensive mobility and engaged in other communities at different levels of inclusiveness and participation, as we will see in the case of women from Elamma's family.

For the purposes of our discussion, *mobility* is defined as a social process culturally located and experienced differently by different individuals in society (Cresswell 2006). Mobility can be interpreted as a broader continuum of the general fact of movement of individuals or groups, a perspective that avoids reducing our understanding of mobility to particular definitions of migration (i.e. permanent residential translocation, see discussion in Burmeister 2017; Furholt 2018). The members of the same merchant Assyrian family have access to significant translocal mobility between Anatolia and Mesopotamia. That occurred, mainly, by means of donkey caravans.[3] Then, to consider the spatiality between Anatolia and Mesopotamia as translocal is to embrace different geographies, but also to integrate the social interactions and the impacts that are produced from the contact between different communities.

While the movement of things and people can be framed as an empirical reality *per se*, the *means of mobility* is always particular and situated. Mobility of women goes beyond linear dislocation from one place to another. The access by these women to means of transportation and communication available within the

---

3 The idea of *translocality* has been applied in anthropology and archaeology to think about mobility and migration (including of ancient societies) from a postcolonial point of view. The concept arises from the phenomena of globalization, international mobility, and transnational communities (Greiner & Sakdapolrak 2013).

networks they found themselves in impacted directly the 'reach' of their participation and place in multiples CoPs. Their active and continuous engagement in interaction and mobility made of networks a web of connections of dispersed (translocal) places, a cross-community context of membership and identification that traversed physical distances (e.g. between Assyria and Anatolia) and 'create socially more heterogeneous local residences communities' (Furholt 2018, 307).

The women in Elamma's family had a high level of mobility, lived and circulated among translocal social spaces, as we can see in Figure 6.2, which schematizes a model of socio-spatial composition of three generations of women from Elamma's family: his wife, three daughters, and one granddaughter.

Lamassutum, Ištar-lamassī, and Šalimma, for example, spent, for different reasons, part of their lives in Kaneš. Lamassutum, wife of Elamma, at some point in her life moved from Aššur to Kaneš together with her husband. Ištar-lamassī married an Assyrian merchant and also moved with him to Kaneš. As time went on, she became a widow and married for a second time, to an Anatolian man. Both women died in Kaneš. Šalimma, on the other hand, remained married to her Assyrian husband and moved without him to Kaneš, resulting in a family quarrel. Despite marrying and joining their husband's family group, the contact with their primary CoP, that is, their family group of origin, was maintained.

Ummī-Išhara, daughter of Lamassutum and Elamma, and Šīmat-Ištar, daughter of Ištar-lamassī (second and third generation), remained in Aššur throughout their lives and became part of the CoP of consecrated women, the *gubabtum* community.[4] A summary of the *gubabtum*-consecrated women was compiled by Michel (2009b). She was able to recognize about thirty of these women in the available documentation; of whom only a dozen were recognized by name.[5] These women had a high social status, were even owners of their own houses, and shared the same religious practice. In spite of living in Aššur, Ummī-Išhara and Šīmat-Ištar had agents working in Anatolia. They also managed to keep in touch with the original family group, as we can see from the exchange of correspondence and the sending of goods between Aššur and Kaneš.

The women in Elamma's family also established their own trading alliances, carrying out their own transactions with individuals — both Assyrians and Anatolians — who were not part of the family group. Their integration into the trading networks can thus be interpreted in the interaction of these women with different residential groups — or family groups based on Aššur or Kaneš, or even other places in Anatolia.

The physical distance between these individuals forced a reconfiguration of kinship dynamics and adoption of strategies for the maintenance of ties of belonging. The mobility of these women is even keener in documents such as transport and debit contracts and memoranda. In the following sections, I will present the case of three women from this family to highlight the extent of activities of women from merchant families and their mobility. Our corpus allows us to observe their interaction and belonging in different communities at inter-relatable levels.[6]

Feminine Mobility and Long-Distance Trade Networks: Lamassutum

Lamassutum[7] appears in forty-one known documents, thirty-three documents in Elamma's archive. They indicate her articulation in the different networks she was part of. To begin with, Lamassutum sent from Kaneš to Aššur small amounts of silver to her daughter, Ummī-Išhara. This gesture can be understood as a contact maintenance strategy. According to Veenhof (2017), these small amounts of silver (*šēbultum*) would represent gifts. The shipment of quantities of silver to the temple in Aššur is mentioned as well, reinforcing a continuous effort by Lamassutum to maintain her relation-

---

4 The CAD (U, 33) defines a *gubabtum* (*ugbabtum*) as 'a female devotee of a male deity'. Since we do not know about their specific religious duties in this community, we follow Michel's suggestion (2009b, 148) to use *femmes consacrées* instead of *priestesses*.

5 On the economic role of the *gubabtum* in the Old Babylonian period see Klengel 1971. For a general view see Hirsch 1972, 56–57.

6 Part of the information about these women, systematized in Tables 6.1 to 6.11 below, is indebted to the courtesy of Cécile Michel, Leyla Umur, Gojko Barjamovic, and Jan-Gerrit Dercksen towards Klaas R. Veenhof, who published the translation and/or brief excerpts/information about these documents in KT 8 (2017).

7 The name Lamassutum has homonyms in the Old Assyrian corpora (Veenhof 2017, 213). It is impossible then to identify our Lamassutum in KT 6a 12 and KT 6e 1061 and 1062, for example. The identification of *awīltum*-the lady as Lamassutum in also uncertain in KT 8 72, 97, 220, 252.

Table 6.1: Shipping of silver from Lamassutum to the city of Aššur.

DOCUMENT	SHIPPING	TO
KT 8 7	15 shekels of gold together with Aššuriš-tikal, thereof: ½ mina 5 shekels of silver of her ⅓ mina 5 shekels of [silver] (as *ikribū*)	temple
KT 8 8	4 shekels of silver	Ummī-Išhara
KT 8 10	½ mina of silver (*ikribū*) 1 ⅔ shekels of silver	temple Ummī-Išhara

ship with the religious rituals performed in Aššur (Table 6.1). Lamassutum had a crucial role not only in the family organization, of which more below, but also in the trade networks.[8]

In some letters and caravan reports, written to inform Elamma about shipment arrivals, Lamassutum acted as a receiver, taking (*laqā'um*) textiles in Kaneš (Table 6.2). In Kaneš, Lamassutum received pieces of textiles, quantities of metals, and other objects from trading partners, including women from other families (*ana Lamassatim; ana Lamassitim; ana awīltim*). The shipments arrived from Aššur and also from other parts of Anatolia, showing then unbroken continuity of her connections with residential groups in Aššur as well as the enlargement of her networks beyond the Aššur–Kaneš axis (Table 6.3).

Table 6.2: Lamassutum as a receiver of merchandise.

DOCUMENT	TAKE (*laqā'um*)
KT 8 23	1 textile 1 textile (*šūrum*)
KT 8 42	2 textiles (*šūrum*)
KT 8 46	7 textiles (*kutānum*)
KT 8 85	3 textiles

---

8 In addition to the documents referenced in this section, Lamassutum is mentioned as addressee on two envelopes: KT 8 163 and, along with Šalimma, in KT 8 207. She played an important role in the division of Ištar-lamassī's inheritance (KT 8 180, 181, 182, 183, and 185); she appeared in a verbal process after Elamma's death (RA 60, 126–31, *lu aššat awīlim*) and in a verdict of house purchase (KT 8 210bis). It is important to note that KT 8 210bis (=Kt 86/k 155A/B) was not found in Elamma's house. Her participation in trade can also be deduced from assets left after her death (KT 8 164, 176, and 323a).

Table 6.3: Lamassutum receiving metals, textiles, and objects in Kaneš.

DOCUMENT	RECEIVING	FROM
KT 8 30	1 *kusītum*-woollen garment 1 cauldron [from Aššur]	Elamma Tahsi
KT 8 95	1 shawl [from Aššur]	ᶠNerāmtum
KT 8 174	2 minas 15 shekels of silver	Ēnah-ilī in the name of Elamma after his dead
KT 8 323	1 shekel of silver	?
KT 8 327[9]	2 minas [of copper] 2 minas [of copper] 45 shekels [of copper] ½ mina [of copper] + ½ jar of wheat + ½ mina [of copper]	? Šamaš-bāni Šamaš-bēlī Šamaš-bāni
Kt 93/k 73[10]	3 shekels of silver	
Kt 93/k 513[11]	100 (breads) 1 brad-*kubbušum*	?
Kt 94/k 543[12]	1 mina 10 shekels of sealed silver; 3 shekels of silver (as *šēbultum*) [from Anatólia]	?

Lamassutum gave instructions to solve problems concerning a shipment of textiles (KT 8 166). She was involved in trade issues with her son-in-law, Ir'am-Aššur (KT 8 193, 195 and 206). She made an agreement and was involved in contracts about silver (Kt 94/k 123 and KT 8 160). She acquired an Anatolian servant (a girl named Kuzizi) for 15 shekels of silver from Anatolians (KT 8 157). The conditional sale of a girl features in Kt 94/k 127, probably connected with a loan contract where the girl would be her father's pledge (Veenhof 2017, 213). Lamassutum also acted as a creditor in Kaneš for Assyrians as well as Anatolians, suggesting that she was a trustworthy person who has achieved important status in both communities (Table 6.4). And last but not least, KT 8 159 and 164 may point to the possibility that she also manufactured textiles in Kaneš. In the first document, Aššur-taklāku, son of Huliya, owes (*išā'um*) to

---

9 The quantities mentioned in the document are designed for *awīltum*-the lady. There remains a possibility that the document refers to Lamassutum, Ištar-lamassī, or Šalimma. Based on the context, I consider that the document refers to Lamassutum.

10 Unpublished document. Transliteration by Cécile Michel.

11 Lines 12–15 cited by Michel (2016, 229).

12 Unpublished document. Transliteration by M. T. Larsen, to be published by G. Barjamovic. Lines 4–6 are cited by Veenhof (2017, xxxii).

Table 6.4: Lamassutum acting as creditor.

DOCUMENT	QUANTITY	DEBTOR
KT 8 154	20 minas of refined copper (price of an Anatolian servant, a girl named Kukra)	Šamaš-abī (*išā'um*)
KT 8 158	(x) minas of refined silver	Aššur-lamassī (*išā'um*)
KT 8 161	15 shekels of refined silver	Walhišna, Peruwa, and ᶠTuwatuwi (*išā'um*) — Anatolians
KT 8 162	13 shekels of silver	Ilī-bāni (*išā'um*)
Kt 94/k 120[13]	⅔ mina of silver	Dadaya

Lamassutum '30 minas of soft wool for making the wef (*šakākum*)'. In the second one, Pilah-Ištar was supposed to trade Lamassutum's textiles.[14]

Ummī-Išhara

Ummī-Išhara's connections revealed by the documentation provide another interesting take on trade networks. She appears in twenty-one documents (twenty documents in Elamma's archive) and we can identify her seal stamped on the envelope KT 8 207 (Veenhof 2017, pl. 41).[15] As a consecrated woman, she spent her entire life in Aššur. Nevertheless, she was also involved in the trade networks and family decisions in Kaneš. She had the intention of sending from Aššur to Kaneš consignments of textiles and tin to her brother, Pilah-Ištar (Table 6.5).[16] An agreement settled in Kaneš concerning the division of her father's inheritance, names Ir'am-Aššur as her representative (KT 8 175).[17] Her proximity

---

13 Unpublished document. Transliteration by Cécile Michel.

14 KT 8 164:20–22, *9 túg pí-ri-kà-ni ù 1 túg a-bar-ni-am a-na Pi-lá-ah-Ištar a-na ši-a-ma-tim a-dí-in*[1] — 9 *pirikannum*-textiles and 1 textile of Abarnian type I gave to Pilah-Ištar for making purchases.

15 She has at least one homonym, Ummī-Išhara, wife of Šuppi-niman (KT 6d 735). It is impossible to connect our woman with Ummī-Išhara from Kt c/k 608.

16 She was also involved in the division of inheritance of her father and her mother in KT 8 164 (as *gubabtum*-religious women), 176, 177 (together with her sister, as *ahatīšu*-his sisters), 178 (as *ṣuhārtum*-the girl), in the division of inheritance of her sister Ištar-lamassī (KT 8 180 and 181), and in KT 8 87 (as *ṣuhārtum*-the girl, the excerpt concerning Ummī-Išhara is very fragmented).

17 Despite the fact that Ir'am-Aššur, Šalimma's husband, lived in Aššur, the documentation allows us to observe that he travelled frequently between Mesopotamia and Anatolia, spending some periods in Kaneš (Veenhof 2017, 271–94).

Table 6.5: Shipping from Ummī-Išhara to the city of Kaneš.

DOCUMENT	SHIPPING	TO
KT 8 165	2 high quality textiles (*wabālum*) intention to send tin (amount of 1 mine silver) (*wabālum*)	Pilah-Ištar

Table 6.6: Ummī-Išhara receiving silver in Aššur.

DOCUMENT	RECEIVING IN AŠŠUR	FROM
KT 8 7	1 ½ mina of silver	for her textiles?
KT 8 8	5 shekels of silver (as *šēbultum*); 4 shekels of silver; 3 shekels of silver; 1 (x); 2 shekels of silver	for her textiles? (*ša*) Lamassutum Laqēpum (*wabālum*) [PN], son of Kunnaya (*wabālum*) for her textiles?
KT 8 10	10 shekels of silver (as *šēbultum*); 4 shekels of silver; 1 ⅔ shekels of silver	for her textiles? [PN] (*ša*) Lamassutum
KT 8 13	6 shekels of silver (as *šēbultum*);	for her textiles?
KT 8 35	6 shekels of silver (*laqā'um*)	yield from her father's investments
KT 8 139	5 ½ shekels of silver	for her textiles?

to her brother-in-law becomes immediately noticeable from the content of the letter KT 8 206 (that will be discussed in detail below).

Unlike other historical contexts in Mesopotamia, in the Old Assyrian period the order of sender and addressee in the letterhead can vary. The position can be an indicator of status or age of those involved, or even a matter of the subject discussed in the missive.[18] Ummī-Išhara's name appears in a verdict of Kaneš before the name of her brothers (KT 8, 173).[19] The function of consecrated women entailed high status within Assyrian society and the occupation of this position predicts that she 'prend part

---

18 On Old Assyrian letterhead, see Adelhofer 2020.

19 KT 8, 173:16–27, *mer'at Elamma u mer'ū Elamma* — the daughter of Elamma and the sons of Elamma.

à toute décision familiale d'importance' (Michel 2009b, 159). Also, after Elamma's death, she helped her brother Ennam-Aššur in the liquidation of her father's business in Aššur, as demonstrated by Veenhof (2017, 280–83) from the interpretation of KT 8 189, 190, and 191.[20]

By taking into consideration all the pieces of information from Tables 6.5 and 6.6, it can be concluded that she produced textiles for both family members and other trading partners. Moreover, small amounts of silver are shipped by her mother, probably as a gift. It is also important to mention that her shipment is delivered together with the consignment of several other people, including a large number of women.

Šalimma

Šalimma built another female network of activity that the documents of this family allow us to reconstitute.[21] She appears in eighteen documents, eight in this archive. She lived both in Kaneš and Aššur. This fact enabled her to engage in trade networks in both localities: she sent merchandise to Kaneš and received silver when she was in Aššur (Tables 6.7 and 6.8); she received textiles in Kaneš from a shipment that had been sent to her husband (Table 6.9). The letter KT 8 189 shows us that she could take shipments with herself while travelling: 'If your sister goes to the City (of Aššur), give the silver, the price the textiles yielded, to her and let her come here.' Finally, she acted as a creditor in Kaneš for Anatolians — men and a woman (Table 6.10).[22]

In addition to her participation in the family firm, she conducted her own transactions. She had her own tablet coffer and a tablet coffer with her seal (KT 8 208, 237).[23] Šalimma also figures in the purchase of a house and a servant (Table 6.11).[24]

Table 6.7: Šalimma receiving silver in Aššur.

DOCUMENT	RECEIVING IN AŠŠUR	FOR
Kt c/k 30[25]	10 shekels [of silver] (as *šēbultum*)	Šalimma and Masātum

Table 6.8: Shipping from Šalimma to the city of Kaneš.

DOCUMENT	SHIPPING	TO
Kt 94/k 543[26]	8 ⅔ shekels of sealed silver [from Aššur]	Aššur-ṭāb [in Kaneš]

Table 6.9: Šalimma as a receiver of merchandise.

DOCUMENT	TAKE (*laqā'um*)
Kt 94/k 351[27]	2? textile

Table 6.10: Šalimma acting as creditor.

DOCUMENT	QUANTITY	DEBTOR
KT 8 209[28]	15 shekels of silver	fIšhašara and Ali'ahšušar owe to her (*išā'um*) — Anatolians
Kt 94/k 137[29]	15 shekels of silver	Dalaš, Kikaršan, and Taliya — Anatolians
Kt 94/k 554[30]	1 sack and 2 jars of wheat; 1 sack and jars of malt; the removal of the chair of her mother	fAnana became indebted (*ḫabbulum*)

---

20 She is also the addressee of Kt f/k 11 together with her brother, Šu-Bēlum. In this unpublished letter, Ummī-Išhara figures taking care of the assets left by her father in Aššur (Veenhof 2017, 231).

21 There are other references to the same name, but it is impossible to connect them with this woman, as in: KT 6a 14; KT 6d 786, 787; Kt k/k 100; Kt 91/k 134; Kt 94/k 362, 382, 438, 464, 501, and 1001; TPAK 1 175.

22 KT 8 189:33–35 leads us to believe that she could make journeys with merchandise by herself, *šu-ma a-ha-at-kà a-na A-lim*ki *ta-lá-kam kù-babbar ší-im túg*hi-a *dí-ší-ma* [*lu*] *ta-li-kam*.

23 KT 8 208:6–8, *tamalākī ša ṭuppēa pitiā-ma* — open (pl.) my tablet coffer; KT 8 237:20–22, *ta-ma-/lá-kà-*[x] *ša ikkunukkē ša Šalimma* — the tablet box sealed with the seals of Šalimma.

24 In addition to the documents in the tables, she appears in: Kt c/k 128 and Kt 91/k 238 (due to its fragmentary state of preservation, they were not included in the current analysis); KT 8 177 (together with her sisters as *ahatīšu*-his sisters), KT 8 206 (will be addressed below), KT 8 207 (a reverse of an envelope), and Kt 93/k 513 (an unpublished list of bread distribution, where she is referred to as Elamma's daughter, Michel 2016, 229; Veenhof 2017, 295).

25 Unpublished document. Transliteration by J.-G. Dercksen.

26 Unpublished document. Transliteration by M. T. Larsen, to be published by G. Barjamovic. Lines 4-6 are cited by Veenhof (2017, xxxii).

27 An unpublished letter from Enna-Suen and Kulumaya to her husband, Ir'am-Aššur (Veenhof 2021, 182). Transliteration by M. T. Larsen, to be published by G. Barjamovic.

28 This tablet was found with a small piece of its envelope.

29 Unpublished document. Transliteration by Cécile Michel.

30 Unpublished document. Transliteration by M. T. Larsen, to be published by G. Barjamovic. Lines cited by Veenhof (2017, 261).

Table 6.11: Šalimma's own business.

DOCUMENT	SUBJECT
KT 8 210	a house is sold (*tadānum*) to her for 2 ½ minas of silver
KT 8 210bis (=Kt 86/k 155A/B)	verdict about the dispute over the purchase of the house
Kt 94/k 181[31]	buys a servant from an Anatolian family

Taken all together, the documentation highlights the autonomy of these three women in trade within and outside the family network in Aššur and Kaneš. The existence of women's networks is not limited to female members of the same family or living in the same city. The exchange of information among multiple partners and family members stands in for their mobility through translocal communities that pivoted around kinship organization. This means that the women of this network-like system of intercommunication established their contacts and social ties through family networks. That is precisely the reason why the maintenance and proper functioning of the primary CoP, i.e. the family group, is essential for the insertion of these women in business practices. Putting differently, the maintenance of this vast and dynamic social space depended on active engagement and continuous negotiation among its members.

Mobilizing Language

Individuals involved in Old Assyrian trade can engage in common practices and cultivate their membership in a CoP even though they are not physically close to each other, as an in-person interaction between individuals is not a necessary condition for the maintenance of a CoP. The prime means of interaction across this translocal space is the exchange of letters. Writing language counteracted the physical dispersion (mobility) of these individuals.

Language has been extensively considered as part of the practices recognized and commonly shared by all the members of a CoP (Eckert & McConnell-Ginet 1995, 470). By assuming that a CoP is 'the social fabric of learning' (Wenger 1998, 251) and that literacy in the Old Assyrian period initially took place within familial contexts, the mobilization of writing language — materialized in clay letters — is also a practice that emerges in the core of the family and is intrinsically embedded in kinship structures. It follows from this that a letter cannot be reduced to a mechanical communication device.

Gender, Literacy and the Old Assyrian Period

Literacy is a phenomenon that involves a large number of agents and variables such as the social spatial context of communication and social context of the document's production as well as the relationship between who writes, why he/she does so, and for whom. The starting point for thinking about literacy in the Old Assyrian period is taking into account that the function of writing in this society is closely intertwined with a long-distance communication system between Mesopotamia and Anatolia. Since a merchant might not have had a full-time scribe at his disposal, literacy would be essential for successful commercial operations, intercommunication, and inter-community mobility. Beyond that, the characterization of Old Assyrian cuneiform as an easy-to-learn writing system led specialists to challenge the idea that training and mastering of writing took place only in formal educational frameworks, especially when one considers merchant families.[32]

One of the features that makes the Old Assyrian cuneiform script a 'user friendly' system is its simplified writing system, featuring archaic signs that enable them to be represented more easily and make the writing system 'within hands' reach'. Another feature is the not-so-common use of consonant-vowel-consonant (CVC) signs in the documents of the period, and not a very large number of logograms. These features support the view that 'le syllabaire en usage reste relativement simple et ne comporte pas plus de 150 à 200 signes' (Michel 2008, 254) comprising syllabic, logographic, and determinative signs. Keeping these observations in mind, it is quite plausible that merchants had a degree of literacy and hence sufficient knowledge to write and read their own tablets.

As a matter of fact, literacy was probably also learned within the kinship *milieu*, including literacy training for women (as well as operational knowledge of measurement systems), as discussed recently by Cécile Michel

---

31 Kt 94/k 181 is an unopened envelope to be published by Cécile Michel with the 1993 tablets and it is quoted by Veenhof (2017, 253; 295). This damaged envelope is sealed by seven individuals (kišib PN), including Ištar-lamassī, Elamma's daughter, but it only carries the imprint of three seals (courtesy C. Michel).

32 On Old Assyrian literacy, see Larsen 1989, 132–33; 2001, 277; Michel 2001, 39; 2008, 353–54; Kryszat 2008; and Kouwenberg 2017.

and Wiebke Beyer.³³ By studying the Assyrian women of merchant families, Michel (2020, 333; 2023, 228) points out that in the Old Assyrian letters no scribe is mentioned as responsible for writing women's letters. The letters could have been written by the women themselves or by a literate family member living nearby.³⁴

A recent palaeographical analysis carried out by Wibke Beyer (2019) revealed a strong relationship between members of the same family and literacy practices.³⁵ Literacy training was probably provided by a family member, such as a father, an uncle, or an older brother. Beyer evidenced styles of handwriting and writing habits shared by some members of the same family: specific patterns of writing are detected, including a deliberative choice of certain signs and their peculiar execution. A family stylistic pattern can be seen even in the materiality of the table: its shape and preparation before writing can point to group-specific practices.³⁶ Women are included as well in Beyer's insights on degrees of literacy, as Ummī-Išhara, Elamma's daughter, who will be discussed presently.³⁷

Concerning letter writing, women's names are present in 10 to 15 per cent of published letters, as senders and addressees (Michel 2023, 229). In Elamma's archive, the women members of the family appear in 6.5 per cent of the letterheads.³⁸ By analysing these letters, it is only possible to carry out a study of Ummī-Išhara's handwriting. This is the only woman who appears as the only sender in more than one letter.

Looking at the two known letters that introduce Ummī-Išhara as the sender (KT 8 165 and 206), Beyer (2019, 254–59) noted a clear difference between the two tablets. The tablets are of very similar size, KT 8 206 has twice the number of lines and almost four times the number of signs when compared to KT 8 165.³⁹ KT 8 206 has been written carefully and even the very small writing may point to a professional job. The second one, KT 8 165, on the other hand, with much less standardized signs, could have been written by Ummī-Išhara herself. By comparing KT 8 165 with the tablets of Ennam-Aššur, her brother, Beyer concluded that besides presenting the same variants of some signs, the siblings present a similar peculiar and rare execution of three of them (DÍ, KÙ, and TIM), and this may indicate 'someone with a similar educational background' (2019, 258).

The spread of female literacy in the Old Assyrian period can also be argued from the active participation of women in trade (Michel 2009a). Women act as creditors in loan contracts, they possess their own documents, and they have their own seals to validate the transactions. Participation in trade also included the necessity of safekeeping documents and organizing archives.⁴⁰ Tablets were stored in specific spaces inside merchants' houses, and many of them were related to ongoing transactions. Loan contracts, for example, were carefully stored until the debt had been repaid. So, this means that it might be necessary to retrieve any tablets from inside the archive at some point. In this sense, the women who stayed in Aššur or those who lived in Kaneš had a role in taking care of and controlling access to the stored tablets (Michel 2020, 315–21, 333–35).⁴¹ Therefore, a sufficient degree of literacy was needed for anyone who had to find and remove the right tablet.

---

33 Michel 2008; 2010b; 2015; 2020 and Beyer 2019; 2021a; 2021b.

34 Even though some members of the merchant families had had scribal training, as is the case of the son of the well-known merchant Pūšu-kēn, it is quite likely that most of the merchants had learned in a kinship environment.

35 See Stratford 2015 for studies on the scribe's hand and literacy practices in the Old Assyrian period.

36 I consider these patterns shared by members of the same family as *habitus*. According to the socio-theory of learning, *habitus* is 'an emerging property of interacting practices rather than their generative infrastructure' (Wenger 1998, 96).

37 An analysis of the writing of three Assyrian women (Lamassī, wife of Pūšu-kēn; Tarām-Kūbi, wife of Innaya, and Tariša, daughter of Ali-ahum) based on the examination of the materiality of the letters can be found in Michel 2023. Guido Kryszat (2004, 31) has also proposed a relationship between female literacy and intra-family literacy practices by analysing the choices of signs employed by Zizizi, daughter of the merchant Imdī-ilum, in a group of documents that belonged to members of that same family.

38 They feature in seven headings of 109 letters in this archive. In total, Lamassutum, Ištar-lamassī, Ummī-Išhara, Šalimma, and Šīmat-Ištar appear in fifty-four documents in the archive (either their names, or references such as 'PN's wife' or 'the lady-*awīltum*').

---

39 Comparing the two letters, Beyer (2019, 255) established 605 versus 157 total signs, being sixty-four versus forty-six different signs. Photos in Veenhof 2017, pl. 31; pl. 40 and Beyer 2019, 38.

40 The archives could store a vast number of tablets. For example, as of 1994 *c*. 1100 tablets were found in the house of Šalim-Aššur. The archive was edited by Larsen (KT 6, 5 volumes).

41 Three examples of this type in documents of Elamma's archive are here provided: KT 8 195:25–28 'Are my tablets with Lamassutum or does someone from my representatives have them in his possession?' (a letter from Ir'am-Aššur); KT 8 208:5–11 'Please, my son, open my tablet coffer and take out of it the tablet of the debt of Ilī-bāni' (a letter from Šalimma); KT 8 237:20–23 'His debt-note is in the tablet box that is sealed with the seals of Šalimma'.

Letters Sent by Women from Elamma's Family: A General Analysis

The writing of a letter is made possible by sufficient knowledge of the writing language being communicated. Even though we are often unable to establish if the handwriting is that of the sender, in the Old Assyrian period reading and writing skills were widespread among the members of merchant families (Michel 2023, 238). Women, as member of merchant families, were able to structure a message, manifest their demands, and make themselves understood in their very own way. Based on all the aspects discussed above, one can fairly propose that these women also had access to some degree of literacy.

In the context of high circulation of people and things, continuous and intense contact sustained through a system of exchanging letters is paramount not just for the functioning of trade, but also for keeping the ties alive between members of the community. The assumption that effective communication through letters is crucial for a well-oiled system implies equally that it is indispensable to ensure one is being understood correctly. By effectivity I mean a mutual understanding beyond the proper reading of written signs or what is explicitly expressed through linguistic strategies — such as the choice of vocabulary. The mutual understanding stems from a *mutual* engagement in practices that includes what is explicit and 'all the implicit relations, tacit conventions, subtle cues, untold rules of thumb, recognizable intuitions, specific perceptions, well-tuned sensitivities, embodied understandings, underlying assumptions, and shared world views' (Wenger 1998, 47).

Do these women position themselves in specific ways depending on what they communicate and with whom they interact? In what ways are social relations embedded in the written language of commerce? How do gender roles vary in the carousel of subjective positions in a communication system? A systematic analysis of the letters from these women enhances our comprehension of how they position themselves in sets of relationships in collectives, established and maintained bonds, as well as how they negotiated their own social roles. That is why, in what follows, I would like to move my analysis to the letters sent by women from Elamma's family in order to observe the different ways in which they used written language in their favour. Table 6.12 shows the letters in which these women figure as addressees and/or senders.

Table 6.12: Letters sent and/or received by women from Elamma's family.[42]

PUBLICATION	SENDER	ADDRESSEE
KT 8, 165	**Ummī-Išhara**	Pilah-Ištar
KT 8, 166	Bēlānum and **Lamassutum**	Šamaš-bāni and Pilah-Ištar
KT 8, 180	**Lamassutum**, Puzur-Aššur, and Ennam-Aššur	Ataya, Ir'am-Aššur, **Ummī-Išhara**, and **Šīmat-Ištar**
KT 8, 181	**Lamassutum**, Puzur-Aššur, and Ennam-Aššur	Ataya, Ir'am-Aššur, **Ummī-Išhara**, and **Šīmat-Ištar**
KT 8, 195	Ir'am-Aššur	Ikuppī-Aššur, **Lamassutum**, and Ennam-Aššur
KT 8, 206	**Ummī-Išhara**	**Lamassutum** and **Šalimma**
KT 8, 208	**Šalimma**	Šu-Ištar and Aššur-imittī

Ummī-Išhara has her siblings as the main addressees, while Šalimma sent a letter to her sons. Even enjoying great social status, Ummī-Išhara appears as second in the heading of both letters, perhaps suggesting a strategy of humbleness for the request she presented to her addressee. Šalimma, in contrast, is placed first, evoking a hierarchical relationship of a mother towards her sons. By bringing up the relationship of sisterhood with Šalimma and Pilah-Ištar, that is to say, of equal status inside kinship organization, Ummī-Išhara made use of two different strategies. In the first (KT 8 206), she expects — and compels — Šalimma to return home and threatens the disruption of the existing relationship: 'if you are my sister' (do what I am asking for) and (if not) 'you are no longer my sister'. In the second example (KT 8 165), she inverts the strategy, since she is the one who is in debt with Pilah-Ištar (her brother). To defend herself and seek reconciliation, she put her brother in a privileged position: 'please, my brother, don't stay angry, you are the only brother I have' and promises to send, along with the metal shipment, a textile for his personal use.[43]

Widespread literacy among members of Old Assyrian merchant's families allowed the composition of many documents outside the framework of professional writ-

---

42 Ummī-Išhara also figures in another letter as an addressee. In Kt f/k 11, an unpublished letter, she is the addressee together with her brother Šu-Bēlum (lines 5 to 22 are mentioned by Veenhof 2017, 231).

43 KT 8 166:9–13, *a-hi a-ta li-bi-kà lá tù-lá-ma-an a-lá-nu-kà a-ha-am ša-ni-[a-a]m ú-lá i-šu.*

ing, which resulted in letters with a vocabulary close to the spoken language (Larsen 2001, 277). The analysis of letters belonging to a set of documents produced by members of the same family made it possible to investigate the habits of a group of individuals regarding the materiality of the tablets and the materiality of the writing, and also their preferences concerning linguistic habits. As Larsen (2001, 275–76) notes, 'it can be hardly a coincidence [...] that certain words appear exclusively in letters written by one individual or small group of related persons', such as the use of the adjective *saklum* in Elamma's archive. The adjective occurs in the expression *the man is stupid* (*awīlum sakil*), written once in one letter from all Elamma's archive, KT 8 166, sent by Bēlānum and Lamassutum.[44]

Especially in the letters written by the women of the merchant families, it is possible to notice the use of linguistic devices such as unusual vocabulary of everyday life and 'un ton très direct dans les manifestations émotionnelles, souvent proche de la langue parlée' (Michel 2009a, 266), because most of the letters written by men deal mainly with trade issues, while the letters sent by women cover topics that also refer to everyday family concerns (Michel 2023, 234–35). We can then advance as a hypothesis that women from Assyrian merchant families highlight kinship relations and a familiar language when they communicate by letters, relying on a network of trust and proximity in order to influence their recipients.

As commercial demands are permeated by family affairs and conflicts, requests are often intensified through the description of emotions, many of them negative. These aspects of personal suffering are expressed through the choice of a very specific vocabulary, employing many figures of speech.[45] In the case of the family this study places focus on a series of expressions used in women's letters alongside the *libbum*-heart. To do so, I rely on the works of Larsen (2001, 278–79) and Michel (2010a, 306–07), who have extensively discussed the use of expressions containing the substantive *libbum*-heart in the Old Assyrian context:[46]

- + *emmum* (hot): KT 8 165:7–8, 'my feeling too ran high';[47]
- + *ḫad'āum* (D, be/make happy): KT 8 165:25, 'make us happy';[48]
- + *lamānum* (to be bad, be in heat): KT 8 165:3–4, 'you left angry'; 165:10, 'don't stay angry';
- + *marāṣum* (to be disappointed): KT 8 206:39, 'he felt very unhappy';[49]
- + *marāṣum* (Št, to be troubled): KT 208:27 'he has offended me very seriously';[50]
- + *ṣarāpum* (Gtn, to irritate): KT 8 206:6, 'he became irritated';[51]
- + *šanā'um* (to change one's mind): KT 8 206:36, 'before the gentleman changes his mind'.[52]

Some of these expressions, such as *libbum* + *marāṣum*, occur in men's letters in the Elamma corpus. However, all of them are exclusively linked to requests involving commercial issues. Other expressions, specifically with *emmum*, *ḫad'āum*, *ṣarāpum*, and *šanā'um*, appear only in the passages indicated above. Finally, a case that draws our attention is the idiomatic expression *libbum* + *lamānum*, quite common in the Old Assyrian corpus (Larsen 2001, 279). It features in seven other letters sent by men and one letter sent by a woman, Nerāmtum, probably an aunt of Elamma's (Veenhof 2017, 141–42). Only in KT 8 165 and Nerāmtum's letter is the expression connected with demands that permeate the family sphere.

In letters sent by women, they constantly bring trade relations into the family sphere and the commercial demands always come together with a very personal request or complaint expressed through everyday language. This does not imply an essentialist view of a typical feminine language; rather, as pointed out by Michel (2023, 238), it should be stressed 'that certain words and expressions, and the combination of these, are preferred by one gender or the other'. What I want to highlight here is how and in what situations these

---

44 KT 8 166:17, *a-wi-lúm sà-ki-il₅*. The adjective *saklum* designates a simpleton and it has few occurrences in the Old Assyrian corpus (CAD S 81; Veenhof 2017, 234).

45 The use of figures of speech in Old Assyrian letters has been addressed by Veenhof 1987; Larsen 2001 and Michel 2010a.

46 In his article 'Affect and Emotion', Larsen (2001) also analyses discourses on emotion that do not use the substantive *libbum*. These expressions are less common. One of them, *nazāmum* (D,

complain violently) is used by Ummī-Išḫara in KT 8 165:23, 'they complain' (*unazzumū*).

47 *li-bi₄-i [e]-mu-ú*.

48 *l[i-ba-am] /ḫa-dí*. A request that closes the letter after she expresses her displeasure with the situation.

49 *li-bu-šu im-ra-aṣ-ma*.

50 *li-bi₄-i da-ni-iš uš-ta-am-ri-iṣ*.

51 *li-bu-šu : i-ta-na-aṣ-/ra-áp*. (cf. Veenhof 2007, 294; 301–02).

52 *li-bu-šu : iš-ni-ú*.

women used aspects of language to negotiate their participation, foster interactions, and thus expand their potential for mobility inside the networks they participate in. In order to do so, in the last part of this article I would like to focus on the analysis of one episode that had women playing the main role in the development of the events: Šalimma Runs Away to Kaneš (KT 8 206).[53]

Šalimma Runs Away to Kaneš

Ištar-lamassī, the older daughter of Elamma, spent at least ten years of her life in Kaneš. The possibility of moving to another city was enabled by the security of going to a place in which her family — including at least one woman, i.e. Lamassutum — was already established (a family support network). The desire to leave is not sufficient; they needed access to means of mobility, i.e. technology and security to be able to move, as well as emotional and material support to settle in a new place. The establishment of the family in a translocal space and the fact that they belonged to a merchant family (CoP) enables cross-community movement of these women.

A similar movement was made by another of Elamma's daughters, Šalimma. Šalimma, married to the Assyrian merchant Ir'am-Aššur, travelled to Anatolia after the death of her father to spend some time with her mother, Lamassutum. Her stay in Kaneš was apparently extended enough to buy a house in this city (KT 8 210 and 210bis). During this period, her husband and children continued to live in Aššur. From the moment Šalimma decided not to return, an episode of tension grew in family affairs.

The unexpected attitude of this woman caused her husband to mobilize the people around him to bring his wife back to Aššur. The last resort was apparently a long letter (KT 8 206), forty-nine lines long, sent by Ummī-Išhara to her sister Šalimma and her mother Lamassutum. As a *gubabtum*-religious woman, Ummī-Išhara held not only a prestigious position in Assyrian society, but also a very influential place among her siblings (Michel 2009b, 159). She used her social capital as a consecrated woman and her kin proximity as a sister to act as mediator and negotiate Šalimma's return. In terms of structure, it is interesting to note that this is not a letter written in haste, but a message that required extensive planning to be composed. This missive presents a high level of thematic organization and division into units of arguments — which I seek to follow in my analysis. It is clear that the sender expected that her arguments would affect the addressee towards what she thought to be the right direction to be taken.

In the beginning, after the letterhead, the subject is introduced by a direct speech (*umma sūtma*) informing that Ir'am-Aššur tried several times to get Šalimma back to Aššur. Through the use of a rhetorical question, the distress of Ir'am-Aššur's is emphasized. He had no further arguments to persuade Šalimma: 'I talked to him several times, but every time he became angry, saying: "Several letters of mine went to her, but she refused to come here! What else could I write to her in my various letters that I have already sent before?"'[54]

A first block of arguments deals with the commercial relations established between the members of the family of Elamma and Ir'am-Aššur. At this moment, kinship ties are highlighted in an attempt to raise her sister's awareness of the commercial problems her departure may cause. Ummī-Išhara made her point by describing the way in which her sister's attitude will implicate other family members, bringing to the fore trade connections. Firstly, the direct speech device is used twice to put in evidence the seriousness of the situation: 'The gentleman has become very annoyed by the matter and said: "Since she refuses to come, you must not speak to me again!"';[55] and 'You have brought me into conflict with the gentleman, (who said) as follows: "Since (she doesn't act like) my wife, she refuses to come here, you must not mention her name to me again or you will no longer be my sister!"'[56] The crises provoked by Ummī-Išhara's sister would extend to her own personal sphere, since Ir'am-Aššur, Šalimma's husband, was an important trading partner of the family and figured as Ummī-Išhara's representative in an inheritance agreement (KT 8 175). If family relations are not in harmony, they endanger trade relations and, consequently, lead to the disruption of an already established system of

---

53 This well-known letter was edited and analysed by Veenhof in 2007 and published together with the other documents from Elamma's archive in 2017. In addition to Veenhof's edition, KT 8 206 has been edited and published in: Michel 2014, 209–10; Kienast 2015, 47b; Michel 2020, 264. As part of my undergoing PhD work, this letter was translated into Portuguese and French.

54 KT 8, 206:5–10, *a-dí ma-lá ú ši-ni-šu aq-bi-šu-ma li-bu-šu : i-ta-na-aṣ-/ra-áp um-ma šu-ut-ma : a-dí : ma-lá : ú ši-ni-šu na-áš-pé-er-tí : i-li-ik-ši-im-ma a-lá-kam lá ta-mu-a : ša a-ša-pá-ru-ší-ni-ba i-ṣé-er na-áš-pé-ra-tí-a iš-té-et : ú ši-ta : ša i-li-kà-/ši-ni.*

55 KT 8 206:11–13, *a-wi-lúm: a-wa-tim: i-ta-ah-dar [u]m-ma šu-ut-ma iš-tù : a-lá-kam : lá ta-mu-ú lá ta-tù-ri-ma : lá ta-qá-bi-im.*

56 KT 8 206:27–31: *i-na pá-ni : a-wi-lim : tù-uš-ta-zi-zi um-ma šu-ut-ma iš-tù-ma lá am-tí-ni : ší-it a-lá-kam :*

solidarity among these individuals. If Šalimma is not to return to Aššur, she must no longer demand silver from Ir'am-Aššur as she will not be his responsibility anymore. She will have to beg her mother and brothers for her survival. Meanwhile, the family's support network is also disrupted.

The second moment consists in a strategy used by Ummī-Išhara to criticize Šalimma's moral conduct, showing us that she deviated from gender expectations. Once again, using rhetorical questions, the speaker uses language to reiterate her disappointment: 'Why are others taking care of your children and your household, while you are staying there?'[57] The negative aspects of her sister's attitude of neglecting her responsibilities had consequences in the lives of her children and husband: 'do not let your children waste away. [...] The day Pilah-Ištar arrived here, since you did not come with him, he (Ir'am-Aššur) felt very unhappy and for five days he did go out.'[58] Šalimma's decisions also reflected on her personal life: 'do not take me away from the gentleman's house.'[59] In an urgent fashion, Ummī-Išhara made it clear that Šalimma could still reverse the decision: 'If there is a possibility for you to come here, get ready and leave for here before the gentleman changes his mind.'[60]

The letter closes with an ultimatum concerning Šalimma's decision in a very sarcastic tone: 'If you are looking for another husband, write to me to let me know.'[61] The pressure for a decision follows a list that repeats and organizes the five negative consequences in case Šalimma decides to not return: 'If you do not come here, (1) you will bring me into conflict with the gentleman (2) **and** you will let your children perish (3) **and I**, I will **never** mention your name again. (4) **And** you will **no** longer be my sister, (5) **and** you must **not** write to me anymore' (summarization and emphasis added).[62]

In this moment, various strategies are applied to emphasize the urgency of the matter and to express Ummī-Išhara's dissatisfaction through negative emotions. From a grammatical point of view — as highlighted in the excerpt — the clauses are connected in the form of syndetic coordination connected with *and* (*u*). Generally speaking, when more than two coordinated sentences are present, the *u* is placed only in the last of them (Kouwenberg 2017, 757). However, the continuous use of this resource is noted by repeating the connection in all of the sentences. Textual emphasis is also achieved by placing (clause 3) an independent pronoun of first person singular *I* (*anāku*) plus a verb that is already conjugated in the first person (Veenhof 2007, 301). Finally, the prohibitive (*lā* plus a verb in present tense or *ula* in the nominative clause) is employed to express exhortation (clauses 3 to 5).

Sentences 1 and 2 bring back the consequences that Šalimma's attitude will bring to the lives of her relatives. There is a change of tone in sentences 3 to 5 where kinship vocabulary is used to mark boundaries of belonging. The relationship of sisterhood involves trust and equality. By threatening never to mention Šalimma's name again, Ummī-Išhara evoked the possibility of her obliteration — a threat that also came from her husband ('you must not mention her name to me again').[63] Fear of the name's annihilation was quite present in the Mesopotamian imaginary. Naming is a meaningful act directly associated with the essence that will be attached to an individual who will carry the name during life. But not only. As Bahrani (1995, 377) reminds us, 'the naming of a thing was tantamount to its existence, and that a thing did not exist unless it was named'. To erase her name is to vanish the seed of her offspring. By considering the possibility of the disruption of kinship ties, Ummī-Išhara makes it clear to Šalimma that her breaking out of the network may represent her 'social suicide'. She will not be recognized among her peers anymore, resulting in her family disconnection and her isolation from the community.

Conclusion

Space is an incertitude to be conquered relentlessly, George Perec (1974) once said. The women of Assyrian merchant families were part of the trade networks and circulated in an extensive socio-geographical space

---

lá ta-am-tù-a-ni : lá ta-tù-ar-ma šu-um-ša : lá ta-za-kà-ri-im : ú a-tí lá a-ha-tí.

57 KT 8 206:31–33, *mì-šu-um šé-re-ki ú é bé-et-ki ša-ni-ú-tum : i-bé-e-lu : ú a-tí : a-ma-kam wa-áš-ba-tí.*

58 KT 8 206:33, *šé-re-ki : lá tù-ha-li-qí́*; KT 8 206:37–40, *i-na* ᵈ*utu*ˢⁱ *: Pí-lá-ah-Ištar : e-ru-ba-ni ki-ma iš-tí-šu : lá ta-li-ki-ni : li-bu-šu im-ra-aṣ-ma : 5 u₄-me-e : a-na ki-dim lá ú-ṣí.*

59 KT 8 206:34, *ú i-a-tí : i-na é a-wi-lim : lá tù-re-qí-ni.*

60 KT 8 206:35–36, *šu-ma : a-lá-ki : i-ba-ší : tí-ib-e-ma a-tal-ki-im lá-ma a-wi-lúm li-bu-šu : iš-ni-ú.*

61 KT 8 206:40–42, *šu-ma : mu-tám : ša-ni-a-am ta-šé-e-i : šu-up-ri-ma : lu i-dí šu-ma ki a-am : tí-ib-<e>-ma a-tal-ki-/im.*

62 KT 8 206:43–49, *šu-ma : lá ta-li-ki-im i-a-tí: i-na pá-ni : a-wi-lim tù-ša-zi-zi ú šé-re-ki : tù-ha-li-q[í́] ú a-na-ku lá a-tù-ar-ma : šu-um-ki lá*

a-za-kà-ar ú-lá a-ha-tí : a-tí ú mì-ma i-a-tí lá ta-ša-pí-ri-im.

63 KT 8 206:30, *šu-um-ša : lá ta-za-kà-ri-im.*

between Mesopotamia and Anatolia. To conquer this translocal space, they depended on knowledge of trade practices and access to means of mobility. These were accessible from their participation as members of CoPs, that is, of a merchant family. The relationship between the members of a family is not static, neither is it contained exclusively by biological ties. In the Old Assyrian period, family and trade networks were fostered on a daily basis. That is why women's membership in these networks is constantly negotiated and renegotiated, and this had a direct impact on the achievement of their social integration.

Access to literacy practices was probably learned by these women within the family sphere. Writing letters was a strategy of communication through social network's channels that enabled physical and social mobility in socio-geographical space. In the hands of these women, it was an active instrument of interaction for producing new spaces within evolving trade relationships between Anatolia and Mesopotamia. Lamassutum, Ištar-lamassī, Ummī-Išhara, Šalimma, and Šīmat-Ištar used written language as a means of maintaining ('keeping in touch') kinship ties. Literacy practice and membership of a CoP together entailed a cross-community movement and interaction of these women.

Acknowledgements

I wish to express my gratitude to the São Paulo Research Foundation (FAPESP) for my PhD scholarships (grantee no. 2019/12945-6 and 2020/07395-4). Also, I would like to thank both my thesis advisors, Cécile Michel and Marcelo Rede, for their valuable support. I am particularly grateful for the help provided by Renan Falcheti Peixoto not only with the theoretical discussions but also for the countless readings that have increased the readability of this paper. I also would like to thank the anonymous reviewer for his/her precious suggestions. Finally, my colleagues from LAOP (Ancient Near East Research Group at the University of São Paulo), in particular Leandro Ranieri and Thais Rocha, for all the comments when this text was just an idea.

Abbreviations

CAD *The Assyrian Dictionary of the Oriental Institute of the University of Chicago*. Oriental Institute, Chicago, 1956–2006.

KT 6a-e See Larsen 2010–2021.

KT 8 See Veenhof 2017.

TPAK 1 See Michel & Garelli 1997.

Bibliography

Adelhofer, Matthias
2020 'On the Old Assyrian Letter Heading. Playing with Social Hierarchy for Rhetorical Effect', *Chatreššar* 2: 5–18.

Bahrani, Zainab
1995 'Assault and Abduction: The Fate of the Royal Image in the Ancient Near East', *Art History* 18: 363–82.

Beyer, Wiebke
2019 'The Identification of Scribal Hand' (unpublished doctoral thesis, University of Hamburg).

2021a 'Teaching in Old Babylonian Nippur, Learning in Old Assyrian Aššur?', in Stefanie Brinkmann, Giovanni Ciotti, Stefano Valente & Eva Maria Wilden (eds), *Education Materialised: Reconstructing Teaching and Learning Contexts through Manuscripts*. De Gruyter, Berlin: 15–32.

2021b 'The Transmission of the Scribal Art in the Old Assyrian Period – A Paleographic Analysis', in Fikri Kulakoğlu, Guido Kryszat & Cécile Michel (eds), *Cultural Exchange and Current Research in Kültepe and its Surroundings: Kultepe, 1-4 August 2019* (Kültepe International Meetings 4, Subartu 46). Brepols, Turnhout: 197–208.

Burmeister, Stefan
2017 'The Archaeology of Migration: What Can and Should It Accomplish?', in Harald Meller, Falko Daim, Johannes Krause & Roberto Risch (eds), *Migration und integration von der Urgeschichte bis zum Mittelalter*. Landesmuseum für Vorgeschichte, Halle: 57–68.

Carsten, Janet
1995 'The Substance of Kinship and the Heat of the Hearth: Feeding, Personhood and Relatedness among Malays of Pulau Langkawi', *American Ethnologist* 22/2: 223–41.

2000 *Cultures of Relatedness: New Approaches to the Study of Kinship*. Cambridge University Press, Cambridge.

2004 *After Kinship*. Cambridge University Press, Cambridge.

Cresswell, Tim
2006 *On the Move: Mobility in the Modern Western World*. Routledge, London.

Eckert, Penelope & McConnell-Ginet, Sally
1992 'Think Practically and Look Locally: Language and Gender as Community-Based Practice', *Annual Review of Anthropology* 21: 461–90.

Furholt, Martin
2018 'Translocal Communities – Exploring Mobility and Migration in Sedentary Societies of the European Neolithic and Early Bronze Age', *Praehistorische Zeitschrift* 92: 304–21.

Garcia-Ventura, Agnès
2014 'Mano de obra y relaciones de parentesco en Mesopotamia: madres trabajadoras versus hombres "ganadores de pan"', *Arenal: Revista de historia de las mujeres* 21/1: 297–316.

Garelli, Paul
1966 'Tablettes Cappadociennes de collections diverses', *Revue d'assyriologie et d'archéologie oriental* 60 (= RA 60): 93–152.

Greiner, Clemens & Sakdapolrak, Patrick
2013 'Translocality: Concepts, Applications and Emerging Research Perspectives Geography Compass', *Geography Compass* 7/5: 373–84.

Hirsch, Hans
1972 *Untersuchungen zur altassyrischen Religion* (Archiv für Orientforschung 13–14). BiblioVerlag, Osnabrück.

Kienast, Burkhart
2015 *Das altassyrische Eherecht: Eine Urkundenlehre* (SANTAG 10). Harrassowitz, Wiesbaden.

Klengel, Horst
1971 'Horst Drei altbabylonische Urkunden betreffend Felder von ugbabtum-Priesterinnen', *Journal of Cuneiform Studies* 23/4: 124–29.

Kogan, Leonid
2014 *Genealogical Classification of Semitic: The Lexical Isoglosses*. De Gruyter, Berlin.

Kouwenberg, Norbert J. C.
2017 *A Grammar of Old Assyrian* (Handbook of Oriental Studies). Brill, Leiden.

Kryszat, Guido
2004 *Zur Chronologie der Kaufmannsarchive aus der Schicht 2 des Kārum Kaneš: Studien und Materialien* (Old Assyrian Archives. Studies 2). Nederlands Instituut voor het Nabije Oosten, Leiden.
2008 'The Use of Writing among Anatolians', in Jan Gerrit Dercksen (ed.), *Anatolia and the Jazira during the Old Assyrian Period* (Old Assyrian Archives. Studies 3). Nederlands Instituut voor het Nabije Oosten, Leiden: 231–38.

Larsen, Mogens Trolle
1989 'What They Wrote on Clay', in Karen Schousboe & Mogens Trolle Larsen (eds), *Literacy and Society*. Akademisk Forlag, Copenhagen: 121–48.
2001 'Affect and Emotion', in Wilfred van Soldt, Jan Gerrit Dercksen, Norbert J. C. Kouwenberg & Theo Krispijn (eds), *Studies Presented to Klaas R. Veenhof on the Occasion of his Sixty-Fifth Birthday*. Nederlands Instituut voor het Nabue Ooste, Leiden: 275–86.
2007 'Individual and Family in Old Assyrian Society', *Journal of Cuneiform Studies* 59: 93–106.
2010–2021 *Kültepe Tabletleri VI (AKT 6 a-e): The Archive of the Salim-Assur Family*, 5 vols. Türk Tarih Kurumu, Ankara.

Lave, Jean & Wenger, Etienne
1991 *Situated Learning: Legitimate Peripheral Participation*. Cambridge University Press, Cambridge.

Michel, Cécile
2001 *Correspondance des marchands de Kaniš au début du IIe millénaire avant J.-C.* (Littératures anciennes du Proche-Orient 19). Éditions du Cerf, Paris.
2008 'Écrire et compter chez les marchands assyriens du début du IIe millénaire av. J.-C.', in Taner Tarhan, Aksel Tibet & Erkan Konyar (eds), *Mélanges en l'honneur du professeur Muhibbe Darga*. Sadberk Hanım Museum Publications, Istanbul: 345–64.
2009a 'Les Femmes et l'écrit dans les archives paleo-assyriennes', in Françoise Briquel-Chatonnet, Saba Farès, Brigitte Lion & Cécile Michel (eds), *Femmes, cultures et sociétés dans les civilisations méditerranéennes et proche-orientales de l'Antiquité* (Topoi Orient Occident, supplément 10). De Boccard, Paris: 253–72.

2009b 'Les filles consacrées des marchands assyriens', in Françoise Briquel-Chatonnet, Saba Farès, Brigitte Lion & Cécile Michel (eds), *Femmes, cultures et sociétés dans les civilisations méditerranéennes et proche-orientales de l'Antiquité* (Topoi Orient Occident, supplément 10). De Boccard, Paris: 145–63.

2010a 'Le langage figuré dans les lettres paléo-assyriens. Expressions relatives à l'homme et à la nature', in Leonid E. Kogan, Natalia Koslova, Sergey Loesov & Serguei Tishchenko (eds), *Proceedings of the 53rd Rencontre Assyriologique Internationale: Language in the Ancient Near East*, I.1. Penn State University Press, University Park: 347–76.

2010b 'Writing, Counting and Scribal Education in Aššur and Kaniš', in Fikri Kulakoğlu & Selmin Kangal (eds), *Anatolia's Prologue Kültepe Kanesh Karum: Assyrians in Istanbul*. Avrupa Kültür Baskent, Istanbul: 82–93.

2014 'Old Assyrian Kaniš (Akkadian Texts: Women in Letters)', in Mark Chavalas (ed.), *Women in the Ancient Near East: A Sourcebook*. Routledge, London: 205–12.

2015 'Women in the Family of Ali-ahum son of Iddin-Suen (1993 Kültepe Archive)', in Fikri Kulakoğlu & Cécile Michel (eds), *Proceedings of the 1st Kültepe International Meeting, Kültepe, 19-23 September, 2013: Studies Dedicated to Kutlu Emre* (Kültepe International Meetings 1, Subartu 35). Brepols, Turnhout: 85–93.

2016 'Women and Real Estate in the Old Assyrian Texts', *Orient* 51: 83–94.

2020 *Women of Assur and Kanesh: Texts from the Archives of Assyrian Merchants* (Writings from the Ancient World). SBL, Baltimore.

2023 'Gendered Private Letters: The Case of the Old Assyrian Correspondence (Nineteenth Century BC)', in Madalina Dana (ed.), *La correspondance privée dans la méditerranée antique: sociétés en miroir* (Scripta antiqua). Ausonius, Bordeaux: 223–41.

Michel, Cécile & Garelli, Paul

1997 *Tablettes paléo-assyriennes de Kültepe* (TPAK 1). De Boccard, Paris.

Nielsen, John P.

2011 *Sons and Descendants: A Social History of Kin Groups and Family Names in the Early Neo-Babylonian Period (747-626 BC)* (Culture & History of the Ancient Near East 43). Brill, Leiden.

Olabarria, Leire

2020 *Kinship and Family in Ancient Egypt: Archaeology and Anthropology in Dialogue*. Cambridge University Press, Cambridge.

Perec, George

1974 *Espèces d'espaces*. Galilée, Paris.

Rede, Marcelo

2007 *Família e patrimônio na antiga Mesopotâmia*. Mauad, Rio de Janeiro.

2009 'Héritage, dot et prestations matrimoniales en Babylonie ancienne', *Dialogues d'histoire ancienne* 35/2: 13–44.

Schneider, David

1984 *A Critical Study of Kinship*. University of Michigan Press, Ann Arbor.

Stratford, Edward

2015 'Old Assyrian Literacy: Formulating a Method for Graphic Analysis and Some Initial Results', in Fikri Kulakoğlu & Cécile Michel (eds), *Proceedings of the 1st Kültepe International Meeting, Kültepe, 19-23 September 2013: Studies Dedicated to Kutlu Emre* (Kültepe International Meetings 1, Subartu 35). Brepols, Turnhout: 117–28.

Veenhof, Klaas R.

1987 '"Dying Tablets" and "Hungry Silver". Elements of Figurative Language in Akkadian Commercial Terminology', in Murray Mindlin, Markham J. Geller & John E. Wansbrough (eds), *Figurative Language in the Ancient Near East*. Routledge, London: 41–75.

2007 'Sisterly Advice on an Endangered Marriage in an Old Assyrian Letter', in Martha Roth, Walter Farber, Matthew Stolper & Paula von Bechtolsheim (eds), *Studies Presented to Robert D. Biggs, June 4, 2004: From the Workshop of the Chicago Assyrian Dictionary*, II. Oriental Institute of the University of Chicago, Chicago: 285–304.

2014 'Families of Old Assyrian Traders', in Lionel Marti (ed.), *La Famille dans le Proche-Orient ancien: réalités, symbolismes, et images; Proceedings of the 55th Rencontre Assyriologique International at Paris, 6-9 July 2009*. Eisenbrauns, Indiana: 341–74.

2015 'The Archive of Elamma Son of Iddin-Suen and his Family', in Fikri Kulakoğlu & Cécile Michel (eds), *Proceedings of the 1st Kültepe International Meeting, Kültepe, 19-23 September 2013: Studies Dedicated to Kutlu Emre* (Kültepe International Meetings 1, Subartu 35). Brepols, Turnhout: 73–83.

2017 *Kültepe Tabletleri 8 (AKT 8): The Archive of Elamma, Son of Iddin-Suen, and his Family (Kt. 91/k 285-568 and Kt. 92/k 94-187)*. Türk Tarih Kurumu, Ankara.

2021 'Chroniques bibliographiques 24. "Kültepe Texts" 1990–2010–2020 – Part 2', *Revue d'assyriologie et d'archéologie orientale* 115: 175–202.

Wenger, Etienne

1998 *Communities of Practice*. Cambridge University Press, Cambridge.

7. The Hand of a Woman?

Wiebke Beyer

Women and Literacy

In the ancient city of Kaneš, more than 22,000 tablets from the Old Assyrian period have been excavated so far. Thousands are letters concerning mainly the business and daily affairs of men. Many were presumably also written by them.[1] However, among this large number of tablets, there are several letters sent by women. But who wrote them?

Considering the situation of the merchant families, one could assume that women were also literate. While traders were travelling, women took care of house, family, and business matters. Furthermore, it is known from several letters that they were in charge of the tablet collections stored in their houses. Many of these texts address both men and women — wives, mothers, sisters — to handle cuneiform tablets.[2] In TPAK 1, 32, Kuzum asks Šumī-abya and Maka to store a document safely in a container with other tablets: 'Concerning the tablet of the house sale on which my father's name is written, as you are my mother, that very tablet, you yourself and Šumī-abiya open the tablet (container) and place (it) with my tablets' (Michel 2020, 328). In AKT 3, 84, Ennam-Aššur instructs a colleague and his wife Nuhšatum to send him a specific tablet: 'I have drawn up a certified tablet at the Gate of the God [...] and it is placed in the ṣiliānum-container with the tablets of the Gate of the God. Look for (this) tablet, sealed with the seal of Aššur-ṭāb and Enna-Suen and take it out' (Michel 2020, 323). Even though a closer look at these texts, as Veenhof noted in his detailed study of Nuhšatum's letters (2015), suggests that women were more likely to be responsible for guarding the strongroom and men for handling the tablets, one might still wonder why women are addressed directly in the letters if they could not read.

Another indication of the literacy of women might be the verb *lapātum* which means 'to write down, write out' in Old Assyrian. It can be found in several letters sent by women, and its use could imply that the sender actually wrote the message, unlike other verbs that refer only to sending or transporting tablets. For example, in BIN 6, 93, Hattītum writes to Zikri-Elka 'you have written angry words to me' (Michel 2020, 336–37).[3] In CCT 4, 8a, Abaya reminds her brother-in-law that she is able to draw the accounts: 'Do not blame me for the fact that I might write down for you as owed by him more or less!' (Michel 2020, 337).

Direct evidence on women's literacy such as this is sparse and does not allow for general conclusions. Therefore, other approaches need to be explored. One of them is the analysis of handwriting. What can palaeographic studies of women's letters tell us about the writers? In the following, various letter corpora sent by women are examined for their handwriting and com-

---

1 Features such as a relatively low number of cuneiform signs, the different levels of writing skills, and, but not least, the situation of the travelling merchants indicate widespread literacy (see Larsen 1976, 305; Michel 2008a).

2 For an extensive list of these texts, see Michel 2020, 333–38.

3 For a discussion of the term *awātum himṭātum* ('heated/angry words'), see Hirsch 1967 and Larsen 2001, 280–81. For the discussion of the same term in combination with *lapātum*, see Michel 2020, 334–35.

Wiebke Beyer (wiebeyer@gmail.com) PhD from the University of Hamburg

pared with those of male family members to identify any familial characteristics.

Ummī-Išhara, the Daughter of Elamma

Ummī-Išhara was the daughter of Elamma and Lamassutum. She was probably the couple's oldest daughter and lived as a *gubabtum*-priestess in Aššur. She is mentioned in a few texts as the recipient of small amounts of silver. The tablet collection found in her family's house in Kaneš, excavated in 1991 and published by K. R. Veenhof in KT 8, contains two letters sent by her: KT 8, 165 (Kt 91/k 508) is addressed to one of her brothers, Pilah-Ištar; KT 8, 206 (Kt 91/k 385) is a long text to her mother and Šalimma, one of her sisters. Two tablets are not sufficient to identify the hand of a writer. Nevertheless, they can tell us something about him or her. The case of Ummī-Išhara's two tablets is interesting because they are entirely different.[4]

The tablet KT 8, 165 probably broke into two parts already in ancient times, but they fit together quite well. Even though some signs are missing from the broken edges,[5] the rough shape of the tablet and the irregular writing are clearly visible. The different heights of the lines and the uneven orientation and position of the cuneiform signs are noticeable at first glance. The space between the signs as well as between the wedges of a sign and the depth of their impression is also irregular. A clear example is the obverse's second line, which reads *um-ma Um-mì-Iš-ha-ra-ma* (Fig. 7.1).

Figure 7.1: The second line on the obverse of KT 8, 165 shows many irregular or uneven elements, such as the different heights of the line and uneven spacing between signs and wedges. Anadolu Medeniyetleri Müzesi. Photo: Cécile Michel.

The upper ruling of this line is wavy, while the one below is relatively straight. Therefore, the height of the line changes accordingly. The space between the signs is generous at the beginning of the line and becomes smaller towards the end. The signs also show some peculiar features: for example, the two occurrences of the sign UM are written with different numbers of vertical wedges; a third horizontal of the sign MA (in *um-ma*) is hardly visible; all the necessary wedges of HA seem to be there, but their order is curious; and the impression of the wedges, in general, differs significantly. While the final verticals are often impressed deeply, filling wedges are thin, small, and appear to be written hesitantly (e.g. the filling verticals of the second UM and the *Winkelhaken* of HA). These elements indicate a writer who does not have much experience.

The second letter naming Ummī-Išhara as the sender is KT 8, 206. The tablet is complete and the opposite of the aforementioned letter. The tablet is slightly larger than KT 8, 165 but while the latter contains twenty-five lines, the text on KT 8, 206 consists of forty-nine lines, which is due to significantly smaller writing (Fig. 7.2).

Figure 7.2: Comparison of KT 8, 165 (right) and 206 (left). Anadolu Medeniyetleri Müzesi. Photo: Wiebke Beyer.

KT 8, 206 is the prime example of a tablet: neatly shaped and fully inscribed. The ruling is slightly oblique, the lines show basically the same height, and the space is filled in consistently. Although barely 2 mm in size, the script is evenly impressed and clearly legible. The second line reads *um-ma Um-mì-Iš-ha-<ra->ma a-dí-ma na-áš-pé-er-tim* and is a good example of careful handwriting (Fig. 7.3). The quality of both the tablet and the writing indicates a very well trained and most likely professional scribe.

Figure 7.3: The second line on KT 8, 206. Anadolu Medeniyetleri Müzesi. Photo: Cécile Michel.

While the elements discussed highlight the different skill levels of the two writers of Ummī-Išhara's letters, a comparison of sign variants on these two tablets and typical variants on the tablets of the father and one of

---

4 The study of Ummī-Išhara is based on Beyer 2019, 254–61 and Beyer 2021a, 22–30.

5 See for images of both sides and the missing parts KT 8, pl. 31.

7. THE HAND OF A WOMAN

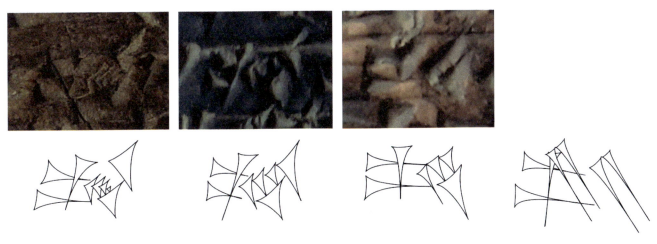

Figure 7.4: Examples of the sign AM on tablets of Ummī-Išhara (KT 8, 165 and 206), Ennam-Aššur (KT 8, 190), and Elamma (KT 8, 80). Anadolu Medeniyetleri Müzesi. Photo: Cécile Michel.

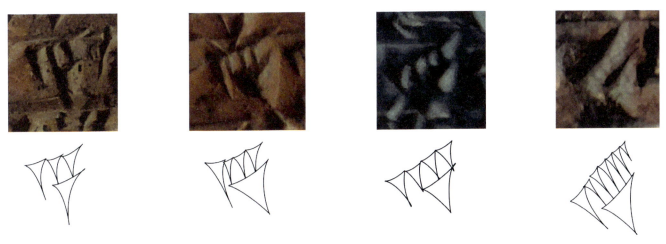

Figure 7.5: Examples of the sign DÍ with the protruding first upper *Winkelhaken* on KT 8, 165, 206, 190, and 79. Anadolu Medeniyetleri Müzesi. Photo: Cécile Michel.

the brothers also shows intriguing results.[6] First of all, the writing styles of these four people are very similar. There are no unusual sign forms on any of the tablets, and the sign variants are often quite similar. An example of this is AM. The main discriminating element of this sign is the *Winkelhaken* cluster, including the number of triangular wedges and their position. The variations preferred by the four writers show differences regarding both characteristics. Another element, which can vary greatly, is always the same: the size and position of the vertical wedge (Fig. 7.4).

Another example is DÍ. Among the four handwriting styles, the number of *Winkelhaken* varies between three and five wedges in the upper row. However, their arrangement is always the same, i.e. the first *Winkelhaken* of the upper row protrudes past the lower one (Fig. 7.5).

Furthermore, many signs have been written similarly by two or more writers. For example, the writers of the tablets of Ummī-Išhara and Ennam-Aššur wrote BA and IM in the same way, while the writer of Elamma's tablets preferred other variations. The writers of Ummī-Išhara's rough tablet and Ennam-Aššur's tablets have several sign variants in common, which are written differently on KT 8, 206 and Elamma's tablets: DÍ (showing both the same arrangement and number of wedges), GA, ḪA, MA, and TIM (Fig. 7.6).

Little is known about how and from whom children learned to write in the Old Assyrian period. In the let-

---

6 Neither the hand of the father Elamma nor his son Ennam-Aššur could be identified yet. However, at least three out of seven letters of Elamma were presumably written by the same person (i.e. KT 8, 79, 80, and 82). Therefore, they are used for comparison. Only three letters are preserved from Ennam-Aššur, and all of them show the same handwriting (i.e. KT 8, 189, 190, and 191). For more information, see Beyer 2021a.

Figure 7.6: Examples of the signs DÍ, GA, ḪA, MA, and TIM on KT 8, 165 and tablets of Ennam-Aššur (KT 8, 190, 189, 190, 189, 189). Anadolu Medeniyetleri Müzesi. Photo: Cécile Michel.

ter CCT 4, 6e, a boy names a DUB.SAR, i.e. a professional scribe, as his teacher.[7] A palaeographic case study has shown that the brothers Aššur-nādā and Ilī-ālum must have learned the art of writing from the same teacher, who was not their father (Beyer 2021b). However, it is not known whether they were taught by their siblings, a relative, or a professional scribe. Likewise, little is known about the circumstances of the teaching. Perhaps the children went to a scribe in the neighbourhood and learned together with other children, or perhaps a scribe was employed to teach the children of the family. It may have varied from case to case.

In the case of Ummī-Išhara, the similarities between the handwriting on KT 8, 165 and Ennam-Aššur's tablets could perhaps indicate a situation in which the siblings Ennam-Aššur and Ummī-Išhara learned together or from the same teacher or model. But there is still no clear answer to this (Beyer 2021a).

The case of Ummī-Išhara is interesting and difficult. Any interpretation of the observations is based on speculation. The daughter of Elamma is not the only woman who sent letters to her family in Anatolia.

Tariša, the Daughter of Ali-ahum

Tariša was the daughter of Ali-ahum, whose house in Kaneš was excavated in 1993 (Michel 2008b, 2015, and 2018). It is known from the texts that she was originally living in Aššur and only moved to Kaneš following the death of her father, where she possibly lived with the family of her brother, Aššur-taklāku. Nothing is known about her status, for example, whether she was married or a priestess. Seven intact letters remain, which she had sent from Aššur to Kaneš. All of them are addressed to her brother: three letters name Tariša as the sole sender, and four were sent by a group of people.

All seven tablets make a consistent and neat impression.[8] The quality of the tablets and the writing on them is high. The wedges are evenly impressed and have a sharp outline so that the writing is clearly legible. The rulings are not necessarily straight, but the lines are consistently filled in, and the spacing between signs and wedges is even.

The handwriting on the seven tablets indicates that they were written by the same writer, as noticed by

---

7 See for the text Larsen 1976, 305 n. 47 and Michel 1998, 250 and n. 2.

8 For a description of Tariša's tablets and writing, see Michel 2015, 89–91.

Michel (2015, 89). They must have been skilled because the diagnostic signs show astonishing similarity and consistency. Figure 7.7 presents an example of IM from each of the seven tablets. The main discriminating element here is the *Winkelhaken* cluster, specifically its number of wedges, their size, and positioning. On all tablets of Tariša, the *Winkelhaken* cluster consists of three wedges in the upper row and one at the bottom. The last one of the upper row protrudes past the one at the bottom and tends to be slightly enlarged and/or offset towards the upper right.

Comparison with the hands of her brother Aššur-taklāku and her father Ali-ahum shows mixed results. Several diagnostic signs like BA, IR, MA, and Ù are basically written in the same way by the writers of the three letter corpora. Especially the first three of these signs generally show little variation. In contrast, the signs AM, DU, GA, KÙ, LI, and ZI on Tariša's tablets are written differently than those of her family members. This could indicate that the writer of Tariša's letters did not learn the same writing tradition as her brother and father. Then again, for most of these diagnostic signs, the tablets of father and son also show different variations: either a different number of wedges or different arrangement.[9] Thus, neither Ali-ahum nor Aššur-taklāku nor the writer of Tariša's tablets seems to have learned the art of writing from the same person or in the same writing style.

While there are writing styles, there are also family traditions, i.e. writing habits, that were passed down within the family. With only two generations of the family for comparison, the term 'tradition' is questionable. Nevertheless, particularities of writing that several family members share could point in the direction of such family writing habits. Two of them can be observed on the tablets of father and son. One is the writing of *um-ma* ('thus, as follows', but also found in the combination of the name Ali-ahum and the enclitic particle *-ma*). The two signs can be combined with a ligature. In this case, the last vertical wedge of UM is also the first vertical of MA. On the tablets of Ali-ahum and Aššur-taklāku, the sign combination is usually written with a ligature, while on the tablets of Tariša, both signs are clearly separated (Fig. 7.8).

Another more explicit example is the writing of the name Aššur-taklāku. It can be written with the sign TÁK or the sign combination *ta-ak*. With only very few exceptions, Ali-ahum and Aššur-taklāku use the sign

Figure 7.7: Examples of IM on Kt 93/k 143, 198, 301, 352, 543, 564, and 722. Anadolu Medeniyetleri Müzesi. Photo: Cécile Michel.

Figure 7.8: The sign combination *um-ma* on Kt 93/k 303 (Ali-ahum), Kt 93/k 489 (Aššur-taklāku), and Kt 93/k 143 (Tariša). Anadolu Medeniyetleri Müzesi. Photo: Cécile Michel.

---

9 This is not the case for LI and ZI, where Aššur-taklāku frequently used the same variant as his father.

TÁK. On the tablets of Tariša, however, TÁK is used only on two tablets, while all other instances have *ta-ak* (Beyer 2021b, 206). Whether these differences indicate an unknown scribe or that Tariša learned from a different teacher than her brother cannot yet be determined by the observations.

Šīmat-Ištar, a Lady from the Kt c/k Archive

Šīmat-Ištar may have been the daughter of Ali-ahum of the Kt c/k archive, excavated in Kaneš in 1950 (Dercksen 2015). Not much is known about her yet, only that she lived in Aššur. Seven of her letters remained in the archive. In six of them, she is the sole sender, and all are addressed to Ali-ahum. The seventh letter, Kt c/k 113, was sent by a group of people, including Šīmat-Ištar and one son of Ali-ahum, Aššur-malik, and it is addressed to another son, Aššur-bēl-šadue. This is the only letter of Šīmat-Ištar written by a different hand. Therefore, it is not included in the following discussion.

The six letters of Šīmat-Istar show very consistent handwriting. Most of the seventeen diagnostic signs[10] analysed for the handwriting comparison are written similarly on the six tablets with only slight differences or additional variations. For example, the sign AM is usually written with the vertical wedge positioned at the beginning of the two parallel horizontals and a *Winkelhaken* cluster consisting of two small wedges framed by two larger ones. On several tablets, however, we find an additional variant where the framing large *Winkelhaken* are changed to intersecting oblique wedges (Fig. 7.9).

Apart from the remarkable consistency in the handwriting on Šīmat-Ištar's tablets, the most striking features are signs with more wedges than usual. For example, the most common variant of the signs LI and ZI have a *Winkelhaken* cluster with two larger wedges at the bottom and four or more smaller *Winkelhaken* in an upper row. On the tablets of Šīmat-Ištar, on the other hand, LI and ZI are written with at least three *Winkelhaken* in the lower row and also three or more in the upper one. Furthermore, the sign NA is written in a rather unusual way. While the most common variants of this sign have a large vertical wedge followed by a combination of one or two *Winkelhaken* and a small vertical, the variant on the tablets of Šīmat-Ištar has mainly three, sometimes even four *Winkelhaken*. Lastly, the sign Ù consists of a

---

10 The diagnostic signs are AM, BA, DÍ, DU, GA, IM, IR, KI, KÙ, LI, MA, NA, ŠA, ŠUR, TIM, Ù, and ZI.

Figure 7.9: Two variations of the sign AM on Kt c/k 127. Anadolu Medeniyetleri Müzesi. Photo: Jan Gerrit Dercksen.

Winkelhaken and vertical wedge combination, followed by a box construction, usually consisting of three verticals and several horizontals. On Šīmat-Ištar's tablets, however, the 'box' is mainly constructed with four or even five vertical wedges (Fig. 7.10).

A comparison with the handwriting of other people of the Kt c/k archive proves difficult. Firstly, the handwriting on the tablets of Ali-ahum and his sons is not as consistent as on the tablets of Šīmat-Ištar. None of them could be identified yet as the writer of (some of) their tablets. Secondly, several tablets of Ali-ahum and his son Aššur-malik seem to have been written by the same person. So the situation regarding handwriting, family traits, and traditions is very unclear. Nevertheless, a general comparison is possible, especially in regard to the above-mentioned signs, which stand out because of the number of wedges.

As it turns out, on the tablets of Ali-ahum and Aššur-malik, written by the same person, the signs LI and ZI are also written with usually three *Winkelhaken* at the bottom and three to four in the upper row. Thus, the same or a similar variant of these signs was used by that writer and is therefore not a unique feature of the writer of Šīmat-Ištar's hand in this archive.

There are other distinguishing elements. One is the variant of the sign AM with the oblique wedges instead of *Winkelhaken*. This feature for the sign AM cannot be found on the tablets of the male members of the family. In general, it is not a unique trait. However, the oblique wedges are usually considered an archaizing way of writing. Its frequent use — even when mixed with variants with *Winkelhaken* — may point to a more formal or older/earlier education. The use of more wedges than usual for the signs NA and Ù is also not unique but is not found on the other tablets of the family.

Two additional features set the writing and the tablets of Šīmat-Ištar apart from the tablets of the other family members: one concerns the use of signs. In the Old Assyrian script, the use of several homophone alternatives is common, especially for sounds like /bi/, /la/,

7. THE HAND OF A WOMAN

Figure 7.10: Examples of sign variants: the sign LI on Kt c/k 272, ZI on Kt c/k 266, NA on Kt c/k 272, and Ù on KT c/k 44. Anadolu Medeniyetleri Müzesi. Photo: Jan Gerrit Dercksen.

or /šur/.[11] On the tablets of Ali-ahum's family, both BI and BE (bi_4) are used for the sound /bi/. It is thus noteworthy that on the tablets of Šīmat-Ištar, only BI was used. Furthermore, on three of the tablets (Kt c/k 43, 127, and 272), the sign LA is used in addition to LÁ which cannot be found on the tablets of the other family members.

The second outstanding feature is the shape of the tablets. Pointy or even squeezed corners are a very prevalent feature of the tablets of all male members of the family. The tablets of Šīmat-Ištar, on the other hand, have rounded corners (Fig. 7.11).

Although no family member's handwriting could be identified yet, the comparison of the hands of Šīmat-Ištar's tablets with the ones on the tablets of the male family members shows apparent differences. Particularly worth mentioning are the rounded corners of the tablets, as the consistency of this feature is remarkable in itself. Additionally, the lack of homophone alternatives may indicate that the writer of Šīmat-Ištar's tablets may not have been a member of the core family of the c/k archive and therefore did not learn the writing tradition of the family.

The Women of the Kt 94/k Archive

In 1994, a house was excavated in the Lower Town of Kaneš that contained more than 1100 tablets. Among

Figure 7.11: The typical edges of the tablets of Ali-ahum (Kt c/k 249), Aššur-bēl-šadue (Kt c/k 208), Aššur-malik (Kt c/k 801), and Šīmat-Ištar (Kt c/k 272). Anadolu Medeniyetleri Müzesi. Photo: Jan Gerrit Dercksen.

them are the small letter corpora of three women of the family (Mogens T. Larsen in KT 6a-e, 2010–2021).

Lamassī

Lamassī, a daughter and probably the eldest child of Šalim-Aššur, belonged to the fourth known generation of the family and was the sister of Ennam-Aššur, the principal owner of the house in Kaneš. It is known from the texts that she lived as a priestess in Aššur. Seven of eight letters from her show the same handwriting.[12] Three of these tablets were sent by multiple senders, including Lamassī, the other four by her alone. All the letters were addressed to her brothers, especially Ali-ahum.

The writing on her tablets testifies to skill and experience. The diagnostic signs are written in a very consistent way, and only in a few cases can one find more than one variant of a sign. In these cases, however, the difference is usually in the number of wedges, while the formation remains the same. The sign DÍ, for example, is usually written with five *Winkelhaken* in the upper row. The first is larger and protrudes past the one at the bottom. But on two tablets, there are only four *Winkelhaken* in the upper

---

11 Guido Kryszat (2015, 111–12) has worked on writing traditions and noticed that there seems to be an earlier and a later writing tradition regarding homophone alternatives. The signs LA, BI, and ŠÙR belong to the earlier tradition, while in the later, LÁ, BE, and ŠUR were preferred. Both traditions are not strictly separated and often intermingle.

12 The situation of the eighth tablet, KT 6a 170, is unclear. The most significant diagnostic signs are missing. Thus, it is not clear whether the same person wrote this tablet.

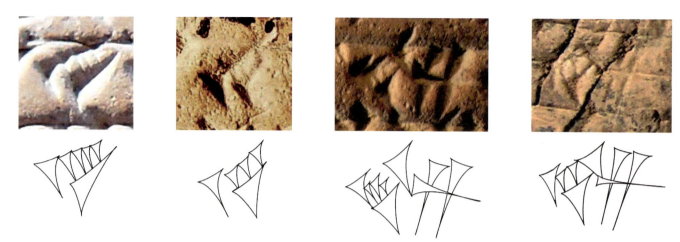

Figure 7.12: Examples of DÍ on KT 6a, 237 und KT 6b, 533, and IM on KT 6a, 235 and 245; in both cases, the number of wedges differs, but not their arrangement. Anadolu Medeniyetleri Müzesi. Photo: Mogens Trolle Larsen.

Figure 7.13: The sign AM on KT 6a, 236 shows the gap between the small *Winkelhaken* and the large one at the top. Anadolu Medeniyetleri Müzesi. Photo: Mogens Trolle Larsen.

row. The protruding first one can still be noticed. A similar case is the sign IM. Here, as with DÍ, the difference is not in the arrangement of the *Winkelhaken*, but in their number (Fig. 7.12). In both signs, IM and DÍ, the number of these wedges is remarkable. While three *Winkelhaken* in the top row are typical for this type of formation, five wedges, as seen in Lamassī's tablets, are noteworthy.

Another notable writing habit can be observed for the sign AM. The *Winkelhaken* cluster of this sign consists of three, sometimes four, small *Winkelhaken* in a row, followed and framed by two large ones. Interestingly, the small *Winkelhaken* are shifted into the space between the parallel horizontal wedges. Thus, only the last one or two small *Winkelhaken* are connected to the large one at the bottom (usually, most are overlapped by this one), and there is a gap between the last small *Winkelhaken* and the large one at the top (Fig. 7.13).

The handwriting of her closest family members, i.e. her father Šalim-Aššur and her two brothers, is difficult. The elder of the brothers, Ennam-Aššur, was certainly the writer of his tablets (Beyer in preparation). Part of the corpus of his brother, Ali-ahum, was also written by one person, but whether this is Ali-ahum has not yet been established beyond doubt.

The corpus of the father's letters can be divided into three groups. One part of the corpus was written by Ennam-Aššur (Beyer in preparation), and the other two groups were written by two unidentified persons. The writer of Group 2 could not have been Šalim-Aššur, since another tablet was written by the same hand only after his death (KT 6a, 250). Several tablets of Group 3 could have been sent from Aššur, but the writer's identification has not been possible so far.

A comparison with the hands on the tablets of her male family members shows that the hand on Lamassī's tablets is unique — as are those on the tablets of the three men. Each hand can be distinguished by different sign variants, and there is little overlap. Lamassī's letters bear the most similarities to Ali-ahum's tablets. Several signs such as DU, KÙ, LI, ŠA, and ZI are written with the same variants, and it can be noted that these variants, although generally quite common, do not or hardly appear on the tablets of the other family members.

On the other hand, there is also a feature that the writer of Lamassī's tablets shares with her other brother and the writer of her father's tablets (Group 2): the sign AM on the tablets of Lamassī and the two men's tablets is not exactly the same, but they all have in common the gap between the small and the large *Winkelhaken*. The writing of AM with this gap is not unique to the family of the Kt 94/k archive; it is also found on tablets of other families. It is remarkable, though, how consistently this sign variant was written on the tablets of the three family members (Fig. 7.14).

To sum up, the handwriting on Lamassī's tablets is very consistent. While some sign forms correspond to those of the younger brother Ali-ahum, other signs such

Figure 7.14: The sign AM with the gap on KT 6a, 236 (Lamassī), KT 6a, 136 (Šalim-Aššur), and KT 6a, 231 (Ennam-Aššur). Anadolu Medeniyetleri Müzesi. Photo: Mogens Trolle Larsen.

as DÍ, IM, KI, and NA are written in a way that is hardly found on tablets of any family member. Therefore, the writer of her tablets was probably taught in a different writing tradition. Lamassī was a priestess, but we know little about her daily life or duties. Therefore, we cannot assess whether writing was one of Lamassī's frequently performed tasks. The person who wrote the tablets was a skilled writer. Whether it was Lamassī cannot yet be said.

Šāt-Aššur

Šāt-Aššur was another daughter of Šalim-Aššur. She lived in Anatolia with her husband, an Anatolian named Šuppinuman. Five letters remained in the Kt 94/k archive, all sent by her alone. They are addressed alternately to her brothers or a business partner of her brothers.

A major problem in analysing the handwriting on Šāt-Aššur's tablets is that the texts are quite short, and there are hence not many signs to compare. In particular, many of the typical diagnostic signs are missing. Thus, it is mainly the tablets that are examined, their form and layout. The analysis of the few cuneiform characters supports the evaluation.

The two tablets KT 6b, 317, and 319, look very similar. Their shape is somewhat rough, i.e. the edges are rather irregular. The ruling is primarily straight, but the height of the lines is uneven, and the writing is not always on one level, with varying space between the signs, wedges, and the ruling. As far as a comparison is possible,[13] the signs on both tablets show similar variations. Two diagnostic signs, AM and DÍ, are written in variants that do not appear on the tablets of other family members. The other diagnostic signs, however, resemble a mix of variants written on the tablets of her three siblings Ennam-Aššur, Ali-ahum, and Lamassī. For example, the signs BA and KI are written in the same way as on the tablets of Ennam-Aššur. The variants of KÙ, LI, and NA are identical to those on the tablets of Ali-ahum and partly Lamassī.

Three other letters from Šāt-Aššur seem to have been written by three different people. KT 6c, 554 is interesting because AM is written with a gap, the same variant as on the tablets of Ennam-Aššur. The other diagnostic signs are again written in variants found on the tablets of various family members. The letter KT 6b, 318 was sent to Ennam-Aššur and specifically to Damiq-pī-Aššur, an acquaintance of the family. There are not many diagnostic signs on this tablet, but the few signs and the tablet's shape indicate that Ennam-Aššur wrote it.

The last tablet of Šāt-Aššur, KT 3b, 316, is another interesting case, as both the tablet and the writing indicate that an inexperienced writer made it. The shape of the tablet is uneven, and the edges are strongly curved so that the tablet appears almost oval. The impression of the lines and wedges is wobbly, and their depth and length are uneven. Moreover, in signs like ŠA and TA, the *Winkelhaken* are replaced by intersecting oblique wedges. The very few diagnostic signs are even more problematic than on the other four tablets. Only seven of the seventeen signs are to be found. Five of these are the same variants found on Ali-ahum's and Lamassī's tablets.

The case of Šāt-Aššur is difficult. While the corpus of letters is not much smaller than Lamassī's, at least four different writers were involved. Ennam-Aššur almost certainly wrote one tablet; the other four letters appear to have been written by individuals writing in a similar style to Šāt-Aššur's siblings. However, their shape and writing, in general, show different levels of writing ability. An identification of Šāt-Aššur as the writer of these tablets is not yet possible.

Anna-anna

Anna-anna was the Anatolian wife of Ennam-Aššur. She managed the household in Kaneš and seems to have supported her husband's business because she collected outstanding debts with Laqēpum (Larsen 2013, 13).

She is named as the sender in six letters, alone or with others. She and her husband sent KT 6b, 313, and it shows the typical handwriting of the latter. It is, therefore, not included in the following analysis. Four letters are addressed to Ennam-Aššur, and one was addressed

---

13 Four diagnostic signs are not written on these tablets, and four additional ones are only written on one tablet or the other. Thus, there are only eight of the usual diagnostic signs to compare.

to Šāt-Aššur and two men. In these five letters, Anna-anna was the sole sender.

The handwriting can be divided into three groups. None of them stands out with fancy or unusual sign forms, and they all have several sign variants in common. That they were nevertheless not written by the same person can be concluded, among other things, from the shape of the tablets and the layout. KT 6a, 239 has slightly rounded corners; the layout shows very straight rulings and much space between the signs, wedges, and lower lines. The two tablets KT 6a, 238 and KT 6b, 314, also have slightly rounded corners, but the writing and lineation are tight. The other two tablets, KT 6b, 299, and 302, have pointed and sometimes even squeezed corners and tight writing (Fig. 7.15).

Some diagnostic signs such as AM, BA, DÍ, DU, and GA are written in different variations on the five tablets. Other signs such as KI, MA, NA, ŠA, and TIM are written similarly. This observation could lead to the interpretation that the tablets were written by the same hand, while the differences may be due to the passage of time. While this is generally possible,[14] it is unlikely for Anna-anna's tablets. At least the contents of letters KT 6a, 238, and 239 suggest that they were written at more or less the same time. However, the two tablets are shaped differently and have diagnostic signs with different variants. Therefore, different writers are more likely.

Comparing the three hands on Anna-anna's tablets with the tablets of the family members, it is striking that these hands show the most similarities with Group 3 of Šalim-Aššur. This is especially true for the signs, which are written in the same way on most her tablets — with few exceptions: on Šalim-Aššur's tablets, some of these signs show more complicated variants, i.e. the number of wedges is higher. For example, the *Winkelhaken* cluster of the signs LI and ZI are written with four *Winkelhaken* at the bottom. Furthermore, the sign IM is usually formed with an arrangement of *Winkelhaken* or oblique wedges, followed by a fixed combination with a horizontal wedge crossed by two vertical ones. On the tablets of Šalim-Aššur's Group 3, however, an additional vertical wedge is added to the *Winkelhaken* cluster. For all three signs, IM, LI, and ZI, the writer of Anna-anna's tablets chose simplified variants with fewer wedges (Fig. 7.16).

In general, Anna-anna's situation is similar to that of Šāt-Aššur: her small letter corpus seems to have been

Figure 7.15: The different corner types of Anna-anna's tablets: KT 6a, 239 vs. KT 6a, 238 + KT 6b, 314 vs. KT 6b, 299 + 302. Anadolu Medeniyetleri Müzesi. Photo: Mogens Trolle Larsen.

written by several people. The different hands show the closest resemblance, if any, to the handwriting of the father-in-law. However, these signs are, at the same time, very typical sign variants. The analysis of the handwriting does not allow us to determine the identity of the scribes or Anna-anna.

The Hands of the Women's Letters of the Kt 94/k Archive

The hands on the letter corpora of the three women from the Kt 94/k archive are very interesting. They have some variations and unique elements that distinguish them from the other hands. However, there are also similarities between the hands on the tablets of the women and their male family members.

The following table summarizes the observations discussed above. It contains a selection of the diagnostic signs analysed and the variants written on the tablets of the three women. It gives an overview of the variants and variations written on the different tablets. Each row represents a tablet, and each column a sign such as AM or BA. The sign variants found on the tablets have been numbered consecutively for ease of presentation. These numbers are noted in the cells. Therefore, the same

---

14 See Koppenhaver 2007, 12.

7. THE HAND OF A WOMAN

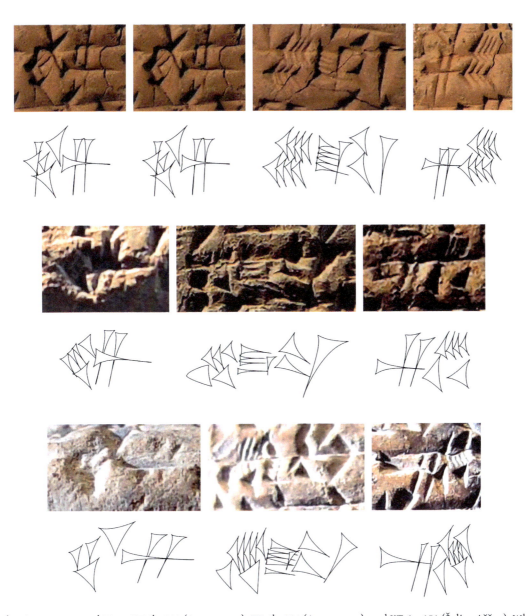

Figure 7.16: The signs IM, LI, and ZI on KT 6b, 302 (Anna-anna), KT 6b, 314 (Anna-anna), and KT 6a, 151 (Šalim-Aššur). While the signs on Anna-anna's tablets are written with very common and simple variants, the ones on Šalim-Aššur's tablets are more complex. Anadolu Medeniyetleri Müzesi. Photo: Mogens Trolle Larsen.

number in the cells of a row means that the same sign variant was used on the corresponding tablets. The colours are a tool to emphasize that the writers basically used different signs. For example, the signs marked in red are mainly used by one of the scribes of Šāt-Aššur's tablets but are hardly found on the tablets of the others.

In addition to the tablets of the three women, the three male family members presented are also included. However, no specific tablets are noted in their case, but their typical sign variants.[15]

Table 7.1 clearly shows how different the hands are on the tablets of all the family members. Among the women of the family, it is striking how consistent the writing is on the tablets of the eldest daughter and how different the hands are on the tablets of Šāt-Aššur and Anna-anna, especially when compared to the living situation of the three women. Lamassī was a priestess who lived in Aššur. Her sister Šāt-Aššur probably grew up in Aššur but later moved to Anatolia. Anna-anna was Anatolian and lived in Kaneš. Their corpora are almost the same size, but while the same person wrote

---

15 Group 1 of Šalim-Aššur is not mentioned since the texts were written by Ennam-Aššur. The same goes for Anna-anna's letter KT 6b, 313 which was also written by her husband Ennam-Aššur.

Table 7.1: Sign variants according to letter authors and tablets.

Name	Tablet	AM	BA	DÍ	DU	IM	KI	KÙ	LI	MA	NA	Ù	ZI
Lamassī	KT 6a, 235	1	2	1	1	1	3	5	2	1	3	2	2
	KT 6a, 236	1	2	1	1	1	3	5	1	1	3	2	3,1
	KT 6a, 237	-	2	1	1	1	3	5	?	1	3	3	3
	KT 6a, 244	1	2	1	1	1	3	5	1	1	3	2	1
	KT 6a, 245	1	2	1	1	2	1	5	2,1	1	-	3	1
	KT 6a, 247	1	2	2	1	1	3	5	-	1	3	3	1
	KT 6a, 533	1	2	2	1	3	3	2	1	1	3	2	1
Šāt-Aššur	KT 6b, 316	-	-	-	-	-	2	5	1	2	3	-	-
	KT 6b, 318	-	-	2	-	-	1	4	-	2	1	-	-
	KT 6b, 554	4	2	2	1	7,8	2	10	2	1	2	-	-
	KT 6b, 317	2	2	3,6	-	4	1	5	-	1	-	-	-
	KT 6b, 319	2	2	3,7	-	-	1	5	1	1	1	-	-
Anna-anna	KT 6a, 239	5	2	4,5	3	4	2	1	1	1	2	-	3
	KT 6b, 299	3	2	5,2	-	-	2	-	1	1	2	1	1
	KT 6b, 302	3,6	2	5	2	5	2	2	2	1	2	2	1
	KT 6a, 238	7	1	4	1	6	2	-	-	1,2	2	-	2
	KT 6b, 314	8	1	4	1	6	1	2	3	1	2	-	1
Šalim-Aššur (Group 2)		1	1	1	2	4	2	2	6	1,4	1	4	3
Šalim-Aššur (Group 3)		9	9	1	5	4	9	2	2	4	1	2	2
Ennam-Aššur		4	4	2	4	5,6	4,9	1	4	5	2	2	4
Ali-ahum		3	3	1	5	1	10	1	5	1	1	3	2,3

Lamassī's letters, the corpora of the other two women are written by several people. Moreover, on Lamassī's tablets, more elaborate variants are used, like those of DÍ and IM. On the other hand, the signs on the tablets of Šāt-Aššur and Anna-anna are written mainly with common variants and fewer wedges. Thus, there is some qualitative difference between the tablets of the woman in Aššur and the two in Kaneš.

Assuming women learned the art of writing as children, just like men, then Lamassī and Šāt-Aššur may have had the same educational background. Indeed, at least Šāt-Aššur's two tablets, KT 6b, 317, and 319, show several sign forms that are also found on the tablets of her sister and the tablets of her two brothers, especially Ali-ahum. This could indicate a similar writing tradition. In contrast, the few diagnostic signs on KT 6b, 316, a tablet evidently written by an untrained person, also show a high degree of similarity to the tablets of their siblings.

The case of the Anna-anna tablets is even trickier. On the one hand, several writers could be identified. On the other hand, these tablets are similar to those of Group 3 of Šalim-Aššur. Both corpora stand out from the tablets of the other family members because of 'non-family' sign variants.

The Women of Aššur and Kaneš

For the present study, the palaeographic aspects of six women's letter corpora were analysed. When looking at the individual women, none of them could be identified with certainty as the writer of their texts — or completely ruled out as such. Even the comparison with the hands of male relatives did not yield the desired result, for on the one hand, there were very often significant differences, such as the unusual tablet form of Šīmat-Ištar or the divergent spelling of names in Tariša's texts. On the other hand, there are also many similarities, especially with regard to the sign forms.

However, if one takes a step back and looks at the corpora of women together, one can discover something else. Four women lived in Aššur, while two — at least at the time they sent the letters — lived in Anatolia. From three women from Aššur, namely Tariša, Šīmat-Ištar, and Lamassī, we have corpora of seven or more letters, and the majority of these tablets were each written by the same writer. These writers were skilled and well trained. Furthermore, the texts are written with steady and consistent hands and show here and there remarkable sign variations with rather unusual numbers of wedges or formations.

On the other hand, the letter corpora of the two women living in Anatolia were each written by several people with different levels of writing skills. The sign variants used are among the common ones and are simpler variants, i.e. with fewer wedges. This means there is a clear qualitative difference between the letters from Aššur and Anatolia.

Any further interpretation is only based on speculation, as there is insufficient evidence to date. There were undoubtedly many professional scribes in Aššur. Regardless of whether they were literate or not, women (and men) would have had the possibility to turn to such a scribe, for example, if they wanted to send a letter to their family members in Anatolia. It is also possible that one had a particular scribe whom one always commissioned, whether because he lived in the neighbourhood or perhaps was connected to the family in some way, perhaps even employed. If our women living in Aššur did not write their texts themselves, this would explain the uniformity and the high quality of the letters. The two women in Anatolia did not have this luxury and perhaps turned to relatives or colleagues who happened to be there to write their letters. Therefore, their letters are characterized by various hands with different levels of skill.

This does not mean that women could not read and write. Ummī-Išhara could be an example of this. As a woman in Aššur, she could hire a scribe. However, in special cases, she might have preferred to write herself.

Acknowledgements

The research for this paper was funded by the Deutsche Forschungsgemeinschaft (DFG, German Research Foundation) under Germany's Excellence Strategy — EXC 2176 'Understanding Written Artefacts: Material, Interaction and Transmission in Manuscript Cultures', project no. 390893796. The research was conducted within the scope of the Centre for the Study of Manuscript Cultures (CSMC) at Universität Hamburg. My thanks go especially to Jan Gerrit Dercksen, Mogens Trolle Larsen, and Cécile Michel, who allowed me to study the tablets of the archives Kt c/k, Kt 94/k, and Kt 93/k and also provided me with the photos. Without them, this work would not have been possible.

Abbreviations

AKT 3   Bilgiç, Emin & Cahit Günbattı, *Ankaraner Kültepe-Texte*, III: *Texte der Grabungskampagne 1970* (Freiburger altorientalische Studien 3). Stuttgart: Steiner, 1995.

BIN 6   Stephens, Ferris J., *Old Assyrian Letters and Business Documents* (Babylonian Inscriptions in the Collection of James B. Nies 6). Yale University Press, New Haven, 1944.

CCT 4   Smith, Sidney, *Cuneiform Texts from Cappadocian Tablets in the British Museum*, IV. British Museum, London, 1925.

KT 6a-e   see Larsen, 2010–2021.

KT 8   see Veenhof 2017.

TPAK 1   Michel, Cécile & Paul Garelli (eds), *Tablettes paléo-assyriennes de Kültepe*, I: *Kt 90/k*. De Boccard, Paris, 1997.

Bibliography

Beyer, Wiebke

2019   'The Identification of Scribal Hands on the Basis of an Old Assyrian Archive' (unpublished doctoral thesis, University of Hamburg) <https://ediss.sub.uni-hamburg.de/handle/ediss/8815> [accessed 1 November 2023].

2021a   'Teaching in Old Babylonian Nippur, Learning in Old Assyrian Aššur?', in Stefanie Brinkmann, Giovanni Ciotti, Stefano Valente & Eva Maria Wilden (eds), *Education Materialised: Reconstructing Teaching and Learning Contexts through Manuscripts* (Studies in Manuscript Cultures 23). De Gruyter, Berlin: 15–32.

2021b   'The Transmission of the Scribal Art in the Old Assyrian Period – A Palaeographic Approach', in Fikri Kulakoğlu, Guido Kryszat & Cécile Michel (eds), *Cultural Exchange and Current Research at Kültepe and its Surroundings: Kültepe, 1-4 August, 2019* (Kültepe International Meetings 4, Subartu 46). Brepols, Turnhout: 197–208.

in preparation   'Traces of Handwriting in an Archive – The Case of Ennam-Aššur'.

Dercksen, Jan Gerrit

2015   'The Archive of Ali-ahum (I). The Documents Excavated in N-O-P/20 in 1950', in Fikri Kulakoğlu & Cécile Michel (eds), *Proceedings of the 1st Kültepe International Meeting, Kültepe, 19-23 September, 2013: Studies Dedicated to Kutlu Emre* (Kültepe International Meetings 1, Subartu 35). Brepols, Turnhout: 47–58.

Hirsch, Hans

1967   'Zornige Worte', *Zeitschrift für Assyriologie* 58: 104–09.

Koppenhaver, Katherine M.

2007   *Forensic Document Examination: Principles and Practice*. Humana: Totowa.

Kryszat, Guido

2015   'Old Assyrian Writing and the Secret of the Kültepe Eponym List A', in Fikri Kulakoğlu & Cécile Michel (eds), *Proceedings of the 1st Kültepe International Meeting, Kültepe, 19-23 September, 2013* (Kültepe International Meetings 1, Subartu 35). Brepols, Turnhout: 111–15.

Larsen, Mogens Trolle

1976   *The Old Assyrian City-State and its Colonies* (Mesopotamia 4). Akademisk Forlag, Copenhagen.

2001   'Affect and Emotion', in Wilfried H. van Soldt, Jan Gerrit Dercksen, N. J. C. Kouwenberg & Theo J. H. Krispijn (eds), *Veenhof Anniversary Volume: Studies Presented to Klaas R. Veenhof on the Occasion of his Sixty-Fifth Birthday* (PIHANS: Uitgaven van het Nederlands Historisch-Archaeologisch Instituut te Istanbul 89). Nederlands Instituut voot het Nabije Oosten, Leiden: 275–86.

2010 *The Archive of the Šalim-Aššur Family: The First Two Generations* (Kültepe Tabletleri 6a). Türk Tarih Kurumu Basımevi, Ankara.

2013 *The Archive of the Šalim-Aššur Family: Ennam-Aššur* (Kültepe Tabletleri 6b). Türk Tarih Kurumu Basımevi, Ankara.

2014 *The Archive of the Šalim-Aššur Family: Ali-ahum* (Kültepe Tabletleri 6c). Türk Tarih Kurumu Basımevi, Ankara.

2018 *The Archive of the Šalim-Aššur Family: Texts concerning Non-Family Members* (Kültepe Tabletleri 6d). Türk Tarih Kurumu Basımevi, Ankara.

2021 *The Archive of the Šalim-Aššur Family: Anonymous Texts and Fragments* (Kültepe Tabletleri 6e). Türk Tarih Kurumu Basımevi, Ankara.

Michel, Cécile

1998 'Les marchands et les nombres: l'example des Assyriens à Kaniš', in Jiří Prosecky (ed.), *Intellectual Life of the Ancient Near East: Papers Presented at the 43rd Rencontre Assyriologique Internationale, Prague, July 1-5, 1996*. Academy of Sciences of the Czech Republic, Prague: 249–67.

2008a 'Écrire et compter chez les marchands assyriens du début du IIe millénaire av. J.-C.', in Aksel Tibet, Erkan Konyar & Taner Tarhan (eds), *Muhibbe Darga Armağanı*. Sadberk Hanim Muzesi Yayini, Istanbul: 345–64.

2008b 'The Alāhum and Aššur-taklāku Archives Found in 1993 at Kültepe Kaniš', *Altorientalische Forschungen* 35: 53–67.

2015 'Women in the Family of Ali-ahum Son of Iddin-Suen (1993 Kültepe Archive)', in Fikri Kulakoğlu & Cécile Michel (eds), *Proceedings of the 1st Kültepe International Meeting, Kültepe, 19-23 September, 2013* (Kültepe International Meetings 1, Subartu 35). Brepols, Turnhout: 85–93.

2018 'Constitution, Contents, Filing and Use of Private Archives: The Case of Old Assyrian Archives Nineteenth Century BCE)', in Alessandro Bausi, Christian Brockmann, Michael Friedrich & Sabine Kienitz (eds), *Manuscripts and Archives: Comparative Views on Record-Keeping* (Studies in Manuscript Cultures 11). De Gruyter, Berlin: 43–70.

2020 *Women of Assur and Kanesh: Texts from the Archives of the Assyrian Merchants* (Writing from the Ancient World 42). SBL Press, Atlanta.

Veenhof, Klaas R.

2015 'Nuhšatum, the Wife of an Old Assyrian Trader. Her Status, Responsibilities and Worries (with Two New Letters)', in İrfan Albayrak, Hakan Erol & Murat Çahır (eds), *Cahit Günbattı'ya Armağan: Studies in Honour of Cahit Günbattı*. Ankara Üniversitesi Dil ve Tarih-Coğrafya Fakültesi, Ankara: 271–88.

2017 *The Archive of Elamma, Son of Iddin-Suen, and his Family (Kt. 91/k 285-568 and Kt. 92/k 94-187)* (Kültepe Tabletleri 8). Türk Tarih Kurumu Basımevi, Ankara.

8. Invoking Relations in Old Assyrian and Old Babylonian Letters

The Rhetoric of *Aḫī Atta*, *Abī Atta*, etc.

Matthias Adelhofer

Introduction

In order to facilitate the long-distance trade between Aššur and Kaneš in the Middle Bronze Age, the Assyrian merchants entered into a vast web of correspondence whose remnants allow us to consider this era of antiquity that is amongst the best documented. Typically, more than one third of an Old Assyrian merchant's archive consists of letters, constituting the largest single genre of documentation. This situation is unlike that of many other merchant, or generally speaking, private archives from other periods and places, in which letters appear as a minor, ephemeral part of the documentation. Letters in Old Babylonian archives, for instance, principally were 'intended for practically instantaneous long distance communication' and would regularly be sorted out of the archives (Charpin 2014, 27). A superficial search on *Archibab* renders *c.* 31 per cent of the available texts as letters. However, the Mari palace archives contribute significantly to this number, with about a third of the archive being letters, still outnumbered by accounting documents (see Charpin 2014, 39). Subtracting the Mari letters yields *c.* 18 per cent letters. Also in the Neo-Babylonian period 'private archives with a significant component of letters are very rare' (Jursa 2005, 49). The Old Assyrian merchants used their letters to report on the trade, on the one hand, and, more often than not, to request aid in their endeavours gone awry, on the other (for a synopsis on correspondence, see Michel 2008). Herein, correspondence not only takes on the important role of *aide-mémoire*. A regular trade caravan, one of the standard modes of sending letters, may take several weeks, perhaps more than a month, to traverse the distance of roughly one thousand kilometres between Kaneš and Aššur; there were of course also faster means for urgent messages (cf. Veenhof 1988, 249; Barjamovic 2011, 15–17; Stratford 2017, 163–74). It is also not uncommon for letters to readdress matters only several months or even years later, when they had become more pressing (e.g. KT 8, 169; KT 6a, 115). Correspondence also gains an important legal value as evidence, albeit secondary to contracts and debt notes (Hertel 2013, 143–51). Previous letters are often cited in complaints when actions resolving a given problem with the trade have been delayed, or they are used to legitimize a certain course of action as according to the letter instructions (*ammala tîrtim*). This is only the briefest of historical contexts for the fashioning of letters in the Old Assyrian world.

One particular aspect of the rhetoric for conveying instructions in specific situations shall be the topic of the present paper and how it relates as an overarching cultural artefact also to Old Babylonian letters. The most frequent rhetorical figure, used in more than one third of Old Assyrian letters (for such statistical statements about

Matthias Adelhofer (matthias.adelhofer@univie.ac.at) PhD student, University of Vienna, Austria

Old Assyrian letters, see Adelhofer in preparation),[16] refers in a set of stock phrases to the relations among the merchants, mostly but by no means exclusively based on kinship terms, and suggests urgency for the matter at hand. We suggest calling this figure 'invocation of relation'. The present paper expounds on this specific figure and compares it with its cognate in Old Babylonian epistolary practices, in order to derive inferences on the differing social values underlying its utilization. The Old Babylonian evidence, being only in small part truly contemporary to the Old Assyrian one,[17] still gives plentiful grounds for comparison, not least since the two dialect groups and their scribal traditions share a common cultural horizon in Sumer and Akkad.

Old Assyrian Rhetoric and Invoking Relations

We take rhetoric in the letters as elaboration for persuasion,[18] deriving the 'peculiarly constraint-free force of the better argument', as J. G. Habermas (1984, 28) puts it, from the social context and gaining validity from the social acceptability and expectation. Certain situations may be deemed to require more elaboration than framing a request as a plain imperative, which is the basic phrasing in the case of the letters and is what we take as basis for comparison. Any embellishment or ornament, to use a cover term suggested by R. Barthes (1985),[19] truly works only in its particular social setting that determines it. Furthermore, for making our interpretations as overt as possible, we take certain liberties in translation to convey the sense transposed into English as we see it. While we would neither want to go so far as to rewrite the letters in the guise of a modern English one, nor give a 'literal' translation which easily runs the risk of merely reflecting interpretations and the reduction of the Akkadian lexicon to ostensible base meanings of words, we shall attempt a precarious tightrope walk. The original text in its transcription (an interpretation already in and of itself) must serve as corrective and comparative device for the reader, together with the brief contextual descriptions.

The aforementioned most frequent rhetorical figure, the invocation of relation, is most commonly expressed through the stock phrase *aḫī atta* 'You are my brother', *abī atta* 'You are my father', etc., featuring in more than a third of all letters. This quantitative margin, in our opinion, adds to its historical value as piece of rhetoric, not so much for its stylistic sophistication but for its overt social acceptability. Trustworthy relations are pivotal to the Assyrians' trade ventures and by explicitly referencing this fact their letters gain persuasive power. Family being the foremost unit of social interaction, such relational rhetoric is most often framed around it. This abstracted conception is neatly put by a group of trade partners when the head of their firm, Šalim-Aššur, passes away and his eldest son must take over the role, first of all in settling the financial aftermath of the death.

> KT 6, 209: 3–9: *lā libbi ilimma abūni mēt. lā Šalim-Aššur abūni. atta abūni.*
>
> (Unfortunately, our father has died. Not Šalim-Aššur is our father, but you are our father.)

Only the particular shape of the Old Assyrian stock phrase is new, while the underlying notion is, of course, much older and is well established also in Sargonic times.

> FAOS 19, Ki 1: *enma Abbāya ana Duduʾa mīnum ulā abī atta? mā ana 10 gur šeʾam ulā taqippanni? bītum ʿeri? šumma kaspam yeʾrišūka [a]na 20 gur [šal]ša šiqil lusābil[a]kkum. šumma a[na] qaqqadim qaqqadam lusā[b]i<la>kkum. [a]tta šūṣiʾam u merʾaka šup[r]amma [...] lišmeʾ!*
>
> (Abbāya says the following to Duduʾa: Why are you not my father? Alas, you do not trust me with 10 gur of barley? Is the house empty? If they ask silver of you, I would send you a third shekel for 20 gur. If it is for the total, I shall send you the total. Now you send me word! And send your son here so he may hear [...])

Only a handful of terms, taken mostly from the family setting, are used for describing relations of varying social hierarchical constellations. In the letters, the Assyrians use them especially if urgency is of essence.

---

16 The statistics are based on a corpus of *circa* one thousand letters from various merchant archives in Kaneš.

17 For the time frame of most of the Old Assyrian evidence from Kaneš, see Barjamovic et al. 2012, 55–73. Much of the Old Babylonian material starts a few generations after the main period of the *kārum* Kaneš. The Old Assyrian evidence from the Lower Town level Ib is not considered here, since it remains largely unpublished and since the texts pale in their numbers of fewer than one thousand compared to those of level II of more than twenty thousand.

18 This approach, of course, in its first instance goes back to Aristotle in Rhet. I.2., 1355b26.

19 In order to be able to better abstract a concept of rhetoric, R. Barthes (1985, 156–58) declares against what he calls the 'rage taxonomique' of rhetorical forms: 'Ce que nous appelons d'un terme générique les figures de rhétorique, mais qu'en toute rigueur historique, et pour éviter l'ambiguïté entre *Tropes et Figures*, il vaudrait mieux appeler les "ornements", a été pendant des siècles et est aujourd'hui encore l'objet d'une véritable rage de classement, indifférente aux railleries qui ont cependant très tôt surgi.'

Abum takes on the meaning of someone of higher social rank. *Aḫum* means someone of the same rank and is also used by those of higher standing towards those of a lower one. Almost always only in combination with one of these two terms, *bēlum* 'lord' is used to indicate a degree of subservience towards the addressee and reliance on their good graces. In the same way, when addressing women *ummum* 'mother' and *aḫātum* 'sister' are used, together with the rare *bēltum* 'lady, mistress'. Evidence coming from and pertaining to women is underrepresented in relation to men due to the male-dominated trade. In her thorough investigation of Old Assyrian women Cécile Michel estimates that 'letters addressed or received by women represent approximately 20 percent of the letters excavated at Kültepe available in transliterations up to now' (Michel 2020, 27). The use of this rhetorical figure by and towards women, nevertheless, largely conforms *mutatis mutandis* to that among men. Apart from these terms, others are used only very occasionally. *Merʾum* 'son' is either demeaning and used only to slight someone, or in cases of very close quasi-paternal relationship as a form of endearment. For very personal matters or very strong emphasis of one's dependence on the addressee, versions like *ebrī atta* 'You are my friend', or the unique *šamšī atta* 'You are my sun' (OAA 1, 127:17) may be used, but always in combination with one of the main address forms.

Formally, the rhetorical device is used in rather limited constructions. The most common one is the simple nominal sentence reaffirming the relation between the correspondents. It always precedes the statements or parts of the letter that it modifies. In the following example, the letter author feels kept uninformed about his assets and now reaches out to some of his other trade partners for information. He introduces his request with an invocation of relation.

> OAA 1, 78: 30–36: *ṭuppam našpartam ulā ublūnim. umma Iddin-Aššurma lapātam lā imūʾū. abbaʾūa : attunu. werīʾī mala tadnu šīm maškī u pirikannī : mala itbulūni šitti kaspim : mala išittanni tîrtakunu ana Durḫumit lillikam.*[20]

(They did not bring me a letter tablet. Iddin-Aššur said: 'They do not want to write one.' You are my fathers. Send me the report about my copper, how much was sold, about the price of the hides and the *pirikannum*-textiles, how much they fetched, and about the remainder of the silver, how much is left for me, to Durḫumit!)

Here the letter author complains heavily about the lack of correspondence from his associates and is reiterating his request for a favour for a trade partner. He prefaces this request with a humble invocation of relation.

> CCT 3, 11: 3–22: *anāku annakam ana tîrtikunu naḫdāku. aššumi Lipit-Ištar mera Dagan-malkim adi mala u šinīšu ašpurakkunūtima tîrtaknu lā illikam. annakam sikkī iṣṣanabbutū u kutuātiya iktanattuʾū. aḫḫūa bēlūa attunu. kaspum u ṣibātušu ištēat awīlam [gimlā]ma kaspam m[ala tal]eʾʾāni šašqilāma ana mera ummiānim kēnim piqdāma aššumišu eqlam lētiqam.*

(I always pay attention to your instructions here. Concerning Lipit-Ištar, Dagan-malkum's son, I wrote to you several times, but no notice of yours ever came to me. Here, they keep holding onto my hem (i.e. pestering me) and holding my possessions under lock. You are my brothers, my lords. Concerning the silver and its first rates of interest, do the gentleman a [favour][21] and have as much silver paid as you can, then entrust it to a trustworthy affiliated trader, so it is transported overland under his name.)

For expressing even greater urgency, there are two other stock phrases that also invoke relations. One is a *šumma*-phrase of the same pattern as above, e.g. *šumma aḫī atta* 'if you are my brother', *šumma abī atta* 'if you are my father'. Typically, it occurs in the same conversational context which may be introduced by *aḫī atta*. It is even used seemingly asyndetically to preface a statement which the *šumma*-clause cannot connect to semantically (e.g. KT 6b, 364). This is a difference to the identical Old Babylonian phrase, which stands as an entirely independent stock phrase for particular contexts. In the following example, the double negation with the vetitive *ē lā* in combination with the adverb *assurre*[22] and the emotion reference *libbī ē imraṣ*[23] in the (common rhetor-

---

20 The standard formula for referring to the sending of letters is *tîrtum/našpertum alākum*. It appears as an indirect request only strictly in a grammatical sense, but not pragmatically. The logical subject, however, remains the agent and is, as a matter of course, taken up also grammatically in all following or preceding requests. A simple example is the frequent collocation with *uznam patāʾum* 'to inform', e.g. in CCT 3, 33a:10–12: *tîrtaka appāniya lillikamma uznī pite* 'Send me a report and keep me informed!' Thus, we opt to translate it with the standard phraseology in English as 'sending'.

21 Since this is a common rhetorical device which is taken up again later in the same letter, M. Ichisar's (1981, 371) emendation fits very well.

22 For the vetitive with the negation *lā* as 'strong exhortation', see Kouwenberg 2017, 639, and for *assurre* always in collocation with the vetitive, see Kouwenberg 2017, 407.

23 Forms of *libbum marāṣum* are the most frequent and most basic references to negative emotion, possibly translated through a range

ical figure of the) repetition of the request show clear emphasis.

> KT 8, 254:5–16: *lullam kunukkīya u arzallam ša ēzibakkunni šumma aḫī atta lullam kunukkīya u arzallam ana Dadaya din! assurre lullam u arzallam ana Dadaya e lā taddinma libbī e imraṣ!*
>
> > (Concerning the antimony under my seal and the *arzallum* that I left with you: if you are my brother, give the antimony under my seal and the *arzallum* to Dadaya! Do by no means fail to give the antimony and *arzallum* to Dadaya so I shall not need to get upset!)

The other one is used in situations of high emotions, demonstrated through an overall higher number of rhetorical ornaments as well as oftentimes explicit references to emotion terms (cf. Larsen 2001, with important caveats about interpreting such references, e.g. in Jaques 2017). It shows a higher degree of variation in its wording, but a typical example would be *allānukka aḫam šaniam ulā īšu* 'Besides you I do not have another brother' (KT 8, 165:11–13). All three of these stock phrases are used in the same way within a letter, serving to anticipate an urgent request or unpleasant news, but vary in their degree of urgency and emotionality, with *aḫī atta* being the base stock phrase, as well as the basic rhetorical ornament in letters altogether.

Old Babylonian Invocations of Relation

The same framing of relations was, of course, also important outside the distinct group of Old Assyrian merchants. The concept is pervasive in Babylonia of around the same time as well, although with some marked differences in the epistolography of private letters (Kraus 1973, 59; Klengel 1993, 155–57). In his seminal investigation of Old Babylonian epistolary practices, W. Sallaberger (1999, 55–73) observes a very similar distribution of relational terms as in the Old Assyrian corpus. Especially important are family terms, *abum* and *ummum*, *aḫum* and *aḫātum*, as well as *bēlum* and *bēltum*. New among the common terms are the relatively late entries into the repertoire of address forms *šāpirum* 'master' and *awīlum* 'gentleman', the latter of which does not take the first person possessive suffix, unlike all others. Both become more regular only in Late Old Babylonian letters (Sallaberger 1999, 59, 64).

---

between uneasiness, unhappiness, sorrow, or distress; cf. Larsen 2001, 278 n. 12.

The invocation of relation does, however, differ in its formal use from the Assyrian practice. Already in the address, where the Assyrians exclusively use personal names, simple relational terms can be used, or a personal name with the rare addition of such an attribute (Sallaberger 1999, 33–36).

Introduced later, around the formation of the dynasty of Ḫammurabi, the formal element of greetings (Sallaberger 1999, 25), which does not exist in Old Assyrian letters, can also invoke relations. Especially where this is already the case in the address, greetings would reiterate the same relation (Sallaberger 1999, 40).

Apart from the address in the letter heading, there are two main instances of invoking relations in the letter body. First, there is the *šumma* stock phrase, *šumma abī atta*, etc., only in Early Old Babylonian use (courtesy of the blind referee). The earliest examples of the invocation of relation within the letter body that all take this form are roughly contemporary with the Old Assyrian evidence and come from Ešnunna. They feature *abum* (Whiting 1987, nos 34, 35, 37, 40, 55), *aḫum* (Whiting 1987, nos 10, 11, 15, 36, 53), and *bēlum* (Whiting 1987, nos 34, 41).

Second, as the practice of addressing one's correspondents in the second person, as opposed to the third person as in Sumerian practice, becomes the norm around the same time (Sallaberger 1999, 53–55), the simple combination of personal pronoun with relational term, in the way of *aḫī atta*, etc., apparently becomes widespread only later. The earliest clear example (AbB 3, 7) may only be dated to Samsu-iluna's reign (according to Sallaberger 1999, 55). At this point, a striking syntactical difference to the Old Assyrian phrase points to a different understanding of the seemingly identical wording. Where Assyrian *abī atta* is an independent nominal phrase, Babylonian *abī atta* (and corresponding grammatical derivations) becomes part of a longer clause in an appositional construction as reference to the addressee and typically corresponding to the grammatical subject of the sentence; for example, in the final statement of the indignant letter of a daughter to her father.

> AbB 3, 7:23–27: *šumma wardam abī atta lā ḫašḫāti idīšu ša ebūrim idnamma šanûmma līguršu.*
>
> > (If you, my father, do not need the slave, send me his wage for the harvest, so another may hire him!)

Neatly showing the different uses of the invocation of relation, the following Late Old Babylonian letter is an example of its maximum use, in address, greeting, and letter body (in the petition).

> AbB 7, 132: *ana abīya qibīma umma* Warad-Kūbī*ma*. Šamaš u Marduk *abī kâta dāriš ūmī liballiṭū. abī atta lū šalmāta lū baltāta. ilum nāṣirka rēška ana damiqtim likīl. ana šulum abīya kâta ašpuram. šulum abīya kâta maḫar* Šamaš u Marduk *lū dari. ana alpī ṭarādim kīam taqbiam umma attama ṭēmka šupramma alpī lilqūnikkum. annîtam taqbiam. inanna* Warad-Marduk *mār* Šēlebu *zeʾpī uštābilakku. alpū ša ālim illakū. abī atta alpī ṭu<r>damma eqlum lā innaddi. ina annîtim abbūtka lūmur.*

> (Speak to my father, thus says Warad-Kūbī: Šamaš and Marduk shall grant you, my father, life for all days. You, my father, may you be well, may you be healthy. May your protective god be favourably disposed to you. I am writing for my father's health, for yours. May my father's health, yours, be eternal before Šamaš and Marduk. About sending oxen, you said the following: 'Send me your request, then they shall fetch oxen for you.' This you said. Now, I have Warad-Marduk, Šēlebu's son, bring you my notice. The oxen of the town will leave. You, my father, send the oxen, so that the field shall not lie fallow. Through this, I shall witness your fatherly manner.)

While the address as *abum* is consistently employed throughout the greeting section and is dependent on the letter address, *umma* PNa-*ma ana* PNb *qibīma*, that frames the entire piece of correspondence, within the letter body the invocation of relation features — rhetorically quite similarly to the Old Assyrian practice — as part of the direct request. Thus, the invocation of relation can still have an immediate functional aspect for the purpose of argument, as is the case for Old Assyrian letters. However, its usage is for the most part more broadly dictated by the social standing and proximity of the correspondents to one another and the need to express it under the correct and proper circumstances. There are different levels of address in Old Babylonian epistolography that can convey notions of politeness. By the Late Old Babylonian period a tripartite system of address was developed: the basic form is a simple direct address in the second person, then there is the politer variant with the invocation of relation in the second person for a closer relationship, and, lastly, a respectful form of indirect address in the third person that uses relational terms by necessity (Sallaberger 1999, 52–55). Diachronically, the simple address in the second person became the norm after the Ur III period, as is the case with Old Assyrian letters. Old Babylonian letters are again composed in the third person around the reign of Ḫammurabi. The apposition of second person pronoun and relational noun is the youngest form of address in Old Babylonian letters.

Rhetoric and Politeness in Old Assyrian and Old Babylonian Letters

It is noteworthy that '(i)n den Alltagsbriefen des Corpus ist *aḫī* die seltenste der üblichen Anredeformen' (Sallaberger 1999, 62). In contrast, it is the most common one in Old Assyrian letters, appearing more than twice as often as the next most common one in *abum*. This difference must also be owed to the particular corpus of Old Assyrian documentation that we possess today comprising the textual remains of a distinct group of people — albeit perhaps the most significant part of Old Assyrian society — i.e. merchants operating in close-knitted partnership networks. This goes so far that even the Assyrian king can act as a private merchant (as 'une sorte de marchand magnifié, *primus inter pares*', Garelli 1963, 199), who is not so aloof as to not also author letters that use the invocation of relation as rhetorical device in case of troubles with the trade (Adelhofer 2020, 14–16).

Still, this fact corresponds very well with the observation that the main purpose of the invocation of relation in Old Babylonian letters is to establish contact properly and reconfirm the relationship between the correspondents, as it is often used in address and greeting (Sallaberger 1999, 31). In contrast, Old Assyrian letters only use it for specific persuasive purposes, reminding, as it were, their correspondents of their relationship or further nuancing it according to the situation. Thus, also peers, i.e. with reference to *aḫum*, may employ the invocation of relationship regularly, whereas in Old Babylonian letters an address with *aḫum* is often unnecessary. It follows, that such rhetorical embellishment would rather be needed when talking to people of higher standing.

The address containing *bēlum*, with the letter subsequently kept in the third person, appears already in the earliest Old Babylonian letters; a practice already found in Sargonic letters (Sallaberger 1999, 56; with FAOS 19, Ad 3, 4, Eš 6 as Sargonic examples). For Old Assyrian letters, where there would never be added such markers in the address itself, *bēlum* is only a nuancing addendum to *abum* or *aḫum*.

Here, the notion of politeness needs to re-enter the discussion. The choice of additions in the Old Babylonian letter address characterizes the letter as a whole and dictates the form of greeting and also uses of invocations of relation in the letter body (Sallaberger 1999, 41). Thereby it is a form of positive politeness, according to the terminology of Brown & Levinson (1987, 61–74). The Assyrians, on the other hand, are terse and to the point, any rhetorical embellishment serves only an immediate purpose and no additional effort is made to establish and frame the contacting via letter as a whole. Directness, perhaps also by the motto of 'time is money' of *kaspum lā ibarre?* 'silver must not grow hungry' (e.g. in OAA 1, 17:27–30), is most valued.

Conclusions

While the stock phrase *šumma aḫī atta* and its variants are part of the shared rhetorical inventory in Old Assyrian and Old Babylonian letters of the same time, harking back to the Sargonic period, the simple form *aḫī atta* appears to be an Old Assyrian innovation. It represents well the direct approach to matters favoured by the Assyrians, where an indirect address of one's correspondent is unthinkable. The Old Babylonian development moves in exactly that direction of more indirectness: letters use the invocation of relation as apposition to the personal pronoun or are written in the third person altogether (again).

What Old Assyrian and Old Babylonian private correspondence share is that correspondents may only be addressed in terms of equal or higher rank, while it is improper for a person of higher rank to rhetorically mark their correspondent as lower. Incidentally, only in the letter address, do the Assyrians clarify hierarchical constellations, mentioning the very highest ranking person in first position, regardless of whether this person may be among the authors or addressees (Lewy 1926, 61 n. *; Hirsch 1981).

Extrapolating further from the case of the invocation of relation, social interaction through the letters has a clear structure to be followed and for the Assyrian merchants entails that little redressive, polite action (bald on record after Brown & Levinson 1987, 60) is desired. Rather, any rhetorical embellishment serves to emphasize the urgency of any given request, by drawing on their own socially contingent norms. Old Babylonian conventions crystallize in time to the effect of using more active forms of (especially positive) politeness.

Abbreviations

AbB 3 — Frankena, Rintje, *Briefe aus der Leidener Sammlung* (Altbabylonische Briefe 3). Brill, Leiden, 1968.

AbB 7 — Kraus, Fritz R., *Briefe aus dem British Museum* (Altbabylonische Briefe 7). Brill, Leiden, 1977.

Archibab — *Archives babyloniennes (XXe-XVIIe siècles av. J.C.)*. Online catalogue and search engine of Old Babylonian archival texts: <https://www.archibab.fr> [accessed 24 January 2023].

KT 6a — Larsen, Mogens Trolle, *Kültepe Tabletleri VI-a: The Archive of the Šalim-Aššur Family*, I: *The First Two Generations* (Kültepe Tabletleri 6a). Türk Tarih Kurumu Basımevi, Ankara, 2010.

KT 6b — Larsen, Mogens Trolle, *Kültepe Tabletleri VI-b: The Archive of the Šalim-Aššur Family*, II: *Ennam-Aššur* (Kültepe Tabletleri 6b). Türk Tarih Kurumu Basımevi, Ankara, 2013.

KT 8 — Veenhof, Klaas Roelof, *Kültepe Tabletleri VIII: The Archive of Elamma, Son of Iddin-Suen, and his Family (Kt. 91/k 285-568 and Kt. 92/k 94-187)* (Kültepe Tabletleri 8). Türk Tarih Kurumu Basımevi, Ankara, 2017.

CCT 3 — Smith, Sidney, *Cuneiform Texts from Cappadocian Tablets in the British Museum*, III. Trustees of the British Museum, London, 1925.

FAOS 19 — Kienast, Burkhart & Konrad Volk, *Die sumerischen und akkadischen Briefe* (Freiburger altorientalische Studien 19). Steiner, Stuttgart, 1995.

OAA 1 — Larsen, Mogens Trolle, *The Aššur-nādā Archive* (Old Assyrian Archives 1). Nederlands Instituut voor het Nabije Oosten, Leiden, 2002.

Bibliography

Adelhofer, Matthias

2020 'On the Old Assyrian Letter Heading: Playing with Social Hierarchy for Rhetorical Effect', *Chatreššar* 2020/2: 5–18.

in preparation 'Old Assyrian Epistolography: Materiality, Form, Rhetoric, Mentalities, and Norms' (unpublished doctoral thesis, University of Vienna).

Barjamovic, Gojko

2011 *A Historical Geography of Anatolia in the Old Assyrian Colony Period* (Carsten Niebuhr Institut Publications 38). Museum Tusculanum Press, Copenhagen.

Barjamovic, Gojko; Hertel, Thomas Klitgaard & Larsen, Mogens Trolle

2012 *Ups and Downs at Kanesh: Chronology, History and Society in the Old Assyrian Period*. Nederlands Instituut voor het Nabije Oosten, Leiden.

Barthes, Roland

1985 'L'ancienne rhétorique', in Roland Barthes, *L'aventure sémiologique*. Éditions du Seuil, Paris: 85–164.

Brown, Penelope & Levinson, Stephen C.

1987 *Politeness: Some Universals in Language Usage* (Studies in Interactional Sociolinguistics 4). Reissued edn. Cambridge University Press, Cambridge.

Charpin, Dominique

2014 'The Historian and the Old Babylonian Archives', in Heather D. Baker & Michael Jursa (eds), *Documentary Sources in Ancient Near Eastern and Greco-Roman Economic History: Methodology and Practice*. Oxbow, Oxford: 24–58.

Garelli, Paul

1963 *Les assyriens en Cappadoce*. Maisonneuve, Paris.

Habermas, Jürgen

1984 *The Theory of Communicative Action*, I: *Reason and the Rationalization of Society*, trans. Thomas McCarthy. Beacon, Boston.

Hertel, Thomas Klitgaard

2013 *Old Assyrian Legal Practices: Law and Dispute in the Ancient Near East* (Old Assyrian Archives Studies 6). Nederlands Instituut voor het Nabije Oosten, Leiden.

Hirsch, Hans

1981 'Über den Briefbeginn in der Korrespondenz der altassyrischen Kaufleute', in Roswitha G. Stiegner (ed.), *Al-Hudhud: Festschrift; Maria Höfner zum 80. Geburtstag*. Karl-Franzens-Universität Graz, Graz: 79–93.

Ichisar, Metin

1981 *Les archives cappadociennes du marchand Imdilum* (Recherche sur les grandes civilisations 3). Éditions A.D.P.F., Paris.

Jaques, Margaret

2017 'The Discourse on Emotion in Ancient Mesopotamia. A Theoretical Approach', in S. Kipfer (ed.), *Visualizing Emotions in the Ancient Near East* (Orbis biblicus et orientalis 285). Vandenhoeck & Ruprecht, Fribourg: 185–205.

Jursa, Michael

2005 *Neo-Babylonian Legal and Administrative Documents: Typology, Contents and Archives* (Guides to the Mesopotamian Textual Records 1). Ugarit, Münster.

Klengel, Horst

1993 'Verhaltens- und Denkweisen im Alltag Mesopotamiens nach altbabylonischen Briefen', in Julia Zabłocka & Stefan Zawadzki (eds), *Šulmu*, IV: *Everyday Life in Ancient Near East: Papers Presented at the International Conference Poznań, 19-22 September, 1989*. Wydawnictwo Naukowe UAM, Poznań: 151–59.

Kouwenberg, Norbertus J. C.

2017 *A Grammar of Old Assyrian* (Handbuch der Orientalistik 118). Brill, Leiden.

Kraus, Fritz R.

1973 *Vom mesopotamischen Menschen der altbabylonischen Zeit und seiner Welt*. North-Holland Publishing Company, Amsterdam.

Larsen, Mogens T.

2001 'Affect and Emotion', in Wilfred H. van Soldt (ed.), *Veenhof Anniversary Volume: Studies Presented to Klaas R. Veenhof on the Occasion of his Sixty-Fifth Birthday*. Nederlands Instituut voor het Nabije Oosten, Leiden: 278–86.

Lewy, Julius

1926 *Die altassyrischen Texte vom Kültepe bei Kaisarīje* (Keilschrifttexte in den Antiken-Museen zu Stambul 1). Antike Museen zu Stambul, Istanbul.

Michel, Cécile

2008 'La correspondance des marchands assyriens du XIXe s. av. J.-C. De l'archivage des lettres commerciales et privées', in Laure Pantalacci (ed.), *La lettre d'archive: communication administrative et personnelle dans l'antiquité proche-orientale et égyptienne; actes du colloque de l'Université de Lyon 2, 9-10 juillet 2004* (Topoi Supplément 9). Institut français d'archéologie orientale, Cairo: 117–40.

2020 *Women of Assur and Kanesh: Texts from the Archives of Assyrian Merchants* (Writings from the Ancient World 42). SBL Press, Atlanta.

Sallaberger, Walther

1999 *'Wenn Du mein Bruder bist, …': Interaktion und Textgestaltung in altbabylonischen Alltagsbriefen* (Cuneiform Monographs 16). Styx, Groningen.

Stratford, Edward

2017 *A Year of Vengeance*, I: *Time, Narrative, and the Old Assyrian Trade* (Studies in Ancient Near Eastern Records 17/1). De Gruyter, Berlin.

Veenhof, Klaas R.

1988 'Prices and Trade. The Old Assyrian Evidence', *Altorientalische Forschungen* 15/2: 243–63.

Whiting, Robert M.

1987 *Old Babylonian Letters from Tell Asmar* (Assyriological Studies 22). Oriental Institute, Chicago.

9. The Seals of the Šalim-Aššur Family (94/k)

Agnete W. Lassen

Introduction

The house of the family of the Assyrian merchant Šalim-Aššur, son of Issu-arik, was excavated in 1994 in the Lower Town of Kültepe. The building consisted of a two-storey courtyard house with nine rooms, covering an area of 115 m². In the rooms numbered 5 and 6, archaeologists found an archive of more than 1200 cuneiform tablets (Fig. 9.1). These records had been kept on wooden shelves, most originally packed in bags, but some tablets were discovered in pots placed along the walls. In addition to the cuneiform tablets were found twenty-six *bullæ*, nineteen of them carrying seal impressions. The archive, spanning six generations, has been edited by Mogens Trolle Larsen in five separate volumes, published in the *Kültepe Tabletleri* series (Larsen 2010; 2013; 2014; 2018; 2021).

A few early texts date from the time of Issu-arik, but most of the archive dates to the years REL 86–110.[1] The texts reflect activities of three generations: Issu-arik, Šalim-Aššur, and his sons, Ennam-Aššur and Ali-ahum and their families (Fig. 9.2). Issu-arik and Šalim-Aššur (and possibly Ali-ahum) owned multiple properties and it is clear that collection of texts discovered in the 94-house does not represent complete archives of any one of the inhabitants of the house (Larsen 2008; Veenhof 2013).

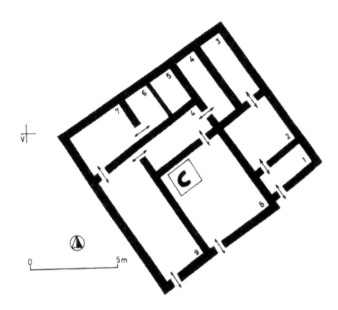

Figure 9.1: The Šalim-Aššur family house, excavated in 1994 (plan from Larsen 2010, 3). Reproduced with permission from author.

It is unclear if the house was ever Issu-arik's primary residence. Šalim-Aššur certainly lived there for a while. At some point during his life, Šalim-Aššur moved to Durhumit. During that time, the Kaneš house was inhabited by his oldest son, Ennam-Aššur, and his wife, Anna-anna. After Ennam-Aššur's death, the house seems to have been inhabited by Ali-ahum, his younger brother.

The focus of this paper are the seals belonging to the members of the Šalim-Aššur family. Of these, only three are already available in the literature, those of Issu-arik, Iddin-abum, Ennam-Aššur. The rest will be presented and discussed here for the first time.

---

1 For an overview of the chronology of the dated texts, see Barjamovic et al. 2012.

Agnete W. Lassen (agnete.lassen@yale.edu) Associate Curator of the Babylonian Collection at the Yale Peabody Museum; Lecturer, Department of Near Eastern Languages and Civilizations, Yale University

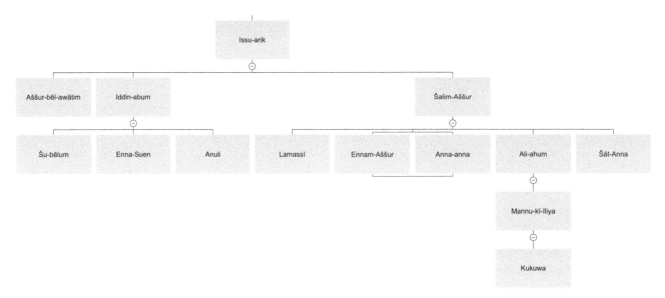

Figure 9.2: The Šalim-Aššur family tree. Individuals with identified seals are marked in bold. By author.

No actual seal stones were found in the Šalim-Aššur family house. Instead, the glyptic evidence discussed here is attested through impressions on the envelopes and *bullae* found in Rooms 5 and 6. The corpus consists of 337 separate impressions made by 196 different cylinder seals and two ring seals. These impressions were found on letter envelopes, *bullae*, and debt notes, as well as documents drawn up in connection with legal procedures, such as witness statements, verdicts, and administrative orders. Most of the seals in the archive are attested only once and most cannot be identified with certainty. Almost three-quarters of the seals in this archive are not attested among previously published material.

The two most active sealers in the archive were Šalim-Aššur and his oldest son, Ennam-Aššur. Šalim-Aššur's seal occurs exclusively on opened letter envelopes. These letters were addressed to his two sons Ennam-Aššur and Ali-ahum, either alone or along with other people. The letters were likely sent while Šalim-Aššur was in Durhumit. Šalim-Aššur's seal is so far not attested outside of this archive.

The seal of Ennam-Aššur also appears on letter envelopes. Most are just small fragments with no writing. The few better-preserved envelopes were addressed to his wife or his representatives or business partners. For whichever reason, these letters were opened in Ennam-Aššur's house, not in the houses of the partners. Ennam-Aššur's seal also appears on two of the *bullae* discovered in the house, including one (KT 6, 520) originally placed on a container that held 'my encased tablets, copies and memoranda' (Özgüç & Tunca 2001, 347; Larsen 2008). It is likely that the arrangement of the archive as it was discovered reflects mostly the practices of Ennam-Aššur. Unlike his father's, his seal is attested outside of the archive, including among the a/k and n/k texts (Özgüç & Özgüç 1953, no. 691; Özgüç 2006, CS 222).

Also the seal of Iddin-abum, Salim-Aššur's older brother, is very well represented in the 94-archive, albeit not on letters. Instead, his impressions are on debt notes in which he appears as the debtor, as well as a contract concerning 2 minas of gold for investment in his joint-stock capital. The loan documents were likely filed together as is indicated by the *bulla* KT 6, 16: 'Tablets concerning our Iddin-abum's debt' and may have been stored in the house in connection with the settling of debts after Iddin-abum's death. Iddin-abum's seal also occurs in several different archives and was recarved at least once during its use life. This will be discussed further below.

The Seals of the Family

The earliest identifiable seal belonged to Issu-arik, the father of Šalim-Aššur. Like the other seals discussed here, the actual seal stone has not been recovered, and it is attested only through its impressions in clay. Only a few texts in the archive mention Issu-arik, but his seal is attested on CTMMA 1, 85 and 86 and on ICK 3, 10. It shows an introduction scene in which a worshipper wearing a cap and a long, hemmed dress is led by an interceding goddess towards a bearded figure in a brimmed cap, seated on a stool (Fig. 9.3). Behind the worshipper is a six-locked hero. Water streams surround his body. The water may be emanating from a vase held in his hands, following an Akkadian and Ur III tradition, or it may be flowing from his shoulders and body, as is sometimes seen on other Old Assyrian seals. Behind the hero are two additional figures wearing caps and hemmed dresses. Filling motifs include ball-and-staff and a vessel.

The seal belongs to the Old Assyrian style, but lacks some of the typical attributes, like the distinctive fork-like hands. The arrangement of the figures in the scene is also uncharacteristically irregular with some figures taller than others. Similar features can be seen in early Old Assyrian style seals, e.g. the seals of Imdī-ilum and Puzur-šadu'e s. Šu-Ištar,[2] and this seal is likely part of that early group.

Figure 9.3: Drawing of the seal of Issu-arik. Drawing by author on the basis of CTMMA 1, pl. 129, seal 34. No CS number; Teissier no. 227.

Issu-arik had at least three sons. The oldest, Aššur-bēl-awātim, held the title of *laputtā'um*, a high-ranking office in Assur and was only marginally involved in the overland trade. He is rarely mentioned in the available texts, and it has not been possible to identify his seal. Similarly, I have not been able to identify the seals of any of his three known sons, Bēlum-bāni, Anina, and Šu-Kūbum. Yet, the important title held by Aššur-bēl-awātim speaks to the importance of the family in the social hierarchy of Assur.[3]

Iddin-abum

Issu-arik's second son, Iddin-abum, had a seal that stands out in the entire corpus of Cappadocian seals because of its exceptional quality and innovative use of frontality and symmetry (Fig. 9.4).[4] The seal shows a symmetrical composition with a seated figure at the centre receiving a libation from the right and an offering from the left. First known to scholars from an impression on an envelope from the Louvre Museum published in 1923 (Delaporte 1923), the seal was then also identified on an envelope kept in the Arkeoloji Müzeleri in Istanbul published in 1952 (ICK 1, 36B). On the basis of these two impressions, the seal was included in Teissier's catalogue in 1994 as no. 582a+b. An attestation of it was found in the excavations of the Lower Town of Kültepe in 1962 and it appears as CS 606 in Nimet Özgüç's 2006 catalogue of the seals in the d/k and n/k archives (Özgüç 2006). In addition to these scattered attestations, the seal belonging to Iddin-abum is found most prominently in the Šalim-Aššur archive with dozens of impressions on eight different envelopes. These additional attestations have allowed previously unnoticed details to become apparent, including a saw and two aryballoi held by figures in the scene.

Figure 9.4: Drawing of the seal of Iddin-abum s. Issu-arik, CS 606. Drawing by author.

What makes this seal remarkable is the use of the full-frontal view, showing a seated and a standing figure entirely from the front. In the art of ancient Western Asia, most human figures carved in bas relief are shown in full or mixed profile, in which parts of the body, such as head and lower body are in profile, although the shoulders and chest are regularly shown frontally. For certain monsters and female gods, a mixed (sometimes called twisted) profile was used, in which head and upper body were shown frontally, but the lower body still in profile. The so-called nude goddess is a rare

---

2 Teissier 1994, no. 231 and Teissier 1994, no. 147. When available, I refer to the so-called 'CS' or 'Teissier numbers' for the seals. These numbers refer to the system of identifying each unique seal or composite seal excavated at Kültepe instituted by Nimet Özgüç in 2001 (Özgüç & Tunca 2001) and the number of the catalogue of Old Assyrian seal impressions by Beatrice Teissier (Teissier 1994).

3 For this title, see Dercksen 2004, 65–72.

---

4 As a group, I refer to the seals attested on documents written in the Old Assyrian dialect and most frequently found in central Anatolia, as 'Cappadocian', rather than Old Assyrian. This is to avoid confusion between seals carved in Old Assyrian style and the corpus in general.

Figure 9.5: Seal impression of Iddin-abum's seal on A 847/TC 1, 64 held at the Louvre Museum. © 2008 Musée du Louvre / Thierry Ollivier.

Figure 9.6: Top, crop of the inscription of Iddin-abum's seal from A 847 (© 2008 Musée du Louvre / Thierry Ollivier.) and kt n/k 1836 (bottom, from Özgüç 2006, pl. 215), flipped horizontally and turned 90 degrees counterclockwise.

case in which the entire body is shown *en face* (Sonik 2013; Bahrani 2001, 131–33). However, the feet of the nude goddess are still usually shown in profile, either both pointing to one side or individually to each side. The seal of Iddin-abum, on the other hand, features two frontal figures where even the feet are shown as seen from the front.

Fine, modelled carvings characterize the seal. Bodies are well proportioned with careful rendering of musculature and physical detail, for example in the knees, where the kneecap and surrounding muscles are clearly visible. The faces show a finely defined nose and a round eye. Costume (dress and jewellery) is shown in detail and different types of fabric, hems, and fringes

can be distinguished. Exactly the quality of the carving and 'bold innovation' made Henri Frankfort claim that Iddin-abum's seal, while impressed on an Old Assyrian envelope, could only be of Babylonian origins (Frankfort 1939, 245). Frankfort's 'Babylon-centric' view is today outdated, and there is no doubt that the seal was part of a Syrian production of the early second millennium BC, albeit a particularly well-made example.[5]

The seal is inscribed and reads: *I-dí-a-bu-um* DUMU *I-sú*-SUD$_x$ 'Iddin-abum son of Issu-arik.' The inscription is mirrored in impressions, as was the norm for most Cappadocian seals. The seal appears with this inscription on all attestations in the Šalim-Aššur archive (Fig. 9.4).

However, on the envelopes kt n/k 1836 and TC 1, 64 (see Fig. 9.5), the seal has a different inscription, this one also in mirror writing: *I-ku-uš-mu* DUMU *I-ra-am-Da-gan* 'Ikūn-UŠMU son of Irâm-Dagan' (see Fig. 9.6).[6]

From the text on TC 1, 64 it is clear that Iddin-abum was using the seal even when it had an inscription that did not read his name. TC 1, 64 is undated but must have been written before the inscription on the seal was changed to read Iddin-abum's name. The seal was thus used by at least one other person before Iddin-abum acquired it and had the inscription updated.

A significant detail of the seal is the peak on the top of the headdress of the central figure. It could be argued that this represents the frontal rendering of the so-called 'peaked cap' (Teissier 1993), which is otherwise shown in profile view. According to Teissier, the peaked cap was worn by the Eblaite ruler and is shown in several other Old Syrian seals, for example on the seals of Irma-Aššur (CS 1148, Teissier 527) and Aššur-nādā

---

[5] e.g. Özgüç 2006, CS 606, Teissier 1994, no. 582a+b. See also Pinnock 2004. Seals in this style are variously called Syro-Cappadocian, Syrian Colony, or Old Syrian style and are sometimes divided into substyles, including 'elaborate', 'linear', drilled, Old Syrian I and II, *Šakkanakku*, see Porada 1985; Teissier 1994; Özgüç 2006; Porter 2001. I have suggested three subdivisions, which align with those used by N. Özgüç in 2006, with the one exception that I lump together her 'linear' and 'drilled' styles into one single group. Syr 1, corresponds to Özgüç's elaborate style; Syr 2, which is technically simpler and cruder and with visible tool marks, but which relates to the iconography of Syr 1; and Syr 3, which is a so-called 'popular' group which is independent of the first two groups. Iddin-abum's seal was part of the Syr 1 group.

[6] A name written *I-ku-uš-mu* is not otherwise attested in the onomasticon, but the element I-KU — *Ikūn* — does occur regularly in the Eblaite sources and is also attested at Mari (Krebernik 1988, 202). While Irâm-Dagan — 'beloved of Dagan' — poses no issues, I am unable to suggest a reading for *I-ku-uš-mu*.

(CS 819, Teissier 529), both of which mention the title of the Eblaite ruler, the *mekum*, in the seal inscription. However, on Iddin-abum's seal the figure wearing the special headdress is a god and not a king: he is placed under the divine sun disc-in-crescent symbol and, receiving libation and an offering, he is the object of ritual attention. A more likely identification of the figure is thus the Storm God, who also wears a peaked headdress. On a seal belonging to the son of a later Eblaite king, for example, the Storm God is shown in profile, but wearing a helmet or cap with a pronounced peak at the top (Collon 2005, no. 545).

Whatever the significance of the peaked headdress here, the seal is stylistically similar to the peaked cap seals, which Teissier argues were Eblaite (see also Pinnock 2004; Teissier 1993). One may also note that the Mariote *Šakkanakku* seals (Beyer 1985; Colonna d'Istria 2020; Colonna d'Istria & Beyer 2015), all have correctly oriented seal inscriptions, whereas the seals mentioning the Eblaite *mekum* have mirrored inscriptions, as was also the case with the original inscription of Iddin-abum's seal.

At the same time, however, the theophoric element in the name of the original inscription 'Dagan', seems more at home in the Mariote royal and royal-adjacent onomasticon than in the Eblaite. One may also note the dress worn by the frontal divinity to the left of the inscription in Iddin-abum's seal is identical in detail to that worn by the statue mentioning the Mariote king Puzur-Ištar (see Fig. 9.7).

Similarly, the detailing of the knees of the two figures in cut-away robes is similar to that on a servant seal of the *Šakkanakku* Iṣi-Dagan discovered on a sealing in the city of Assur (Bär 2003, pl. 45, S6).

Whether Mariote, Eblaite, or from somewhere else, Iddin-abum's seal is of rare artistic quality. The texts offer no indication that Iddin-abum had any particular connection to Syria and there is no mention of how and when he acquired his seal. The change in the seal inscription makes it clear the seal was reused at least once, but it may have had more than the two owners.

Ennam-Aššur

Ennam-Aššur, Šalim-Aššur's oldest son, also had an Old Syrian seal (Fig. 9.8). Like that of his uncle, this seal is of a high craftmanship. It is finely modelled and with careful detailing of costume and body. It shows iconography which references an Akkadian tradition, such as

Figure 9.7: Statue mentioning Šakkanakku of Mari, Puzur-Ištar. Museum of the Ancient Orient, Istanbul. Photo courtesy Giovanni Dall'Orto, 2006.

the two-faced Isimu/Usmu divinity, as well as uniquely Syrian motifs, such as the so-called Syrian Lady and ascending male god with a streamer headdress, likely the Storm God (Williams-Forte 1983). This is typical of the Old Syrian style, which used well-established, recognizable divine or human actors, indicated by consistent use of emblems, posture, and dress. In this way, this style seals differ from the Old Assyrian style where many figures are generic and represented without any distinguishing characteristics. It should also be pointed out that the Old Syrian seals incorporate Akkadian motifs and tropes to a much higher degree than the Old Assyrian.

Figure 9.8: Drawing of the seal of Ennam-Aššur, CS 222. By author.

Figure 9.9: Drawing of Ennam-Aššur's other seal, CS 1317. By author.

Ennam-Aššur's seal shows the ruler with the Eblaite peaked cap mentioned above and his seal was included as her example no. 2 in Teissier's treatment of this motif (Teissier 1993). As in other examples, the peaked cap is worn by a male figure wearing a fleece-like mantel and who is either approaching a seated deity in a cultic/ritual scene or is himself seated.

Smaller scale figures appear commonly on Old Syrian and Old Assyrian seals, particularly right in front of a seated deity, against whom they usually lean. Or they seem to be dancing or are holding small implements. Such a small figure is also seen on Ennam-Aššur's seal. Here, the figure is holding what may be a brush or perhaps a brazier or incense burner. Unique to this seal are the two small figures with crossing legs, supporting on their backs the sundisc-in-crescent symbol in the upper field in front of the seated god.

The seal carries no detectable traces of recarving and it may be that Ennam-Aššur was the first owner/user of this seal, which likely was of Eblaite origins, or, at least, sports Eblaite royal iconography.

Ennam-Aššur also used another seal, this one in Old Babylonian style. In the documentation available to me, Ennam-Aššur used his Old Syrian seal more than a dozen times. However, on one letter in the archive, KT 6, 292, Ennam-Aššur uses a different seal.[7] He used the same seal on POAT 23. The KIŠIB list is broken off from the envelope fragment, but he appears as the last person mentioned in the witness list on the tablet. POAT 23 is dated to REL 95. None of the documents where he uses his Old Syrian seal is dated. But it seems that he used the two seals at the same time albeit with a preference for the Syrian one.

Ennam-Aššur's Old Babylonian style seal shows a contest scene (Fig. 9.9). It has a pair of *bull-men*, each with a large dot or drillhole in their beard. This distinct feature makes the seal easy to recognize. It also has a circle with a cross motif which is unique.

Šāt-Anna and Kukuwa

Šāt-Anna was Šalim-Aššur's youngest child. Her name has an Anatolian theophoric element, Anna, which could suggest she was born in Anatolia. Šāt-Anna lived most of her life in Anatolia, where she was an active and independent agent operating along with her brothers in the overland trade. Šāt-Anna herself travelled across Anatolia with silver and copper (KT 6, 307), and we also hear that she did spend some time in Aššur (KT 6, 319). She married at least twice and is attested with a husband with a Hittite name into the level Ib period. Like her uncle and older brother, Šāt-Anna had an Old Syrian seal. Šāt-Anna was as mobile as her male family members, and while we have no information about how she acquired her Syrian seal, she could have picked it up herself during her travels. Her seal was carved in a simpler version of the Old Syrian style (Syr 2, see n. 4) with distinctly visible tool marks. It is unfortunately only attested in one, badly preserved, impression (KT 6, 553) and the imagery cannot be completely reconstructed (Fig. 9.10).

Her seal shows a supplication scene in which what is likely a ruler, wearing a cut-away robe, approaches a seated, male deity. The seal also shows seven dots located in the upper field. This motif, usually arranged in three pairs and a single dot, is sparsely attested in the second millennium, but becomes common in the first millennium on Neo-Assyrian seals and in the Levant, where it is identified with the Sebitti, representing the Pleiades and the Seven Sages (Verderame 2016; Wiggermann 2010). Its earliest attestation is on the Old Syrian seals.

---

7 Note that there is just one seal impressed several times on the KT 6, 292A, not two, as stated in KT 6a.

9. THE SEALS OF THE ŠALIM-AŠŠUR FAMILY (94/k)

Figure 9.10: Drawing of the seal of Šāt-Anna, Šalim-Aššur's youngest daughter, CS 1293. By author.

Figure 9.11: Drawing of the seal of Kukuwa, CS 1310. By author.

Figure 9.12: Left: drawing of CS 42. Right: drawing of CS 88, the seal of Šu-Kūbum s. Qayātum. Drawings by author.

A series of horizontal and oblique lines in a frame behind the seated figure evokes a seal inscription, although it does not contain legible signs. The seal shows no sign of being reworked.

The seal of Kukuwa, the great-grandson of Šalim-Aššur, was also in Old Syrian style of the same type as Šāt-Anna. It shows an introduction scene (Fig. 9.11). His seal is particularly interesting because of its inscription. A vertical line cuts across its entire length and some 'signs' are just jumbled lines and dots. One could imagine that the two elements in the middle were badly jumbled /ku/-signs written by an illiterate seal carver, but, more likely, this represents pseudo-writing.

There are clearer examples of pseudo-writing, as seen in Figure 9.12, Right where the inscription consists of dots and horizontal and vertical lines. On the seal in Figure 9.12, Left, there is a vertical line running down the middle and similarities in stylistic details of this seal and the 'sign-forms' in Kukuwa's seal could suggest that the same hand cut the two cylinders. The 'inscriptions' on these seals were first and foremost of symbolic or ornamental importance. Genuine inscriptions and pseudo-inscriptions are common in this simpler group of Old Syrian seals, and almost half of the seals have inscriptions — legible or not. That is twice the average inscription frequency in the corpus of Cappadocian seals as a whole.

Šalim-Aššur and Lamassī

Šalim-Aššur and his oldest daughter, Lamassī, both had seals in the Old Assyrian style (Fig. 9.13 and Fig. 9.14). This style consists of a number of clearly distinguishable substyles. One of these substyles represents a 'classic' tradition and both seals fall into this category.

The classic Old Assyrian seals have a standardized image repertoire based heavily on the introduction scene. Both seals show a seated figure wearing a flounced dress and a brimmed cap and holding up a vessel. Both seals show a procession of human and divine figures, and both have a sun-disc-in-crescent before the seated figure. In the terminal, behind the introduction scene, both have a secondary element. On Šalim-Aššur's seal, this is a single rampant lion; on Lamassī's seal, it is a bull-man facing a human worshipper placed above a pair of *kusarikku*s, divine bull-men.

Unfortunately, the use of the introduction scene in the Old Assyrian style is not well understood. In the Ur III prototype, the seated figure is a ruler (Winter

1986) and the approaching human is meant to represent the seal owner (Mayr 2011). However, in the Old Assyrian corpus, the scene is also found on the royal seals in the same configuration and one may then question if the actors are to be interpreted in the same way as in the Ur III model: if the seated figure with the brimmed headdress is the king, then who is the standing human figure on the royal seals?[8]

It is also worth noting that Lamassī's seal shows a male figure in audience, so if the standing human is meant to refer to the seal owner, the representation is only in the most general and stereotypical terms and without reference to aspects of the seal owner's identity, such as gender. There are examples of women in audience in the Old Assyrian corpus (Teissier no. 472), but I am not aware of any examples in which a female seal owner had a seal with a woman in audience.

Lamassī had the status of *gubabtum*, consecrated woman, which meant that she had been placed under the protection of a god and would live her life unmarried (Michel 2009; 2020, 376–81). We do not know the circumstances of how Lamassī acquired her seal, but the last will and testament of Ištar-lamassī, daughter of the merchant Elamma (KT 8, 179) mentions that her seal should go to her daughter, Šīmat-Ištar, who is also a *gubabtum*. More than a dozen consecrated women are known by name, but of these only Lamassī's seal has been identified.[9] Regardless, it does not seem that the personal seals of *gubabtum* women were designed to reflect their special status or their gender.

We have no indication that Lamassī ever left the city of Assur. I have elsewhere suggested that the classic Old Assyrian seals were produced in Assur (Lassen 2014) and Lamassī could have acquired it from new (it shows no signs of reworking) in the city. It may, of course, also be an heirloom from her mother or another relative.

The imagery on Šalim-Aššur's seal is very typical: while there are no exactly identical seals, the general scene is well attested. The introduction scene in the Cappadocian glyptic tradition exists in two basic con-

Figure 9.13: Top: drawing of the seal of Šalim-Aššur, CS 1278. By author. Bottom: impression of CS 1278 on KT 6, 141A. Photo: Kültepe Archaeological Archives.

Figure 9.14: Drawing of the seal of Lamassī, Šalim-Aššur's oldest daughter, CS 1308. By author.

---

8 See Eppihimer's (2013) thorough exploration of the meaning of the introduction scene on the Old Assyrian royal seals.

9 Note a tentative identification of CS 1147 (published in KT 8) with Ummī-Išhara daughter of Elamma by Klaas Veenhof. The seal is carved in Anatolian style and does not show the same scene or symbols as the seal of Lamassī. The seal of a *kumrum* priest of Ištar, named Iddin-abum, has also been identified as CS 1083 (published in KT 5). This seal is also in Anatolian style. It shows a libation scene and other religious/cultic imagery but does not show Ištar. There is a star in the upper field, which could be a reference to this goddess.

9. THE SEALS OF THE ŠALIM-AŠŠUR FAMILY (94/k)

figurations: the 'introduction', in which the worshipper is led by the hand, and the 'audience' (or 'supplication' in N. Özgüç's terminology), in which there is no contact between the intercessor and the worshipper. Šalim-Aššur's seal is an example of the former and Lamassī's seal is an example of the latter. The former type is most commonly attested in the earlier seals and the latter is a later development which gradually replaces the older type.

Variations in the terminal and in the selection of filling motifs (in Šalim-Aššur's seal, three dots, star and scorpion, and a ball-and-staff) differentiate these uninscribed seals. In some contexts, the scorpion symbol is connected to the female gender (Lassen 2020), but as scorpions frequently occur on seals belonging to men in the Cappadocian corpus, the connection here is either indirect or non-existent. Rather than functioning as a rebus alluding to the identity of the seal owner (Collon 1995), filling motifs in the Old Assyrian period perform the function of creating variation for differentiation of seals.

An exception to this rule may be the vertical crescent placed behind the head of the worshipper in Šalim-Aššur's seal. This unusual and poorly understood motif appears on the Old Assyrian royal seals, on those of certain Assyrian officials including the *laputtā'um*, as well as on those of a few traders. It is unclear why this motif appears on Šalim-Aššur's seal. One may speculate that he could have inherited this seal from his older brother, Aššur-bēl-awātim, who held the title of *laputtā'um*, but further study of the distribution of the motif is required.

Anna-anna

Anna-anna or Annanna (the etymology of the name is unclear but incorporates the theophoric element 'Anna') was an Anatolian woman married to Ennam-Aššur. They lived together in the Šalim-Aššur house, at least until her husband died and her brother-in-law Ali-ahum moved in. Anna-anna dealt mostly with domestic affairs, but occasionally had to represent her husband in negotiations with other merchants (Michel 2020, 472–81). Her seal is known from at least one envelope found in the archive containing a letter sent from her to her husband. It is unclear where she was when she sent the letter.

Her seal (Fig. 9.15) is carved in Old Assyrian style like that of her father- and sister-in-law. The seal has few filling motifs, just two triangular crescents in the upper field.

Figure 9.15: Drawing of the seal of Anna-anna, CS 1269. By author.

The main imagery shows an introduction scene of the audience type and a secondary element in two registers consisting of an incense burner (or brazier) in front of a bull-altar with a bird on its back. Below a separating line is a scorpion. I have argued elsewhere that the bull-altar is a representation of the god Aššur (Lassen 2017). The incense burner points to the concrete and tangible nature of the motif as a statue set in an actual ritual space and one may note the find of comparable tall, grooved, cylindrical stands in the Ištar Temple in the city of Aššur (Bär 2003, pls 76, 78).

Compared with the seals of Šalim-Aššur and Lamassī, the figures on Anna-anna's seal are short and stocky. The details of dress and body are stylized and almost cartoon-like. Her seal is part of a locally produced Old Assyrian style (Lassen 2014) which were owned by several other Anatolians as well as other Assyrians. The imagery on these seals was so standardized that some seals were identical except for a few tiny details. They are very rarely inscribed and are quite small. There are extant examples of seals of this type, frequently made of an iron-oxide like hematite (e.g. Buchanan 1981, no. 1102; Doğan-Alparslan, Alparslan & Özdemir 2010, 92).

Figure 9.16: Drawing of the seal of Ali-ahum, CS 1270. By author.

Ali-ahum

Only one family member, Ali-ahum (Šalim-Aššur's youngest son) had an Anatolian seal. There is general agreement that Anatolian style seals were carved in Anatolia, which is then presumably where Ali-ahum acquired his seal.

Ali-ahum's seal shows a rich and tightly packed composition with a series of figures engaging in libations or other cultic activity balancing atop a frieze of animals, birds, and a bull-altar (Fig. 9.16). Stars, animal heads, and fish occupy any sliver of empty space, except for a small area in front of a seated deity. All elements are carved in minute detail. The two figures approaching the seated god alludes to the introduction scene, but the original idea of that scene was modified to a point where it is hardly recognizable as such. Instead, Ali-ahum's seal shows two parallel libations: 1) two figures approach the seated deity with a teapot-type vessel and behind them another figure holding a teapot approaches an Anatolian hunt god, who is standing on a stage and holding a hare and bird in one hand and a weapon in the other. Ceramic vessels of the type depicted in Anatolian style seals have been recovered archaeologically at Kültepe and in central Anatolia, but not at Assur.

Anatolian style cylinder seals were used by both Anatolians and Assyrians. In fact, the Anatolian style seals that can be connected to a specific owner belonged predominantly to Assyrians, although these seals contained imagery that might not have been immediately understandable or significant for them (Larsen & Lassen 2014). While seals of this type are common in the Cappadocian corpus, they were rare in the Šalim-Aššur family.

The Seals of Iddin-abum's Sons

While not part of the Šalim-Aššur's nuclear family, it is also worth mentioning the seals of Iddin-abum's three sons, Šu-Bēlum, Enna-Suen and Anuli. Šu-Bēlum and Anuli both owned Old Syrian seals, both of the simpler group, like Šat-Anna and Kukuwa. Šu-Bēlum's seal shows a bent-straw drinking scene, a typical Syrian motif, and a bull on a pedestal. Anuli's seal shows an introduction scene as well as a bull on a pedestal (see Fig. 9.17).

Enna-Suen's seal is in Old Assyrian style and shows procession in which a goddess, the sun god Šamaš, and a bald human figure approach a seated ruler wearing a flounced dress and a brimmed hat and holding a small vessel in his right hand. Behind the main scene is a statue of a frontal female deity placed on a low pedestal. The divine statue wears a flounced dress and layered, conical headdress (perhaps a variation of the horned headdress also worn by Šamaš) and is receiving worship by a human figure in a skullcap and a cut-away robe (Fig. 9.18).

The seal is carved in Old Assyrian style, but has several features, both iconographic and stylistic, that distinguish it from the seals of Lamassī and Šalim-Aššur. Firstly, Enna-Suen's seal shows identifiable major deities, rare in the classical Old Assyrian style. In the seal, one of the major gods, Šamaš, has been integrated into a presentation scene. Secondly, the use of hatching on the brim of the seated ruler's headdress and on the pedestal of the statue of the goddess, as well as a distinctive upper garment, which is drawn over the shoulders and join around the waist.

Porada and Collon see these exact features as defining of a particular Late (level 1b) Old Assyrian style with Babylonian influence (Porada & Collon 2016, 2; Porada 1980), a group earlier called 'Provincial Babylonian' by Porada (Porada 1948, 109–10). Otto considers these ele-

Figure 9.17: Left: drawing of the seal of Šu-Bēlum, CS 1283. Right: drawing of the seal of Anuli, CS 1355. Drawings by author.

9. THE SEALS OF THE ŠALIM-AŠŠUR FAMILY (94/k)

Figure 9.18: Left: Drawing of the seal of Enna-Suen, CS 1280. By author. Right: Impression of Enna-Suen's seal on KT 6, 71. Courtesy M. T. Larsen.

ments part of a particular northern Mesopotamian/Assyrian expression (Otto 2004, 63–64). Regardless, the presence of Enna-Suen's seal on level II envelopes clearly shows that these features were present together on seals already in the level II period and are not just a later development of the Old Assyrian style.

A Diverse Portfolio

The seals owned by the members of the Šalim-Aššur family belong to a variety of styles: Old Assyrian, Old Syrian, Anatolian, and Old Babylonian. Across the generations, there is a shift away from seals carved in Aššur toward seals from Syria or Anatolia, with a particular preference for Old Syrian seals. Of the thirteen seals discussed here, six are Old Syrian. As Old Syrian seals represent less than 20 per cent of the general corpus of Cappadocian seals, the prevalence in the Šalim-Aššur family is remarkable. There is nothing in the texts indicating that the family or even individual family members had a particular connection to Syria. As merchants, they passed through when they were travelling between Assur and Kaneš, but so did everybody else. A single purchase may account for the bias toward Old Syrian seals: one could imagine that Iddin-abum may have purchased a whole group of seals at one point, keeping the best one for himself and distributing the other seals when there was a particular need for a seal, but this is, of course, speculation.

There does not seem to have been any family preference for iconography. Several seals show variations of the introduction scene, but this is in line with general trends in the corpus.

The seals discussed here are almost all uninscribed. There are just two inscribed examples, of which one was a pseudo-legend. The other, the seal of Iddin-abum, first carried the name of an original owner, which was then changed to read the name of Iddin-abum. Apart from the name, Iddin-abum made no changes to the imagery of his seal.

Overall, there is little stylistic or iconographic coherence in the seals in the Šalim-Aššur family, nothing showing that this was a family. There is nothing that indicates gender — the seals of Lamassī, Šāt-Anna, or Anna-anna do not show women and they share no motif or symbol that might hint at their gender. There is nothing to indicate cultural or political belonging: going by the peaked cap iconography you would think that Ennam-Aššur was part of the Eblaite elite, which he obviously was not. Anatolian Anna-anna had an Old Assyrian seal with Assyrian imagery whereas Assyrian Ali-ahum had an Anatolian seal with an Anatolian hunt god. While one may easily draw a negative conclusion on this background — that nothing relates to anything, that people got their seals at random. This may indeed be the case. But, at the same time, this happy mix of styles and religious iconography perfectly matches the highly mobile, cosmopolitan, and entangled merchant families, who seem to have priced and treasured their seals more for their prestige, quality (and possibly material, although that can't be determined on the basis of impressions) than for their capabilities to communicate aspects of familial or personal identity.

Seal Catalogue

Owner	CS No.	Teissier No.	Description	Drawing
Issu-arik	NA	227	Old Assyrian style; introduction scene	See Fig. 9.3
Iddin-abum s. Issu-arik	606		Old Syrian style; offering and libation	See Fig. 9.4
Šu-Bēlum S. Iddin-abum	1283		Old Syrian introduction, bent straw	See Fig. 9.17, left
Enna-Suen s. Iddin-abum	1280		Old Assyrian introduction	See Fig. 9.18
Anuli s. Iddin-abum	1355		Old Syrian introduction	See Fig. 9.17, right
Šalim-Aššur s. Issu-arik	1278		Old Assyrian introduction	See Fig. 9.13, top
Lamassī d. Šalim-Aššur	1308		Old Assyrian introduction	See Fig. 9.14
Ennam-Aššur s. Šalim-Aššur	222	530	Old Syrian introduction	See Fig. 9.8
Ali-ahum s. Šalim-Aššur	1270		Anatolian presentation	See Fig. 9.16
Šāt-Ana d. Šalim-Aššur	1293		Old Syrian presentation	See Fig. 9.10
Anna-anna wife of Ennam-Aššur	1269		Old Assyrian presentation	See Fig. 9.15
Kukuwa	1310		Old Syrian presentation	See Fig. 9.11
Ennam-Aššur s. Šalim-Aššur	1317	276	Old Babylonian contest	See Fig. 9.9

Acknowledgements

I would like to thank Mogens Trolle Larsen for help and guidance on this project and for sharing his own work and images so generously with me. I would also like to thank Fikri Kulakoğlu for allowing me to publish the seal impressions from the 94-archive, as well as Cécile Michel and the anonymous reviewer for helpful comments.

Abbreviations

94/k	inventory numbers of texts excavated in 1994 in the Lower Town of Kültepe.
a/k	inventory numbers of texts excavated in 1948 in the Lower Town of Kültepe.
CS	Kültepe Cylinder Seal.
CTMMA	Corpus of Cuneiform Texts in the Metropolitan Museum of Art.
d/k	inventory numbers of texts excavated in 1951 the Lower Town of Kültepe.
ICK 1	Hrozný, Bedrich, *Inscriptions cunéiformes du Kultépé*. Státní pedagogické nakladatelství, Prague, 1952.
ICK 3	Matouš, Lubor & Marie Matoušová-Rajmová, *Kappadokische Keilschrifttafeln mit Siegeln: Aus den Sammlungen der Karlsuniversität in Prag*. Karlsuniversität, Prague, 1984.
KT 5	Veenhof, Klaas R., *Kültepe Tabletleri*, 5. Türk Tarih Kurumu Basımevi, Ankara, 2010.
KT 6	Larsen, Mogens Trolle. *Kültepe Tabletleri*, 6. Türk Tarih Kurumu Basımevi, Ankara 2010/2013/2014/2018/2021.
KT 8	Veenhof, Klaas R., *Kültepe Tabletleri*, 8. Türk Tarih Kurumu Basımevi, Ankara, 2017.
n/k	inventory numbers of texts excavated in 1962 in the Lower Town of Kültepe.
POAT	Gwaltney, W. C., *The Pennsylvania Old Assyrian Texts*. Hebrew Union College, Cincinnati, 1983.
REL	Revised Eponym List.
TC 1	Contenau, George, *Tablettes cappadociennes*. Geuthner, Paris, 1920.

Bibliography

Bahrani, Zainab
2001   *Women of Babylon: Gender and Representation in Mesopotamia*. Routledge, London.

Bär, Jürgen
2003   *Die älteren Ischtar-Tempel in Assur* (Wissenschaftliche Veröffentlichungen der Deutschen Orient-Gesellschaft 105). Saarbrücker Druckerei und Verlag, Saarbrücken.

Barjamovic, Gojko, Thomas Hertel & Larsen, Mogens Trolle
2012   *Ups and Downs at Kanesh: Chronology, History and Society in the Old Assyrian Period* (Publications de l'Institut historique-archéologique néerlandais de Stamboul 120). Nederlands Instituut voor het Nabije Oosten, Leiden.

Beyer, Dominique
1985   'Nouveaux documents iconographiques de l'époque des shakkanakku de Mari', *Mari* 4: 173–89.

Buchanan, Briggs
1981   *Early Near Eastern Seals in the Yale Babylonian Collection*. Yale University Press, New Haven.

Collon, Dominique
1995   'Filling Motifs', in Uwe Finkbeiner, Reinhard Dittmann & Harald Hauptmann (eds), *Beiträge zur Kulturgeschichte Vorderasiens: Festschrift für Rainer Michael Boehmer*. Von Zabern, Mainz: 69–76.
2005   *First Impressions: Cylinder Seals in the Ancient Near East*, 2nd rev. edn. British Museum Press, London.

Colonna d'Istria, Laurent
2020   'Du nouveau chez les Šakkanakkus de Mari: nouvelles lectures des empreintes ME64, ME196, et ME14', *Journal of Cuneiform Studies* 72: 35–46.

Colonna d'Istria, Laurent & Beyer, Dominique
2015   'Erra-kibrī, ŠABRA D'Iddin-Ilum et ses collègues', *Journal of Cuneiform Studies* 67: 23–38.

Delaporte, Louis
1923   *Catalogue des cylindres, cachets et pierres gravées de style Oriental*, II: *Acquisitions*. Paris: Hachette.

Dercksen, Jan Gerrit
2004   *Old Assyrian Institutions* (MOS Studies 4). Nederlands Instituut voor het Nabije Oosten, Leiden.

Doğan-Alparslan, Meltem; Alparslan, Metin & Özdemir, Celal
2010   'Amasya Müzesi'nde Bulunan Bir Grup Mühür', in Sevket Dönmez (ed.), *Veysel Donbaz'a Sunulan Yazılar DUB. SAR É.DUB.BA.A / Studies Presented in Honour of Veysel Donbaz*. Ege Publications, Istanbul: 91–96.

Eppihimer, Melissa
2013   'Representing Ashur: The Old Assyrian Rulers' Seals and their Ur III Prototype', *Journal of Near Eastern Studies* 72/1: 35–49.

Frankfort, Henri
1939   *Cylinder Seals: A Documentary Essay on the Art and Religion of the Ancient Near East*. Macmillan, London.

Krebernik, Manfred
1988   *Die Personennamen der Ebla-Texte: eine Zwischenbilanz* (Berliner Beiträge zum Vorderen Orient 7). Reimer, Berlin.

Larsen, Mogens Trolle
2008   'Archives and Filing Systems at Kültepe', in Cécile Michel (ed.), *Old Assyrian Studies in Memory of Paul Garelli* (Old Assyrian Archives Studies 4). Nederlands Instituut voor het Nabije Oosten, Leiden: 77–88.
2010   *The Archive of the Šalim-Aššur Family*, I: *The First Two Generations* (Kültepe Tabletleri 6a). Türk Tarih Kurumu, Ankara.
2013   *The Archive of the Šalim-Aššur Family*, II: *Ennam-Aššur* (Kültepe Tabletleri 6b). Türk Tarih Kurumu, Ankara.
2014   *The Archive of the Šalim-Aššur Family*, III: *Ali-ahum* (Kültepe Tabletleri 6c). Türk Tarih Kurumu, Ankara.
2018   *The Archive of the Šalim-Aššur Family*, IV: *Texts concerning Non-family Members* (Kültepe Tabletleri 6d). Türk Tarih Kurumu, Ankara.
2021   *The Archive of the Šalim-Aššur Family*, V: *Anonymous Texts and Fragments* (Kültepe Tabletleri 6e). Türk Tarih Kurumu, Ankara.

Larsen, Mogens Trolle & Lassen, Agnete Wisti
2014   'Cultural Exchange at Kültepe', in Michael Kozuh, Wouter F. M. Henkelman, Charles E. Jones & Christopher Woods (eds), *Extraction and Control: Studies in Honor of Matthew W. Stolper* (Studies in Ancient Oriental Civilization 68). Oriental Institute of the University of Chicago, Chicago: 171–88.

Lassen, Agnete Wisti
2014   'The Old Assyrian Glyptic Style. An Investigation of a Seal Style, its Owners and Place of Production', in Levent Atici, Fikri Kulakoğlu, Gojko Barjamovic & Andrew Fairbairn (eds), *Current Research at Kültepe/Kanesh: An Interdisciplinary and Integrative Approach to Trade Networks, Internationalism, and Identity*. American Schools of Oriental Research, Boston: 107–21.
2017   'The "Bull-Altar" in Old Assyrian Glyptic: A Representation of the God Assur?', in Fikri Kulakoğlu & Gojko Barjamovic (eds), *Movement, Resources, Interaction: Proceedings of the 2nd Kültepe International Meeting, Kültepe, 26-30 July 2015*. Brepols, Turnhout: 179–95.
2020   'Women and Seals in Ancient Mesopotamia', in Agnete W. Lassen & Klaus Wagensonner (eds), *Women at the Dawn of History*. Yale Babylonian Collection, New Haven: 25–37.

Mayr, Rudy
2011 'The Figure of the Worshipper in the Presentation Scene', in David Owen (ed.), *Garšana Studies* (Cornell University Studies in Sumerology and Assyriology 6). CDL Press, Bethesda: 227–32.

Michel, Cécile
2009 'Les filles consacrées des marchands assyriens', in Françoise Briquel-Chatonnet, Saba Farès, Brigitte Lion & Cécile Michel (eds), *Femmes, cultures et sociétés dans les civilisations méditerranéennes et proche-orientales de l'Antiquité* (Topoi Orient Occident, supplément 10). De Boccard, Paris: 145–63.

2020 *The Women of Assur and Kanesh: Texts from the Archives of Assyrian Merchants* (Writings from the Ancient World 42). SBL Press, Atlanta.

Otto, Adelheid
2004 *Siegel und Siegelabrollungen* (Ausgrabungen in Tall Bi'a/Tuttul 4). Saarbrücken, Berlin:

Özgüç, Nimet
2006 *Kültepe-Kaniš/Neša: Seal Impressions on the Clay Envelopes from the Archives of the Native Peruwa and Assyrian Trader Uṣur-ša-Ištar Son of Aššur-imittī* (Türk Tarih Kurumu Yayınları 5/50). Türk Tarih Kurumu Basımevi, Ankara.

Özgüç, Nimet & Tunca, Önhan
2001 *Kültepe-Kaniš: Sealed and Inscribed Clay Bullae* (Türk Tarih Kurumu Yayınları 5/48). Türk Tarih Kurumu Basımevi, Ankara.

Özgüç, Tahsin & Özgüç, Nimet
1953 *Kültepe Kazısı Raporu, 1949: Ausgrabungen in Kültepe; Bericht über die im Auftrage der Türkischen Historischen Gesellschaft, 1949 durchgeführten Ausgrabungen* (Türk Tarih Kurumu Yayınlarından 5/12). Türk Tarih Kurumu Basımevi, Ankara.

Pinnock, Frances
2004 'Change and Continuity of Art in Syria Viewed from Ebla', in Jan-Walke Meyer & Walther Sommerfeld (eds), *2000 v. Chr. Politische, wirtschaftliche und kulturelle Entwicklung im Zeichen einer Jahrtausendwende*. Harrassowitz, Berlin: 87–118.

Porada, Edith
1948 *The Collection of the Pierpont Morgan Library* (Corpus of Ancient Near Eastern Seals in North American Collections 1). Pantheon, Washington, D.C.

1980 'Kaniš kārum. C. Die Glyptik', in Ernst Wiedner & Wolfram von Soden (eds), *Reallexikon der Assyriologie und vorderasiatischen Archäologie*, III: *Fabel - Gyges*. De Gruyter, Berlin: 369–89.

1985 'Syrian Seals from the Late Fourth to the Late Second Millennium', in Harvey Weiss (ed.), *Ebla to Damascus: Art and Archaeology of Ancient Syria; An Exhibition from the Directorate General of Antiquities and Museums of the Syrian Arab Republic*. Smithsonian Institution, Washington, D.C.: 90–104.

Porada, Edith & Collon, Dominique
2016 *The Second Millennium BC: Beyond Babylon* (Catalogue of the Western Asiatic Seals in the British Museum, Cylinder Seals 4). British Museum, London.

Porter, Barbara A.
2001 'Old Syrian Popular Style Cylinder Seals' (unpublished doctoral thesis, Columbia University).

Sonik, Karen
2013 'The Monster's Gaze: Vision as Mediator between Time and Space in the Art of Mesopotamia', in Lluis Feliu, Jaume Llop, Adelina Millet Albà & Joaquin Sanmartín (eds), *Time and History in the Ancient Near East: Proceedings of the 56th Rencontre Assyriologique Internationale at Barcelona, 26–30 July 2010*. Eisenbrauns, Winona Lake: 285–300.

Teissier, Beatrice

1993 'The Ruler with the Peaked Cap and Other Syrian Iconography on Glyptic from Kültepe in the Early Second Millennium BC', in Machteld J. Mellink, Edith Porada & Tahsin Özgüç (eds), *Aspects of Art and Iconography: Anatolia and its Neighbors; Studies in Honor of Nimet Özgüç*. Türk Tarih Kurumu Basimevi, Ankara: 601–12.

1994 *Sealing and Seals on Texts from Kültepe Kārum Level 2* (Publications de l'Institut historique-archéologique néerlandais de Stamboul 120). Nederlands Instituut voor het Nabije Oosten, Leiden.

Veenhof, Klaas R.

2013 'The Archives of Old Assyrian Traders: Their Nature, Functions and Use', in Michele Faraguna (ed.), *Archives and Archival Documents in Ancient Societies: Legal Documents in Ancient Societies IV, Trieste 30 September – 1 October 2011*. EUT Edizioni Università di Trieste, Trieste: 27–71.

Verderame, Lorenzo

2016 'Pleiades in Ancient Mesopotamia', *Mediterranean Archaeology and Archaeometry* 16/4: 109–17.

Wiggermann, Frans A. M.

2010 'Siebengötter (Sebettu, Sebittu, Sibittu)', in Dietz Otto Edzard (ed.), *Reallexikon der Assyriologie und vorderasiatischen Archäologie*, XII: *Šamuḫa – Spinne*. De Gruyter, Berlin: 459–66.

Williams-Forte, Elizabeth

1983 'The Snake and the Tree in the Iconography and Texts of Syria during the Bronze Age', in Leonard Gorelick & Elizabeth Williams-Forte (eds), *Ancient Seals and the Bible*. Undena, Malibu: 18–43.

Winter, Irene

1986 'The King and the Cup: Iconography of the Royal Presentation Scene on Ur III Seals', in Marilyn Kelly-Buccellati (ed.), *Insight through Images: Studies in Honour of Edith Porada* (Bibliotheca Mesopotamica 21). Undena, Malibu: 253–68.

OF HUMANS AND ANIMALS

10. A First Attempt to Assess Activity Patterns at Kültepe

Studying Entheseal Changes in the Bronze Age Skeletal Sample

Donald Kale, Handan Üstündağ, Semih Özen, Doruk Cafer Özgü & Fikri Kulakoğlu

Introduction

Human bioarchaeology, an interdisciplinary field combining the approaches of archaeology and biological anthropology, offers new perspectives on traditional research subjects, such as daily life in past societies. Besides written sources and archaeological artefacts, the study of human skeletal remains can also contribute greatly to our understanding of this subject. For example, physical activities that are part of an individual's daily routine can lead to some modifications on the skeletal system. These activities may be related to manual labour or occupation (e.g. textile production, metalworking), subsistence (e.g. agricultural work, animal husbandry), environmental conditions (e.g. carrying water, shovelling snow), household tasks (e.g. food preparation, cutting firewood), construction work, and transportation (e.g. horseback riding, canoeing). It should be emphasized that only activities involving repetitive movements performed regularly over a period of time, such as many years, can result in changes in bone structure. This explanation is based on the assumption that changes of a bone's structure are the result of a response to mechanical loading and is called 'bone functional adaptation' (Ruff et al. 2006). Bioarchaeologists suggest that through a careful study of these changes, it may be possible to reconstruct activity patterns, as well as gain some insights into the division of labour and social roles within a population. The studies of so-called 'activity-related skeletal changes' constitute an advanced field of research in human bioarchaeology and have led to a large amount of literature. There have been studies linking various markers in the skeleton, such as osteoarthritis (degenerative changes in joints), cross-sectional bone geometry, and entheseal changes (EC) to long-term repetitive activities (for a detailed review see Knüsel 2000; Jurmain et al. 2012; Villotte 2023). The examination of EC, also called musculoskeletal stress markers, has been the increasingly favoured method utilized by researchers in recent years to study activity patterns in past populations. There are numerous published studies on EC which have been conducted on various archaeological as well as modern (with known and identified demographics) skeletal collections (e.g. Dutour 1986; Hawkey & Merbs 1995; Robb 1998; Eshed et al. 2004; Molnar 2006; Villotte

---

Donald Kale (dkale309@gmail.com) Department of Archaeology, Graduate School of Social Sciences, Anthropology Laboratory, Faculty of Humanities, Anadolu University, 26470 Eskişehir, Türkiye

Handan Üstündağ (hustunda@anadolu.edu.tr) Department of Archaeology, Anthropology Laboratory, Faculty of Humanities, Anadolu University, 26470, Eskişehir, Türkiye

Semih Özen (semihoozen@gmail.com) Department of Biology, Institution of Graduate Schools, Eskişehir Technical University, 26555, Anthropology Laboratory, Faculty of Humanities, Anadolu University, 26470, Eskişehir, Türkiye

Doruk Cafer Özgü (dorukozgu@gmail.com) Anthropology Laboratory, Faculty of Humanities, Anadolu University, 26470, Eskişehir, Türkiye

Fikri Kulakoğlu (kulakoglu@ankara.edu.tr) Department of Protohistory and Near Eastern Archaeology, Faculty of Languages and History-Geography, Ankara University, 06430, Ankara, Türkiye

et al. 2010; Havelková et al. 2011; Santana-Cabrera et al. 2015; Schrader 2015; Carballo-Pérez & Schrader 2023).

Entheses are areas where muscles attach to the bone. It has been suggested that some distinctive alterations, such as new bone formation or bone destruction, may occur in the entheses due to the intensive and prolonged use of the attached muscle (Jurmain et al. 2012). By observing these changes, researchers try to determine muscle use and estimate the repetitive movements that lead to the changes on the bone. However, due to some etiological, methodological, and interpretative difficulties, these estimations are not straightforward. To suggest that an individual is involved in certain activities or occupations simply by observing changes on the bone is now highly criticized and outdated (for a critical evaluation of the literature see Meyer et al. 2011; Jurmain et al. 2012; Villotte 2023). First of all, activity is not the only cause of EC. Various other factors that may affect EC development must also be taken into account, such as ageing (Mariotti et al. 2004; 2007; Alves Cardoso & Henderson 2010; Villotte et al. 2010; Milella et al. 2012; Henderson et al. 2017b; Villotte & Santos 2023), body mass (Weiss 2003), and sex hormones (Mariotti et al. 2007; Niinimäki 2012; Weiss et al. 2012).

To avoid any subjectivity, activity-related bone changes should be systematically recorded and statistically analysed. Researchers have put great efforts into developing standard recording methods for EC and to find the most appropriate entheses that can be best accurately and reliably associated with activity (Hawkey & Merbs 1995; Mariotti et al. 2004; 2007; Villotte 2006; Santana 2011; Henderson et al. 2013; 2016). Attention is also paid to the nature of the enthesis (whether it is fibrous or fibrocartilaginous). In recent years, many researchers seem to agree on using fibrocartilaginous entheses in activity-related studies, as they are less affected by ageing (Villotte et al. 2010; Henderson et al. 2013; 2016; 2017b; Michopoulou et al. 2017). Recently, new quantitative 3D-based methods have also been proposed for EC research (Karakostis & Harvati 2021). In EC studies applying the correct statistical analysis is also important to accurately interpret the data. Most of the studies use non-parametric correlation tests (e.g. Mann–Whitney U test, Spearman's Rho test), but some researchers suggest the application of multivariate analysis to show the interaction of multiple muscles and the effects of various factors (Millela et al. 2015; Karakostis & Harvati 2021).

Within the scope of the Kültepe excavations, human skeletal remains belonging to a total of 285 individuals have been recovered since 2005. These remains come from three main chronological periods; the Early Bronze Age (EBA) (n=24), Middle Bronze Age (MBA) (n=94), and Hellenistic-Roman periods (n=167). Osteological research has been carried out on these skeletons and partially published (see Üstündağ 2009, 2014). The research project 'A Multidisciplinary Analysis of the Biological and Social Structure of the Kültepe-Kaneš Population', which is funded by TÜBİTAK, was initiated in 2020. This ongoing project aims to understand the Kültepe-Kaneš Bronze Age population in terms of gender, ethnicity, and social status variations, by using different bioarchaeological methods. As one of these methods, the examination and analysis of EC were used to assess potential activity differences in the population. However, as it does not seem possible for now to clearly distinguish subgroups regarding ethnicity and status, here we only analysed the differences of EC among age, sex, period, and burial type groups.

Material

The settlement of Kültepe is located in the Kayseri Plain north-east of the modern city of Kayseri, Türkiye. The site has been recurrently excavated since its discovery in the late nineteenth century, and since 2005 excavations are directed by F. Kulakoğlu. The mound and the Lower Town together constitute the site of Kültepe. The mound is comprised of eighteen cultural levels, with the earliest occupation of the mound beginning during the EBA. The Lower Town was inhabited during MBA and consists of four cultural levels. It functioned as a commercial and residential centre. The site appears to have been unoccupied during the Late Bronze Age, then being resettled in the Iron Age. The last cultural levels at Kültepe belong to the Hellenistic and Roman periods (Özgüç 2005; Kulakoğlu 2011).

Skeletal remains used in this research were recovered from both the mound and the Lower Town and are dated to the EBA and MBA. EC studies can only be performed in adult individuals, and, therefore, EC were recorded in a group of fifty-two adult individuals for this study. There are fourteen individuals from the EBA (more precisely the EBA III period, dated to between 2350–2020 cal BC) which were recovered during the 2017–2020 excavation seasons. Thirty-eight individuals from the MBA were also studied. These MBA individuals were recovered during the 2005–2013 excavation seasons from levels Ia/Ib of the Lower Town (dated to 1750–1690 cal BC), with exception of one individual who comes from the mound (dated to 2019 cal BC).

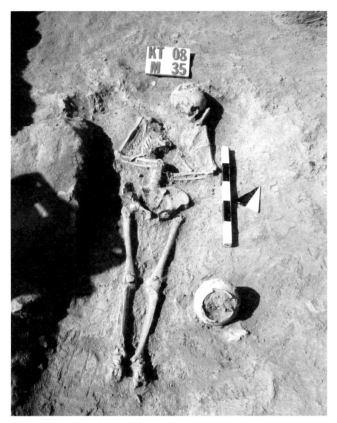

Figure 10.1: A simple inhumation from the Lower Town. © Kültepe-Kanesh Excavations Archive, reproduced with permission of Fikri Kulakoğlu.

Figure 10.2: A stone cist burial from the Lower Town. © Kültepe-Kanesh Excavations Archive, reproduced with permission of Fikri Kulakoğlu.

Skeletons were buried under buildings' floors or in open areas, in most cases accompanied by a variety of mortuary objects. There were three main burial types; simple inhumations (n=17; Fig. 10.1), stone cists (n=20; Fig. 10.2), and jars/'bathtubs' (n=13; Fig. 10.3 and 10.4). However, mortuary objects were not used for correlation purposes, as their classification is quite problematic. We know that the graves were opened by the relatives of the buried at that time and new burials were made. In fact, the mortuary objects left in the grave to the one buried first were taken from their original places and placed next to the one who was buried later.

The skeletal remains were fragmentary and only some of them were well-enough preserved for recording EC. Damaged entheses that might lead to confusion when recording EC were excluded. Accordingly, less than half of the entheses from the sub-sampled fifty-two individuals were suitable for observation of EC. The bones showed some degradation due to prolonged exposure to the underground burial environment, but no specific taphonomic changes associated with human or animal activities were observed.

Methodology

Sex and Age-at-Death Estimation

Standard morphological methods were used to estimate the sex and age-at-death of the sample group. Morphological traits of the pelvis and cranium were used for sex estimation (Phenice 1969; Buikstra & Ubelaker 1994). Pubic symphysis morphology (Brooks & Suchey 1990), sternal rib end changes (İşcan et al. 1984; 1985), and dental attrition (Lovejoy et al. 1985) were used for estimating the age-at-death. The sample population was grouped into three age categories following Buikstra & Ubelaker (1994); young adults (twenty–thirty-four years), middle adults (thirty-five–forty-nine years), and old adults (fifty years and older). An age group could not be assigned to all individuals, therefore, five of them (n=5) were categorized only as adults. As a result of this the sample population was further reduced to forty-seven individuals during correlation tests between age and EC scores. It was not possible to estimate the sex for seven individuals, who were then excluded from correlation tests between sex and EC scores. The sex and age-at-death distribution of the EBA and MBA individuals are presented in Table 10.1.

Figure 10.3: A jar burial from the Lower Town. © Kültepe-Kanesh Excavations Archive, reproduced with permission of Fikri Kulakoğlu.

Figure 10.4: A bathtub burial from the Lower Town. © Kültepe-Kanesh Excavations Archive, reproduced with permission of Fikri Kulakoğlu.

Table 10.1: Sex and age-at-death distribution of the sample group.

Period	Sex	Young Adult	Middle Adult	Old Adult	Adult	Total
EBA	Males	1	1	0	1	3
	Females	4	2	0	0	6
	Indeterminate	1	2	0	2	5
	Total	6	5	0	3	14
MBA	Males	4	7	2	0	13
	Females	12	5	6	0	23
	Indeterminate	0	0	0	2	2
	Total	16	12	8	2	38
All Bronze Age	Males	5	8	2	1	16
	Females	16	7	6	0	29
	Indeterminate	1	2	0	4	7
	Total	22	17	8	5	52

Recording Process

The Coimbra Method (which was the method applied in this study to examine and record EC) utilizes fibrocartilaginous entheses, and six defined features are recorded (for details see Henderson et al. 2013; 2016; 2017a). According to this method, entheses are divided into two zones: Zone 1 (Z1), which is the outer margin of the attachment site; and the entheseal surface where the muscle attaches which is demarcated as Zone 2 (Z2). Features are characterized as enthesophytic, porotic, or lytic changes. Bone formation (BF) is an enthesophytic change and is recorded in both zones of the enthesis (Fig. 10.5). Erosion (ER) is a lytic change that occurs in both zones and appears in the form of irregular depressions. The rest of the features are recorded only in Z2 of the enthesis. Textural change (TC) manifests as an irregular coarse striated surface with an appearance similar to sandpaper. The rest of the features are of porous nature. Fine porosity (FPO) is defined as a smooth-edged cavity up to 1 mm wide (Fig. 10.5). Macro-porosity (MPO) is defined as cavities larger than 1 mm with an unapparent floor (Fig. 10.5). Cavitation (CA) manifests as a hole, and contrary to MPO has an apparent floor. Features are scored as absent or in two degrees of expression, either slight (degree 1) or severe (degree 2). However, TC is only scored as present (degree 1) or absent (degree 0).

For this study, eleven fibrocartilaginous entheses located on the upper and lower limbs (both right and left sides) and the pelvic girdle (described in Table 10.2) were examined. We intended to record 176 variables (eight features on twenty-two entheses) for the fifty-two individuals. Due to the fragmentary state of the skeletal remains, it was not possible to record all of the entheses. The number of actually observed entheses is presented in Table 10.3. The recording process took place in the Anthropology Laboratory of Anadolu University in Eskişehir. Following the method's guidelines, for each skeletal individual, the data were collected independently by four observers (the first four authors of this paper). The observers became acquainted and trained with the method before applying it to the sample population. Independent recording was performed on purpose in order to test interobserver agreement (IOA) among the observers (for details see Kale et al. 2023). IOA tested by using Fleiss's kappa on three entheses (subscapularis, common extensor, and biceps brachii) indicated a moderate agreement according to Landis and Koch (1977). The degree of expression for each feature was calculated based on the mean of the four observers' given values.

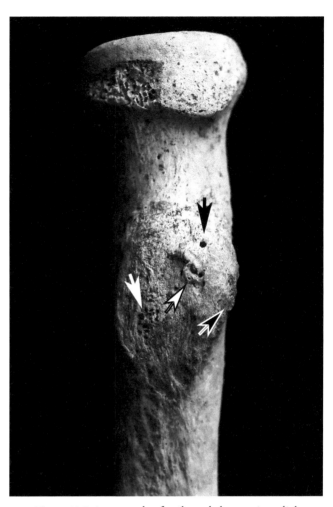

Figure 10.5: An example of entheseal changes in radial tuberosity: bone formation in Zone 1 (black-filled arrow with white border), bone formation in Zone 2 (white-filled arrow with black border), fine-porosity in Zone 2 (white arrow), and macro-porosity in Zone 2 (back arrow). Figure by Handan Üstündağ, reproduced with permission of Fikri Kulakoğlu.

Statistical Data Analysis

The data obtained from this study were processed in a database created in IBM SPSS Statistics software version 26.0. Mean score and Spearman's Rho correlation statistics were used for data analysis. The statistical significance was defined by a probability level of $p<0.05$. Age-at-death, sex, chronological period, and burial type were the available variables for which we could perform correlation tests. In order to control for the age factor, only young and middle adults were included in the correlation tests, with the exception of the EC-age correlation tests (n=36). Considering the small sample size in this study, individuals from the EBA and MBA were pooled together during correlation tests. EC scores of males and females were correlated with period and burial type, both pooled together and also separately.

Table 10.2: The observed entheses and related muscles of the upper and lower limbs and the pelvic gridle, and their actions (anatomical descriptions adapted from Standring 2021).

Bone	Muscle	Enthesis & Attachment site	Action
Humerus	Supraspinatus	Superior facet of the greater tubercule	Arm abduction and stabilization
	Infraspinatus	Middle facet of the greater tubercule	Lateral rotation, transverse arm abduction and stabilization
	Subscapularis	Lesser tubercule of the humerus	Medial arm rotation and stabilization
	Common Extensor	Lateral epicondyle of the humerus	Hand and wrist extension and abduction
	Common Flexor	Medial epicondyle of the humerus	Hand and wrist flexion and abduction
Radius	Biceps Brachii	Radial tuberosity	Forearm supination and flexion
Ulna	Triceps Brachii	Superior end of the olecranon of the ulna	Extends forearm at the elbow joint
Os coxae	Biceps femoris	Ischial tuberosity, line aspera, and lateral supracondylar line	Leg flexion and lateral rotation; thigh extension
	Semitendinosus	Inferior aspect of the posterior portion of the ischial tuberosity	
	Semimembranosus	Lateral aspect of the posterior portion of the ischial tuberosity	
Femur	Gluteus minimus	Antero-lateral aspect of the greater trochanter of the femur	Medial rotation and abduction of the thigh
	Gluteus medius	Lateral aspect of the greater trochanter of the femur	Medial rotation and abduction of the thigh
	Iliopsoas (iliacus & psoas major)	Lesser trochanter of the femur	Thigh flexion, trunk flexion; hip stabilization
Calcaenus	Triceps surae (Achilles tendon)	Posterior aspect of the calcaneus	Foot plantar-flexion

Table 10.3: Number (n) of observed entheses (Z: zone).

Bone	Enthesis	Right Z1 n	Right Z2 n	Left Z1 n	Left Z2 n
Humerus	Supraspinatus & Infraspinatus	15	17	10	12
	Subscapularis	14	14	16	15
	Common Extensor	18	21	18	18
	Common Flexor	17	24	19	21
Radius	Biceps Brachii	22	22	25	25
Ulna	Triceps Brachii	18	18	23	23
Os coxae	Biceps femoris & Semitendinosus & Semimembranosus	24	25	19	19
Femur	Gluteus minimus	22	24	19	21
	Gluteus Medius	18	19	19	20
	Iliopsoas (iliacus & psoas major)	21	21	24	22
Calcaneus	Triceps surae (Achilles tendon)	14	13	17	13

Table 10.4: Significant results for correlation between EC scores and age groups (Z: zone, n: number, MS: mean score).

Related Joint	Enthesis	Side	Z	Feature	Young Adult		Middle Adult		Old Adult		Spearman's Rho	
					n	MS	n	MS	n	MS	r_s	p value
Shoulder	Supraspinatus & Infraspinatus	Right	2	ER	11	0	4	0.25	2	1	0.725	0.001
Hip	Gluteus minimus	Right	1	BF	12	0	8	0.13	2	1.00	0.587	0.004
	Gluteus medius	Right	1	BF	9	0	8	0.13	1	1	0.479	0.044
	Gluteus medius	Left	1	BF	8	0	6	0.50	4	0.75	0.671	0.003
	Iliopsoas	Left	1	BF	9	0	11	0.36	3	0.67	0.524	0.010
Ankle	Triceps surae	Right	1	BF	6	0.33	6	1	2	1	0.614	0.020
	Triceps surae	Left	1	BF	8	0.13	7	0.86	2	1	0.702	0.002

Table 10.5: Significant results for correlation between EC scores and sex (Z: zone, n: number, MS: mean score).

Joint	Enthesis	Side	Z	Feature	Sex	n	MS	Spearman's Rho	
								r_s	p value
Shoulder	Subscapularis	Right	2	CA	Male	4	0.50	-0.624	0.040
					Female	7	0.00		
	Subscapularis	Left	2	BF	Male	2	0.50	-0.667	0.035
					Female	8	0.00		
Elbow	Common extensor	Left	1	BF	Male	5	0.40	-0.561	0.024
					Female	11	0.00		

Results

Correlation tests were performed for age-at-death, sex, period, and burial type for twenty-two entheses including eight features, with a total of 176 variables. Only significant results are presented in the following tables, due to the impossibility of presenting all results as four enormous tables. The data supporting this study are available from the corresponding authors upon request.

Age-at-Death

Both sexes were pooled to conduct correlation tests between age groups and EC scores. In this test seven entheses (right m. supraspinatus & infraspinatus, right m. gluteus minimus, right and left m. gluteus medius, left m. iliopsoas, and right and left m. triceps surae attachment sites) showed statistically significant results (Table 10.4). ER in Z2 of m. supraspinatus and infraspinatus enthesis, which is related to the shoulder joint, demonstrated an increase with age. Other significant cases showing a clear increase with age are represented by BF in Z1 of the entheses related to the hip and ankle joints (Table 10.4).

Sex

For the correlation tests between sex and EC scores, the exclusion of old adults (to control for the age factor) reduced the sample to thirty-six individuals. When young and middle adults were pooled, only three entheses showed a significant difference in EC scores between males and females. These results indicate that CA in the right m. subscapularis enthesis, BF in Z2 of the left m. subscapularis enthesis, and BF in Z1 of the m. common extensor enthesis were observed in almost half of the male individuals, while females exhibited no changes at all (Table 10.5). However, if we look at the age groups of these individuals, we can see that the majority of females belong to the young adult group, whereas males were mostly middle adults, and therefore age may be a factor.

Chronological Period

For analysing chronological period differences of EC scores, the sample was analysed in two ways; with the sexes pooled as well as separately (with all old adults excluded). There was only one statistically significant

Table 10.6: Significant results for correlation between EC scores and chronological periods (Z: zone, n: number, MS: mean score).

Joint	Enthesis	Side	Z	Feature	Chronological Period	Sex	n	MS	Spearman's Rho	
									r_s	p value
Elbow	Triceps brachii	Left	1	BF	Early Bronze Age	Male	1	0.67	-0.624	0.007
						Female	5			
					Middle Bronze Age	Male	5	0.00		
						Female	6			

value (BF in Z1 of the left m. triceps brachii enthesis) when both sexes were pooled together. This enthesis is related to the left elbow joint, and, therefore, it seems like the individuals (both males and females) from the EBA developed some changes on the left elbow joint while those from the MBA exhibited no EC at all (Table 10.6).

Burial Type

Correlation analysis between EC scores and individuals from different burial types was conducted with sex groups pooled and also separated (with all old adults excluded). There were only two statistically significant results; one for both sexes pooled, and one for the male group. No statistically significant correlation was found between the burial types and EC scores for female individuals. When both sexes are pooled a significant correlation was found for the right m. gluteus minimus enthesis related to the hip joint. In this case the mean values indicate that individuals (male and female, young and middle adult) recovered from simple inhumations exhibit some changes (ER in Z2) on the right m. gluteus minimus enthesis, whilst individuals from jar/'bathtub' and stone cist burials exhibit no EC (Table 10.7). The significant example within the males indicates that there is a relationship between EC scores and burial type for the left m. iliopsoas enthesis. Males from simple inhumations show some EC (BF in Z1), while the rest do not exhibit any changes (Table 10.8). Both of these results indicate that individuals (in this sample population) recovered from simple inhumations developed more changes in the entheses related to the hip joints than individuals from the other two burial types.

Discussion

Several previous studies have presented age as an influential factor for EC (Weiss 2003; 2007; Mariotti et al. 2004; 2007; Molnar 2006; 2010; Alves Cardoso & Henderson 2010; Jurmain et al. 2012; Milella et al. 2012; Niinimäki 2012; Henderson & Nikita 2016; Michopoulou et al. 2015; Henderson et al. 2017b; Villotte & Santos 2023). In our study, only seven entheses showed a statistically significant increase in EC scores with advancing age. Most of the features on these seven entheses were BF in Z1. It is also apparent that changes, particularly in entheses related to hip and ankle joints, are positively correlated with age. These findings demonstrate once again that age is a prominent factor in the development of EC. Therefore, to avoid any misinterpretation caused by ageing, this is why we decided to exclude old adults from the rest of the correlation tests.

There is a discussion among researchers on the influence of sex in the development of EC. Many studies have pointed out that higher scores of EC are evident in males (Weiss 2003; 2007; Mariotti et al. 2004; 2007; Molnar 2006; 2010; Villotte et al. 2010; Jurmain et al. 2012; Niinimäki 2012; Alonso-Llamazares et al. 2022). Higher EC scores in males are attributed either to sexual dimorphism (sex hormones, body mass) and/or sexual division of labour. In our study, the correlation between sex and EC scores indicates that males developed more EC than females in two entheses (in three features) of the upper limb. Yet, in all these cases there is a dominance in young adult females, whilst male individuals with EC are mostly middle-aged. This demographic bias is particularly evident in the MBA group (Table 10.1). As our results are clearly influenced by age, it is unreasonable to discuss any other factor for the difference found between the sexes.

There was only one significant difference regarding EC scores between EBA and MBA individuals. EBA individuals developed more EC exhibited as BF in Z1 of the left m. triceps brachii enthesis. The triceps brachii muscle is involved in arm extension. However, drawing a difference in activities between individuals of the two

Table 10.7: Significant results for correlation between EC scores and individuals from different burial types, both sexes pooled (Z: zone, n: number, MS: mean score).

Joint	Enthesis	Side	Z	Feature	Burial Type	Sex	n	MS	Spearman's Rho	
									r_s	p value
Hip	Gluteus minimus	Right	2	ER	Simple Inhumation	Male	2	0.43	-0.504	0.028
						Female	5			
					Jar/'bathtub'	Male	1	0.00		
						Female	4			
					Stone Cist	Male	2	0.00		
						Female	5			

Table 10.8: Significant results for correlation between EC scores and individuals from different burial types, only males (Z: zone, n: number, MS: mean score).

Joint	Enthesis	Side	Z	Feature	Burial Type	Age Group	n	MS	Spearman's Rho	
									r_s	p value
Hip	Iliopsoas	Left	1	BF	Simple Inhumation	Middle Adult	2	1	-0.837	0.019
					Jar/'bathtub'	Young Adult	1	0.00		
						Middle Adult	1			
					Stone Cist	Middle Adult	3	0.00		

periods based only on this result could be misleading and erroneous.

According to the statistical analysis, only two entheses from the lower limbs, the gluteus minimus and the iliopsoas, exhibited significant differences within the different burial groups. These differences resulted from the presence of these EC only in individuals from simple inhumations, while the rest exhibit no changes. The medical literature may provide some insight into the discussion of the underlying causes of these EC. Although the cases presented in the medical literature are pathological conditions and therefore are probably not the same as EC recorded in this study, they may still provide some explanation about the causes of the biomechanical stress at the enthesis.

The pathological condition which occurs in the m. triceps brachii enthesis is called *triceps tendonitis* and mainly affects males. It is thought to be caused by forceful repetitive elbow extension activities, such as throwing sports (Jafarnia et al. 2001). We do not associate the EC in our sample with a pathologic condition, but this information may provide a clue that excessive arm extension may be caused by an activity such as throwing.

In the case of the m. gluteus minimus enthesis, changes were observed in both males and females from simple inhumations. The gluteus minimus muscle, which attaches on the antero-lateral aspect of the greater trochanter of the femur, is involved in the medial rotation and abduction of the thigh. In the medical literature, the most common pathological condition causing modifications at this attachment site is labelled as *gluteal tendinopathy* or *greater trochanteric pain syndrome* (including both the m. gluteus medius and m. gluteus minimus) (Bird et al. 2001; Grimaldi et al. 2015; Grimaldi & Fearon 2015; Canosa-Carro et al. 2022). It is reported as being more common in females than males, and the risk increases for females over forty years of age (Bird et al. 2001; Grimaldi et al. 2015; Grimaldi & Fearon 2015; Canosa-Carro et al. 2022). The causes of gluteal tendinopathy may be excessive hip adduction during static or dynamic postures (e.g. squatting, lunging, sit-to-stand, climbing, descending, single-leg stance, hop, landing) (Grimaldi et al. 2015). If we check the age groups of the individuals that exhibited EC on the gluteus minimus enthesis we observed that they are in a young adult female, an early middle adult female, and a middle adult male. So, it can be argued that individuals from simple inhumations remain outside the risk category of developing gluteal tendinopathy. However, similar biomechanical causes, such as excessive hip adduction, may have also affected the occurrence of non-pathological changes in the m. gluteus minimus enthesis of individuals from simple inhumations.

Significant correlation between scores of the m. iliopsoas enthesis and burial type was found only in males. The iliopsoas muscle attaches to the lesser trochanter of the femur and is involved in hip and trunk flexion, hip stabilization, and external rotation of the femur (Johnston et al. 1998; Anderson 2016). The pathological condition causing modifications on this enthesis is called *iliopsoas bursitis and tendinitis* or *iliopsoas tendinopathy* (Johnston et al. 1998; Visco & Rittenberg 2010). This condition is very common among athletes, although it may also occur in non-athletic individuals, and risk increases after the age of thirty (Visco & Rittenberg 2010). Rheumatoid arthritis, acute trauma, and overuse injury (acute or chronic occupational trauma) are remarked as being the main causes of iliopsoas tendinopathy (Johnston et al. 1998). It has been also inferred by Johnston et al. (1998) that heavy labour or excessive mechanical stress (e.g. intense training, running, jumping, throwing, and rowing) may lead to this condition. In our sample, the two male individuals from simple inhumations exhibiting changes in the iliopsoas enthesis are both middle adults. Since these individuals are in the age group at risk for this condition, the changes may have similar causes such as heavy labour or excessive mechanical stress, but also may have been caused simply by ageing.

Conclusions and Future Directions

There were some limitations that we encountered while conducting this research. The main problem was the sample size, which limited statistical analysis. Although the Kültepe Bronze Age skeletal assemblage is not large (n=118), it can be considered sufficient for osteological studies. However, since we only examined adult individuals in this study, the number of individuals was considerably reduced. Moreover, due to the fragmentary nature of the skeletal remains, only half of the adult individuals presented observable entheses. Furthermore, when groups were separated for correlation purposes, we encountered much smaller subgroups which resulted in insignificant statistical results. Likewise, unequal demographic distribution affected some of the correlation tests, as we mentioned in the discussion.

No sufficient evidence was found to distinguish any differences between males and females regarding EC. The uneven demographic distribution between the sexes, both in terms of the total number of individuals and age distribution, seem to have played an important role in this outcome. There is only one significant EC difference between EBA and MBA individuals, which is related to left arm extension movement. However, this finding is far from sufficient evidence to show activity differences between the two periods. Taking into account the burial type variables, only individuals from simple inhumations revealed some changes of the hip-related entheses, while the rest showed no changes at all. This finding suggests that individuals from simple inhumations may have participated more regularly in physically demanding activities, especially those involving the overuse of hip-related muscles. Additional studies can be conducted using other methods to support these preliminary results with more data and statistics.

A further limitation originates from the method used in this study. The new Coimbra Method is advised, as an appropriate and useful method, for assessing EC. However, this method was developed and tested in relatively modern and well-preserved skeletal assemblages. It has been demonstrated that the Coimbra Method indicates the most specific recording criteria and the lowest general trends of EC scores among similar standard methods (Perez-Arzak et al. 2022). In a relatively large sample population with good skeletal preservation, and where we can distinguish individuals according to specific occupations based on archaeological or written sources, this method is likely to yield good results. However, we do not encounter such osteoarchaeological assemblages very often. Most assemblages from relatively early periods, such as our sample population, usually have a small sample size, naturally fragmentary skeletal remains, and there is no or little other evidence about individuals' occupations. Archaeological artefacts and literary sources from Kültepe indicate some activities related to the manufacturing and merchandising of metal and textile products (Kulakoğlu 2011) and grinding grain for women (Michel 2020). However, it is problematic to distinguish personal identities/occupations based on grave goods or literary sources alone. The grave goods may cause ambiguous interpretations due to many multiple burials or disturbed ones. It should also not be forgotten that grave goods may not directly indicate personal identity, but carry symbolic meanings.

This study marks the first trial of activity-related research on the Kültepe Bronze Age population. In the future, other promising methods can be applied to study activity-related skeletal changes, such as more advanced statistical tools (e.g. multivariate analysis), cross-sectional bone geometry, and quantitative 3D-based methods. Another research proposal would be to examine EC in the Hellenistic and Roman period skeletons from the Lower Town and compare the results with those from the Bronze Age population to investigate the diachronic differences in activity patterns between these periods. Meanwhile, the possibility of enlarging the sample size is probable as excavation at the site continues, which may also further help to advance these studies.

Acknowledgements

We thank Dr Benjamin Irvine for English language editing. We are also grateful to Prof. Dr Cécile Michel for her valuable comments and suggestions on our paper. This study was funded by 'Türkiye Bilimsel ve Teknolojik Araştırma Kurumu (TÜBİTAK)' under project no. 219Z060, and by 'Anadolu Üniversitesi Bilimsel Araştırma Projeleri (BAP)' under project no. 2106E083.

Bibliography

Alonso-Llamazares, Carmen; Lopez, Belen & Pardiñas, Antonio F.
2022 'Sex Differences in the Distribution of Entheseal Changes: Meta-analysis of Published Evidence and its Use in Bayesian Paleopathological Modeling', *American Journal of Biological Anthropology* 177/2: 249–65.

Alves Cardoso, F. & Henderson, Charlotte Y.
2010 'Enthesopathy Formation in the Humerus: Data from Known Age-at-Death and Known Occupation Skeletal Collections', *American Journal of Physical Anthropology* 141/4: 550–60.

Anderson, Christian N.
2016 'Iliopsoas: Pathology, Diagnosis, and Treatment', *Clinics in Sports Medicine* 35/3: 419–33.

Bird, Paul A.; Oakley, Stephen P.; Shnier, Ron & Kirkham, Bruce W.
2001 'Prospective Evaluation of Magnetic Resonance Imaging and Physical Examination Findings in Patients with Greater Trochanteric Pain Syndrome', *Arthritis & Rheumatism: Official Journal of the American College of Rheumatology* 44/9: 2138–45.

Brooks, Sheilagh & Suchey, Judy M.
1990 'Skeletal Age Determination Based on the Os Pubis: A Comparison of the Acsádi-Nemeskéri and Suchey-Brooks Methods', *Human Evolution* 5: 227–38.

Buikstra, Jane E. & Ubelaker, Douglas (eds)
1994 *Standards for Data Collection from Human Skeletal Remains* (Arkansas Archaeological Survey Research Series 44). Arkansas Archaeological Survey, Fayetteville.

Canosa-Carro, Lorena; Bravo-Aguilar, Maria; Abuin-Porras, Vanesa; Almazan-Polo, Jaime; Garcia-Perez-de-Sevilla, Guillermo; Rodriguez-Costa, Isabel; Lopez-Lopez, Daniel; Navarro-Flores, Emmanuel & Romero-Morales, Carlos
2022 'Current Understanding of the Diagnosis and Management of the Tendinopathy: An Update from the Lab to the Clinical Practice', *Disease-a-Month* 68/10: 101314.

Carballo-Pérez, Jared & Schrader, Sarah A.
2023 'Embodied Labors during the State Formation of Egypt and Nubia (ca. 4800–1750 BCE): Elucidating Transformations in Behavioral Patterns with Entheseal Changes', *International Journal of Osteoarchaeology*: 1–17.

Dutour, Olivier
1986 'Enthesopathies (Lesions of Muscular Insertions) as Indicators of the Activities of Neolithic Saharan Populations', *American Journal of Physical Anthropology* 71/2: 221–24.

Eshed, Vered; Gopher, Avi; Galili, Ehud & Hershkovitz, Israel
2004 'Musculoskeletal Stress Markers in Natufian Hunter-Gatherers and Neolithic Farmers in the Levant: The Upper Limb', *American Journal of Physical Anthropology* 123/4: 303–15.

Grimaldi, Alison & Fearon, Angela
2015 'Gluteal Tendinopathy: Integrating Pathomechanics and Clinical Features in its Management', *Journal of Orthopaedic & Sports Physical Therapy* 45/11: 910–22.

Grimaldi, Alison; Mellor, Rebecca; Hodges, Paul; Bennell, Kim; Wajswelner, Henry & Vicenzino, Bill
2015 'Gluteal Tendinopathy: A Review of Mechanisms, Assessment and Management', *Sports Medicine* 45: 1107–19.

Havelková, Petra; Villotte, Sébastien; Velemínský, Petr; Poláček, L. & Dobisíková, Miluše
2011 'Enthesopathies and Activity Patterns in the Early Medieval Great Moravian Population: Evidence of Division of Labour', *International Journal of Osteoarchaeology* 21/4: 487–504.

Hawkey, Diane E. & Merbs, Charles F.
1995 'Activity-Induced Musculoskeletal Stress Markers (MSM) and Subsistence Strategy Changes among Ancient Hudson Bay Eskimos', *International Journal of Osteoarchaeology* 5/4: 324–38.

Henderson, Charlotte Y.; Mariotti, Valentina; Pany-Kucera, Doris; Villotte, Sébastien & Wilczak, Cynthia
2013 'Recording Specific Entheseal Changes of Fibrocartilaginous Entheses: Initial Tests Using the Coimbra Method', *International Journal of Osteoarchaeology* 23/2: 152–62.
2016 'The New "Coimbra Method": A Biologically Appropriate Method for Recording Specific Features of Fibrocartilaginous Entheseal Changes', *International Journal of Osteoarchaeology* 26: 925–32.

Henderson, Charlotte Y.; Mariotti, Valentina; Santos, Frederic; Villotte, Sébastien and Wilczak, Cynthia A.
2017b 'The New Coimbra Method for Recording Entheseal Changes and the Effect of Age-at-Death', *Bulletins et mémoires de la Société d'anthropologie de Paris* 29/3–4: 140–49.

Henderson, Charlotte Y. & Nikita, Efthymia
2016 'Accounting for Multiple Effects and the Problem of Small Sample Sizes in Osteology: A Case Study Focussing on Entheseal Changes', *Archaeological and Anthropological Sciences* 8/4: 805–17.

Henderson, Charlotte Y.; Wilczak, Cynthia & Mariotti, Valentina
2017a 'Commentary: An Update to the New Coimbra Method for Recording Entheseal Changes', *International Journal of Osteoarchaeology* 27/3: 521–22.

İşcan, M. Yaşar; Loth, Susan R. & Wright, Ronald K.
1984 'Age Estimation from the Rib by Phase Analysis: White Males', *Journal of Forensic Sciences* 29/4: 1094–1104.
1985 'Age Estimation from the Rib by Phase Analysis: White Females', *Journal of Forensic Sciences* 30/3: 853–63.

Jafarnia, Kourosh; Gabel, Gerard T. & Morrey, Bernard F.
2001 'Triceps Tendinitis', *Operative Techniques in Sports Medicine* 9/4: 217–21.

Johnston, Christopher A. M.; Wiley, J. Preston; Lindsay, David M. & Wiseman, David A.
1998 'Iliopsoas Bursitis and Tendinitis: A Review', *Sports Medicine* 25: 271–83.

Jurmain, Robert; Alves Cardoso, Francisca; Henderson, Charlotte & Villotte, Sébastien
2012 'Bioarchaeology's Holy Grail: The Reconstruction of Activity', in Anne L. Grauer (ed.), *A Companion to Paleopathology*. Wiley-Blackwell, Chichester: 531–52.

Kale, Donald; Üstündağ, Handan; Özen, Semih & Özgü, Doruk C.
2023 'Testing the Guidelines of the New Coimbra Method for Recording Entheseal Changes via Interobserver Agreement in a Bronze Age Skeletal Sample from Kültepe-Kanesh, Türkiye', *International Journal of Osteoarchaeology* 33/3: 479–88.

Karakostis, Fotios A. & Harvati, Katerina
2021 'New Horizons in Reconstructing Past Human Behavior: Introducing the "Tübingen University Validated Entheses-Based Reconstruction of Activity" Method', *Evolutionary Anthropology: Issues, News, and Reviews* 30/3: 185–98.

Knüsel, Christopher
2000 'Bone Adaptation and its Relationship to Physical Activity in the Past', in Margaret Cox & Simon Mays (eds), *Human Osteology in Archaeology and Forensic Science*. Cambridge University Press, Cambridge: 381–401.

Kulakoğlu, Fikri
2011 'Kültepe-Kaneš: A Second Millennium B.C.E. Trading Center on the Central Plateau', in Sharon R. Steadman & Gregory McMahon (eds), *The Oxford Handbook of Ancient Anatolia*. Oxford University Press, Oxford: 1012–30.

Landis, J. Richard & Koch, Gary G.
1977 'The Measurement of Observer Agreement for Categorical Data', *Biometrics* 33/1: 159–74.

Lovejoy, C. Owen; Meindl, Richard S.; Pryzbeck, Thomas R. & Mensforth, Robert P.
1985 'Chronological Metamorphosis of the Auricular Surface of the Ilium: A New Method for the Determination of Adult Skeletal Age at Death', *American Journal of Physical Anthropology* 68/1: 15–28.

Mariotti, Valentina; Facchini, Fiorenzo and Belcastro, Maria G.
2004 'Enthesopathies – Proposal of a Standardized Scoring Method and Applications', *Collegium antropologicum* 28/1: 145–59.
2007 'The Study of Entheses: Proposal of a Standardised Scoring Method for Twenty-Three Entheses of the Postcranial Skeleton', *Collegium antropologicum* 31/1: 291–313.

Meyer, Christian; Nicklisch, Nicole; Held, Petra; Fritsch, Barbara & Alt, Kurt W.
2011 'Tracing Patterns of Activity in the Human Skeleton: An Overview of Methods, Problems, and Limits of Interpretation', *Homo* 62/3: 202–17.

Michel, Cécile
2020 *Women of Assur and Kanesh: Texts from the Archives of Assyrian Merchants*. SBL Press, Atlanta.

Michopoulou, Efrossyni; Nikita, Efthymia & Henderson, Charlotte Y.
2017 'A Test of the Effectiveness of the Coimbra Method in Capturing Activity-Induced Entheseal Changes', *International Journal of Osteoarchaeology* 27/3: 409–17.

Michopoulou, Efrossyni; Nikita, Efthymia & Valakos, Efstratios D.
2015 'Evaluating the Efficiency of Different Recording Protocols for Entheseal Changes in Regards to Expressing Activity Patterns Using Archival Data and Cross-Sectional Geometric Properties', *American Journal of Physical Anthropology* 158/4: 557–68.

Milella, Marco; Alves Cardoso, Francisca; Assis, Sandra; Perréard Lopreno, Geneviève & Speith, Nivien
2015 'Exploring the Relationship between Entheseal Changes and Physical Activity: A Multivariate Study', *American Journal of Physical Anthropology* 156/2: 215–23.

Milella, Marco; Belcastro, Maria G.; Zollikofer, Christoph P. & Mariotti, Valentina
2012 'The Effect of Age, Sex, and Physical Activity on Entheseal Morphology in a Contemporary Italian Skeletal Collection', *American Journal of Physical Anthropology* 148/3: 379–88.

Molnar, Petra
2006 'Tracing Prehistoric Activities: Musculoskeletal Stress Marker Analysis of a Stone-Age Population on the Island of Gotland in the Baltic Sea', *American Journal of Physical Anthropology* 129/1: 12–23.
2010 'Patterns of Physical Activity and Material Culture on Gotland, Sweden, during the Middle Neolithic', *International Journal of Osteoarchaeology* 20/1: 1–14.

Niinimäki, Sirpa
2012 'The Relationship between Musculoskeletal Stress Markers and Biomechanical Properties of the Humeral Diaphysis', *American Journal of Physical Anthropology* 147/4: 618.

Özgüç, Tahsin
2005 *Kültepe/Kaniš-Neša*. Yapı ve Kredi Bankası Yayınları, Ankara.

Perez-Arzak, Uxue; Villotte, Sébastien; Arrizabalaga, Alvaro & Trancho, Gonzalo J.
2022 'Looking for the Most Suitable Method for the Study of Entheseal Changes: Application to Upper Limb's Fibrocartilaginous Entheses in a Human Medieval Sample', *International Journal of Osteoarchaeology* 32/3: 595–606.

Phenice, Terrell
1969 'A Newly Developed Visual Method of Sexing in the Os Pubis', *American Journal of Physical Anthropology* 30: 297–301.

Robb, John E.
1998 'The Interpretation of Skeletal Muscle Sites: A Statistical Approach', *International Journal of Osteoarchaeology* 8/5: 363–77.

Ruff, Christopher; Holt, Brigitte, & Trinkaus, Erik
2006 'Who's Afraid of the Big Bad Wolff?: "Wolff's Law" and Bone Functional Adaptation', *American Journal of Physical Anthropology* 129: 484–98.

Santana-Cabrera, Jonathan
2011 'El trabajo fosilizado: patrón cotidiano de actividad física y organización social del trabajo en la Gran Canaria prehispánica' (unpublished doctoral thesis, Universidad de Las Palmas de Gran Canaria).

Santana-Cabrera, Jonathan; Velasco-Vázquez, Javier & Rodríguez-Rodríguez, Amelia
2015 'Entheseal Changes and Sexual Division of Labor in a North-African Population: The Case of the Pre-Hispanic Period of the Gran Canaria Island (11th–15th c. CE)', *Homo* 66/2: 118–38.

Schrader, Sarah A.
2015 'Elucidating Inequality in Nubia: An Examination of Entheseal Changes at Kerma (Sudan)', *American Journal of Physical Anthropology* 156/2: 192–202.

Standring, Susan (ed.)
2021 *Gray's Anatomy E-book: The Anatomical Basis of Clinical Practice.* Elsevier Health Sciences, Amsterdam.

Üstündağ, Handan
2009 'Kültepe/Kanesh (Turkey), Season 2007', *Bioarchaeology of the Near East* 3: 31–35.
2014 'Human Remains from Kültepe-Kanesh: Preliminary Results of the Old Assyrian Burials from the 2005–2008 Excavations', in Levent Atıcı, Fikri Kulakoğlu, Gojko Barjamovic & Andrew Fairbairn (eds), *Current Research at Kültepe-Kanesh: An Interdisciplinary and Integrative Approach to Trade Networks, Internationalism, and Identity* (Journal of Cuneiform Studies Supplemental Series 4). Lockwood, Atlanta: 157–76.

Villotte, Sébastien
2006 'Connaissances médicales actuelles, cotation des enthésopathies: Nouvelle méthode', *Bulletins et mémoires de la société d'anthropologie de Paris* 18/1–2: 65–85.
2023 'Activity-Related Skeletal Changes', in *Reference Module in Social Sciences*. Elsevier: 892–900. <https://doi.org/10.1016/B978-0-323-90799-6.00016-1>.

Villotte, Sébastien & Santos, Frédéric
2023 'The Effect of Age on Entheseal Changes: A Study of Modifications at Appendicular Attachment Sites in a Large Sample of Identified Human Skeletons', *International Journal of Osteoarchaeology*: 1–13.

Villotte, Sébastien; Castex, Dominique; Couallier, Vincent; Dutour, Olivier; Knüsel, Christopher J. & Henry-Gambier, Dominique
2010 'Enthesopathies as Occupational Stress Markers: Evidence from the Upper Limb', *American Journal of Physical Anthropology: The Official Publication of the American Association of Physical Anthropologists* 142/2: 224–34.

Visco, Christopher J. & Rittenberg, Joshua D.

2010 'Iliopsoas Tendinopathy', in William Micheo (ed.), *Musculoskeletal, Sports and Occupational Medicine*. Demos, New York: 104–05.

Weiss, Elizabeth

2003 'Understanding Muscle Markers: Aggregation and Construct Validity', *American Journal of Physical Anthropology* 121/3: 230-40.

2007 'Muscle Markers Revisited: Activity Pattern Reconstruction with Controls in a Central California Amerind Population', *American Journal of Physical Anthropology: The Official Publication of the American Association of Physical Anthropologists* 133/3: 931–40.

Weiss, Elizabeth; Corona, Leslie & Schultz, Bobbie

2012 'Sex Differences in Musculoskeletal Stress Markers: Problems with Activity Pattern Reconstructions', *International Journal of Osteoarchaeology* 22/1: 70–80.

11. Reconstructing Bronze Age Diet from Stable Isotopes Analysis

Preliminary Results from Kültepe-Kaneš

Kameray Özdemir, Handan Üstündağ, Turhan Doğan, Furkan Kulak & Fikri Kulakoğlu

Introduction

The reconstruction of the dietary habits of past populations has attracted the interest and attention of researchers from various fields, including archaeologists and anthropologists. They often utilize different sources of knowledge to obtain traces of past human dietary habits, such as historical written or visual documents and sources, archaeological findings connected with food processing and cooking, faunal and botanical remains from sites, pathological investigations of individual human bones and dentition, and biochemical analysis of food residues and human remains such as stomach contents and coprolites (Keegan 1989; Larsen 1997; 2018; Katzenberg & Waters-Rist 2018; Papathanasiou & Richards 2015). Although these sources are all valuable for reconstructing past dietary habits, they tend to only supply indirect evidence (Keegan 1989; Larsen 1997). More direct evidence, however, can come from bone biogeochemical composition analysis since their accumulation patterns often demonstrate a relation with the consumed food sources (DeNiro & Epstein 1978; Schoeninger & DeNiro 1984; Sandford 1992; Larsen 2018; Lee-Thorp 2008; Schwarcz & Schoeninger 2011). Therefore, the determination of the relative ratio and proportion of elements and stable isotopes — for example, stable isotopes of carbon (C) and nitrogen (N) — within bones can reflect the sources of dietary input over the lifetime of individuals and help us to understand variations at intra- and inter-population levels (Faure & Mensing 2005; Fernandes et al. 2012; Lee-Thorp 2008; Pollard et al. 2007; Schwarcz & Schoeninger 2011; Szpak et al. 2013).

Stable carbon and nitrogen isotope analysis applied to bulk bone collagen is the most commonly utilized isotopic method in paleodiet reconstruction studies. Stable isotope analysis from bulk bone collagen provides direct evidence of dietary protein sources in the last c. 10 years average 'before death' (Richards et al. 2003). The basic principles of this method rely on the fact that characteristic ratios of stable isotopes of carbon ($^{13}C/^{12}C$, expressed relative to an international standard as $\delta^{13}C$ values) and nitrogen ($^{15}N/^{14}N$, expressed relative to an international standard as $\delta^{15}N$ values) are found between both different food types and different consumers, and accumulate in human bodies with some fractionation due to their trophic levels (Faure & Mensing 2005; Lee-

Kameray Özdemir (kameray.ozdemir@hacettepe.edu.tr) Department of Anthropology, Faculty of Letters, Hacettepe University, Ankara

Handan Üstündağ (hustundag@anadolu.edu.tr) Department of Archaeology, Faculty of Humanities, Anadolu University, Eskişehir

Turhan Doğan (turhandogan@hotmail.com) TÜBİTAK-Marmara Araştırma Merkezi, İklim Değişikliği ve Sürdürülebilirlik Başkan Yardımcılığı, Gebze-Kocaeli

Furkan Kulak (furkan.kulak@tubitak.gov.tr) TÜBİTAK-Marmara Araştırma Merkezi, İklim Değişikliği ve Sürdürülebilirlik Başkan Yardımcılığı, Gebze-Kocaeli

Fikri Kulakoğlu (kulakoglu@ankara.edu.tr) Department of Protohistory and Near Eastern Archaeology, Faculty of Languages and History-Geography, Ankara University, Ankara

Thorp 2008; Pollard et al. 2007; Schwarcz & Schoeninger 2011).

The measurement of stable carbon isotopes from bone collagen can help to identify and distinguish the contribution of plant proteins (in human diets; either directly or via an animal vector), particularly related to whether they were plants following C_3 or C_4 photosynthetic pathways (DeNiro & Epstein 1978; DeNiro 1985; Faure & Mensing 2005; Fernandes et al. 2012; Papathanasiou 2015; Pollard et al. 2007; Schwarcz & Schoeninger 2011; Szpak et al. 2013). C_3 plants include temperate grasses, all trees and shrubs, all fruits and nuts, and cultivated roots and tubers, which constitute the majority of flora of Europe and Anatolia (Hoefs 2009; Still et al. 2003; Richards et al. 2003). They have $δ^{13}C$ values ranging from approximately -35‰ to -26‰ (Ambrose 1986; 1993; DeNiro 1987; Katzenberg 2000). However, C_4 plants are more commonly arid-adapted plants and grasses, such as sorghum and millet, with $δ^{13}C$ values around -12‰ (Herrscher et al. 2018; Miller et al. 2016; Murphy 2016; Nesbitt & Summers 1988; Riehl 2009). Sorghum and millet are common C_4 domestic cultivars from the 'Old World' — specifically originating in East Asia before moving westwards and there is, currently, no evidence that they were cultivated in Anatolia in the early second millennium BC. Wild C_4 grasses do grow in Anatolia though (Herrscher et al. 2018; Irvine et al. 2019; Richards et al. 2003; Rudov et al. 2020). Stable carbon isotope ratios can also be used to investigate the proportional contribution of marine and terrestrial protein sources to dietary intake, particularly when examined in conjunction with stable nitrogen isotope values (Schoeninger & DeNiro 1984; Papathanasiou 2015; Pollard et al. 2007).

Stable nitrogen isotope ratios from bone collagen reflect the trophic level of an organism, with a fractionation factor of about 2.5–3‰ per trophic step (Schoeninger & DeNiro 1984; Müldner & Richards 2005; Faure & Mensing 2005; Pollard et al. 2007). An estimation as to whether an individual's dietary input came mostly from plant or animal sources can be made as $δ^{15}N$ values are usually always lower in plants than animals. Therefore, due to the fractionation effects up the food web, an individual with a predominantly vegetarian diet will have lower $δ^{15}N$ values than an individual with a mixed plant-animal diet, and particularly lower than an individual whose main dietary input came from animal proteins (Schoeninger & DeNiro 1984; Faure & Mensing 2005; Pollard et al. 2007). Furthermore, due to the step-wise trophic enrichment of $δ^{15}N$ values, marine (and to a certain extent freshwater, although there is a significant overlap between terrestrial and freshwater $δ^{15}N$ values) environments produce higher $δ^{15}N$ values than terrestrial ones as they often have more trophic levels (i.e. more chance for trophic enrichment of $δ^{15}N$). Organisms towards the top of marine ecosystems, or humans consuming mostly marine food sources can have $δ^{15}N$ values *c.* 16±2‰, whilst in freshwater ecosystems they can be *c.* 12±2‰ respectively (Schoeninger & DeNiro 1984; Budd et al. 2013). Thus, $δ^{15}N$ values in an individual, and population, can be useful for examining potential, and relative, contributions of marine and freshwater resources in the dietary habits (Schoeninger & DeNiro 1984; Ambrose 1986; Minagawa & Wada 1984; Katzenberg 2000). Stable nitrogen isotope ratios can also be used to examine sociocultural variation, such as examining breastfeeding patterns and the weaning process (Katzenberg et al. 1996; Dupras & Tocheri 2007). To a certain extent, the type of plant material (beyond simply C_3 or C_4 plants) can be hypothesized with legumes having lower $δ^{15}N$ values (due to them being nitrogen fixers) than non-legume plants (Keegan 1989; Katzenberg 1992).

Stable carbon and nitrogen isotope analysis from bulk bone collagen has been applied in order to investigate and greater understand subsistence behaviour of past people globally. A growing body of research has focused on sample populations from Anatolia in the last couple of decades (Richards et al. 2003; Lösch et al. 2006; 2014; Pearson et al. 2010; Fuller et al. 2012; Budd et al. 2013; Benz et al. 2016; Pickard et al. 2016; 2017; Itahashi et al. 2017; 2021; Özdemir 2018; Özdemir et al. 2019; Irvine et al. 2019; 2020; Iacumin et al. 2020). Stable isotope research has provided information on almost all time periods in Türkiye, from the Epipaleolithic to the Middle Byzantine period with a predominant focus on the Neolithic and Early Bronze Age periods (Irvine & Özdemir 2020). Up to now, however, no Anatolian Middle Bronze Age population's dietary habits have been thoroughly examined isotopically or published yet. Thus, with Kaneš being an important Middle Bronze Age centre, it is the ideal place to conduct isotopic research to investigate past dietary habits; allowing us to contribute in a meaningful way to our understanding not only of the settlement and its inhabitants, but also more generally of dietary habits and subsistence practices in ancient Anatolia.

Table 11.1: List of Kültepe samples for carbon and nitrogen analysis.

Number	Skeleton Code	Genus/Species	Number	Skeleton Code	Genus/Species
1	KT'06-10	*Homo sapiens*	37	KT'13-25	*Homo sapiens*
2	KT'07-79-2	*Homo sapiens*	38	KT'13-26-1	*Homo sapiens*
3	KT'07-84-4	*Homo sapiens*	39	KT'13-26-2	*Homo sapiens*
4	KT'08-34-2/3	*Homo sapiens*	40	KT'13-27-1	*Homo sapiens*
5	KT'08-36-1	*Homo sapiens*	41	KT'13-27-2	*Homo sapiens*
6	KT'08-36-2	*Homo sapiens*	42	KT'13-27-3	*Homo sapiens*
7	KT'10-1	*Homo sapiens*	43	KT'13-27-5/6	*Homo sapiens*
8	KT'13-1	*Homo sapiens*	44	KT'13-28-1	*Homo sapiens*
9	KT'13-2	*Homo sapiens*	45	KT'13-30-1	*Homo sapiens*
10	KT'13-3	*Homo sapiens*	46	KT'13-30-2	*Homo sapiens*
11	KT'13-4	*Homo sapiens*	47	KT'13-30-5	*Homo sapiens*
12	KT'13-5	*Homo sapiens*	48	KT'17-2-1	*Homo sapiens*
13	KT'13-6	*Homo sapiens*	49	KT'17-14	*Homo sapiens*
14	KT'13-7-1	*Homo sapiens*	50	KT'17-1-1	*Homo sapiens*
15	KT'13-7-2	*Homo sapiens*	51	KT'17-8-1	*Homo sapiens*
16	KT'13-7-3	*Homo sapiens*	52	KT'18-3	*Homo sapiens*
17	KT'13-8	*Homo sapiens*	53	KT'19-2	*Homo sapiens*
18	KT'13-9	*Homo sapiens*	54	KT'19-3	*Homo sapiens*
19	KT'13-10	*Homo sapiens*	55	KT'20-2	*Homo sapiens*
20	KT'13-11	*Homo sapiens*	56	KT'20-3	*Homo sapiens*
21	KT'13-12-1	*Homo sapiens*	57	KT'20-4	*Homo sapiens*
22	KT'13-12-2	*Homo sapiens*	58	KT'20-5	*Homo sapiens*
23	KT'13-13-1	*Homo sapiens*	59	KT'20-6	*Homo sapiens*
24	KT'13-15-1	*Homo sapiens*	60	KT'20-7-1	*Homo sapiens*
25	KT'13-15-2	*Homo sapiens*	61	KT'20-7-2	*Homo sapiens*
26	KT'13-16-1	*Homo sapiens*	62	KT'20-11	*Homo sapiens*
27	KT'13-16-2	*Homo sapiens*	63	KT'20-14	*Homo sapiens*
28	KT'13-17	*Homo sapiens*	64	KT'20-15	*Homo sapiens*
29	KT'13-18	*Homo sapiens*	65	KT'20-16-1	*Homo sapiens*
30	KT'13-19-1	*Homo sapiens*	66	2018 Dog 1	*Canidae*
31	KT'13-21	*Homo sapiens*	67	2018 Dog 2	*Canidae*
32	KT'13-23-1	*Homo sapiens*	68	2018 Dog 3	*Canidae*
33	KT'13-23-2	*Homo sapiens*	69	2017 Sheep/Goat 1	*Ovis/Capra*
34	KT'13-24-1	*Homo sapiens*	70	2008 Sheep/Goat 2	*Ovis/Capra*
35	KT'13-24-2	*Homo sapiens*	71	2017 Sheep/Goat 3	*Ovis/Capra*
36	KT'13-24-3	*Homo sapiens*	72	2020 Sheep/Goat 4	*Ovis/Capra*

This study was carried out within the scope of a research project supported by TÜBITAK, which started in 2020 and is still ongoing. The aim of this project, which is called 'A Multidisciplinary Analysis of the Biological and Social Structure of the Kültepe-Kaneš Population', is to better understand the intra-population variations by examining the skeletal remains found at Kültepe with different bioarchaeological methods. Stable isotope analysis is one of the methods employed by the project with the primary aim of investigating the dietary habits of the Bronze Age population at Kaneš. This paper presents the preliminary results of stable carbon and nitrogen isotope analysis of humans and associated animal remains from the Early Bronze Age (EBA) to Middle Bronze Age (MBA) contexts (third and second millennia BC) at Kültepe. In addition to the characterization of dietary habits, this study also aims to explore potential sociocultural internal variations in dietary habits; i.e. by sex or age group, etc.

Materials

Kültepe is located in central Anatolia in the province of Kayseri. Excavations at Kültepe have been undertaken since its discovery in the late nineteenth century, and since 2005 they have been continued under the direction of Fikri Kulakoğlu (Ankara University). Together, the mound and the Lower Town constitute the site of Kültepe. The mound has eighteen cultural levels, with the earliest occupation of the mound beginning during the EBA. It was the seat of the regional Anatolian administrative centre and residence. The Lower Town was inhabited during the MBA and consists of four cultural levels. The Lower Town was the centre of the trade network between Anatolia and northern Mesopotamia in the first quarter of the second millennium BC and was a place where merchants lived and traded (called a *kārum*). The site appears to have been unoccupied during the Late Bronze Age, but resettled in the Iron Age. The last cultural levels at Kültepe belong to the Hellenistic and Roman periods (Özgüç 2005; Kulakoğlu 2011).

The skeletal remains analysed in this study were recovered from both the mound and the Lower Town and date to the EBA and MBA. The EBA individuals (more precisely EBA III, dated to between 2350–2020 cal BC) were recovered during the 2017–2020 excavation seasons. The MBA individuals were recovered during the 2005–2013 excavation seasons mainly from levels Ia/Ib (dated to 1750–1690 cal BC) of the Lower Town, with only a few coming from the mound. Individuals were buried under the floors of buildings or in open areas and, in most cases, were accompanied by mortuary objects. There were three main burial types employed at the site; simple inhumations, stone cists, and jars. The anthropological examinations of the skeletal remains were conducted by Handan Üstündağ (for skeletal remains recovered between 2005 and 2008 see Üstündağ 2009; 2014).

A total of seventy-two samples were sent to the Earth and Marine Sciences Institute of the TÜBİTAK Marmara Research Centre for stable carbon and nitrogen isotope analysis (Table 11.1). Sixty-five of these samples were from humans and seven of them from animals. Four of the animal samples are from sheep/goat, with the other three being from dogs.

Twenty-nine (out of the total sample population of fifty-seven human samples) are from adults, whilst twenty-eight samples came from sub-adults. Studies into past human dietary habits utilizing stable isotope analyses are generally performed on adult individuals (>fifteen years of age) so as to prevent any confusion in interpretation of the isotopic values due to the weaning process, or any potential discreet dietary habits and patterns in childhood. The distribution of adult individuals by sex and age group is presented in Table 11.2.

Table 11.2: Distribution of Kültepe samples according to the variables used in the study (samples that do not meet the collagen quality criteria are not included). N: number of samples.

Variables	Sub-variables	N
Age Groups	Young Adult	12
	Middle Adult	11
	Old Adult	6
	Total Adult (age ≥15)	29
	Total Subadult (age <15)	28
Sex (Adult)	Female	18
	Male	8
	Unknown	3

The sample population consists of twelve Young Adult (YA), ten Middle Adult (MA), and seven Old Adult (OA) individuals. Of the twenty-nine sampled adult individuals eighteen are female and eight are male individuals, with the sex of three of the individuals being undetermined (Table 11.2).

Methods

Collagen Extraction and Isotopic Analysis

Collagen extraction and stable isotope analysis was conducted at the National 1MV AMS Laboratory of Türkiye, housed in the Earth and Marine Science Institute at the TÜBİTAK-Marmara Research Centre in Gebze (Doğan et al. 2021). The bone samples were first subjected to physical cleaning including washing with pure water and a brush, washing in an ultrasonic bath, and sandblasting, after which they were cut with a handheld drill. Collagen was extracted following the protocol described by Doğan et al. (2023). Bone samples were demineralized in 1 M HCl. The samples were then gelatinized at 70 °C for twelve hours and this was then filtered and freeze-dried to obtain collagen samples. Macromolecules over 30,000 Dalton were collected with an ultrafiltration step (Brown et al. 1988) before freeze-drying. Approximately 1 mg of collagen (for $\delta^{13}C$ and $\delta^{15}N$) was weighed into tin capsules (4 × 6 mm) before being run through the stable isotope ratio mass spectrometer. Carbon and nitrogen isotope analysis of pre-weighed collagen samples was undertaken by Elemental Analysis – Isotope Ratio Mass Spectrometry (the Europa Scientific 20–20 IRMS).

All stable isotope values in this study are given in parts per mil (‰) and the isotopic ratios are relative to the appropriate standards; V-PDB for $\delta^{13}C$ and AIR for $\delta^{15}N$ (Schoeninger & DeNiro 1984).

Sex and Age-at-Death Estimation

Sex and age-at-death estimation of the human skeletons was made by H. Üstündağ using standard osteological methods. Morphological characteristics of the pelvis and cranium were used for sex estimation (Phenice 1969; Buikstra & Ubelaker 1994). For estimating the age-at-death, pubic symphysis morphology (Brooks & Suchey 1990), sternal rib end changes (İşcan et al. 1984; 1985), and dental attrition (Lovejoy et al. 1985) were used. The sample population was grouped into three age categories following Buikstra & Ubelaker (1994) young adults (twenty–thirty-four years), middle adults (thirty-five–forty-nine years), and old adults (fifty years and older).

Statistics

The statistical analysis covers the descriptive statistics (mean, standard deviation, minimum and maximum values), t test ($p < 0.05$), and analysis of variance (ANOVA) in order to recognize variation in subgroups.

Results

Quality Criteria and Collagen Preservation

Biological diagenesis, as well as being exposed to physical and chemical changes over time in the burial environment affects archaeological bones. Therefore, the obtained collagen sometimes reflects contaminant values.

It is well established that collagen with atomic C:N ratio values lower than 2.9 or higher than 3.6 is altered, contaminated, or affected by diagenesis and should be discarded from future study (DeNiro 1985; however, see also Guiry & Szpak 2021). Furthermore, collagen yields above 2 per cent are considered to have good collagen preservation. If the other quality criteria (comparison of C:N ratio and nitrogen value) of the samples with a collagen yield between 1 per cent and 2 per cent are within acceptable limits, it should be considered that the collagen is intact (Ambrose & Norr 1993).

Samples that do not meet the quality criteria were excluded from further analysis and statistical evaluations. Considering the collagen quality criteria mentioned above, eight human samples and one animal sample did not meet the collagen quality criteria and were discarded from further investigation.

Adult Humans and Local Fauna

The $\delta^{13}C$ values of all adult individuals range from -19.51‰ to -18.32‰ (mean = -18.86 ± 0.30‰, see Tables 11.3 and 11.4). The $\delta^{15}N$ values range between 8.86‰ and 11.58‰ (mean = 10.46±0.69‰, see Tables 11.3 and 11.4). The analysed isotope values plot in a narrow range (Fig. 11.1) with the difference between the highest and lowest $\delta^{13}C$ values being 1.19‰, and for $\delta^{15}N$ the calculated range of values is 2.72‰.

Sample 'Sheep/Goat 4' has the lowest $\delta^{15}N$ (5.93‰) and $\delta^{13}C$ (-20.08‰) values of the sampled fauna (Table 11.3). As can be seen from Table 11.3, 'Sheep/Goat 2' and 'Sheep/Goat 3' have relatively high $\delta^{15}N$ values (the expected $\delta^{15}N$ value for terrestrial C_3 herbivores, especially for sheep/goats is usually around 5 to 6‰). The $\delta^{13}C$ values of the three dogs analysed are close to -18‰, while the $\delta^{15}N$ values cluster around 9‰ (Table 11.3), and the dogs plot close to the humans (Fig. 11.1).

Sex and Age Groups

The stable carbon and nitrogen isotope values of the sex and age groups are presented in Figures 11.2 and 11.3 and

Table 11.3: $\delta^{13}C(‰)$ and $\delta^{15}N(‰)$ results of Kültepe adult human and animal samples. EBA: Early Bronze Age; MBA: Middle Bronze Age.

Number	Skeleton Code	Sex	Age Group	Time Period	Burial Place	$\delta^{13}C(‰)$	$\delta^{15}N(‰)$	C(%)	N(%)	C:N
1	KT'10-1	Male	Middle Adult	MBA	Tepe	-18.93	9.69	44.6	15.9	3.0
2	KT'13-5	Male	Old Adult	MBA	Lower Town	-19.31	9.36	43.2	15.5	3.0
3	KT'13-8	Female	Young Adult	MBA	Lower Town	-18.95	10.24	43.7	16.2	2.9
4	KT'13-11	Female	Young Adult	MBA	Lower Town	-19.00	9.18	44.7	16.1	3.0
5	KT'13-12-1	Male	Young Adult	MBA	Lower Town	-18.48	10.95	42.8	15.8	2.9
6	KT'13-12-2	Male	Middle Adult	MBA	Lower Town	-18.60	10.84	43.1	15.9	2.9
7	KT'13-15-1	Male	Middle Adult	MBA	Lower Town	-18.78	10.64	46.0	16.9	2.9
8	KT'13-15-2	Female?	Young Adult	MBA	Lower Town	-18.32	11.08	43.3	15.8	2.9
9	KT'13-16-1	Female	Young Adult	MBA	Lower Town	-18.86	10.11	42.5	15.4	3.0
10	KT'13-21	Female	Old Adult	MBA	Lower Town	-18.77	9.55	43.4	15.9	2.9
11	KT'13-24-1	Female	Old Adult	MBA	Lower Town	-19.14	10.16	45.7	16.9	2.9
12	KT'13-24-3	Male	Young Adult	MBA	Lower Town	-18.46	11.58	44.4	16.2	2.9
13	KT'13-26-1	Male	Middle Adult	MBA	Lower Town	-18.96	10.63	43.7	16.2	2.9
14	KT'13-27-1	Female	Old Adult	MBA	Lower Town	-18.84	10.99	43.9	16.1	2.9
15	KT'13-27-2	Female	Old Adult	MBA	Lower Town	-18.80	11.24	46.2	17.1	2.9
16	KT'13-27-3	Female	Young Adult	MBA	Lower Town	-19.02	10.26	45.8	16.9	2.9
17	KT'13-30-1	Unknown	Middle Adult	MBA	Tepe	-18.51	11.17	43.5	16.3	2.9
18	KT'13-30-2	Female	Middle Adult	MBA	Tepe	-18.82	10.73	43.5	16.1	2.9
19	KT'13-30-5	Unknown	Old Adult	MBA	Tepe	-18.53	11.07	44.3	16.4	2.9
20	KT'17-14	Female	Middle Adult	EBA	Tepe	-18.99	8.86	44.1	16.5	2.9
21	KT'17-1-1	Female	Middle Adult	EBA	Tepe	-19.26	10.84	43.9	16.4	2.9
22	KT'18-3	Male?	Young Adult	EBA	Tepe	-18.78	10.88	45.5	16.3	3.0
23	KT'19-2	Female	Middle Adult	EBA	Tepe	-18.90	10.00	44.2	16.6	2.9
24	KT'20-2	Female	Middle Adult	EBA	Tepe	-19.30	10.59	45.5	17.1	2.9
25	KT'20-3	Female	Middle Adult	EBA	Tepe	-18.45	10.78	43.9	16.2	2.9
26	KT'20-4	Female	Young Adult	EBA	Tepe	-19.51	10.41	45.8	17.0	2.9
27	KT'20-7-1	Female	Young Adult	EBA	Tepe	-19.16	10.22	43.1	16.0	2.9
28	KT'20-14	Unknown	Young Adult	EBA	Tepe	-18.46	11.43	45.5	16.9	2.9
29	KT'20-16-1	Female	Young Adult	EBA	Tepe	-19.07	9.74	42.1	15.7	2.9
30	2018 Dog 1	-	-	-	-	-18.39	9.34	42.1	15.7	2.9
31	2018 Dog 2	-	-	-	-	-18.02	9.07	42.9	16.1	2.9
32	2018 Dog 3	-	-	-	-	-18.42	9.72	42.9	15.8	2.9
33	2008 Sheep/Goat 2	-	-	-	-	-18.56	8.68	43.1	15.9	2.9
34	2017 Sheep/Goat 3	-	-	-	-	-19.31	7.33	42.6	15.9	2.9
35	2020 Sheep/Goat 4	-	-	-	-	-20.08	5.93	41.5	15.5	2.9

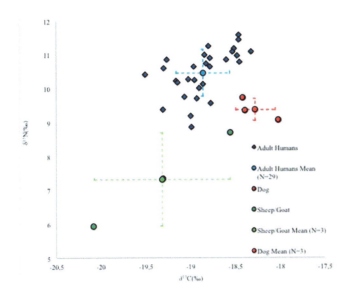

Figure 11.1: Adult individuals and local fauna scatter plot graph. Mean values with standard deviation.

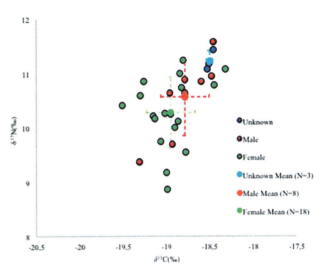

Figure 11.2: Scatter plot graph by sex groups. Mean values with standard deviation.

are summarized in Table 11.4. Male and female means for $\delta^{13}C$ were -18.79‰±0.28‰ and -18.95‰±0.28‰, respectively. For $\delta^{15}N$, the means of males and females are 10.28‰±0.65‰ and 10.57‰±0.65‰, respectively. The mean values for both $\delta^{13}C$ and $\delta^{15}N$ are very similar between the sexes. There is no statistically significant difference between the means of male and female individuals (*t* test, $p = 0.182$ for $\delta^{13}C$, $p = 0.310$ for $\delta^{15}N$). The standard deviation for $\delta^{15}N$ is higher than the standard deviation of $\delta^{13}C$ for both sexes. The $\delta^{15}N$ values of the three individuals whose sex could not be determined are the highest values in the sample population.

Variation in stable carbon and nitrogen isotope values according to age groups coincides with the picture revealed by examining differences between the sexes. The mean values for both isotope ratios are very close to each other between age groups. The standard deviation of $\delta^{15}N$ is higher than for $\delta^{13}C$, and there are no statistically significant differences between the means (ANOVA, $p = 0.647$ for $\delta^{13}C$, $p = 0.167$ for $\delta^{15}N$).

Discussion

When the isotope values of all analysed adults are evaluated together, it is possible to say that the dietary habits of the sampled population are mixed but predominantly indicates a C_3-based terrestrial diet (Ambrose 1993; Schoeninger & DeNiro 1984). However, high $\delta^{15}N$ values indicate significant protein input in the diets of individuals, likely through the consumption of terrestrial animal protein (Camin et al. 2008; Irvine & Erdal 2020).

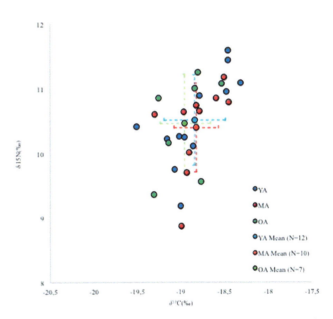

Figure 11.3: Scatter plot graph by age groups. Mean values with standard deviation. YA: Young Adult; MA: Middle Adult; OA: Old Adult.

The adult sample population $\delta^{13}C$ values are also close to the -18‰ threshold that indicates a greater consumption of C_4 plants (Richards et al. 2003; Lösch et al. 2006; 2014; Fuller et al. 2012; Pickard et al. 2016; Propstmeier et al. 2017). In this case, the reason for these values is likely due to the consumption of herbivorous animals that consume/graze on wild C_4 plants, given the period to which the population is dated — there is currently no evidence for the cultivation of C_4 crops in the Early to Middle Bronze Ages in Anatolia (Herrscher et al. 2018; Miller et al. 2016; Murphy 2016; Nesbitt & Summers 1988;

Table 11.4: Descriptive statistics of Kültepe carbon and nitrogen results according to the studied variables. N: number of samples; SD: standard deviation value; Max.: maximum value; Min.: minimum value.

Variable	Subvariable	δ^{13}C(‰)					δ^{15}N(‰)			
		N	Mean	SD	Max.	Min.	Mean	SD	Max.	Min.
Age Group	Young Adult	12	-18.84	0.35	-18.32	-19.51	10.51	0.70	11.58	9.18
	Middle Adult	10	-18.82	0.25	-18.45	-19.30	10.39	0.68	11.17	8.86
	Old Adult	7	-18.95	0.08	-18.53	-19.31	10.46	0.77	11.24	9.36
	Total	29	-18.86	0.30	-18.32	-19.51	10.46	0.69	11.58	8.86
Sex	Female	18	-18.95	0.28	-18.32	-19.51	10.28	0.65	11.24	8.86
	Male	8	-18.79	0.28	-18.46	-19.31	10.57	0.72	11.58	9.36
	Unknown	3	-18.50	0.04	-18.46	-18.53	11.22	0.19	11.43	11.07
Animal	Herbivore	3	-19.32	0.76	-18.56	-20.08	7.31	1.38	8.68	5.93
	Omnivore	3	-18.28	0.22	-18.02	-18.42	9.38	0.33	9.72	9.07

Riehl 2009). A general homogeneity is also observed in the δ^{13}C and δ^{15}N values with the majority of the adults' isotope value ranges of 1–2‰ for δ^{13}C and 3‰ for δ^{15}N and this can be considered an indication that the adult humans in the sample population were consuming food sources from the same level in the food chain (trophic level). Therefore, the close clustering of the isotope values can be accepted as an indication that the nutritional habits of the sampled individuals, and the food sources they consume are similar. However, this is not strictly true, as δ^{13}C values provide minimal information about levels of the food chain/trophic levels. Rather the homogeneous isotopic values suggest that all sampled individuals were consuming similar food resources from similar sources — i.e. homogeneity in the isotopic values of the consumed food resources is reflected in homogeneity of the isotopic values of the consumer (human) tissues (collagen).

Although there are only three sheep/goat specimens in the faunal sample population, there is a relatively large range in their δ^{13}C and δ^{15}N values. It is difficult to interpret this reliably with such a small sample size, but the wide spread in isotopic values could be considered an indicator of different herding/feeding/herd management strategies for sheep/goats at the site. The more positive δ^{13}C value of the 'Sheep/Goat 2' sample, compared to the other sheep/goat samples, could possibly be explained by the fact that there was a contribution of (likely wild) C_4 plants in its diet, which may indicate that it was grazing/herded on grasslands away from the settlement. In other words, it could be argued that this animal was herded farther than the other two sheep/goats sampled and, therefore, is indicative of a different management strategy. However, its δ^{13}C value is not

>-18‰ meaning that it still had a significant C_3 component in its diet. This combined with its higher δ^{15}N (relative to the other sheep/goat in the sample population) may actually suggest that it was foddered or grazing on plant material (including crops) from manured (or nitrogen-rich) fields (Bogaard et al. 2007; Budd et al. 2013; Müldner et al. 2014; Irvine & Erdal 2020). This would, conversely, suggest that it was actually herded closer to the settlement than its relatively more positive δ^{13}C value would suggest. However, for now, with such a small faunal sample population and the fact that isotopic values from bulk bone collagen provide an average over an individual's lifetime, we cannot say anything with certainty and the hypotheses presented above remain only speculation. From the data that we have, it would seem that sheep/goat contributed a significant proportion of animal protein input in the dietary habits of the humans. However, as no other domestic or wild animals were sampled for this study this remains only conjecture and an initial observation.

The dogs sampled in this study have some of the most positive δ^{13}C values, and whilst plotting close to the sampled adult humans, they actually have even more positive δ^{13}C values than some of the sampled human adult individuals (Fig. 11.2). In effect, the dogs appear to have had similar dietary habits with a portion of the adult humans, perhaps even sharing food or feeding on food waste from the humans. Whilst, again, it is difficult to say this with certainty, the isotopic values of the dogs may act as a proxy for further suggesting the different management of sheep/goats (at least) if we follow the hypothesis that a large part of their protein input came from animals consuming C_4 plants. Alternatively, they may have had a protein input from wild animals from a more C_4 plant dominated environment, although this remains only speculation as we currently have no wild animal isotope values to compare them with.

No significant differences in dietary habits by sex and/or age group at Kültepe were revealed in the stable isotope data of this study. This could possibly be explained by the homogeneity of acquired dietary habits due to social group or family life. However, as Bourbou & Richards (2007) have noted, if there was any difference in diet according to sex, it may have been subtle (e.g. different cuts of meat, different proportions in meals, or priority in eating) and not detectable by isotopic analysis of bulk bone collagen.

The palynological, zoological, historical, and archaeological research conducted at Kültepe has revealed some information into subsistence strategies and animal usage. The palynological study, which investigated the vegetation and climate history of the last 2300 years, following an examination of sedimentary cores from Lake Engir near Kültepe has revealed that pine forests became dominant around Lake Engir between the years 2300 and 1930 BP (Şenkul et al. 2018). In the period known as the Beyşehir Occupation Phase (c. 1850 BP) agricultural activities were intensely performed and people cut down the pine forests to open up agricultural land and to use the wood as fuel. During this intensified agricultural period cereal species (*Cerealia*), grapes (*Vitis vinifera*), walnuts (*Juglans regia*), and olive (*Olea europaea*) were the main agricultural products (Şenkul et al. 2018). Studies on the cuneiform tablets written in an Old Assyrian dialect have revealed the exploitation of a variety of animals, including cattle, sheep, and donkeys for various uses (Atıcı 2014). The texts show that cattle, ploughs, carts, and wagons played a substantial role in both intensifying agricultural production and creating grain surpluses to feed the local population and to facilitate the political agendas of the Anatolian and Assyrian elites (Atıcı 2014).

Conclusion

The dietary habits revealed by stable isotope analysis of bulk bone collagen from the Kültepe assemblage suggest a largely C_3-based terrestrial diet. This is what would have been expected following the palynological, zoological, historical, and archaeological information from the site. There was no isotopic evidence for sex or age group-based variation in the dietary habits of the sample population. This is consistent with many similar studies within Anatolia (Irvine et al. 2019); however, sex-based variation in diet, not observable in the isotopic values, cannot be ruled out entirely and this must be taken into account when considering the limitations that accompany stable isotope analysis. Although it is too early to definitively say whether this reflects a true representation of dietary patterns at Kaneš, more analysis needs to be done on the dataset for further conclusions to be drawn.

Future Perspectives

This preliminary assessment of the stable isotope data is based on the analysis of twenty-nine human adult individuals. The small sample size has limited the statistical analysis. To overcome this issue, the stable carbon and nitrogen isotopes results of another, independent, study done on the Kültepe skeletons will be evaluated together for future investigations. Following this, the statistical analyses will be reassessed. The scope of the study will also evolve to investigate variations in isotopic values and indicated dietary habits with relation to social structure. Potential variations within the sample will also be examined by performing Principal Components Analysis and Hierarchical Cluster Analysis. Deep sequencing (aDNA) results and previously conducted strontium (Sr) isotope analysis will also be evaluated together with the principal components and clustering analyses to further investigate variations and social status within the Bronze Age population of Kaneš. The number of animal samples will also be increased to gain a better understanding of animal management strategies at Kaneš in the Bronze Age.

Acknowledgements

This study was supported by the Turkish Scientific and Technical Research Council (TÜBITAK- 1001 project number: 219Z060). The authors would like to thank to Dr Benjamin Irvine for his valuable comments on and interpretations of the data, and for editing the English edition of the text. The authors would also like to thank to Donald Kale, Semih Özen, and Doruk Cafer Özgü from Anadolu University for their help with collecting the bone samples. Data is available on request from the corresponding author.

Bibliography

Ambrose, Stanley H.

1986 'Stable Carbon and Nitrogen Isotope Analysis of Human and Animal Diet in Africa', *Journal of Human Evolution* 15/8: 707–31.

1993 'Isotopic Analysis of Paleodiets: Methodological and Interpretive Considerations', in Mary K. Sandford (ed.), *Investigations of Ancient Human Tissue: Chemical Analyses in Anthropology*. Langhorne: Gordon and Breach: 59–130.

Ambrose, Stanley H. & Norr, Lynette

1993 'Experimental Evidence for the Relationship of the Carbon Isotope Ratios of Whole Diet and Dietary Protein to Those of Bone Collagen and Carbonate', in Joseph B. Lambert & Gisela Grupe (eds), *Prehistoric Human Bone: Archaeology at the Molecular Level*. Springer, Berlin: 1–37

Atıcı, Levent

2014 'The Secondary Products Revolution in Light of Textual Evidence from Kültepe/Kanesh, Central Turkey', in Haskel J. Greenfield (ed.), *Animal Secondary Products: Domestic Animal Exploitation in Prehistoric Europe, the Near East and the Far East*. Oxbow, Oxford: 233–52.

Benz, Marion; Fecher, Marc; Scheeres, Mirjam; Alt, Kurt W.; Erdal, Yılmaz S.; Şahin, Feridun & Özkaya, Vecihi

2016 'Results of Stable Isotopes from Körtik Tepe Southeastern Turkey', *Arkeometri Sonuçları Toplantısı* 31: 231–52.

Bogaard, Amy; Heaton, Tim H. E.; Poulton, Paul & Merbach, Ines

2007 'The Impact of Manuring on Nitrogen Isotope Ratios in Cereals: Archaeological Implications for Reconstruction of Diet and Crop Management Practices', *Journal of Archaeological Science* 34/3: 335–43.

Bourbou, Chryssa & Richards, M. Phillip

2007 'The Middle Byzantine Menu: Palaeodietary Information from Isotopic Analysis of Humans and Fauna from Kastella, Crete', *International Journal of Osteoarchaeology* 17/1: 63–72.

Brooks, Sheilagh & Suchey, Judy M.

1990 'Skeletal Age Determination Based on the Os Pubis: A Comparison of the Acsádi-Nemeskéri and Suchey-Brooks Methods', *Human Evolution* 5: 227–38.

Brown, Thomas A.; Nelson, D. Erle; Vogel, John S. & Southon, John R.

1988 'Improved Collagen Extraction by Modified Longin Method', *Radiocarbon* 30/2: 171–77.

Budd, Chelsea; Lillie, Malcolm C.; Alpaslan-Roodenberg, Songül; Karul, Necmi & Pinhasi, Ron

2013 'Stable Isotope Analysis of Neolithic and Chalcolithic Populations at Aktopraklık, Northern Anatolia', *Journal of Archaeological Science* 40: 860–67.

Buikstra, Jane E. & Ubelaker, Douglas (eds)

1994 *Standards for Data Collection from Human Skeletal Remains* (Arkansas Archaeological Survey Research Series 44). Arkansas Archaeological Survey, Fayetteville.

Camin, Federica; Perini, Matteo; Colombari, Gianni; Bontempo, Luana & Versini, Giuseppe

2008 'Influence of Dietary Composition on the Carbon, Nitrogen, Oxygen and Hydrogen Stable Isotope Ratios of Milk', *Rapid Communications in Mass Spectrometry* 22: 1690–96.

DeNiro, Michel J.

1985 'Postmortem Preservation and Alteration of *in vivo* Bone Collagen Isotope Ratios in Relation to Paleodietary Reconstruction', *Nature* 317: 806–09.

1987 'Stable Isotopy and Archaeology', *American Scientist* 75: 182–91.

DeNiro, Michel J. & Epstein, Samuel
1978 'Influence of Diet on the Distribution of Carbon Isotopes in Animals', *Geochimica et cosmochimica acta* 42: 495–506.

Doğan, Turhan; İlkmen, Erhan & Kulak, Furkan
2021 'A New National 1 MV AMS Laboratory at TÜBİTAK MRC in Turkey, Nuclear Instruments and Methods in Physics Research Section B', *Beam Interactions with Materials and Atoms* 509: 48–54.
2023 'Radiocarbon Analysis and Status Report from Türkiye: 1mv National Ams Laboratory (TUBITAK-AMS)', *Radiocarbon* 65/2: 375–88.

Dupras, Tosha L. & Tocheri, Matthew W.
2007 'Reconstructing Infant Weaning Histories at Roman Period Kellis, Egypt Using Stable Isotope Analysis of Dentition', *American Journal of Physical Anthropology: The Official Publication of the American Association of Physical Anthropologists* 134/1: 63–74.

Faure, Gunter & Mensing, Teresa M.
2005 *Isotopes Principles and Applications*, 3rd edn. Wiley, Hoboken.

Fernandes, Ricardo; Nadeau, Marie-Josée & Grootes, Pieter M.
2012 'Macronutrient-Based Model for Dietary Carbon Routing in Bone Collagen and Bioapatite', *Archaeological and Anthropological Sciences* 4: 291–301.

Fuller, Benjamin T.; Du Cupere, Bea; Marinova, Elena; Van Neer, Win; Waelkens, Marc & Richards, Michael P.
2012 'Isotopic Reconstruction of Human Diet and Animal Husbandry Practices during the Classical-Hellenistic, Imperial, and Byzantine Periods at Sagalassos, Turkey', *American Journal of Physical Anthropology* 149: 157–71.

Guiry, Eric J. & Szpak, Paul
2021 'Improved Quality Control Criteria for Stable Carbon and Nitrogen Isotope Measurements of Ancient Bone Collagen', *Journal of Archaeological Science* 132: 105–416.

Herrscher, Estelle; André, Guy; Bodet, Catherina; Chataigner, Christine; Decaix, Alexia; Goude, Gwenaëlle; Hamon, Caroline; Le Mort, Françoise; Lyonnet, Bertille; Martin, Lucie; Messager, Erwan; Oberlin, Chritine; Ollivier, Vincet; Poulmarc'h, Modwene; Sermet, Christian & Vila, Emmanuelle
2018 'The Origins of Millet Cultivation in the Caucasus: Archaeological and Archaeometric Approaches', *Préhistoires Méditerranéennes* 6 <doi.org/10.4000/pm.1367>.

Hoefs, Jochen
2009 *Stable Isotope Geochemistry*, 6th edn. Springer, Berlin.

Iacumin, Paola; Di Matteo, Antonietta; Macrì, Antonella & Galli, Elisa
2020 'Late Chalcolithic Population in Arslantepe: Stable Isotope Reconstruction of Diet and Subsistence Strategies', *Origini* 44: 51–64.

Irvine, Benjamin & Erdal, Yılmaz S.
2020 'Analysis of Dietary Habits in a Prehistoric Coastal Population (İkiztepe, North Anatolia), Using Stable Isotopes of Carbon, Nitrogen, and Sulphur', *Journal of Archaeological Science: Reports* 29: 102067.

Irvine, Benjamin; Erdal, Yılmaz S. & Richards, Michael P.
2019 'Dietary Habits in the Early Bronze Age (3rd Millennium BC) of Anatolia: A Multi-isotopic Approach', *Journal of Archaeological Science: Reports* 24: 253–63.

Irvine, Benjamin & Özdemir, Kameray
2020 'Biogeochemical Approaches to Bioarchaeological Research in Turkey: A Review', *Journal of Eastern Mediterranean Archaeology & Heritage Studies* 8/2: 174–99.

İşcan, M. Yaşar; Loth, Susan R. & Wright, Ronald K.
1984 'Age Estimation from the Rib by Phase Analysis: White Males', *Journal of Forensic Sciences* 29/4: 1094–1104.
1985 'Age Estimation from the Rib by Phase Analysis: White Females', *Journal of Forensic Sciences* 30/3: 853–63.

Itahashi, Yu; Miyake, Yutaka; Maeda, Osamu; Kondo, Osoma; Hongo, Hitomi; Van Neer, Win; Chikaraishi, Yoshito; Ohkouchi, Naohiko & Yoneda, Minoru
2017 'Preference for Fish in a Neolithic Hunter-Gatherer Community of the Upper Tigris, Elucidated by Amino Acid δ 15 N Analysis', *Journal of Archaeological Science* 82: 40–49.

Itahashi, Yu; Stiner, Mary C.; Erdal, Omur Dilek; Duru, Güneş; Erdal, Yılmaz S.; Miyake, Yutaka; Güral, Demet; Yoneda, Minoru & Özbaşaran, Mihriban
2021 'The Impact of the Transition from Broad-Spectrum Hunting to Sheep Herding on Meat Consumption: Multi-isotopic Analyses of Human Bone Collagen at Aşıklı Höyük, Turkey', *Journal of Archaeological Science* 136: 105505.

Katzenberg, M. Anne
1992 'Advances in Stable Isotope Analysis of Prehistoric Bones', in Shelley R. Saunders & M. Anne Katzenberg (eds), *Skeletal Biology of Past Peoples: Research Methods*. Wiley-Liss, New York: 105–19.
2000 'Stable Isotope Analysis: A Tool for Studying Past Diet, Demography, and Life History', in M. Anne Katzenberg & Shelley R. Saunders (eds), *Biological Anthropology of the Human Skeleton*. Wiley-Liss, New York: 305–28.

Katzenberg, M. Anne; Herring, D. Ann & Saunders, Shelley R.
1996 'Weaning and Infant Mortality: Evaluating the Skeletal Evidence', *American Journal of Physical Anthropology: The Official Publication of the American Association of Physical Anthropologists* 101(S23): 177–99.

Katzenberg, M. Anne & Waters-Rist, Andrea L.
2018 'Stable Isotope Analysis: A Tool for Studying Past Diet, Demography, and Life History', in M. Anne Katzenberg & Anne L. Grauer (eds), *Biological Anthropology of the Human Skeleton*. Wiley-Liss, New York: 467–504.

Keegan, William F.
1989 'Stable Isotope Analysis of Prehistoric Diet', in M. Yaşar İşcan & Kenneth A. R. Kennedy (eds), *Reconstruction of Life from the Skeleton*. Liss, New York: 223–36.

Kulakoğlu, Fikri
2011 'Kültepe-Kaneš: A Second Millennium B.C.E. Trading Center on the Central Plateau', in Sharon R. Steadman & Gregory McMahon (eds), *The Oxford Handbook of Ancient Anatolia*. Oxford University Press, Oxford: 1012–30.

Larsen, Clark S.
1997 *Bioarchaeology: Interpreting Behavior from the Human Skeleton*. Cambridge University Press, Cambridge.
2018 'Bioarchaeology in Perspective: From Classifications of the Dead to Conditions of the Living', *American Journal of Biological Anthropology* 165: 865–78.

Lee-Thorp, Julia A.
2008 'On Isotopes and Old Bones', *Archaeometry* 50: 925–50.

Lösch, Sandra; Grupe, Gisela & Peters, Joris
2006 'Stable Isotopes and Dietary Adaptations in Human and Animals at Pre pottery Neolithic Nevalı Çori, Southeast Anatolia', *American Journal of Physical Anthropology* 131: 181–93.

Lösch, Sandra; Moghaddam, Negahnaz; Grossschmidt, Karl; Risser, Daniele U. & Kanz, Fabian
2014 'Stable Isotopes and Trace Element Studies on Gladiators and Contemporary Romans from Ephesus (Turkey, 2nd and 3rd, Ct. AD) – Implications for Differences in Diet', *PLOS ONE* 9/10: 1–17.

Lovejoy, C. Owen; Meindl, Richard S.; Pryzbeck, Thomas R. & Mensforth, Robert P.
1985 'Chronological Metamorphosis of the Auricular Surface of the Ilium: A New Method for the Determination of Adult Skeletal Age at Death', *American Journal of Physical Anthropology* 68/1: 15–28.

Miller, Naomi F.; Spengler, Robert N. & Frachetti, Michael
2016 'Millet Cultivation across Eurasia: Origins, Spread, and the Influence of Seasonal Climate', *The Holocene* 26/10: 1566–75.

Minagawa, Masao & Wada, Eitaro
1984 'Stepwise Enrichment of 15N Along Food Chains: Further Evidence and the Relation between $\delta^{15}N$ and Animal Age', *Geochimica et cosmochimica acta* 48: 1135–40.

Müldner, Gundula; Britton, Kate & Ervynck, Anton
2014 'Inferring Animal Husbandry Strategies in Coastal Zones through Stable Isotope Analysis: New Evidence from the Flemish Coastal Plain (Belgium, 1st–15th Century AD)', *Journal of Archaeological Science* 41: 322–32.

Müldner, Gundula & Richards, Michaell P.
2005 'Fast or Feast: Reconstructing Diet in Later Medieval England by Stable Isotope Analysis', *Journal of Archaeological Science* 32: 39–48.

Murphy, Charlene
2016 'Finding Millet in the Roman World', *Archaeological and Anthropological Sciences* 8: 65–78.

Nesbitt, Mark & Summers, Geoffrey D.
1988 'Some Recent Discoveries of Millet (*Panicum miliaceum* L. and *Setaria* (L.) P. Beauv.) at Excavations in Turkey and Iran', *Anatolian Studies* 38: 85–97.

Özdemir, Kameray
2018 'Bizans Dönemi Kovuklukaya Topluluğunun (Boyabat, Sinop) Beslenme Alışkanlıklarının Yeniden Yapılandırılması: Sabit İzotop Oranı Analizlerinin Öncül Sonuçlari', *Hitit Üniversitesi Sosyal Bilimler Enstitüsü Dergisi* 11/2: 1155–75.

Özdemir, Kameray; Erdal, Yılmaz S.; Itahashi, Yu & Irvine, Benjamin
2019 'A Multi-faceted Approach to Weaning Practices in a Prehistoric Population from Ikiztepe, Samsun, Turkey', *Journal of Archaeological Science: Reports* 27: 101982.

Özgüç, Tahsin
2005 *Kültepe/Kaniš-Neša*. Ankara, Yapı ve Kredi Bankası Yayınları.

Papathanasiou, Anastasia & Richards, Michael P.
2015 'Summary: Patterns in the Carbon and Nitrogen Isotope Data through Time', in Anastasia Papathanasiou, Michael P. Richards & Sherry C. Fox (eds), *Archaeodiet in the Greek World: Dietary Reconstruction from Stable Isotope Analysis*. American School of Classical Studies at Athens, Princeton: 195–203

Pearson, Jessica A.; Hedges, Robert E. M.; Molleson, Theya I. & Özbek, Metin
2010 'Exploring the Relationship between Weaning and Infant Mortality: An Isotope Case Study from Aşikli Höyük and Çayönü Tepesi', *American Journal of Physical Anthropology* 143: 448–57.

Phenice, Terrell
1969 'A Newly Developed Visual Method of Sexing in the Os Pubis', *American Journal of Physical Anthropology* 30: 297–301.

Pickard, Catriona; Caldeira, Claudia; Harten, Ninke; Schoop, Ulf-Dietrich; Üstündağ, Handan; Bartosiewicz, Laszlo & Schachner, Andreas

2017 'Reconstructing Iron Age to Roman Period Diet from Bioarchaeological Remains: Preliminary Results from Boğazköy, North-Central Anatolia', in Andreas Schachner (ed.), *Innovation versus Beharrung: Was macht den Unterschied des hethitischen Reichs im Anatolien des 2. Jahrtausends v. Chr.?* Istanbul: Ege Yayınları: 239-55.

Pickard, Catriona; Schoop, Ulf-Dietrich; Dalton, Alan; Sayle, Kerry L.; Channell, Ian; Calvey, Kevin; Thomas, Jayne-Leigh; Bartosiewicz, Laszlo & Bonsall, Clive

2016 'Diet at Late Chalcolithic Çamlıbel Tarlası, North-Central Anatolia: An Isotopic Perspective', *Journal of Archaeological Science* 5: 296-306.

Pollard, Mark; Batt, Catherine; Stern, Ben & Young, Suzanne M. M.

2007 *Analytical Chemistry in Archaeology.* Cambridge University Press, Cambridge.

Propstmeier, Johanna; Nehlich, Olaf; Richards, Michael P.; Grupe, Gisela; Müldner, Gundula & Teegen, Wolf-Rüdiger

2017 'Diet in Roman Pergamon: Preliminary Results Using Stable Isotope (C, N, S), Ostearchaeological and Historical Data', in J. Rasmus Brandt, Erica Hagelberg, Gro Bjørnstad & Sven Ahrens (eds), *Life & Death in Asia Minor in Hellenistic, Roman & Byzantine Times: Studies in Archaeology & Bioarchaeology.* Oxbow, Oxford: 237-49.

Richards, Micheal P.; Pearson, Jessica A.; Molleson, Theya I.; Russell, Nerissa & Martin, Louise

2003 'Stable Isotope Evidence of Diet at Neolithic Çatalhöyük, Turkey', *Journal of Archaeological Science* 30: 67-76.

Riehl, Simone

2009 'Archaeobotanical Evidence for the Interrelationship of Agricultural Decision-Making and Climate Change in the Ancient Near East', *Quaternary International* 197: 93-114.

Rudov, Alexander; Mashkour, Marjan; Djamali, Morteza & Akhani, Hossein

2020 'A Review of C_4 Plants in Southwest Asia: An Ecological, Geographical and Taxonomical Analysis of a Region with a High Diversity of C_4 Eudicots', *Frontiers in Plant Science* 11: 546518.

Sandford, Mary K.

1992 'A Reconsideration of Trace Element Analysis in Prehistoric Bone', in M. Anne Katzenberg & Shelley R. Saunders (eds), *Biological Anthropology of the Human Skeleton.* Wiley-Liss, New York: 79-103.

Schoeninger, Margaret J. & DeNiro, Michel J.

1984 'Nitrogen and Carbon Isotopic Composition of Bone Collagen from Marine and Terrestrial Animals', *Geochimica et cosmochimica acta* 48: 625-39.

Schwarcz, Henry P. & Schoeninger, Margaret J.

2011 'Stable Isotopes of Carbon and Nitrogen as Tracers for Paleo-Diet Reconstruction', in Baskaran Mark (ed.), *Handbook of Environmental Isotope Geochemistry*, I. Springer, Heidelberg: 725-42.

Still, Christopher J.; Berry, Joseph A.; Collatz, James G. & DeFries, Ruth S.

2003 'Global Distribution of C_3 and C_4 Vegetation: Carbon Cycle Implications', *Global Biogeochemical Cycles* 7/1: 1006-13.

Szpak, Paul; White, Christine D.; Longstaffe, Fred J.; Millaire, Jean François & Vasquez, Sanchez Victor F.

2013 'Carbon and Nitrogen Isotopic Survey of Northern Peruvian Plants: Baselines for Paleodietary and Paleoecological Studies', *PLoS One* 8/1: 1-28.

Şenkul, Çetin; Ören, Aziz; Doğan, Uğur & Eastwood, Warren John

2018 'Late Holocene Environmental Changes in the Vicinity of Kültepe (Kayseri), Central Anatolia, Turkey', *Quaternary International* 486: 107-15.

Üstündağ, Handan

2009 'Kültepe/Kanesh (Turkey), Season 2007', *Bioarchaeology of the Near East* 3: 31–35.

2014 'Human Remains from Kültepe-Kanesh: Preliminary Results of the Old Assyrian Burials from the 2005–2008 Excavations', in Levent Atıcı, Fikri Kulakoğlu, Gojko Barjamovic & Andrew Fairbairn (eds), *Current Research at Kültepe-Kanesh: An Interdisciplinary and Integrative Approach to Trade Networks, Internationalism, and Identity* (Journal of Cuneiform Studies Supplemental Series 4). Lockwood, Atlanta: 157–76.

12. Of Lions and Sheep: Animal Exploitation at Kültepe and in Central Anatolia during the Middle Bronze Age

New Data from Recent Excavations

Fikri Kulakoğlu, Luca Peyronel & Claudia Minniti

Introduction

This paper aims to present the preliminary results of the analysis of animal remains retrieved at Kültepe in the south-western sector of the mound and associated with a large semi-subterranean building, labelled the Stone Building, dated to the late Middle Bronze Age. Since 2019, excavations have restarted in this part of the ancient town with the main objective of investigating the sequence of occupation spanning from the late third millennium BC to the Iron Age (Kulakoğlu & Peyronel 2022). Previous archaeological research conducted in the fifties and sixties of the last century brought to light a large stone-paved square, the so-called Palace on the Southern Terrace, and a ceremonial precinct with two allegedly sacred buildings with a series of ancillary structures, datable between the very end of the third and the beginning of the second millennia BC (phases 10–17 of the mound roughly corresponding with the phases II and Ib of the Lower Town, Özgüç 1999).

Immediately to the west of the southernmost temple (Temple II), a monumental stone building has been discovered by the team of the University of Milan, consisting of two adjacent underground chambers, (Kulakoğlu & Peyronel 2023; Kulakoğlu & Peyronel in this volume). A large number of vessels including two exceptional pithoi with applied reliefs have been found in the fillings over the rooms together with a huge number of animal remains. The building is preserved only in the basement, serving as a warehouse, and must have had at least an upper floor of which no traces remain. The presence of fillings rich in materials over the collapsed layers have been considered a probable ritual closure of the building that might have happened shortly after the sudden collapse of the structures, possibly in relation to a natural event such as an earthquake, although the hypothesis needs further elements to be confirmed. The pottery retrieved in all the stratigraphy associated with the building is completely homogeneous and attributable to a late horizon of the Middle Bronze Age sequence, indicatively datable to the eighteenth century BC, also on the basis of ceramic comparisons and radiocarbon datings. The monumental building therefore seems connected to the adjacent sacred area, and can be framed in the last phase of occupation of the site immediately preceding its abandonment at the turn of the eighteenth and seventeenth centuries.

Fikri Kulakoğlu (kulakoglu@yahoo.com) Director of Kültepe excavations, University of Ankara

Luca Peyronel (luca.peyronel@unimi.it) Head of the Italian Archaeological Project at Kültepe, University of Milan (Italy)

Claudia Minniti (claudia.minniti@uniroma1.it) Zooarchaeologist of the Italian Archaeological Project at Kültepe, Sapienza University of Rome (Italy)

Material and Method

The animal remains coming from multiple layers associated with the Stone Building's filling, collapsed structures, and floor levels are here preliminarily discussed together, to gain detailed information on the husbandry practices and the animal exploitation at Kültepe in the eighteenth century BC. The sample is particularly significant due to its excellent preservation.

All animal remains were identified, but the mammal and bird remains were recorded and counted in the quantification analysis according to a selective diagnostic zone recording protocol (Davis 1992; Albarella & Davis 1994); all parts of the skeletons were instead used in the ageing analysis. The scientific nomenclature of domestic animals refers to Gentry et al. (2004).

The sheep/goat distinction was attempted using the criteria described in Boessneck (1969), Kratochvil (1969), Payne (1985), Halstead et al. (2002), Zeder & Lapham (2010), and Zeder & Pilaar (2010). Horse was differentiated from donkey and hybrids according to Davis (1980) and Johnstone (2004). Pigs and wild boars were sexed on the basis of canines and canine alveoli shape. Information on the state of epiphyseal fusion for all long bones was undertaken using Silver (1969) for cattle, Bull & Rackham (1982) for caprines, and Bull & Payne (1982) for pigs. Wear stages were recorded following Grant (1982) for cattle mandibular, Grant (1982), Bull & Payne (1982) for pig teeth, Payne (1973; 1987) for sheep/goats mandibular. Measurements of bones were taken following the criteria described in Albarella & Davis (1994), Albarella & Payne (2005), Davis (1992), von den Driesch (1976), and Payne & Bull (1988).

Discussion

Species Frequency

Over 4400 animal remains, corresponding to c. two-thirds of the entire sample collected so far, were identified according to class, species, anatomical element, sex, and age. The results document that most animal remains are from mammals; the other animal classes that were identified, such as birds, fish, reptiles, and molluscs were represented by a lower number of finds (Table 12.1).

Table 12.1: Numbers of identified animal remains (NISP) per species.

Species	NISP
Horse — *Equus cab.*	29
Donkey — *Equus as.*	2
Equids — *Equus* sp.	6
Cattle — *Bos taurus*	1408.5
Goat — *Capra hircus*	163.5
Sheep — *Ovis aries*	725.25
Caprines — *Ovis/Capra*	1636.5
Pig — *Sus domesticus*	111.5
Dog — *Canis familiaris*	29
Red deer — *Cervus elaphus*	63
Mouflon — *Ovis orientalis*	6
Bezoar — *Capra aegagrus*	3
Wild boar — *Sus scrofa*	12.25
Bear — *Ursus arctos*	4.5
Hyena — *Hyaena hyaena*	1
Wolf — *Canis lupus*	1
Fox — *Vulpes vulpes*	34.5
Marten — *Martes/Foina*	1
?Lion — *Panthera* sp.	8.75
Beaver — *Castor fiber*	1
Hare — *Lepus capensis*	31.5
Birds — Aves ind.	34
Tortoise — *Testudo* sp.	2
Fish — Pisces ind.	1
Sea Molluscs — Mollusca ind.	146
Freshwater Molluscs — Mollusca ind.	5
Total identified	**4466.75**
Ribs	2087
Vertebrae	1133
Total	**7686.75**

Domestic Species

The remains of the main domestic animals exploited as food source, cattle, sheep, goats, and pigs, are predominant in the sample with the 95 per cent of identified rests. In addition to them, dog and equid remains have been also identified. Wild species are present with a certain variability but are less in number, with only 5 per cent of identified remains.

Sheep and goats dominate the sample with 62 per cent of the remains of the three main categories, while cattle follow with 35 per cent of remains. Pig remains have been identified, but this species is very rarely represented with only 3 per cent of remains. These results reflect what is commonly found in the samples from the Lower Town previously investigated at Kültepe: the main domestic mammals dominate the two samples coming from the Lower Town (*kārum*) level II (Atici 2014), where the sample from the houses is formed in order of importance by the remains of caprines (64 per cent), cattle (31 per cent), and pigs (5 per cent). The sample from the streets is comprised of a higher percentage of caprine remains (87 per cent), followed by those of cattle (10.6 per cent) and pigs (2.5 per cent). Similar frequencies were also observed in other Middle and Late Bronze sites of Anatolia such as e.g. at Ḫattuša (Hollenstein & Middea 2016), where various faunal samples were collected in the Square Buildings of the valley west of Sarıkale, the Lower City (von den Driesch & Boessneck 1981), Büyükkaya (von den Driesch & Pöllath 2004), and Kesikkaya (Adcock 2020), at Çadır Höyük (Arbuckle 2009; Adcock 2020), and at Kaman-Kalehöyük (Hongo 1996; Atici 2003; 2006).

In the sample found at Kültepe in the Middle Bronze Age monumental Stone Building, the proportion of cattle that had reached skeletal maturity before death was high. According to the epiphyseal fusion analysis, 75 per cent of cattle bones belonged to animals that reached and exceeded the third year of age. They were slaughtered only in a secondary stage, between the first and the third year of age (23 per cent), and very few animals (2 per cent) did not pass the first year of life. Tooth wear stage analysis, performed on 150 mandibles, confirms the mentioned results, but shows a major percentage of adult and elderly cattle and a minor percentage of young animals. All these data suggest that cattle were mainly used as draught and ploughing animals and slaughtered in adult age after the exploitation for secondary products (milk in case of females and traction power). The interest in beef production for which young and immature animals are usually exploited was minor.

Among caprines, the vast majority of remains were identified as sheep with a ratio of 4:1. Mortality data derived from the analysis of epiphysial fusion of bones show that caprines were mainly after their third year of life (66 per cent), and secondarily between the first and the third years (27 per cent) and before one year of age (6 per cent).

The results of tooth wear stage are more significant as they allow for a separate interpretation of the use of sheep and goats, which may have been exploited for different purposes (Fig. 12.1). Sheep were exploited mainly for mutton and for wool production. Milk seems to be less important even if the exploitation of milk without killing very young lambs within two months of life (category A, according to Payne 1973) could be suggested by a high mortality rate from two to four years (categories E–F, according to Payne 1973) which could include females that were culled at the period of the decrease of milk production. Goats were more exploited for meat and after prolonged use of fleece. Their exploitation in the production of dairy products remains more important than that of sheep.

The pig remains that have been found show a slaughtering pattern addressed in a balanced way to all age categories, with animals slaughtered before reaching the first year of life, presumably for obtaining tender meat, some killed between the first and the third year, in the period of achievement of the maximum meat yield, and others slaughtered after the third year of life and their use for reproduction. Both sexes are well represented in the sample.

Many worked/modified sheep and goat astragali and a few pig astragali were found in the filling layers of the Stone Building. They are usually smoothed on several sides but in two cases they have also been perforated and filled with lead. Similar finds are rather common in other MB and LBA settlements in Anatolia and the Levant, such as at Ebla, Ḫattuša, Alalakh, Ugarit (Minniti & Peyronel 2005; Hollenstein & Middea 2016, 176–77). Their interpretation is controversial, and symbolic/ritual (divination) to utilitarian functions (weights, gaming pieces) have been proposed.

Figure 12.1: Goat (above) and sheep (below) mortality profiles according to the model of Helmer et al. (2007). Age classes according to Payne (1973). Total goat mandible/teeth: 63; total sheep mandible/teeth: 361.

Wild Species

One of the most striking pieces of evidence in the sample is the occurrence of a wide variety of wild mammals. They include red deer, wild sheep and wild goat, boar, bear, hyena, wolf, fox, lion, marten, beaver, and hare. The variety of wild animal species suggests the exploitation of different habitats from foothills to mountain valleys and plateaus, to areas covered with dense forest vegetation and areas near rivers (beaver, freshwater molluscs — *Unio* sp., mallard).

Of the larger wild mammals red deer provided the greatest number of remains. Most remains belonged to non-meat-bearing parts (such as teeth, phalanges, metapodials) and therefore represent butchery waste, but some good meat-bearing parts are also represented (such as scapula, humerus, pelvis, and femur). The presence of different body parts suggest that deer hunting was with no doubt practised. A few fragments of antler with working marks and a meaningful arrowhead made of antler clearly document the practice of antler working.

Bear is also well represented by some remains belonging to two individuals. The identification of a scapula excludes the possibility that only bear furs were present, a situation which is usually supported by the linked parts of head and the extremities of legs (Fig. 12.2).

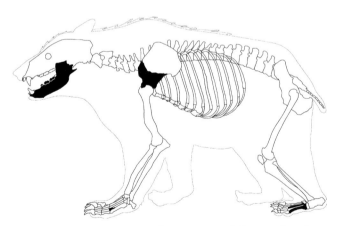

Figure 12.2: Representation of bear anatomical elements found in the monumental Stone Building at Kültepe. By Arch. Maurizio Rocca.

Among the wild bird remains that have been identified at species level so far, mallard and eagle are well documented. It is interesting to point out that eagles are mentioned several times in pre-Hittite and Hittite texts and figurative documents describing rituals or oracle acts (Görke & Kozal 2018).

Many flat oysters (*Ostrea edulis*), very few limpets (*Patella* sp.), and a specimen of sea snail belonging to the turbinate monodont (*Phorcus turbinatus*) document the arrival of sea food at Kültepe. Oysters and limpets were commonly found from both the Mediterranean Sea and the Black Sea; by contrast, the turbinate monodont is widespread only in the Mediterranean. No perforated specimens of oyster were found at Kültepe, unlike at Ḫattuša, where three valves that had been perforate are attested (Hollenstein & Middea 2016, 175). The holes made on the margins of the oyster shells can be associated with the methods of transportation and the need to preserve their freshness.

A fragment of mandible belonged to striped hyena. This animal is considered to have occurred in western Anatolia, up to the late seventies and the early eighties of the last century (Kasparek et al. 2004).

Of utmost importance is also the discovery of the remains of several big cats. Large carnivores were present in Anatolia in antiquity, most of them now extinct. In order of size from smallest to largest, these were the Eurasian lynx, the Asian cheetah, the Anatolian leopard, the Asiatic lion, and the Caspian tiger. Currently, the Asiatic cheetah is a very rare subspecies and is considered an endangered animal in central Asia (Iran), but some records from Türkiye testify its ancient presence in Anatolia (Albayrak et al. 1997; Siracusano 2012); the Anatolian leopard is the largest surviving wild cat species in Türkiye and it is still present in north-eastern Anatolia (Masseti 2007; Sarı et al. 2020).

Tigers expanded westward in central and western Asia to eastern Türkiye and eastward to the Russian Far East. The Caspian tiger had a particularly large geographical range, extending from eastern Türkiye through much of central Asia, and it was reported from the easternmost parts of Anatolia up to the seventies of the last century (Schnitzler & Hermann 2019).

Türkiye was certainly occupied by the Asiatic lion. According to some testimonies, a population of lions still occurred in southern Türkiye until the middle of the eighties, but now it is extinct almost everywhere (Kasparek 1986).

The remains (axis, two mandibles, distal humerus, two distal radius, pelvis, distal tibia, third metatarsal, third phalanx) that have been found until now at Kültepe most probably belonged to lion (Figs 12.3-12.4). A distal humerus was subjected to dating with the radiocarbon method at the Nuclear Dating and Diagnostic Centre (CEDAD) of the University of Salento (Lecce,

Italy) confirming the chronology of sample (1895–1674 cal BC at probability of 94.2 per cent). The *taxon* identification of these lion remains was made looking at the morphological characters of the bones (Onwuama et al. 2021; Sohel et al. 2021) and comparing biometric data with some metric data of African lion and leopard (derived from Plug 2014) and with those of tiger skeletons from the north-east Tibet Plateau (Ren et al. 2015). Although lion and tiger skeletons are quite similar, most of the remains from Kültepe should belong to lion. Three remains (axis, distal radius, distal tibia) were also characterized by the presence of several tiny cut marks that could be aimed at the recovery of the skin. The identification of two left mandibles and two distal radii of different size suggests the presence of at least two or three individuals of different size.

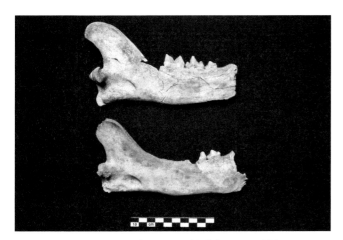

Figure 12.3: Two fragmented left lion mandibles.

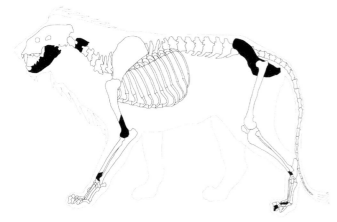

Figure 12.4: Representation of lion anatomical elements found in the monumental Stone Building at Kültepe. By Arch. Maurizio Rocca.

According to the review of finds of lion and its distribution during the Holocene made by Schnitzler (2011), other bones were found in variously dated levels of Kilise Tepe (Baker 2006), Ḫattuša, Norsuntepe (Vila 1998), Arslantepe (Bökönyi 1983; Bartosiewicz 1998) and Lidar Höyük (Vila 1998). At Ḫattuša several bones belonging to the same individual were found in the buildings in the valley west of Sarıkale and are dated to the sixteenth and fifteenth centuries BC (Hollenstein & Middea 2016, 176). A metacarpal of a lion was found in the Architectural Complex of Hirbemerdon Tepe along the River Tigris, near Diyarbakir, and is dated to the Middle Bronze Age, but is considered part of a skin that may have been imported (Berthon 2011, 74). The mandible of lion found at Kaman-Kalehöyük is instead dated to the Iron Age (phase IId, twelfth–eighth centuries BC) (Hongo 1996, 85). Schnitzler (2011) mentions the possibility that many finds may relate to imported animals from Syria. However, the hypothesis that these animals were hunted at not too great a distance from the Anatolian sites must be considered, and actually now becomes reliable considering the new evidence from Kültepe.

The archaeozoological research that has been carried out so far at the site, suggests that the variety of wild species seems to be a peculiar trait of the sample found in the Middle Bronze Age monumental Stone Building discovered in the southern sector of the Upper Town. The two samples previously studied coming from the Lower Town have yielded few remains of wild animals, corresponding to 4 per cent of the identified remains and only belonging to red deer, wild boar, and hare (Atici 2014, 203). Lions and other wild animals, such as bear, hyena, and wolf, were certainly hunted to protect humans and their livestock, but they could also be hunted for symbolic reasons. In the well-known and much discussed Anitta's text (Neu 1974) all these species are mentioned as prey of a royal hunt, following the conquest of Kaneš/Neša by the king of Kuššara, certainly describing not a utilitarian act but a strongly ideological action related to the royal power.

Conclusion

The analysis of animal remains found at Kültepe in the monumental Stone Building dated to the Middle Bronze Age allowed a preliminary outline of the animal exploitation carried out at the site during the eighteenth century BC.

The sample is represented by a high number of identified remains, offering data that are statistically significant, although preliminary, and suggesting a scenario that is partially consistent with those of other contemporary sites. The results show that the primary economy was mainly based on sheep/goat husbandry, followed by cattle, while pig husbandry had a marginal role. Sheep and goat husbandry was aimed at meat consumption and the exploitation of secondary products (mainly wool and fleece), while cattle were used mainly for ploughing. Similar results are documented in other contemporary sites of central Anatolia.

Hunting was a secondary activity, but a significant variety of wild species of animals is documented, reflecting a wide range of habitats that were exploited. Of particular interest is the presence of some species of wild animals, such as lion that could have had a particular and/or symbolic role and could be strictly linked to royal hunting actions.

The abundance of animal remains, their excellent state of preservation, the variety of identified species, and the presence of particular animals associated with a particular building that is located in a highly significant area of the site, point towards something previously unknown at Kültepe, adding important data to the knowledge of animal exploitation in the period immediately preceding the Old Hittite kingdom.

Acknowledgements

The research at Kültepe carried out by the Italian team of the University of Milan is supported by the Italian Ministry of Foreign Affair and International Cooperation, the Italian Ministry of University and Research (Project PRIN 2017 'Big Data and Early Archives'), and the University of Milan. The Italian project at Kültepe is part of an agreement between the University of Milan and the University of Ankara, under the scientific coordination the Director of the Kültepe Expedition. The introduction is written by Fikri Kukakoğlu and Luca Peyronel, the conclusion is jointly written by all the authors, while the other parts are by Claudia Minniti, to whom is entrusted the zooarchaeological analysis of the Italian Project.

Bibliography

Adcock, Sarah Ellen

2020   'After the End: Animal Economies, Collapse, and Continuity in Hittite and Post-Hittite Anatolia' (unpublished doctoral thesis, University of Chicago, Chicago).

Albarella, Umberto & Davis, Simon J. M.

1994   'The Saxon and Medieval Animal Bones Excavated 1985–1989 from West Cotton, Northamptonshire' (unpublished AML report 17/94, English Heritage, London).

Albarella, Umberto & Payne, Sebastian

2005   'Neolithic Pigs from Durrington Walls, Wiltshire, England: A Biometrical Database', *Journal of Archaeological Science* 32/4: 589–99.

Albayrak, İrfan; Pamukoğlu, Nahit & Aşan, Nursen

1997   'Bibliography of Turkish Carnivores (Mammalia: Carnivora)', *Communications Faculty of Sciences University of Ankara Series C-Biology* 15: 1–20.

Arbuckle, Benjamin S.

2009   'Chalcolithic Caprines, Dark Age Dairy, and Byzantine Beef. A First Look at Animal Exploitation at Middle and Late Holocene Çadır Höyük, North Central Turkey', *Anatolica* 35: 179–226.

Atici, Levent A.

2003   'Early Bronze Age Fauna from Kaman-Kalehöyük (Central Turkey): A Preliminary Analysis', *Anatolian Archaeological Studies* 12: 99–10.

2006   'Who Let the Dogs out? Bone Destruction and its Broader Implications in Interpreting Bronze Age Pastoral Economies at Kaman-Kalehöyük', *Anatolian Archaeological Studies* 15: 121–31.

2014   'Food and Ethnicity at Kültepe-Kanesh: Preliminary Zooarchaeological Evidence', in Levent Atici, Fikri Kulakoğlu, Gojko Barjamovic & Andrew Fairbairn (eds), *Current Research at Kültepe/Kanesh: An Interdisciplinary and Integrative Approach to Trade Networks, Internationalism, and Identity* (Journal of Cuneiform Studies Supplement Series 4). Lockwood, Atlanta: 195–211.

Baker, Polydora

2006   'Economy, Environment and Society at Kilise Tepe, Southern Central Turkey – Faunal Remains from the 1994–1998 Excavations', in *Archaeozoology of the Near East VIII: actes des Huitièmes Rencontres Internationales d'Archéozoologie de l'Asie du Sud-Ouest et des régions adjacentes* (Travaux de la Maison de l'Orient et de la Méditerranée 49). Pouilloux, Lyon: 407–30.

Bartosiewicz, Làszló

1998   'A Lion's Share of Attention: Archaeozoology and the Historical Record', *Acta archaeologica* 60/1: 1–15.

Berthon, Rémi J.-P.

2011   'Animal Exploitation in the Upper Tigris River Valley (Turkey) between the 3rd and the 1st Millennia BC' (unpublished doctoral thesis, University of Kiel).

Boessneck, Joachim

1969   'Osteological Differences between Sheep (*Ovis aries* Linné) and Capra (*Capra hircus* Linné)', in Don Brothwell & Eric S. Higgs (eds), *Science in Archaeology*. Thames & Hudson, London: 331–58.

Bökönyi, Sandór

1983   'Late Chalcolithic and Early Bronze I Animal Remains from Arslantepe (Malatya), Turkey', *Origini* 12: 581–98.

Bull, Gail & Payne, Sebastian

1982 'Tooth Eruption and Epiphyseal Fusion in Pigs and Wild Boar', in Bob Wilson, Caroline Grigson & Sebastian Payne (eds), *Ageing and Sexing Animal Bones from Archaeological Sites* (British Archaeological Reports, British Series 109). BAR, Oxford: 55–72.

Bull, Gail & Rackham, James D.

1982 'Epiphyseal Fusion and Tooth Eruption of Feral Goats from Moffatdale, Dumfries and Galloway', in Bob Wilson, Caroline Grigson & Sebastian Payne (eds), *Ageing and Sexing Animal Bones from Archaeological Sites* (British Archaeological Reports, British Series 109). BAR, Oxford: 73–80.

Davis, Simon J. M.

1980 'Late Pleistocene and Holocene Equid Remains from Israel', *Zoological Journal of the Linnean Society* 70/3: 289–312.

1992 'A Rapid Method for Recording Information about Mammal Bones from Archaeological Sites' (unpublished AML report 19/92, English Heritage, London).

Driesch, Angela von den

1976 *A Guide to the Measurements of Animal Bones from Archaeological Sites* (Peabody Museum Bulletin 1). Peabody Museum of Archaeology and Ethnology, Cambridge, MA.

Driesch, Angela von den & Boessneck, Joachim

1981 *Reste von Haus- und Jagdtieren aus der Unterstadt von Boğazköy-Hattuša* (Boğazköy-Ḫattuša Ergebnisse der Ausgrabungen 11). Mann, Berlin.

Driesch, Angela von den & Pöllath, Nadja

2004 *Vor- und frühgeschichtliche Nutztierhaltung und Jagd auf Büyükkaya in Boğazköy-Ḫattuša, Zentralanatolien.* Von Zabern, Mainz.

Gentry, Anthea; Clutton-Brock, Juliet & Groves, Colin P.

2004 'The Naming of Wild Animal Species and their Domestic Derivatives', *Journal of Archaeological Science* 31: 645–51.

Görke, Susanne & Kozal, Ekin

2018 'Birds of Prey in Pre-Hittite and Hittite Anatolia (c. 1970–1180 BCE): Textual Evidence and Image Representation', in Karl-Heinz Gersmann & Oliver Grimm (eds), *Raptor and Human: Falconry and Bird Symbolism throughout the Millennia on a Global Scale* (Advanced Studies on the Archaeology and History of Hunting 1/1–1/4), 4 vols. Wachholtz, Kiel: IV, 1667–90.

Grant, Annie

1982 'The Use of Tooth Wear as a Guide to the Age of Domestic Ungulates', in Bob Wilson, Caroline Grigson & Sebastian Payne (eds), *Ageing and Sexing Animal Bones from Archaeological Sites* (British Archaeological Reports, British Series 109). BAR, Oxford: 91–108.

Halstead, Paul; Collins, Paul & Isaakidou, Valasia

2002 'Sorting the Sheep from the Goats: Morphological Distinctions between the Mandibles and Mandibular Teeth of Adult *Ovis* and *Capra*', *Journal of Archaeological Science* 29: 545–53.

Helmer, Daniel; Gourichon, Lionel & Vila, Emmanuelle

2007 'The Development of the Exploitation of Products from Capra and Ovis (Meat, Milk and Fleece) from the PPNB to the Early Bronze in the Northern Near East (8700 to 2000 BC cal.)', *Anthropozoologica* 42/2: 41–69.

Hollenstein, Daria & Middea, Geraldine

2016 'The Faunal Remains from the Square Building Horizon in the Valley West of Sarikale, Boğazköy-Ḫattuša, Turkey (16th/15th Century BC)', in Andreas Schachner & Jürgen Seeher (eds), *Ausgrabungen und Forschungen in der westlichen Oberstadt von Ḫattuša*, I (Boğazköy-Ḫattuša Ergebnisse der Ausgrabungen 24). De Gruyter, Berlin: 147–225.

Hongo, Hitomi
1996 'Patterns of Animal Husbandry in Central Anatolia from the Second Millennium BC through the Middle Ages: Faunal Remains from Kaman-Kalehöyük, Turkey' (unpublished doctoral thesis, Harvard University).

Johnstone, Cluny J.
2004 'A Biometric Study of Equids in the Roman World' (unpublished doctoral thesis, University of York).

Kasparek, Max
1986 'On a Historical Occurrence of the Lion, *Panthera leo*, in Turkey', *Zoology in the Middle East* 1: 9–10.

Kasparek, Max; Kasparek, Aygün; Gözcelioğlu, Bülent & Çolak, Ercüment
2004 'On the Status and Distribution of the Striped Hyaena, *Hyaena hyaena*, in Turkey', *Zoology in the Middle East* 33: 93–108.

Kratochvil, Zdnêk
1969 'Species Criteria on the Distal Section of the Tibia in *Ovis ammon* F. *aries* L. and *Capra aegagrus* F. *hircus* L.', *Acta veterinaria* 38: 483–90.

Kulakoğlu, Fikri & Peyronel, Luca
2022 'L'organizzazione dello spazio pubblico e privato a Kültepe tra Bronzo Medio ed Età del Ferro. Nuovi dati dal settore meridionale dell'insediamento/ Kültepe'de Orta Tunç ve Demir Çağı'nda kamusal ve özel alanların organizasyonu. Yerleşim alanının güney bölümüne ait yeni veriler', in *Lo spazio pubblico, lo spazio privato: XI Convegno contributo delle missioni archeologiche italiane a scavi, ricerche e studi in Turchia; Atti del Convegno 2020 / Kamusal alan, özel alan. XI Türkiye'deki arkeolojik çalışmalara eğitim, araştırma ve kazı'da İtalya katkısı sempozyumu. Sempozyum bildirileri 2020*. Istituto italiano di cultura, Istanbul: 31–44.
2023 'L'arte del vasaio in Anatolia antica. Il repertorio figurativo della ceramica di Kültepe durante il periodo delle colonie assire: nuovi dati dagli scavi recenti/Eski Anadolu seramik sanatı. Kültepe'de Asur Ticaret Kolonileri Çağı tasvirli seramik sanatı: son kazılardan yeni bilgiler', in *Arte, funzione e simboli nella cultura materiale dell'Anatolia Antica: XII Convegno sul contributo a scavi, ricerche e studi nelle missioni archeologiche in Turchia; Atti del Convegno 2021 / XII Türkiye'deki arkeolojik çalışmalara eğitim, araştırma ve kazı'da İtalya katkısı sempozyumu. Sempozyum bildirileri 2021*. Istituto italiano di cultura, Istanbul: 67–81.

Masseti, Marco
2007 'Ancient Historical Faunae of Continental and Insular Asia Minor, and their Relations with the Western Mediterranean, with Particular Reference to the Italian Peninsula', *International Journal of Anthropology* 22/3–4: 177–95.

Minniti, Claudia & Peyronel, Luca
2005 'Symbolic or Functional Astragali from Tell Mardikh-Ebla (Syria)', *Archaeofauna* 14: 7–26

Neu, Erich
1974 *Der Anitta-Texts* (Studien zu den Boğazköy-Texten 18). Harrassowitz, Wiesbaden.

Onwuama, Kenechukwu T.; Zubair, Alhaji J.; Salami, Sulaiman O. & Kigi, Esther S.
2021 'Morphological Studies on the Axial Skeleton of the African Lion (*Panthera leo*)', *International Journal of Veterinary Science and Animal Husbandry* 6/2: 9–14.

Özguç, Tahsin
1999 *Kültepe-Kaniš/Neša Saraylari ve Mabetleri / The Palaces and Temples of Kültepe-Kaniš/Neša* (Türk Tarih Kurumu Yayınları 5/46). Türk Tarih Kurumu Basimevi, Ankara.

Payne, Sebastian

1973 'Kill-off Patterns in Sheep and Goats: The Mandibles from Aşvan Kale', *Anatolian Studies* 23: 281-303.

1985 'Morphological Distinctions between the Mandibular Teeth of Young Sheep, *Ovis*, and Goats, *Capra*', *Journal of Archaeological Science* 12: 139-47.

1987 'Reference Codes for Wear States in the Mandibular Cheek Teeth of Sheep and Goats', *Journal of Archaeological Science* 14: 609-14.

Payne, Sebastian & Bull, Gail

1988 'Components of Variation in Measurements of Pig Bones and Teeth, and the Use of Measurements to Distinguish Wild from Domestic Pig Remains', *ArchaeoZoologia* 2: 27-66

Plug, Ina

2014 *What Bone Is That? A Guide to the Identification of Southern Africa Mammal Bones*. Rosslyn, Pretoria.

Ren, Lele; Wang, Yiru; Li, Guoqiang; Li, Qilu; Ma, Zhanting & Dong, Guanghui

2015 'Discovery of a Tiger (*Panthera tigris* (L.)) Skeleton from the Little Ice Age Buried on the Shore of Qinghai Lake, Northeast Tibet Plateau', *Quaternary International* 355: 145-52.

Sarı, Alptuğ; Gündoğdu, Ebubekir; Başkaya, Şağdan & Arpacık, Ahmet

2020 'Habitat Preference by the Anatolian Leopard (*Panthera pardus tulliana* Valenciennes, 1856) in North-Eastern Anatolia, Turkey', *Belgian Journal of Zoology* 150: 153-68.

Schnitzler, Annik E.

2011 'Past and Present Distribution of the North African-Asian Lion Subgroup: A Review', *Mammal Review* 41/3: 220-43.

Schnitzler, Annik E. & Hermann, Luc

2019 'Chronological Distribution of the Tiger *Panthera tigris* and the Asiatic Lion *Panthera leo persica* in their Common Range in Asia', *Mammal Review* 49/4: 340-53.

Silver, Ian A.

1969 'The Ageing of Domestic Animals', in Don Brothwell & Eric S. Higgs (eds), *Science in Archaeology*. Thames & Hudson, London: 283-302.

Siracusano, Giovanni

2012 'An Amazing Discovery at Arslantepe (East Anatolia): Unusual Find of a Cheetah in an EBA III Level', in Christine Lefèvre (ed.), *Proceedings of the General Session of the 11th International Council for Archaeozoology Conference at Paris 2010* (British Archaeological Reports, International Series 2354). BAR, Oxford: 165-81.

Sohel, Shahrian H.; Islam, K. H. Nurul & Rahman, Mohammad L.

2021 'Anatomical Features of Some Bones of the Forelimbs of Lions (*Panthera leo*)', *International Journal of Morphology* 39/2: 378-85.

Vila, Emmanuelle

1998 *L'exploitation des animaux en Mésopotamie aux IVᵉ et IIIᵉ millénaires avant J.-C.* (Monographies du C.R.A. 21). CNRS Éditions, Paris.

Zeder, Melinda A. & Lapham, Heather A.

2010 'Assessing the Reliability of Criteria Used to Identify Postcranial Bones in Sheep, *Ovis*, and Goats, *Capra*', *Journal of Archaeological Science* 37/11: 2887-2905.

Zeder, Melinda A. & Pilaar, Suzanne E.

2010 'Assessing the Reliability of Criteria Used to Identify Mandibles and Mandibular Teeth in Sheep, *Ovis*, and Goats, *Capra*', *Journal of Archaeological Science* 37/11: 225-42.

RECENT DISCOVERIES AT KÜLTEPE AND ITS VICINITY

13. Discovering the Late Chalcolithic Period at Kültepe

Excavation of the Central Trench (2021–2022)

Fikri Kulakoğlu, Ryoichi Kontani & Yuji Yamaguchi

Introduction

The approximately 23,000 clay tablets discovered at the Kültepe site were included in the UNESCO Memory of the World register in 2015. In 2014 the entire site was added to the UNESCO World Heritage tentative list. To demonstrate the importance of the site, which is attracting attention from many quarters, a visitor centre was set up near the dig-house and opened to the public in 2022. In addition, a new museum, tentatively called the Kültepe Museum, is under construction approximately four kilometres south-east of the site.

Considering these circumstances, one issue yet to be elucidated at the Kültepe site is the presence or absence of a Chalcolithic cultural layer. Excavations were started in 2015 in two trenches located at the northern and western sides of the Kültepe site aiming at establishing a pre-Bronze Age cultural chronology (Kulakoğlu et al. 2020; Yamaguchi 2022; Shimogama 2022). However, we were unable to discover a reliable Chalcolithic layer in either trench due to groundwater and the presence of massive Early Bronze Age architectural complexes. In 2021, a new research area called the Central Trench, was established in the southern part of the Waršama Palace in the centre of the Kültepe mound, where the Late Chalcolithic cultural layer was finally discovered (Kontani et al. 2022; 2023).

Much work remains to be done in studying Chalcolithic chronology in central Anatolia (Schoop 2011), starting with pioneering investigations at Alişar Höyük carried out more than eighty years ago (Osten 1937). What were the factors that led to the urbanization of the Kültepe site, which was not located in a large agricultural area? Understanding the origins of urban civilizations in West Asia, compared with northern and southern Mesopotamia, which were based on agriculture, are essential (Kontani & Kulakoğlu 2022). However, first it is necessary to clarify the material culture of the Chalcolithic period in Anatolia.

Central Trench at Kültepe

The new Central Trench is located at the southern end of the 'Waršama Palace' (Fig. 13.1), which dates back to the eighteenth century BC. The palace measures approximately 100 m × 100 m and is thought to have had at least two storeys at that time (Özgüç 1999; 2003). Accordingly, the foundation stone is over 2 m wide and dug deep into the ground. Topographically, the central part of the mound, the site of the 'Waršama Palace', is considerably higher than the surrounding area. It is approximately 7 m higher than the area around the south-western trench of the mound, where large-scale buildings from the latter part of Early Bronze Age have

---

Fikri Kulakoğlu (kulakoglu@ankara.edu.tr) Department of Near Eastern Archaeology, Ankara University

Ryoichi Kontani (kontani@post.ndsu.ac.jp) Faculty of Literature, Notre Dame Seishin University

Yuji Yamaguchi (yujiyamaguchi@cc.okayama-u.ac.jp) Research Institute for the Dynamics of Civilizations, Okayama University

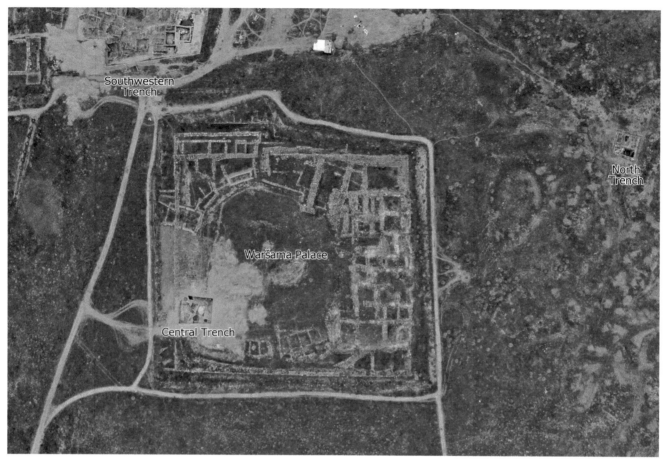

Figure 13.1: Location of central trench (north on the right). Created by authors.

been discovered (Kulakoğlu 2017). The central part of the mound commands a panoramic view of Mount Erciyes, making it a suitable place for the ruling class to establish a monument. In fact, as if to prove this point, there is a large oval-shaped architectural complex surrounding the central part of the mound, which belongs to the Early Bronze Age II, located directly below the 'Waršama Palace' (Özgüç 1999, 2003). Furthermore, there is a large depression in the central part of the mound, where a survey by B. Hrozný destroyed many architectural layers (Özgüç 1999; 2003). Based on the above, it was decided to establish a new Central Trench here, since it is highly probable that a cultural layer dating back to the Chalcolithic period exists beneath the 'Waršama Palace' and that this cultural layer can be investigated (Kontani et al. 2022; 2023).

Figure 13.2: Plan of large zigzag building. Created by authors.

Figure 13.3: Black burnished pottery with white-filled incision. Created by authors.

Figure 13.4: Burial jar from south-west part of Room 1. Created by authors.

Figure 13.5: Burial jar from north-east part of Room 1. Created by authors.

Large Zigzag Building

An excavation of the Central Trench to approximately 2.5 m below the surface in 2022, revealed two building layers. This section describes the large zigzag-plan building extending in an east–west direction, which was discovered in the lower layer (Fig. 13.2).

The building consists of mud-brick walls more than 1.5 m wide, and preserved up to 2 m above the floor level in some places. The walls and floors are carefully plastered. The foundation stones of the walls have not been identified at this stage. Large-sized pottery jars, bowls, and pots have been retrieved, including a type of Red-Black Pottery and black burnished pottery with white-filled incisions (Fig. 13.3). Few faunal remains have been found in the associated layers.

In Room 1, three floor levels can be identified, supported by a pivot on each floor level on the west side

Figure 13.6: Horseshoe-shaped hearth in Room 1 (north on the right). Created by authors.

Table 13.1: AMS ¹⁴C dates from Central Trench. Created by authors.

Lab no.	Sample type	¹⁴C date (BP)	Calibrated dates(1σ)	Calibrated dates(2σ)	Context
PLD-47874	Charcoal	4464±25	3325–3233 cal BC (44.14%) 3180–3157 cal BC (9.21%) 3108–3091 cal BC (7.61%) 3054–3034 cal BC (7.31%)	3335–3212 cal BC (51.28%) 3192–3075 cal BC (32.67%) 3065–3026 cal BC (11.49%)	Horseshoe-shaped hearth in Room1
PLD-47873	Charcoal	4932±23	3709–3666 cal BC (52.99%) 3664–3651 cal BC (15.28%)	3768–3721 cal BC (19.90%) 3715–3646 cal BC (75.55%)	Around red burnished pottery from deep sounding

of the room. Interestingly, large jars were buried in the corners of the room (south-west and north-east) as artefacts associated with the surface of the lowest floor. Within these, a small pot and a small bowl were excavated in a nested state (Figs 13.4 and 13.5). A horseshoe-shaped hearth, more than 2 m wide, was also identified in the south-western part of the room (Fig. 13.6). Radiocarbon dating of samples from this hearth correspond to 3335–3026 cal BC (2σ) (Table 13.1).

Small rooms with mud-brick walls were excavated, arranged regularly around Room 1. A large jar, a cup with a handle, and flint stone blades (Canaan blades) were found in the eastern small room (Figs 13.7 and 13.8).

Deep Sounding

The deep sounding measuring approximately 4 m × 4 m was investigated in the north-western part of the Central Trench. The aim was to identify a cultural layer even older than the large zigzag building. Although no clear building was identified, there were significant changes in the pottery found. While most of the pot-

Figure 13.7: Burial jar in eastern small room. Created by authors.

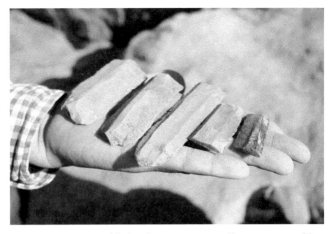

Figure 13.8: Canaan blades from eastern small room. Created by authors.

tery excavated from the large zigzag building was black burnished pottery, the ratio of red burnished pottery increased in the lower layers. Radiocarbon dating of the samples recovered from the surroundings of the red burnished pottery excavated at the deepest level of the area at this point corresponds to 3768–3646 cal BC (2σ) (Table 13.1).

Concluding Remarks

Excavations in the Central Trench have reached the oldest cultural layer at the Kültepe site so far. The large building with a zigzag plan dates to the late fourth millennium BC according to the ^{14}C data, and corresponds to the Late Chalcolithic period. Considering its plan, scale, and excavated artefacts, it is thought that this structure may be unique. In future, it will be necessary to clarify the overall picture of this structure. There are many similarities between the pottery from this trench and that of the Late Chalcolithic period to Early Bronze Age I period pottery excavated at Büyük Güllücek (Koşay & Akok 1957; Orthman 1963) and Alişar Höyük (Osten 1937). These artefacts could provide a potential solution to the problematic distinction between the Late Chalcolithic and Early Bronze Age I in the central Anatolian chronology. Furthermore, considering that the deep sounding has not yet reached virgin soil, it is highly likely that cultural layers existed at Kültepe prior to the Late Chalcolithic period. Continued research and investigation should be undertaken to resolve these issues.

Acknowledgements

This work was supported by JSPS KAKENHI Grant Number JP20K01097, MEXT KAKENHI Grant Number JP21H00009, The Mitsubishi Foundation, The Takanashi Foundation for Historical Science, and the FY 2022 Joint Research Project of RIDC. We also would like to thank Editage (www.editage.com) for English language editing.

All photos in this paper were taken by the authors.

Bibliography

Kontani, Ryoichi & Kulakoğlu, Fikri

2022 'Urbanization of Kültepe: The Origin of a Mega-City in Central Anatolia', *Journal of West Asian Archaeology* 23: 137–44 (in Japanese).

Kontani, Ryoichi; Yamaguchi, Yuji & Kulakoğlu, Fikri

2022 'Investigation towards the Understanding of the Chalcolithic Period in Central Anatolia: Excavations at the Central Trench, Kültepe, Turkey (2021)', in Japanese Society for West Asian Archaeology (ed.), *Proceedings of the 29th Annual Meetings of Excavations in West Asia: Japanese Society for West Asian Archaeology*. Japanese Society for Western Asian Archaeology, Tsukuba: 97–99 (in Japanese).

2023 'Investigation towards the Understanding of the Chalcolithic Period in Central Anatolia: Excavations at the Central Trench, Kültepe, Turkey (2022)', in Japanese Society for West Asian Archaeology (ed.), *Proceedings of the 30th Annual Meetings of Excavations in West Asia: Japanese Society for West Asian Archaeology*. Japanese Society for Western Asian Archaeology, Tsukuba: 22–25 (in Japanese).

Koşay, Hâmit & Akok, Mahmut

1957 *Büyük Güllücek Kazısı: 1947 ve 1949'daki Çalışmalar Hakkında İlk Rapor*. Türk Tarih Kurumu, Ankara.

Kulakoğlu, Fikri

2017 'Early Bronze Age Monumental Structure at Kültepe', in Fikri Kulakoğlu & Gojko Barjamovic (eds), *Proceedings of the 2nd Kültepe International Meeting: Kültepe, 26-30 July, 2015; Studies Dedicated to Klaas Veenhof* (Kültepe International Meetings 2, Subartu 39). Brepols, Turnhout: 217–26.

Kulakoğlu, Fikri; Kontani, Ryoichi; Uesugi, Akinori; Yamaguchi, Yuji; Shimogama, Kazuya & Semmoto, Masao

2020 'Preliminary Report of Excavations in the Northern Sector of Kültepe 2015–2017', in Fikri Kulakoğlu, Cécile Michel & Güzel Öztürk (eds), *Investigative Approaches to the Archaeology and History of Kültepe-Kaneš, Kültepe, 4-7 August 2017* (Kültepe International Meetings 3, Subartu 45). Brepols, Turnhout: 9–88.

Orthman, Winfried

1963 *Die Keramik der Frühen Bronzezeit aus Inneranatolien* (Istanbuler Forschumgen 24). Mann, Berlin.

Osten, Hans H. von der

1937 *The Alişar Hüyük: Seasons of 1930-1932*, I (Researches in Anatolia 7). University of Chicago Press, Chicago.

Özgüç, Tahsin

1999 *Kültepe-Kaniš / Neša Saraylari ve Mabetlari / The Palaces and Temples of Kültepe Kaniš / Neša*. Türk Tarih Kurumu, Ankara.

2003 *Kültepe Kaniš / Neša: The Earliest International Trade Center and the Oldest Capital City of the Hittites*. Middle Eastern Culture Center in Japan, Tokyo.

Schoop, Ulf-Dietrich

2011 'The Chalcolithic on the Plateau', in Gregory McMahon & Sharon Steadman (eds), *The Oxford Handbook of Ancient Anatolia: 10000-323 B.C.E.* Oxford University Press, Oxford: 150–73.

Shimogama, Kazuya

2022 'Ceramic Production at Early Bronze Age Kültepe in Light of Technological Changes and Urbanization Process in Anatolia', *Journal of West Asian Archaeology* 23: 111–26 (in Japanese).

Yamaguchi, Yuji

2022 'Red-Black Pottery in Kültepe, Central Anatolia: Inter-regional Relations from 4th to 3rd Millennium BC', *Journal of West Asian Archaeology* 23: 101–10 (in Japanese).

14. Changes in the Settlement Plan at the End of the Third Millennium BC in Kültepe-Kaneš

New Data on the Transition from Public Buildings to Private Workshops

Yılmaz Rıdvanoğulları, Güzel Öztürk, Cihan Ay, Elif Genç & Fikri Kulakoğlu

Introduction

Kültepe (ancient Kaneš) is located 21 km north-east of Kayseri, at the foot of Mount Erciyes (3917 m), the highest mountain in central Anatolia, in the centre of a fertile plain and at a key point at the intersection of natural trade routes that easily connected northern Syria and Mesopotamia (Özgüç 1963, 28; 2005, 7–8) (Fig. 14.1). The important roads from the Kayseri Plain to the Cilician Plain, which were used both in the early and late periods, are the most compelling evidence of this (Özgüç 1950, 9–10). Kayseri is the starting point of these routes, which descend southwards through the main passes of the difficult mountainous terrain of the Central Taurus Mountains. Therefore,

Yılmaz Rıdvanoğulları (yilmazridvanogullari@ktb.gov.tr) PhD Candidate, Ankara University — Archaeologist, Republic of Türkiye Ministry of Culture and Tourism, Kayseri Archaeology Museum, Kayseri/Türkiye

Güzel Öztürk (guzelozturk@gmail.com; guzel.ozturk@balikesir.edu.tr) Assist. Prof., Balıkesir University, Architectural Restoration Program, Ayvalık/Balıkesir, Türkiye

Cihan Ay (cihanay09@gmail.com) PhD Candidate, Ankara University, Faculty of Language, History, and Geography, Department of Near Eastern Archaeology, Ankara/Türkiye

Elif Genç (egenc@cu.edu.tr) Assoc. Prof., Çukurova University, Faculty of Science and Letters, Department of Archaeology, Adana/Türkiye

Fikri Kulakoğlu (kulakoglu@ankara.edu.tr; kulakoglu@yahoo.com) Prof., Ankara University, Faculty of Language, History, and Geography, Department of Near Eastern Archaeology, Ankara/Türkiye

Anatolia, whose natural richness is well known by the neighbouring regions, has always been the centre of attention of the neighbours in the south through these roads.

The discovery of Ubaid pottery during the excavations carried out by Tahsin Özgüç in the mound across the Fraktin Rock Relief is extremely important in terms of showing the relations of central Anatolia with Syria and Mesopotamia since the early periods (Özgüç 1956, 63). Kültepe, which is located in the Central Taurus region and very close to silver deposits (Yener & Özbal 1986; Yener et al. 1991), such as Bolkardağ and Aladağ (Fig. 14.2), which are referred to as the 'Silver Mountains' (Dercksen 1996, 149; Barjamovic 2019, 77) in later texts quoting the Akkadian Empire, gained a dominant place in the international trade established between Anatolia and distant regions since the second half of the third millennium and was one of the main interlocutors of this trade in Anatolia. Thanks to these trade relations that continued uninterrupted until the end of the third millennium, Kültepe was adorned with monumental buildings in the Early Bronze Age (EBA) III period. In addition, cylinder seals and jewellery made of precious metals and stones, which are indicative of contacts extending to southern Mesopotamia, show that the intellectual world of Kültepe developed and reached high living standards in this period (Özgüç 1986). However, by the end of the third millennium, with the emergence of new dynamics affecting almost all of Anatolia, the monumental buildings built

■ Great EBA Trench ■ EBA II Trench ■ West Trench ■ North Trench ■ Late Chalcolithic Trench

Figure 14.1: Kültepe-Kaneš mound, view from the east. © Kültepe-Kanesh Excavations Archive.

in accordance with the pre-planned settlement model in the mound area were replaced by modest buildings with simple plans.

Scientific excavations carried out to date have revealed that the simple planned architectural structures built in the early third millennium (i.e. those contemporary with the EBA I–II periods in Anatolian chronology) were replaced by monumental structures in the second half and last quarter of the age (EBA III). In addition, recent studies by Fikri Kulakoğlu at the mound constitute significant improvements in the settlement plan, as evidenced by the modest buildings, which are thought to have been used as private workshops, built immediately after the end of this rich phase, which dates to the last quarter of the third millennium at Kültepe and is represented by monumental buildings as well as imported finds that can be considered as evidence of international relations (Kulakoğlu 2017, 217). The data shedding light on these developments were obtained during the excavations carried out in the south-west of the mound. These new structures, which were built right on top of the fire debris of the monumental building dated to level 11b of Kültepe are very remarkable in that they appear to date to the end of the third millennium. In the light of the available data, it is possible to say that these buildings, which are dated to level 11a of Kültepe and thereafter, had more than one construction phase and had expanded to the south and turned into a large interconnected complex. These buildings, which were apparently not exposed to any fire, have the character of private workshops and have mud-brick walls with foundations made of small stones that have been constantly repaired. In this study, salient developments and changes in the settlement plan of Kültepe will be emphasized from the second half of the third millennium to the beginning of the second millennium, and the dynamics that triggered them will be evaluated in the light of new data.

Stratigraphy and Chronology

The results of the excavations carried out in the mound area of Kültepe in recent years have provided compelling new data on the stratigraphy and chronology of Kültepe. In this context, a cultural layer dating to the Late Chalcolithic period was identified in the area excavated for the first time in 2021 (2021 — Trench03) on the south-eastern slope of the Waršama Palace. This layer is represented by monumental architecture characterized by mud-brick walls. The first excavations and research to understand the strata and cultures dating to the third millennium were carried out by Özgüç between 1953–

1986. Özgüç determined that the third-millennium cultures at the mound are represented by level 18 (EBA I), the earliest of which dates to the beginning of the third millennium, and level 11, with two sub-building levels (a-b) which dates to the end of this millennium (EBA III) (Özgüç 1999, 5). Levels 17–14 of Kültepe represent the second or middle phase of the EBA.

The architectural data of levels 18 and 17 are unfortunately limited due to the narrow area of the excavations (Kulakoğlu 2015, 11). These levels are characterized by handmade, monochrome red burnished pottery as well as red on buff painted and fluted pottery (Kulakoğlu 2015). In addition, the excavations carried out between 2015–2017 in the area called the 'North Trench' on the northern part of the mound revealed levels that are likely to be dated to the beginning of the third millennium (Kulakoğlu et al. 2020, 15–16). Radiocarbon analyses from these levels, which are represented by stone-based structures, yield early dates of the third millennium (Kulakoğlu et al. 2020, 10, table 2.1).

Levels dating to the middle of the third millennium (levels 15–16) and the end of this phase (level 14) at Kültepe show an increase in the number of ceramics imported from the Upper Euphrates region (Özgüç 1986, 37). The wheel-made Syrian bottles, known from contemporary settlements in south-eastern Anatolia and northern Syria, were found in the stone cist graves and on the floor of the rooms belonging to level 15. In addition to this, the examples of 'Darboğaz Ware/Metallic Ware' found in Kültepe from level 14 onwards have an essential place in this group which has an interregional distribution in this period (Kulakoğlu 2015, table 1). One of the imported pottery examples of this level are the horizontal grooved beakers, which are also well known from the EBA II Tarsus-Gözlükule (Özgüç 1986, 38, figs 3-19, 3-20). Headless idols made of alabaster shed light on the belief world of third-millennium Anatolia, the earliest examples of which are found in level 15 and have a style unique to Kültepe (Öztürk 2015, 158–60, figs 1–4).

New data from the middle of the third millennium have been obtained from the 'Great EBA Trench' in the mound, which has been excavated since 2010, and from recent investigations on the eastern slope of the Waršama Palace and on the western slope of the mound. The buildings dated to the early and mid-third millennium exposed in the 'Great EBA Trench' could only be investigated in a narrow area since they were under the monumental buildings dated to the later phase (i.e. second half and last quarter of the third millennium). Nevertheless, the finds yielded crucial clues for understanding the characteristic features of this period (Özgüç 1986; Kulakoğlu 2015, 11). In the light of the studies carried out to date, the 'Radial Planned Building' discovered on the south-eastern slope of Waršama Palace and dated to the end of the middle phase of the third millennium (level 14), provides new and important data not only for Kültepe but also for this period of central Anatolia (Kulakoğlu 2015, 12).

The building complex unearthed during the excavations carried out by Özgüç in 1981–1982 and 1986 by Kulakoğlu in 2009 on the eastern slope of the citadel where the Waršama Palace was built and dated to level 14 of EBA II clearly shows that it was built in a similar architectural character with the advanced examples we know from the building levels of Demircihöyük (Korfmann 1983, 222, Abb. 343), Bademağacı (Duru & Umurtak 2011, 10–13, Res. 1), Küllüoba (Fidan 2013), and other settlements in central western Anatolia (Fig. 14.2), especially those dating to the I-II periods of the EBA, which were first defined as 'Anatolian Settlement Scheme' by Korfmann in the archaeological literature (Kulakoğlu 2017, 217). However, this complex unearthed at Kültepe was not built on the entire mound but on one of the multiple hills on the mound, which makes it different from the other centres. Built in two phases, the complex has a series of connected rooms with common walls and a secure entrance with a stone-paved ramp and door sockets. These findings suggest that the building was once a private area on the top of the mound used by the local ruling class (Kulakoğlu 2015, 12). Apart from Kültepe, the architectural finds unearthed in the EBA levels of Ahlatlıbel (Koşay 1934, 7), Koçumbeli (Tezcan 1966, 7; İlgezdi-Bertram & Bertram 2012, 118–19), and Resuloğlu (Yıldırım 2013, pl. 1; Yıldırım & Kısa 2015, 100, fig. 1), which reflect a similar settlement pattern in central Anatolia, clearly show that this settlement pattern is not unique to central western Anatolia (Fidan 2013) and the Aegean (Gündoğan 2020), but was also applied in central and northern Anatolia. These fundamental findings point out that this model may have been applied in Kültepe and other central Anatolian centres in earlier periods. Unfortunately, the monumental buildings covering a large part of the EBA settlement at Kültepe do not allow the investigation of earlier levels in this large area. Therefore, it would not be correct to attribute the origin of this model to any region or centre, by ignoring the large centres such as Kültepe, where the existence of this model has been proven and research is still ongo-

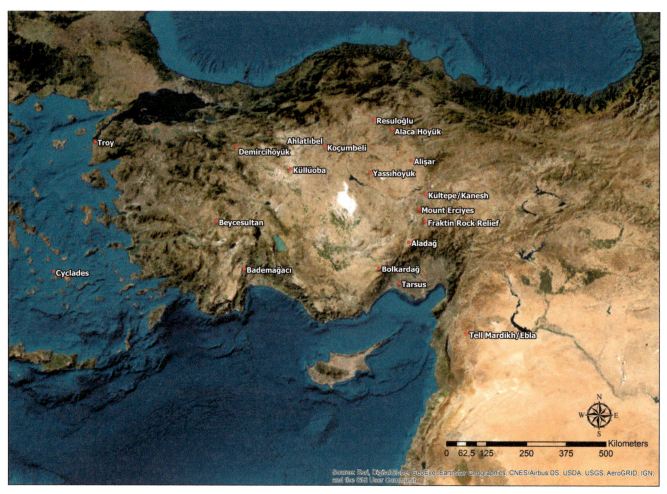

Figure 14.2: Centres mentioned in the text. Map produced by Y. Rıdvanoğulları using ArcGIS/ArcMap World Imagery.

ing. One of the prime dynamics underlying the popular preference of this settlement model in Anatolia during this period is the defence mechanism. Especially at the end of this period, the exploitation of mineral resources by certain control mechanisms accelerated the formation of a hierarchical order and led to the emergence of political principalities with centres surrounded by a defence system (Şahoğlu 2004, 247–48). In this context, Kültepe, which established cultural and commercial links with Syria and Mesopotamia through Cilicia, must have started to take its first steps towards becoming a powerful kingdom in this period.

Settlement Models of the Second Half of the Third Millennium BC

The building levels at Kültepe, dating to the second half of the third millennium (levels 13, 12, and 11a-b), are characterized by monumental buildings built on top of each other, each destroyed by severe fires, and by local and imported ceramic and small finds. These findings not only provide information about the rich indigenous culture of Kültepe in the second half of the third millennium, but also shed light on the understanding of regional–interregional relations with surrounding cultures. In this period, a similar building model was found in three different building levels in Kültepe. All of these monumental and public or religious buildings have a pre-planned scheme. However, simple cell structures and silos built in the middle of the third millennium, when monumental structures were still in existence, are not included in the settlement model and they are evaluated under a separate heading.

Palatial Complex at Level 13

Built at the beginning of the second half of the third millennium, this building (Fig. 14.3) measures 70 m east–west and 55 m north–south and is the largest building known from this period in Anatolia, although only a part of it has been exposed as a result of the excavations carried out in 2010–2015 (Kulakoğlu 2017, 219–22, figs 2–6; Kulakoğlu et al. 2013, 46–49, fig. 2). The complex, which has been documented in three phases, currently consists of two different structures. According to the findings, although the northern building unit is earlier, the most dominant part of the complex consists of a series of large rooms on the southern facade. The length of the rooms in this part of the complex increases from east to west, while their width (about 5 m) is almost the same. The length of the easternmost room is 7 m, while towards the west the rooms increase up to 8.5 m. The reason for this situation is not clear, it is most likely an irregularity caused by errors in architectural planning. The rooms have a hard floor of compacted clay with sand and gravel underneath. The walls are approximately 1.60 m thick, suggesting that the building may have two storeys. Considering the dimensions of the complex and the construction plan, it is highly probable that this was the northern wing of a large palace and that these building units were used for storage.

The results of ^{14}C analyses (2460 BC (86.8 per cent) 2279 BC) of samples taken from the remains of a burnt beam found in situ in one of the doorway thresholds of the complex prove that the building is one of the oldest monumental structures built on the mound. Excavations in the rooms of the complex yielded, with some exceptions, very little pottery and few artefacts, indicating that the impending danger was recognized in advance and the rooms were evacuated before the great fire that destroyed the entire complex. Although rare, some finds discovered in situ in some rooms provide important data about the ceramic culture of this period. This large building of level 13 represents one of the first buildings constructed according to the pre-planned layout. Shortly after the destruction of this building by fire, the monumental buildings of levels 12 and 11b were gradually constructed towards the south.

Figure 14.3: Palatial complex of level 13. Orthomosaic produced by Yuichi Hayakawa, 2015. © Kültepe-Kanesh Excavations Archive.

The Monumental Building at Level 12

Just south of the level 13 complex, two monumental buildings were unearthed during the excavations carried out by Özgüç in the stratigraphically higher level trenches (Kulakoğlu 2017, 222). The first of these is the monumental building dated to level 12, which Özgüç labelled as 'so-called megaron' due to its similarity in plan to the megaron structures unearthed in western Anatolian settlements such as Troy and Beycesultan in the same period, and interpreted as a temple due to the sacred objects found inside (Özgüç 1963, 35). During his excavations in the same area, he uncovered a series of rooms belonging to the same stratigraphic level just south of this monumental building and considered them outbuildings belonging to the structure in question. It is evident that this monumental building of level 12 continued to the west, but unfortunately, just like the complex dated to level 13, a large part of this building extending to the west was destroyed by the a 'Large Grain Silo' and a refuse the 'Great Pit' dated to a later period. Within the scope of the new period excavations conducted under the direction of Kulakoğlu, new excavations were carried out in 2022 in order to understand the westward extension of this monumental building. The latest excavations revealed that the building continued westwards in the form of long rectangular rooms from the point where it was cut by the 'Large Grain Silo', and that it formed a huge complex together with the group of buildings that Özgüç had uncovered in the south and interpreted as the outbuildings of the this building. It is still being investigated as to whether these long rooms consisting of plastered stone walls/foundations about 2 m high were used as storerooms.

After the destruction of the northern complex, which apparently belongs to the level 13, this area of the town was not abandoned; on the contrary, it was shifted towards the south and a new construction was formed. This situation shows that the same political power or its successors in Kültepe recovered from the situation immediately and interregional relations continued intensively on the same scale without interruption. The clearest evidence of this is the continuation of certain cultural traditions in this phase of level 13 without any change. When the model of the level 12 complex is carefully analysed, it is seen that it was built with the same orientation and with the same ideas and purposes as the level 13 complex.

The only difference in this complex so far is that it has a large hall with a hearth, the roof of which is supported by four pillars around it, where religious rituals or meetings were probably held. In order to fully understand the construction plan and function of both buildings, and thus to clearly reveal the settlement pattern of the city in this period, it is necessary to reveal the large courtyards, administrative and private units of both buildings, and the city wall, which is at least as important as these, during the ongoing excavations. The part of this monumental building excavated by Özgüç, has a very large ceramic and artefact repertoire. The excavations in this level yielded a group of Intermediate Ware vessels and a group of locally produced ceramics that show the strong relations with western Anatolia. Painted *depas* produced in accordance with the painted ceramic traditions of the Kayseri Plain, bowls painted with red cross motifs, red slipped bowls previously known from Troy II, and a large amount of wheel-made 'Troy A2 Type' simple ware plates belonging to the plain ware group were found. Besides these, wheel-made double-handled goblets, imported ceramics from Cilicia, and Syrian alabastron-shaped bottles show Kültepe's intensive relations with its neighbours to the south (Özgüç 1963; 1986, 34, 38–39, 41).

The Monumental Building with Pilasters at Level 11b

Immediately after the destruction of the 'Monumental Building of Level 12' by fire, a monumental building was built directly on top of it, which Özgüç calls the 'The Building with Pilaster' due to the fact that its walls were supported both internally and externally by mudbrick pilasters to help carry the upper cover (Özgüç 1986, 31–34). Measuring 22.5 × 25 m, this building is one of the largest monumental structures built in Anatolia during this period, although it has not been completely unearthed.[1] The large inner hall of the building, measuring 10.5 × 17 m, has a hearth with a diameter of 4.3 m and is similar to the hall of the 'Monumental Building of Level 12'. Although the exact plan is still unknown, Özgüç (1986, 34) states that the building differs from the modest architecture of contemporary central Anatolia and that it may have been a temple or a palace. The building can be compared with the monumental building/palace (2260–2135 BC) discovered at Yassıhöyük east of the Kızılırmak River (Omura 2013, 316; 2015, 304–06). This building, which was constructed immediately after the destruction of the 'Monumental Building of Level 12' by fire, shows with its construction plan and architectural arrangements that the political power

---

[1] For reviews of contemporary monumental buildings in western Anatolia, see Perello 2015.

that dominated the mound from the second half of the third millennium onwards, just like its predecessors, reflected the ideas inspired from outside influences in the architecture by characterizing them with the local Anatolian culture.

The Burnt 'Idol Room' and the 'Kitchen' Installation at Level 11b

Level 11b, dating to the last quarter of the third millennium at Kültepe, is characterized by the 'Monumental Building with Pilasters', as well as the large building with a room called the 'Idol Room' discovered in 2018, and a kitchen outbuilding. This level is a continuation of the previous level from a cultural standpoint, but architecturally it belongs to a higher building level. Intermediate Ware painted and plain ceramics, painted *depas*, 'Troy A2 Type' plates, and alabastron-shaped Syrian bottles continue to be used intensively in this level. The religious contexts belonging to this phase yielded large quantities of Kültepe type alabaster idols and statuettes and special vessels thought to have been used for ritual purposes. No cultural change was detected.

Since 2015, the excavations carried out gradually towards the south of the mound have uncovered rooms belonging to a large monumental structure underneath the modest structures dated to the late third millennium. Just like the monumental buildings of the previous phases, the most important feature that distinguishes this building, which was completely burnt down, from the others is the presence of the belongings of the rooms in situ, since the inhabitants did not have time to empty the rooms. Especially this room, which was discovered in the south-east part of the trench in 2018–2021 and called the 'Idol Room' due to the presence of nearly a hundred idols and statuettes inside, makes this building special (Fig. 14.4).

To the west of this room are two long rectangular rooms belonging to the same building, which are thought to have been used for different functions. The vessels found in situ, scattered throughout the room as a result of the great fire, offer a very wide and rich repertoire. This building, which is thought to have been burnt down during the Akkadian period (*c.* 2350–2150 BC) according to the results of the analysis of carbon samples taken from the interior of the room (2352–2201 BC (83.7 per cent). The building, which houses one of the largest known collections of ritual objects from this period in the Near East, not only reflects the belief and socio-economic structure of the period, but also is

Figure 14.4: A view of the south-western part of the 'Idol Room' with its plastered walls and benches. © Kültepe-Kanesh Excavations Archive.

the last representative of the pre-planned architectural model understanding that started in the second half of the third millennium at Kültepe.

Just to the north of this building, excavations in 2015 uncovered a large 'kitchen' with a total of seven hearths in a keyhole-shaped form (Kulakoğlu 2017, 223, fig. 6:E). This kitchen, which is thought to be a special building where food or health services were produced for the elite class living in monumental buildings in Kültepe during this period, is extremely important in terms of understanding the settlement model of Kültepe in every aspect. The large number of burnt wood remains discovered at the mouth of the hearths forming the kitchen structure is a clear indication of the intensive activities carried out here. The most significant finds that make this building special are undoubtedly the *depas* recovered in considerable numbers. This vessel form, which was found in various contexts belonging to building levels 12 and 11b in Kültepe, was found in situ in various parts of the kitchen. The considerable amount of seed grains found in one of these vessels is extremely important in terms of understanding the function of both this vessel form and the kitchen structure.

Analyses of the *depas* discovered in the EBA settlement of Küllüoba in central-western Anatolia have revealed that this vessel form may have been used as a drinking vessel during a celebration or ritual, or it may have been used in some medical activities (Türkteki et al. 2022). Outside Anatolia, evidence for such medical activities during this period comes from the Ebla G Palace at Tell Mardikh in Syria (*c.* 2400–2300 BC). In a room belonging to this palace (Room L.2890), a kitchen equipped with hearths was unearthed, just like in Kültepe (Matthiae

& Marchetti 2013, 53–54, fig. 2.15). In this room, which was equipped with a total of eight hearths and was not a normal kitchen, many wild plants were found in the soil samples obtained from this room and almost all of them were found to have medicinal properties as a result of the analyses (Peyronel et al. 2016, 3). These wild seeds are thought to have been deliberately collected for the preparation of medicinal substances, infusions, or medicines (Peyronel et al. 2016). In the context of these outstanding examples, it should be noted that the Kültepe kitchen may have been a specially constructed building not only for food production but also for medical services. The fact that the kitchen building is immediately adjacent to the north of the 'Idol Room' suggests that this outbuilding may be related to the large building to which this room belongs. The fact that both structures belong to the same period stratigraphically as well as the similar vessel forms recovered from both structures support this idea.

Settlement Model of the End of the Third Millennium BC: Transition from Public Buildings to Modest Dwelling and Private Workshops at Level 11a

Level 11a at Kültepe is characterized by modest structures built on the fire debris of the 'Idol Room', which spread southwards into a multi-phased architecture. With level 11a, which is considered contemporary with the end of EBA III in the Anatolian chronology, a new tradition of paint decorated ceramics called Alisar III emerged in this phase, when the cultural traditions defined as the third millennium in Kültepe gradually began to decline. Moreover, as the excavations carried out so far have shown, the idols and statuettes defined as 'Kültepe type' in the archaeological literature were not used in level 11a and this tradition has completely ended (Öztürk 2015, 165).

In the last century of the third millennium, very important changes occurred in the settlement model understanding of Kültepe. This period also corresponds with the emergence of new dynamics affecting the whole of Anatolia and with important developments in both cultural and socio-economic structure. During the excavations carried out on the south-western part of the mound between 2015–2021, modest multi-stage structures, which gradually evolved towards the south, were unearthed just above the room named the 'Idol Room' which is dated to building level 11b. This extensive architecture, documented by excavations in an

Figure 14.5: Kültepe-Kaneš Late EBA III Modest Workshops. The earliest phase of the complex (in violet). Rooms A1 and A2. © Kültepe-Kanesh Excavations Archive.

area of approximately 30 × 15 m, has at least three main architectural phases and their subphases. The construction plan and technical features of the structures unearthed here prove that the people living in Kültepe in this period led a more modest life and carried out this steadily without being exposed to any threat.

The earliest phase of this architectural construction is represented by the at least four rooms (Figs 14.5, 14.23; Rooms A1 and A2 in violet on the plan) built directly on the fire debris of the 'Idol Room'. Measuring 7.90 × 3.30 m of these rooms have been excavated, which were built with simple, local andesite stones and have plastered walls about 40 cm thick. The interior width dimensions of the rooms are close to each other. While the width of the room in the east was 3.5 m, it was limited to 3 m in the west. Although most of the rooms were destroyed by the pits of the upper levels, floor remains were found in a limited area in both rooms.

The findings unearthed in Room A1 in the west provide invaluable information about the function of these early phase rooms. An oven partially destroying the western wall (W07) of the room, and therefore apparently belonging to a upper phase of the room, and a bronze needle and a clay crucible (Fig. 14.6) containing metal slag (copper/bronze?) found in the cultural fill of the room prove that this room was used as a workshop.[2] Apart from these two rooms, some walls and architectural elements belonging to the rooms in the north-west

---

[2] Samples were taken to be analysed to determine the type and proportion of minerals inside the mine remains found in the crucible and to reveal more specifically the function of the room.

and north-east of these rooms (Fig. 14.23, Room B1 and the room north-east of B4 (in dark green on the plan)) were found to be built directly on the walls of level 11b, and therefore it is thought that these rooms may have been used in the early phase.

In addition, a dense ash level and small pieces of wood were documented in the section of the level to which these significant findings belong. It is noteworthy that sherds belonging to some ceramic forms seen in levels 12 and 11b continue to be seen in this area, albeit in small quantities. Especially the sherds of handmade, red slipped plates produced in the local Anatolian tradition found in building levels 11b and earlier. In addition most of the ceramics are handmade pieces, wheel-made pieces are also not few. The wheel-made sherds belong to the form known in the literature as 'Troy A2 Type' plate. Handmade, coarse sherds were recovered in and around the oven unearthed in the western room.

In the middle and late phase, a much more widespread architectural formation is encountered. This modest-looking complex, presents a new model with its architectural features, consisting of rectangular and irregular square planned rooms lying adjacent to each other in two parallel building groups on the east–west axis. According to the present data, this group of buildings continues both eastwards and westwards, consisting of at least six rooms with multiple phases (Figs 14.7, 14.23; Rooms B1–B6 in plan). In almost every room, ovens where mine smelting activities were carried out, and the discovery of important finds such as crucibles indicate the presence a large industrial complex. These buildings, which are far from monumental as in the early phase, have mud-brick walls with stone foundations. The lowest row of foundations consists of large worked stones, while the other foundation stones rising above them are smaller. The plastered mud-brick walls rising on a stone foundation are of the same character in all rooms and have a thickness of approximately 40–45 cm. The final phase of all rooms is covered with a white coloured, organic floor. Room B3 in the northeast distinguishes itself from the others by a different floor application which appears to have three different phases of use. Separated from the room to the north by a mud-brick partition wall built in the early phase this room, the floor in the top phase of the room is covered with a white organic layer as in the other rooms, while below it there is a stone pavement with two phases (Figs 14.7, 14.23). Scattered hand and wheel-made painted and simple ware potsherds, and stone tools were discovered in situ in the uppermost phase of the room. On the stone pavement floor representing the early phase of the room, a group of ceramics was found in situ. Among these, a handmade buff slipped bowl (Fig. 14.8), a wheel-made, simple ware two-handled cup, and painted decorated potsherds are highlights of these wares.

In the narrower room to the north of Room B3 (middle phase of Room A1), handmade, painted decorated, 'Gritty Ware' jar sherds (Fig. 14.9), fragments of handmade 'Local Anatolian Type' plates (Fig. 14.10) with the entire inside and part of the outside (only outer part of the rim) painted in dark reddish brown, and wheel-made simple ware plate fragments known from EBA III were found.

Figure 14.6: A clay crucible containing metal slag found in Room A1. © Kültepe-Kanesh Excavations Archive.

Figure 14.7: Kültepe-Kaneš Late EBA III Modest Workshops with oven installations. *Room is labelled as 'B' in the Figure. © Kültepe-Kanesh Excavations Archive.

Figure 14.8: Handmade buff slipped bowl found in the early phase of Room B3. © Kültepe-Kanesh Excavations Archive.

Figure 14.9: Gritty Ware sherds found in the middle phase of Room A1. © Kültepe-Kanesh Excavations Archive.

Figure 14.10: 'Local Anatolian Type' plate fragments. © Kültepe Excavations Archive.

Figure 14.11: A clay crucible containing metal slag found in the middle phase of Room A1. © Kültepe-Kanesh Excavations Archive.

Four ovens,[3] one hearth and one so-called tandoor were unearthed in these interconnected workshops built on the east–west axis. The ovens in Rooms A1 and B2 were cancelled out by the walls of the upper phase during later repairs or renovations.[4] In the south-east corner of Room A1 (middle phase of room), right next to the oven cut by the wall of the upper phase, two crucibles containing metal slag were found in situ (Fig. 14.11). A similar oven was discovered in the west of Room B2. Like the oven in Room A1, this oven was cut off by a wall belonging to the upper phase.

The so-called tandoor unearthed in Room B1 and located at the intersection of the east and north walls of the room draws attention (Fig. 14.12). The open top tandoor has two openings on the west and south sides. It is clearly seen that the interior of the tandoor, which was unearthed together with the igniter and ash pit on the south face, was exposed to a severe fire due to intense use. Since no finds were found in and around the tandoor, its actual function is not known. However, the data obtained from the neighbouring rooms suggest that this installation also had an industrial function. In addition, the fact that the tandoor and the early phase of the walls of this room were built directly on the debris of level 11b suggests that the activities in this room may have been carried out since the early phase and that the walls were repaired and renovated over time.

---

3 Although there is no evidence of smelting activities in some of these ovens, it is thought that they may have been used for the same purpose as they have the same technical and formal characteristics as the other samples containing finds.

4 The walls shown in light green (third phase of level 11a) on the plan represent the middle and late phase of the modest complex of buildings in this area. These walls cut through some of the earlier ovens.

A considerable number of baked and unbaked loom weights and spindle whorls were discovered from the floor of some rooms, proving that weaving producing activities were carried out. The pottery found in the late phase of the rooms shows that the old traditions were gradually abandoned and a new culture emerged in this phase.

The emergence of paint decorated ceramic culture, is seen for the first time gradually in this phase, which is known as *Alisar III* in the literature due to its dense presence in cultural level III of Alişar, one of the first settlements excavated for EBA in central Anatolia, and which was confirmed to originate from the Kayseri Plain as a result of the excavations and research carried out in and around Kültepe in the following periods.

A cache of ceramics found in situ on the floor of Room B5, in the south-west part of the complex (Fig. 14.13), which contains important findings (Fig. 14.14) indicating that ceramic activities were carried out during the same phase, yielded secondary use of paint decorated sherds belonging to the EBA III Intermediate (Fig. 14.15) tradition as well as paint decorated vessels of Alişar III (Fig. 14.16). These critical findings are extremely important as they prove that the end of a tradition overlaps at some point with the beginning of a new tradition (Özgüç 1963, 24, 34).

This tradition of painted ceramics, which spread from the Kayseri Plain to the surrounding cultural regions (especially in the Kızılırmak arc), was popular at Kültepe until the Karum II period, after which it disappeared. In addition to these important findings, a thin layer of unbaked clay on a white organic floor that cov-

Figure 14.12. The so-called tandoor unearthed in Room B1. © Kültepe-Kanesh Excavations Archive.

Figure 14.14: A ceramic group found on the floor of the late phase of Room B5. © Kültepe-Kanesh Excavations Archive.

Figure 14.13: Kültepe-Kaneš Late EBA III Modest Workshops. The multi-phase rooms in the south-west part of the complex excavated in 2019–2021. *Room is labelled as 'B' in the Figure. © Kültepe-Kanesh Excavations Archive.

Figure 14.15: Paint decorated sherds of vessel with Intermediate tradition, found on the floor of the late phase of Room B5. © Kültepe-Kanesh Excavations Archive.

Figure 14.16: Alişar III ware cup and a vessel fragment found on the floor of the late phase of Room B5 ©Kültepe-Kanesh Excavations Archive.

Figure 14.17: The multi-phase unused oval kiln and a pile of baked and unbaked pottery over northern upper wall. © Kültepe-Kanesh Excavations Archive.

ers almost the entire room, which belongs to the late phase of the room, and an unbaked clay pithos left on the eastern wall of the room, indicate that this room may have been a workshop where pottery production activities were carried out. Just west of Room B5 is a room with two ovens side by side, but only part of it has been excavated.

A multi-phase unused oval kiln, which seems to have been built later in Room B2 of the complex, attracts attention with its architectural design and the finds discovered from it (Fig. 14.17). The exterior of this special structure, which was built in the middle of the large room in the northern part of the complex, is formed by a series of medium-sized stones with a total of three different phases (Fig. 14.18). The stones are raised in an oval shape from the bottom to the top and filled with raw earth mortar. The interior of the structure consists of seventeen rows of plastered unbaked mud-brick blocks, approximately 2 m high, placed in an oval shape from the lowest level to the top.

The ceramic pile of baked and unbaked clay vessels and the carbonized seed grains found next to them, which partially destroyed the northern upper part of the 'Unused Oval Kiln' which resembles a ceramic kiln in terms of its architectural design, are remarkable. These finds which were found in grey, soft fill cutting part of the structure, suggest that this part of the mound, including the 'Unused Oval Kiln' and Room B5 located to the south-west of it, may have been used for pottery activities. The following were among the finds of the earlier periods recovered during the excavations inside the kiln, a painted decorated pot (Fig. 14.19) reflecting the characteristic Intermediate tradition of EBA III, an alabastron-shaped Syrian bottle (Fig. 14.20) well known from level 11b (Özgüç 1986, 34–36), a stone idol[5] (Fig. 14.21) and amulet (?) (Fig. 14.22), various stone weights, loom weights, and a bone spindle, show that the structure lost its basic function in the last phase of use and turned into an oval-shaped trash pit.

In the same area, the remains of some buildings were unearthed, which are dated to levels 10 and 9 respectively, but which do not give a proper plan according to the current data. After these phases, a stone-paved structure (Fig. 14.23, in dark blue) was built dating to the early second millennium. According to available data this stone structure supported by two pilasters is stratigraphically the latest example of architectural structures in this area.

As a result, the modest structures, which are completely different from the monumental structures unearthed in the northern and central parts of the 'Great EBA Trench', have led to two different hypotheses: in this context, the first hypothesis that comes to the fore is that the public buildings, which were continuously constructed in the same area from the second half to the last quarter of the third millennium, may have shifted or moved to different parts of the mound during this period. The second hypothesis is that

---

5 Alabaster and clay examples of this type of idols were found in the early strata of the EBA. For more detailed information see Öztürk 2015, 158–60, figs 1–4.

14. CHANGES IN THE SETTLEMENT PLAN AT THE END OF THE THIRD MILLENNIUM BC IN KÜLTEPE-KANEŠ

Figure 14.18: The multi-phase unused oval kiln. View of the exterior of the structure from the east. © Kültepe-Kanesh Excavations Archive.

Figure 14.19: A pot with painted decoration in Intermediate style from 'Unused Oval Kiln'. © Kültepe-Kanesh Excavations Archive.

Figure 14.20: Alabastron-shaped Syrian bottle from 'Unused Oval Kiln'. © Kültepe-Kanesh Excavations Archive.

Figure 14.21: Stone idol from 'Unused Oval Kiln'. © Kültepe-Kanesh Excavations Archive.

Figure 14.22: Stone amulet (?) from 'Unused Oval Kiln'. © Kültepe-Kanesh Excavations Archive.

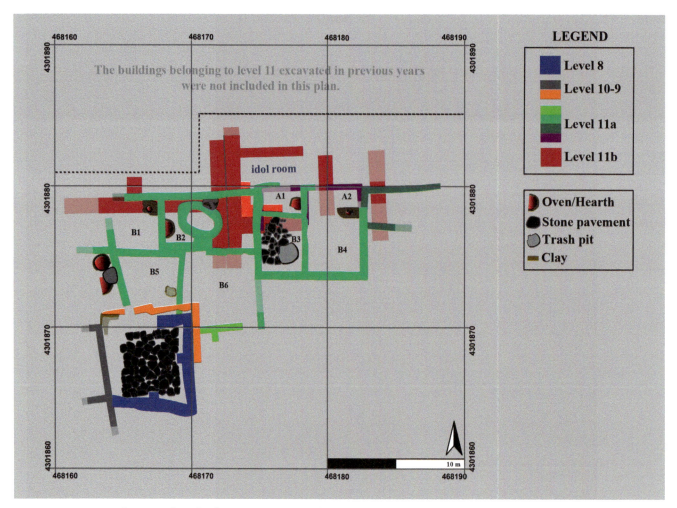

Figure 14.23: Schematic plan of Kültepe Late EBA III workshops and other later level buildings. Plan produced by Yılmaz Rıdvanoğulları using AutoCAD and ArcGIS/ArcMap.

Kültepe's trade with distant regions may have been disrupted after the great fire that destroyed building level 11b, where the last monumental buildings were constructed, and that as a result the prosperous level of life seen throughout EBA III may have declined until level 8, when large public buildings reappear on the mound thanks to the international trade relations established with Assyria in the early second millennium.

Stone Cells and Silos/Storage Pits of the Last Quarter of EBA III

During the 2010 excavation season, the excavations carried out in the north of the 'Great EBA Trench' revealed multifunctional cell-type structures and silos/storage pits which were apparently built on the debris and walls of the monumental complex dating to level 13. These structures, which are dated to levels 12 and 11b based on the finds and ceramics found inside them, are most probably the architectural reflection of a precaution taken against an approaching danger. In the last quarter of the third millennium, when the last monumental buildings are represented on the south-western part of the mound, Kültepe probably faced a political (?) or climatic threat, and small structures of this type began to be built, mostly probably for grain storage. The most interesting of these structures is undoubtedly the square cell-type underground room discovered in 2010 (Fig. 14.24). In this room, which was almost entirely constructed of local andesite stones, statuettes of gods/goddesses and very special ritual vessels were found, which were the characteristic belief elements of Kültepe and dated to level 12 of EBA III. This collection, which most likely belonged to the rooms of monumental buildings dating to level 12, was stored in this small but secure cell to prevent it from being damaged or stolen in the event of an attack or fire-like disaster.

Immediately to the north-east of this building, we encountered rectangular cell-planned stone structures and round stone silos (Fig. 14.25) built on the walls and debris of the building belonging to level 13. These structures, which are dated to EBA III based on the material found in them, are also indicative of a measure taken during this period, just like this above-mentioned cell.

Figure 14.24: The cell-type underground room of level 12. © Kültepe-Kanesh Excavations Archive.

Figure 14.25: Round and cell-planned stone structures of EBA III. © Kültepe-Kanesh Excavations Archive.

These small stone structures, which were probably built during the period when the last monumental buildings were abandoned, are undoubtedly important signals of the great danger that would end the bright period of prosperity seen in Kültepe from the second half of the third millennium.

The appearance of a pre-planned architectural model at Kültepe from the second half of the third millennium onwards must have been the result of the transfer of ideas and technology within the scope of the intensive trade and cultural relations Kültepe established with its neighbours to the south during this period. The monumental buildings built at Kültepe were inspired by the planned urban centres and monumental buildings designed in Syria and Mesopotamia, and are at a level that can compete with the contemporary buildings in these regions in terms of size and plan.[6] The excavations and research carried out so far in the 'Great EBA Trench' have shown that these monumental buildings were not modest. This not only proves the existence and continuity of a very strong administrative authority at the mound, but also proves that Kültepe was ruled and controlled by the same political power or its successors till to the last century of EBA III.

Conclusion and Discussion

This study examines the development and differences in the settlement plan of Kültepe from the second half of the third millennium to the beginning of the second millennium, and reveals architectural models with different construction plans and functions. The transformation of Kültepe from a simple EBA settlement into a metropolitan city was the result of intensive trade and cultural relations with northern Syria and Mesopotamia, where complex urban centres emerged in the second half of the fourth millennium. In this context, these relations, which were not very intense in the middle and late phases of the EBA II, gradually increased and as a result, the settlement grew uninterruptedly until the last quarter of the third millennium. Given the size of

---

[6] For detailed information on contemporary monumental buildings in the Jezirah, see Pfälzner 2011.

the Kültepe mound (c. 21 hectares) and the scale of the EBA excavations and research, it is difficult to know the exact point at which this expansion began at the end of EBA II. The fact that some of the structures unearthed in various parts of the mound and dated to the same period have quite different depth levels from each other shows that the contemporary communities that settled on the mound had different opinions about where to settle. In this context, some buildings were constructed on the hills above the mound, while others were built on lower levels and slopes.

Since the second half of the third millennium, metallurgical technology, which developed with a significant acceleration, led to the establishment of a systematic trade network between distant regions to meet the need for raw materials and the emergence of a homogenous culture in these regions.[7] It has been suggested by researchers that mining in the Middle Taurus Mountains, which started in the middle of the third millennium, may have been one of the triggers of this trade network that emerged in the second half of the third millennium. The new data obtained by recent research have provided a better understanding of the extent and nature of cultural relations, especially in this period when metal technology and state formation began to take shape (Yener et al. 2015, 607; Kulakoğlu 2015, 13). During this period, a wide trade network emerged from Mesopotamia and northern Syria to central Anatolia to the north through the Cilicia region, to northern-western Anatolia and Thrace through the Eskişehir-Afyon region, and from the coastal area of western Anatolia to the Cyclades and continental Greece (Şahoğlu 2004, 246). Thanks to its strategic location, Kültepe was able to take its place among the administrative control mechanisms that organized this extensive trade network, and thanks to this special advantage, the settlement grew rapidly during the EBA III period and turned into a metropolis equipped with rich monumental buildings.

Archaeological excavations at Kültepe revealed that all building levels dating to the second half and last quarter of the third millennium (i.e. early to late 13–12–11b, respectively) were destroyed by major fires. The results of the excavations carried out in recent years in the limited area to the south-west of the mound clearly show that after building level 11b, where the last major fire occurred, modest buildings with industrial functions were built at Kültepe-Kanesh instead of monumental buildings. Immediately after the level 11b fire, these buildings were constructed directly above the monumental complex of which the 'Idol Room' was a part, rising from east to west according to the condition of the underlying rubble. This architectural configuration has been transformed into a multi-stage complex by continuous renovation and repair within the same spatial arrangement over a not very long period of time.

Paleoclimatic studies covering the time period of 2250–2000 BC in Anatolia revealed that a major climate change may have occurred at the end of EBA III and this event may have caused the administrative mechanisms in these regions to lose control and enter into a major conflict (Wiener 2014; Massa & Şahoğlu 2015). As a result of these conflicts, which may have been caused by a major drought crisis, it has been suggested that the major centres in western Anatolia shrank, while in central Anatolia there was a gradual transition towards MBA territorial city-states. Considering the ^{14}C dates and the findings obtained from the modest buildings of level 11a built on the wreckage of the burnt building of level 11b, the critical changes in Kültepe during this phase can be discussed under this hypothesis. The last great fire at Kültepe in late EBA III not only destroyed monumental buildings but also brought the urban culture of the settlement to an end. ^{14}C dates from burnt wood samples found in the 'Idol Room' suggest that this level is contemporary with the Akkadian period. Although the Akkadians may have not been directly responsible for this great destruction, they may have indirectly triggered this crisis. Kültepe, which maintained its prosperous urban structure during the intensive commercial relations with northern Syria and Mesopotamia from the second half of the third millennium onwards, may have suffered intermittent stoppages due to the blockage of the trade network as a result of the political and climatic crises (Fiorentino et al. 2008, 52–53; Sallaberger 2007) in these regions during this period, and may have been targeted by rival kingdoms in Anatolia. Especially the campaigns of the Akkadians against the most important centres of northern Syria may have caused the collapse of the communication network established between northern Syria and Anatolia. In addition, it is also possible that the Akkadians may have been the direct cause of the great fires and destructions that took place in Kültepe-Kanesh and other major contemporary centres during this period. At this point, the texts of *šar tamhari* and *The Legend of Narām-Sîn* are particularly important sources of reference (Westenholz 1997). The *šar-tamhari* texts of Sargon's exploits contain details of Sargon's campaign against the Anatolian city

---

[7] For detailed information see Mellink 1989; Şahoğlu 2004; Efe 2007.

of Purušhanda (Acemhöyük?) following a complaint by Akkadian merchants (Westenholz 1997, 102–39). *The Legend of Narām-Sîn* documents the details of the battle in which Sargon's grandson Naram-Sin defeated a coalition of seventeen kings, including the king of Kaneš Zippani and Pampa the king of Hatti.

The construction plan and function of the modest buildings constructed in the south-west of the mound after these crises and destructions suggest that they should be evaluated from a broader perspective. All these buildings are more like private workshops, equipped with ovens and hearths, than simple dwellings. It is therefore difficult to regard them as conclusive evidence of a stagnation following the crises and destructions of the last quarter of the third millennium. On the other hand, the stylistic features of the four lapis lazuli cylinder seals dated to the Post-Akadian period and the two lapis lazuli cylinder seals dated to the Ur III period found in Kültepe (Öztürk 2019b, figs 3–8) prove that Kültepe maintained connections with distant regions during this period and that foreign merchants continued to exist in Kültepe within the framework of these connections (Öztürk 2019a, 58–60; 2019b, 199–200). In addition to this evidence, the Old Palace, which according to available data was probably built in 2020 BC (Barjamovic et al. 2012, 34, fig. 11), and the South Terrace Palace, which was probably built somewhat earlier (Özgüç 1999, 67), prove that Kültepe re-emerged in this period with a much stronger trade network.

Bibliography

Barjamovic, Gojko
2019 'Silver, Markets and Long-Distance Trade in the Konya Region, 2400–1700 BCE', in Çiğdem Maner (ed.), *Crossroads: Konya Plain from Prehistory to the Byzantine Period; 9th International Anamed Annual Symposium*. Ege Yayınları, Istanbul: 71–81.

Barjamovic, Gojko; Hertel, Thomas & Larsen, Mogens Trolle
2012 *Ups and Downs at Kanesh: Chronology, History, and Society in the Old Assyrian Period*. Nederlands Instituut voor het Nabije Oosten, Leiden.

Dercksen, Jan Gerrit
1996 *The Old Assyrian Copper Trade in Anatolia*. Nederlands Historisch-Archaeologisch Instituut te Istanbul, Istanbul.

Duru, Refik & Umurtak, Gülsün
2011 'Excavations at Bademağacı in 2010', *Anadolu Akdenizi Arkeoloji Haberleri Bülteni* 9: 7–15.

Efe, Turan
2007 'The Theories of the "Great Caravan Route" between Cilicia and Troy: The Early Bronze Age III Period in Inland Western Anatolia', *Anatolian Studies* 57: 47–64.

Fidan, Erkan
2013 'Anadolu Yerleşim Planı Üzerine Yeni Bir Değerlendirme [An Up-to-Date Evaluation of "Anatolian Settlement Plan" (Anatolishes Siedlungsschema)]', *Arkeoloji Dergisi* 18: 113–25.

Fiorentino, Girolamo; Caracuta, Valentina; Calcagnile, Lucio; D'Elia, Marisa; Matthiae, Paolo; Mavelli, Fabio & Quarta, Gianluca
2008 'Third Millennium B.C. Climate Change in Syria Highlighted by Carbon Stable Isotope Analysis of ^{14}C-AMS Dated Plant Remains from Ebla', *Palaeogeography, Palaeoclimatology, Palaeoecology* 266: 51–58.

Gündoğan, Ümit
2020 'The "Aegean Settlement Pattern" in Coastal Western Anatolia from the Neolithic Age to the End of the 3rd Millennium BC', *TÜBA-AR* 27: 29–43.

İlgezdi-Bertram, Gülçin & Bertram, Jan Krzysztof
2012 'Ankara Bölgesi'nde İlk Tunç Çağı Yerleşimleri', in Ali Akın Akyol & Kameray Özdemir (eds), *Türkiye'de Arkeometrinin Ulu Çınarları: Prof. Dr Ay Melek Özer ve Prof. Dr Şahinde Demirci'ye Armağan*. Homer Kitabevi, Istanbul: 117–24.

Korfmann, Manfred
1983 *Demircihüyük: Die Ergebnisse der Ausgrabungen 1975-1978; Architektur, Stragraphie und Befunde*, I. Von Zabern, Mainz.

Koşay, Hamit Zübeyr
1934 'Ahlatlıbel Hafriyatı', *Türk Tarih, Arkeologya ve Etnografya Dergisi* 2: 3–101.

Kulakoğlu, Fikri
2015 'Current Research at Kültepe', in Fikri Kulakoğlu & Cécile Michel (eds), *Proceedings of the 1st Kültepe International Meeting: Kültepe, 19-23 September, 2013; Studies Dedicated to Kutlu Emre* (Kültepe International Meetings 1, Subartu 35). Brepols, Turnhout: 9–21.

2017 'Early Bronze Age Monumental Structures at Kültepe', in Fikri Kulakoğlu & Gojko Barjamovic (eds), *Movement, Resources, Interaction: Proceedings of the 2nd Kültepe International Meeting Kültepe; 26-30 July 2015* (Kültepe International Meeting 2, Subartu 39). Brepols, Turnhout: 217-26.

Kulakoğlu, Fikri; Emre, Kutlu; Kontani, Ryoichi; Ezer, Sabahattin & Öztürk, Güzel

2013 'Kültepe-Kaniş, Turkey: Preliminary Report on the 2012 Excavations', *Bulletin of the Okayama Orient Museum* 27: 43-50.

Kulakoğlu, Fikri; Kontani, Ryoichi; Uesugi, Akinori; Yamaguchi, Yuji; Shimogama, Kazuya & Semmoto, Masao

2020 'Preliminary Report of Excavations in the Northern Sector of Kültepe 2015-2017', in Fikri Kulakoğlu, Cécile Michel & Güzel Öztürk (eds), *Integrative Approaches to the Archaeology and History of Kültepe-Kaneš, Kültepe, 4-7 August 2017* (Kültepe International Meetings 3, Subartu 45). Brepols, Turnhout: 8-88.

Massa, Michele & Şahoğlu, Vasıf

2015 'The 4.2 ka BP Climatic Event in West and Central Anatolia: Combining Palaeoclimatic Proxies and Archaeological Data', in Harald Meller, Roberto Risch, Reinhard Jung & Helge W. Arz (eds), *2200 BC - Ein Klimasturz als Ursache für den Zerfall der Alten Welt? / 2200 BC - A Climatic Breakdown as a Cause for the Collapse of the Old World? Mitteldeutscher Archäologentag vom 23. bis 26. Oktober 2014 in Halle (Saale)*. Halle: 61-78.

Matthiae, Paolo & Marchetti, Nicolò

2013 *Ebla and its Landscape: Early State Formation in the Ancient Near East*. Left Coast, Walnut Creek.

Mellink, Machteld Johanna

1989 'Anatolian and Foreign Relations of Tarsus in the Early Bronze Age', in Barthel Hrouda, Kutlu Emre, Machteld J. Mellink & Nimet Özgüç (eds), *Anatolia and the Ancient Near East; Studies in Honor of Tahsin Özgüç*. Anadolu Medeniyetleri Araştırma ve Tanıtma Vakfı Yayınları, Ankara: 319-31.

Omura, Masako

2013 'Yassıhöyük Kazıları 2011', *34. Kazı Sonuçları Toplantısı* 1: 313-22.

2015 'Yassıhöyük Kazıları 2013', *36. Kazı Sonuçları Toplantısı* 2: 301-12.

Özgüç, Tahsin

1950 *Türk Tarih Kurumu Tarafından Yapılan Kültepe Kazısı Raporu 1948 / Ausgrabungen in Kültepe Bericht über die im Auftrage der Türkischen Historischen Gesellschaft, 1948 durchgeführten Ausgrabungen* (Türk Tarih Kurumu Yayınları 5/10). Ankara.

1956 'Fraktin Kabartması Yanındaki Prehistorik Ev', *Anadolu/Anatolia* 1: 59-64.

1963 'Early Anatolian Archaeology in the Light of Recent Research. Yeni Araştırmaların Işığında Eski Anadolu Arkeolojisi', *Anadolu/Anatolia* 7: 1-42.

1986 'New Observations on the Relationship of Kültepe with Southeast Anatolia and North Syria during the Third Millennium B.C.', in Jeanny V. Canby, Edith Porada, Brunilde S. Ridgway & Tamara Stech (eds), *Ancient Anatolia: Aspects of Change and Cultural Development; Essays in Honor of Machteld J. Mellink*. University of Wisconsin Press, Wisconsin: 31-47.

1999 *Kültepe-Kaniš/Neša Sarayları ve Mabetleri: The Palaces and Temples of Kültepe-Kaniš/Neša* (Türk Tarih Kurumu Yayınları 5/46). Türk Tarih Kurumu Basımevi, Ankara.

2005 *Kültepe-Kaniš/Neša*. Yapı Kredi Yayınları, Istanbul.

Öztürk, Güzel

2015 'Representations of Religious Practice at Kültepe: Alabaster Idols of Early Bronze Age', in Fikri Kulakoğlu & Cecile Michel (eds), *Proceedings of the 1st Kültepe International Meeting: Kültepe, 19-23 September, 2013; Studies Dedicated to Kutlu Emre* (Kültepe International Meetings 1, Subartu 35). Brepols, Turnhout: 155-70.

2019a 'Post-Akkadian and Ur III Features on Cylinder Seals from Kültepe-Kanesh: An Iconographic and Stylistic Analysis', *Adalya* 22: 46–67.

2019b 'Kültepe Seal and Seal Impressions at the End of the 3rd Millennium BC and Early 2nd Millennium BC in the Light of New Excavations' (unpublished doctoral thesis, Ankara University).

Perello, Bérengère

2015 'Architecture de prestige et matérialisation du pouvoir en Anatolie occidentale au Bronze ancien (IIIe millénaire)', in Cécile Michel (ed.), *De la maison à la ville dans l'Orient ancien: la ville et les débuts de l'urbanisation* (Cahiers des Thèmes transversaux d'ArScAn 12). ArScA, Nanterre: 151–59.

Peyronel, Luca; Vacca, Agnese & Wachter-Sarkady, Claudia

2016 'Food and Drink Preparation at Ebla, Syria. New Data from the Royal Palace G (c. 2450–2300 BC)', *Food & History: European Institute for the History and Culture of Food* 12/3: 3–38.

Pfälzner, Peter

2011 'Architecture', in Marc Lebeau (ed.), *Jezirah* (Associated Regional Chronologies for the Ancient Near East and the Eastern Mediterranean 1). Brepols, Turnhout: 137–200.

Sallaberger, Walther

2007 'From Urban Culture to Nomadism: A History of Upper Mesopotamia in the Late Third Millennium', in Catherine Kuzucuoğlu & Catherine Marro (eds), *Sociétés humaines et changement climatique à la fin du troisième millénaire: une crise a-t-elle eu lieu en Haute Mésopotamie? Actes du Colloque de Lyon, 5–8 décembre 2005* (Varia Anatolica 19). Institut français d'études anatoliennes-Georges Dumézil. De Boccard, Paris: 417–56.

Şahoğlu, Vasıf

2004 'Erken Tunç Çağı'nda Anadolu Ticaret Ağı ve İzmir Bölgesi', *I. - II. Ulusal Arkeolojik Araştırmalar Sempozyumu* (Anadolu / Anatolia: Ek Dizi 1). Üniversitesi Basımevi, Ankara: 245–62.

Tezcan, Burhan

1966 *1964 Koçumbeli Kazısı Koçumbeli Excavation in 1964* (Arkeoloji Yayınları No. 3). Orta Doğu Teknik Üniversitesi, Ankara.

Türkteki, Murat; Tarhan, İsmail; Kara, Hüseyin & Tuna, Yusuf

2022 'Possible Uses of Depas Amphikypellon from Küllüoba in Western Central Anatolia through Gc-Ms Analysis of Organic Residues', *Mediterranean Archaeology and Archaeometry* 22/1: 127–54.

Westenholz, Joan Goodnick

1997 *Legends of the Kings of Akkade*. Eisenbrauns, Winona Lake.

Wiener, Malcolm H.

2014 'The Interaction of Climate Change and Agency in the Collapse of Civilizations ca. 2300–2000 BC', *Radiocarbon* 56: 1–16.

Yener, Kutlu Aslıhan & Özbal, Hadi

1986 '29. Bolkardağ Mining District Survey of Silver and Lead in Ancient Anatolia', in Jacqueline S. Olin & M. James Blackman (eds), *Proceedings of the 24th International Archaeometry Symposium*. Smithsonian Institution Press, Washington, D.C.: 309–20.

Yener, Kutlu Aslıhan; Sayre, Edward V.; Joel, Emile C.; Özbal, Hadi; Barnes, Ivan Lynus & Brill, Robert H.

1991 'Stable Lead Isotope Studies of Central Taurus Ore Sources and Related Artifacts from Eastern Mediterranean Chalcolithic and Bronze Age Sites', *Journal of Archaeological Science* 18: 541–77.

Yener, Kutlu Aslıhan; Kulakoğlu, Fikri; Yazgan, Evren; Kontani, Ryoichi; Hayakawa, Yuichi S.; Lehner, Joseph W.; Dardeniz, Gonca; Öztürk, Güzel; Johnson, Michael & Hacar, Abdullah
2015 'The Discovery of New Tin Mines and Production Sites near Kültepe, Ancient Kaneş in Turkey: A Third Millennium BC Highland Production Model', *Antiquity* 89/345: 596–612.

Yıldırım, Tayfun
2013 'Resuloğlu 2012 Yılı Çalışmaları', *3. Çorum Kazı ve Araştırmalar Sempozyumu*. Çorum İl Kültür ve Turizm Müdürlüğü, Çorum: 5–11.

Yıldırım, Tayfun & Kısa, Aslı
2015 'Çorum/Resuloğlu 2014 Yılı Çalışmaları', *5. Çorum Kazı ve Araştırmalar Sempozyumu*. Çorum İl Kültür ve Turizm Müdürlüğü, Çorum: 97–104.

15. The Settlement Sequence of Kültepe from the Late Early to the Middle Bronze Age

Stratigraphic and Ceramic Periodization from Recent Excavations in the Southern Sector of the Mound

Fikri Kulakoğlu, Luca Peyronel, Valentina Oselini & Agnese Vacca

Stratigraphy and Architectural Sequence

The Italian Archaeological Project at Kültepe (PAIK), which started in 2019 as an international collaboration of the Turkish Archaeological Expedition at Kültepe directed by Fikri Kulakoğlu, is carrying out excavations in the south-western mound of Kültepe (Açma/Operations 01, 05 and 08), a key area that is providing an almost undisturbed sequence of Iron Age, Middle Bronze, and late Early Bronze Age periods (Kültepe mound levels/periods 4-10) (Kulakoğlu & Peyronel 2022; 2023).

In this article the most recent discoveries of the PAIK expedition are illustrated following a chrono-stratigraphic outline, discussing the stratigraphic and architectural sequence, as well as the ceramic assemblage, taking the view of intra-site developments, as well as comparing the Kültepe horizons with other contemporary sites in central Anatolia.

Fikri Kulakoğlu (kulakoglu@yahoo.com) Director of Kültepe excavations, University of Ankara

Luca Peyronel (luca.peyronel@unimi.it) Head of the Italian Archaeological Project at Kültepe, University of Milan (Italy)

Agnese Vacca (agnese.vacca@unimi.it) Field Director of the Italian Archaeological Project at Kültepe, University of Milan (Italy)

Valentina Oselini (valentina.oselini@unimi.it) Pottery Supervisor of the Italian Archaeological Project at Kültepe, University of Milan (Italy)

The Burnt Room

The Burnt Room shows a similar layout and orientation as the rooms pertaining to the so-called Palace on the Southern Terrace excavated by T. Özgüç in 1954–1967. The excavated portion of the room is located on the western wing of the latter architectural complex, immediately to the north of the large rectangular Room B12. The Palace on the Southern Terrace is comprised of an eastern and a western wing — with rooms arranged in two rows — on each side of a 50 m south–north long passageway, stone-paved in the northern part and covered by wooden planks to the south (Özgüç 1999, 106–16) (Fig. 15.1). It ended in a large open space paved with stone slabs. According to T. Özgüç the complex might be considered as a palace of level/period 8 and level II of the Lower Town of Kaneš (Özgüç 1999, 79–105), dated to the Middle Bronze I (c. 1950–1835 BC). However, the construction of this architectural complex could date back to an earlier phase, as also noticed by T. Özgüç, based on the pottery assemblages retrieved in the rooms of the building that show some 'unusually archaic traits' (Özgüç 1999, 109–10). This would mean that the complex was likely constructed during the Early Bronze-Middle Bronze Age transition and remained in use in MB I (mound levels/periods 9–10 through 8) to be ultimately destroyed by a severe fire that has been related to that which occurred around 1835 BC in the Lower Town II phase (Barjamovic et al. 2012, 46). However, a

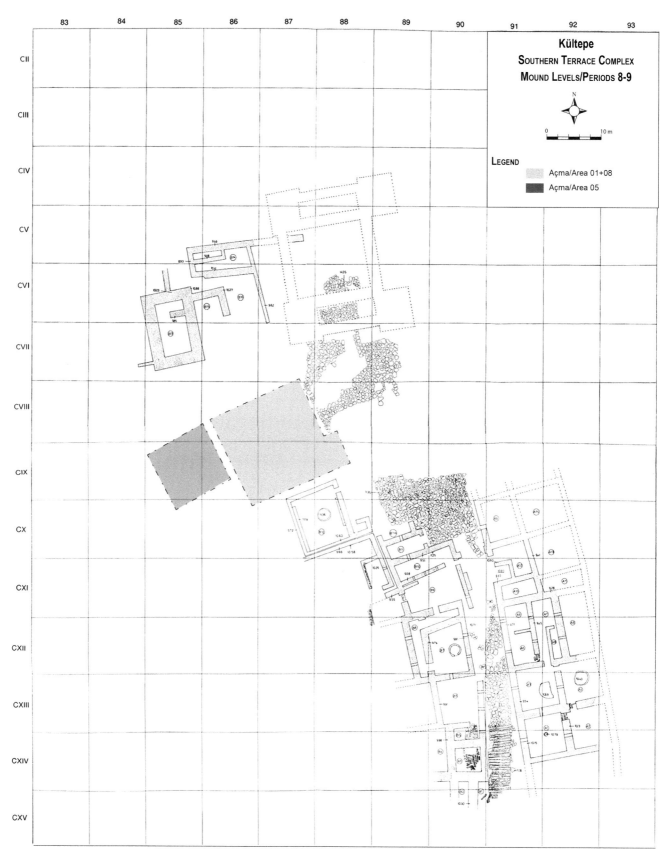

Figure 15.1: Kültepe, southern terrace complex, mound levels/periods 8–9 with indication of Açma/Operations excavated by the PAIK in 2019–2022. © Kültepe Expedition.

precise correlation between the two events needs to be assessed based on a thorough sequence anchored to radiocarbon dating.

In general, it is reasonable to consider the architectural complex on the southern terrace as a composite public area in which administrative activities like storage and exchange of commodities, proven by cuneiform tablets and sealings, were carried out (Kulakoğlu 2011). The complex was presumably located close to the southern gate giving access to the upper mound of Kaneš. According to Naumann (1971, 271, 275) the complex should be part of a corridor-like gate connected with the fortification wall, which is almost completely buried under the later Hellenistic/Roman fortification with the exception of a small portion of what has been tentatively identified as a casemate tower (Rooms B1–2 according to Makowski 2014, 96).

The long stone-paved street led to the 'plaza', a wide square located at the centre of the upper mound. The architectural arrangement of this open space and of the adjacent buildings is unfortunately little known due to the poor state of preservation of most of the structures which were affected by later MBA construction activities at this spot (Özgüç 1999, 108). In the southern sector of the complex no traces of reconstruction are instead documented, and the burnt remains of the final architectural phase (mound level/period 8) are immediately covered by Iron Age structures (mound levels/periods 4–5, Özgüç 1999, 110).

According to Özgüç, Room B12 — located to the south of the renewed excavations by the PAIK team — is the only one that shows at least two rebuilding phases. The earliest is assigned by the excavator to the level/period 8 complex and consists of a large rectangular room (8.5 × 9 m) with stone foundations and mud-brick walls plastered with red coating, benches arranged along the inner east and west walls, and a large hearth, full of ash, in the middle of the room. The later phase of use has been assigned to level/period 7 and consists of stone walls built directly on top of the burnt mud-brick walls of the previous period (Özgüç 1999, 108).

The relationship with the stone-paved court is not clear since the andesite slabs of the square are largely missing in the area immediately to the east of Room B12. Overall, it seems that the court was in use for a long period of time, as demonstrated by re-flooring of worn slabs documented at some spots and resulting in two superimposed levels of stone pavement (Özgüç 1999, pl. 53:1). In level/period 7, the stone pavement is partly destroyed, partly obliterated by the construction of the temple and other buildings assigned by T. Özgüç to level/period 7, including the *temenos* that was accessed through a western entrance.

Excavations carried out in 2020–2021 brought to light an additional large room pertaining to the complex on the southern terrace in Açma/Operations 01 and 08, which is located on the western wing of the architectural compound, immediately to the north of the large rectangular Room B12 (Kulakoğlu & Peyronel, in this volume). The structure was extensively cut on its northern portion by the construction of the semi-subterranean monumental Stone Building that is considered contemporary with mound level/period 7 temples (see *infra*). The preserved portion of the Burnt Room with its 0.7 m wide walls measures 5 m east–west and 4 m north–south (Fig. 15.2).

The construction technique is comparable to that documented in other rooms of the complex and consists of mud-brick walls resting upon andesite stone foun-

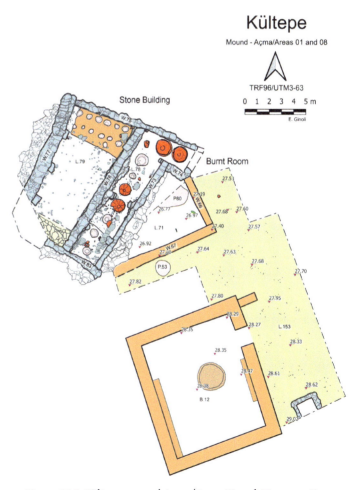

Figure 15.2: Kültepe, mound Açma/Areas 01 and 08, excavations 2020–2022 with the Burnt Room (periods/levels 8–9/10) and the Stone Building (period/level 7). © Kültepe Expedition.

dations with crossed wooden beams inserted into the wall structure alternating with vertical poles. The use of beams led the final conflagration to be severe, causing the melting of mud-bricks that turned into yellow and orange hard slag. Two overlapping floors are documented (L.70 and L.71); they are beaten earth floors with a mat covering that has left traces of organic fibre residues. The two floors differ *c.* 0.40 m from each other. The two rooms yielded scanty pottery, bronze and bone pins, as well as crescent-shaped clay loom weights.

To the south of the Burnt Room, a floor level (L.153) was identified and belongs to a probable outdoor space, extending to the south and placed on a slightly higher terrace, *c.* 0.35 m higher than L.71 and 0.20 m than L.70. This arrangement made it possible to overcome the difference in height of the stone-paved court. The latter has a difference in elevation of *c.* 2.9 m over 35 m, e.g. from the beginning of the plaza towards its northern edge (Özgüç 1999, 109, plan 4 CIX/89 to CVI/88). The outdoor area shows two overlapped compact beaten earth floors (L.153 and L.151) partially extending immediately to the south of the Burnt Room (20.t 08.Mk.03 and 05), both of which yielded few and scattered pottery materials fully comparable to those retrieved over the two floor levels L.70 and L.71.

Overall, ceramics associated with the Burnt Room and related layers seem to date to an Early–Middle Bronze Age Transitional horizon (mound levels/periods 9–10), thus pertaining to an earlier occupational phase of the complex on the southern terrace that was continuously occupied throughout level/period 8 (contemporary with level II in the Lower Town). However, excavations did not allow the identification of substantial architectural levels dating to level/period 8 at this spot, probably also due to later building activities related to the construction of the Stone Building that deeply affected the stratigraphy (see *infra*). Ongoing investigations and reopening of older sectors planned for the next excavation campaigns in Operations 01+08 will make it possible to clarify the occupational history of the area, as well as the stratigraphic relationship of the Burnt Room with the complex on the southern terrace.

The Stone Building

Immediately to the north of the Burnt Room a large semi-subterranean building, labelled the Stone Building, was brought to light (Fig. 15.2). This monumental structure is related to reconstruction activities dated to level/period 7 of the mound (MB II, *c.* eighteenth century BC) involving for instance the erection of the Waršama Palace on the citadel above the Old Palace (level/period 8), and the reconfiguration of the area around the stone-paved court with the construction of two monumental temples. The erection of the Stone Building has entailed large construction works, including excavating and levelling activities that caused the complete loss of the most recent phase of occupation of the complex on the southern terrace, which instead seems to be preserved on a higher terrace located about 5 m further west.

The Stone Building shows a completely different orientation (north-east/south-west) with respect to the previous architecture of levels/periods 8–10 (displaying a prevalent east–west orientation) and has been interpreted as a ceremonial building related to the sacred area occupied in level/period 7 by two monumental temples (see Kulakoğlu & Peyronel in this volume).

Excavations brought to light the basement of the building, consisting of two adjacent Rooms (L.78 to the south-east and L.79 to the north-west) delimited by stone walls made of local volcanic rock with roughly squared faces on the inner sides, while the exterior facade was directly leaned against the cut made in the ground (and therefore not visible). Both Rooms L.78 and L.79 were filled with about 4 m of superimposed layers corresponding to a single destruction event, possibly related to an earthquake. Different collapsing layers were separated, each characterized by a different direction and inclination corresponding to the destruction of given walls and architectural features which had fallen inside the room in a chaotic manner.

Room L.79 is a large hall (12 × 5.2 m) with a floor made of small stones coated with a layer of clay and covered by a reed mat. The lowest collapse layer directly above the floor (22.t 01.Mk05) is characterized by small and medium size stones, fragmented mud-bricks, and thousands of pottery fragments belonging to broken vessels concentrated along the northern and southern walls of the room (probably originally stored on shelves). A large concentration of broken vessels is also found above a wide low clay bench, placed along the eastern side of the room, and furnished with shallow hollows intended to hold vessels. Conversely, while moving towards the centre of the room the quantity of materials drops and the matrix appears more clayey with fewer inclusions. The collapse and accumulation layers immediately above are characterized by the presence of stone blocks and fragmented vessels; the latter are mainly found up to a height of 1.5 m and they likely pertain to the assemblage originally stored in the basement level, crushed, and scattered throughout by the stones when the walls collapsed inside the rooms. The uppermost layers (from 1.5 to *c.* 2.70 m) are characterized by a very large number of collapsed stone blocks extending over both Room L.78 and L.79 and yielded a large quantity of pottery, including several fragments pertaining to two decorated pithoi, suggesting the presence of spaces for storing vessels also on the ground level (Kulakoğlu & Peyronel in press; see also Kulakoğlu & Peyronel in this volume).

In the south-eastern L-shaped Room L.78, a long storeroom (12 × 2.3 m) equipped with nine big pithoi, the arrangement of collapse layers is similar, with large and medium size blocks found at different heights from the floor level up to 2.50 m, mixed with large fragments of pithoi blown up and scattered throughout. Room L.78 features a beaten earth floor spaced at intervals by large flat slabs and small and medium-large stones placed around the base of the pithoi to make them stand up. The filling layer covering the floor is characterized by a thick silty-clay matrix with small charcoals, and calcium carbonate concretions, that would suggest a humid environment probably due to the presence of water or liquids (contained in the pithoi?), and quite a high number of fragmented vessels.

The last level related to the building is an artificial filling rich in pottery sherds and animal bones that covered the collapse levels of the building. It has been tentatively interpreted as a deliberate closure that happened shortly after the last phase of use (Kulakoğlu & Peyronel; Kulakoğlu, Peyronel & Minniti in this volume).

Overall, the collapse layers of the building and the subsequent artificial filling are concentrated exclusively within the perimeter of the structure. Conversely, excavation in the area immediately outside the Stone Building did not allow the recognition of collapse layers related to the destruction of the walls that stood above the ground level, probably due to later levelling activities of the whole area. The stratigraphic position of the Stone Building and its relative chronology is confirmed by its relationship with the layers and structures directly affected by the cut for its construction. In fact, as previously mentioned, the northern portion of the Burnt Room has been completely removed by the construction of the massive stone walls of the south-eastern Room L.78. A similar situation, although not excavated yet, is observable along the western and northern limits of the building, where MBA I burnt levels emerge and are clearly cut by the Stone Building structures.

The Pottery Assemblage of the Burnt Room

The pottery assemblage of the Burnt Room can be assigned to the Early–Middle Bronze Age transition or to the very beginning of the Middle Bronze Age period (twenty-first–early twentieth century BC). With respect to the local sequence a dating to periods/levels 9–10 of the mound can be suggested based on ceramic parallels. Overall, pottery materials retrieved in the Burnt Room and related layers are quite scanty, as already noted by Özgüç (1999, 109) for the complex on the southern terrace that is said to have been partially emptied during the conflagration.

The pottery assemblage encompasses four main ware classes. Simple Ware (48 per cent out of 234 diagnostic fragments) is the most attested category, followed by Painted Ware (23 per cent), Red Slip Ware (21 per cent), and Cooking Ware (8 per cent). Painted Ware encompasses dark brown to faded black painted motifs applied either on self-slip and smoothed surfaces or on red/orange slipped and polished surfaces.[8]

Simple Ware is the most attested ware category and includes hand-made vessels manufactured with coarse red/orange or brown-coloured fabrics with abundant vegetal and grit inclusions, and wheel-finished vessels manufactured with light coloured pastes, mineral tempered. The former mainly encompasses inverted-rim bowls slightly carinated or with rounded incurving rim (Fig. 15.3:1–3), large shallow bowls or trays with thickened inside rim (Fig. 15.3:4), and jars with offset necks and with everted rims and rounded lips with or without vertical handles (Fig. 15.3:11–12). The outer surfaces are generally smoothed or polished. Conversely, vessels in Simple Ware manufactured with light coloured, mineral tempered pastes, include truncated-conical goblets with string-cut bases, large shallow bowls with simple rounded rim, and hemispherical bowls with rounded rim (Fig. 15.3:6–10). Comparable is the Simple Ware repertoire from the complex on the southern terrace, as well as from the Old Palace where similar Simple Ware types are documented (Özgüç 1999, figs C.1, C.16, B.95, B.97–98). In particular, drinking cups and goblets with thin walls are found in great quantity in all of the stratigraphic units associated with the Burnt Room phase. They are wheel made (as also suggested by the string-cut bases) and characterized by mineral tempered fab-

---

8 The study of the pottery assemblage of the Burnt Room is in progress and the percentage of the different classes is currently still provisional although reflecting a preliminary picture of the main categories attested and their relative occurrence.

rics fired at high temperatures. These types initially appear in level IV of the Lower Town (Emre 1989, 114) and in level/period 10 of the mound (Özgüç 1999, 110, fig. B.98) and continue to be manufactured in level II, being common also in levels 9 to 8 of the mound.

Red Slip Ware is quite common in these levels, featuring pinkish or buff fabrics covered by a thick red or brownish slip which is usually horizontally burnished, although vertical and diagonal strokes of burnishing can be also noticed. The repertoire encompasses a few recurrent shapes such as bowls with inverted rim and bowls with thickened and rounded rim and flattened or ring base. Generally, they are handleless although exemplars with cylindrical or triangular handles can be found (Fig. 15.3:13–14, 16–17). Other recurrent shapes are pitchers with a short and sharp spout (Fig. 15.3:15), jars with offset neck (Fig. 15.3:18), and pedestal bases likely pertaining to fruit-stands (although the latter are very rare). In a few cases plastic decorations also occur in the shape of bars, or crescents applied on the outer surface of the vessel (Özgüç 1999, fig. C.14–15). Red Slip Ware displays a thick red coating applied on the inner and outer surface of the vessel or on the outer surface and on the inner rim (Fig. 15.3:16–17). In one case the inner walls are decorated with intersecting red painted bands reminiscent of the Intermediate Ware tradition of the EB III period (Fig. 15.3:16). The repertoire of shapes shows comparisons with level III of the Lower Town where red slipped and brightly polished vessels are quite common (Emre 1989, fig. AII, 1–12), with several types, especially bowls, that are long-lived shapes attested in contexts of Lower Town level/period II and in the Old Palace (Özgüç 1999, fig. B.15–25).

Painted Ware is quite frequent, representing a significant percentage of the assemblage. It is characterized by a coarse fabric with both vegetal and mineral inclusions. Fabrics show colours ranging from light orange to red-brownish and the surfaces can be buff, yellowish, or reddish slipped and polished (in some cases also coarsely burnished). The repertoire of shapes includes a standardized set of vessels. These involve deep bowls with elongated vertical rim and thinned lip (Fig. 15.4:1) or bowls with rounded profile, short, everted rim and, in some cases, cylindrical handles (Fig. 15.4:2–5). Bowls with inverted rim and handled jars (with two or four handles) with flaring elongated rim also occur (Fig. 15.4:6–8, 10–11). Further to this, other common painted shapes are shallow bowls with thickened and bevelled rim or with short, everted rim, decorated with a thick red painted band applied on the inner and outer rim (Fig. 15.4:9). Decorations encompass geometric designs in a black matt paint, such as parallel lines, zigzags, triangles, chequer-patterns, and rhombus often with a metope-shaped outline.

Painted Ware with geometric designs has been labelled in the literature Alişar III (von der Osten 1937), a distinctive pottery style of the central Anatolian plateau that continues the tradition of the local painted ware of the EB III period (e.g. Intermediate Ware), and typically documented in the area to the south of the Kızılırmak River (Manuelli & Mielke 2022, 6–7 for an overview about pottery terminology).

Hence, Alişar III originates from the previous tradition of EB III local painted wares developing during the final stage of this period, around the twenty-second century BC, and continuing to be also produced in the early second millennium BC with the introduction of elements characteristic of the Early to Middle Bronze Age transition. At Kültepe/Kaneš Alişar III pottery appears from level 11a of the mound sequence, at the end of the third millennium BC, and continues to be produced until level/period 8, at around the mid-nineteenth century BC (Kulakoğlu 2015, 15–18; Rıdvanoğulları et al. in this volume). In the sequence excavated in Trench 1 in the northern sector of the mound, this ware occurs in level I in association with wheel-finished Simple Ware plates (or A2 Trojan plates) and handmade Red Slip Ware (Kulakoğlu et al. 2020, figs 2:14–15). A single ^{14}C dating from level I suggests a 2σ range comprised between 2148–2027 cal BC (Kulakoğlu et al. 2020). Alişar III is also well attested in levels/periods IV and III of the Lower Town and continues in level/period II although it is much less common (Emre 1989, 117–19). The repertoire of shapes documented in the Burnt Room and associated layers is largely comparable with the assemblage excavated in levels III and IV of the Lower Town, such as bowls with inverted rims, one-handled cups, jugs and large jars with flaring rim and vertical handles (Emre 1989, figs 19–62).

Interestingly, rare painted sherds from the Burnt Room are manufactured with a lighter coloured pink-yellowish mineral tempered paste and have a white polished coating over which black painted geometric motifs are applied (Fig. 15.4:1). These rare fragments recall the so-called 'Wavy Line' pottery of the MB I well attested in level/period II of the Lower Town and level/period 8 of the mound (see Manuelli & Mielke 2022, 7).

Overall, the ceramic assemblage from the Burnt Room seems to overlap with the one documented in levels 9–10 of the mound and levels III–IV of the Lower

15. THE SETTLEMENT SEQUENCE OF KÜLTEPE FROM THE LATE EARLY TO THE MIDDLE BRONZE AGE

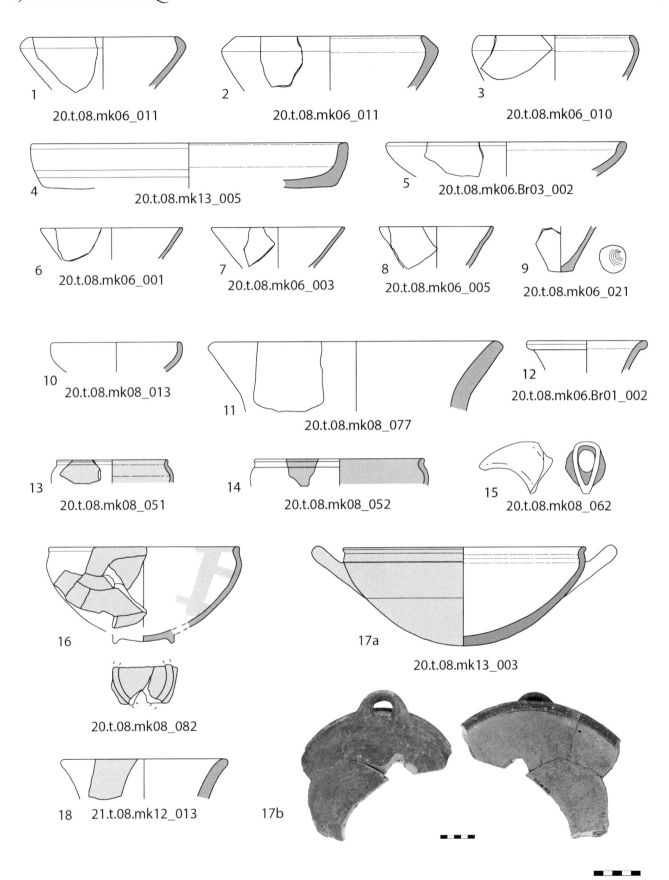

Figure 15.3: Pottery from the Burnt Room: Simple Ware, open and closed shapes (1–12); Slip and Burnished Ware (13–18). © Kültepe Expedition.

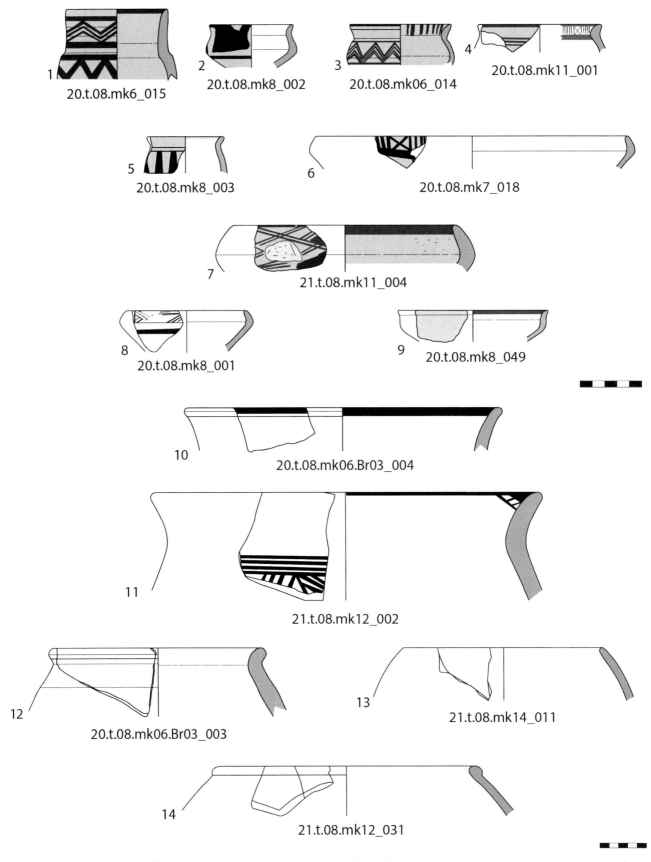

Figure 15.4: Pottery from the Burnt Room: Painted Ware, open and closed shapes (1–11); Cooking Ware, closed shape (12–14). © Kültepe Expedition.

Town, while a partial overlap can be also seen with the Old Palace and the complex on the southern terrace, and with the Lower Town level/period II. For instance, the simultaneous occurrence of two different traditions — e.g. Alişar III Painted Ware and Red Slipped Ware — characterizes the pottery assemblage of the Burnt Room. According to Emre (1989, 112) this is a major element in distinguishing Lower Town levels III–IV and II respectively. In levels IV the two wares are equally attested, while in level III Alişar III Painted Ware decreases, with a trend continuing in level II when painted pottery becomes rarely attested (Özgüç & Özgüç 1953, 188; Emre 1963, 87; 1989, 112).

Cooking Ware is documented by a limited number of types manufactured with grey coloured fabrics rich in mineral inclusions (mica and quartz) and mainly consisting of globular pots with thickened and flared out rim and hole-mouth pots with rounded or thickened outside rim (Fig. 15.4:12–14).

While most of comparisons point to an Early to Middle Bronze Age transition, other shapes that can be considered long-lived types find parallels in contexts of the Old Palace, suggesting a strong continuity and a gradual development of the local assemblage.

When we enlarge the perspective at a regional and interregional level, parallels for the Burnt Room horizon can be seen at Alişar III, especially in phase 6M on the mound and phase 12 on the terrace (von der Osten 1937, 240; Schmidt 1932, 194–202; see also Öktü 1973), and at Boğazköy in level IVd of Büyükkaya (Fischer 1963).

The Pottery Assemblage of the Stone Building

The destruction and filling layers of the Stone Building yielded a large amount of smashed pottery vessels, most of them with a very high level of fragmentation. The assemblage is chronologically homogeneous and was part of the equipment of the building, with a clear stratigraphic distinction between vessels kept in the basement storerooms and specimens that might pertain to the ground level which collapsed with the walls inside the structure. During the 2021 and 2022 fieldwork seasons, 2736 diagnostic sherds pertaining to the upper and lower collapses and to the accumulation levels of Rooms L.78 and L.79, together with 1383 sherds from the artificial fillings covering the collapse of the building have been filed. In order to gain a complete overview of the assemblage, the study of which is still in progress, selected layers were processed at first.

Three principal ware classes have been identified: Simple Ware, Red Slip Ware, and Cooking Ware. An additional class which includes the large storage vessels/pithoi has been considered independently. Painted potsherds are very rare, corresponding to 1 per cent of the total. The pottery assemblage encompasses serving vessels and tableware, storage vessels and cooking pots.

Simple Ware represents 68 per cent of the total. It is characterized by a monochrome pale brown or pinkish fabric with very fine mineral inclusions and sand. Surfaces are mostly smoothed or scraped. Simple Ware shapes are bowls with conical, hemispherical, sinuous, or carinated bodies, handled bowls and mugs, pitchers, jars/*hydrias*, globular pots, and miniaturized vessels.

Conical bowls with simple rims (Fig. 15.5:1–2) and hemispherical bowls with slightly thickened and inverted rims (Fig. 15.5:3–6) represent the most common types in the assemblage. They are mainly wheel-thrown and smoothed on the surface of the upper body, while the lower part is usually scraped with a spatula. Conical and hemispherical bowls have small bases, which vary between rounded, pointed, or flattened. Among the slightly thickened and inverted rim bowls, we can roughly distinguish between two standard sizes: a smaller one of *c.* 14–18 cm in diameter, and a larger one, about 20 to 25 cm in diameter. They have been found in very high quantities throughout the layers, from the floors to the upper fillings that closed the collapse level, attesting to a standardized production well known in the late phases (levels/periods Ib-a) of the Lower Town and in association with the buildings of period/level 7 of the Upper Town, as testified e.g. by specimens found in the Waršama Palace and in the Official Storage Building of the temples (Özgüç 1999, 85; figs A; E: 1–9). The bowls with a slightly thickened and inverted rim are common in the Middle Bronze Age also at Boğazköy-Ḫattuša and continue there during the Old Hittite period (Schoop 2006, 227, fig. 5:F, G; Strupler's contribution in Schachner 2011, 56; fig. 32:h, i; Schoop 2011: 243–46, fig. 1:A–C). This shape is also frequent in the early Late Bronze Age repertoires, e.g. in different layers of Building D (levels 2b and 2a) at Kayalıpınar (Müller-Karpe & Müller-Karpe 2020, fig. 9:10–17; fig. 10:2–3; fig. 13:15–16).

Other Simple Ware open shapes from the Stone Building are the deep bowls with a sinuous profile and an out-flared rim (Fig. 15.5:7), characterized by pinkish fabric and dark core as well as the carinated bowls (Fig. 15.5:8–10). This last category consists of various types, including specimens with sinuous profile or

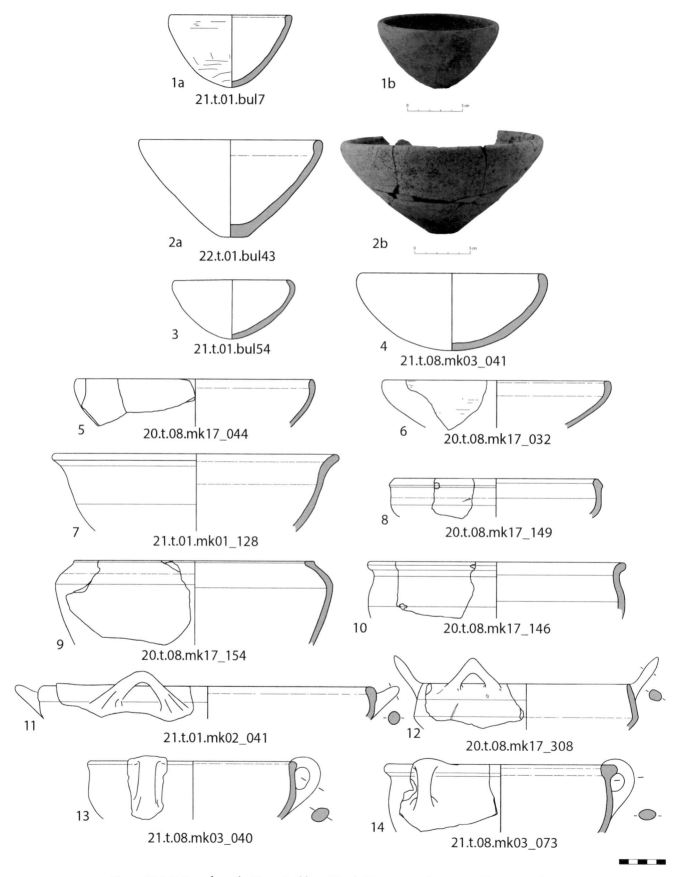

Figure 15.5: Pottery from the Stone Building: Simple Ware, open shapes. © Kültepe Expedition.

sharper carination and a thickened, everted, or outwardly protruding rim. Carinated bowls have occasionally horizontal arch-shaped or triangular handles applied on the carination or in the upper part of the body (Fig. 15.5:11–12). Handled carinated bowls also recur within the Red Slip Ware assemblage. Mugs are wheel-thrown and show a sinuous profile, simple rim, and vertical tubular handle applied between the rim and the body (Fig. 15.5:13–14). Handled bowls and mugs occur since the level II period, in both the Lower Town contexts and in the Old Palace level/period 8 (Özgüç 1999, 98–99; fig. B:1–5, 7, 23, 25, 29).

Well represented among closed shapes are the pitchers with narrow neck and handle, characterized sometimes by beak-shaped spouts and, rarely, by trefoil-mouth (Fig. 15.6:1). Beak-shaped pitchers are one of the types that are well known in Kültepe, as well as in Boğazköy-Ḫattuša also during the Old Hittite period (see Strupler's contribution in Schachner 2011, 53; fig. 31:g–i; Schoop 2011, 251). A large number of bird-shaped spouts may suggest the presence of teapots, of which a miniaturistic specimen was found completely preserved (Fig. 15.6:2). Teapots represent an element of continuity between the Lower Town level II and the later Hittite period. In fact, they have been found in the Palace of the Southern Terrace at Kültepe, level/period 8 (Özgüç 1999, fig. B:11), and are still common within the assemblage of the Hittite building D at Kayalıpınar, level 2a (Müller-Karpe & Müller-Karpe 2020, fig. 13:1).

Jars are differentiated between necked jars with out-flared slightly thickened rims (Fig. 15.6: 3–6), and funnel-like necked jars with an inwardly ridged rim (*hydrias*) (Fig. 15.6:7, 9). The latter appears in Lower Town level II and continues during the Lower Town level Ib as testified by examples from the Waršama Palace (Özgüç & Özgüç 1953, 174, figs 233; 236; Özgüç 1999, 85, fig. A:22–26). A valuable comparison for the funnel-like necked jars found in the Stone Building comes from the excavation in the Lower Town at Boğazköy-Ḫattuša, specifically in the *kārum* period at Kesikkaya (Schachner 2020, 22–23; fig. 21).

Also frequent are examples of hole-mouth jars with thickened rims (Fig. 15.6: 8) and globular jars with a single or double handle, often characterized by a white slip and polishing treatment (White Slip Ware) (Fig. 15.6:10). Decorations on Simple Ware specimens are occasionally attested, especially on jars and storage vessels, i.e. incised lines and rope-motif impressions, as well as plastic decorations, including a bull's head in relief (Fig. 15.7).

Red Slip Ware, which corresponds to 19 per cent of the total production, is characterized by a monochrome pale brown or pinkish fabric with mineral inclusions, a red slip coating, and a burnished or polished treatment of the surface. This ware is typical of north-central Anatolia and is mainly attested in the Lower Town levels from III to Ib, encompassing the entire Middle Bronze Age. The slip is usually applied on the outer surface and sometimes on the inside; it mainly covers the upper part of the body and, less frequently, the entire shape. The colour of the coating varies between a range of dark red-purple, bright red, and reddish orange. In some cases, the red slip is severely eroded and poorly preserved, and a bright component can be seen on the surface of the vessels, possibly related to mica inclusions within the clay lining. The presence of mica in the vessel's surface slip is a characteristic that appears associated with the Red Slip Ware since the Lower Town level/period Ib (Özgüç & Özgüç 1953, 153–54; Emre 1963, 93).

Open shapes include a few shallow bowls with thin walls (Fig. 15.8:1–2), deep bowls with thickened rims (Fig. 15.8:3–4), carinated bowls (Fig. 15.8:5–6), and carinated bowls with triangular handles (Fig. 15.8:7–8). The latter represent an element of continuity with the Burnt Room phase as well as with level/period 8 of the Old Palace, and Lower Town level II (Özgüç 1986, figs 42–44; 1999: 99; fig. B:22–23; 25–26). As already mentioned by Emre, a firm continuity links the handled carinated bowls of levels/periods II and Ib (Emre 1963, fig. 11). Closed shapes include beak-spouted pitchers (Fig. 15.8:9–10), necked jars with simple or thickened rims (Fig. 15.8: 11–12), jars with out-flared and thickened rim (Fig. 15.8: 13), hole-mouth jars with thickened and ridged rims (Fig. 15.8:15–16), and jars with out-flaring neck and thickened and inwardly ridged rims (Fig. 15.8:14). A well-preserved example of a jar shows a short out-flaring neck, an inwardly ridged rim, at least two triangular handles on the shoulder and a rounded base. The slip is reddish-orange and covers three-quarters of the vessel, leaving the lower part uncoated (Fig. 15.9:1). Beak-shaped spout pitchers and necked jars with a red slip coating are part of the assemblage of the *kārum* period contexts at Boğazköy-Ḫattuša (see Strupler's contribution in Schachner 2011, 52; 2012, 89; figs 8, 9).

Another remarkable dark red-purple slipped jar with out-flaring neck and inwardly ridged rim is decorated with grooved horizontal lines and protruding studs (Fig. 15.9:2). This style is well known in Kültepe,

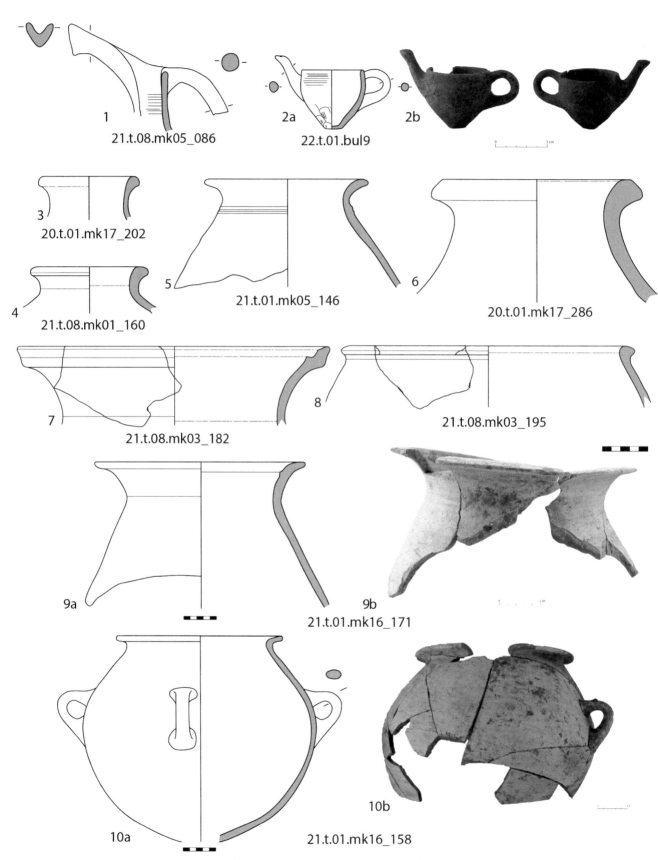

Figure 15.6: Pottery from the Stone Building: Simple Ware, closed shapes. © Kültepe Expedition.

Figure 15.7: Pottery from the Stone Building: an applied bull's head decoration on a Simple Ware jar. © Kültepe Expedition.

occurring on small pots with decorations in the shape of grapes, of which a specimen comes from the official storage building of the temples on the citadel, level/period 7 (Özgüç 1999, fig. E:12).

Among the Red Slip Ware, fragments of fruit-stand bases have been occasionally found (Fig. 15.8:17). They are characterized by a thickened edge and are often red slipped and burnished, especially on the outer surface.

Decorations on Red Slip Ware shapes include horizontal ridges and grooves, protruding studs, plastic application of concentric circles, and the motif of the *signe royal* (Fig. 15.9:3), which was stamped on pottery from the Lower Town level/period Ib (Emre 1963, 94). Jars with *signe royal* have been found in the Lower Town level/period Ib, in the Waršama Palace, and in the official storage building of the temple, level/period 7 (Özgüç & Özgüç 1953, 174; fig. 131; Özgüç 1999, figs A:18, 19, 21; E:11). Moreover, examples of zoomorphic protomes, representing cattle, caprids, and felines possibly pertaining to *rhyta* or jars with applied decorations have been frequently attested (Fig. 15.9:4).

Cooking Ware represents 12 per cent of the sample and it is characterized by a porous brownish-black or grey matrix with frequent large visible mineral inclusions. Cooking Ware is almost exclusively associated with cooking pots, which are easily recognizable within the ceramic assemblages because of their peculiar pale brown or pinkish surface and darker core. Surfaces are smoothed and darker traces of secondary burning are frequent. The bulk of the cooking pots have a globular shape, which made them more resistant when placed on a fire or hot coals, and an outwardly thickened rim, often characterized by a double ridge (Fig. 15.10:1-4). Most of the examples have two applied vertical handles on the shoulder (Fig. 15.10:5). Globular shape and vertical handles also represent an element of continuity with the later Hittite repertoire, possibly suggesting a long-standing tradition in culinary practices (Schoop 2011, 249; Glatz 2015, 193-94).

The long narrow room of the Stone Building was equipped with at least nine big pithoi, set into the floor, as large storage vessels. Two of them have been found entirely preserved and located in their original place (see Kulakoğlu & Peyronel in press and in this volume). They are *c*. 175-180 cm high with a capacity of more than two thousand litres. They have large mouths with thick protruding rims, flattened on the top and on the outer profile, and the shoulder decorated with a row of round pommels, *c*. 7-8 cm in diameter. The pithoi have a cylindrical shape that progressively contracts towards the base, which is flat and 25 cm in diameter. The lower part of the body is decorated with irregular rope impressions. The pithoi are characterized by a pinkish fabric, with a grey core and mineral fine inclusions; the surface is coated with a very pale brown layer of clay. Visible traces in the fractures indicate that the pithoi were built by joining regular clay slabs, *c*. 3.5-4 cm thick. The two pithoi in situ were also both restored in antiquity considering the presence of several lead notches and plaques.

Large cylindrical storage vessels with applied pommels are very rare at Kültepe and are also only occasionally attested in other contemporary sites, such as at Boğazköy-Ḫattuša, where a very similar specimen has been found in the north-east sector of the town (Schachner 2020, figs 3-4).

Many fragments belonging to two pithoi characterized by applied plastic decorations alternated with incisions and impressions, have been found scattered in the upper levels of the collapsed structures of the building, suggesting that the vessels were originally kept at ground level. All the pieces are *c*. 3-3.2 cm thick and are characterized by a pinkish-brown fabric, with a grey core. The surface is coated with a very pale brown slip. The two pithoi slightly differ in the shape of the rims and the decorative scenes portrayed on the sur-

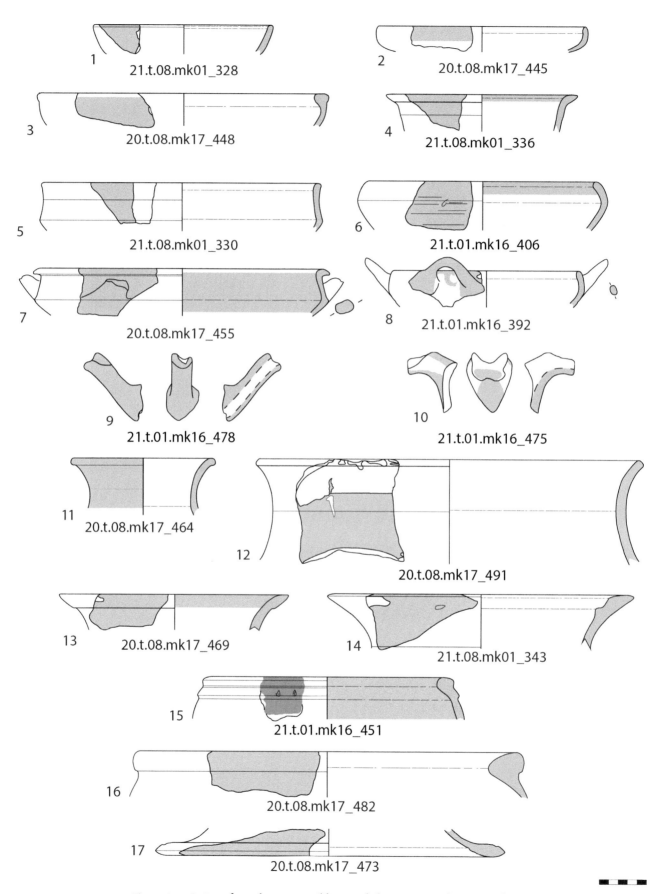

Figure 15.8: Pottery from the Stone Building: Red Slip Ware. © Kültepe Expedition.

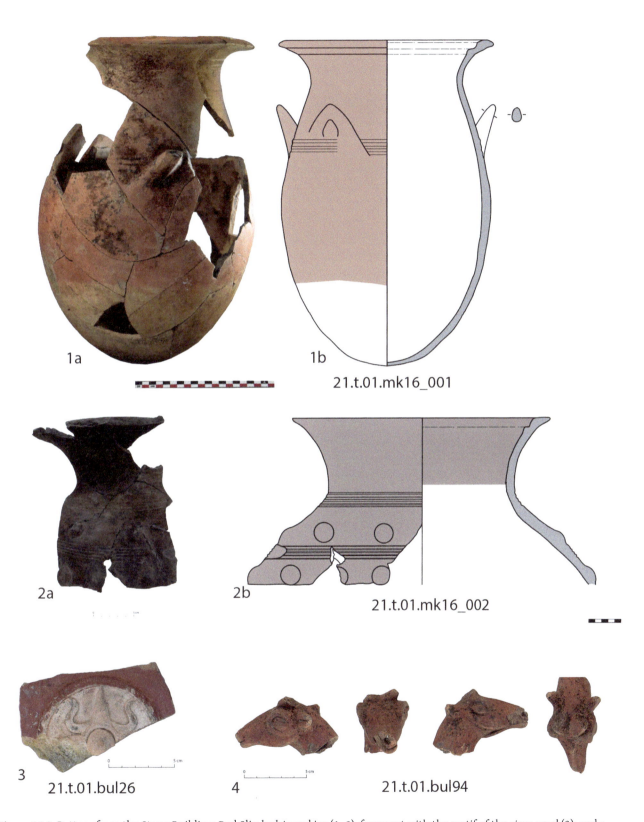

Figure 15.9: Pottery from the Stone Building: Red Slip *hydria* and jar (1–2), fragment with the motif of the *signe royal* (3); and a fragment with plastic animal's head (4). © Kültepe Expedition.

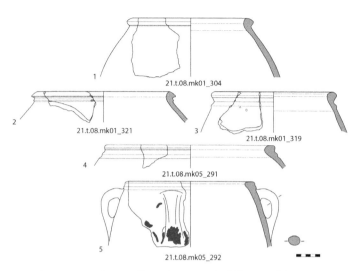

Figure 15.10: Pottery from the Stone Building: Cooking Ware. © Kültepe Expedition.

Figure 15.11: A detail of the plastic geometric decoration applied on pithos 20.t 08.mk17_647. © Kültepe Expedition.

face. The first pithos has a thickened and protruding edge and is provided with a spout. Below the rim, various decorative motifs are organized into three different registers separated by flattened horizontal ridges 5 cm thick. The registers are subdivided into metopes by applied vertical ridges. Simple dots about 1.5 cm in diameter are the recurring motif on the background. Concentric circles and lunettes, 'ladder' motifs, triangles and parallel strips, wide diamonds filled with dots and circles, as well as composite motifs are alternated on the surface of the vessel. This pithos was also provided with triangular handles, located at the centre of the body. The figurative scene in the second register is of great interest, which includes various animals and humans (for a wider discussion and figures see Kulakoğlu & Peyronel 2023 and in this volume).

The second pithos has a simple rim, and, as in the former case, is characterized by geometric motifs realized with applied plastic decorations. These are distributed over three horizontal registers. The upper and lower registers are subdivided into several metopes, c. 15 × 9 cm each, while the central register has different and wider patterns (Fig. 15.11). The style of the decorations is comparable to the one on the first pithos, including applied dots, concentric circles, triangles, crosses, or rays. In both vessels, the lower part is lacking applied elements and provided with rope-impressions.

Up to now, no strict comparisons are known in Anatolia, although some exemplars of large pithoi with plastic geometric patterns come from the Great Temple I at Boğazköy-Ḫattuša (Schachner 2021, fig. 68).

The pottery assemblage of the Stone Building shows a high standardization of shapes and techniques. The assemblage includes *longue durée* types, i.e. Simple Ware narrow conical bowls with pointed bases, Red Slip Ware jars, teapots and carinated bowls with handles, which are used also in the mound level/period 8, as well as new shapes that appeared in the mound level/period 7 and Lower Town level/period Ib. Simple Ware bowls with inverted rims have been found in a huge quantity and show strict typological comparisons with exemplars from the Waršama Palace, and from the official storage building near the temples on the mound. Among the Red Slip Ware shapes, jars with the *signe royale*, are usually typical of the Lower Town level Ib phase/level 7. The assemblage from the Stone Building at Kültepe also finds comparisons with some coeval and later contexts at Boğazköy and Kayalıpınar.

The sharing of similar pottery types that starts at the beginning of the second millennium BC and continues until the Old Hittite period within such a wide region clearly indicates the development of a common tradition of pottery production. As pointed out by Emre (Emre 1963, 95), this phenomenon needs to be better explored, starting with a detailed re-examination of the ceramic material.

Conclusions

The recent excavations carried out in the southern sector of the mound shed new light on the development of the town from the end of the third millennium BC to the end of the second millennium BC occupation at Kültepe. The presence of sequence of overlapping architectural phases makes it possible to check and refine the overall periodization of the mound levels/periods 10–6. The materials from the Burnt Room have confirmed the dating of the first construction of the complex on the southern terrace excavated by Özgüç to the very late third millennium BC, or at the transition between the EB and MB periods, before the first implanting of the Assyrian merchants at the site (mound levels/periods 10–9). The destruction of the building should probably be ascribed to the same event that affected the Old Palace and the Lower Town II, during the second half of the nineteenth century BC, and the results from currently ongoing ^{14}C analysis from samples collected in the layers over the floors would give additional data to fix its absolute chronology. The Burnt Room was cut by the foundation of the monumental Stone Building to the north. The latter is dated to the late nineteenth–eighteenth centuries BC by radiocarbon dating and chrono-typology of associated pottery materials. The large number of complete and restorable vessels related to the original assemblage of the basement's building therefore offered a unique occasion to elaborate a coherent and well dated chronology for level/period 7 of the mound. The repertoire shows the strong continuity of the pottery tradition throughout the *kārum* period and, at the same time, the changes and development that are comparable with those evidenced by materials from other coeval reliable contexts of the upper mound, such as the Waršama Palace, and the Lower Town Ib houses and tombs. However, it is probable that the building ended abruptly sometime before the end of the level/period 7, which is marked by a fierce destruction of the town (Kulakoğlu & Peyronel in this volume). This is in fact suggested by the lack of a destruction layer in the Stone Building and by the presence of an artificial closure indicated by levelling/fillings that sealed the collapse of the structures. The fillings atop the building are very rich in pottery fragments pertaining to the very same ceramic horizon as the vessels found over the floors, thus suggesting the short time that elapsed between the collapse and the closure. The excavations planned for the next seasons in the western part of the area would add further evidence to the articulated sequence of the second millennium BC, allowing for a better understanding of the terracing system towards the fortification and its chronology during the *kārum* period.

The study of the pottery assemblages combined with the stratigraphic sequence of building phases is making it possible to build a solid relative chronology anchored to absolute dating, which is necessary for a better understanding of the development of the material culture at the site. It might then be framed in a wider regional dimension, as well as evaluated in a longer diachronic perspective, to investigate how the following ceramic tradition of the Old Hittite period was rooted and directly linked with the pottery production of Kültepe.

Acknowledgements

The research at Kültepe carried out by the Italian team of the University of Milan are supported by the Italian Ministry of Foreign Affair and International Cooperation, the Italian Ministry of University and Research (Project PRIN 2017 'Big Data and Early Archives') and the University of Milan. We wish to warmly thank the members of the PAIK expedition (<https://orienteantico.unimi.it/it/paik/>) and of the Turkish Mission at Kültepe for their precious work on the field and the documentation. We also wish to thank the anonymous reviewers for their suggestions. This article is the result of a joint work carried out by the authors. A. Vacca, L. Peyronel, and F. Kulakoğlu wrote the paragraphs on stratigraphy and architecture, A. Vacca dealt with the pottery from the Burnt Room, and V. Oselini with the pottery from the Stone Building; conclusions were written jointly.

Bibliography

Barjamovic, Gojko; Hertel, Thomas, Larsen & Mogens Trolle

2012 *Ups and Downs at Kanesh: Observations on Chronology, History and Society in the Old Assyrian Period* (Publications de l'Institut historique archéologique néerlandais de Stamboul 120). Nederlands Instituut voor het Nabije Oosten, Leiden.

Emre, Kutlu

1963 'The Pottery of the Assyrian Colony Period according to the Building Levels of Kanis Karumu', *Anadolu/Anatolia* 7: 87–99.

1989 'Pottery of Levels III and IV at the Kārum of Kanesh', in Kutlu Emre, Machteld Mellink, Barthel Hrouda & Nimet Özgüç (eds), *Anatolia and the Ancient Near East: Studies in Honour of Tahsin Özgüç*. Türk Tarih Kurumu Basımevi, Ankara: 111–28.

Fisher, Frank

1963 *Die Hethitische Keramik von Boğazköy-Hattusa* (Wissenschaftliche Veröffentlichungen der Deutschen Orient-Gesellschaft 75). Mann, Berlin.

Glatz, Claudia

2015 'Plain Pots. Festivals and Feasting in Late Bronze Age Anatolia', in Claudia Glatz (ed.), *Plain Pottery Traditions of the Eastern Mediterranean and Near East: Production, Use, and Social Significance*. Left Coast, Walnut Creek: 183–214.

Kulakoğlu, Fikri

2011 'Kütepe-Kanes: A Second Millennium B.C.E. Trading Center on the Central Plateau', in Sharon R. Steadman & Gregory McMahon (eds), *The Oxford Handbook of Ancient Anatolia 10,000-323 B.C.E.* Oxford University Press, Oxford: 1012–30.

2015 'Current Research at Kültepe', in Fikri Kulakoğlu & Cécile Michel (eds), *Proceedings of the 1ˢᵗ Kültepe International Meeting Kültepe 19-23 September 2013* (Kültepe International Meetings 3, Subartu 35). Brepols, Turnhout: 9–21.

Kulakoğlu, Fikri; Kontani, Ryoichi; Uesugi, Akinori; Yamaguchi, Yuji; Shimogama, Kazuya & Semmoto, Masao

2020 'Preliminary Report of Excavations in the Northern Sector of Kültepe 2015–2017', in Fikri Kulakoğlu, Cécile Michel & Güzel Öztürk (eds), *Integrative Approaches to the Archaeology and History of Kültepe-Kaneš. Kültepe 4-7 August 2017* (Kültepe International Meetings 3, Subartu 45). Brepols, Turnhout: 9–97.

Kulakoğlu, Fikri & Peyronel, Luca

2022 'L'organizzazione dello spazio pubblico e privato a Kültepe tra Bronzo Medio ed Età del Ferro. Nuovi dati dal settore meridionale dell'insediamento', in *Lo spazio pubblico, lo spazio privato: XI Convegno contributo delle missioni archeologiche italiane a scavi, ricerche e studi in Turchia; Atti del Convegno 2020 / Kamusal alan, özel alan: XI Türkiye'deki arkeolojik çalışmalara eğitim, araştırma ve kazı'da İtalya katkısı sempozyumu; Sempozyum bildirileri 2020*. Istituto italiano di cultura, Istanbul: 31–44.

2023 'L'arte del vasaio in Anatolia antica. Il repertorio figurativo della ceramica di Kültepe durante il periodo delle colonie assire: nuovi dati dagli scavi recenti/Eski Anadolu seramik sanatı. Kültepe'de Asur Ticaret Kolonileri Çağı tasvirli seramik sanatı: son kazılardan yeni bilgiler', in *Arte, funzione e simboli nella cultura materiale dell'Anatolia Antica: XII Convegno sul contributo a scavi, ricerche e studi nelle missioni archeologiche in Turchia; Atti del Convegno 2021 / XII Türkiye'deki arkeolojik çalışmalara eğitim, araştırma ve kazı'da İtalya katkısı sempozyumu; Sempozyum bildirileri 2021*. Istituto italiano di cultura, Istanbul: 67–81.

Makowski, Maciej

2014 'The Road to the Citadel of Kanesh. Urban Structure and Spatial Organization of the City during the Assyrian Colony Period', in Piotr Bieliński, Michał Gawlikowski, Rafał Koliński, Dorota Ławecka, Arkadiusz Sołtysiak & Zuzanna Wygnańska (eds), *Proceedings of the 8th International Congress on the Archaeology of the Ancient Near East 30 April – 4 May 2012, University of Warsaw*, I. Harrassowitz, Wiesbaden: 93–111.

Manuelli, Federico & Mielke, Dirk Paul

2022 'Introduction – Throwing Some Colour on a Plain World', in Federico Manuelli & Dirk Paul Mielke (eds), *Late Bronze Age Painted Pottery Traditions at the Margins of the Hittite State: Papers Presented at a Workshop Held at the 11th ICAANE (München 4 April 2018) and Additional Contributions*. Archaeopress, Oxford: 1–20.

Müller-Karpe, Andreas & Müller-Karpe, Vuslat

2020 'Untersuchungen in Kayalıpınar 2019', *Mitteilungen der Deutschen Orient-Gesellschaft zu Berlin* 152: 191–236.

Naumann, Rudolf

1971 *Architektur Kleinasiens von ihren Anfängen bis zum Ende der hethitischen Zeit*. Wasmuth, Tübingen.

Öktü, Armağan

1973 *Die Intermediate Keramik in Kleinasien*. Salzer, Munich.

Osten, Hans Henning von der

1937 *The Alişar Hüyük Season of 1930-32*, I (Oriental Institute Publications 28). Oriental Institute of the University of Chicago, Chicago.

Özgüç, Tahsin

1986 *Kültepe-Kaniš*, II: *New Researches at the Trading Center of the Ancient Near East*. Türk Tarih Kurumu Yayınları, Ankara.

1999 *Kültepe-Kaniš/Neša Sarayları ve Mabetleri / The Palaces and Temples of Kültepe-Kaniš/Neša* (Türk Tarih Kurumu Yayınlarından 5/46). Türk Tarih Kurumu Yayınları, Ankara.

Özgüç, Tahsin & Özgüç, Nimet

1953 *Kültepe Kazisi Raporu 1949/Ausgrabungen in Kültepe* (Türk Tarih Kurumu Yayınları 5/12). Türk Tarih Kurumu Yayınları, Ankara.

Schachner, Andreas

2011 'Die Ausgrabungen in Boğazköy-Ḫattuša 2010', *Archäologischer Anzeiger*: 31–86.

2012 'Die Ausgrabungen in Boğazköy-Ḫattuša 2011', *Archäologischer Anzeiger*: 85–137.

2020 'Die Ausgrabungen in Boğazköy-Ḫattuša 2019', *Archäologischer Anzeiger*: 11–66.

2021 'Die Ausgrabungen in Boğazköy-Ḫattuša 2020', *Archäologischer Anzeiger*: 1–95.

Schmidt, Erich F.

1932 *The Alishar Hüyük Seasons of 1928 and 1929*, I (Oriental Institute Publications 28). Oriental Institute of the University of Chicago, Chicago.

Schoop, Ulf-Dietrich

2006 'Dating the Hittites with Statistics: Ten Pottery Assemblages from Boğazköy-Ḫattuša', in Dirk Paul Mielke, Ulf-Dietrich Schoop & Jürgen Seeher (eds), *Structuring and Dating in Hittite Archaeology: Requirements, Problems, New Approaches* (BYZAS 4). Ege Yayınları, Istanbul: 215–339.

2011 'Hittite Pottery: A Summary', in Hermann Genz & Dirk Paul Mielke (eds), *Insights into Hittite History and Archaeology* (Colloquia antiqua 2). Peeters, Leuven: 241–73.

16. Šamuha and Kaneš

Andreas Müller-Karpe

Introduction

Until now, most of the Old Assyrian trading stations mentioned in the archives of Kaneš cannot be located with certainty. One of the few exceptions is Šamuha. The decisive tablet, which proves the localization of Šamuha at Kayalıpınar, was discovered in 2014 at this site (Rieken 2014). The city had its heyday and epoch of greatest historical importance in the Middle Hittite period and the Hittite empire period, i.e. mainly in the fourteenth and thirteenth centuries BC. Although most of the ruins uncovered so far can be dated to this period, remains from Early Hittite/Old Assyrian times have also been found. These are the remains that belong to the same Šamuha trading station that was mentioned in eighteen of the Kültepe texts (Barjamovic 2011, 151). Compared to other places, this number is relatively small. However, this does not indicate a low importance, but rather, it reflects the fact that Šamuha was not located on one of the main trade routes controlled by Kaneš. In particular, the movement of goods from Aššur to Kaneš did not pass through Šamuha. On the contrary, it was a station on the so-called 'narrow track', i.e. smuggler's route, which connected the ore rich Pontic Mountain region, especially in copper production, with Aššur, bypassing Kaneš (Barjamovic 2011, 169–79, map). Nevertheless, there were also direct connections between Kaneš and Šamuha, but they were within the framework of regional goods traffic, whereby the trade in wool seems to have played an important role (Barjamovic 2011, 153). Both cities, Kaneš and Šamuha, were connected by a 175 km long caravan trail, with stopovers at Sultanhanı, Yeniçubuk, and Şarkışla (Fig. 16.1). The distance between these places is always a day trip of 30–35 km. The route will therefore have taken four days. It did not lead along the River Maraššanta (modern Kızılırmak), as there are no relevant archaeological sites.

In Kaneš, according to current knowledge, it was mainly the family of Aššur-taklāku, son of Ali-ahum, who had frequent connections with Šamuha, as can be seen from the evidence in the archive discovered in the house of this Assyrian.[1] But, for example, two legal documents issued in Šamuha were also found in the house of Šalim-Aššur, son of Issu-arik, which are as of yet unopened (Larsen 2021, 159, nos 978, 979). Kültepe tablets also reveal the names of two Assyrian merchants who lived at least temporarily in Šamuha: Šalim-ahum and Amur-Šamaš (Barjamovic 2011, 153). Two fragments of Old Assyrian tablets found in Kayalıpınar also list several Anatolian names, who may have been merchants as well: Tamura, [T]atali, [ ]-uman, [Ḫa]ššui, and [Ḫa]puala (Sommerfeld 2006; Kryszat 2014; 2019).

However, it is not clear from the written sources whether or not Šamuha was politically dependent on Kaneš in the nineteenth/eighteenth century BC. The mention of a palace in Šamuha should probably be interpreted that a more or less independent city-state or principality existed here in this period.[2] Economically,

---

Andreas Müller-Karpe (muekarpe@uni-marburg.de) Philipps Universität Marburg, Germany

---

[1] Michel 2008, 235, 239, 241, 242; Barjamovic 2011, 153; Hertel 2014, 47, house no. 57/58.

[2] Concerning the general situation in central Anatolia: Barjamovic et al. 2012, 43: 'The merchant records produce a consistent image of a competitive political landscape of independent micro-states.'

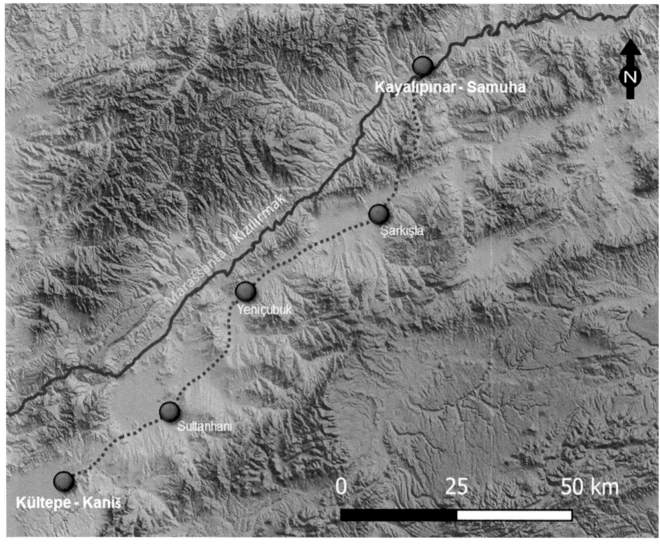

Figure 16.1: Reconstruction of the caravan route between Šamuha and Kaneš with intermediate stops (daily stages).

on the other hand, the *wabartum* Šamuha, which is repeatedly mentioned in Kültepe tablets, was subordinate to the *kārum* Kaneš. This at least concerns the situation in the time of the level *kārum* Kaneš II. After Kaneš had lost its dominant role for the Assyrian Anatolian trade in the time of the level *kārum* Kaneš Ib, there is now also a mention of a *kārum* Šamuha in a text of this era (Balkan 1965, 155), which suggests an increased economic importance.

But how is the situation reflected in the archaeological record? The excavations that began in Kayalıpınar in 2005 provide some information. The time of the *kārum* Kaneš II and Ib layers corresponds roughly to layers 6 and 5 in Kayalıpınar. When comparing the two sites, it should be taken into account that in Kayalıpınar this period has so far only been excavated on an area of 0.1 ha while in Kültepe, in the Lower Town alone more than 9 ha with about three hundred houses have already been uncovered (Hertel 2014, 30, 34).

Architecture

In Kayalıpınar, traces of six or seven houses from layer 5 have been recorded during the excavations so far. The ground plans of only two buildings can be reconstructed with some degree of reliability (Müller-Karpe et al. 2014, 13–17). The older layer 6 was only investigated in a very small section, in which a wall remnant about two metres long was recorded. Therefore, concrete statements can only be made about layer 5, in which at least three different construction phases can be distinguished.

Because of the discovery of an Old Assyrian clay tablet fragment mentioning the name Tamura, we call the western building 'House of Tamura', the eastern one:

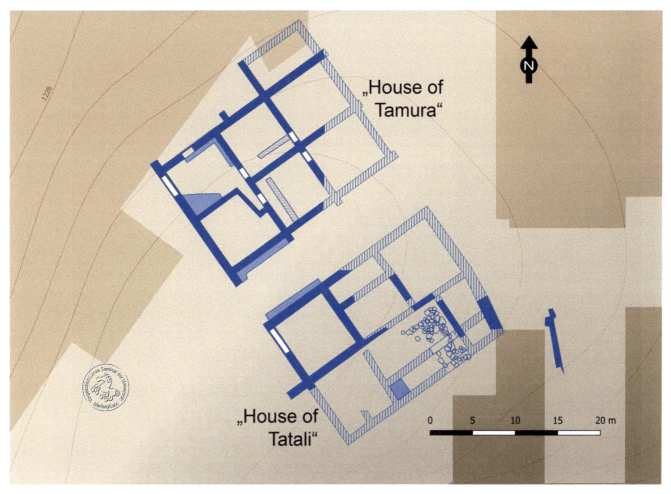

Figure 16.2: Kayalıpınar level 5.

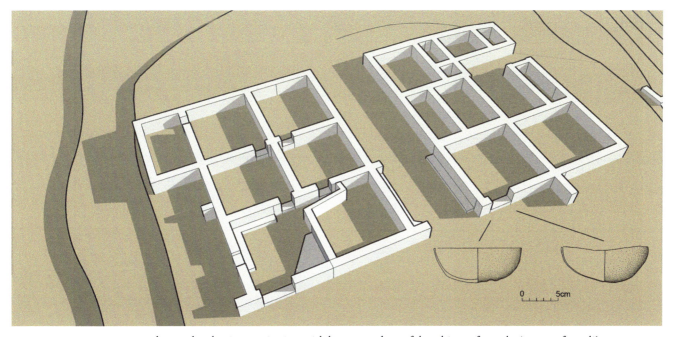

Figure 16.3: Kayalıpınar level 5, isometric view with bronze sockets of door hinges from the 'House of Tatali'.

'House of Tatali' (Fig. 16.2). The construction method of the houses corresponds to that in Kültepe as well as to what is usually seen in Anatolia in this epoch: the foundation consists of rubble stones with a superstructure of mud-bricks. However, in contrast to the common construction method in Mesopotamia, the mud-brick walls are not solid but always have struts of wooden beams. It was thus a half-timbered construction method using considerable amounts of wood. Some of the mud-brick walls are still about 1.3 m high in the present day.

The doorways of the buildings in Kayalıpınar were also designed the same as those in Kültepe. The remains of wooden door thresholds and door frames were still detectable. At the exterior gate of the 'House of Tatali', the bronze sockets of the door hinges of a two-winged gate came to light (Fig. 16.3). The walls are usually arranged orthogonally. Several rooms show a square floor space of about 7.5 m on each side (Fig. 16.4). This length seems to have been the basic unit on which the construction of the buildings was organized. Presumably, the site was initially parcelled out in this way. The ground plans of the buildings would have been staked out with pegs and cords in order to lay the foundations. Therefore, the basic measurement will probably not have been a foot, but a cubit (Akkadian *ammatu*, Hittite *gipessar*) of about 50 cm. The grid thus had a side length of 15 cubits each. Since 30 cubits corresponds to one IKU, it would mean that this unit of measurement would have been crucial here. It is now striking that some buildings of the Lower Town in Kaneš fit into this system well, e.g. the house of Šalim-Aššur (Fig. 16.4).[3] In addition, not only are the proportions between the

---

3 Further information about this house: Michel 2014, 75 f.

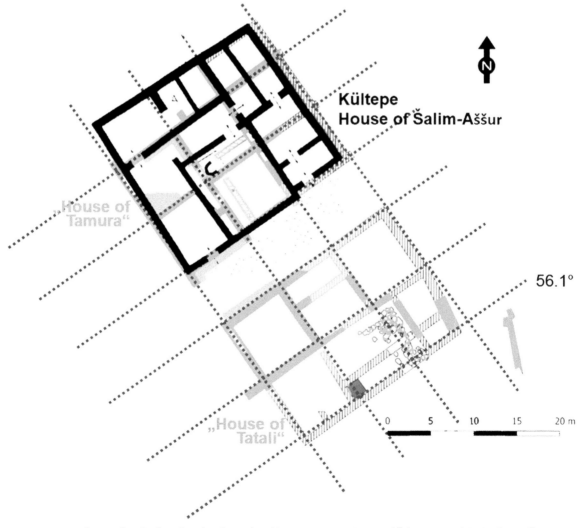

Figure 16.4: Kayalıpınar, level 5 (grey) and Kültepe, level *kārum* Kaneš II, house of Šalim-Aššur (black after T. Özgüç 2003).

Figure 16.5: Kayalıpınar level 5. Virtual reconstruction of the situation at sunrise at the summer solstice. The walls of the houses are exactly in line with the first rays of the sun.

buildings of Kaneš and Kayalıpınar comparable, but their orientations also match exactly. In Kayalıpınar, some walls excavated to the north-east of the 'House of Tamura' and the 'House of Tatali' as well as structures found during the geomagnetic survey, show the same orientation: the angle is 56.1° east. In Kültepe, the house of Šalim-Aššur is not the only house to have this orientation. However, there was possibly such an original parcelling here as well, which was then no longer adhered to so strictly in the course of urban development.[4] But the basic orientation of the buildings is, with some variations, quite comparable between the Lower Town of Kültepe and level 5 in Kayalıpınar.

Is this just a coincidence? In Kültepe, the buildings on the citadel are all orientated differently. Their orientation obviously played no role in the construction of the Lower Town, the so-called kārum-Kaneš. Why do urban districts in Kaneš and Šamuha show a similar alignment? It could be for the same reason, the same idea, for example an orientation to the course of the sun. With the help of NASA's Horizons Web Interface, calculations can be made on a wide variety of constellations of celestial bodies in the past. And indeed: the sun's northernmost rising point, the summer solstice, was in Kayalıpınar during the early second millennium BC at 56°.361 east. This matches nearly perfectly with the orientation of the buildings.[5] As a

---

[4] T. Özgüç (2003, 78) also emphasizes the planned structure of the Lower Town: 'regular quarters [...] clearly oriented streets.' In contrast to this Schachner 1999, 167: 'vegetative, addierende Entwicklung der Siedlung'; Hertel 2014, 26: 'The lower town seems to have been an organically grown urban space.' Regarding the kārum Hattuš K. Bittel (1983, 49) remarks: 'Die Ansiedlung läßt hier deutlich einige Regelmäßigkeit erkennen. Alle Bauten sind einheitlich von Nordosten nach Südwesten orientiert.'

[5] Calculations were made with <https://ssd.jpl.nasa.gov/horizons/> on basis of the geographical setting: 36° 31'41"E 39°

result it can be stated: there are strong indications, that the summer solstice played the decisive role for the planning of the *kārum* Šamuha and *kārum* Kaneš (Fig. 16.5). But why should simple residential areas be orientated towards the summer solstice? A solution might be, for example, a temple here in these districts with this special orientation. Then, the normal houses were erected in accord with the temple. Such temples have not yet been uncovered, they may have existed. It is just a hypothesis, but we have evidence that in this period the solstice was indeed important for the orientation of sacred buildings: the ziggurat in Aššur, erected during the reign of Šamšī-Adad I, is aligned exactly with the point on the horizon where the sun rises on the day of the summer solstice.[6] Such a huge construction project requires careful planning. Everything had a meaning in a sacred building, therefore the orientation of the ground plan certainly had one too. This is not only found in Mesopotamia either, as we have some examples for solstice-orientated buildings in Hittite Anatolia too (A. Müller-Karpe 2013).

Pottery

Between Kültepe and Kayalıpınar there are also strong parallels regarding the inventory of the buildings, as is seen with the pottery. Large quantities of pottery were recovered during the excavations, of which only one typical assemblage will be presented here. It was found in the destruction layer on the floor immediately in front of the main entrance of the Tatali House (Figs 16.6–16.9). All vessels belong together, they are from the same phase. First, four high-quality beaked jugs, which have a typical polished red slip, are to be quickly mentioned (Fig. 16.8:1–4). In Kültepe, the best parallels come from the house of Adad-ṣululī, but the matches are not exact (T. Özgüç 1950, 173 Lev. 36; Kulakoğlu 2010, 190, no. 49). The slight deviations could be related to the fact that the pieces from Kayalıpınar are somewhat younger than the examples, most of which are from the *kārum* Kaneš II layer. In addition to the jugs, two hemispheri-

Figure 16.6: Kayalıpınar level 5, pottery in situ during the excavation.

Figure 16.7: Kayalıpınar level 5, pottery after restoration.

cal drinking bowls were found (Fig. 16.8:5.6). Besides the tableware, big storage vessels were uncovered (Fig. 16.9:1–6). They belong to long-lived types that cannot be dated more precisely. The same problem applies to the large cooking pots (Fig. 16.7, 16.9:9) and beer vessels (Fig. 16.7; 16.9: 8.10). In addition, no regional peculiarities can be identified; such a vessel inventory could also have been found in Kültepe. However, it is difficult to draw a clear parallel with one of the three *kārum* period layers, as there are relatively few published pottery inventories from the *kārum* Kaneš layers Ib and Ia.[7]

Glyptics

There are also clear parallels between Kültepe and Kayalıpınar in the field of glyptics.[8] In the con-

---

37'11"N, horizon 0° 1229 m MSL, time: 1800 BC; Kültepe: 35°38'05"E 38°51'03"N 1100 m MSL horizon -0.5° (seen from the citadel) 1900 BC, result: 57.316° i.e. one degree further south, because Kültepe lies further south than Kayalıpınar. The sunrise point depends on the latitude, the further south, the bigger the angle.

6 Orientation of the ziggurat (according to google maps): 59.9°. Location: 43°15'40.4"E 35°27'35.0"N time: 1800 BC, result: rising point of sun at summer solstice: 59.203° (calculation <https://ssd.jpl.nasa.gov/horizons/>).

---

7 In addition, there are difficulties concerning the stratigraphic classification of some find complexes in Kültepe. Garelli 1963, 51: 'La distinction archéologique entre les couches doit être examinée avec précaution et l'on ne saurait s'y fier aveuglément.'

8 This section was written using documents from my late wife, Dr Vuslat Müller-Karpe, who herself had planned a publication on the subject.

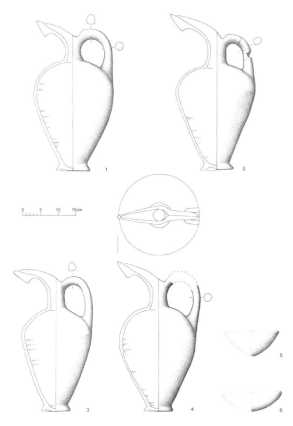

Figure 16.8: Kayalıpınar level 5, beak-spouted pitchers and drinking bowls.

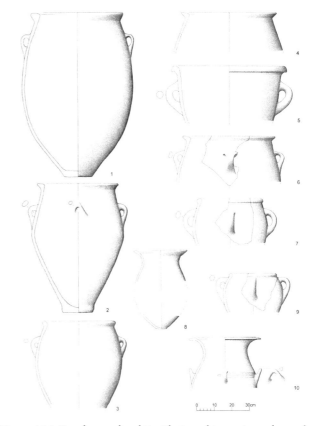

Figure 16.9: Kayalıpınar level 5, pithoi, cooking pots, and vessels.

text of layer 5 in Kayalıpınar, two cylinder seals and seventy-two clay sealings have been found so far. Various glyptic styles can be distinguished here, all of which are also represented in Kültepe. Most of the specimens belong to the Anatolian style group. The first subgroup contains purely geometric motifs. Figure 16.10:1.2 shows a partially preserved imprint of a stamp seal with quatrefoil shape with S-spirals as a motif. Nimet Özgüç (1968, 28, 67, pl. XVI A) published a similar impression from a tablet, found in level *kārum* Kaneš Ib (Fig. 16.10:3). Another example is Figure 16.10:4: a clay stopper with four imprints of a round stamp seal with radial lines in the centre (a rosette?), framed by a ladder band. A terracotta stamp seal with a comparable motif was also found in 'the debris covering level Ib' in Kültepe (N. Özgüç 1968, 73, pl. XXXVII:6).

The second subgroup includes depictions of animals, single ones or combinations of several animals. A typical example is Fig. 16.11:1: On a clay sealing, one impression of the lower half of the image and separately one of the upper half have been preserved, so

that it can be seen that both parts complement each other. The motif is a lion attacking a sheep or a goat, a very popular motif in Anatolian glyptic (Fig. 16.11:2). In the centre of the picture is a lion facing left with its tail raised in excitement and its mouth half-opened aggressively with pointed teeth. He is leaping onto the back of the sheep (?) shown below him, whose head is not preserved. Above the lion is a bird of prey with a curved beak, probably a vulture, speculating on a remnant of the prey.

A variant of the same motif is represented in Figure 16.12:1.2: In the centre, again, a lion with an exaggeratedly long tail is tearing at a goat or gazelle. In this case, however, the scene is supplemented by a hunter holding a lance (V. Müller-Karpe 2009). Above them is possibly a seated monkey and a circular object. Pictures of stamp- and cylinder-seals from level *kārum* Kaneš II offer similarities (Fig. 16.12:3–5).

An unusual composition is seen in Figure 16.13:1.2. The picture has no fixed orientation, but can be viewed from different sides. The central motif, a representation of cattle, is shown in a kind of top view, with the legs folded

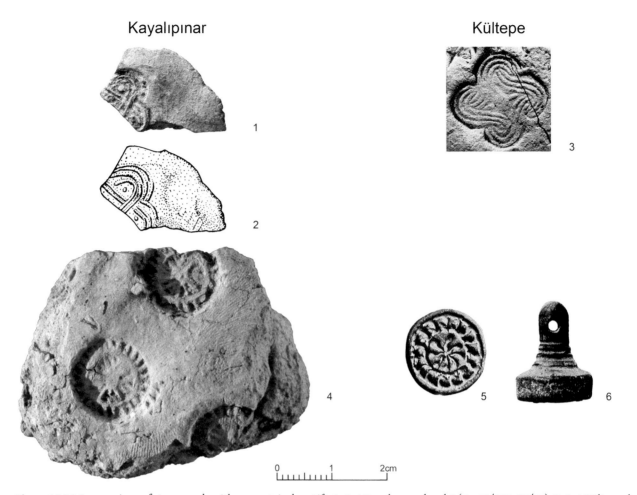

Figure 16.10: Impressions of stamp seals with geometrical motifs: 1, 2, 4 Kayalıpınar level 5 (Kp 06/152; 07/74); 3, 5, 6 Kültepe, level *kārum* Kaneš Ib (after N. Özgüç 1968, 9, 28, 46, 67, pls VI A, XXXVII:6).

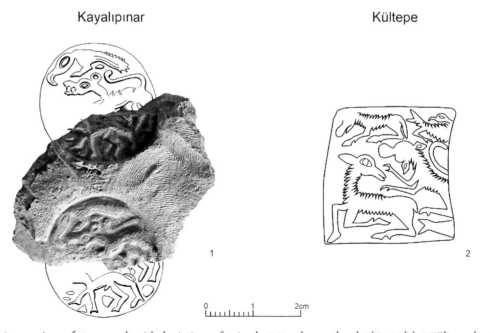

Figure 16.11: Impressions of stamp seals with depictions of animals: 1 Kayalıpınar level 5 (Kp 08/5); 2 Kültepe, level *kārum* Kaneš II (after N. Özgüç 2006, pl. 15 Kt.d/k 48B St 104).

to the side and bent. The other animals, probably goats and a bird (goose?) arranged in a circle around the cattle, were usually shown in profile. On the left edge is a single unarmed human figure, possibly a shepherd. Again, good parallels can be recognized in the individual and the animals in top-down view motifs in Kültepe (Fig. 16.13:3 middle bottom; 4 left side). Nevertheless, slight stylistic differences can still be discerned. On the other hand, the examples from Kayalıpınar are very similar to each other, indicating a local seal workshop here. Typical are coarse, particularly expressive and dynamic images.

One of the most important glyptic finds from layer 5 in Kayalıpınar is a clay sealing with impressions of two stamp seals, one of which shows a motif of a heraldic double-headed eagle framed by a spiral band. The best comparative pieces for this were found in the Waršama Saray in Kaneš, which is paralleled with layer Ib of the Lower Town (Fig. 16.14; V. Müller-Karpe 2009).

Beside the examples of several Anatolian glyptic styles in layer 5 of Kayalıpınar, there is also evidence for the Mesopotamian glyptic tradition. As would be expected in an Assyrian trading settlement, it is the Old Assyrian style. Agnete Wisti Lassen (2014) distin-

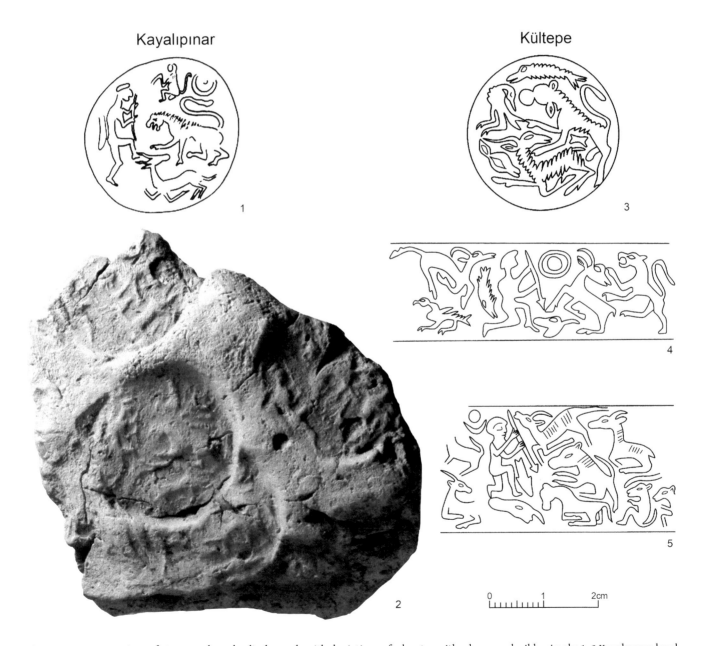

Figure 16.12: Impressions of stamp seals and cylinder seals with depictions of a hunter with a lance and wild animals: 1, 2 Kayalıpınar level 5 (Kp 07/44); 3–5 Kültepe, level *kārum* Kaneš II (after N. Özgüç 2006, pl. 114, Kt.d/k 48A St 103; 19 Kt.n/k 1703; 37 Kt.n/k 1779B CS481).

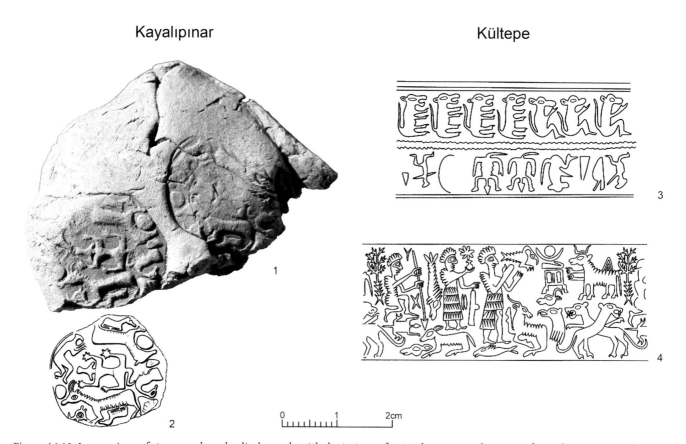

Figure 16.13: Impressions of stamp seals and cylinder seals with depictions of animals, among others seen from above: 1, 2 Kayalıpınar level 5 (Kp 08/101); 3, 4 Kültepe, level kārum Kaneš II (after N. Özgüç 2006, pl. 10, Kt.d/k 28A CS 301; 17 Kt.c/k 1636A CS 345).

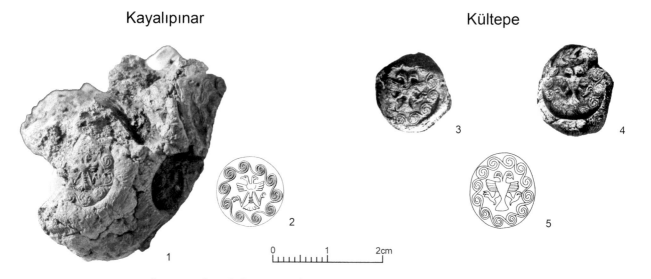

Figure 16.14: Impressions of stamp seals with depictions of a double-headed eagle: 1, 2 Kayalıpınar level 5 (Kp 08/6); 3–5 Kültepe, Waršama Saray (after Özgüç & Tunca 2001, pl. 18. 76 Kt.v/t 22, 43 St 39).

guishes two substyles here: 'Classic Old Assyrian' (OA1) and 'Assyro-Cappadocian' (OA2). Since OA2 developed from OA1, OA2 tends to be somewhat younger, but seals from both substyles were used side by side in Kültepe over a longer period of time. Their simultaneous use is also shown by examples from Kayalıpınar: clay sealings from the 'House of Tamura' show impressions of a OA1-cylinder seal as well as of an OA2 one (Figs 16.15:1; 16.16:1). In the upper half is the imprint of a quite high-quality seal of the 'Classic Old Assyrian' substyle,

16. ŠAMUHA AND KANEŠ

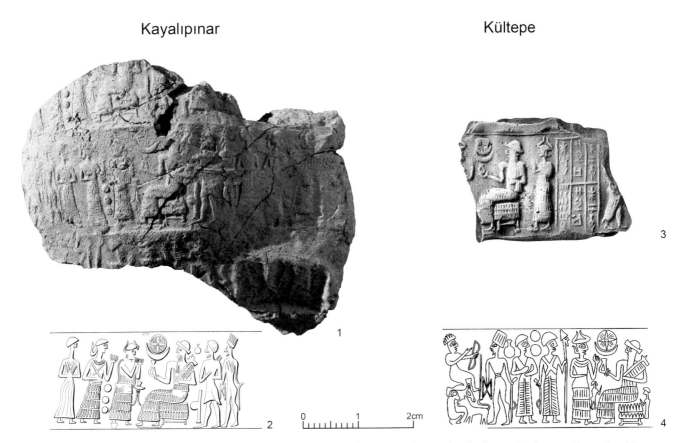

Figure 16.15: Impressions of cylinder seals, Classic Old Assyrian Style: 1, 2 Kayalıpınar level 5 (Kp 08/109); 3, 4 Kültepe, level *kārum* Kaneš II (after T. Özgüç 2003, 19; N. Özgüç 2006, 288 Kt.n/k 1956 C Pl. 82).

of which there are also further partial imprints from other sealings of this find context. The occupant of the house must therefore have received several shipments of goods from the same sender, before the entire settlement was destroyed in a major fire disaster. Purely theoretically, another option would be that this seal could have also belonged to the house owner who sealed outgoing goods here. In this case, finds of intact sealings would have been expected, however, such objects are missing. Like most of the other clay sealings discovered in layer 5, they were intentionally broken, and thus originate from delivered and opened containers.

Let's now take a closer look at this seal image: it shows an introduction scene with a seated human figure in the centre. Due to the fact that he wears a semispherical cap with a broad rim, he might be interpreted as a ruler, not a deity. He holds a conical cup in his right hand. It is a drinking cup, typical for this period in contrast to the standard drinking cup in the following period of the Hittite kingdom, a semispherical bowl. Over his shoulder is an axe, the shaft of which he holds with his left hand. The type of the axe, a so-called *Nackenkammaxt* (axe with a comb-like three-pointed

socked decoration) is known from Mesopotamia as well as from Anatolia (A. Müller-Karpe 1994, pl. 45 f.). He wears a flounced dress with vertical striations; the basket-woven chair he sits on, is depicted in the same way. In front of him are three persons, the first of them a *Lamassu* with a horned cap, leading two female persons to the ruler. Between the seated ruler and the *Lamassu* are the disc-in-crescent symbol (moon and sun) and an offering table. Behind him two armed male persons. One of them has a tower crown and an ox-hide shield in his right hand. Comparable scenes are known from a lot of Kültepe seals (Fig. 16.3:4).

The second seal image at the lower edge of the clay sealing is only partially preserved here. However, since there are several partial impressions of this cylinder seal on various clay-sealing fragments from the 'House of Tatali', it was possible to reconstruct the entire seal image (Fig. 16.16:2). It turned out to be a typical representation of the Assyro-Cappadocian substyle as defined by A. W. Lassen. Characteristic is the stronger stylization of the figures (Lassen 2014, 113–14). In the centre of the seal image is a deity standing on a lion. In one hand it holds an axe raised up, which, despite

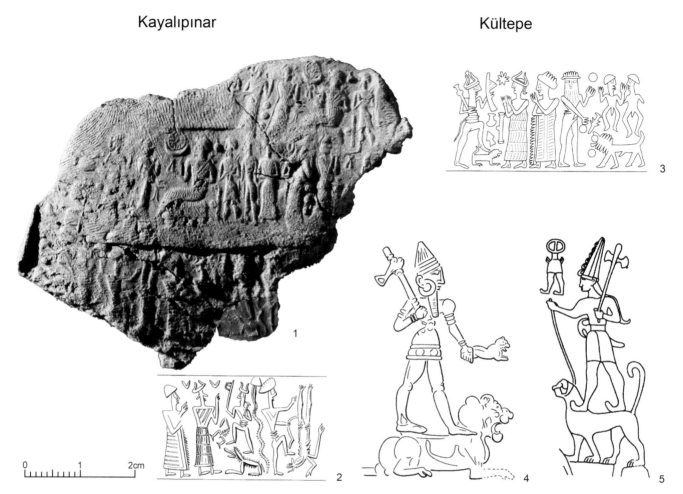

Figure 16.16: Impressions of cylinder seals, Old Assyrian Style (top left) and Old Assyro-Cappadocian Style (bottom left and top right) with the motif God of War on Lion: 1, 2 Kayalıpınar level 5 (Kp 08/16. 17. 108); 3 Kültepe, level *kārum* Kaneš II (N. Özgüç 2006, pl. 60 Kt.n/k 1851 CS 641). Parallels of the motif: 4 gold folio from Kültepe (Kulakoğlu 2008); 5 Yazılıkaya (after Seeher 2011, 64, fig. 62).

the tiny format of the depiction and the correspondingly strong stylization, can be determined as a fenestrated axe. Axes of this type are widespread throughout the Near East in this period and were also produced in Kültepe (Erkanal 1977, 22–26; A. Müller-Karpe 1994, pl. 48, 5–7). In the other hand the deity holds a second weapon, which is laid over his left shoulder. It looks like a hammer, but cannot be identified more precisely. The weapons identify the deity as a god of war (ZABABA, *hattic*: Wurunkatte).

The deity wears a horned crown on his head, but of the clothing, only three horizontal lines are indicated in the hip area, a very abbreviated depiction of a belt and short apron, as they are typical for war deities. Two persons stand in front of the god with one hand raised in a gesture of greeting or adoration. They wear different long robes and headdresses. The first is identified as another deity by a horned crown and is usually inter-

preted as *Lamassu*, the second wears a semicircular cap. Between the two deities, halfway up, is a scorpion.

A second scene is depicted behind the war god: a hero is chopping the hind legs of a (dead) lion with one hand stretched upwards, so that the body of the animal hangs vertically downwards. The other hand holds the tail and one foot is placed on the lion's head. This motif of the lion tamer is very common in Mesopotamian glyptic and is found in our example in a highly stylized form. A snake-like structure is inserted between the war god and the hero. The way the hands are depicted, angled fork-like with only three fingers, as well as the arms, is typical of the OA2 substyle (Lassen 2014, 113). The motif of the war deity on a lion deserves special attention. In various forms, this motif is represented in Kültepe glyptics (Fig. 16.16:3 left side), but especially on the famous gold folio discovered in 2006 (Fig. 16.16:4; Kulakoğlu 2008). The motif then lives on in the period of the Hittite empire, as shown, for example, by the rock

16. ŠAMUHA AND KANEŠ

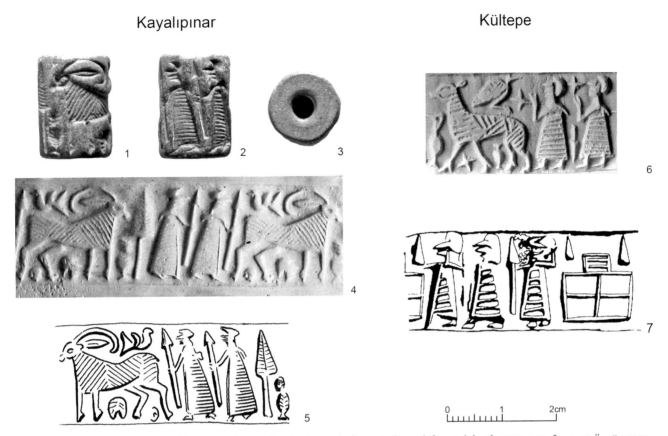

Figure 16.17: 1–5 Cylinder seal from Kayalıpınar level 5 (Kp 07/45); 6, 7 Kültepe (after Kulakoğlu 2010, 150, fig. 6; N. Özgüç 1968, pl. 28:2).

relief of Šarruma in Yazılıkaya, which was created in the thirteenth century BC (Fig. 16.16:5).

Another example of the OA2 substyle from layer 5 at Kayalıpınar was already published by Vuslat Müller-Karpe (2014a, 31–33). It is a cylinder seal depicting two scenes: 1. a seated male deity with a horned crown and a long robe, holding a goblet in one hand. In front of him is a male, also wearing a long, but somewhat less carefully crafted robe and a hat with a wide, double brim. The hand raised in the usual gesture of greeting or adoration goes directly into the shoulder, the arm starts anatomically incorrectly in the hip area, like the hands, which again consist of only three fingers, these are characteristic features of this substyle. Between the two figures is the schematic representation of a fish. The second scene on the seal image offers the motif of animal combat: an erected lion against a goat (?) in the same posture. Between the two animals there is once again a fish. The similarities with numerous examples from Kültepe are so great that one would like to think of products from the same seal workshop. Whether this workshop was located in Kültepe or Aššur or whether mobile seal cutters worked in Aššur or Anatolia cannot be determined. No Anatolian influence can be detected in either motif.

A second cylinder seal was found in layer 5 at Kayalıpınar. It is made of a dark red stone (Fig. 16.17:1–5). It depicts a wild goat with a long, curved horn being pursued by two hunters with lances. A tree with a pointed triangular crown and two bushes indicates the landscape. A bird flies above the animal's back. The style is clearly different from all other glyptic products from Kayalıpınar discussed so far. Characteristic is the strong stylization of roughly cross-hatched bodies. The human figures, which often dominate the seal image in a stereotypical sequence, usually carry vertical lances with triangular tips in front of them. There are examples of this style group from Kültepe as well as from other Anatolian sites, but most of the pieces come from the Syrian-Levantine area (Figs 16.17, 6, 7; 16.18). It was therefore thought that they originated in this region (Mazzoni 1975). An Anatolian origin should not be ruled out, however, as there are striking similarities in the type of body representations with lead figures or the

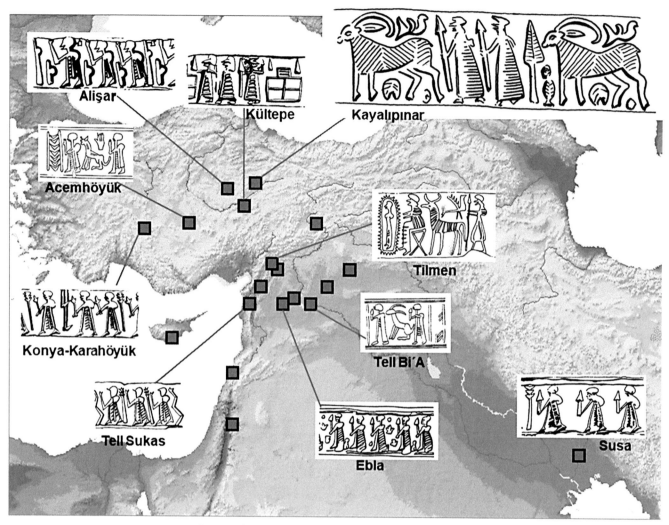

Figure 16.18: Distribution of cylinder seals like Fig. 16.17 (after Mazzoni 1975 with additions).

corresponding casting moulds from the *kārum* period/ early Hittite complexes (A. Müller-Karpe 1994, pl. 60). Narrow cross-hatched lines set at angles are used here in the same way. It is quite possible that seals of this type were produced in workshops that also made moulds for the votive lead figures.

Chronology and Historical Implications

The good correspondences between the finds from Kayalıpınar and Kültepe prove the contemporaneity of the two sites. In addition to the archaeological findings, there are also some results of scientific investigations. From the burned layer below the level of the floor of the 'House of Tamura' (layer 6) three samples of charred plant seeds were taken and analysed with the radiocarbon method (Fig. 16.19): the results are with a probability of 95.4 per cent: 1765–1751 cal BC, 2022–1795 cal BC, 2017–1799 cal BC. The data are therefore too inaccurate to be used for more precise chronological statements. They only show in general that layer 6 belongs to the older *kārum* period, which was already known on the basis of its stratigraphical position. Concerning the following layer 5 in Kayalıpınar, the situation is somewhat better. Several parts of charred wooden beams, some of them relatively well preserved, were found in the fire debris of this layer. It can be assumed that they were part of the construction of the houses. Later, when the Hittite palace complex was erected (layer 4), some of the fire debris from layer 5 was used for levelling measures in the area of Building A. From this context (Room 9) came some pieces of beams with a total of sixty-four annual rings. Here, samples of different annual rings were taken, analysed with the radiocarbon method, followed by a wiggle-matching analysis of the data[9] (Fig. 16.20). The result with the highest probability is the year 1839 BC for the last preserved tree ring. The date can thus be regarded as a *terminus post quem* for the construction of the building. The diameter of the beam and its surface structure suggest that only a few years are missing until the bark. Accordingly, the buildings of layer 5 will have been erected at the beginning of the last third of the nineteenth century BC. The situation is very similar for the Waršama Saray in Kültepe. According to dendrochronological investigations, it was built in 1835/1832 BC and last repaired in 1776/1771 BC (Newton & Kuniholm 2004, 168 f.). Before the construction of this building, the 'Eskisaray/Old Palace' was destroyed. Layer 2 of the Lower Town also ended in the same fire disaster.[10] In Kayalıpınar, the buildings of layer 6 were burned down as well. The destruction of Kaneš and Šamuha in the 1830s could thus have belonged to the same historical event. However, it is also possible that the destructions occurred a few years apart from each other. If there was a time gap between the two events at all, it will not have been very long.

The end of the Lower Town level II is associated with a campaign by Uhna, king of Zalpa on the Black Sea. Trevor Bryce (1998, 34) suspects this as the reason: 'Nesa may have provoked it by over-exploiting its position at the centre of Assyrian merchant system, perhaps closing off, or threatening to close off, the routes leading to the more northerly Anatolian kingdoms.' In this case, it would not necessarily be expected that Šamuha was also a party to the conflict. However, there were also frequent armed conflicts in the period that could have led to the destruction of Šamuha. As in Kaneš, Šamuha was also rebuilt (layer 5) and the record of the wooden beams mentioned are connected with this event. Inar, father of Waršama, was the ruler in Kaneš during this time. In the case that the merchant Tamura mentioned in the Kayalıpınar text Kp 05/120 (Sommerfeld 2006) is identical with the Tamuria mentioned in the Kültepe text Kt n/k32 (which is possible, but not certain), then there would even be a direct reference to the reign of Inar. Barjamovic, Hertel & Larsen (2012, 35) refer to Kt n/k32 as 'A key-text for the succession of the early king of Kaneš', since it contains other ruler names: *Hurmeli* and *Hapatiwa* are mentioned alongside *Inar* and *Šamnuman*. *Hapatiwa* and *Šamnuman* are interpreted as *rabi simmiltim*, although Kryszat (2014, 37) considers it possible that the latter name could be restored in the Kayalıpınar text Kp 14/113 Vs 4'. The two Old Assyrian

---

9   The wiggle matching is owed to R. Süssenguth.

10 T. Özgüç 2003, 131; Barjamovic et al. 2012, 31: 'destruction of the lower town around REL 138'; 43: 'local event that destroyed Kaneš after 1835 BC.'

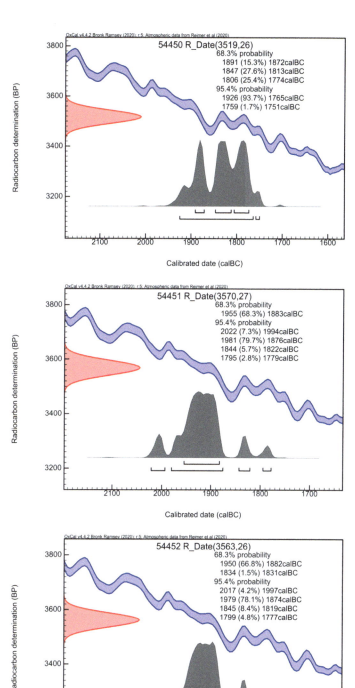

Figure 16.19: Kayalıpınar level 6, radiocarbon dates from three samples of charred grains (Curt-Engelhorn-Zentrum Archäometrie, Mannheim).

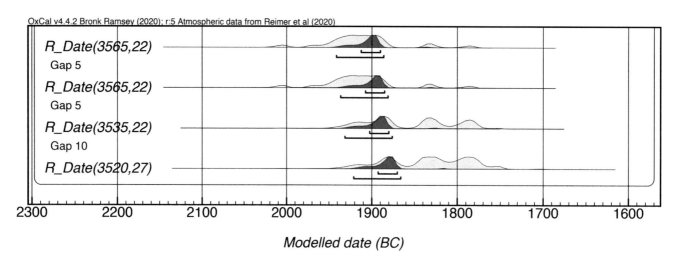

Figure 16.20: Kayalıpınar level 5, radiocarbon dates of four different annual rings of a charred wooden beam. The light grey area indicates the calibrated age without wiggle matching, the dark grey area the calibrated age with wiggle matching (Curt-Engelhorn-Zentrum Archäometrie, Mannheim).

tablet fragments would then have to be dated to the early period of layer 5, the late nineteenth century BC. The palaeography does not contradict this. While in the first publication of the fragment from the 'House of Tamura' W. Sommerfeld described the ductus as typical of the *kārum* Kaneš II stratum, G. Kryszat (2019, 111) noted that the character forms deviate sporadically from what is normally known from the *kārum* Kaneš II layer. He noticed that the writing in the fragment from the 'House of Tatali' was also unusually large and had been written by a 'very inexperienced scribe'. He considered a 'dating parallel to the end of layer 2 or beginning of 1 b possible' (Kryszat 2014, 38). The archaeological context is now to be paralleled with *kārum* Kaneš Ib according to the results of the wooden beam mentioned above.

Although several phases of modifications of the buildings can be identified in layer 5 at Kayalıpınar, it was not possible to classify archaeological finds according to these individual phases. During the excavation, layer 5 appeared to be a thick stratum of fire debris. In the area of the two excavated houses and the adjoining open space to the south, the layer consisted of burnt mud-brick chunks, the lintel of the buildings, and ashes and pottery on the still preserved floors. The finds recovered here thus belong to the youngest phase of layer 5, reflecting the period of destruction.

Even though there are good parallels to the pottery from the *kārum* Kaneš II layer, no break in the development of pottery between *kārum* Kaneš II and Ib can be detected in Kültepe. The pottery does not yet offer any clear clues for a detailed chronological determination, as relatively few examples from a secure stratigraphic context of layer 1b have been published.

In the case of glyptic, too, a sharp distinction between seals of the older and the younger *kārum* period has only been possible in a few stylistic elements and motifs. Among the stylistically earliest examples is the sealing Figure 16.15:1.2. The piece belongs to the 'Classic Old Assyrian' style (OA 1), which according to A. W. Lassen (2014, 115–19) dominates on Kültepe tablets dated by eponyms between REL 31–90 (MC 1942–1833 BC), but is also attested later, albeit much more rarely. The cylinder seal impressed on the two clay sealings found in the 'House of Tamura' is thus likely to have been several generations old. The use of ancient seals is a well-known phenomenon: in Kültepe, for example, an Ur III period seal was still used (Götze 1957, 70) and already in the Hittite song of *Ullikummi* it is said: 'And let them bring the old fathers' seal and let them seal them (the seal houses) again with it' (Güterbock 1948, 128).

The examples of seals of the 'Assyro-Cappadocian' substyle (OA2) attested in Kayalıpınar also find good parallels already in layer II of the lower city of Kaneš (Fig. 16.16), although such seals only occur with certainty from REL 81 (MC 1892 BC) onwards; most of the evidence comes from the decade REL 101–10 (MC 1872–1863 BC, Lassen 2014, 11).

For the seals of the Anatolian style, a detailed chronological study is still lacking. But here too, the best parallels to most examples from Kayalıpınar are available from layer II of the lower city of Kaneš (Figs 16.11–16.13). Stamp seals with spiral band, loop band, or braided-band frames also appear for the first time in the *kārum* Kaneš Ib layer. Seals with such frames dominate in the glyptic of the Old and Middle Hittite kingdom, but the beginnings here lie in the younger *kārum* period. The proportion of stamp seals with such a frame is 13 per cent in the seals in the *kārum* Kaneš Ib layer published by N. Özgüç (1968), 38 per cent in Konya-Karahöyük (Alp 1968), and as much as 65 per cent in the finds of Waršama-Saray (T. Özgüç 1999, pls 70–75). In Kayalıpınar, only one clay sealing with impressions of two different stamp seals with a spiral band frame is available from a secure context of layer 5 (Fig. 16.14). It is probably the most recent seal find from this context. The best parallels are two pieces from the Waršama Saray (T. Özgüç 1999, pl. 71; Özgüç & Tunca 2001, pl. 18. 76 Kt. v/t 22, 43). They are impressions on conical clay *bullae* that were probably hardened by the fire when the palace was destroyed. They can therefore be dated to the end of the palace's period of use. A good comparison piece comes from the *kārum* Hattuš (Beran 1967, 21, pl. 4, 36). It is one of the few specimens from a secure context of the Lower City 4 stratum in Boğazköy, the end of which is associated with the conquest by Anitta. The change of government from Anitta to Zuzu took place in REL 248 (MC 1725 BC), the destruction of Hattuš will have taken place before that, *c.* 1730 BC (Barjamovic et al. 2012, 40). The last year attested on a *līmum* list found at Kültepe (REL. 255) is 1718 BC according to the middle chronology (Barjamovic et al. 2012, 23, 29, 97). At least four to seventeen younger year eponyms can be traced from other texts (Çayır 2015), which indicate that the destruction of the city and undoubtedly also the Waršama Palace probably took place around the turn of the eighteenth to the seventeenth centuries BC. The fire catastrophe in which the buildings of layer 5 in Kayalıpınar came to an end does not necessarily have to have occurred at the same time as the end of layer 1b in Kültepe. It is possible that the destruction in Kayalıpınar took place later, in the course of the early seventeenth century BC. Other stylistically very late finds from Kayalıpınar layer 5 can be regarded as indications of a somewhat later destruction: impressions of cylinder seals from the 'House of Tamura', which show rows of highly stylized monkeys, as well as impressions of a round stamp seal with antithetic lion depictions, which also have equivalents in Konya-Karahöyük and on the Tyskiewicz seal (V. Müller-Karpe 2014b).

The end of layer 5 in Kayalıpınar was undoubtedly caused by military conquest, systematic plundering, and subsequent pillaging. The archaeological evidence clearly shows that the houses were emptied very hastily and that inventory was also deliberately smashed. Metal objects are almost completely missing. They were certainly looted. But not even pottery inventory was found in situ in the rooms of the two houses. Instead, a number of more or less complete vessels lay on the open space in front of the entrance gate of the 'House of Tatali'. It seems that the vessels (with their contents) were carried out of the building for removal, but then partly remained there. Logically, when a city was looted, it would hardly have been possible to remove everything. The remaining vessels, however, were smashed and thrown about.

The perpetrators are unknown, but this event could have been connected with the rise of the Hittite kingdom. According to the Zalpa text, 'The [grand]father of the king [gave] the city of Hurma to the father of the old king' (Otten 1973, 8–9). Hurma/Hurama is often mentioned in connection with Šamuha, so it was probably not too far away, but in any case it was south of Šamuha. Since Ḫattuša lies to the north-west of Šamuha, it can be assumed that the passage refers to a time when Šamuha already belonged to the Hittite domain, i.e. it was ruled from Ḫattuša and accordingly its conquest had taken place before. However, it is disputed who the mentioned 'grandfather of the king' was: Huzzia '0' or Tudhaliya I is discussed (Beal 2003, 21, 34–35). The crucial point is that the text passage in any case refers to the time about three generations before Hattušili I, whose reign is assumed to have begun around 1650 BC (MC).

Concluding Remarks

The comparison of the archaeological finds from layer 5 of Kayalıpınar with objects from layers *kārum* Kaneš II and Ib showed very strong similarities. These finds represent the same culture, but how should we describe it? Many different terms are used by scholars: Middle Bronze Age culture, culture of the old Assyrian colonies/Colony culture, *kārum* culture, pre-Hittite or early Hittite culture.

The term Middle Bronze Age is neither wrong nor quite useful, because some scholars include the Hittite Old Kingdom, others don't. And the Middle Bronze Age culture, i.e. in Beycesultan or Tarsus, is not the same as in Kültepe and Kayalıpınar. 'Colonial' period or culture is a very problematic expression as well. As Cécile Michel (2014, 80) pointed out: 'The Old Assyrian *kārum*s in Anatolia, are arguably unique, and their designation by the word "colonies" is not satisfactory, as this term denotes some kind of domination of a state over a foreign territory.' But in many publications the early second millennium BC in Anatolia is still referred to as the 'Colonial period'. This term derives from a time when it was thought that Kaneš and Cappadocia were part of the Assyrian empire. This idea was developed by Eduard Meyer in 1909[11] and was followed by Julius Lewy in 1923.[12] At that time, the colonization of territories was something positive from a European point of view. A quarter of the globe was ruled from London alone, when scholars introduced the term 'Colonial period' in Assyriology and Anatolian archaeology. But times changed. Today we have a more critical view of colonialism as part of European imperialism and have become aware of its criminal side. There is a worldwide discussion about the problematic aftermath of colonialism. By applying the term 'colonial period' to the early second millennium BC in Anatolia, a false historical parallel is drawn.[13] There are alternatives: during his excavations in Alişar (1927–1932) Hans Henning von der Osten did not hesitate to call this period 'Hittite'. He took the tablets into account, but linked them to the rest of the material culture of the strata in which they were found: 'On the Büyük Kale at Boğazköy tablets which dated from the end of the New Hittite Empire were associated with cultural remains of the same style as those associated on the Alişar mound with tablets of the Cappadocian type. Hence this cultural period began around the twentieth century B.C., probably earlier, and ended approximately within the twelfth century B.C.' (von der Osten 1937, 1). His argumentation was an archaeological one. He had understood that there was no cultural break between the time of the Cappadocian (Old Assyrian) tablets and that of the 'New Hittite' tablets and therefore rightly counted the two stages as a common 'cultural period'. In this respect, the archaeological picture has not changed since then; on the contrary, it has become increasingly clear that regarding architecture, art, metal crafts, and pottery production, a continuous development can be observed from the early second millennium to the period around 1200 BC. Moreover, it is now known that Hittite was spoken in the streets of Kaneš/ Neša and that the Hittites themselves derived the name of their language from this city (nesili).

The discovery of the gold folio with the god on a lion in Kültepe (Fig 16.16:4), the logo of the symposium published in this volume, once again demonstrates this cultural continuity. Kültepe is not only home of the forerunners of Hittite art. Pieces like the gold folio are representatives of real Hittite art, even in an already developed, mature form. Unfortunately, however, scholars often confuse political history and cultural history. Accordingly, Hittite art and culture are thought to have begun at the same time as Hittite kingship (Schachner 2012). Archaeological finds from the time before the Hittite kingdom are therefore generally called 'pre-Hittite'. But the Hittite kings were neither the inventors of the Hittite language nor of Hittite art and culture. Of course, Luwians,[14] Hattians, and other groups also had a share in the development of this culture, which we nevertheless can call Hittite.[15] This culture is primarily an Anatolian one. It is not a colonist culture or a colonial culture. There is no question that important influences came from Aššur, but apart from writing and aspects of the glyptic, the cultural imprint is Anatolian-Hittite and not a Mesopotamian one. There are thus good reasons to call the culture of the first third of the second millennium BC in central Anatolia 'Early Hittite'.

Figure Credits and Acknowledgements

Unless otherwise stated, the drawings are by the author. The graphic editing was done by Katja Bieber, Vorgeschichtliches Seminar der Philipps Universität Marburg, photographs: Kayalıpınar project. I am grateful to Andrew Tesja for corrections to my English text.

---

11 In the second edition of his famous *Geschichte des Altertums*, for the first time he phrased the thought of an 'assyrische Herrschaft und Kolonisation' in Cappadocia (Meyer 1909, 595). In the following third edition of the same work, Kültepe is mentioned for the first time as the capital of an Assyrian colony in Anatolia: 'So wird es sich hier doch wohl um eine von Assyrien ausgehende Kolonie handeln, deren Hauptstadt der Hügel Kültepe bedeckt' (Meyer 1913, 612).

12 He was convinced 'daß Aššur und die assyrischen Siedlungen in Kleinasien [...] eine politische Einheit, ein Reich bildeten' (Levy 1923, 538; 1925), in contrast to Sidney Smith and Budge: 'The [Cappadocian] Tablets make it quite clear, that a brisk trade was carried on between these Semites and Assyria, but all proof that they were subject to Assyria is waiting' (Smith 1921, 1). Benno Landsberger also rejects the idea of an Assyrian empire reaching as far as Anatolia and speaks for the first time of Assyrian trading colonies and 'Die assyrischen Kolonisten sind durchweg Kaufleute' (Landsberger 1924, 225).

13 Michel 2014, 71: 'Today, everyone agrees a "colonial system" does not describe the Assyrian kārum system in Anatolia, but even so, many colleagues still use the word colony to translate the word kārum.'

14 Archi (2018, 136) makes an apt comment on the tendencies in recent research to valorise the importance of the Luwians for cultural development: 'An attempt (conditioned by our contemporary feelings) to redeem the Luwians from a sad destiny of exclusion imposed by presumed imperialistic practices would be, however, anachronistic. Anatolian society did not discriminate ethno-linguistic groups, but was organized into social classes.'

15 Numerous ethnic groups were involved in the development of Roman culture, inhabitants of the city of Rome were a minority. But no one denies the existence of Roman culture.

Bibliography

Alp, Sedat

1968 *Zylinder- und Stempelsiegel aus Karahöyük bei Konya* (Türk Tarih Kurumu yayınlarından 5/26). Türk Tarih Kurumu, Ankara.

Archi, Alfonso

2018 'Boekbesprekingen- Hettitologie: Mouton, A., Rituels, mythes et prières hittites', *Bibliotheca Orientalis* 75/1–2: 133–40.

Balkan, Kemal

1965 Review of Matuš: Inscriptions cuneiforms du Kültépé, II, *Orientalistische Literatur-Zeitschrift* 60/3–4: 146–62.

Barjamovic, Gojko

2011 *A Historical Geography of Anatolia in the Old Assyrian Colony Period* (Carsten Niebur Institute Publications 38). Museum Tusculanum Press, Copenhagen.

Barjamovic, Gojko; Hertel, Thomas & Larsen, Mogens T.

2012 *Ups and Downs at Kanesh: Chronology, History and Society in the Old Assyrian Period* (Publications de l'Institut historique archéologique néerlandais de Stamboul 120). Nederlands Instituut voor het Nabije Oosten, Leiden.

Beal, Richard H.

2003 'The Predecessors of Ḫattušili I', in Gary Beckman, Richard Beal & Gregory McMahon (eds), *Hittite Studies in Honor of Harry A. Hoffner Jr. on the Occasion of his 65th Birthday*. Eisenbrauns, Winona Lake: 13–35.

Beran, Thomas

1967 *Die hethitische Glyptik von Boğazköy, I: Die Siegel und Siegelabdrücke der vor- und althethitischen Perioden und die Siegel der hethitischen Großkönige* (Wissenschaftliche Veröffentlichungen der Deutschen Orient-Gesellschaft 76). Mann, Berlin.

Bittel, Kurt

1983 *Hattuscha: Hauptstadt der Hethiter; Geschichte und Kultur einer altanatolischen Großmacht*. DuMont, Cologne.

Bryce, Trevor

1998 *The Kingdom of the Hittites*. Clarendon, Oxford.

Çayır, Murat

2015 'İki Kültepe tableti ve iki yeni līmum', in İrfan Albayrak, Hakan Erol & Murat Çayır (eds), *Cahit Günbattı'ya Armağan: Studies in Honour of Cahit Günbattı*. Ankara Üniversitesi yayınları, Ankara: 39–48.

Erkanal, Hayat

1977 *Die Äxte und Beile des 2. Jahrtausends in Zentralanatolien* (Prähistorische Bronzefunde 11/8). Beck, Munich.

Garelli, Paul

1963 *Les Assyriens en Cappadoce* (Bibliothèque archéologique et historique de l'Institut français d'archéologie d'Istanbul 19). Maisonneuve, Paris.

Götze, Albrecht

1957 *Kleinasien* (Handbuch der Altertumswissenschaft 3/1/3, Kulturgeschichte des alten Orients 3/1). Beck, Munich.

Güterbock, Hans Gustav

1948 'The Hittite Version of the Hurrian Kumarbi Myths: Oriental Forerunners of Hesiod', *American Journal of Archaeology* 52: 123–34.

Hertel, Thomas Klitgaard

2014 'The Lower Town of Kültepe: Urban Layout and Population', in Levent Atıcı, Fikri Kulakoğlu, Gojko Barjamovic & Andrew Fairbairn (eds), *Current Research at Kültepe-Kanesh: An Interdisciplinary and Integrative Approach to Trade Networks, Internationalism, and Identity* (Journal of Cuneiform Studies Supplemental Series 4). Lockwood, Atlanta: 25–54.

Kryszat, Guido

2014 'Ein altassyrisches Tontafelfragment der Grabungskampagne 2014 aus Kayalıpınar', in Andreas Müller-Karpe, Vuslat Müller-Karpe & Guido Kryszat (eds), 'Untersuchungen in Kayalıpınar 2013 und 2014', *Mitteilungen der Deutschen Orient-Gesellschaft* 146: 35–38.

2019 'Bemerkungen zu den altassyrischen Fragmenten KpT 1.2 und KpT 1.35', in Elisabeth Rieken (ed.), *Keilschrifttafeln aus Kayalıpınar, I: Textfunde aus den Jahren 1999-2017* (Documenta antiqua Asiae Minoris 1). Harrassowitz, Wiesbaden: 111–12.

Kulakoğlu, Fikri

2008 'A Hittite God from Kültepe', in Cécile Michel (ed.), *Old Assyrian Studies in Memory of Paul Garelli* (Old Assyrian Archives, Studies 4; PIHANS: Uitgaven van het Nederlands Instituut voor het Nabije Oosten te Leiden 112). Leiden, Nederlands Instituut voor het Nabije Oosten: 13–19.

2010 *Anatolia's Prologue Kültepe Kanesh Karum: Assyrians in Istanbul* [catalogue of the exhibition in Istanbul 29 December 2010–26 March 2011] (Kayseri Büyükşehir Belediyesi kültür yayınları 78). Kayseri Büyükşehir Belediyesi, Istanbul.

Landsberger, Benno

1924 'Über die Völker Vorderasiens im dritten Jahrtausend', *Zeitschrift für Assyriologie*, n.s. 35: 213–38.

Larsen, Morgens

2021 *Kültepe Tabletleri VI-e: The Archive of Šalim-Aššur Family, V: Anonymous Texts and Fragments.* (Türk Tarih Kurumu Yayınları 6/33), Türk Tarih Kurumu, Ankara.

Lassen, Agnete Wisti

2014 'The Old Assyrian Glyptic Style: An Investigation of a Seal Style, its Owners, and Place of Production', in Levent Atıcı, Fikri Kulakoğlu, Gojko Barjamovic & Andrew Fairbairn (eds), *Current Research at Kültepe-Kanesh: An Interdisciplinary and Integrative Approach to Trade Networks, Internationalism, and Identity* (Journal of Cuneiform Studies Supplemental Series 4). Lockwood, Atlanta: 107–22.

Lewy, Julius

1923 'Zur Geschichte Assyriens und Kleinasiens im 3. und 2. Jarhrtausend v. Chr.', *Orientalistische Literaturzeitung* 26/11: 533–44.

1925 'Der *karrum* der altassyrisch-kappadokischen Städte und das altassyrische Großreich', *Zeitschrift für Assyriologie*, n.s. 36: 19–29.

Mazzoni, Stefania

1975 'Tell Mardikh e una classe glittica siro-anatolica del period di Larsa', *Annali Istituto Universitario Orientale, Napoli: Rivista del Dipartimento di Studi Asiatici e del Dipartimento di Studi e Ricerche su Africa e Paesi Arabi* 35: 21–43.

Meyer, Eduard

1909 *Geschichte des Altertums, I.2: Die ältesten geschichtlichen Völker und Kulturen bis zum sechzehnten Jahrhundert*, 2nd edn. Cotta, Stuttgart.

1913 *Geschichte des Altertums, I.2: Die ältesten geschichtlichen Völker und Kulturen bis zum sechzehnten Jahrhundert*, 3rd edn. Cotta, Stuttgart.

Michel, Cécile

2008 'Nouvelles données de géographie historique anatolienne d'après des archives récentes de Kültepe', in Karl Strobel (ed.), *New Perspectives on the Historical Geography of Anatolia in the II and I Millennium B.C.* (Eothen 16). LoGisma, Florence: 235–52.

2014 'Considerations on the Assyrian Settlement at Kanesh', in Levent Atıcı, Fikri Kulakoğlu, Gojko Barjamovic & Andrew Fairbairn (eds), *Current Research at Kültepe-Kanesh: An Interdisciplinary and Integrative Approach to Trade Networks, Internationalism, and Identity* (Journal of Cuneiform Studies Supplemental Series 4). Lockwood, Atlanta: 69–84.

Müller-Karpe, Andreas

1994 *Altanatolisches Metallhandwerk* (Offa-Bücher 75). Wachholtz, Neumünster.

2013 'Einige archäologische sowie archäoastronomische Aspekte hethitischer Sakralbauten', in Kai Kaniuth, Anne Löhnert, Jared L. Miller, Adelheid Otto, Michael Roaf & Walther Sallaberger (eds), *Tempel im Alten Orient: 7. Internationales Colloquium der Deutschen Orient-Gesellschaft, 11.–13. Oktober 2009, München*. Harrassowitz, Wiesbaden: 335–53.

Müller-Karpe, Vuslat

2009 'Frühhethitische Siegelabdrücke', in Andreas Müller-Karpe & Vuslat Müller-Karpe (eds), 'Untersuchungen in Kayalıpınar und Umgebung 2006–2009', *Mitteilungen der Deutschen Orient-Gesellschaft* 141: 193–200.

2014a 'Glyptische Funde der frühhethitischen Schicht 5', in Andreas Müller-Karpe, Vuslat Müller-Karpe & Guido Kryszat (eds), 'Untersuchungen in Kayalıpınar 2013 und 2014', *Mitteilungen der Deutschen Orient-Gesellschaft* 146: 30–36.

2014b 'Kayalıpınar'da bulunmuş üç silindir mühür baskısı üzerine değerlendirmeler', in Nazlı Çınardalı-Karaaslan, Ayşegül Aykurt, Neyir Kolankaya-Bostancı & Yiğit H. Erbil (eds), *Anadolu Kültürlerine Bir Bakış: Armağan Erkanal'a Armağan / Some Observations on Anatolian Cultures: Compiled in Honor of Armağan Erkanal*. Hacettepe Üniversitesi, Ankara: 309–18.

Müller-Karpe, Andreas & Müller-Karpe, Vuslat

2019 'Untersuchungen in Kayalıpınar 2017 und 2018' with contributions by Mert Özbilgin, Daniel Scherf & Riko Süssenguth, *Mitteilungen der Deutschen Orient-Gesellschaft* 151: 219–70.

Müller-Karpe, Andreas; Müller-Karpe, Vuslat & Kryszat, Guido

2014 'Untersuchungen in Kayalıpınar 2013 und 2014', *Mitteilungen der Deutschen Orient-Gesellschaft* 146: 11–41.

Newton, Maryanne W. & Kuniholm, Peter Ian

2004 'A Dendrochronological Framework for the Assyrian Colony Period in Asia Minor', *Türkiye Bilimler Akademisi Arkeoloji Dergisi* 7: 165–76.

Osten, Hans Henning von der

1937 *The Alishar Hüyük: Seasons of 1930–32*, II (Oriental Institute Publications 29). University of Chicago, Chicago.

Otten, Heinrich

1973 *Die althethitische Erzählung um die Stadt Zalpa* (Studien zu den Boğazköy-Texten 17). Harrassowitz, Wiesbaden.

Özgüç, Nimet

1968 *Kaniş Karumu Ib Katı Mühürleri ve Mühür Baskılar / Seals and Seal Impressions of Level IB from Karum Kanish* (Türk Tarih Kurumu Yayınlarından 5/1/25). Türk Tarih Kurumu, Ankara.

2006 *Kültepe-Kaniš/Neša: Yerli Peruwa ve Aššur-imittī'nin oğlu Aššur'lu Tüccar Uṣur-ša-Ištar'ın Arşivlerine ait Kil Zarfların Mühür Baskı / Seal Impressions on the Clay Envelopes from the Archives of the Native Peruwa and Assyrian Trader Uṣur-ša-Ištar son of Aššur-imittī* (Türk Tarih Kurumu Yayınları 5/50). Türk Tarih Kurumu, Ankara.

Özgüç, Nimet & Tunca, Önhan
2001 *Kültepe-Kaneš Mühürlü Yazılı Kil Bullalar / Sealed and Inscribed Clay Bullae* (Türk Tarih Kurumu Yayınları 5/48). Türk Tarih Kurumu, Ankara.

Özgüç, Tahsin
1950 *Türk Tarih Kurumu tarafından yapılan Kültepe kazısı raporu 1948 / Ausgrabungen in Kültepe: Bericht über die im Auftrage der Türkischen Historischen Gesellschaft, 1948 durchgeführten Ausgrabungen* (Türk Tarih Kurumu yayınları 5/10). Türk Tarih Kurumu, Ankara.

1999 *Kültepe-Kaniš/Neša Sarayları ve Mabetleri / The Palaces and Temples of Kültepe-Kaniš/Neša* (Türk Tarih Kurumu Yayınları 5/46). Türk Tarih Kurumu, Ankara.

2003 *Kültepe Kaniš/Neša: The Earliest International Trade Center and the Oldest Capital City of the Hittites*. Middle Eastern Culture Center in Japan, Istanbul.

Rieken, Elisabeth
2014 'Ein Kultinventar für Šamuḫa aus Šamuḫa und andere Texte aus Kayalıpınar', *Mitteilungen der Deutschen Orientgesellschaft* 146: 43–54.

Schachner, Andreas
1999 *Von der Rundhütte zum Kaufmannshaus. Kulturhistorische Untersuchungen zur Entwicklung prähistorischer Wohnhäuser in Zentral-, Ost- und Südostanatolien* (British Archaeological Reports, International Series 807). Archaeopress, Oxford.

2012 'Gedanken zur Datierung, Entwicklung und Funktion der hethitischen Kunst', *Altorientalische Forschungen* 39: 130–66.

Seeher, Jürgen
2011 *Götter in Stein gehauen: Das hethitische Felsheiligtum von Yazılıkaya*. Ege yayınları, Istanbul.

Smith, Sidney
1921 *Cuneiform Texts from Cappadocian Tablets in the British Museum*, I. British Museum, London.

Sommerfeld, Walter
2006 'Ein altassyrisches Tontafelfragment aus Kayalıpınar', in Andreas Müller-Karpe, 'Untersuchungen in Kayalıpınar 2005' with contributions by Vuslat Müller-Karpe, Elisabeth Rieken, Walter Sommerfeld, Gernot Wilhelm & Manuel Zeiler, *Mitteilungen der Deutschen Orient-Gesellschaft* 138: 231–33.

17. Two New Tablets from the House of Kuliya, Son of Ali-abum, and One Broken Envelope

2022 Kültepe Texts (Kt 22/k 02–03, 05)

Adam Anderson

Introduction

This article includes an edition and description of two tablets and an envelope, discovered in the 2022 season. All three artefacts are to be included in the archive of Kuliya, which was excavated in 1989 and 1992 and published by Professor Klaas Veenhof in 2010 (abbreviated here as KT 5, nos 1–76 and which includes texts Kt 92/k 188–263).[1]

The first tablet (Kt. 22/k 02) was found on the southern surface of the mud-brick wall in Kuliya's archive room. The tablet was split in half, with the obverse sitting face up, and the reverse on the ground just below the southern wall of the archive room. Upon further inspection, the second tablet (Kt. 22/k 03) was found in perfect condition, also on the ground near the reverse half of the first tablet, underneath a loose rock. The inscribed and sealed envelope (Kt. 22/k 05) was found the following day, 7 August 2022. This find-spot suggests that the tablets were previously located in the wall, which had apparently disintegrated to some degree since the 1992 excavation. This would also explain why they were not found with the other texts in Kuliya's archive during the excavation.

The content of the two tablets makes clear that both are debt-notes, and that they were redeemable for some value. The first is a fairly straightforward debt of 3 shekels, which was to be repaid with interest in Hattum. The stipulation of the location of repayment could indicate that Hattum was where Kuliya was located at that time, as expressed in another document in Kuliya's archive, the text KT 5, 19. The second tablet can be identified as one of eight debt-notes itemized in another tablet, KT 5, 69: ṭup-pu-um ša 10 ma-na kù-babbar ša Puzur$_2$-A-šur ù Puzur$_2$-^{d}IŠKUR (Veenhof 2010, 182). It was no doubt listed among Kuliya's records due to the value of the tablet, similar to a bearer's cheque. As indicated by the verb in line 6 (maškattam), the text included a joint liability clause, which bound the brothers Puzur-Aššur and Puzur-Adad to repay their debt with the revenue of the merchandise. The text included a clause for the delivery of 10 minas of refined silver to Kuliya's amtum-wife, which suggests that Kuliya himself was not present in Kaneš at that time. The amount of 10 minas was apparently written as an addendum, positioned just below the main line of text on line 4, but it is unclear what this amount is referencing. If it is meant as an indication of the price of the textiles, they would cost 17 1/2 shekels a piece, far too much for Aššur and too little for Anatolia.

The second tablet is dated to month VIII of eponym year 136, which according to the revised eponym list is

---

1 Tarik Öğreten, Adam Anderson, and Anita Fattori were all present when the tablets were found between 6–7 August 2022. The following photos, summaries, transliterations, translations, and commentaries were made by Adam Anderson, and any errors are his responsibility.

Adam Anderson (adamganderson@gmail.com), PhD from Harvard University, director of the FactGrid Cuneiform project (<https://database.factgrid.de/wiki/FactGrid:Cuneiform_Project>)

Kültepe at the Crossroads between Disciplines: Society, Settlement and Environment from the Fourth to the First Millennium BC, ed. by Fikri Kulakoğlu and Cécile Michel, Subartu, 51 (Turnhout, 2024), pp. 249–255.
DOI 10.1484/M.SUBART-EB.5.136352

year 136 (REL 136, *c.* 1837 BC). This date is noteworthy for two reasons. First, it was the same month and year attested in AKT 5, 39, in which a debt of 10 minas of silver was to be repaid to Kuliya by his servant Asānum, which may provide an explanation as to why Puzur-Aššur and Puzur-Adad were delivering the 10 minas of refined silver to Kuliya's estate. Secondly, according to Veenhof (2010, 19) this is both the last date recorded in Kuliya's archive, as well as the closest date of the destruction of Kültepe Lower Town level II.

The broken envelope was found lying in the road just outside of the north-eastern wall of Kuliya's house. At least one of the names on the envelope contains a patronymic attested in Kuliya's archive, suggesting that although the envelope was found in the street, it most likely belonged to Kuliya's archive as well. The inscription has hardened dirt filled into many of the wedges, suggesting that it was discarded in antiquity.

17. TWO NEW TABLETS FROM THE HOUSE OF KULIYA, SON OF ALI-ABUM, AND ONE BROKEN ENVELOPE

Kt 22/k 02

Measurements: 3.56 × 2.69 × 1.16 cm

Debt-note

Obv.

1	3 gin₂ ku₃-babbar i–*li-/bi*	(1) 3 shekels of silver on
	Ú-ṣú-ur-ša-A-šùr	(2) Uṣur-ša-Aššur
	dumu *Puzur₄-A-šùr*	(3) son of Puzur-Aššur,
	Ku-li-a i-šu 6 gin₂ ku₃-babbar	(4) Kuliya has a claim. 6 shekels of silver
5	[*i*]-*na Ḫa-tim*	(5) [i]n Hattum
	[*i*]-*ša-qal*	(6) he will pay.
	[ig]i *Ku-ra* dumu *Šu-A-nim*	(7) [Witn]ess: Kura son of Šu-Anum

Rev.

8	igi *Ma-al-ku-um-/i-šar*	(8) Witness: Malkum-išar
9	dumu *Am-ra-a*	(9) son of Amraya

(remainder uninscribed)

Translation

Kuliya has a claim of 3 shekels of silver on Uṣur-ša-Aššur son of Puzur-Aššur. He will pay 6 shekels of silver in Hattum.

KT 22/k 03

Measurements: 5 × 4.82 × 1.05 cm

Contract for a caravan shipment

Eponym: REL 136 (c. 1837 BC)

Obv.

1	35 túg^(hi-a) sig₅^(tim)	(1) 35 textiles of top
	wa-at-ru-tim : mì-iš-lim	(2) quality, half of which are
	A-bar-ni-ú mì-iš-lim	(3) *abarnī'um*-textiles, half of which are
	ku-ta-nu : 10 ma-na / 3 anše^(hi-a)	(4) *kutānu*-textiles / 10 mina \ 3 donkeys
5	ṣa-lá-mu : mì-ma : a-nim	(5) black, all of this
	ma-áš-kà-tám ša Ku-li-a	(6) was laid claim by Kuliya,
	dumu A-lá-bi-im	(7) son of Alābum
	a-na Puzur₄-A-šùr	(8) to Puzur-Aššur
	dumu A-ḫu-wa-qar	(9) son of Aḫu-waqar
10	ù Puzur₄-^(d)im	(10) and Puzur-Adad
lo.e.	a-ḫi-šu : i-dí-in-šu?-nu?	(11) his brother, he gave them.

Rev.

12	10 ma-na kù-babbar ṣa-ru-pá-am	(12) 10 minas of refined silver
	a-na geme₂-šu	(13) to his *amtum*-wife
	i-ša-qú-lu : kù-babbar	(14) they will pay. For the silver
15	i-na qá-qá-ad šál-mì-šu-nu	(15) they are jointly liable,
	ù ke-ni-šu-nu ra-ki-is	(16) and it is bound to the one who is solvent.
	Iti-kam Qá-ra-a-tim	(17) Month VIII, Qarrātum.
	li-mu-um En-na-Sú-en₆	(18) Eponym: Enna-Suen
	dumu I-dí-a-bi₄-im	(19) son of Iddin-abum
20	igi Du-du dumu Šu-Bé-lim	(20) Witness: Dudu son of Šu-Bēlum
	igi Šu-Sú-en₆	(21) Witness: Šu-Suen
	dumu I-tur₄-dingir	(22) son of Itūr-ilī

Translation

1–5) 35 textiles of top quality, half of which are *abarnī'um*-textiles, half of which are *kutānu*-textiles, 10 minas, (and) three black donkeys.

5–11) All of this Kuliya, son of Alābum, gave to Puzur-Aššur, son of Aḫu-waqar, and Puzur-Adad his brother.

12–14) They will pay 10 minas of refined silver to his *amtum*-wife.

14–16) They are jointly liable for the silver, and it is bound to the one of them who is solvent.

17–19) The eighth month (Qarrātum) in the eponym year of Enna-Suen, son of Iddin-abum.

20–22) Witnesses: Dudu, son of Šu-Bēlum, Šu-Suen, son of Itūr-ilī.

Kt 22/k 05

Measurements: 6.95 × 4.12 × 0.93 cm

Inscribed and sealed envelope

(two different seal impressions without inscriptions, both are Assyrian style presentation scenes)

1 [....... dumu] Šu-A-nim
2 [......... En-na-]Sú-en₆ dumu A-šùr-ma-lik
3 [kà-ru-um Kà-]né-eš₁₅ i-dí-ni-a-tí-ma
4 [igi gír ša A-]šùr ší-bu-tí-ni ni-dí-in

(remainder uninscribed)

Translation

1 [... son of]Šu-Anum
2 [... Enna-]Suen son of Aššur-malik
3 [the *kārum* of Ka]neš gave to us.
4 We gave our testimony [before the dagger of A]ššur.

Acknowledgements

Thanks goes to Cécile Michel and her doctoral student, Anita Fattori, who read the edition and provided helpful feedback, as well as to Klaas Veenhof, who provided additional notes about the unique features of these particular texts. Many thanks also to Fikri Kulakoğlu, who allowed for these unexcavated tablets to be published, as well as all those who helped in making a prompt edition of the texts.

Bibliography

Veenhof, Klaas R.

2010 *The Archive of Kuliya, Son of Ali-abum (Kt. 92/k 188–263)* (Ankara Kültepe Tabletleri 5). Türk Tarih Kurumu, Ankara.

18. Recent Excavations on the Mound of Kültepe

A New Public Building from the End of the Karum Period at Kaneš-Neša

Fikri Kulakoğlu & Luca Peyronel

The South-Western Sector of the Kültepe Mound during the Middle Bronze Age

The urban layout of Kültepe has been investigated primarily for the Middle Bronze Age period/Karum period, roughly covering the first three centuries of the second millennium BC, thanks especially to the long-term exploration carried out since 1948 by the Turkish expedition led by Tahsin and Nimet Özgüç, Kutlu Emre, and currently by Fikri Kulakoğlu. At least by the end of the third millennium BC the site included a large circular mound of 570 m (N-S) × 500 m (E-O) (*c.* 30 ha), more than 20 m high, corresponding to an Upper Town where palatial buildings, ceremonial areas, and domestic sectors were located, and an extended Lower Town, which surrounded the mound (Özgüç 1999; 2003; Kulakoğlu 2011). The precise extension and organization of the Lower Town has not yet been precisely established (Barjamovic 2014), while its eastern part has been extensively excavated. Here, large quarters of dwellings and workshops together with houses of the Assyrian merchants were discovered (Özgüç 1986; Hertel 2014).

However, the history of the settlement began much earlier, as has been revealed by the excavations carried out especially during the last fifteen years in the central and southern part of the mound. Below the initial Middle Bronze levels, structures pertaining to an articulated occupation of the Early Bronze Age III testify to the development of a flourishing urban centre already during the second half of the third millennium BC (Kulakoğlu 2017). Three architectural phases consisting of an articulated monumental complex with various independent units have been brought to light. Each phase ends in destruction with a violent fire as demonstrated by thick layers with collapsed burnt bricks, wooden beams, and ashes. Without any striking parallels in Anatolia in regard to their dimensions and plan, these public buildings might have been inspired by northern Levantine or Mesopotamian palaces. These elements reveal that Kültepe was a powerful kingdom in central Anatolia which had close interactions with its neighbours, as attested by imported pottery and materials (Peyronel & Vacca 2021) together with local assemblages and artistic productions, such as the alabaster idols and statuettes found in a large number at the site (Kulakoğlu et al. 2022). The sequence of the overlapped architectural phases made it possible to recognize a transition from the monumental public compound to a specialized handicraft complex at the very end of the third millennium BC, possibly indicating a shift in the monumental public quarter towards the area later occupied by the citadel during the Middle Bronze Age (Rıdvanoğulları, Öztürk, Ay, Genç & Kulakoğlu in this volume). A sounding at the northern edge of the mound also made it possible to build up an uninterrupted stratigraphic sequence covering the whole third millennium BC at the periphery of the Early Bronze settlement and the new excavations south of the palace have showed clear evidence of a Late Chalcolithic occupa-

---

Fikri Kulakoğlu (kulakoglu@yahoo.com) Director of Kültepe excavations, University of Ankara

Luca Peyronel (luca.peyronel@unimi.it) Head of the Italian Archaeological Project at Kültepe, University of Milan (Italy)

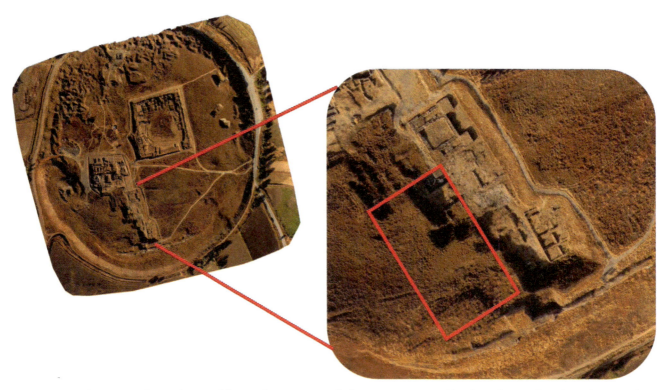

Figure 18.1: Kültepe mound. Aerial view of the southern sector with the area investigated by the Italian Archaeological Project (PAIK) of the University of Milan. © Kültepe Expedition.

tion (Kulakoğlu et al. 2020; 2022; Kulakoğlu, Kontani & Yamaguchi in this volume).

Since 2019 new excavations on the south-western sector of the mound have been carried out by the Italian Archaeological Project at Kültepe (PAIK) of the University of Milan, as a part of the programme of international collaborations of the Kültepe Expedition.

The area was carefully selected to offer the best choices to link the previously investigated levels with a new complete fine-tuned stratigraphic sequence from the Iron Age occupation (levels/periods 4–5) to the Middle Bronze (levels 6–9) and the late Early Bronze Age (level 10), in order to build up a reliable chronological sequence anchored to radiocarbon dates and diagnostic pottery types of each phase (Kulakoğlu & Peyronel 2022) (Fig. 18.1). The excavations are in fact located immediately to the west of a wide excavated sector of the mound investigated by the Turkish mission between 1954 and 1967, where important official public buildings dated to the end of the Early Bronze Age and the Middle Bronze Ages were brought to light (Özgüç 1999) (Fig. 18.2). This sector of the Middle Bronze Age town included to the north a complex with two buildings interpreted as temples ('Temples' I and II; E and F in Fig. 18.2), other independent structures (level/period 7, C and D in Fig. 18.2), and a large stone-paved courtyard (the 'plaza', B in Fig. 18.2) connected with the so-called 'Palace on the Southern Terrace' (levels/periods 8–9, A in Fig. 18.2). The latter building is composed of an eastern and a western wing — with rooms arranged in two rows — on each side of 47 m long south–north passageway, which was stone-paved in the northern part (towards the plaza) and covered by wooden planks to the south (Özgüç 1999, 106–16). It is reasonable to consider the southern complex as an official building in which administrative activities — testified by the presence of some tablets and sealings — storing and exchange of commodities were carried out (Makowski 2014; Larsen 2015, 34–36). It was located just inside the town, presumably near one of the gates, and it led to an open area (the paved 'plaza') in the middle of the town. The new excavations in the south-western sector of the mound discovered some structures related to the western wing of a complex, with a well-preserved large room and an outdoor area. Pottery materials retrieved in the layers over two overlapping floors of the room pertain to a horizon that can be assigned to the Early–Middle Bronze Age transition and to the very beginning of the Middle Bronze Age period, pointing to a strong continuity and a gradual development of the local assemblage. Thus, the stratigraphic evidence seems to confirm the

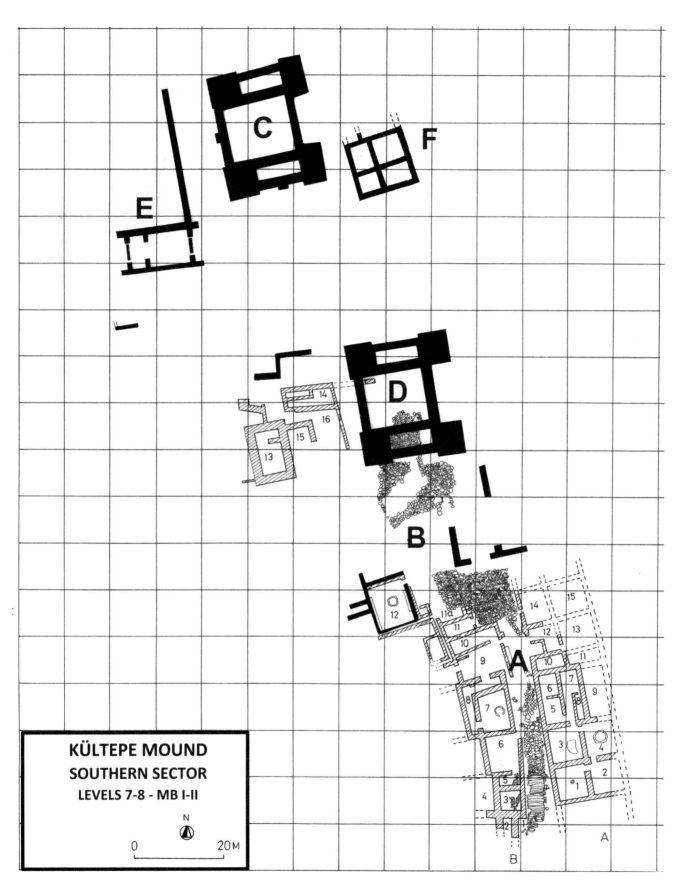

Figure 18.2: Schematic plan of the Middle Bronze I–II (mound levels/periods 7–8) building in the central-southern sector of the Upper Town of Kültepe. (A) Southern Terrace Building Complex, (B) Stone-Paved Plaza, (E) Warehouse, (F) Square Building, (C–D) Temple I and II. © Kültepe Expedition.

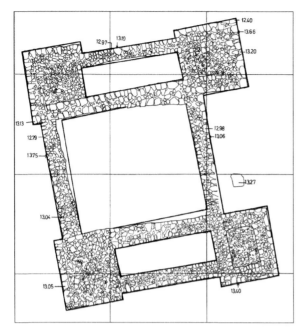

Figure 18.3: Plan and view from the north of Temple II of Kültepe. © Kültepe Expedition.

foundation of the Southern Building Complex at the end of the third millennium BC, and its use until the second half of the nineteenth century BC, when it was destroyed in a violent conflagration (Kulakoğlu, Oselini, Peyronel and Vacca in this volume).

Notwithstanding some difficulties in the precise stratigraphic correlation between the various architectural structures, the building on the southern terrace can be dated between the end of the third millennium BC and the end of the nineteenth century BC (EB–MB transition and MB I; mound levels/periods 8–9), when it was definitely destroyed and abandoned. According to Özgüç the complex might be contemporary with the level 8 palatial compound (the so-called 'Old Palace'), discovered below the 'Waršama' Palace of level 7 in the central part of the mound, although he did not exclude an earlier date for its first construction, being aware of some unusually 'archaic' traits observed in the pottery materials from the building's assemblages (Özgüç 1999, 109–13). Thus, the conflagration which marked the last building phase may have been contemporary with the destruction of the Old Palace and it might also be correlated with the same destruction in the eastern Lower Town which ended the first phase of the Karum period (level II of the Lower Town). Although ^{14}C and dendro-chronological datings are not available for the building, the tree-ring chronology established for the two palaces on the citadel indicated that the earlier palatial complex used timber from trees that were felled in 2027–2024 BC, while the juniper wood associated with the construction of the later palace gave a dating of 1835–1832 BC (Newton & Kuniholm 2004; *contra* Manning et al. 2016, in which the tree-ring chronology has been revised proposing dates thirteen–sixteen years earlier than previously suggested, thus implying no direct relation between the destructions of Lower Town phase II and mound level/period 8). Moreover, this evidence fits very well with the historical data gathered from the cuneiform texts, where the last attested eponyms of the *karum* II tablets can be dated to REL 138, and the intervals between phase II and Ib of the *karum* could lasted only a few years, between REL 138 and 141 (Barjamovic et al. 2012, 28–40).

After the abandonment of the southern complex, the area underwent a complete re-organization in level/period 7 (MB II, *c*. eighteenth century BC) with the creation of what could be considered a ceremonial district centred on two monumental buildings interpreted as temples, and including also the nearby so-called warehouse (in CII–CIII/82–83) and a four-room square building (in C–CI/87–88) to the west (Özgüç 1999, 117–28; Makowski 2014, 97–99, fig. 9).

The temples are identical in plan with massive angular protruding buttresses, lateral recesses delimited by double walls and a central square room (12 × 13 m). Their ceremonial/cultic function is probable, notwithstanding the lack of installations and cultic paraphernalia, since only the foundations have been preserved (Fig. 18.3).

Figure 18.4: Kültepe mound. The Stone Building in the southern sector of the Upper Town. © Kültepe Expedition.

However, a rock crystal lion statuette, a gold cup, bronze vessels including two cauldrons, and a small hoard of small gold ingots coming from badly preserved structures to the west of Temple II (in squares CIV-V/85-86), show indeed the importance of this area (Özgüç 1999, 121). To the west of Temple I lies a two-room rectangular building (c. 18 × 7.5 m) that was intended in a first phase as the entrance to the precinct from the west and which in its last use might have been changed in function becoming a sort of official warehouse. More than three tons of obsidian blocks and a few worked pieces were in fact stored in it. The famous bronze dagger bearing the Akkadian inscription 'palace of Anitta, the king', found together with a bronze vessel in the filling layer over the floor of the main room, suggests that the building was directly controlled by the royal power, although the presence of such a prestige item inside it is somehow puzzling (Özgüç 1956; Kulakoğlu & Kangal 2011, 172-73, no. 1).

This wide and articulated programme of urban renewal also affected the palatial area, which was radically transformed by the construction of the new palace (the so-called Palace of Waršama) over the ruins of the Old Palace (Özgüç 1999, 79-94; Barjamovic 2014; Makowski 2014; Michel 2015; 2019). The two MBA palatial citadels have in fact completely different arrangements with the earlier building showing independent units and a circular fortification wall, while the last palace of Kaneš was square in shape (measuring 100 × 110 m) and surrounded by a substantial wall (2-4.5 m in thickness). It was organized with a central courtyard flanked by rows of small rooms and ended in a fierce destruction that is particularly evident on the northern side, where the still 2 m high walls are completely melted and vitrified. The timber and the timber impressions on the bricks preserved very well the tree-ring sequences, making it possible to date the construction (1835-1832) and two phases of different repairs (1810 and 1774-1771) prior to the destruction (Newton & Kuniholm 2004, 168-69).

Thus, according to the available evidence, since the end of the nineteenth century the Upper Town was organized with a citadel occupied by the imposing square palace and by a ceremonial district immediately to the south. In this period the main gate leading to the Upper Town might have been on the eastern side, possibly changing the overall orientation of the urban layout which previously would have been organized according to a south–north main axis starting from a city gate at the end of the southern complex.

As is the case for the Waršama Palace, the buildings related to the ceremonial sector were also preserved only at the foundation level, without any clear evidence of floor level. Özgüç has excluded the possibility that the stone-paved square of level 8 would have still been partially used during the later MB phase, although he noticed the presence in some parts of two overlapping stone-paved floors. Since the plaza is *c.* 1 m lower than the corridor of the southern building, it could be possible that an intervention levelling the area to arrange the new ceremonial district was carried out shortly after the level 8 destruction.

The Stone Building in the South-Western Sector of the Kültepe Mound

The major result of the new excavations in the south-western sector of the mound is related to the discovery of a large, monumental stone building already identified in 2015, defined in its stratigraphic relations in 2020, and almost completely excavated between 2021 and 2022 (Fig. 18.4).

The building is oriented north-east/south-west and is composed of two adjacent underground chambers, which have been interpreted as the building's basement: the southern one (L.78) is a long storeroom of 11.7 × 2.5 m, with a 'L' recess at its north-eastern end; the northern one (L.79) is a large hall measuring *c.* 11.2 × 5.4 m, without any direct connection to the other at floor level (Fig. 18.5).

The stone walls are built using unworked and worked blocks of local volcanic andesite rocks, set in place with clay mortar. The larger blocks dress in quite regular rows the lower part of the inner facades. The walls had no outer faces at their underground level, since the stones were abutted directly against the earlier stratigraphy cut by the foundation trenches, as is evident

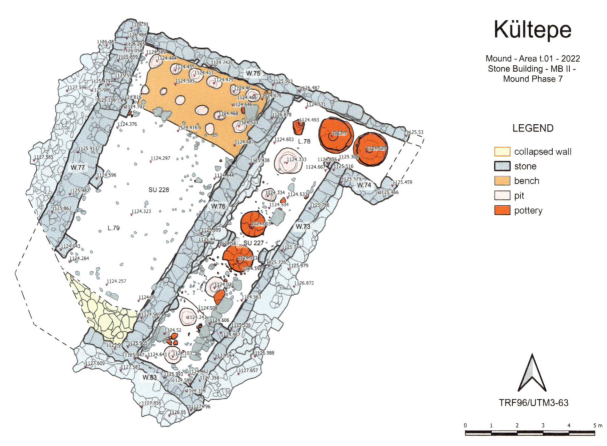

Figure 18.5: Kültepe mound. Plan of the Stone Building of the Upper Town. © Kültepe Expedition.

Figure 18.6: Kültepe mound. Stone Building. View of Room L.79 from the north. © Kültepe Expedition.

Figure 18.7: Kültepe mound. Stone Building. Section with the level of collapsed stones in Room L.79 from the north. © Kültepe Expedition.

Figure 18.8: Kültepe mound. Stone Building. The bench in Room L.79 from the south. © Kültepe Expedition.

Figure 18.9: Kültepe mound. Stone Building. Detail of the mat over the floor in Room L.79. © Kültepe Expedition.

especially on the western and south-western sides. The southern, northern, and western rear walls, *c.* 3 m in thickness, had the structural function of sustaining the upper terrace/floor in addition to containing the thrust of the earth, while the eastern wall apparently was only 0.5 m thick, since it does not have a major static function (Fig. 18.6). The western wall is the best-preserved one, reaching more than 3.5 m at the south-eastern corner, as well as the western one, which is 3 m high, although it is conceived in a different manner, as a double-wall with a passageway to access to the main hall from above.

Hundreds of stones have been found fallen inside the two rooms, appearing immediately beneath an upper filling layer rich in animal bones and pottery sherds (Fig. 18.7). Scattered among these were some blocks worked with a semicircular hollow that could be functional for housing the beams supporting the ground/upper floor, as also suggested by one block still in its original position on the partition wall at *c.* 1.8 m high from the floor. The entrance to the basement of the building is not unequivocally identified: the most reliable possibility is a staircase located in the north-western corner made by stone steps set parallel to the northern wall. The staircase made it possible to reach from the outside a walkway along the wall with three doors leading inside the large room. These entrances, only 1 m wide, were placed at 2.3 m intervals, in the correspondence of flat stones on the floor.

The northern room is equipped with a large low bench on the eastern side in which several medium-sized vessels were set (Fig. 18.8), while the rest of the floor was covered by a reed mat that has been found mineralized in situ (Fig. 18.9).

Tens of bowls and cups were originally aligned and stored upside down along the southern wall (Fig. 18.10). On the bench and along the other walls many other vessels have been retrieved crushed on the floor, including craters, pitchers, spouted bowls, and medium-sized jars. Fine Red Slip Ware with or without burnishing appears also in a good amount (*c.* 20–30 per cent) especially with the types of cups and bowls and jugs with beaked spouts. The extremely large amount of pottery — amounting to hundreds of pieces according to a preliminary estimation — has been found in a very fragmentary condition crushed by the stone blocks of the walls collapsed inside the room. They pertain to the very same ceramic horizon that can be assigned to level 7 and tentatively dated to the eighteenth century (Kulakoğlu, Peyronel, Oselini & Vacca in this volume).

Figure 18.10: Kültepe mound. Stone Building. Detail of bowl over the floor in Room L.79. © Kültepe Expedition.

The same time span is suggested by the small finds, which include bronze pins, rings, and small tools, lead rings, sheets and a plaque, thin bone hairpins, and a lead figurine of a female deity. A series of radiocarbon datings from charred seeds and bones gave a range from the mid-nineteenth to the beginning of seventeenth centuries, thus confirming the chronological attribution (Fig. 18.11).

The southern parallel room of the stone building is a long storeroom equipped with nine big pithoi: two of them are almost complete and still set into the floor, while only the bases and the circular depressions in the floor of the others are preserved, with numerous fragments scattered around and in the collapsed level of the structures (Fig. 18.12). They were 175–180 cm high (with a capacity of *c.* 2200 litres) with a thick square or

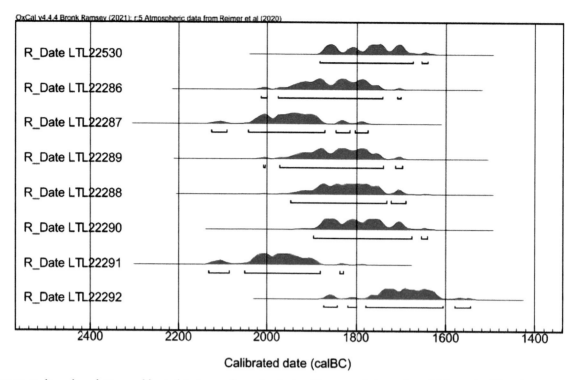

Figure 18.11: Radiocarbon datings calibrated 2-sigma of samples (animal bones and charred seeds) from the filling layers of the Stone Building. © Kültepe Expedition.

Figure 18.12: Kültepe mound. Stone Building. The pithoi in Room L.78 from the west. © Kültepe Expedition.

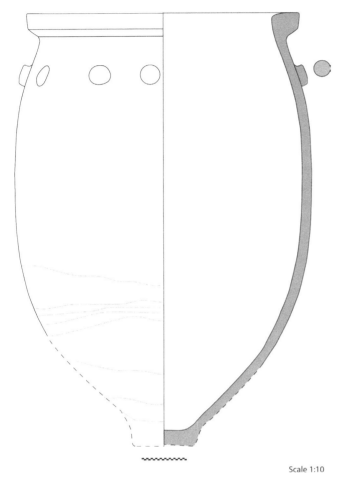

Figure 18.13: Pithos Kt.22.t 01.Mk4.P_2 from Room L.78. © Kültepe Expedition.

round rim and a decoration formed by a row of round pommels on the shoulder and rope impressions in the lower part of the body (Fig. 18.13). Two pithoi have been restored in autumn 2022 and this was the occasion for an accurate documentation of the vessels. They both show striking evidence for repairs done at the time of their use with drills and application of lead clasps. In one case a kind of stitching technique was used to repair a vertical fracture with lead clasps inserted alternately from the inside and outside.

Two other big jars characterized by an extraordinary plastic decoration, might have been kept at the ground-floor level of the building, since the fragments were found scattered from the uppermost layers of both rooms (Figs 18.14–18.15).

They are without comparison at the site and in MBA Anatolia and might be related to ceremonial activities performed in association with the building (Kulakoğlu & Peyronel 2023). Thanks to the ongoing restoration work, it was possible to ascertain their shape and dimensions. One pithos is 103 cm high (maximum preservation, *c.* 125 cm reconstructed height) with ovoidal body and round thickened rim, the other is more globular, 90 cm high (maximum preservation, *c.* 115 cm reconstructed height), and *c.* 110 cm wide, with a similar rim. Differently from the other exemplar, it has a large spout at the mouth and triangular oblique handles. Both vessels are characterized by applied decoration in the upper part up to the ridges below the rim, comprised of three broad bands (24–30 cm) separated by lintels, with a series of metopes densely decorated by means of recurring elements, including small globes, lozenges, festoons, single or multiple circular elements, crescents, and scale motifs. The spouted pithos featured a central frieze in which figurative elements are arranged in two scenes: a lioness probably attacking a long-horned rampant caprid holding a cub on its hind legs and, after an area with a large circular relief element, a lyre player and two figures — one of whom is ityphallic — represented in the act of dancing which appear in succession on a background filled by globular elements (Fig. 18.14). This is a very special narrative-type composition, the meaning of which certainly seems to be ceremonial or ritual, providing a valuable element for the interpretation of the building. The presence of the images also constitutes an important link with the later Old Hittite production of polychrome vessels with figurative reliefs, attested in several Anatolian centres dated between the late seventeenth and sixteenth centuries, with the most complete specimens found at İnandıktepe, Hüseyındede, and Bitik (Özgüç 1957; 1988; Sipahi 2000; Yıldırım 2005; 2008). In these exceptional specimens, which are true masterpieces of Hittite ceramic art, the morphology recalls four-handled types known at Kültepe (Özgüç 2003, fig. 187), which are also strictly related to a vessel from Eskiyapar characterized by a device with bull's heads, demonstrating that Kaneš was one of the centres of the earliest elaboration in an uninterrupted development of libation vessels during the first half of the second millennium (Kulakoğlu & Peyronel 2023).

The very rich decoration of these vessels is organized in parallel friezes with ritual scenes and processions in which a large number of figures appear. The interpretation of the various representations is certainly very complex and debated, both in the individual figurative elements and in the overall scenes (Strupler 2012; Gates 2017). Male and female characters with musical instruments, including lyre players, are frequent in the processions (Şare 2017; Schwemer 2020).

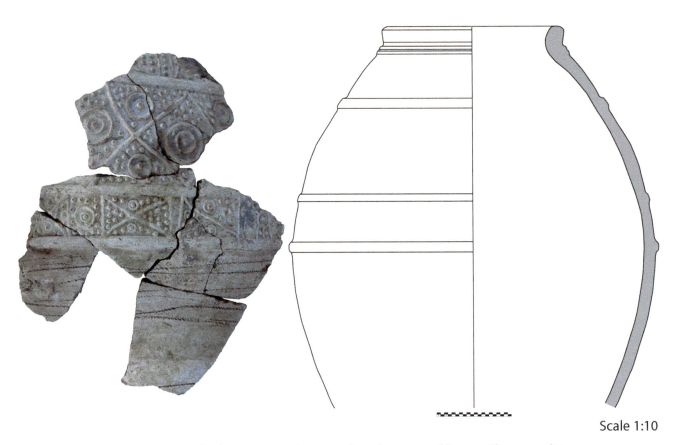

Figure 18.14: Decorated pithos Kt.20.t 08.Mk17.P_647 from the Stone Building. © Kültepe Expedition.

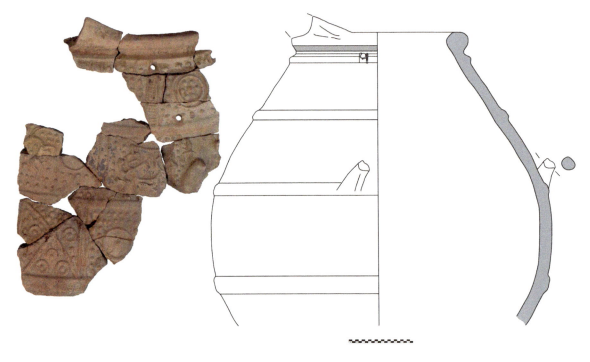

Figure 18.15: Decorated pithos Kt.20.t 08.Mk17.P_648 from the Stone Building. © Kültepe Expedition.

18. RECENT EXCAVATIONS ON THE MOUND OF KÜLTEPE

Figure 18.16: Detail of the figurative frieze of decorated pithos Kt.20.t 08.Mk17.P.647. © Kültepe Expedition.

Figure 18.17: Detail of the lyre player of the Inandik vase and Kültepe pithos Kt.20.t 08.Mk17.P.647. © Kültepe Expedition.

The structure of the instrument with sinuous sides and snake- or lion-head terminations, which is represented both in a small version and in a larger one, played by two personages, turns out to be identical to that depicted in the frieze of the Stone Building's pithos discovered in Kültepe, although the stylistic rendering is very different (Fig. 18.15).

It should be strongly emphasized that the similarity between the stringed instruments of Kültepe and İnandıktepe, testifies to the existence of an uninterrupted cultural tradition linking the Anatolian principalities and the Old Hittite kingdom during the Middle Bronze Age (Özgüç 1988).

Although the presence of lyre players is quite rare in the Middle Bronze glyptics from Anatolia and the Levant, it is documented by a few cylinder seals and seal impressions from Kültepe and other sites, dated to the eighteenth century BC. A seal found at Tarsus-Gözlükule shows a lyre player with a bird-like head, similar to the personage depicted in the Kültepe pithos, together with animals, like scorpions, a lion, and two caprids (Goldman 1956, 235, 239, pl. 400 n. 35). In addition, a similar animal mask, which is believed to have been worn by people during religious ceremonies, is seen on a relief vase fragment from Boğazköy (Boehmer 1983, 28–29, pls IX–X). Thus, the bird (?)-headed lyre-playing figure from the Kültepe pithos would be a forerunner of this tradition. In another seal, allegedly from Mardin and now in the British Museum, a horizontally placed lyre is played by a personage associated with friezes of birds and quadrupeds (Rimmer 1969, 28, pl. 8a). However, in both seals the cordophone instrument is a round soundbox bottom lyre with double curved arms placed in a horizontal position (Li Castro & Scardina 2011). While stringed instruments are not attested in the so-called Anatolian group of seals from Kültepe, they do appear occasionally in Old Syrian seal impressions, such as in the sealing from Acemhöyük, depicting a seated person (a god or the king) in front of a female figure holding a five-strings lyre (Özgüç, N. 2015, 123–24, fig. 95).

Conclusions

The recent discovery of the monumental Stone Building in the southern sector of the Kültepe mound adds a new important piece of evidence to strengthen the functional interpretation of the area as a ceremonial/religious district of the Upper Town during the last Middle Bronze occupation at the site. The interpretation of the building as related to feasting and commensality can be proposed on the basis of multiple evidence, pointing at its complementarity with the surrounding structures, especially the so-called Temple II, located just a few metres to the east.

Only the basement of the Stone Building is preserved and its plan and the materials retrieved on the floor level indicate that it was used for storing foodstuffs in large pithoi lined up in the long and narrow room, and for keeping serving and table wares in the other room, where a large quantity of bowls, cups, jugs, jars have been found lined along the walls and set on a low clay bench. This pottery was probably distributed for the consumption of liquids and food at the ground floor or immediately outside the building. In the layers pertaining to the collapse of the structures, a large quantity of pottery was found as well, suggesting the presence of spaces for storing vessels also at the ground level. From these layers come the two decorated pithoi, which might have been visible to the audience in order to make explicit the ritual meaning evocated by their exceptional decoration. Immediately covering the level of the collapse of the building an artificial filling rich in pottery sherds has been interpreted as a deliberate closure that happened shortly after the last phase of use, which possibly ended with a collapse caused by a natural event such as an earthquake. In the filling layers a huge amount of animal bones has been collected (Kulakoğlu, Peyronel & Minniti in this volume). Over 4400 animal remains were identified as domestic mammals (mainly sheep and goat, cattle) and an unusual high number of wild species, including lions, bears, boars, wolf, hyena, wild goat, and deer have also been found in the assemblage. This situation appears to be markedly different from other contexts at the site, and it could be related to the ceremonial function. In this respect, the presence of lion, bear, boar, and deer immediately recalls the famous passage of the Anitta-text in which the ruler of Kuššara explicitly reported about his religious building activities and mentioned a hunting expedition. He lists several animals including two lions, seventy boars, one boar of the canebrake, and 120 other wild animals, whether leopards, lions, mountain sheep, or wild sheep that were brought by him to Neša (Hoffner 1997). The chronological range of the Stone Building roughly corresponded with the period of the Kanešite kings known from written documents, spanning from the beginning to the end of the eighteenth century BC, with Anitta and his father Pithana ruling from *c*. 1750 to 1725, succeeded by the last king attested in the texts, Zuzu (Barjamovic et al. 2012, 31–40; Larsen 2015, 32–34). A direct relation between the animals mentioned by Anitta and these faunal remains is nothing more than a fascinating speculation, although it cannot be denied that the Stone Building presents various elements suggesting the performance of ritual and ceremonial activities and the animal remains in the fillings testify to animal consumption and/or animal sacrifices.

The building presents some singularities that are difficult to explain at the moment. Firstly, its orientation is completely different from that of the other coeval structures and in particular with that of the two hypothetical sacred buildings (Temples I and II). Although the basement of the stone building should not have been visible, it does not seem possible that on the ground floor it had a different orientation. It is likely that the choice depended on static requirements for the pre-existing stratigraphy within which the structure was founded. It is very difficult to propose the appearance of the elevation above ground level, although the presence of hundreds of stone blocks collapsed inside both rooms seems to be compatible with a significant elevation of the structures even above ground level. The major problem is the complete lack of preservation of any traces of floors or an outdoor area around the building. The burnt remains of walls and the destruction level of the previous phase of occupation (period/level 8 of the mound, Middle Bronze I) appear everywhere to the west, east and north-east, while to the south the building is cut into the stone paved plaza excavated by Özgüç. Therefore, the urban layout of this sector of the town during the Middle Bronze II (periods/levels 7–6) is still unclear, due to the almost complete lack of the original floor level inside and outside the buildings.

Notwithstanding this, the presence of several interrelated buildings in this part of the town, with a clear ceremonial and religious connotation, testified also by materials, such as the two pithoi with relief decoration retrieved in the Stone Building, allow us to point out how much the later Hittite rituality — highly structured and strongly linked to ceremonies connected to the sacred buildings — rather than being seen as an innovation, was deeply rooted in earlier experiences, which were re-elaborated and then embedded in the context of Hittite centralized power.

The discovery of the monumental Stone Building thus provided results that make a surprising contribution to our knowledge of a crucial phase in the cultural and artistic development of Middle Bronze Age Anatolia, on the threshold of the emergence of the Hittite state. An in-depth analysis of the last phase of the Middle Bronze Age occupation at the site is now possible thanks to the new evidence from the mound, although future excavation campaigns will undoubtedly provide further valuable data in an attempt to understand an era of decisive historical transformations in the Anatolian plateau.

Acknowledgements

We wish to thank all the Kültepe members involved in the excavations conducted in the south-western sector of the mound and in the processing and study of the materials. We are especially grateful to Agnese Vacca (deputy director of the PAIK team) and Valentina Oselini (responsible for the pottery data management). The research at Kültepe carried out by the Italian team of the University of Milan is supported by the Italian Ministry of Foreign Affairs and International Cooperation, the Italian Ministry of Universities and Research (Project PRIN 2017 'Big Data and Early Archives'), and the University of Milan. The Italian project at Kültepe is part of an agreement between the University of Milan and the University of Ankara, under the scientific responsibility of Fikri Kulakoğlu and Luca Peyronel. The first paragraph and conclusions are written jointly by both the authors, the paragraph on the Stone Building is by L. Peyronel.

Bibliography

Barjamovic, Gojko

2014 'The Size of Kaneš and the Demography of Early Middle Bronze Age Anatolia', in Levent Atici, Fikri Kulakoğlu, Gojko Barjamovic & Andrew Fairbairn (eds), *Current Research in Kültepe/Kanesh: An Interdisciplinary and Integrative Approach to Trade Networks, Internationalism, and Identity during the Middle Bronze Age* (Journal of Cuneiform Studies Supplemental Series 4). Lockwood, Atlanta: 55–68.

Barjamovic, Gojko; Hertel, Thomas & Larsen, Mogens Trolle

2012 *Ups and Downs at Kanesh: Observations on Chronology, History and Society in the Old Assyrian period* (Publications de l'Institut historique archéologique néerlandais de Stamboul 120). Nederlands Instituut voor het Nabije Oosten, Leiden.

Boehmer, Rainer Michael

1983 *Die Reliefkeramik von Boğazköy: Grabungskampagnen 1906-1912, 1931-1939, 1952-1978* (Boğazköy-Hattuša 13). Mann, Berlin.

Gates, Marie-Henriette

2017 'Gods, Temples, and Cult at the Service of the Early Hittite State', in Yağmur Heffron, Adam Stone & Martin Worthington (eds), *At the Dawn of History: Ancient Near Eastern Studies in Honour of J. N. Postgate*. Penn State University Press, Philadelphia: 189–210.

Goldman, Hetty

1956 *Excavations at Gözlü Kule, Tarsus*. Princeton University Press, Princeton.

Hertel, Thomas Klitgaard

2014 'The Lower Town at Kültepe/Kanesh: The Urban Layout and the Population', in Levent Atici, Fikri Kulakoğlu, Gojko Barjamovic & Andrew Fairbairn (eds), *Current Research in Kültepe/Kanesh: An Interdisciplinary and Integrative Approach to Trade Networks, Internationalism, and Identity during the Middle Bronze Age* (Journal of Cuneiform Studies Supplemental Series 4). Lockwood, Atlanta: 25–54.

Hoffner, Harry A. Jr.

1997 'Hittite Canonical Compositions – Historiography. Proclamation of Anitta of Kuššar', in William W. Hallo & K. Lawson Younger, Jr. (eds), *The Contexts of Scripture*, I: *Canonical Composition from the Bible World*. Brill, Leiden: 182–84.

Kulakoğlu, Fikri

2011 'Kültepe-Kaneš: A Second Millennium B.C.E. Trading Center on the Central Plateau', in Sharon R. Steadman & Gregory McMahon (eds), *The Oxford Handbook of Ancient Anatolia: 10,000–323 B.C.E.* Oxford University Press, Oxford: 1012–30.

2017 'Early Bronze Age Monumental Structures at Kültepe', in Fikri Kulakoğlu & Gojko Barjamovic (eds), *Movement, Resources, Interaction: Proceedings of the 2nd Kültepe International Meeting; Kültepe, 26-30 July 2015; Studies Dedicated to Klaas Veenhof* (Kültepe International Meetings 2, Subartu 39). Brepols, Turnhout: 215–24.

Kulakoğlu, Fikri; Genç, Elif; Kontani, Ryoichi; Peyronel, Luca; Masatçıoğlu, Nilgün; İpek, Önder; Öztürk, Güzel; Hacar, Abdullah; Öğreten, Mehmet Tarık; Tüysüz, Burcu

2022 '2019–2020 Yılı Kültepe Kaniş Kazıları', in Adil Özme (ed.), *2019-2020 Yılı Kazı Çalışmaları* (CİLT 4). T.C. Kültür Varlıkları ve Müzeler Genel Müdürlüğü, Ankara: 209–21.

Kulakoğlu, Fikri & Kangal, Selmin (eds)

2011 *Anatolia's Prologue: Kultepe Kanesh Karum; Assyrians in Istanbul*. Kayseri Metropolitan Municipality, Istanbul.

Kulakoğlu, Fikri; Kontani, Ryoichi; Uesugi, Akinori; Yamaguchi, Yuji; Shimogama, Kazuya & Semmoto, Masao

2020 'Preliminary Report of Excavations in the Northern Sector of Kültepe 2015–2017', in Fikri Kulakoğlu, Cécile Michel & Güzel Öztürk (eds), *Integrative Approaches to the Archaeology and History of Kültepe-Kaneš: Kültepe 4–7 August 2017* (Kültepe International Meetings 3, Subartu 45). Brepols, Turnhout: 9–97.

Kulakoğlu, Fikri & Peyronel, Luca

2022 'L'organizzazione dello spazio pubblico e privato a Kültepe tra Bronzo Medio ed Età del Ferro. Nuovi dati dal settore meridionale dell'insediamento', in *Lo spazio pubblico, lo spazio privato: XI Convegno contributo delle missioni archeologiche italiane a scavi, ricerche e studi in Turchia; Atti del Convegno 2020 / Kamusal alan, özel alan: XI Türkiye'deki arkeolojik çalışmalara eğitim, araştırma ve kazı'da İtalya katkısı sempozyumu; Sempozyum bildirileri 2020*. Istituto italiano di cultura, Istanbul: 31–44.

2023 'L'arte del vasaio in Anatolia antica. Il repertorio figurativo della ceramica di Kültepe durante il periodo delle colonie assire: nuovi dati dagli scavi recenti/Eski Anadolu seramik sanatı. Kültepe'de Asur Ticaret Kolonileri Çağı tasvirli seramik sanatı: son kazılardan yeni bilgiler', in *Arte, funzione e simboli nella cultura materiale dell'Anatolia Antica: XII Convegno sul contributo a scavi, ricerche e studi nelle missioni archeologiche in Turchia; Atti del Convegno 2021 / XII Türkiye'deki arkeolojik çalışmalara eğitim, araştırma ve kazı'da İtalya katkısı sempozyumu; Sempozyum bildirileri 2021*. Istituto italiano di cultura, Istanbul: 67–81.

Larsen, Mogens Trolle

2015 *Kanesh: A Merchant Colony in Bronze Age Anatolia*. Cambridge University Press, Cambridge.

Li Castro, Emiliano & Scardina, Placido

2011 'The Double Curve Enigma', *Music in Art* 36: 203–17.

Makowski, Maciej

2014 'The Road to the Citadel of Kanesh. Urban Structure and Spatial Organization of the City during the Assyrian Colony', in Piotr Bieliński, Michał Gawlikowski, Rafał Koliński, Dorota Ławecka, Arkadiusz Sołtysiak & Zuzanna Wygnańska (eds), *Proceedings of the 8th International Congress on the Archaeology of the Ancient Near East 30 April – 4 May 2012, University of Warsaw*, I. Harrassowitz, Wiesbaden: 93–111.

Manning, Sturt W.; Griggs, Carol B.; Lorentzen, Brita; Barjamovic, Gojko; Bronk Ramsey, Christopher; Kromer, Bernd & Wild, Eva Maria

2016 'Integrated Tree-Ring-Radiocarbon High-Resolution Timeframe to Resolve Earlier Second Millennium BCE Mesopotamian Chronology', *PLoS ONE* 11: e0157144 <https://www.doi.org/ 10.1371/journal.pone.0157144>.

Michel, Cécile

2015 'L'organisation du palais de Kaneš d'après la documentation textuelle', *Cahiers des thèmes transversaux d'ArScAn* 12: 161–74.

2019 'Palaces at Kaneš during the Old Assyrian Period', in Dirk Wicke (ed.), *Der Palast im antiken und islamischen Orient: 9. Internationales Colloquium der Deutschen Orient-Gesellschaft 30. März – 1. April 2016*. Harrassowitz, Wiesbaden: 121–38.

Newton, Maryanne W. & Kuniholm, Peter Ian

2004 'A Dendrochronological Framework for the Assyrian Colony Period in Asia Minor', *Türkiye Bilimler Akademisi Arkeoloji Dergisi* 7: 165–76.

Özgüç, Tahsin

1956 'The Dagger of Anitta', *Türk Tarih Kurumu Belleten* 77: 33–36.

1957 'Bitik Vase', *Anatolia* 2: 57–85.

1986 *Kültepe-Kaniš*, II: *New Researches at the Trading Center of the Ancient Near East* (Turk Tarih Kurumu Yayınlarından 5/41). Türk Tarih Kurumu Yayınları, Ankara.

1988 *İnandıktepe, Eski Hitit Çağında Önemli Bir Kült Merkezi*. Türk Tarih Kurumu Yayınları, Ankara.

1999 *Kültepe-Kaniş/Neşa Sarayları ve Mabetleri / The Palaces and Temples of Kültepe-Kaniš/Neša* (Türk Tarih Kurumu Yayınlarından 5/46). Türk Tarih Kurumu Yayınları, Ankara.

2003 *Kültepe, Kaniš/Neša: The Earliest International Center and the Oldest Capital of the Hittites*. Middle Eastern Culture Center in Japan, Tokyo.

Özgüç, Nimet

2015 *Acemhöyük / Burushaddum, I: Silindir Mühürler ve Mühür Baskılı Bullalar / Cylinder Seals and Bullae with Cylinder Seal Impressions*. Türk Tarih Kurumu Yayınları, Ankara.

Peyronel, Luca & Vacca, Agnese

2021 'When Different World Meet: Exchange Networks in Anatolia and the Northern Levant during the Third Millennium BC', in Fikri Kulakoğlu, Guido Kryszat & Cécile Michel (eds), *Cultural Exchange and Current Researches at Kültepe and its Surroundings: Kültepe 1-4 August, 2019* (Kültepe International Meetings 4, Subartu 46). Brepols, Turnhout: 23–50.

Rimmer, Joan

1969 *Ancient Musical Instruments of Western Asia in the Department of Western Asiatic Antiquities*. British Museum, London.

Schwemer, Daniel

2020 'Fest und Feierlichkeit, Euphorie und Ektase Musik im Kult des hethitischen Anatolien', in Florian Leitmeir, Dahlia Shehata & Oliver Wiener (eds), *Mus-ic-on! Klang der Antike: Begleitband zur Ausstellung im Martin von Wagner Museum der Universität Würzburg 10. Dezember 2019 bis 12. Juli 2020*. Würzburg University Press, Würzburg: 103–12.

Sipahi, İbrahim Tunç

2000 'Eine Althetische Reliefvase vom Hüseyindede Tepesi', *Istanbuler Mitteilungen* 50: 63–85.

Strupler, Néhémie

2012 'Reconstitution des vases à reliefs monochromes d'Alaca Höyük et d'Eskiyapar', *Anatolia antiqua* 20: 1–12.

Şare, Tuna

2017 'Women and Music in Ancient Anatolia: The Iconographic Evidence', in Ekin Kozal, Murat Akar, Yağmur Heffron, Çiler Çilingiroğlu, Tevfik Emre Şerifoğlu, Canan Çakırlar, Sinan Ünlüsoy & Eric Jean (eds), *Questions, Approaches, and Dialogues in Eastern Mediterranean Archaeology: Studies in Honor of Marie-Henriette and Charles Gates*. Ugarit, Münster: 555–80.

Yıldırım, Tayfun

2005 'Hüseyindede Tepesinde Bulunan Yeni bir Kült Vazosu', in Aygül Süel (ed.), *V. Uluslararası Hititoloji Kongresi Bildirileri: Acts of the Vth International Congress of Hittitology*. Çorum İl Özel İdaresi, Ankara: 761–78.

2008 'New Scenes on the Second Relief Vase from Hüseyindede and their Interpretation in the Light of Hittite Representative Art', *Studi Micenei ed Egeo-Anatolici* 50: 837–50.

19. Studies on Kültepe Hellenistic Period

Preliminary Evaluations on 2022 Excavations

Burcu Tüysüz & Yılmaz Rıdvanoğulları

Introduction

Kültepe is located 20 km north-east of Kayseri city centre in central Anatolia. It lies within the boundaries of the Cilicia province in the area known as Cappadocia during the Hellenistic period, which spans between 330–30 BC in Anatolia's historical continuum.[1] At that time, the mound served as a settlement encircled by a 5 m high and 2.5 m wide city wall, while the Lower Town was mostly utilized as a necropolis. The Hellenistic settlement represented by the building level 3 in the Kültepe stratigraphy[2] is known as Anisa[3] (Cumont 1932; Hild & Restle 1981, 193; Alp 1997, 45; Mitford 2000, 986; Barjamovic 2015; Kulakoğlu 2017). According to the *Anisa Tablet*, Anisa settlement is a small Cappadocian city with institutions reflecting the Greek city order, such as *demos*, *boule*, *archon*, and *prytaneis*, affiliated to Eusebeia, the capital of the Cappadocia Kingdom.

The systematic excavations began at Kültepe in 1948 under the direction of Tahsin Özgüç. It was possible to reach Hellenistic period structures and data linked to these structures during his excavations. However, during the excavations led by Tahsin Özgüç, which was focusing mainly on the Middle Bronze Age, the Hellenistic period settlement was quickly excavated to reach the earlier layers. Additionally, the results of these excavations were presented briefly to the scientific world in small number of publications (Taner 1971; 1974; Zoroğlu 1981). New excavations began in 2006 under the direction of Fikri Kulakoğlu with the scope of completing the stratigraphy of both the mound and Lower Town. These excavations also revealed Hellenistic–Roman period layers, and works in this direction were initiated. Excavations conducted periodically in various areas of the mound have indicated that the Hellenistic settlement persisted uninterruptedly from the last quarter of the fourth century BC until the end of the first century BC. The excavations in grid-squares 84–85–86/XCVII–XCVIII–XCIX, brought to light a building complex covering approximately 350 m², that is allowing a better understanding of the settlement's architectural structure, ceramic culture, religious traditions, commercial relations, and trade routes (Fig. 19.1).

Three architectural phases have been identified in the building, and its multiroom architecture generally consists of interconnected rectangular spaces. The spaces are defined by walls constructed using both regular and irregular masonry systems, consisting of neatly and roughly cut stones of varying sizes. As can be understood from the floors that are preserved in some places, the floors are covered with beaten earth or stone pavement. The architectural characteristics

---

[1] Strabon *Geographika*, XII, 1, 1–4.

[2] For Kültepe stratification, see Özgüç 1999, 4; Kulakoğlu 2010, 41; 2017; 2018.

[3] The name Anisa is found on a bronze tablet inscribed in Greek. For detailed information about the tablet, see Cumont 1932, 135–36; Güterbock 1956; Barjamovic 2015.

Burcu Tüysüz (burcutuysuz@nevsehir.edu.tr) Nevsehir Hacı Bektaş Veli University

Yılmaz Rıdvanoğulları (yilmaz.rdvn1@gmail.com) Ankara University

Figure 19.1: Sites excavated in 2009–2020 and geophysical studies in 2022. Kültepe Excavation Archive.

Figure 19.2: Goddess statue and bull's head. Kültepe Excavation Archive.

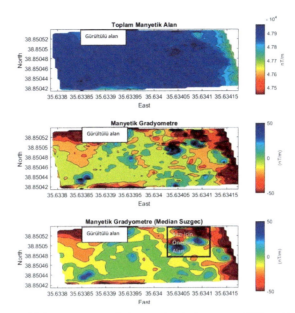

Figure 19.3: Sites with intense anomaly in geophysical surveys. Kültepe Excavation Archive.

of the phases are structurally similar. Small architectural changes between the phases are manifested by raising the ground levels and rearranging the interior architectural elements. This suggests that the building, constructed during the early phase, was reused in later phases with modifications, where most of the original walls were retained and some unnecessary areas were eliminated or new spaces were added as required, as evidenced by its architectural continuity.

Among the remarkable discoveries in the room with a later-added door are a statue of a goddess holding a pomegranate, a bull's head protome, and four dog burials in the corners of the walls. These finds suggest that the excavated area was related to a religious function (Kulakoğlu 2017, XIV–XV). The goddess statue holding a pomegranate also indicates the existence of a goddess cult and provides a clue about the Hellenistic period religious life of Kültepe (Fig. 19.2). Significant pottery finds found in the structure were produced in western Anatolia and Pergamon, from different geographies of Anatolia. Attic ceramics and sealed amphora handle fragments also suggest commercial relations with the Aegean and Mediterranean regions (Tüysüz 2021 and 2022, 122–218). In addition to these, the Kızılırmak Basin Ceramics found in the structure are also indicative of the local production, revealing valuable insights into the production potential, technical skills, and artistic vision of the local potters.

While the studies conducted in the building provided valuable insights into the Hellenistic settlement of Kültepe, it's important to note that only a limited portion of the structure was actually excavated. In the 2022 excavation season, the focus was on studying the north of the structure, which had not been explored before. The aim was to gain a deeper understanding of the building itself, as well as the cultural traits of the era it belongs to, while shedding new light on the Hellenistic settlement of Kültepe. This article presents preliminary evaluations of the studies conducted in the northern section of the aforementioned structure, as well as the results obtained during the 2022 excavation season.

Geophysical surveys constitute the first stage of the research on the area in 2022. In order to determine the distribution of the remains, an area of 500 m² in the northern part of the building was prospected with magnetic gradiometer and direct current resistivity-DCR (Fig. 19.3).[4] As a result of the scans, the residue density that regularly gives anomalies was found in the 86–87/XCVI grid-squares in the north-east of the area. Based on the results obtained from the surveys, an excavation area of 5 × 10 m was determined in this grid-square (Fig. 19.4). The Hellenistic period layer with a height of more than 2 m was excavated in this area called Trench 4 in the Kültepe excavation system. Excavations in this area revealed two cultural phases (early and late).

---

4 Prof. Dr M. Emin Candansayar, a faculty member of Ankara University's Faculty of Engineering, Department of Geophysical Engineering, conducted the geophysical measurements. We would like to thank Prof. Dr Emin Candansayar for his contributions to Kültepe studies.

Figure 19.4: Trench 4 excavation site. Kültepe Excavation Archive.

Later Phase

A series of structures and associated deposits that have been related to the last phase of Hellenistic occupation have been revealed (Fig. 19.5). The plan of the architectural remains could not be fully understood due to the limited excavation area. Despite this, it was possible to reveal certain walls and rooms of the architectural spaces within the excavated area.

Within the excavated area, three different rooms (Mk02, Mk03, and Mk04) that use common walls were identified. These walls are labelled as Dv01, Dv02, and Dv03. Dv01 extends in a north-west–south-east direction and has regular stone masonry. Its height is 1.20 m and its thickness is about 65 cm. Dv02 abuts Dv01 and extends eastwards in a regular pattern up to a certain point. However, it then continues as a 'masonry wall' with an irregular and ruinous appearance. Dv02 is preserved up to a height of about 1 m. From its intersection with Dv01, it extends 2.70 m to the east. Afterwards, it continues southwards as a new wall (Dv03), making a corner and defining the eastern boundary of the room. Dv03, whose western face was exposed as a result of the works carried out in the eastern section of the trench, has a regular stone pattern just like Dv01. The 1.10 m extension of this wall, which was preserved up to a height of approximately 1.15 m, towards the south was exposed and it was determined that the wall in question continued in the same direction.

Due to partial excavation of the rooms, no definitive information regarding their dimensions could be obtained. Nonetheless, the widths of some rooms that could be measured were 5.30 × 4.90 m for Mk02, 3 × 1.90 m for Mk04, and 4.20 × 2.90 m for Mk03. The floors are made of packed earth. In the large room (Mk02) to the west of the structure, almost all the floor is well preserved. However, in some parts it collapsed inward. In the other two rooms to the east of the structure, the floor was partially destroyed. Dv01, which forms the eastern border of the western room, rises about 20 cm from the floor in a row of stones.

Towards the south-west of Dv01, a row of uniformly sized stones measuring around 1.25 m wide was discovered. Two large and thick blocks[5] resembling neatly cut cubes were also found, along with the remains of a damaged jar or tandoor leaning against them. The row of stones, which is believed to belong to this structure, is laid directly on the floor and extends towards the south. Unfortunately, as the area has not been fully excavated, there is not enough data available to determine the function of this particular architectural installation.

The orientation of the entrance to the building has not been determined yet. Nonetheless, an inverted jamb measuring approximately 45 cm, located in the north-west of the room to the north and adjacent to Dv01, can be seen as significant information for future evaluations regarding the orientation of the building's entrance. The jamb stone in question suggests that there was a doorway in this area.

The absence of any mud-brick or wooden remains associated with the structure implies that the building was constructed entirely from stone.

At this stage, it is not possible to make any definitive statements regarding the functions of the different areas within the structure. Nevertheless, the discovery of the in situ pithos, along with seed remains in Mk03, suggests that the storage of goods may have taken place in this particular area of the structure.

The excavation of the deposits associated with the late phase of the building revealed a significant number of ceramics, as well as six spindle whorls and two beads.

Initial studies on ceramics have revealed that the pottery from this phase can be divided into two groups: local and imported. Kızılırmak Basin Ceramics, which are a local production, constitute the majority within the group. In addition to these, another group of samples were identified, which may have been imported as they differ from local production in terms of their paste-slip characteristics. Ceramics, which can be considered as imported vessels of this phase, have red and brown paste-slip characteristics (Fig. 19.6:1–2).

---

5 Both block stones have a height of 45 cm. However, their widths are different. One is 55 cm and the other 65 cm wide.

19. STUDIES ON KÜLTEPE HELLENISTIC PERIOD

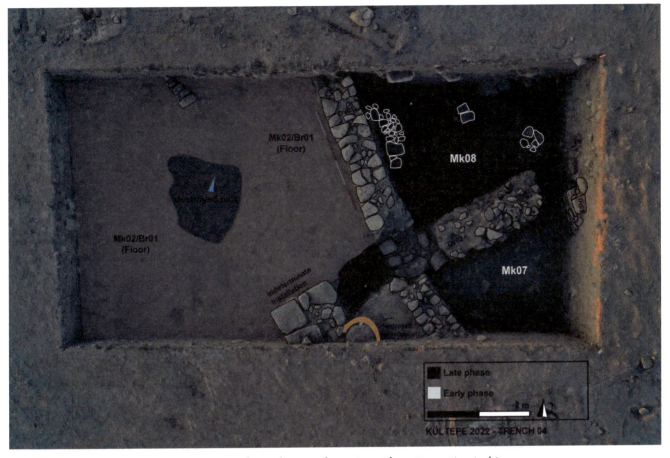

Figure 19.5: Trench 4 architectural remains. Kültepe Excavation Archive.

The red slipped samples in the imported ceramics exhibit a high degree of purity in their well-tempered paste, with very low amounts of mica and lime, and boast a range of distinct red shades in their paste-slip colours. Its forms consist of different types of bowl. The most prevalent type of bowl in this collection are those with a deep-bodied form, as shown in Figure 19.6:1. The rims of these specimens are noticeably inverted. Mouth diameters vary between 12–14 cm. We have discovered profiles that are remarkably similar, to the extent that they could be grouped together, in Cappadocia Komana. The samples from Komana, categorized as Form 1, have been dated to the late first century BC and the first century AD (Körsulu 2014, figs 16–18). Another similar example was found in the Hellenistic period level of Aşvan Castle (Mitchell 1980, fig. 31:300, fig. 35:398). A bowl with a similar profile was also found in the building levels of Tille mound, dated to the late first century BC and first century AD (French et al. 1982, fig. 12:1).

Another form group among the imported ceramics is the fish plate (Fig. 19.6:2). It is distinguished by its brown slip and pinkish-grey paste. The piece was found as a pedestal-body and the pedestal diameter is 8 cm. The saucer pit features a relief profile around its perimeter with a low circular base. The pottery exhibiting the aforementioned paste-slip qualities is commonly found alongside local sigillata in the region of Hadrianopolis, dating back to the first century BC and first century AD (Kan Şahin 2019, 140–57). Samples exhibiting similar paste-slip properties were identified in Kültepe and classified as Brown Slipped Ceramics based on the Hadrianopolis samples (Tüysüz 2022, 194–97). These samples were discovered in contexts dating back to the latter half of the second century BC and the first century BC (Tüysüz 2022, 195–96, Lev. 21, 132–33). The plate's convex profile and pedestal shape are reminiscent of the Form 1 fish plates described by Hayes, which are believed to date back to before 100 BC (Hayes 1985, Rev. 1, 1).

The samples categorized as local production comprise samples from the Kızılırmak Basin Ceramics group, as classified by the Kültepe Hellenistic period ceramic typology. The clays of the ceramics of the group are not completely purified. The clay content of these samples

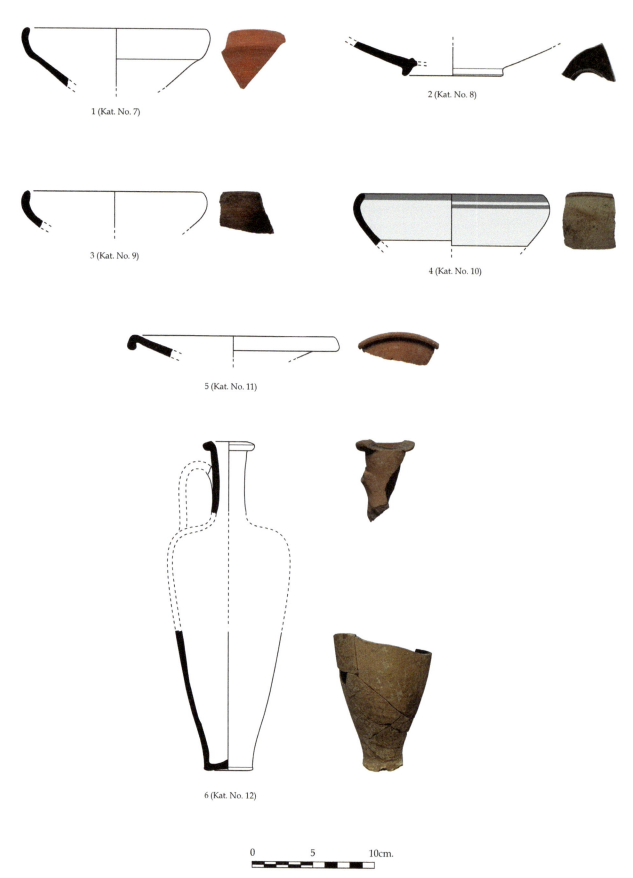

Figure 19.6: Ceramic samples unearthed in the late phase, drawings and photographs. Kültepe Excavation Archive.

always contains dense grains of mica, lime, and grit. The paste of these samples varies in shades of red, brown, and grey, with the slips either matching the colour of the paste or appearing in light and dark tones. These samples come in a variety of forms, including different types of bowls, fish plates, pots, *lekanes*, and pithos.

The bowls with incurving rims (Figs 19.6:3–4) are the most prevalent shape among the samples. All of the samples consist of rim and body parts. Mouth diameters vary between 12 cm and 14 cm. Their bodies come in either a shallow or deep form. Based on intact specimens, these samples typically have either a low circular base or a raised flat bottom (Tüysüz 2022, Lev. 27, 174–75, Lev. 29, 201, Lev. 34, 244, 247). The body of the object shown in Figure 19.6:4 features band decoration both on the inside and outside. Figure 19.6:3 is similar to the examples in the Type 4c group, dated to the second century BC based on their context at Kültepe, among the evaluated bowls (Tüysüz 2022, Lev. 29, 191–95). Bowls with similar form characteristics, which are common in different settlements, mostly belong to the second and first centuries BC.[6] A similar specimen to Figure 19.6:4, found in Kültepe, was classified as Type 5a.1 and dated to the second century BC based on its context.[7]

Another frequently encountered shape among the Kızılırmak Basin Ceramics of the late phase is the fish plate (Fig. 19.6:5). Examples belonging to this group were recovered as rim-body or pedestal-body fragments. This group of examples can be associated with the Attic fish plate form, characterized by its turned-down rim, and it is likely that they were produced by local potters who were inspired by fish plates imported to the region.[8] Fish plates of local production with similar forms, collected under the title of Type 22 in the form repertoire of Kültepe's Kızılırmak Basin Ceramics, were found in the contexts of structures dated to the middle of the second century BC and the first century BC (Tüysüz 2022, Lev. 50, 362–64). In the Hellenistic period settlements of central Anatolia, regional or local fish dishes with similar forms have been dated to the second and first centuries BC.[9]

The jugs, which were primarily used for service and transportation purposes, are also among the most numerous categories of ceramics from the late phase (Fig. 19.6:6). Among the samples of jug shapes, most of which are rim and neck fragments, only Figure 19.6:6 was recovered as a rim-neck-handle-bottom fragment, and there are deficiencies in the body part. The mouth diameter is 4.7 cm, bottom diameter is 4.5 cm. The jug has a typologically extended rim and a narrow long neck. Its body, which narrows towards the bottom, ends with a flat bottom. Its single handle protrudes from the neck and probably rests on the shoulder. Forms with this type of rim are known from Topaklı, Aşvan Castle, İmikuşağı, and Kurul Castle.[10] Late Hellenistic period structures at Topaklı mound and Aşvan Castle have yielded significant findings, while fragments from Kaman-Kalehöyük dating between 300 BC and 100 BC were discovered in phase IIa1–2. Additionally, İmikuşağı examples from the first century BC were found at building level 4a. A vessel with a similar rim and neck profile found in the Kurul Castle, and having a single handle, was also dated to the end of the second century BC and the first half of the first century BC.

A pithos was found in situ in the room associated with Mk03 (Fig. 19.7), provides information about the activities that took place in the area, while its sturdiness reveals details about its original shape and form. In addition to these, a significant number of carbonized seed samples found in the pithos provide clues as to the

---

6 Pergamon: Schäfer 1968, Taf. 1, A3; Topaklı: Pecorella 1975, fig. 20, 6; Aşvan Castle: Mitchell 1980, fig. 27, 173, fig. 28, 192 (Late Hellenistic period); İmikuşağı: Derin 1995, Res. 38, 8, 11 (Late Hellenistic–Early Roman); Ephesus: Meriç 2002, Taf. 1, K4 (second century BC and first century BC); Sivas Ziyaretsuyu: Abdioğlu 2007, Lev. 2, 1–3 (second century BC); Gordion: Stewart 2010, fig. 218, 227, 233, fig. 219, 241, 249 (Middle Hellenistic period); Corinth: James 2018, pl. 25, 171, 172 (late second century BC, early first century BC); Hadrianopolis: Kan Şahin 2019, Lev. 7, 202, 204 (second and first century BC); Kurul Castle: Yorulmaz 2019, Lev. IV, 29, Lev. V, 30–31 (late second century BC, first half of first century BC).

7 Tüysüz 2022, Lev. 34, 245. For different centres, see Hadrianopolis: Kan Şahin 2019, Lev. 10, 272, 278 (second and first centuries BC); Kurul Castle: Yorulmaz 2019, Lev. I, 2, Lev. II, 12 (late second century BC, first half of first century BC); Fatsa-Cıngırt Rock: Erol & Aydın 2021, Lev. 22, 136 (Hellenistic period); Kurul Castle: Yorulmaz 2019, Lev. I, 2, Lev. II, 12 (late second century BC, first half of first century BC).

8 Imported fish plates have been found in Kültepe dating back to the third quarter of the third century BC. Tüysüz 2022, Lev. 6, 28–31.

9 Zengibar Castle: Köker-Gökçe 2017, cat. nos 157, 160, 164 (second and first centuries BC); Kizildag and Gavur Höyük: Bilgin 2004, draw. 15, 2, 4 (second century–first half of the first century BC); Gordion: Stewart 2010, fig. 232 (235–189 BC); Comana of Cappadocia: Körsulu 2011, Lev. XXXVI, 129, Lev. XXXVII, 130 (third century BC); Karatas: Şahin 2014, fig. 5:16–17 (third and second centuries BC); Tarsus: Jones 1950, fig. 178, 23, A.

10 Topaklı: Pecorella 1975, fig. 22, 18, 21, 25; Aşvan Castle: Mitchell 1980, fig. 33, 349, fig. 36, 411, 412; Kaman-Kale mound: Matsumura 2005: Taf. 240, 1390, Taf. 242, 1132, 1188; İmikuşağı: Derin 1995, Res. 40, 6–7; Kurul Castle: Yorulmaz 2019, Lev. XI, 71.

Figure 19.7: In situ pithos unearthed in the late phase. Kültepe Excavation Archive.

type of consumption products stored in the pithos.[11] The pithos in question has an angular rim that is pulled out and thickened on the outside. The body of the pithos expands from the rim towards the belly, creating a rounded profile. The form narrows from the belly towards the bottom and ends with a flat bottom. There are relief profiles on the outer surface of the body. The pithos with similar form characteristics to the evaluated pithos are labelled as Kültepe Type 41 and are generally dated to the second and first centuries BC.[12] Similar to the pithoi, of which many examples are found in Kültepe, they were also encountered in the Hellenistic period settlements of Topaklı, Kaman-Kalehöyük, Sivas Ziyaretsuyu, Gordion, Camihöyük, Kırşehir Merkez Kale mound, Kurul Castle, and Fatsa Cıngırt Rock.[13]

Six terracotta loom weights found near the lower parts of the pithos, are considered a distinct group of artefacts from the late phase (Fig. 19.8). Two of the spindle whorls were found intact and one was found in several fragments. Some of the body parts of the other three spindle whorls were missing or broken. All have a discoid shape. Each features a large hole in the centre of its body. Some were shaped before their outer edges underwent firing (Fig. 19.8:1–2). Figure 19.8:1–3 is fired; Figure 19.8:4–6 is not fired.

One of the two beads constituting the last group of finds of this phase was found broken and missing. The broken specimen is made of blue coloured glass (Fig. 19.9:1), and the other intact specimen is made of frit (Fig. 19.9:2).

---

11 Studies on seed samples have not yet been concluded and are still in progress. Therefore, it is not possible to say anything about the species for now.

12 Tüysüz 2022, Lev. 79, 546, Lev. 80, 551, 554, 555–59, 566, Lev. 81, 570, 572, 573, 574, 576, 578.

13 Topaklı: Pecorella 1975, fig. 24, 8–10; Kaman-Kale mound: Matsumura 2005, Taf. 233, 1200, Taf. 236, 1199; Ziyaretsuyu: Abdioğlu 2007, Lev. 35, 4; Gordion: Stewart 2010, fig. 211, 182, 184, 185, fig. 212, 191; Camihöyük: Uysal Tezer 2011, Lev. 23, 105, Lev. 24, 108; Kırşehir Merkez Kale mound: Bişkin 2019, cat. nos 2, 4, 5, 6, 16, 17, 26, 33, 38, 62, 84–91; Kurul Castle: Yorulmaz 2019, Lev. XXXVI, Lev. XXXVII; Fatsa Cıngırt Rock: Erol & Aydın 2021, Lev. 29, 176–78, Lev. 30, 183, 185, Lev. 31, 186, 187.

19. STUDIES ON KÜLTEPE HELLENISTIC PERIOD

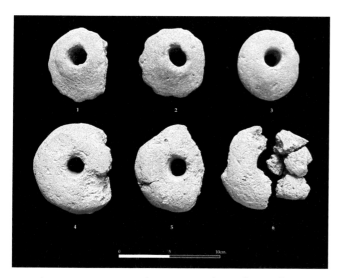

Figure 19.8: Loom weights uncovered in pithos. Kültepe Excavation Archive.

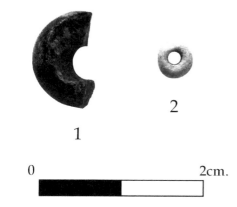

Figure 19.9: Beads. Kültepe Excavation Archive.

The archaeological materials belonging to this phase are significant in identifying the chronological span of the late phase, with ceramics being particularly noteworthy. According to the typological development of the ceramics pre-evaluated above, it is seen that they belong to the second and first centuries BC. Considering this data, we can say that the late phase settlement in Trench 4 stratigraphy can be dated to the second and first centuries BC. Loom weights and beads found in the context material of the late phase can also be dated to the second and first centuries BC.

Earlier Phase

The early phase consists of the architectural remains of the late phase, which were unearthed by descending to the lower level of the damaged floors in the southeast (Mk04) and north-east (Mk03) rooms (Fig. 19.5). As the excavations were conducted within a limited period, no data could be obtained regarding the well-preserved condition associated with the architecture of the aforementioned phase. Nevertheless, there were some discoveries that suggest the high likelihood of a structure/settlement existing during this phase. One of these discoveries is the layer of black burnt material found in the north-eastern part of the site. The layer of burnt material in the Mk08 section is situated beneath the endpoint of the walls' foundations from the later phase, and it appears to cover nearly the entire area. In addition, on the northern edge of the excavated area, burnt clay cells of different shapes, organized from west to east and containing significant amounts of charcoal, were uncovered.

Another architectural discovery made in this phase was a ruined stone wall that stretched for 1.5 m in a north–south direction, uncovered in the western region of the Mk08 section. The final piece of information regarding the architecture of this phase concerns a structural element made of gathered stones, forming a square shape with a thickness of approximately 40 cm. The purpose of this building element is unknown, and it was discovered near the eastern boundary of the same site.

The remnants found in the early phase point towards the existence of a structure/settlement from a period earlier than the late phase in the area. While these findings are indicative of the establishment of a structure during the early phase, they were unable to be fully uncovered due to the conclusion of the excavation.

Although no architectural remains with an identifiable plan were identified during the excavations in the early phase of Trench 4 various pottery items, an appliqué with a goat figure, and two coins were discovered that can be attributed to this phase. Pottery makes up the majority of these discoveries.

In accordance with a preliminary evaluation of the pottery, the samples belonging to this phase were divided into two categories: imported and local production. While imported ceramics are represented by a small number of examples, ceramics of local production constitute the majority.

The imported vessels of this phase are different from the red-brown slipped ceramics of the late phase and have a glossy slip in black tones. The vessels in question are examples of the group known as Black Slip Ceramics in the literature (Fig. 19.10:1–2). The paste-slip characteristics of these pieces indicate that they were produced in western Anatolia. The forms of the group con-

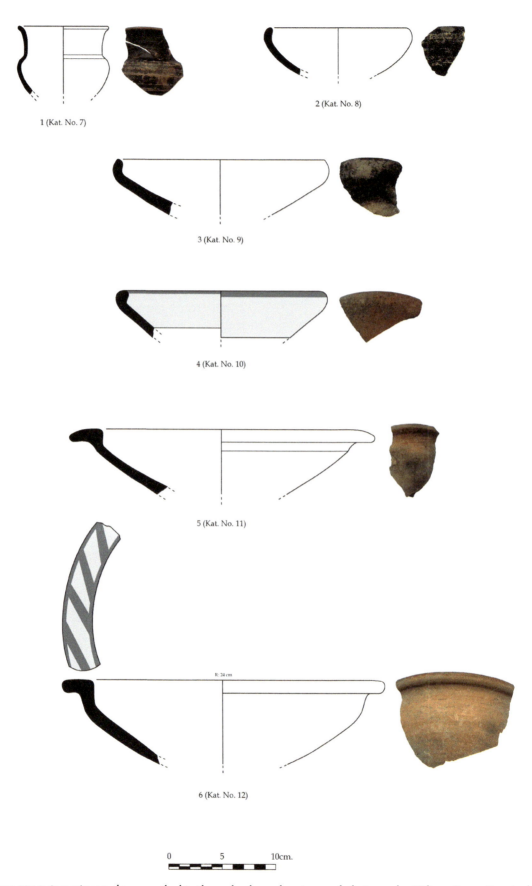

Figure 19.10: Ceramic samples unearthed in the early phase, drawings and photographs. Kültepe Excavation Archive.

sist of kantharoi and bowls. According to the typology of the form, the kantharos artefact found in this phase is a drinking vessel and belongs to the straight-rimmed type (Rotroff 1997, 83–119). This vessel has a flat rim curving outward, a concave neck, and a pronounced shoulder profile (Fig. 19.10:1). The body of the vessel tapers from the shoulder to the bottom and is supported by a profiled foot, according to the solid examples.[14] Kantharos vessels with similar typological features are highly prevalent on the coastlines of Greece, the islands, and Anatolia, and are dated to 325–275 BC based on the context of the finds.[15] The other forms of black slipped ceramics are examples known as 'echinus bowls' in the literature (Fig. 19.10:2). The group's rim curves inward, while the body has a shallow shape, and intact specimens indicate that they terminate with a circular base (Tüysüz 2022, Lev. 3, 13–14, Lev. 8, 44–46). These bowls exhibit similarities with samples found at various archaeological sites that date back to the last quarter of the fourth century BC and the first half of the third century BC.[16]

Kızılırmak Basin Ceramics, which are of local production of the early phase, consist of painted (band decorated) and unpainted samples (Figs 19.10:3–6). The paste-slip properties of this group of ceramics exhibit similarities with those found in the Kızılırmak Basin Ceramics of the late phase.[17] While some vessel types in the late phase continue to be seen in this early phase, there are also new forms that have been encountered for the first time. The forms of this phase are different types of bowls, plates/fruit-stands, bowls, jugs, and cooking utensils.

Incurving rimmed bowls constitute the major group among the forms. All specimens in the group were found as rim-body fragments. Mouth diameters range from 16 cm to 22 cm (Figs 19.10:3–4). In the decorated samples of the group, the decorations are in the form of horizontal bands. Formally, the inner surface of the rims is either rounded or thickened, while the bodies of the objects have a shallow or deep conical shape. According to their intact samples, they should end with a flat bottom or a circular base (Tüysüz 2022; Lev. 27, 174–75; Lev. 29, 201; Lev. 34, 244, 247).

The evaluated bowls display similarities with the ceramic samples categorized as Type 4a and Type 5d.1 in the Kültepe typology of Hellenistic period ceramics, which date back to the third century BC.[18] Moreover, bowls with incurving rims, which are similar in form to the evaluated samples, are the most characteristic form of the Hellenistic period ceramics and are prevalent in almost all settlements across the region.[19]

The most common form group are the vessels with extended rims (Figs 19.10:5–6). These samples, all of which were recovered as rim-body fragments, probably belong to fruit-stand or plate form.[20] Mouth diameters range from 16 cm to 24 cm. The common characteristic of these pieces, which can be further categorized based on their rim shape, is the presence of a broad flat surface on the outer side of the outwardly extending rim. Among the examples, there are also fragments with rim decoration. The decoration in these pieces consists of parallel curved lines delimited by two horizontal bands. Plates and fruit-stands with extended rims, as well as their corresponding fragments, are commonly found in the ceramic repertoire of Kültepe during the Hellenistic period.[21] The fragments, which can be further categorized into subtypes, bear a strong resemblance to the samples recovered from Trench 4, particularly those from the third-century BC contexts. Fruit-stands with similar rims appear in the Hellenistic period layers of Alişar, Topaklı, Sulucakarahöyük, Eskiyapar, Gordion, and Porsuk Zeyve mound as a pre-

---

14 For intact examples, see Kültepe: Tüysüz 2022, Lev. 13, 87; Athens: Rotroff 1997, fig. 4.

15 Smyrna: Cook 1965, 146–47, fig. 3; Pergamon: Schäfer 1968, Taf. 5, C24; Ephesus: Mitsopoulos Leon 1991, Taf. 21, B5–B6 (early third century BC); Athens: Rotroff 1997, fig. 4, 1–14 (325–275 BC); Sardis: Rotroff & Oliver 2003, 20, Pl. 4, 7 (325 BC?); Gordion: Stewart 2010, fig. 207, 154, 155, 159 (333–275 BC); Mount Nif: Bilgin 2017, Lev. 5, 31–33 (325–275 BC); Kültepe: Tüysüz 2022, Lev. 1, 1–3 (first quarter of the third century BC).

16 Antioch: Waage 1948, pl. 2, 70, 73; Ephesos: Mitsopoulos Leon 1991, Taf. 3 A10; Athens Agora: Rotroff 1997, 338–40, fig. 62, 965–66; Kerameikos: Knigge 2005, 199, 220, Abb. 41, 674–887; Mount Nif: Bilgin 2015, 33, pl. III, 22; Bilgin 2017, Lev. 8, 52; Sillyon: Bilgin et al. 2020, pl. 4, 28; Kültepe: Tüysüz 2022, Lev. 3, 11.

17 See cat. nos 7–12.

18 Cat. no. 3: Tüysüz 2022, Lev. 27, 183; cat. no. 4: Lev. 38, 272.

19 For central Anatolia and its surroundings, see cat. no. 3: Alişar: Waage 1937, pl. IX 3367; Kaman-Kalehöyük: Matsumura 2005, Taf. 227, 1100, Taf. 230, 1158, 1117; Sivas Ziyaretsuyu: Abdioğlu 2007, Lev. 3, 1, 2, 5; Gordion: Stewart 2010, fig. 194, 36, 38; Porsuk Zeyve Höyük: Köker Gökçe & Barat 2022: fig. 2a–c (third–second century BC); cat. no. 4: Alişar: Waage 1937, pl. IX, a165, 2807; İmikuşağı: Derin 1995, Res. 31, 6–9, Res. 32, 10 (late third century BC–second century BC); Kaman-Kalehöyük: Matsumura 2005, Taf. 230, 1214; Sivas Ziyaretsuyu: Abdioğlu 2007, Lev. 15, 3, Lev. 16, 6.

20 Fruit-stands with a similar rim profile and plates with flat bottoms or circular bases were found at Kültepe. See Tüysüz 2022, Lev. 43, 327, Lev. 44, 328, Lev. 45, 336, Lev. 46, 337–40.

21 Tüysüz 2022, Lev. 45, 336, Lev. 46, 337, 338, Lev. 47, 341, 342, 344, Lev. 48, 350.

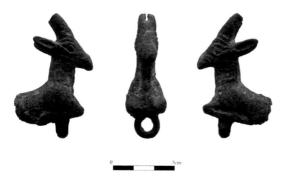

Figure 19.11: Goat-figured appliqué. Kültepe Excavation Archive.

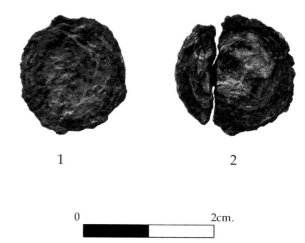

Figure 19.12: Coins. Kültepe Excavation Archive.

ferred form especially in the central Anatolian region.[22] Moreover, plate forms with comparable rims and multicoloured band decorations are predominantly found in Boğazköy, a settlement located in the Kızılırmak Basin.[23]

Among the small finds, a remarkable bronze goat-figured appliqué has been retrieved (Fig. 19.11). This appliqué is produced by casting technique and has a green patina in places. The object portrays a goat in a seated position with its front legs bent at the knee. There is a ring in the lower part of its body between its two feet. The horns placed just above the forehead are broken and missing. The ears are aligned with its eyes and extend backward in a horizontal position. The object highlights prominent details of the eyes and eyebrows. The eyes are depicted as relief dots, while the eyebrows are shown as a relief band. Two thin strips are present on the left and right sides of the neck, extending forward. These strips, which cannot be traced on the front of the neck due to corrosion, are believed to represent the string of the bell hanging on the neck. The transition to the appliqué on the object is provided by the back part of the animal's body and the inside of this part is covered with a layer of lead.[24]

Two bronze coins constitute the last group of finds from the early phase. Unfortunately, both the specimens, which could give important chronological information, are badly preserved and corroded, making their precise identification impossible. Therefore, they were completely destroyed and are unreadable (Figs 19.12:1–2).

The ceramics evaluated above play an important role in determining the historical range of the early phase. Based on the typological characteristics of the examined sherds, they are dated to the last quarter of the fourth century BC and the third century BC. Considering the data obtained from the ceramics, we can say that this phase in the stratigraphy of Trench 4 may belong to the last quarter of the fourth century BC and the third century BC. In addition, the goat-figured appliqué in the context material of the early phase should be dated to the mentioned centuries.

Conclusions

As stated in the introduction, Tahsin Özgüç's research mainly focused on the Protohistoric periods, which resulted in the Hellenistic period settlement being inadequately studied and introduced to the scientific community through only a few publications. Excavations led by Prof. Dr Fikri Kulakoğlu in 2006 aimed to contribute to the understanding of the Hellenistic period of both Kültepe and the central Anatolian region by conducting a detailed study of the settlement of this period. For this

---

22 Alişar: Waage 1937, pl. IX, b704; Topaklı mound: Polacco 1969, 54–71, figs 25–26; Eskiyapar: Bayburtluoğlu 1979, Res. 36; Gordion: Stewart 2010, fig. 228, 336; Porsuk Zeyve mound: Köker Gökçe & Barat 2022, fig. 3a–c; Sulucakarahöyük: Hacı Bektaş Archaeology Museum. For examples with similar rims, see Yassıdağ: Emre 1973, figs 34–36 (third century BC to mid-first century BC); Sulucakarahöyük: Zoroğlu 1978, Lev. XVII, 146 (fourth century BC); İmikuşağı: Derin 1995, Res. 35, 3–14 (late third century BC–second century BC); Gordion: Toteva 2007, pl. 3, 26 (fourth century BC); Stewart 2010, fig. 203, 105, 108, 111 (Early Hellenistic period), fig. 225, 305, fig. 226, 321, fig. 227, 331, fig. 228, 304 (Middle Hellenistic period); Nagidos: Körsulu 2015, cat. nos 18–22; Tarsus-Keşbükü: Körsulu & Kılıç 2021, cat. nos 29–31 (third–second centuries BC); Fatsa Cıngırt Rock: Erol & Aydın 2021, Lev. 18, 106–08.

23 Boğazköy: Maier 1963, Abb. 12; Künhe 1969, 36, pl. 22b–c (second and first centuries BC).

---

24 The study of details on the goat-figured appliqué continues.

purpose, on the one hand, the finds obtained during the Tahsin Özgüç excavations were examined, on the other hand, excavations were carried out on the mound. During this process, the results obtained from the studies started to be introduced to the scientific community.

This article presents preliminary evaluations of the 2022 excavation works conducted in the northern part of the Hellenistic period building, a part of which was excavated in grid-squares 84–85–86/XCVII–XCVIII–XCIX.

The first step of the studies carried out in 2022 was geophysical surveys. In the geophysical surveys, the most intense anomalies were detected in an area measuring 7 × 6 m located in grid-squares 86–87/XCVI, and excavation works were initiated in this area. The excavations in the area revealed two different cultural layers, one belonging to the late phase and the other to the early phase. The upper level of the excavation area consists of late phase architectural remains and finds related to these remains. The architectural remains of this phase are represented by rooms with packed earthen floors, and walls made of neatly and roughly cut stones, some of which can be traced. The finds related to the architectural remains in question consist of ceramics, spindle whorls, and beads.

The lower level, which belongs to the earlier phase, is represented by findings that do not fully reveal a structure due to the limited excavation area but indicate the presence of a structure/settlement. The findings from the lower level consist of a burnt area, a weakly built wall, and some structural elements whose function has not yet been determined. The finds of this phase include a large number of ceramics, a goat-figured appliqué, and two coins.

The most abundant findings recovered in both phases of Trench 4 are ceramics. The evaluation of the ceramics in question enabled the determination of the occupational phasing of the site. At this point, the results obtained from the ceramics show that the structures in Trench 4 were used during the Hellenistic period. Upon a detailed study of the finds, the recovered ceramics from the late phase, dating back to the second–first centuries BC, suggest that the site was inhabited during that particular period. The ceramics discovered from the early phase, which were dated to the last quarter of the fourth century BC and the third century BC, indicate that this phase corresponds to those centuries.

As mentioned in the study's introduction, the excavation of grid-squares 86–87/XCVI aims to investigate the northward expansion and development of a structure that was excavated in the adjacent grid-squares (84–85–86/XCVII–XCVIII–XCIX) in the past few years. The studies carried out in 2022 took place in a limited space and time. Based on the available data, we can conclude that the architectural remains found in grid-squares 86–87/XCVI share similar characteristics with those discovered in the adjacent grid-squares 84–85–86/XCVII–XCVIII–XCIX (Fig. 19.13). In this context, walls with regular and irregular masonry, often built with cut stones, and the rectangular rooms divided by these walls are the common features of the structures found in the mentioned trenches. In contrast, the architecture in the grid-squares 84–85–86/XCVII–XCVIII–XCIX is divided into three phases and provides more detailed sections, while the architecture in the grid-squares 86–87/XCVI is only biphasic and offers more limited information. This can undoubtedly be explained by the fact that the excavations in grid-squares 84–85–86/XCVII–XCVIII–XCIX were carried out at wider and deeper levels. Future excavations in the grid-squares 86–87/XCVI are expected to provide more detailed information about the settlement in this area and may reveal the highly probable connections between the structures identified in these squares.

In addition to the common features mentioned above, it is known that the settlement in the grid-squares under discussion began in the last quarter of the fourth century BC. However, the settlement in the structures found in the grid-squares 86–87/XCVI lasted one century longer than in the other squares, ending in the last decade of the first century BC.[25]

The architectural remains uncovered in various trenches on the mound, dating back to the Hellenistic period, exhibit similarities with the architectural style typical of the Hellenistic period in the central Anatolian region. In this context, the architectural remains under discussion are likely to be representatives of multiphase, interconnected, multiroom architectural structures with stone walls in Kayseri and Kültepe. Such structures are well-known from centres like Niğde Kınık Höyük (Trameri & d'Alfonso 2020, 65–93; d'Alfonso et al. 2020, 25–28), Nevşehir Camihöyük (Uysal-Tezer 2011, 11–23), and Kululu (Özgüç 1971), which have been excavated in the region.

The excavations conducted in Kültepe, and the analysis of the archaeological findings discovered in these

---

25 It was determined that the building in the grid-squares 84–85–86/XCVII–XCVIII–XCIX was abandoned in the second century BC.

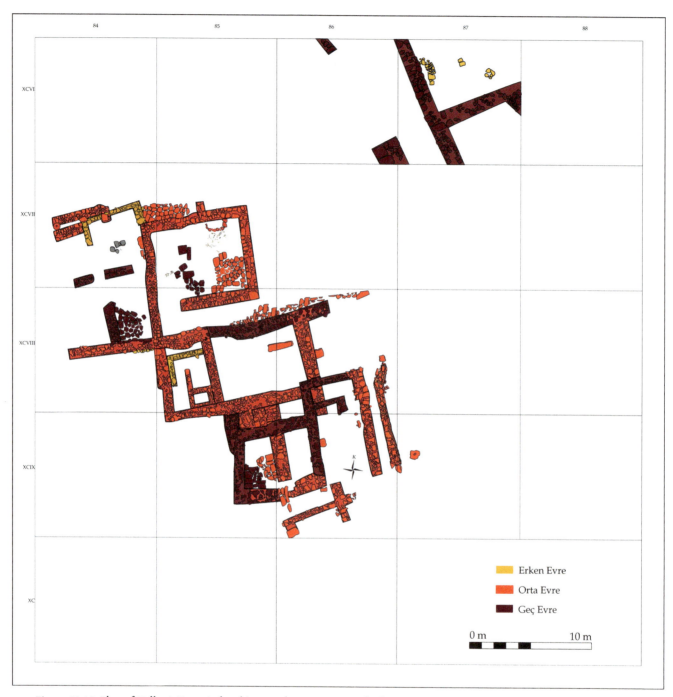

Figure 19.13: Plan of Hellenistic period architectural remains unearthed in 2009, 2020, and 2022. Kültepe Excavation Archive.

excavations hold a crucial position in comprehending the Hellenistic period culture, which remains incompletely understood in the southern region of the Kızılırmak Basin, excluding Kültepe. Studies conducted in the Kültepe region have primarily focused on the Protohistoric periods, leading to a limited number of excavations on Classical period settlements. As a result, Classical period cultures in the region have not been fully recognized, leading to a significant lack of information. In this context, the recent studies on the Hellenistic period culture of Kültepe and the dissemination of their findings to the scientific community undoubtedly make significant contributions to our understanding of the cultural characteristics of the Hellenistic period in the central Anatolian region.

Pottery Catalogue

In this study, Munsell Soil-Color Charts 2009 have been used. Abbreviations: RD: Rim Diameter; H: Height; WT: Wall Thickness; BD: Base Diameter.

Cat. No.: 1 (Fig. 19.6:1)
Place of Find: Trench 04 / Mk01 / Late Phase
Name of the Form: Bowl
Sizes: RD: 14 cm; H: 4.8 cm; WT: 0.3 cm
Description: Rim and body fragment. Light red (2.5YR 6/8) clay is well purified, mica tempered, densely textured, and hard. Inner and outer surfaces are red (10R 5/8) glazed, slightly glossy and slightly rough. It is well fired, wheel made.

Cat. No.: 2 (Fig. 19.6:2)
Place of Find: Trench 04 / Mk02 / Late Phase
Name of the Form: Fish plate
Sizes: BD: 8 cm; H: 2.3 cm; WT: 0.4 cm
Description: Base and body fragment. Grey (10YR 6/1) clay is very little mica, lime tempered, densely textured, and hard. Inner and outer surfaces are dark greyish brown (10YR 4/2) glazed, slightly glossy, and slightly rough. It is well fired, wheel made.

Cat. No.: 3 (Fig. 19.6:3)
Place of Find: Trench 04 / Mk02 / Late Phase
Name of the Form: Bowl
Sizes: RD: 14 cm; H: 2.9 cm; WT: 0.5 cm
Description: Rim and body fragment. Light reddish brown (5YR 6/4) clay tempered with mica, lime, and tiny stones, densely textured and hard. Inner and outer surfaces glazed in the colour of the clay, matt, and slightly rough. It is well fired, wheel made.

Cat. No.: 4 (Fig. 19.6:4)
Place of Find: Trench 04 / Mk04 / Late Phase
Name of the Form: Bowl
Sizes: RD: 14 cm; H: 4.1 cm; WT: 0.4 cm
Description: Rim and body fragment. Brown (7.5YR 5/3) clay, tempered with mica, lime, and tiny stones, densely textured and hard. Inner and outer surfaces pale brown (2.5Y 8/2) glazed, matt, and slightly rough. The rim is decorated with a brown (7.5YR 4/4) band on the inner and outer surfaces. The core of the clay has grey discolouration due to firing. Poorly fired, wheel made.

Cat. No.: 5 (Fig. 19.6:5)
Place of Find: Trench 04 / Mk01 / Late Phase
Name of the Form: Fish plate
Sizes: RD: 16 cm; H: 1.7 cm; WT: 0.6 cm
Description: Rim and body fragment. Reddish yellow (5YR 6/6) clay, tempered with mica, lime, and tiny stones, densely textured, and hard. Inner and outer surfaces glazed in the colour of the clay, matt, and slightly rough. It is well fired, wheel made.

Cat. No.: 6 (Fig. 19.6:6)
Place of Find: Trench 04 / Mk01 / Late Phase
Name of the Form: Single handle jug
Sizes: RD: 3 cm; BD: 4.5 cm; H: 1.7 cm; WT: 0.6 cm
Description: Rim, body, bottom, and handle fragment. Pink (7.5YR 7/3) clay, tempered with mica, lime, and tiny stones, densely textured, and hard. Inner and outer surfaces glazed in the colour of the clay, matt, and slightly rough. There are grey colour changes in the clay core due to firing. Poorly fired, wheel made.

Cat. No.: 7 (Fig. 19.10:1)
Place of Find: Trench 04 / Mk07 / Early Phase
Name of the Form: Kantharos
Sizes: RD: 8 cm; H: 6.1 cm; WT: 0.3 cm
Description: Rim and body fragment. Light reddish brown (2.5YR 7/4) clay, with some mica, mineral, lime tempered, densely textured, and hard. Inner and outer surfaces dark reddish grey (10R 3/1) glazed, slightly shiny, and smooth. It is well-fired and wheel made.

Cat. No.: 8 (Fig. 19.10:2)
Place of Find: Trench 04 / Mk06 / Early Phase
Name of the Form: Bowl
Sizes: RD: 12 cm; H: 4.2 cm; WT: 0.5 cm
Description: Rim and body fragment. Pink (7.5YR 7/4) clay, with some mica, mineral, lime tempered, densely textured, and hard. Inner and outer surfaces black (2.5YR 2.5/1) glazed, slightly shiny, and smooth. It is well fired and wheel made.

Cat. No.: 9 (Fig. 19.10:3)
Place of Find: Trench 04 / Mk06 / Early Phase
Name of the Form: Bowl
Sizes: RD: 19 cm; **H:** 4.9 cm; **WT:** 0.8 cm
Description: Rim and body fragment. Light reddish brown (5YR 6/4) clay, tempered with mica, lime, and tiny stones, densely textured and hard. Inner and outer surfaces glazed in the colour of the clay, matt and slightly rough. There are grey colour changes in the clay core due to firing. Poorly fired, wheel made.

Cat. No.: 10 (Fig. 19.10:4)
Place of Find: Trench 04 / Mk06 / Early Phase
Name of the Form: Bowl
Sizes: RD: 18 cm; **H:** 4.2 cm; **WT:** 0.6 cm
Description: Rim and body fragment. Light red (2.5YR 6/6) clay, tempered with mica, lime, and tiny stones, densely textured, and hard. Inner and outer surfaces glazed in the colour of the clay, matt, and slightly rough. Red (10R 4/6) coloured band around the rim. It is well fired and wheel made.

Cat. No.: 11 (Fig. 19.10:5)
Place of Find: Trench 04 / Mk07 / Early Phase
Name of the Form: Plate / Legged Plate
Sizes: RD: 22 cm; **H:** 5.9 cm; **WT:** 0.5 cm
Description: Rim and body fragment. Light reddish brown (5YR 6/4) clay, tempered with mica, lime, and tiny stones, densely textured, and hard. Inner and outer surfaces red (2.5YR 4/6) glazed, matt, and slightly rough. There are grey colour changes in the clay core due to firing. Poorly fired, wheel made.

Cat. No.: 12 (Fig. 19.10:6)
Place of Find: Trench 04 / Mk07 / Early Phase
Name of the Form: Plate / Legged Plate
Sizes: RD: 24 cm; **H:** 7.3 cm; **WT:** 0.6 cm
Description: Rim and body fragment. Light reddish brown (5YR 6/4) clay, tempered with mica, lime, and tiny stones, densely textured, and hard. Inner and outer surfaces glazed in the colour of the clay, matt, and slightly rough. The rim is decorated with red (10R 4/6) oblique bands parallel to each other between two horizontal bands. It is well fired and wheel made.

Bibliography

Abdioğlu, Esra

2007 'Sivas Ziyaretsuyu Hellenistik ve Roma Dönemi Seramikleri' (unpublished master's thesis, University of Gazi).

Alp, Sedat

1997 'Die Mehrheit der einheimischen Bevölkerung in der Kārum-Zeit in Kaneš/Neša', *Studi Micenei ed Egeo-Anatolici* 39: 35–48.

Barjamovic, Gojko

2015 'Kültepe after Kaneš', in Fikri Kulakoğlu & Cécile Michel (eds), *Proceedings of the 1st Kültepe International Meeting: Kültepe 19-23 September, 2013; Studies Dedicated to Kutlu Emre* (Subartu 35; Kültepe International Meetings). Brepols, Turnhout: 233–42.

Bayburtluoğlu, İnci

1979 'Eskiyapar Phryg Çağı', *VIII. Türk Tarih Kongresinde Sunulan Bildiriler* (Cilt 1). Türk Tarih Kurumu Yayınları, Ankara: 293–303.

Bilgin, Mustafa

2004 'Konya-Karaman İlleri Hellenistik ve Roma Çağı Keramikleri' (unpublished master's thesis, University of Selçuk).

2015 'Pottery Finds from Nif-Olympus', in Ergün Laflı & Sami Patacı (eds), *Recent Studies on the Archaeology of Anatolia* (British Archaeological Reports, International Series 2750). Archaeopress, Oxford: 27–40.

2017 'Keramik Buluntular', in Müjde Peker, Ceren Baykan & Daniş Baykan (eds), *Nif Dağı Ballıcaolluk (2008-2016)*. Homer Kitapevi ve Yayıncılık, Istanbul: 32–110.

Bilgin, Mustafa; Kızıltepe Bilgin, Pınar & Özdemir, Eylem

2020 'Yüzey Araştırmaları Işığında Sillyon Seramikleri Üzerine Ön Değerlendirmeler', in Murat Taşkıran (ed.), *Yüzey Araştırmaları Işığında Sillyon ve Çevresi* (Sillyon Araştırmaları 1). Ege Yayınları, Istanbul: 33–89.

Bişkin, Zehra

2019 'Kırşehir Merkez Kalehöyük Depolama Kaplarının Sınıflandırılması ve Tabakalara Göre Değerlendirilmesi' (unpublished master's thesis, University of Uludağ).

Cook, J. Manuel

1965 'Fourth-Century Black Glaze', *British School at Athens* 60: 143–53.

Cumont, Frantz

1932 'À propos d'un décret d'Anisa en Cappadoce', *Revue des études anciennes* 34: 135–38.

D'Alfonso, Lorenzo; Yolaçan, Burak; Castellano, Lorenzo; Highcock, Nancy; Casagrande Kim, Roberta; Gorrini, Maria E. & Trameri, Andrea

2020 'Niğde Kınık Höyük: New Evidence on Central Anatolia during the First Millennium BCE', *Near Eastern Archaeology* 83/1: 1–29.

Derin, Zafer

1995 '4. Yapı Katı-Çanak Çömlek', in Veli Sevin (ed.), *İmikuşağı*, I. Türk Tarih Kurumu Yayınları, Ankara: 69–74.

Emre, Kutlu

1973 'Yassıdağ Kazısı 1973', *Anadolu (Anatolia)* 17: 43–90.

Ergün, Gürkan
2020 'Late Bronze Age Spindle Whorls and Loom Weights from Beycesultan in Western Anatolia: New Findings, New Observations', *Mediterranean Archaeology and Archaeometry* 20/2: 1–18.

Erol, Ayşe F. & Aydın, Safiye
2021 *Fatsa Cıngırt Kayası – Günlük Kullanım Kapları Işığında Antik Çağda Karadeniz Mutfak Kültürü*. Bilgin Kültür Sanat Yayınları, Ankara.

French, David H.; Moore, John & Russell, Harry F.
1982 'Excavations at Tille 1979–1982: An Interim Report', *Anatolian Studies* 32: 161–87.

Güterbock, Hans G.
1956 'The Deeds of Suppiluliumas as Told by his Son Mursili II', *Journal of Cuneiform Studies* 10: 41–68, 75–98, 109–30.

Hayes, John W.
1985 'Sigillate Orientali, Atlante delle forme ceramiche II. Ceramica fine romana nel bacino mediterraneo', in Giovanni Pugliese Carratelli (ed.), *Atlante delle forme ceramiche*, II: *Ceramica fine romana nel bacino mediterraneo, tardo ellenismo e primo impero* (Enciclopedia dell'arte antica classica e orientale, Supp. 2). Istituto della Enciclopedia italiana, Rome: 9–96.

Hild, Friedrich & Restle, Marcell
1981 *Kappadokien (Kappadokia, Charsianon, Sebasteia und Lykandos)* (Tabula Imperii Byzantini 2). Verlag der Österreichischen Akademie der Wissenschaften, Vienna.

James, Sarah A.
2018 *Hellenistic Pottery: The Fine Wares* (Corinth 7/7). American School of Classical Studies at Athens Press, Princeton.

Jones, F. Follin
1950 'The Pottery', in Hetty Goldman (ed.), *Excavations at Gözlü Kule, Tarsus*, I: *The Hellenistic and Roman Periods*. Princeton University Press, Princeton: 149–209.

Kan Şahin, Gülseren
2019 *Hadrianopolis Seramik Buluntuları*. Türk Tarih Kurumu Yayınları, Ankara.

Knigge, Ursula.
2005 *Kerameikos Ergebnisse der Ausgrabungen*, XVII. Deutsches Archäologisches Institut Press, Munich.

Köker Gökçe, Emine
2017 'Yüzey Araştırmaları Işığında Isaura (Zengibar Kalesi) Seramikleri' (unpublished doctoral thesis, University of Dokuz Eylül).

Köker Gökçe, Emine & Barat, Claire
2022 'Porsuk-Zeyve Höyük Hellenistik Dönem Yerel Üretim ve Geleneksel Boya Bezemeli Seramikleri', *Cedrus* 10: 139–64.

Körsulu, Hatice
2011 'Kappadokia-Komanası Hellenistik ve Roma Dönemi Seramikleri' (unpublished doctoral thesis, University of Mersin).
2014 'Kappadokia Komana'sı Hellenistik Dönem Seramikleri', *Cedrus* 2: 89–133.
2015 'Nagidos Arkaik, Klasik ve Hellenistik Dönem Mutfak ve Pişirme Kapları', *GEPHYRA* 12: 141–77.

Körsulu, Hatice & Kılıç, Tuğba
2021 'Keşbükü Hellenistik ve Roma Dönemi Seramikleri', in Deniz Kaplan (ed.), *Tarsus Araştırmalar*, II: *Keşbükü Buluntuları*. Bilgin Kültür Sanat Yayınları, Ankara: 101–90.

Kulakoğlu, Fikri
2010 'Kültepe Kaniş-Karum: Anadolu'nun En Eski Uluslararası Ticaret Merkezi', in Fikri Kulakoğlu & Selmin Kangal (eds), *Anadolu'nun Önsözü Kültepe Kaniş-Karum, Asurlular İstanbul'da*. Kayseri Büyük Şehir Belediyesi Kültür Yayınları, Istanbul: 40–52.
2017 'Kaniş, Neşa, Anisa, Karye-i Kınış', *Arkeoloji ve Sanat Yayınları* 155: vii–xvi.
2018 'Kaniş Karumu: Eski Asur Ticaretinin Anadolu'daki Başkenti', in Kemalettin Köroğlu & S. Ferruh Adalı (eds), *Asurlular Dicle'den Toroslar'a Tanrı Assur'un Krallığı*. Yapı Kredi Yayınları, Istanbul: 56–83.

Künhe, Hartmut
1969 'Die Bestattungen der Hellenistischen bis Spätkaiserzeitlichen Periode', in *Boğazköy*, IV: *Funde aus den Grabungen 1967 und 1968*. Mann, Berlin: 35–45.

Maier, Ferdinand
1963 'Bemerkungen zur Sogenannten Galatischen Keramik von Boğazköy', *Archäologischer Anzeiger* 78: 218–55.

Matsumura, Kimiyoshi
2005 'Die Eisenzeitliche Keramik in Zentralanayolien Aufgrund der Keramik in Kaman-Kalehöyük' (unpublished doctoral thesis, University of Freien).

Meriç, Recep
2002 *Späthellenistisch-römische Keramik und Kleinfunde aus einem Schachtbrunnen am Staatsmarkt in Ephesos* (Forschungen in Ephesos 9/3). Verlag der Österreichischen Akademie der Wissenschaften, Vienna.

Mitchell, Stephen
1980 *Aşvan Kale Keban Rescue Excavations, Eastern Anatolia*, I: *The Hellenistic, Roman and Islamic Sites* (British Archaeological Reports, International Series 80). Archaeopress, Oxford.

Mitford, Terence B.
2000 'Caesarea-Melitene (1:500.000)-1996', in Richard J. A. Talbert (ed.), *Barrington Atlas of the Greek and Roman World*. Princeton University Press, Princeton: 87–88.

Mitsopoulos-Leon, Veronika
1991 *Forschungen in Ephesos*, IX.2.2: *Die Basilika am Staatsmarkt in Ephesos Kleinfunde*. Verlag des Österreichischen Archäologischen Institut in Wien, Vienna.

Munsell Soil-Color Charts
2009 *Pantone M50215B: Munsell Book of Soil Color Charts*, rev. edn. Munsell Color, Grand Rapids.

Özgüç, Tahsin
1971 *Demir Devrinde Kültepe ve Civarı*. Türk Tarih Kurumu Yayınları, Ankara.
1999 *Kültepe Kaniş/Neşa Sarayları ve Mabetleri*. Türk Tarih Kurumu Yayınları, Ankara.

Pecorella, Paolo E.
1975 'Topaklı. La trincea di sud-ovest', *Studi Micenei ed Egeo-Anatolici* 16: 9–76.

Polacco, Luigi
1969 'Topaklı. Campagna di scavo 1968', *Studi Micenei ed Egeo-Anatolici* 10: 54–71.

Rotroff, Susan I.
1997 *Hellenistic Pottery, Athenian and Imported Wheelmade Table Ware and Related Material* (The Athenian Agora 29). American School of Classical Studies at Athens Press, Princeton.

Rotroff, Susan I. & Oliver, Andrew
2003 *The Hellenistic Pottery from Sardis: The Finds through 1994.* Harvard University Press, Cambridge, MA.

Schäfer, Jörg
1968 *Hellenistische Keramik aus Pergamon* (Pergamenischen Forschungen 2). Deutsches Archäologisches Institut, Berlin.

Stewart, Shannan Marie
2010 'Gordion after the Knot: Hellenistic Pottery and Culture' (unpublished doctoral thesis, University of Cincinnati).

Strabon
2012 Adnan Pekman (Çev.) *Antik Anadolu Coğrafyası (Geographika Kitap: XII-XIII-XIV)*, 6th edn. Arkeoloji ve Sanat Yayınları, Istanbul.

Şahin, Fatma
2014 'Karataş Burnu Yüzey Araştırmasında Bulunan Hellenistik ve Roma Dönemi Keramikleri', *TÜBA-AR* 17: 143-61.

Taner, Saadet
1971 'Kültepe Kazısında Bulunan Sikkeler', *Anadolu / Anatolia* 15: 139-59.
1974 'Kültepe Sikkeleri', *Belleten* 38/152: 583-96.

Toteva, Galya D.
2007 'Local Cultures of Late Achaemenid Anatolia' (unpublished doctoral thesis, University of Minnesota).

Trameri, Andrea & d'Alfonso, Lorenzo
2020 'The "Sacred City" of Kınık Höyük: Continuity and Change in Cappadocia (Turkey) between the Late Achaemenid and Late Hellenistic Periods', in Winfried Held & Z. Kotitsa (eds), *In the Transition from the Achaemenid to the Hellenistic Period in the Levant, Cyprus and Cilicia: Cultural Interruption vs Cultural Continuity? Symposion at Philipps-Universität Marburg, October 12-15, 2017* (Marburger Beiträge zur Archäologie 6). Eigenverlag des Archäologischen Seminars der Philipps-Universität, Marburg: 65-82.

Tüysüz, Burcu
2021 'Preliminary Assessments of Black-Glazed Attic Pottery Found at Kültepe', in Fikri Kulakoğlu, Guido Kryszat & Cécile Michel (eds), *Cultural Exchanges and Current Researches at Kültepe and Surroundings* (Kültepe International Meetings 4, Subartu 46). Brepols, Turnhout: 161-77.
2022 'Kültepe'nin Hellenistik Dönem Seramikleri' (unpublished doctoral thesis, University of Pamukkale).

Uysal-Tezer, Canan
2011 'Nevşehir Camihöyük Hellenistik ve Roma Seramikleri' (unpublished master's thesis, University of Gazi).

Waage, Frederick O.
1937 'Greek, Hellenistic and Roman Pottery from Alişar', in J. Albert Wilson & T. George Allen (eds), *The Alishar Hüyük Season of 1930-32*, III. University of Chicago Press, Chicago: 74-77.
1948 'Hellenistic and Roman Tableware of North Syria', in Frederick O. Waage (ed.), *Antioch on-the-Orontes*, IV.1: *Ceramics and Islamic Coins*. Princeton University Press, Princeton: 1-60.

Yorulmaz, Leyla
2019 'Kurul Kalesi Hellenistik Dönem Seramikleri' (unpublished doctoral thesis, University of Hacı Bayram Veli).

Zoroğlu, K. Levent
1978 'Hellenistik Çağ'da Kızılırmak Havzası Boyalı Kapları' (unpublished doctoral thesis, University of Ankara).
1981 'Kültepe'de Bulunan Hellenistik Çağ'a ait Bir Amphora', *Selçuk Üniversitesi Fen-Edebiyat Fakültesi Dergisi* 1: 239–52.

Index

Page number *in italics* refers to footnotes

Personal Names

Abbāya: *110*
Adad-ṣulūlī: 232
Ali'ahšušar: 81
Ali-ahum (c/k): 98–99
Ali-ahum, son of Iddin-Suen: *6*, *83*, 96–98
Ali-ahum, son of Šalim-Aššur: 16–17, 100–01, 104, 117–18, 125–28
Amur-Šamaš: 227
Anitta: 6, 171, 243, 261, 270–71
ᶠAnna-anna, wife of Ennam-Aššur: 81, 101–04, 117–18, 125, 127–28
Anina, son of Aššur-bēl-awātim: 119
Anuli, son of Iddin-abum: 126, 128
Anum-hirbi: 21
Asānum, servant of Kuliya: 250
Aššur-bēl-awātim, son of Issu-arik: 125
Aššur-idī, son of Amur-Aššur: 35
Aššur-imittī: 36, 84
Aššur-lamassī: 80
Aššur-malik: 98–99, 254
Aššur-nādā: 96, 120
Aššur-taklāku, son of Ali-ahum: *6*, *18*, 96–97, 227
Aššur-taklāku, son of Huliya: 80
Aššur-ṭāb: 81, 93
Ataya: 84

Bahunu: 22
Bēlānum: 84–85
Bēlum-bāni, son of Aššur-bēl-awātim: 119
Buziya, son of Šu-Anum: 36

Dadaya: 80, 112
Dalaš: 81
Dudu, son of Šu-Bēlum: 253
Duduʾa: 110

Elamma: 4, 75–86, 94–96, 124
Ennam-Aššur, son of Elamma: 81, 83–84, 95–96
Ennam-Aššur, son of Šalim-Aššur: 16–17, 99–101, 103–04, 117–18, 121–22, 125, 127–28
Ēnah-ilī: 79
Enna-Suen: *81*, 93
Enna-Suen, son of Aššur-malik: 254
Enna-Suen, son of Iddin-abum: 126–28, 253 (*limum*)
Erišum I: 58
Erišum II: 22
Erum: 41–42

Hapatiwa: 241
Hapuala: 227
Haššui: 227
Hattušili: 68, 243
Hayaša: 66
Hurmeli: 14, 16, 18–20, 22, 241
Huzzia: 243

Iddin-abum, son of Issu-arik: 117–21, 126–28
Ikūn-UŠMU, son of Irâm-Dagan: 120
Ikuppī-Aššur: 84
Ilī-ālum: 96
Ilī-bāni: 80, *83*
Ilu-šūma: 13
Imdī-ilum: *83*, 119
Inar: 241
Ir'am-Aššur: 79–81, *83*, 84, 86–87
Iṣi-Dagan: 121
Issu-arik: 117–20, 128, 227
ᶠIšhašara: 81
ᶠIštar-lamassī, daughter of Elamma: 75–76, 78–83, 86, 88, 124

Kapukkuzi: 65
Kikaršan: 81
Kukuwa, grandson of Ali-ahum: 122–23, 126, 128
Kuliya, son of Ali-abum: 6, 249–54
Kulumaya: *81*
Kunnaya, son of K.: 80
ᶠKuzizi: 79

ᶠLamassī, daughter of Šalim-Aššur: 99–101, 103–05, 123–28
ᶠLamassī, wife of Pūšu-kēn: *83*
ᶠLamassutum: 75–76, 78–80, 83–84, 86, 88, 94
Laqēpum: 80, 101
Lipit-Ištar, son of Dagan-malkum: 111

Malkum-išar, son of Amraya: 251
Masātum: 81
Muršili II: 67
Muršili III: 65
Mutawalli II: 66

Narām-Sîn: 22, 202
ᶠNerāmtum: 79, 85
Ni-mar-ša-ra-ma-té: 56

Pampa, king of Hatti: 202
Peruwa: 66, 68, 80
Pilah-Ištar: 80, 84, 87, 94
Pithana: 6
Pūšu-kēn: 17–18, *83*
Puzur-Adad: 249–50, 253
Puzur-Aššur: 14, *15*, 84, 249–51, 253
Puzur-Ištar: 121
Puzur-Ištar, son of Šu-Anum: 36
Puzur-šadu'e, son of Šu-Ištar: 119

Strabo: 63, 66, 68
Šalim-ahum: 227
Šalim-Aššur, son of Issu-arik: 4, 16, 83, 99–104, 110, 117–18, 121–28, 227, 230–31
ᶠŠalimma: 75–76, 78–79, 81–84, 86–88, 94
Šamaš-abī: 80
Šamaš-bāni: 79, 84
Šamaš-bēlī: 79
Šamnuman: 241
Šamšī-Adad I: 2, 13–14, 18–19, 22–23, *56*, *57*–58

Sargon: 201, 202
ᶠŠāt-Anna, daughter of Šalim-Aššur: 122–23, 126–27
ᶠŠāt-Aššur: 101–04
Šattiwaza: 64, 66
ᶠŠīmat-Ištar, daughter of Ali-ahum (c/k): 98
ᶠŠīmat-Ištar, daughter of ᶠIštar-Lamassī: 75–76, 78, 83–84, 88, 124
Šiwašme'i: 68
Šu-Anum: 36, 251, 254
Šu-Bēlum, son of Iddin-abum: *18*, *81*, *84*, 126, 128, 253
Šu-Ištar: 84, 119
Šu-Kūbum, son of Aššur-bēl-awātim: 119
Šu-Kūbum son of Qayātum: 123
Šuppiluliuma: 64, 66
Šu-Suen, son of Itūr-ilī: 253

Tahsi: 79
Taliya: 81
Tamura: 227–31, 237, 240–43
ᶠTariša, daughter of Ali-ahum: *83*, 96–98, 104–05
ᶠTarām-Kūbi, wife of Innaya: xvii, *83*
Tatali: 229–32, 237, 242, 243
Thutmosis III: 44
Tudhaliya IV: 65, *67*
Tukultī-Ninurta: *67*
ᶠTuwatuwi: 80

Uhna: 241
Ullikummi: 242
ᶠUmmī-Išhara, daughter of Elamma: 75–76, 78–81, 83–88, 94–96, 105, 124
ᶠUmmī-Išhara, wife of Šuppi-niman: 80
Uṣur-ša-Aššur, son of Puzur-Aššur: 251
Uṣur-ša-Ištar, son of Assur-imittī: 36

Walhišna: 80
Wališra: 68
Warad-Kūbi: 113
Warad-Marduk, son of Šēlebu: 113
Waršama: 5, 21, 186, 187, 235, 236, 241, 243
Wiušti: 21

Yahdun-Lim: *56*
Yasmah-Addu: 57

Zimrī-Lîm: 19, 57
Zippani, king of Kaneš: 202
ᶠZizizi, daughter of Imdī-ilum: 83
Zuzu: 6, 243, 270

Divine Names

Adad: *47*, 59
Anna: 125
Anu: 59
Aššur: 2, 36–37, 41, 55–59, 125
Aškašepa (Mount Erciyes): 3, 63–68

Bēl-mātim: 56

Daganzipa: *64*

Enlil: 56–58

Hantašepa: *64*
Hapandaliya: 66
Haš(š)ammeli: 66
Haššušara (MUNUS.LUGAL): 64–67
Hebat: 66
Heptad: *64*
Hilanzipa: *64*
Hilašši: *64*

Isimu: 121
Išpanzašepa: *64*
Ištar: 2, 64
 of Haddarina: 66–67
 MULTARRIHU: *64*
 Venus (MUL DIL.BAD): *64*

Karzi: 66
Kumarbi: 57–58, 68

Maliya: 64, 67
Marduk: 113
Miyatanzipa: *64*, 68

Ninurta: 57–58, *67*
Nisaba: 42

Pap-ul-e-gar-ra: 57–58
Pirwa: 64–68

Sebitti: 122
Seven Sages: 122
Stag God: 64
Storm God: 66, 68, 121
Suen: 59
Sun God: 41–43, 45
Sun God of Heaven: 65
Sun Goddess of Arinna: 68
Syrian Lady: 121
Šamaš: 2, 42–43, 48, 58–59, 113, 126
Šarra-mātān: 3, 56–59

Telipinu: 66

ᴰU.GUR: 64

Zintuhi: 67

Geographical Names (ancient)

Amkuwa (Alişar): *55*, 179, 183, 192, 195–96, 212, 215, 244, 285, *286*
Amurru: 66
Anisa (Kültepe): 6, 275
Apûm: 3
Argaeus: 63–64, 66, 68
Aššur (Qal'at Sherqat): 2–4, 13–23, 45, 47, 57–59, 75, 78–83, 86–87, 94, 96, 98–100, 103–05, 109, 119, 121, 124–27, 227, 232, 239, 244, 249–50
Atarmapa: 67

Burušhattum: 13

Durhumit/Durmitta: 6, 15, 66, 111, 117–18

Ebla (Tell Mardikh): 120–22, 127, 169, 191
Ešnunna: 18–19, 112
Eusebia: 6

Hahhum: 14
Harhara: 3, *63*, 68
Harka/BABBAR: *63*
Harsamna: 16, 18–19
Hurama/Hurma: 15, 243
Hattum: 249, 251
Hatti: 202
Hattuša (Boğazköy/Boğazkale): 64, 66, 68, 169–71, 215, 217, 219, 222, 243–44, 270

Isin: 35, *36*

Kaneš (Kültepe): 1–6, 13–23, 33–34, 37–39, 42–48, 63–68, 75, 78–83, 86, 93–105, 109–10, 117, 127, 136–38, 151–54, 159, 171, 185–202, 207–23, 227–44, 249, 257–71, 275–90
Karahna: 66
Karakin: 23
Kukrin: 15

Larsa: 35, *36*, 45–46
Luhusattiya: 16

Mama: 21
Mari: 18–19, 23, 56, 58, 109, *120*, 121
Mittani: 64, 66
Mount Puškurunuwa: 64, 66
Mount Šummiyara: 66
Mount Tatta: 66

Nahur: 19
Niqqum: 23

Sippar: 35, *36*
Šalušna: 67
Šamuha (Kayalıpınar): 6, 215, 217, 222, 227–43
Šukziya: 67

Tawiniya: 15, 17
Tenizidaša: *65*

Ur: 35
Uršum: 19, 23

Wašhaniya: 15

Zalpa: 14, 16–18, 241, 243

Geographical Names (modern)

Acemhöyük: 22, 45, 202, 270
Aladağ: 185
Ališar: *see* Amkuwa
Arslantepe: 171

Bademağacı: 187
Beycesultan: 190, 243

Boğazköy: *see* Hattuša
   Büyükkaya: 169, 215
   Kesikkaya: 169, 217
Bolkardağ: 185

Demircihöyük: 187

Hirbemerdon Tepe: 171
Hisarcık: 63, 68

Kaman-Kalehöyük: 169, 171, 281–82, *285*
Kayalıpınar: *see* Šamuha
Koçumbeli: 187
Konya-Karahöyük: 243
Kilise Tepe: 171
Küllüoba: 187, 191
Kültepe: see Kaneš

Lidar Höyük: 171

Mardin: 270
Mount Erciyes: 3, 63–68, 180, 185

Norsuntepe: 171

Sultanhanı: 227
Sulusaray: 66
Şarkışla: 227

Tarsus-Gözlükule: 187, 270
Tekirderbent: *63*, 68
Tenizidaša: *65*
Tarsus: 243

Yeniçubuk: 227

Kültepe Sectors and Monuments

Building with Pilaster: 190–91
Burnt Room: 5, 207–15, 217, 222–23

Lower Town: 1–6, 20–23, 33, 38, 46, 75, 99, *110*, 117, 119, 136–38, 145, 154, 156, 167, 169, 171, 207, 210, 212, 215, 217, 219, 222–23, 228–44, 250, 257, 260, 275

Monumental building of level 12: 190

Old Palace: 202, 210–12, 215, 217, 223, 241, 260

INDEX

Southern Terrace: 207–11, 217, 223, 258–60
South Terrace Palace: 202
Stone Building: 5–6, 165–71, 209–11, 215, 217, 219, 222–23, 261–71

Waršama Palace: 5, 179–81, 186–87, 210, 215, 217, 219, 222, 223, 260–62

Words Commented

abarnī'um: 253
abum: 110–14
ahātum: 80–81, 111–12
ahum: 110–14
ālum: 19
amutum: 18
ašium: 17
awīltum: 79
awīlum: 112
awītum: 79, 83

bariga: 43
bēlum: 111–14
bēltum: 111
bīt kittim: 45

dammuqum: 45

ebrum: 111
emmum: 85
erbum: 16
ešartum: 15

gubabtum: 78, 80

habbulum: 81
hadā'um: 85

ikribū: 79
išā'um: 80–81

karpatum: 45
kaspum: 114
kaspum kankum: 45
kārum: 228, 230–38, 240, 242, 243
kišeršum: 18
kubbušum: 79

kumrum: 124
kusītum: 79
kutānum: 16, 79, 253

lamānum: 85
laputtā'um: 119, 125
laqā'um: 79–80
libbum: 85
limum ša še'im: 44

marāṣum: 85
mekum: 121
mer'um: 111
mešēqum: 44–45

našpertum: 111
nazāmum: 85
nihātum: 21
niš'um: 16
nuwā'um: 18

pazzurtum: 17
pirikannum: 21

rabi še'ē: 44
rubā'um: 13–14

saklum: 85
sūtu: 43
ṣarāpum: 85
ṣarrupum: 45
ṣuhārtum: 80
šakākum: 80
šakkanakku: 33, 39, 56, *120*, 121
šanā'um: 85
šāpirum: 112
šar tamhari: 201
šēbultum: 78–81

tadānum: 82
tāmartum: 16
tîrtum: 111

uddu: 45
ummum: 111–12

unuššum: 21
uznam patā'um: 111

wabālum: 80
wabartum: 6, 14–16, 228
waklum: 14

Texts
Akkad
FAOS 19, Ki 1: 110
The Legend of Narām-Sîn: 201, 202

Old Assyrian
AKT 3, 37: 19
AKT 3, 84: 93
Apûm-Aššur Treaty (L.T. 5): 14, 56
ATHE 62: 17
BIN 6, 93: 93
CCT 3, 11: 111
CCT 4, 6e: 96
CCT 4, 8a: 93
CCT 4, 30a: 15
CCT 6, 15b: 15
CTMMA 1, 84a: 20
CTMMA 1, 85: 118
CTMMA 1, 86: 118
ICK 1, 36B: 119
ICK 3, 10: 118
Kayseri 1830: 16
KT 4, 42: 56
KT 5, 19: 249
KT 5, 39: 250
KT 5, 69: 249
KT 6a, 12: 78
KT 6a, 14: 81
KT 6a, 16: 118
KT 6a, 115: 109
KT 6a, 136: 101
KT 6a, 141a: 124
KT 6a, 146: 16
KT 6a, 151: 103
KT 6a, 209: 110
KT 6a, 231: 101
KT 6a, 235: 104
KT 6a, 236: 100–01, 104
KT 6a, 237: 104
KT 6a, 238: 102, 104
KT 6a, 239: 102, 104
KT 6a, 245: 104
KT 6b, 292: 122
KT 6b, 292a: *122*
KT 6b, 302: 103–04
KT 6b, 307: 122
KT 6b, 313: 101, *103*
KT 6b, 314: 102–04
KT 6b, 316: 104
KT 6b, 317: 101, 104
KT 6b, 318: 101, 104
KT 6b, 319: 104, 122
KT 6b, 520: 118
KT 6c, 523: 16
KT 6c, 553: 122
KT 6d, 735: *80*
KT 6d, 771: 17
KT 6d, 786: *81*
KT 6d, 787: *81*
KT 6e, 1061: *78*
KT 6e, 1062: *78*
KT 8, 7: 79–80
KT 8, 8: 79–80
KT 8, 10: 79–80
KT 8, 13: 80
KT 8, 23: 79
KT 8, 30: 79
KT 8, 35: 80
KT 8, 42: 79
KT 8 46: 79
KT 8 72: *78*
KT 8, 80: 95
KT 8, 85: 79
KT 8, 87: *80*
KT 8, 95: 79
KT 8, 139: 80
KT 8, 157: 79
KT 8, 159: 79
KT 8, 160: 79
KT 8, 161: 80

KT 8, 162: 80
KT 8, 163 (envelope): *79*
KT 8, 164: *79, 80*
KT 8, 165: 80, 83–85, 94–96, 112
KT 8, 166: 79, 84–85
KT 8, 169: 109
KT 8, 173: 80
KT 8, 174: 79
KT 8, 175: 80, 86
KT 8, 176: *79, 80*
KT 8, 177: *80–81*
KT 8, 178: *80*
KT 8, 179: 124
KT 8, 180: *79–80*, 84
KT 8, 181: *79–80*, 84
KT 8, 182: *79*
KT 8, 183: *79*
KT 8, 185: *79*
KT 8, 189: *81, 95*
KT 8, 190: 81, 95–96
KT 8, 191: 81
KT 8, 193: 79
KT 8, 195: *83–84*
KT 8, 206: *79–81*, 83–*87*, 94–95
KT 8, 207: 79, 80, *81*
KT 8, 208: 81, *83–85*
KT 8, 209: 81
KT 8, 210: 82, 86
KT 8, 210bis: *79*, 82, 86
KT 8, 220: *78*
KT 8, 237: 81, *83*
KT 8, 252: *78*
KT 8, 254: 112
KT 8, 274: 15
KT 8, 323: 79
KT 8, 323a: *79*
KT 8, 327: 79
Kt c/k 30: 81
Kt c/k 44: 99
Kt c/k 127: 98
Kt c/k 128: *81*
Kt c/k 208: 99
Kt c/k 249: 99

Kt c/k 261: 19
Kt c/k 266: 99
Kt c/k 272: 99
Kt c/k 608: *80*
Kt c/k 801: 99
Kt c/k 839: 20
Kt f/k 11: *81, 84*
Kt f/k 183: 15
Kt g/t 35: 20
Kt g/t 42+z/t 11: 20
Kt h/k 317: 15
Kt k/k 14: 21
Kt k/k 100: *81*
Kt m/k 14: 19
Kt n/k 32: 241
Kt n/k 388: 16
Kt n/k 794: 14, 16
Kt n/k 1836: 120
Kt 85/k 27: 16
Kt 85/t 17: 19–20, 22
Kt 91/k 100: 14, 17, 20
Kt 91/k 134 (envelope): *81*
Kt 91/k 238 (envelope): *81*
Kt 93/k 73: 79
Kt 93/k 143: 97
Kt 93/k 198: 97
Kt 93/k 301: 97
Kt 93/k 303: 97
Kt 93/k 352: 97
Kt 93/k 489: 97
Kt 93/k 513: 17: 79, *81*
Kt 93/k 543: 97
Kt 93/k 564: 97
Kt 93/k 722: 97
Kt 94/k 123: 79
Kt 94/k 127: 79
Kt 94/k 137: 81
Kt 94/k 181: 82
Kt 94/k 351: 81
Kt 94/k 362: *81*
Kt 94/k 382: *81*
Kt 94/k 438: *81*
Kt 94/k 464: *81*

Kt 94/k 501: *81*

Kt 94/k 543: 79, 81

Kt 94/k 554: 81

Kt 94/k 670: 55

Kt 94/k 1001: *81*

Kt 98/k 118: 23

Kt 00/k 6: 3, 14, *16*, 20–21, 63, *64*, 68

Kt 00/k 10: 14, 16

Kt 01/k 217: 20

KTP 14: 15

Liepsner tablet: 14

OAA 1, 17: 114

OAA 1, 51: *18*

OAA 1, 78: 111

OAA 1, 127: 111

OIP 27, no. 2: *56*

POAT 23: 122

RA 60, 126–31: *79*

RIMA 1.A.o.33.1 (Erišum I): *58*

RIMA 1.A.o.33.14 (Erišum I): *58*

RIMA 1.A.o.39.1 (Šamši-Adad I): *57–58*

TC 1, 1: 19

TC 1, 39: 16

TC 1, 40: 14

TC 1, 64: 120

TC 3, 85: 16

TPAK 1, 32: 93

TPAK 1, 175: *81*

Old Babylonian

AbB 3, 7: 112

AbB 7, 132: 113

Amorite and Akkadian Bilinguals: 57

ARM 6, 23: 18

Hittite

CTH 471/Ritual of Ammiḫatna: 57

CTH 586: 67

CTH 670: 66, 68

CTH 744: 67

IBoT 2.131: 65

KBo 1.1: 64

KBo 1.2: 64

KBo 7.38: 66

KBo 10.20: *66*, 67–68

KBo 12.135: 67

KBo 12.53+: *65*

KBo 18.25: *67*

KBo 22.39: 67

KBo 24.118: 67

KBo 25.88: 66

KBo 30.56: 66

KBo 31.69: *67*

KBo 38.50: *67*

KBo 40.210: *67*

KBo 42.5: *65*

KBo 45.27: *67*

KBo 49.54: *64*

KBo 67.186: *64*

KBo 71.81: 21

KUB 1.17: 65

KUB 10.92: *66*

KUB 17.8+: *66*

KUB 2.13 ++: *64*

KUB 25.32: 66

KUB 26.39: 66

KUB 28.108: 67

KUB 35.1: 66

KUB 35.2: 66, 68

KUB 35.4: 66, 68

KUB 38.19: *67*

KUB 51.23: *67*

KUB 51.79: *66*

KUB 54.61: 67

KUB 54.90: *67*

KUB 57.108: *67*

KUB 58.15: *67*

KUB 59.6: *67*

KUB 6.45: *64*

KUB 8.82: 66

VSNF 12.1: 67–68

Seals

CS 42: 123

CS 73: 35

CS 79: 36

CS 88: 123

INDEX

CS 136: *41*
CS 222: 118, 122
CS 270: 37
CS 292: 35
CS 310: *37*
CS 345: 40, 236
CS 502: 37
CS 518: 36
CS 548: 35
CS 560: 35
CS 606: 119, *120*
CS 609: 37
CS 629: 35
CS 631: *41*
CS 662: 40
CS 668: 40
CS 679: 46
CS 744: 37
CS 767: 39
CS 806: 36
CS 819: 120
CS 822: 36
CS 1083: *124*
CS 1147: *124*
CS 1148: 120
CS 1269: 125
CS 1270: 125
CS 1278: 124
CS 1280: 127
CS 1283: 126
CS 1293: 123
CS 1308: 124
CS 1317: 122
CS 1355: 126

Teissier no. 227: 119, 128
Teissier no. 276: 128
Teissier no. 472: 124
Teissier no. 530: 128
Tyskiewicz seal: 243

Thematic Index

activity patterns: 135–45
activity-related skeletal changes: *see* entheseal changes

altar: 34, 36–37, 39, 42, 47
amulet: 34, 196, 198
animals (wild and domestic): 2, 4–5, 66, 126, 135, 137, 152, 154–59, 167–72, 211, 221–22, 233–36, 238–39, 265–66, 270–71, 286
    bear: 5, 168, 170–71, 270
    beaver: 168, 170
    boar: 168, 170–71, 270
    caprines: 168–69
    cattle: 159, 168–69, 172, 219, 235, 270
    deer: 168, 170–71, 270
    donkey: 19, 77, 159, 168, 253
    eagle: 170, 235–36
    goat: 5, 66, 153–56, 158, 168–70, 172, 233, 235, 239, 270, 283, 286–87
    hyena: 168, 170–71, 270
    lion: 168, 170–72, 261, 267, 270
    oysters: 170
    pig: 168–69, 172
    sheep: 5, 66, 153–59, 168–70, 172, 233, 270
    turbinate monodont: 170
architecture: 6, 186, 190–92, 210, 228–32, 244, 275, 283, 287
archive: 3–4, 6–7, 14, 17, 33, 36, 39, 75–88, 98–105, 109, 117–28, 137–38, 227, 249–50

balance: 2, 34, 39, 42, 45, 47
ball-staff: 33, 48
bioarchaeology (human): 135–45, 151–65, 151–65
brother: 80–83, 87, 94–101, 110–12, 117, 122, 125, 249, 253
bull-altar: 36–40, 125–26
burials: 137–38, 142–44

Canaan blades: 182–83
caravan: 3, 13–14, 17–22, 77, 79, 109, 227–28, 253
celebration: 191
city-state: 13–14, 19, 201, 228
communication: 14, 68, 78, 82, 84, 88, 109–10, 201
communities of practices: 75
crescent: 121–25, 210–12, 237, 267
crucible: 192–94

diagnostic sign: 4, 97–104
dimensions, of tablets: 20
diplomacy: 13, 22
drought: 201
dual case: 55–57

elders, of Aššur: 19
envelope: 2, 4, 6, 20, 41, *79–80*, *81-82*, 118–20, 124, 126, 249–50, 254
envoys, messengers: 13, 15, 17–19, 22
entheseal changes: 4–5, 135–45
eponym: 19, 22, *36*, 242–43, 249, 253, 260
estate: 18, 250

father: 110–11

gifts: 15, 19, 21

Hittite rituals: 57, *65*, 271
homophone alternative: 99
hunt god: 126–27
Hurrian rituals: 57

Idols: 187, 191–92, *196*, 257
introduction scene: 43, 118, 123–28, 237
iron, meteoritic: 16, 21

justice: 2, 41–42, 46–48

Lamassu: 237, 238
lapis lazuli: 21–22, 42–43, 47, 202
letters: 4, 109–10
libation: 34, 39, 57, 119, 121, *124*, 126, 128, 267
loom weight: 195–96, 210, 282–83

megaron: 190

lyre: 267, 269–70

measuring (instrument): 34, 42–48
money, blood: 16, 17
month names: 56–57
murder: 17

paleodiet: 5, 151–65
palaeography: 4, 93–105
pantheon: 3, 58, 65
Pleiades: 122
politeness: 113–14
pot, pottery: 167, 181–83, 185–89, 195–97, 207–23, 232–33, 242–44, 257–60, 265, 270, 277–79, 283, 289–90
   Alişar III: 192, 195–96, 212, 215

black burnished: 181, 183
Darboğaz Ware: 187
depas: 190–91
Gritty Ware: 193–94
Intermediate Ware: 190–91, 212
Kızılırmak Basin Ceramics: 277–81, 285
Metallic Ware: 187
pithos/pithoi decorated: 6, 167, 211, 219–22, 267–71
red-black pottery: 181
red Slip/Red Slip Ware: 190, 193, 211–12, 215, 217–22, 232, 265, 279
Syrian bottles: 187, 191
Troy A2 Type plate: 190–93
Ubaid pottery: 185
wheel-made: 187, 190, 193
punishment: 17
purse: 45–48

queen, of Kaneš: 17
queen, of Wahšušana: 16

relations, social: 109–12
rhetoric: 109–10, 113–14
righteousness: 42, 47

sack: 45–48, 81
safety: 16
scorpion: 125, 238, 270
seal, glyptic: 2, 4, 22, 33–48, *63*, 68, 79–83, 93, 112, 117–28, 185, 202, 209, 223, 233–40, 242–44, 249, 254, 258, 270, 277
   (Old) Anatolian style: 34–41, 124–26, 233
   (Old) Assyrian style: 119–28, 236–38, 242
   (Old) Babylonian style: 33, 38, 122
   cylinder: 2, 33–47, 118, 126, 187, 202, 233, 235–39, 242–43, 270
   filling motif: 34–35, 119, 125
   guilloche: 34
   Isin-Larsa: *35*
   ring: 118
   royal: 124–25
   stamp: 34–35, 47, 80, 233–36, 243
   (Old) Syrian style: 34–35, 37, 39–40, *120*, 121–23, 128
   Syro-Cappadocian style: 34, 37–39, *120*
   Ur III: 35
service duty: 21

signe royal: 219, 221–22
skeletal remains: 135–45
slag: 192–94, 210
smuggling: 17, 18
solstice: 6, 231–32
spindle: 196
spindle whorls: 195, 278, 282, 287
stable carbon isotopes analysis: 151–65
stable nitrogen isotopes analysis: 151–65
strickle: 2, 44, 48
supreme authority: 33–48

temple: 6, 20, 44–45, 58, 67, 79, 125, 167, 190, 209, 210, 215, 222, 232, 258–60, 271
textiles: 2, 16–22, 46, 79–81, 111, 249, 253
treaty: 3, 14–23, 55, 59, 63, 66, 68

weight stones: 42, 45–46, 196
women's literacy: 93
women's mobility: 75
worshipper: 34, 42, 48118, 123, 125
wine: 21
writing habit: 83, 97, 100
writing style: 95, 97

SUBARTU

All volumes in this series are evaluated by an Editorial Board, strictly on academic grounds, based on reports prepared by referees who have been commissioned by virtue of their specialism in the appropriate field. The Board ensures that the screening is done independently and without conflicts of interest. The definitive texts supplied by authors are also subject to review by the Board before being approved for publication. Further, the volumes are copy-edited to conform to the publisher's stylebook and to the best international academic standards in the field.

Titles in Series

Stefano Anastasio, *The Archaeology of Upper Mesopotamia: An Analytical Bibliography for the Pre-Classical Periods* (1995)

Farouk Ismail, Walther Sallaberger, Philippe Talon, & Karel Van Lerberghe, *Administrative Documents from Tell Beydar (Seasons 1993-1995)* (1997)

Tell Beydar, Three Seasons of Excavations (1992-1994): A Preliminary Report, ed by Marc Lebeau & Antoine Suleiman (1997)

About Subartu: Studies Devoted to Upper Mesopotamia — Volume I: *Landscape, Archaeology, Settlement*; Volume II: *Culture, Society, Image*, ed. by Marc Lebeau (1998)

Roger Matthews, *The Early Prehistory of Mesopotamia* (2000)

Tell Beydar: Environmental and Technical Studies, ed. by Karel Van Lerberghe & Gabriella Voet (2000)

Olivier Rouault & Markus Wäfler, *La Djéziré et l'Euphrate syriens de la protohistoire à la fin du second millénaire av. J.C. : Tendances dans l'interprétation historique des données nouvelles* (2000)

Maria Grazia Masetti-Rouault, *Cultures locales du Moyen-Euphrate. Modèles et événements (IIe-Ier millénaires av. J.-C.)* (2001)

Tell Boueid II: A Late Neolithic Village on the Middle Khabur (Syria), ed. by Olivier Nieuwenhuyse & Antoine Suleiman (2002)

The Origins of North Mesopotamian Civilization: Ninevite 5 Chronology, Economy, Society, ed. by Harvey Weiss & Elena Rova (2003)

Tell Beydar, The 1995 to 1999 Seasons of Excavations: A Preliminary Report, ed. by Marc Lebeau & Antoine Suleiman (2003)

Lucio Milano, Walther Sallaberger, Philippe Talon, & Karel Van Lerberghe, *Third Millenium Cuneiform Texts from Tell Beydar (Seasons 1996-2002)* (2004)

Atlas of Pre-Classical Upper Mesopotamia including a Supplement to 'The Archaeology of Upper Mesopotamia. An Analytical Bibliography for the Pre-Classical Periods' and an Analytical Repertory of Archaeological Excavations, ed. by Stefano Anastasio, Marc Lebeau, & Martin Sauvage (2004)

Das mittelassyrische Tontafelarchiv von Giricano/Dunnu-Sha-Uzibi. Ausgrabungen in Giricano 1, ed. by Karen Radner (2004)

Tell Beydar, the 2000-2002 Seasons of Excavations, the 2003-2004 Seasons of Architectural Restoration: A Preliminary Report, ed. by Marc Lebeau & Antoine Suleiman (2004)

Si un homme... Textes offerts en hommage à André Finet, ed. by Phillipe Talon & Véronique Van der Stede (2005)

Les espaces syro-mésopotamiens. Dimensions de l'expérience humaine au Proche-Orient ancien Volume d'hommage offert à Jean-Claude Margueron, ed. by Pascal Butterlin, Marc Lebeau, J.-Y. Monchambert, J.L. Montero Fenollós, & B. Muller (2007)

Tell 'Acharneh 1998-2004 : Rapports préliminaires sur les campagnes de fouilles et saison d'études. Preliminary Reports on Excavation Campaigns and Study Season, ed. by Michel Fortin (2006)

Adelheid Otto, *Alltag und Gesellschaft zur Spätbronzezeit: Eine Fallstudie aus Tall Bazi (Syrien)* (2006)

Andreas Schachner, *Bilder eines Weltreichs: Kunst- und kulturgeschichtliche Untersuchungen zu den Verzierungen eines Tores aus Balawat (Imgur-Enlil) aus der Zeit von Salmanassar III, König von Assyrien* (2007)

Tell Beydar, the 2000-2002 Seasons of Excavations, the 2003-2004 Seasons of Architectural Restoration. A Preliminary Report, ed. by M. Lebeau, A. Suleiman (2007)

Beydar Studies 1, ed. by Marc Lebeau & Antoine Suleiman (2008)

Philippe Quenet, *Les Echanges du Nord de la Mésopotamie avec ses voisins proche-orientaux au IIIe millénaire (ca. 3100-2300 Av. J.-C.)* (2008)

À propos de Tepe Gawra, le monde proto-urbain de Mésopotamie ; About Tepe Gawra, a Proto-Urban World in Mesopotamia, ed. by Pascal Butterlin (2009)

Stefano Anastasio, *Atlas of the Assyrian Pottery of the Iron Age* (2010)

Emar After the Closure of the Tabqa Dam: The Syrian-German Excavations 1996-2002 — Volume I: Late Roman and Medieval Cemeteries and Environmental Studies, ed. by Uwe Finkbeiner & Ferhan Sakal (2010)

Alexander Pruss, *Die Amuq-Terrakotten. Untersuchungen zu den Terrakotta-Figuren des 2. und 1. Jahrtausends v. Chr. aus den Grabungen des Oriental Institute Chicago in der Amuq-Ebene* (2010)

Holocene Landscapes through Time in the Fertile Crescent, ed. by Katleen Deckers (2011)

Greta Jans & Joachim Bretschneider, *Seals and Sealings from Tell Beydar/Nabada (Seasons 1995-2001): A Progress Report* (2012)

Khashuri Natsargora: The Early Bronze Age Graves. Publications of the Georgian-Italian Shida Kartli Archaeological Project I, ed. by Elena Rova & Marina Puturidze (2012)

'L'Heure immobile' entre ciel et terre. Mélanges en l'honneur d'Antoine Souleiman, ed. by Philippe Quenet & Mīšāl al- Maqdisī (2012)

Ferhan Sakal, *Die anthropomorphen Terrakotten der Region am syrischen Mittleren Euphrat im 3. Jahrtausend v. Chr.* (2013)

Tell Beydar: Environmental and Technical Studies, Volume II, ed. by Lucio Milano & Marc Lebeau (2014)

Tell Beydar. The 2010 Season of Excavations and Architectural Restoration: A Preliminary Report / Rapport préliminaire sur la campagne de fouilles et de restauration architecturale 2010, ed. by Marc Lebeau & Antoine Suleiman (2014)

Proceedings of the 1st Kültepe International Meeting, Kültepe, September 19—23, 2013. Studies Dedicated to Kutlu Emre. Kültepe International Meetings 1, ed. by Fikri Kulakoğlu & Cécile Michel (2015)

Mille et une empreintes : Un Alsacien en Orient. Mélanges en l'honneur du 65e anniversaire de Dominique Beyer, ed. by Julie Patrier, Philippe Quenet, & Pascal Butterlin (2016)

Emmanuel Laroche, *Études anatoliennes*, ed. by Alfonso Archi & Hatice Gonnet (2016)

At the Northern Frontier of Near Eastern Archaeology: Recent Research on Caucasia and Anatolia in the Bronze Age/An der Nordgrenze der vorderasiatischen Archäologie: Neue Forschung über Kaukasien und Anatolien in der Bronzezeit. Publications of the Georgian-Italian Shida-Kartli Archaeological Project 2, ed. by Elena Rova & Monica Tonussi (2017)

Proceedings of the 2nd Kültepe International Meeting, Kültepe, 26-30 July 2015. Studies Dedicated to Klaas Veenhof. Kültepe International Meetings 2, ed. by Fikri Kulakoğlu & Gojiko Barjamovic (2017)

Barbara Couturaud, *Les incrustations en coquille de Mari* (2019)

Thomas L. McClellan, *El-Qitar: A Bronze Age Fortress on the Euphrates* (2019)

Andreas Schachner, *Die chalkolithische Siedlung von Giricano am Oberen Tigris: Die Ausgrabungen in Giricano II* (2020)

After the Harvest: Storage Practices and Food Processing in Bronze Age Mesopotamia, ed. by Noemi Borrelli & Giulia Scazzosi (2020)

Circular Cities of Early Bronze Age Syria, ed. by Corinne Castel, Jan-Waalke Meyer & Philippe Quenet (2020)

Integrative Approaches to the Archaeology and History of Kültepe-Kaneš: Kültepe, 4-7 August, 2017, ed. by Fikri Kulakoğlu, Cécile Michel & Güzel Öztürk (2020)

Cultural Exchanges and Current Research at Kültepe and its Surroundings: Kültepe, 1-4 August, 2019, ed. by Fikri Kulakoğlu, Guido Kryszat & Cécile Michel (2021)

Interdisciplinary research on the Bronze Age Diyala: Proceedings of the Conference Held at the Paris Institute for Advanced Study, 25-26 June, 2018, ed. by Carlos Gonçalves & Cécile Michel (2021)

Andrea Ricci, *Settlement, Mobility, and Land Use in the Birecik-Carchemish Region: (Fifth-Third Millennium BCE)*

Michel Fortin, *Tell 'Atij, Moyen Khabour (Syrie): Rapport final de fouilles (1986-1993)* (2023)

In Preparation

Akiva Sanders, *Violence and Imagination after the Collapse: Encounters, Identity and Daily Life in the Upper Euphrates Region, 3200-2500* BCE